SCOTLAND'S GLOBAL EMPIRE

Scotland's Global Empire

A Chronicle of Great Scots

Jock Gallagher

Whittles Publishing

Published by
Whittles Publishing Ltd.,
Dunbeath,
Caithness, KW6 6EG,
Scotland, UK

www.whittlespublishing.com

ISBN 978-184995-102-9

Printed by

Latimer Trend & Company Ltd., Plymouth

for Sheenagh

*who may now go to sleep without having to listen to yet another
recitation of the achievements of one great Scot or another*

and for The Chummies

*Margaret and Paul Hill, Ann and Tony McDowell and Marie and John O'Brien,
who had to survive endless dinner parties in similar listening mode*

CONTENTS

AUTHOR'S DISCLAIMER...OR A LAME EXCUSE

Before any of my academic friends decide to exercise their critical faculties, let me stress that this book is essentially superficial. This is no scholarly study of the Scots' role in history. While my researches may have been exhausting, they are far from exhaustive. I have simply gathered information in the course of my trade as an honest hack. Bits and pieces have been picked up here, there and everywhere from myriad sources over nearly half a century...and without intent that I would one day try to piece all the parts together into a kind of patriotic mosaic.

From my history and geography lessons at Greenock High School, I've always had a fair inkling we Scots had done pretty damn well both in and by the world. However, it wasn't until reminiscing, a large glass of amber liquid close to hand, over a mass of scribbles and dodgy shorthand in my dog-eared reporter's notebooks and a substantial collection of fading newspaper cuttings that I slowly become aware of a greater significance than I'd previously recognised.

Indeed the list of Scottish pioneers, inventors, innovators, discoverers and the generally-renowned that emerged is so long that it's difficult to know where to start... especially as I have neither the desire nor the competence to attempt to rank genius. Who am I to relate the invention of the steam engine to the discovery of penicillin or the wonders of television to the humble bike? Instead I seek refuge in chronology and alphabet...and, of course, whimsy!

There are lots of well-kent names - from Andrew Carnegie to John Paul Jones; Alexander Graham Bell to John Logie Baird; Alexander Fleming to Charles Rennie McIntosh - who have had due recognition over the years and of whom it would be difficult to say much more than is already recorded in the volumes of history books, a host of excellent biographies, countless learned magazines and not to mention the ever-burgeoning websites.

While these household names are included to underpin my thesis about the strength and breadth of The Scottish Empire, I have refrained from re-telling tales we all learned at school. Instead, I offer only abbreviated reminders of their achievements so that I have more space to write about those whose talents are, for one reason or another, less celebrated than perhaps should be the case.

Space is again the reason for not adhering to the usual publication practice of including an index. To list all the names included would be the equivalent of adding another large chapter to an already lengthy tome. However, an index of key Scottish names can be downloaded at http://www.whittlespublishing.com/Scotlands_Global_Empire or simply scan the QR code below.

I'm also conscious that there are many more examples of extraordinary human endeavour that simply haven't found a place in the book because of my shortcomings

At the risk of perpetuating the unfairness of the prophets-without-honour-in-their-own-land syndrome, I have also had to exclude all those great Scots whose achievements are more relevant within Scotland and the successful thousands of the second and third generation Scots abroad.

The end result, therefore, is undoubtedly idiosyncratic but I've tried to plug some of the more obvious gaps courtesy of Encyclopaedia Britannica, the Oxford Dictionary of Political Biography, a wide range of other reference books, countless newspapers from around the world but especially The Scotsman, sundry magazines plus, of course, the now omnipresent internet and especially Wikipedia.

Where I do know from whence came any scrap of knowledge, I readily credit the source and I hope the extensive Bibliography will be taken into consideration and underline my indebtedness to others. In all too many instances, however, my memory and my reporter's notes are treacherous aids and to anyone who might feel their work has been plundered, I can only offer genuine apologies and assurances that it has been inadvertent.

Jock Gallagher

1

GENESIS OF AN EMPIRE

 *'We look to Scotland for all
our ideas of civilisation'*
— *Voltaire*

The Scottish Empire is, of course, illusory but the giants who spread their influence across the globe offer tangible evidence that, had they had the mind to make it so, the saltire of St Andrew or the more flamboyant lion rampant might have flown across much of the civilised world and the atlases could have had a very different hue.

This, however, is not an empire of colonisation that diminishes or enslaves those whom it embraces. It involves neither the greed nor the ruthlessness so often inherent in empire-building. It is without condescension: an empire that breaks down barriers rather than creating ownership and, it can be claimed, enhances civilisation. Where would you plant the flag to claim sovereignty of ideas and philosophies?

This is not a recital of the adventures of conquering heroes, although some are included. The empire I have in mind is more an outreach of ideas, the story of human endeavour in its many forms, pushing at the boundaries of the imagination and stretching the accepted order. It sweeps from the foothills of press freedom to the high plains of moral philosophy; from the oceans of ingenuity to the great rivers of physical courage; from the borderlands where determination meets initiative to the mighty mountain ranges of originality. It encompasses everything from the spirit of pioneering to the mystical qualities of leadership. It's luckily not dependent on a seat of power and nor is it affected by the bruising arguments about Scotland's place within the UK or as an independent state.

In building this empire, however inadvertently, its citizens have shown down the centuries extraordinary vision, creativity, innovation, energy, leadership, diplomacy, skill, artistry, sometimes pure genius and, more often, downright doggedness. Voltaire might have over-egged the pudding but in all these areas, I believe, our small nation has punched well above its weight and has earned his generous compliment. A fine conceit? An extravagant claim? Read on before you judge.

These few chapters include, for example, the Scots who...

invented radar, television, the telephone, the forerunner of the fax machine, the pneumatic tyre, the bicycle, the steam engine, the iron ship, gas lighting, the flashing lighthouse, the breech-loading rifle, the electric clock, the mackintosh raincoat, tarmac, the vacuum flask, the Anderson air raid shelter, tubular steel, Telford bridges and hundreds of other essentials... as well as the not-so-essential fountain pen, sticky postage stamp and kaleidoscope;

pioneered medical breakthroughs with penicillin, antiseptics, quinine, anaesthetics, insulin, beta-blockers, a cure for scurvy (which included the consumption of limes and led to British sailors being called 'limeys'), birth control, chloroform, ultrasound, the hypodermic syringe and the MRI scanner;

won Nobel prizes for chemistry (for the discovery of five of the six noble gases), physics, medicine and for other important contributions to the peace of the world;

founded (or reorganised) the modern navies of the United States, Australia, Chile, Russia and Japan, provided admirals for Peru, Brazil and Greece, but also brought terror to the high seas in the shape of the notorious pirate Captain Kidd;

fought gloriously on battlefields across the globe and won hundreds of awards for bravery, including 169 Victoria Crosses;

served as generals and field marshals all across Europe including Holland, France, Prussia and Russia and with the ANZAC forces in the First World War, and helped set up the Royal Flying Corps, the Women's Royal Air Force, the Royal New Zealand Air Force, the Special Operations Executive, the SAS, the Territorial Army and the Royal British Legion;

provided a fistful of prime ministers and other senior politicians for Australia, New Zealand and Canada and nine for Britain (including the first Tory PM), five of India's viceroys, a goodly number of America's founding fathers, and the first secretary general of the League of Nations;

established great educational institutions including America's second college (the William and Mary in Virginia), Princeton in New Jersey, Harvard Medical School, McGill University in Montreal, Imperial College of Engineering in Tokyo, Birkbeck College in London, and the Open University, the world's first distance-learning university;

introduced tea to India and improved the quality of America's coffee;

saved America's buffalo from extinction;

launched the famous Cunard Line, Japan's industrial giant Mitsubishi, Australia's transcontinental railway, America's great Pinkerton Detective Agency (and coined the term 'private eye'), Canada's famous Mounted Police, the Buick Motor Company, San Francisco's famous cable cars and the world's first municipal fire brigade;

created *Encyclopaedia Britannica*, the *Oxford English Dictionary* and *Chambers Dictionary*, the novel, the historical novel and children's picture books;

made the first transatlantic air flight (Sir Arthur Brown of Alcock and Brown)

built the RMS *Queen Mary*, the *Queen Elizabeth*, the *QE2* and a fleet of other famous ships including the paddle steamer *Sirius*, the first steamship to cross the Atlantic non-stop;

discovered the Victoria Falls, the source of the Nile, the Yukon River, the Mackenzie River in Canada, the magnetic North Pole and Nova Scotia;

started the Bank of England, the Commonwealth Bank of Australia, Hong Kong's Jordan Mathie Bank, the great 1794 gold rush in California; and gave the world its very first savings bank and the decimal point;

fathered modern economics, geology, philosophy, freedom of the press, the Labour Party and the great British welfare state;

produced World and Olympic champions in athletics, boxing, swimming, motor racing, cycling, golf, snooker, darts and, improbably, curling;

wrote a vast library of books from *Sherlock Holmes* to *The Thirty-Nine Steps*, *Waverley* (the first historical novel) to *Whisky Galore*, *The Coral Island* to *The Prime of Miss Jean Brodie*, *Kidnapped* to *Treasure Island*, from *Winnie-the-Pooh* to *Peter Pan* and *Dr Finlay's Casebook* to *All Creatures Great and Small*;

inspired Rudyard Kipling's poem 'If', Mendelssohn's *Hebrides Overture* (*Fingal's Cave*) and his *Scottish Symphony*, Malcolm Arnold's *Four Scottish Dances*, and Paul McCartney's 'Mull of Kintyre';

spawned legendary characters including James Bond, Thomas Crown, Horatio Hornblower, Robinson Crusoe, Lieutenant Pinkerton, Dr Jekyll and Mr Hyde, Young Lochinvar, the Admirable Crichton, Professor Moriarty, Dr Watson, Richard Hannay, John Bull, Pooh Bear, Toad of Toad Hall, Peter Pan, Captain Hook, Long John Silver, Wee Willie Winkie, the voice of Mickey Mouse and an array of cartoon heroes – from Desperate Dan to Dennis the Menace – from *The Dandy* and *The Beano* (the world's oldest comic); and

gave birth to the BBC – for me, still the world's greatest broadcasting organisation – and a subsequent stream of television icons like Victor

Meldrew, Rab C Nesbitt, Dr Finlay, Dr Cameron, James Herriot, Taggart, Rebus, Hamish MacBeth and the Laird of Glenbogle.

Down through the centuries, Scots have made the world a better place. Our doctors have made it a healthier place. Our engineers have ingeniously contributed to making it a more efficient place in which to live. Others have been a civilising influence through their writings and political convictions, through economic policies, trade unions, fairness and equality, through concern for the common man, pioneering, questing and, above all, through their restlessness.

Scots are not the most contented spirits. They find it difficult to be passive. The status quo does not feature greatly in our vocabulary. That's not to suggest we are a nation of saint-like marvels. We have more than our fair share of dullards, drunkards, despots, crooks and thugs. However, having thus acknowledged their existence, I unashamedly linger no longer on negatives. There is too much to celebrate.

All the major inventions and the more important discoveries are, of course, well tabulated and while it's important to acknowledge them as part of the totality, I don't need to replicate *those* stories of genius and enterprise. But beyond the names we learned about at school, there is another great raft of ingenuity and perseverance, and a host of heroes about whom much less has been written. Together, the well-known and the not-so-well-known show the Scots' considerable contribution to the world and to my imaginary empire. That's the substance of this commentary, which can only be a series of journalistic snapshots but which may hopefully stimulate readers to dig deeper into some of the personalities. Many of them are worth a book in their own right.

Some of my empire builders made their name working within Scotland, hunched over Bunsen burners, test tubes, blueprints and the brouhaha of invention and reinvention, producing their artefacts, burning the midnight oil, examining and re-examining philosophy, pouring forth their theories and trying to make life better for their fellow men and women. Others achieved it abroad, many after perilous journeys to the far corners of the world: discovering new places, administering new countries, creating new ways of doing things and providing leadership in myriad ways.

As a result of this diaspora, Scottish place names are strewn liberally across the globe in evidence of the Scots propensity to travel hopefully. There are thousands of examples but my favourite is Glasgow in Kentucky. It's a small agricultural centre as different from Scotland's dynamic industrial capital as it's possible to get. It has a population of less than 15,000 but has its own annual Highland Games and is a clear indication that the Scottish travellers never forgot their origins. Perhaps the very best example of this is the United States' recognition of April 6, the anniversary of the signing of the Declaration of Arbroath, as Tartan Day, an occasion when they acknowledge Scotland's huge contribution to their history and celebrate all things Scottish. Would America do that if it weren't for the Scottish influences so deeply embedded in the national psyche?

Although he attributed the emotion to Highlanders, Burns was speaking for most Scots in his poem:

> 'My heart's in the Highlands, my heart is not here,
> My heart's in the Highlands a-chasing the deer;
> Chasing the wild deer, and following the roe,
> My heart's in the Highlands, wherever I go.'

Distance, it seems, was never a deterrent and nor was mode of transport. When it was all that was available to them, they bravely sailed in frail ships across angry seas and raging rivers. They endured severe hardship as they trekked across mean deserts, wild prairies and bleak ice fields. They ignored physical exhaustion as they hacked their way through dense jungles and ingeniously found ways to cross towering mountain ranges. It's easy to see where Harry Lauder got the inspiration for his signature tune, 'Keep Right on to the End of the Road'. And always, the Scots were at the leading edge when it came to the *means* of travel: they helped develop steam engines that made the ships go faster, railways and locomotives that transformed land travel, and they were up there with the pioneers of aviation. Equally awe-inspiring, they made great journeys of the mind via the high tables of Scotland's universities and the lecture rooms of the learned institutions.

My problem has not been, as some sceptical Sassenach friends forecast, a lack of material. More than one gleefully predicted this would be a very short book if it was to be about *great* Scots! In honesty, my struggles have not been in finding names to include but in editing the ever-growing list into something vaguely cohesive. And I have only just scratched the surface: there is but a passing reference to Robert Burns and his vast canon of poems and songs (including 'Auld Lang Syne', sung around the globe almost as often as 'Happy Birthday'), and nothing of the Edinburgh Festivals (launched in 1947 and today one of the world's most lively cultural events) nor much of the Enlightenment.

It's hard to imagine the atmosphere that must have pervaded Scotland during that golden, febrile period – somewhere between 1740 and 1800 – when sharp intellects came together in glorious and unique fusion. It's equally difficult to determine just when the Enlightenment gained its capital 'E' but it was clearly a time when restless minds broke free from academic and social constraints to debate, as never before, in the areas of moral philosophy, social history, economics and the ethics of capitalism, not to mention mathematics and geology and chemistry and every subject under heaven. There was High Table discourse and argument among the most erudite academics in the nation's universities, and the intellectual diet ranged from David Hume's moral philosophy to Adam Smith's economics, from the profundity of James Hutton's geological studies to the original theories of the chemist Joseph Black.

Imagine what it might have been like if they had had today's communication tools – the personal computer, television, radio, the mobile phone and the profusion of social networks. Imagine Mr Hume theorising on a walk through Edinburgh when some thought about moral philosophy strikes him: what if he had been able to access the internet? Imagine how Jeremy Paxman and his television cohorts might have coped with shaping intelligent and illuminating interviews: 'Mr Hume, you say you have to be good to do good: does it follow that if you do good you *are* good?' Hume (born Edinburgh, 1711–1776), probably the leading figure of the Enlightenment, is best known for his *Treatise of Human Nature*. He wrote it when he was 28 and, for the first time, applied scientific reasoning in resolving moral issues. He was able to test many of his ideas in rigorous debate with the Glasgow University philosophy professor Francis Hutcheson. In a 2005 poll, Hume was voted as the Scot who had made the greatest impact on the world in the past 1,000 years.

His young associate, Adam Smith (born Kirkcaldy, 1723–90), had gone to Glasgow University when he was just 14 and by the time he was 23 was lecturing in rhetoric at Edinburgh. There was nothing precocious, however, about his seminal work *The Wealth of Nations*. It took ten years to research and consider before he was ready to publish it in 1776 and is of course said to be the basis for many of today's market economy theories. He later became Lord Rector at Glasgow. James Hutton (born Edinburgh, 1726–97), a one-time gentleman farmer, published his *Theory of the Earth* in 1785 and in it described his ideas about the formation of the Earth's crust. His theory was that the slow processes that had created and shaped the Earth were still ongoing. He was the founder of modern geology and is often described as 'the man who found time'. Like Smith, Joseph Black (born Bordeaux, France, 1728–99) also brought the two great universities together. He was professor of anatomy and chemistry in Glasgow and, later, professor of medicine and chemistry in Edinburgh. Among his many successes, he established the importance of quantitative experiments and invented the first accurate method of measuring heat – indeed, a version of his calorimeter is still in use today. He is regarded as the father of modern chemistry.

There were many other clear minds drawn into the tight, golden circle of the academic intelligentsia, but even outside it the likes of Robert Burns (1759–96) were making their mark. Although Burns was at his most creative during the latter half of the period, Scotland's national bard is not acknowledged as part of the Enlightenment. Yet there's a single poem that, despite his reputation as a womaniser, surely stamps him out as a radical philosopher well ahead of his time. It is 'The Rights of Woman', which he wrote in 1792.

While Europe's eye is fix'd on mighty things,
The fate of empires and the fall of kings;
While quacks of state must each pronounce his plan,
And even children lisp the Rights of Man;
Amid this mighty fuss just let me mention,
The Rights of Woman merit some attention.

First on the sexes' inter-mix'd connexion,
One sacred Right of Woman is protection.
The tender flower that lifts its head, elate,
Helpless, must fall before the blasts of fate,
Sunk on the earth, defac'd its lovely form,
Unless your shelter ward th' impending storm.

Our second Right — but needless here is caution,
To keep that right inviolate's the fashion,
Each man of sense has it so full before him,
He'd die before he'd wrong it — 'tis decorum.
There was, indeed, in far less polish'd days,
A time, when rough, rude man had haughty ways;
Would swagger, swear, get drunk, kick up a riot,
Nay, even thus invade a lady's quiet.

Now, thank our stars! these Gothic times are fled;
Now, well-bred men — and you are all well-bred —
Most justly think (and we are much the gainers)
Such conduct neither spirit, wit, nor manners.

For Right the third, our last, our best, our dearest,
That right to fluttering female hearts the nearest,
Which even the Right of Kings in low prostration
Most humbly own — 'tis dear, dear admiration!
In that blest sphere alone we live and move;
There taste that life of life — immortal love.
Smiles, glances, sighs, tears, fits, flirtations, airs,
'Gainst such an host what flinty savage dares —
When awful Beauty joins with all her charms,
Who is so rash as rise in rebel arms?

But truce with kings and truce with constitutions,
With bloody armaments and revolutions,
Let majesty your first attention summon,
Ah! ça ira! the majesty of woman!

I heard that read with tremendous feeling by a Russian woman at an otherwise bizarre Burns supper in Moscow. She was a professor of English and her impeccable presentation brought a storm of applause from her university colleagues and left British guests in awe. I'd been in the city researching a programme for the BBC when an Irishman, of all people, invited me to propose the immortal memory at a 'little bit of a Burns do' he was organising.

It turned out to be something more than that. There were about 300 guests from the various diplomatic communities and a healthy smattering of Muscovite intelligentsia. When the time came to address the haggis, the great chieftain o' the puddin' race turned out – in a glorious example of Irish initiative – to be an ancient tin of shortbread. The real thing, ordered from Scotland, had fallen foul of the Russian customs officers who, no doubt, had great difficulty in identifying it as an innocent, edible delicacy! It was not easy to keep a straight face as I symbolically scratched the shortbread tin with a borrowed carving knife.

There's little that hasn't been written about Burns' life and lifestyle but I continue to be astonished at his enduring appeal. No other Scot commands such universal acclaim that his birthday is celebrated just about everywhere around the world. The United States has hundreds of Burns Clubs (and not a few St Andrew's and Caledonian Societies) and that's matched pro rata in Canada, Australia, New Zealand and, indeed, any place where more than a half a dozen Scots, Scots' descendants or wannabe Scots are gathered together. I've read reports of Burns suppers to celebrate the bard's birthday being held in many unlikely places around the world, including Beijing: one can only wonder what the 800 guests of the city's Drama Academy made of the haggis!

Burns, very much the people's poet, has clearly influenced many later writers. John Steinbeck, for example, paraphrased one of his lines 'The best laid schemes o' mice and men/Gang aft agley', from 'Ode to a Mouse' for the title of his novel *Of Mice and Men*. More recently, Bob Dylan cited Burns as his greatest inspiration and quoted 'A Red, Red Rose' as the lyric that has had the greatest effect on his life. There is another theory that Burns also gave the Mexicans their *gringo* (meaning American) after hearing a US cavalry unit (supplemented by more than 80 Scots mercenaries) defiantly singing the refrain of the Bard's 'Green Grow the Rashes, O' at the Alamo in 1836. Perhaps the ultimate tribute to Burns came from Abraham Lincoln. He had often said the Scot was his favourite poet and that he could recite most of his work from memory, but when asked to toast the immortal memory, the great man's response was: 'I cannot frame a toast to Burns because I can say nothing worthy of his generous heart and transcending genius.'

Underpinning the cliché of the Scottish doctor is the reality of the medical men who attended everyone from Napoleon to the Duke of Wellington, from the Tsars of Russia to George Washington and of course a long line of British monarchs. Many more Scottish clinicians contributed to the care of ordinary folk around the globe by tending to their needs, devising new therapies and discovering new drugs.

The man who looked after Napoleon and witnessed his death on St Helena in 1821 was Dr Archibald Arnott, from Ecclefechan in Dumfries. He was a Royal Navy doctor and for his services, he received 12 francs, a snuff box and a locket containing some of Napoleon's hair. All the Tsars from Peter II to Nicholas II – stretching over more than 150 years – had Scottish doctors (see Chapter 8: Reaching for the Tsars). George Washington's doctor was Dr James Craik from Arbigland in Dumfriesshire. He was physician general to the United States Army from 1798 to 1800 and served under Washington in his campaigns against the Indians. He diagnosed the president's fatal illness, treated him until his final hours and was remembered in his will: 'To my compatriot in arms and old and intimate friend, Dr Craik, I give my bureau and the cabinet chair, an appendage of my study.'

The first Scottish royal doctor I have found was Arthur Johnston of Caskieben in Aberdeenshire. He was physician to Charles I in 1625. He graduated from Padua University, practised in France, returned to Britain to tend the king and later became rector of Aberdeen University. Sir Andrew Hallidie from Dunfermline was doctor to King William IV and Queen Victoria, while both her personal physician and personal surgeon were also Scots. Sir Robert Christison from Edinburgh looked after her health and still found time to act as chairman of the committee that prepared the first *Pharmacopoeia of Great Britain and Ireland* in 1864. Her surgeon was Sir William Fergusson from Prestonpans, who was also president of the Royal College of Surgeons.

Major General Thomas Menzies from Aberdeen was doctor to King George VI from 1949 to '52. He had served in the Royal Army Medical Corps in both world wars and been appointed professor of tropical medicine at the Royal Army Medical College in 1940. He was also director of medical services at the General Headquarters of the Middle East Land Forces (1948–50). Another army man, Major General Ian Campbell Crawford from Dumfries, had been director of army medicine before becoming physician to Queen Elizabeth II from 1990 to '99; he was a cardiology consultant. It was yet another royal physician and soldier who might be regarded as the father of military medicine. Sir John Pringle, from Stichill in Roxburghshire, was physician to King George III and physician general to the British Army in the Netherlands in 1744.

Although the earliest armies had medical services of a sort, it was he who set out to rationalise the care of soldiers and improve camp sanitation. In 1752, he made rules for the prevention of dysentery, one of the scourges of the day. He had noticed a relation between putrefaction and disease, and his treatment dramatically reduced military deaths. He was elected president of the Royal Society in 1772. The next major step forward came when Sir James McGrigor, from Cromdale, laid the foundations for the establishment of the Royal Army Medical Corps. He was the Duke of Wellington's Surgeon General during the Peninsular War (1808–14) and, in 1815, he undertook a dramatic reorganisation of what was then the Army Medical Department. He read medicine at Aberdeen University and Edinburgh University before joining the army as a surgeon in 1793. He served with the 88th Regiment of Foot in Flanders (1794), the West Indies and India (1799). In 1801, as Superintendent Surgeon in Egypt and despite suffering from malaria himself at the time, he set up an isolation hospital to deal with an outbreak of plague. Following the Battle of Waterloo, he instigated the changes in the Army Medical Department in 1815. He established a system for the evacuation of the wounded and arranged for prefabricated huts to be sent from Britain for use as convalescent depots, which meant that those who recovered quickly could be kept in the field. He further improved the standards of cleanliness and sanitation both in the field and in the barracks, which reduced deaths from cholera, dysentery and typhus. He also introduced the stethoscope to military medical practice and created a specialist ambulance corps to get injured and sick personnel to his field hospitals or back to Britain. He was knighted and appointed director general of the Army Medical Service, a post he held for 36 years.

It was another 40 years, however, before the RAMC was finally created from the merger of the Army Medical Service and the Medical Staff Corps in 1898. One of the early commandants of the Corps was Major General Sir William Grant Macpherson (who was also author of its official history). During the Great War, he served in France as deputy director of General Medical Services, was mentioned in dispatches nine times and received additional honours from France, Italy and the United States. When he died in 1929, an obituary said, 'he was popularly known as 'Tiger Mac', a name not given him on account of anything ferocious or daring in his character but as a tribute to his energy, thoroughness and singleness of purpose.' On a memorial tablet in Edinburgh's St Giles Cathedral, his RAMC colleagues inscribed: 'In humble gratitude for his great and distinguished service.'

It was a former RAMC officer, Professor Ian Aird (born Edinburgh, 1905–62), who developed the kidney transplant in the UK. He carried out the first transplant where donor and recipient were not identical twins. He also hit the headlines in 1953 when, as Professor of Surgery at the University of London, he separated a pair of Nigerian conjoined twins, one of whom survived. It was the first time the operation had been undertaken in Britain. During the Second World War, he served with the Eighth Army in North Africa and was leader of a mobile surgical unit which saved hundreds of lives on the front line. He was twice mentioned in dispatches. According to a piece written by Iain Macintyre in *Surgeons' News* in 2008, Aird operated on a German officer injured in the fighting: 'As the tank warfare ebbed and flowed across the desert, Aird's unit was overrun by a panzer column. The medical officer of the German unit sought the surgeon in charge and when Aird introduced himself, the German doctor asked, "are you Aird of Edinburgh?" When an astonished Aird replied that he was, the German doctor went on to explain that he had read with interest about Aird's work... he was then asked to operate on a senior German officer who had sustained a serious chest wound. After successful resuscitation, Aird performed a thoracotomy... surrounded by a ring of German officers including Field Marshal Rommel himself.' Unfortunately, he was unable to save the man's life but his colleagues were appreciative of Ian Aird's efforts.

More recently, Air Marshall Sir John Alexander Baird from Aberdeen was surgeon general of the Armed Forces (1997–2000), having previously been the RAF's director general of medical services between 1994 and 1997. He is a member of the International Academy of Aviation and Space Medicine.

Scots, doctor, pioneer: these words go together so readily that it's impossible to do more than offer the briefest of tasters about a handful of pioneering Scottish doctors. William Cullen, from Hamilton, became Britain's first chemistry professor (at Glasgow

University) in 1751. He was the foremost medical teacher of his time and was mainly responsible for recognising the important part played by the nervous system in health and disease. He published an edition of the *Edinburgh Pharmacopoeia* in 1776.

Brothers John and William Hunter, from East Kilbride, were a remarkable pair. John, the younger by ten years, was an anatomist and physiologist and the founder of scientific surgery, previously practised by barbers. He was surgeon extraordinary to King George III (1776), surgeon general to the Army (1790) and pioneered tissue grafting and dissection. One English writer said of him, 'as a physiologist, he was equalled by Aristotle but as a pathologist he stands alone.' His *Natural History of Human Teeth* (1771–78) is said to have revolutionised dentistry. Big brother William was also an anatomist and the founder of modern obstetrics, raising the practice of midwifery to a branch of medicine. He was personal physician to Queen Charlotte and attended 11 royal births (from 1762). He was the first professor of anatomy to the Royal Academy (1768) and president of the Royal College of Physicians. He went to Glasgow University when he was 13 and in 1770 built a house with an amphitheatre for lectures and a dissecting room – now the Hunterian Museum – which he bequeathed to Glasgow University with an endowment of £8,000.

Sir Charles Bell, from Doun-in-Monteath, conducted early investigations of the central nervous system, discovered motor, sensory and motor-sensory nerves – the most important discoveries in physiology since Harvey's circulation of the blood – and gave his name to Bell's palsy. He had been a surgeon at Waterloo and in 1824 became the first professor of anatomy and surgery of the College of Surgeons in London. Four years later, he helped found the Middlesex Hospital and Medical School.

In the mid 19th century Scot John Bennett discovered the medicinal use of cod liver oil as a source of vitamins A and D, while surgeon James Braid pioneered the use of hypnosis in medicine. His 1843 paper used the word 'hypnosis' for the first time. In 1847, Sir James Young Simpson from Bathgate pioneered the use of chloroform during childbirth, despite both medical and religious objections. He, too, served as personal physician to Queen Victoria and she allowed him to use chloroform during the birth of Prince Leopold in 1853. He was the first man to be knighted (in 1866) for services to medicine.

In 1854 Edinburgh surgeon James Syme, professor of surgery at Edinburgh University (1833–70), helped found the General Medical Council. He was said to be the greatest surgeon of his time and developed new amputation techniques aimed at reducing trauma in an era before anaesthetics, of which he was also an early advocate. He reduced the time needed to amputate a leg, for example, to a minute and a half and he also experimented with what is now plastic surgery. He had been medical superintendent of Edinburgh's Fever Hospital, where he himself caught typhus in 1820. Two years later, when he was banned from practising at the city's Royal Infirmary, he founded his own medical school to teach anatomy and surgery. He was president of the Royal College of Surgeons of Edinburgh from 1850.

Professor Alexander Bain from Aberdeen was ahead of the field in the study of psychology. He was professor in logic and English at Aberdeen University, 1860–80.

Between 1876 and 1891 he published, at his own expense, *Mind,* the journal that became the primary outlet for English language philosophy. Francis Maitland Balfour from East Lothian was a zoologist and founder of modern embryology and younger brother of Prime Minister Arthur Balfour. His *Treatise on Comparative Embryology* (1880–81) laid the foundations for modern embryology. He died climbing in the Alps. Sir Thomas Lauder Brunton (1844–1916), from Roxburgh in the Borders, a physician best known for his work on the circulation of blood in the body, discovered that amyl nitrite could relieve the agonising pain of angina. His writings, covering the use of digitalis, amyl nitrite and enzymes, were published as *Collected Papers on Circulation and Respiration* in 1907. Gynaecologist Sir Dugald Baird (1899–1986), from Dyce, Aberdeen, was a pioneer of maternity and neonatal care. He publicly supported and advocated therapeutic abortion according to social criteria relating to the wellbeing of the mother. He performed abortions within the NHS from 1950 and advised David Steel MP on drafting the Abortion Act 1967.

More recently, it was another Scot, Sir Kenneth Calman who held the key post of the government's Chief Medical Officer from 1991–98. He had previously been chief medical officer for Scotland, 1989–91. His biggest crisis was the BSE outbreak. In 2006, he was elected chancellor of Glasgow University, where he had graduated, lectured, held the chair in cancer research and was dean of postgraduate medical education. In March 2008 he was appointed chair of the commission to review Scottish devolution.

As evidence of how well the travelling Scot fits into any society, a politician from Falkirk was voted 'The Greatest Canadian of All Time' in a 2004 poll by listeners and viewers of the Canadian Broadcasting Corporation and an Edinburgh-born professor was named 'Australian of the Year' in 2007.

Tommy Douglas (1905–86) was a preacher turned politician and said to be the best prime minister Canada didn't have. He won the 2004 poll because, said the citation, 'he had the most profound impact on the nation'. He earned that accolade for having introduced Canadians to universal medical care, car insurance, the minimum wage, old-age pensions and a mothers' allowance and for having ensured women had the right to drink alcohol in bars. He gave up preaching for full-time politics during Canada's economic depression and was an unsuccessful candidate for the Farmer Labour Party in the 1934 election. He won the following year and served in the national parliament for nine years. He then went back to Saskatchewan, where he became leader of the Co-operative Commonwealth Federation and, at the age of 39, provincial premier of the country's first socialist government. He served five terms, during which he introduced free hospital treatment and universal publicly funded healthcare. In 1964 he also launched the Saskatchewan Power Corporation, which provided energy to more than 65,000 homes.

The Australia Day Committee named immunologist Ian Frazer their 2006 Aussie of the year for his work in cervical cancer treatment and prevention. He developed the vaccine Gardasil, which is said to prevent about 70 per cent of cervical cancer viruses. Professor Frazer emigrated after graduating from Edinburgh University in 1980.

He is currently head of the Diamantina Institute (formerly Centre for Immunology and Cancer Research) at the University of Queensland and acts as an adviser on papilloma vaccines to the World Health Organisation and to the Bill and Melinda Gates Foundation. On receiving his award, he said he would use his new profile to ensure that his cancer vaccine reached those who need it most: women and girls living in poverty. Perhaps ironically, it was Scots who penned both 'Rule Britannia' and 'Advance Australia Fair' and cast the first dollar sign at a Philadelphia type foundry. In James VI, Scotland gave Great Britain its very first monarch. He became James I on the Union of the Crowns in 1606 and promptly introduced the enduring and unifying symbol of the Union Jack. I've had countless arguments over the years with pedants who insist that it should be referred to as the Union Flag but the King James proclamation calls it the Union Jack and that's good enough for me. It isn't for use on ships, incidentally, but can be used anywhere on land without permission (unless you're planning to run it up a particularly grandiose flagpole, in which case you might need planning consent for the pole!). The same royal also gave us, of course, the King James Bible, said by scholars to be a masterpiece of translation.

While we can't – nor would I personally want to – lay claim to the British national anthem, it was a Scot who stimulated its first use in the theatre and subsequently at so many other public gatherings down the years. 'God Save the King' was first sung in public in London in 1745, after Bonnie Prince Charlie had defeated the army of King George II just outside Edinburgh. In a moment of patriotic fervour and to show support for their king, the management of the Theatre Royal had it played at the end of the performance. On impulse, the audience rose to its feet... and a very British tradition was born!

That minor tilt at royalty apart, I have neatly sidestepped the complex royal blood-lines of Scotland as an area for commentary. In any case, I'm sure everyone would agree there is already a sufficiency of excellent books on the subject in the libraries and Hollywood has, for those who need their history to be entertaining, added plenty of cinematic spin to the adventures of Bruce, Wallace, Bonnie Prince Charlie and Rob Roy MacGregor *et al*! These are works with which I could not compete.

Perhaps appropriately for a Scot, Allan Ramsay opened (in Edinburgh in 1725) the first public lending library in the world, making books freely available to those who couldn't afford to buy them. I continue to show my appreciation of the good Mr Ramsay by regularly borrowing books from my local library. He is, I would assert, more than worthy of his place on a plinth in Edinburgh's High Street, and in our empire.

With education being one of Scotland's finest disciplines, it's not surprising that the distinguished educationist Sir Eric Anderson, from Edinburgh, has had a hand in teaching the Prince of Wales (when he was at Gordonstoun), former Prime Minister Tony Blair (at Fettes College) and current Prime Minister David Cameron (at Eton)! Another highly successful teacher was William Garden of Glasgow, who in 1910 invented the revolving blackboard. In 1929 he also, more lucratively, created the tote board, or totalisator, which transformed racehorse betting and saw it in operation for the first time the following year in Carntyne, Glasgow.

It is well known that Scotland has some of the oldest and most respected universities in Europe – St Andrews was founded in 1413, Glasgow in 1451, Aberdeen in 1495, and Edinburgh in 1583 – but it is less widely recognised that it can also lay claim to one of the earliest systems of compulsory education. This dates back to 1496 when, encouraged by Bishop Elphinstone, the founder of Aberdeen University, King James IV passed an Education Act decreeing that the eldest sons of all noblemen should attend school from the age of eight or nine. They were to study Latin and then go on to university to study law for three years. The new act was designed to improve the running of the country by producing well-educated judges to help keep unruly nobles in order, but despite the threat of a £20 fine for non-compliance, it was not widely enforced.

Education, such as it was, continued to be provided by the church. Certainly in the later 16th century, the leaders of the church in Scotland were keen that people should be literate so that they could read the Bible! In 1562, the General Assembly of the Kirk ordered that schools should be established in every parish. Sadly, despite further acts of Parliament in 1633 and 1646, there weren't enough teachers or schools to meet this worthy objective. The turning point came in 1696 when another act, that 'for the settling of schools,' ordered that a school should be set up in every parish and a schoolmaster appointed at an annual salary of up to £140. A number of benefactors also began around this time to establish their own schools to help the children of poor families. For example, George Heriot, the wealthy Edinburgh goldsmith, bequeathed more than £6,000 for the creation of a school in the city for 'poor, fatherless boys.' It was founded in 1628 and is still thriving today, although most of its pupils are fee-paying.

In those early days, the standard of teaching was variable to say the least because there was no recognisable training or assessment. That didn't really change until the 19th century when it was again the Church of Scotland that led the way toward establishing compulsory teacher training in both Glasgow and Edinburgh, although both the Catholic and Episcopal churches were also beginning to develop schools. In 1872, the Education (Scotland) Act established formal education for children from the age of five and brought schools under state control. Today, our schools retain many distinct features and Scotland can still lay claim to having a population that ranks among the highest-educated in the world.

To aid his contemporaries with their literary labours, Peter Roget (not a native Scot but a graduate of Edinburgh University, which paid for the research) devised a masterpiece of helpfulness. *Roget's Thesaurus* is probably the best crib sheet I ever found in my struggle to survive in the world of words. But then, I'm a journalist rather than anything as grand as a writer. I have always seen my role as that of a communicator passing on information. As will be painfully obvious from this book, I have never aspired to be a guardian of language, neither concerned about the splitting of infinitives nor enthusiastic about the conjugating of verbs. However, Mr Roget's work has never been out of print since it was launched in 1852 and that suggests it is of inestimable value to more than the journalists among us!

As a diligent hack, I'm also particularly pleased that it was Andrew Hamilton, an Edinburgh lawyer, who was the pioneer of freedom of the press and firmly established it as an essential plank in modern democracy. He was aided and abetted by fellow Scot and lawyer James Alexander. After he had emigrated with his family to America in 1695, he dabbled in journalism and, together with Benjamin Franklin, also helped found the American Philosophical Society. I hope that, were he still alive, he might nod an acknowledgement of my own recent endeavours to help establish an international Centre for Freedom of the Media.

To show even-handedness, I should perhaps also mention another Scottish émigré, one James Callendar, said to be the father of the less-than-edifying yellow press. He began his new life in America writing political pamphlets for Thomas Jefferson, but ended up muck-raking and libelling various presidents (including his former friend Jefferson) and was jailed for sedition after a libellous attack on President James Adams. In the same inglorious vain, the last firing squad in the UK consisted of eight Scots Guards: it was for the execution of the German spy Josef Jakob in the Tower of London on 15 August 1941.

In more recent times, the ubiquitous Personal Identification Number (PIN) was devised and patented by James Goodfellow, of Paisley, in 1966. He was an engineer in his 20s, working for the Glasgow company of Kelvin Hughes, when he was tasked with finding a way for customers to withdraw money from the bank outside normal hours. His answer was the PIN and he took out the patent in May 1966. Forty years later, he was finally recognised with the award of an OBE in the Queen's Birthday Honours of 2006. Although he had not earned a penny from his invention, Mr Goodfellow was quoted as saying he did enjoy a smile every time he used a cash machine! He added modestly that he 'had only been doing [his] job' when he dreamt up the concept, but the PIN led inevitably to the ATM, liberated us all from the shackles of the seriously limited-hours banking systems and gave us back control of our money – while stocks lasted, of course.

The word 'millionaire' was first coined for Edinburgh's John Law in the early 18th century. He founded the Bank Générale in Paris in 1715 and issued the world's first paper money. Like so many of his compatriots, he was also an inveterate traveller and his wealth was represented not only in ownership of the famous Place Vendôme in Paris and a library of more than 50,000 books but also of vast tracts of America (most of which is now in Arkansas). At one point, reportedly, he had more than £750 million in the bank.

His father, a goldsmith and money lender, died when he was just 12 and the inherited wealth quickly led the young John Law into a fairly dissipated lifestyle. His mother tried to persuade him to go to university but instead he ran off to London. There, he seemed hell-bent on enjoying his new-found freedom and, almost inevitably, wasted much of his inheritance on gambling and the city's pretty young things. He would have found himself in the debtor's prison had his mother not come to his rescue. With this second chance, he set out to regain his position as the popular young blade about town. Over six feet tall, dashingly handsome and extremely well dressed, he revelled in the nickname 'Beau Law'. He played the field of London's fashionable ladies and upset one love rival so much he found himself first in a disastrous sword duel and then in prison, having been found guilty of murder. But young Mr Law, still only 23, had almost as many friends as enemies and they rallied to him and somehow arranged his escape to France. There he met and eloped to Switzerland with a married woman, who he eventually married. It was then that he developed his interest in paper money as a way of overcoming the limitation of gold reserves. He decided to give Scotland the benefit of his brilliance but the bankers of Edinburgh, it appears, were either too sensible or too set in their ways to listen. His 1703 publication *Money and Trade Considered* went largely unread. So after ten years of struggling, it was back again to France, which was then in danger of an economic collapse. He somehow inveigled an association with the infant king's regent, the Duke of Orleans, and persuaded him on the idea of paper money. Soon, he had established what would become the Bank of France and later founded what we now know as New Orleans in the Duke's honour. As part of what was clearly a mutual admiration society, Law was showered with titles and riches by the French court. He was named King's Secretary and elected to the highly prestigious French Academy.

However, given his early reputation in London, it was inevitable that it should all end in tears. His banking system collapsed and, having lost the favour of his French sponsors, he ended up in exile in Venice in 1725. There he survived by gambling and when he died of pneumonia in a lodging house four years later, still only 58, one unflattering epitaph read: 'Here lies that celebrated Scotsman, that peerless mathematician who, by the rules of algebra, sent France to the poorhouse.'

Although the Scottish diaspora has spread, mostly gloriously, across the globe and left indelible marks in the most unlikely places, it's ironic that the two attempts to create something of a geographical empire by establishing colonies both ended in dismal failure.

The Darien venture – launched in 1698 by William Patterson, the Scot who had successfully founded the Bank of England just four years earlier – all but made Scotland bankrupt and saw the death of far too many brave Scots succumbing to the savage conditions in what had been promised as paradise. The Scots who, at the urging of Sir William Alexander and King James, settled in Nova Scotia and established the city of Halifax in 1749, were ignominiously thrown out after only 11 years and the territory returned to the French. It has to be said, however, that the usurpers had the grace to retain the Latin name for New Scotland. In their first occupation in 1604, they had called it Arcadia.

While my concept of the Scottish Empire is essentially about the men and women who have made their mark on the wider world, it would be impossible to overlook the global impact of *things* uniquely Scottish: tartan, kilts, bagpipes, whisky, porage (or porridge, if you prefer), shortbread, butterscotch, haggis, bannocks, oat cakes, black bun, Edinburgh rock, Dundee cake, the digestive biscuit, Irn Bru, Harris tweed, Fair Isle sweaters, Inverness capes, Aberdeen Angus cattle, Border collies, Scotch terriers, Shetland ponies, tossing the caber, curling, sword-dancing, the thistle and lucky white heather.

Then there's the geography. At the heart of my empire, in the auld country, there are place names that resonate with millions around the world. Even if they have never visited Edinburgh, people in the five continents still know about the Forth Bridge, Princes Street, the Castle (and its annual Tattoo, broadcast to millions worldwide), the Edinburgh Festival (launched in 1947 and rightly acknowledged as one of the world's greatest cultural events), even the sickly-sweet Edinburgh rock, unlike any other kind of rock, and the arch, Morningside accent that is unlike any other accent! Rivalling that is Glasgow: Sauchiehall Street, the Broomielaw and the great Clyde shipyards, source of so many of the world's most famous ships, the magnificent Burrell Collection, and the Gorbals, infamously representing the less attractive side of Scotland. There's Aberdeen and its timeless granite face; Paisley, and that pattern; Inverness, its nearby Loch Ness monster and the best English accent in the realm; Silicon Glen, centre of the sunrise industries; Fingal's Cave, its splendours expressed so evocatively in Mendelssohn's *Hebridean Suite*; the Mull of Kintyre, inspiration for Paul McCartney's hit song; and the Cairngorms, Skye, Iona, Loch Lomond, Ben Nevis, Scapa Flow, the Trossachs, St Andrews (home of golf), Gleneagles and Gretna Green, once known only as a haven for runaway brides and their lovers but not too long ago revelling in the up-and-down exploits of its football team!

We've also tossed a fair few of our unique words into the melting pot of the English language including decibel (after Alexander Graham Bell), watt (James Watt), divot (only well-known to golfers but originally the sod used to roof crofts), haver (to talk nonsense), glen, loch, cairn and dunce which derives from the name of the medieval theologian John Duns Scotus (1256–1308). His adherents were known as Dunses but that became a term of ridicule among 16th-century humanists, who mocked them for their theological hair-splitting and their hostility to new ideas. Very un-Scottish!

However, instead of simply asserting claims on behalf of my compatriots, let me offer Winston Churchill's endorsement: 'Of all the small nations on earth, perhaps only the ancient Greeks surpass the Scots in their contribution to mankind.'

2

Nobel Scots

 'He who never made a mistake, never made a discovery'
— *Samuel Smiles*

The ingenuity of my compatriots is truly astonishing. Down the years, Scottish engineers and scientists must have driven their families and friends mad with their anguished wrestling with problems and their manic delight in solving them. As the astute Mr Smiles suggests, there must have been many hiccups along the way but as with other aspects of my empire theory, we appear to have a better-than-average success rate. Most of the major, life-changing inventions are, of course, well tabulated, with libraries of books giving due testament to some of the greatest Scots including James Watt and the steam engine, John Logie Baird and television, John Boyd Dunlop and the pneumatic tyre, John Loudon McAdam and tarmac, Robert Watson-Watt and radar, and Alexander Graham Bell and the telephone. That allows me to simply nod respectfully in their direction and concentrate more on those of whom less has been written.

Apart from the enormous satisfaction of having their creations absorbed into everyday life, some of the brainboxes have also been well rewarded with glittering accolades such as the Nobel Prize. Established in 1901 (under the will of Alfred Nobel, the Swedish pacifist and chemist who, ironically, made his fortune from producing explosives… in a factory in Scotland), the prize honours its laureates 'for outstanding achievements in physics, chemistry, medicine, literature and for work in peace.' That seems to me a fairly solid platform from which to launch this chapter.

Nine Scots have been made Nobel laureates. They are well-kent figures, of course, and their achievements need little elaboration but, courtesy of the diligent reporting of many journalist colleagues at numerous newspapers, I can recount some of the personal details that serve to underline their ingenuity. By following the chronology of their awards, I can neatly sidestep any problem of rating their importance. They are Sir William Ramsay, born Glasgow, 1852–1916 (prize for chemistry, 1904); John McLeod, born Cluny, Perthshire, 1876–1935 (prize for medicine, 1923); Charles Wilson, born Glencorse, Midlothian, 1869–1959 (prize for physics, 1927); Arthur Henderson, born Glasgow, 1863-1935, won the 1934 peace prize; Sir Alexander Fleming, born Lochfield, near Darvel, Ayrshire, 1881–1955 (prize for medicine, 1945); Lord Boyd Orr, born Kilmaurs, near Kilmarnock, 1880–1971 (1949 peace prize for his work on nutrition); Lord Todd, born Glasgow, 1907–97 (prize for chemistry, 1957); Sir James Black, born Cowdenbeath, Fife, 1924-2010 (prize for medicine, 1988) and Professor Sir James Mirrlees, born Minnigaff, Kirkcudbrightshire, 1936, won the 1996 prize for economics.

The first Scot to be honoured by the Nobel foundation was Sir William Ramsay, for his discovery of five of the six noble gases: argon (with Lord Rayleigh), neon, krypton and xenon in 1898 and later, helium (the sixth is radon, discovered by the German Friedrich Dorn). The importance of Sir William's work is evidenced by the astonishing honours heaped upon him by scientific colleagues around the world. He was made an honorary member of the Institut de France, the Royal Academies of Ireland, Berlin, Bohemia, the Netherlands, Rome, Petrograd, Turin, Romania, Vienna, Norway and Sweden, the Academies of Geneva, Frankfurt and Mexico, the German Chemical Society, the Royal Medical and Chirurgical Society of London, the Académie de Médecine de Paris, the Pharmaceutical Society, and the Philosophical Societies of Manchester, Philadelphia and Rotterdam. He also received the Royal Society's Davy Medal, the Royal Society of Chemistry's Longstaff Medal, an honorary doctorate from Dublin University, a prize of $5,000 from the Smithsonian Institution, one worth 25,000 francs from France and the German Chemical Society's 1903 AW Hoffmann Gold Medal. He was knighted in 1902 and was also made a Knight of the Prussian order *Pour le mérite*, a Commander of the Crown of Italy and an Officer of France's *Legion d'Honneur*.

After reading chemistry at Glasgow University, William Ramsay went on to take a doctorate at the University of Tübingen under the renowned German chemist Wilhelm Fittig. He returned to Glasgow as an assistant at the Anderson College before being appointed Professor of Chemistry at Bristol University in 1879. Two years later, he became principal of the university but continued to combine administrative responsibility with active research in organic chemistry and on gases. In 1887, he moved to take the chair of chemistry at University College London, where his most notable discoveries were made.

For farmer's son Charles Wilson, a family holiday on the Isle of Arran and a fortnight as a volunteer at the Ben Nevis Observatory were the inspirations leading to the scientific work which made him the only Scot to win the Nobel prize for physics. He was 15 when he stayed on Arran and, with classic teenage inquisitiveness, soon became enthralled by close-up experiences of the beauty and wonders of nature. Arran, in the

Firth of Clyde between Ayrshire and Kintyre, is less than 20 miles long and only about 10 miles wide but it would be hard not to appreciate the amazing variety of landscapes and seascapes it contains. The coastline, with its sandy fringes, contrasts with the dramatic and rugged mountains to the north and the gently rolling green hills and woods to the south. By the time Wilson went back to college after his holiday, he had already resolved to make his career the study of the natural world in all its glory, and he spent hours in the laboratory looking down a microscope at the tiny specimens he had collected from local ponds.

Ten years later, after a change of direction from biology to physics and two desultory years of uncertainty about his career, he decided to spend a couple of weeks of his summer break from a teaching job acting as a volunteer observer on Ben Nevis. Enduring the routine of recording the weather every hour for a fortnight (to provide the basis of weather forecasts for shipping in the Atlantic), clearly instilled a discipline that was to stand him in good stead later in his career. More importantly, living on the peak of Britain's highest mountain in that September of 1894, he was again gripped not just by the beauty but also the power of the natural world, by the coronas and glories seen through the mist and by the ever-changing cloud formations. Fascinated he might have been, but according to his own recollections in the *Notes and Records* of the Royal Society, he was very much uncertain about his future career path: 'I could not imagine what career I was fitting myself for as there were remarkably few openings for trained physicists. I felt I might be of use as an explorer as I had some knowledge of a wide range of sciences and powers of endurance tested on the Scottish hills. The prospects of gaining admission into an electrical engineering works seemed rather remote.'

In the end, he decided to stay with physics, developing his interest in meteorology and using university resources to reproduce under laboratory conditions the cloud formations he had seen from Ben Nevis. From that eventually came the cloud chamber and the Nobel prize, 'for his method of making the paths of electrically charged particles visible by condensation of vapour.' The cloud chamber became an indispensable detection device in nuclear physics. Wilson studied atmospheric phenomena all his life and his work is said to be the basis of our understanding of what is involved in thunderstorms.

Charles Wilson shares the honour (with two other scientists with the same surname) of having the Wilson Crater on the moon named after him and he also gives his name to the Wilson Society (for natural sciences) at Sidney Sussex College, Cambridge.

As a diabetic, I have a deeply personal interest in John Macleod and his discovery of insulin. It's not exactly great fun jabbing oneself with a needle four times a day but it certainly beats the alternative! (I'm also grateful for the more recent work of two Glasgow scientists, John Ireland and Professor David Wyper, in developing the new pen-style syringe that makes the whole business of injecting insulin as easy as possible.)

A son of the manse, JJR Macleod as he is better known went to grammar school in Aberdeen and then on to study medicine at Marischal College at the city's university.

He graduated in 1898 with honours and the Anderson Travelling Fellowship. With that, he was able to work for a year at the Institute for Physiology in Leipzig. In 1899, then 23, he returned as demonstrator of physiology at the London Hospital Medical School, and was promoted to lecturer three years later. He then won another signal honour, a research studentship of the Royal Society which he held until 1903, when he was appointed professor of physiology at an American university. In 1918 he took up a similar post in Toronto and it was there, in 1921, that he linked up with the young scientist Frederick Banting, with whom he was to jointly receive the Nobel prize for their discovery of insulin. This was universally hailed as one of the most significant advances in medicine and insulin was being mass produced within months.

John Macleod wrote a number of books including *Recent Advances in Physiology* (1905); *Diabetes: its Pathological Physiology* (1925); and *Carbohydrate Metabolism and Insulin* (1926). In 1928, in failing health, he returned to Aberdeen as regius professor of physiology and consultant to the Rowett Institute for Animal Nutrition (created by John Boyd Orr). He died there at the early age of 59.

The University of Toronto named the auditorium of its medical science building after him and, as recently as 2005, Diabetes UK named its London offices in his honour. Among the many other honours bestowed on him, he was elected fellow of the Royal Society of Canada (1919), the Royal Society (1923), the Royal College of Physicians (1930) and the Royal Society of Edinburgh (1932); he was president of the American Physiological Society (1921–23) and of the Royal Canadian Institute (1925–26). He was awarded honorary doctorates of the universities of Toronto, Cambridge, Aberdeen and Pennsylvania, the Western Reserve University and the Jefferson Medical College. He was made an honorary fellow of Italy's Accademia Medica, corresponding member of the Medical and Surgical Societies of Bologna and Rome, a fellow of the Leopoldina Academy of Sciences in Halle, Germany, and Foreign Associate fellow of the College of Physicians, Philadelphia.

Few Nobel prize winners can have had a more varied career than John Boyd Orr. To describe him as a polymath seems a limp understatement. If you were to create a fictional character in his astonishingly dynamic image, no one would believe it.

He started working life before he was 18, as a student teacher at an infant school in Saltcoats, Ayrshire, and augmented his meagre salary of £10 a year by giving night classes in book-keeping and accountancy *and* working the odd day in his father's quarry. He won a Queen's Scholarship to complete his teacher training, and that covered both his classes and accommodation at a Glasgow college. When he finished there, he found teaching really wasn't his bag but he dutifully fulfilled his obligations under the scholarship. After that, he went to university to read biology, but with half an eye on a well-paid career he also studied medicine and qualified as a doctor. A bursary had covered his studies but not his living expenses and he inevitably ran up uncomfortable debts. His solution was to take out a mortgage to buy a small block of flats, which he then rented out! He still had an overdraft when he left university and to pay it off, he worked for four months as ship's surgeon on a merchantman trading between Scotland and West Africa.

Once ashore and debt-free, he took up a post as a family doctor but the lure of pure research proved too much. He gave up practice to go back into academia. Not just any academic job, of course. He went to Aberdeen University as professor of agriculture, in the belief that there was an established institute for animal nutrition. What he found, to his horror, was what he described as 'a wooden laboratory in the wilds of Aberdeenshire'. Undeterred, he set about with his usual energy and enthusiasm both fulfilling his professorial responsibilities and developing, from scratch, an institute for animal nutrition, the first of its kind in Britain.

At the outbreak of the First World War, he quickly saw where his duty lay. He set aside his great plans and signed on with the Army Medical Corps. Initially, he served with a unit assigned to improve sanitary facilities in the emergency training camps around Britain and, characteristically, he pushed through a number of schemes to improve conditions and prevent sickness among the young conscripts. But that was never going to be enough to occupy his febrile mind and he insisted on going to the front. He was attached to the Sherwood Foresters, joined the infantrymen in the trenches and tended the wounded. Again, his wholehearted commitment to the job in hand earned him the admiration of the soldiers and won him the Military Cross on the Somme and the Distinguished Service Order at Passchendaele. That might have been enough grim action for lesser mortals, but not the young Boyd Orr. He transferred to active service in the Royal Navy, where he still found time to undertake a close study of military diets.

He returned to Aberdeen in 1918 and resumed his research on his nutrition project with renewed conviction. There, he showed himself adept – though reluctant – at raising much-needed funds. He persuaded the wealthy businessman John Quiller Rowett, who had financed Shackleton's final polar expedition in 1922, to contribute to the development of the Institute. Equally importantly, he talked the government of the day into match-funding the scheme. In 1920, Mr Rowett provided the money to buy a 41-acre site and another £10,000 towards the building costs, while the government provided the rest. Two years later, the Rowett Institute was opened by Queen Mary.

The one proviso the benefactor had insisted upon was a clause in the raison d'etre of the Institute: if any work on animal nutrition was found to have a bearing on human nutrition, the Institute would be allowed to follow it up. Well, of course it did and, inevitably, John Boyd Orr's focus switched and his research led him into lobbying to improve people's diet. One of his proposals was the introduction of free milk for schoolchildren, an initiative that is credited with ending the problem of rickets.

When he retired from the Institute at the age of 65, he hardly paused for breath. He fought and won a parliamentary by-election in April 1945 and was elected as independent MP for the Combined Scottish Universities. He held the seat at the general election three months later but resigned in 1946... to concentrate on another new and massive job: that of the first director general of the UN's new Food and Agriculture Organisation.

From that strategic position, he advocated a worldwide food policy based on human needs rather than trade interests and he was the architect of many food policies designed to help starving nations. He influenced US policy and is credited with preventing famine in Europe. I almost forgot: he also became rector of Glasgow University and served as president of both the National Peace Council and the World Union of Peace Organisations! When, almost inevitably given his record of achievement, he won the Nobel prize in 1949, he donated the considerable associated money to organisations devoted to world peace and a world government. He was given a well-deserved peerage the same year.

Somewhere along the line, he found time to publish a string of works including *The National Food Supply and Its Influence on Public Health* (1934), *Food and the People* (1943), *Food – the Foundation of World Unity* (1948) and *The White Man's Dilemma* (1953). I once heard him speaking at a conference when I was helping to raise funds for the Freedom from Hunger campaign in the early 1960s. He was already into his 80s and had recently been elected the first president of the World Academy of Art and Science. I remember being inspired to greater efforts by his almost messianic oratory. John Boyd Orr's Nobel medal is in the Hunterian Museum at Glasgow University, where there is also a building named in his honour. There is a memorial to him in the Nobel Peace Centre in Oslo.

Alexander Fleming's discovery of penicillin changed modern medicine; it saved – and is still saving – the lives of millions of people around the world. But genius though he was, much of Fleming's major contribution to our health was due to several accidents of fate.

Like Charles Wilson, he was born on a farm and attended local schools and then, for just a couple of years, Kilmarnock Academy. He went to work as a clerk in a shipping office and was only saved from a mundane life of pen-pushing when, at 20, he was lucky enough to inherit money from an uncle. His brother was a doctor and it was he who suggested that young Alexander consider going into medicine. Thus he headed off in a new direction and got a place in the medical school at St Mary's Hospital in London. That was in 1901 and for the next five years he studied intensely and diligently, passing his exams with flying colours.

He had the option of becoming a surgeon but once again fate intervened. Coincidental with his training, he was also a member of the London Scottish Regiment of the Territorial Army and a keen marksman. That had led to membership of the hospital rifle club, where he again distinguished himself as a crack shot. The club captain, anxious not to lose one of his stars, suggested he had a look at a vacancy in the research department at St Mary's. He agreed. So, at the age of 25, Alexander Fleming became an assistant to one of the country's most eminent bacteriologists, Sir Almroth Wright, the pioneer in vaccine therapy and immunology, and set out on the career path that was to bring him so much success. He gained his BSc with Gold Medal in 1908 and then spent six happy years as a lecturer at the hospital.

When the First World War started, like John Boyd Orr, he immediately signed on as a captain in the Army Medical Corps. He too served in the battlefields of the Western Front and his bravery earned him a mention in dispatches. More importantly, he saw at all-too-close quarters the massive problems caused by wounds becoming seriously infected in the gross conditions. Field hospitals were not exactly the healthiest places on the planet and he watched in horror as thousands of soldiers died of septicaemia. The antiseptics being used appeared to be reducing the effectiveness of patients' immune systems faster than they could kill the bacteria.

After the war, he returned to St Mary's as professor of bacteriology and with a determination to solve the problems he'd faced in France. He quickly established a reputation as a brilliant scientist, but he also suffered a touch from the absent-minded-professor syndrome. Cultures he worked on were sometimes forgotten and his lab often appeared chaotic. Returning from one holiday with a little more perspicacity than usual, he saw some of his culture dishes had grown fungus and dumped them in disinfectant. When he retrieved them, he noticed there was a circle around a fungus where bacteria had not grown. As we now know, it was from that unplanned action came penicillin. Alexander Fleming had actually been trying to find a cure for typhoid fever!

That was 1929, but although he published details of his discovery in the learned journals, no one took much notice and he himself is said to have harboured doubts about its effectiveness. He was convinced enough, however, to try to find a chemist who would see the value of penicillin and have the ability to manufacture it in some quantity. It wasn't until 1933 that he used it successfully on a single patient and not until 1940 that the Oxford pathology team – led by Howard Florey and including Ernst Chain, the two with whom Fleming shared the Nobel prize – finally solved the problem. When he heard about their results, Fleming turned up at Oxford to be greeted with Chain's surprised reaction: 'I thought you were dead'. It took another five years before penicillin was finally stabilised and ready for the mass market.

Alexander Fleming was knighted in 1944 and subsequently showered with honours across the world. He was made an honorary fellow of all the great medical institutions, was awarded doctorates at more than 30 European and American universities and given the freedom of towns and cities by the score. He was even made an honorary chief of the Kiowa Indians. Inevitably, he was feted as a great celebrity towards the end of his life and he was given to presenting people with samples of his life-saving mould (suitably and safely contained in plastic, of course). The recipients are said to have included Marlene Dietrich, who told him penicillin had saved the lives of two of her family. During a visit he made to Spain, matadors knelt in the bullring to pay their tribute to the man who saved so many lives. He died from a heart attack in 1955 and was buried as a national hero in the crypt of St. Paul's Cathedral in London. He donated his Nobel medal to the National Museum of Scotland. In 2005, the readers of the *Scotsman* voted Sir Alexander the country's greatest inventor. He won by a clear margin over James Clerk Maxwell, while Alexander Graham Bell was in third place.

Having married the daughter of one Nobel laureate and studied under another, Alexander Todd may appear to have been an inevitable Nobel winner and this he duly achieved when he was awarded the prize for chemistry in 1957, 'for his work on nucleotides and nucleotide co-enzymes'. I quote out of a sense of minor panic because this part of the commentary takes me well out of my comfort zone in terms of trying to understand the full impact of his work. Fortunately his peers are there to help. At the presentation ceremony in Stockholm, a member of the Swedish Royal Academy of Sciences, addressed the new laureate: 'You have, with a rare tenacity and a wonderful acumen, pushed forward step by step into the enigmatic realm that now fascinates many of the keenest brains working in the field of organic chemistry: that of the fundamental structure of the cells.'

A businessman's son, Alexander Todd attended Allan Glen's School and then Glasgow University before going on to take doctorates in Germany (his thesis was on bile acids) and at Oxford. There he worked with Sir Robert Robinson, who went on to win the 1947 Nobel chemistry prize, on the structure of anthocyanins (pigments of flowers) and married Alison, daughter of 1936 Nobel medicine prize winner Sir Henry Dale. His first teaching post was at Edinburgh University (1934) and three years later he moved to London University. Within the year and at the age of just 30, he was appointed professor of chemistry in Manchester (1938) and then, in 1944, he became professor of organic chemistry and a fellow of Christ's College, Cambridge, where he remained until his retirement in 1971.

His work during that time, which included investigations of vitamins, enzymes and the constituents of cannabis, attracted scores of accolades both from his scientific peers and from admiring academics and politicians. He was awarded honorary doctorates, fellowships, honorary memberships and gold medals by the fistful. In 1952, he was appointed chairman of the Churchill government's Advisory Council on Scientific Policy and continued in that key role throughout the premierships of Sir Anthony Eden and Harold Macmillan until 1964. He was knighted for his services to science in 1954 and appointed to the House of Lords in 1962. In 1977, he was installed in The Order of Merit, the unique honour conferred personally by the Queen on 'individuals of exceptional distinction'. He died in Cambridge at the age of 90.

By his own admission, James Black – whose middle name was Whyte – daydreamed through most of his idyllic schooldays in rural Scotland. It was only his abiding passion for music that instilled any sense of self-discipline in him in the years leading up to the Second World War. It must have been a bit of a shock, therefore, when the colliery manager's son was persuaded by the man he called 'a brilliant and rumbustious teacher' to sit the entrance exam for St Andrews University. In his acceptance speech at the 1988 Nobel ceremony, he recalled: 'This led to an interview with the Vice-Chancellor, the redoubtable Sir James Irvine, flanked by elderly academic worthies, all poking into the mind of a nervous 15-year-old boy.' They obviously liked what they detected during their poking about and he was awarded a residential scholarship. Which is just as well because, as he discovered later, the family budget wouldn't otherwise have been able to cover the costs. So from high school in Cowdenbeath, he found himself transported to one of the world's finest seats of learning. He chose to study medicine and 'in the cold, forbidding, grayness of St Andrews learned, for the first time, the joys of substituting hard, disciplined study for the indulgence of day-dreaming.'

His reward for this conversion to scholarship was a couple of undergraduate prizes, a first-class degree... and a glittering career as one of the world's leading pharmacologists. He developed two major groups of drugs: the beta-blockers used in treating heart disease, and receptor antagonists for treating ulcers. He is also credited with introducing analytical pharmacology to the process of developing new drugs. The beta-blocker is considered to be one of the most important contributions to clinical medicine in the 20th century.

After graduating, he lectured at St Andrews and the universities of Malaya and Glasgow, where his research work on receptor antagonists brought him in touch with ICI's Pharmaceutical Division. In 1958, he joined them to develop his ideas. 'My six years at ICI were some of the most exciting of my life,' he said. 'I was assigned a brilliant chemist, John Stephenson. He taught me about modern deductive organic chemistry; how to be more than merely curious about a molecule with an interesting biological effect: how to ask questions about it. He converted me to pharmacology. Indeed, my whole experience at ICI was an educational tour de force. I had to learn how to collaborate across disciplines, how to change gears when changing from research to development, how to make industry work. In short, how to be both effective and productive.'

In 1964, he returned to academia as professor of pharmacology at University College London where, in 1976, he was elected a fellow of the Royal Society and won one of the most important prizes in medical science, the Lasker Award – the United States' equivalent of the Nobel prize. Two years later he had another spell in the more commercial world as director of therapeutic research for the Wellcome Research Laboratories, before going to King's College, Cambridge in 1984. To add to his glittering and much-deserved heap of prizes, he was knighted in 1981 and appointed by the Queen to the exclusive Order of Merit in 2000.

Significant as it is, the Nobel prize and its noble laureates represent only the tip of the iceberg of Scottish inventiveness and encapsulate only the 20th century. There was no shortage of ideas before then, nor indeed since and there's ample evidence of that in headliners such as Messrs Watt, Baird, Fleming and company and even more in the astonishing raft of less-celebrated personalities and their great ideas.

For no better reason than that it starts with an *a*, let me cite as my first example anaesthetics and the pioneering work of physician James Simpson (born Bathgate, 1811–70). I should confess that being a coward with a serious dislike of pain might just have shaded my judgement! Simpson was a remarkable character who went to Edinburgh University to read medicine when he was 14. He passed all the required exams by the time he was 18 but it was decreed that he was too young to be licensed and he had to wait a further two years before he was able to practise in 1832. Professor of midwifery (we would call it obstetrics today) at his alma mater by the time he was 28, Simpson held the post for 30 years and was a pioneer in the use of chloroform as a general anaesthetic in childbirth. He was also physician to Queen Victoria and it was her trust in him and her readiness to take chloroform during the birth of her son, Prince Leopold (later the Duke of Albany), in 1853 that was crucial in having the practice accepted universally.

He had by that point been developing his theories for several years but in echoes of more recent concerns about embryology, he encountered opposition from some religious groups. Chloroform had been discovered in the early 1830s by an American doctor (Samuel Guthrie), but there were those who believed its use was 'against Nature and the will of God' and some of his medical colleagues were distinctly cool about the idea. James Simpson first examined its properties in a brave personal experiment in 1847: he decided to test the required dosage by administering it to himself. He knew that if he inhaled too much, the overdose would kill him and if he didn't take in enough, it wouldn't knock him out. History records that he got it exactly right and chloroform became the anaesthetic of choice (over ether and nitrous oxide) throughout Europe. He also improved the design of obstetric forceps, fought against the scourge of post-childbirth infection in the genital tract, and was a vociferous advocate of midwives in hospitals.

In 1866, he was the first man to be knighted for services to medicine. Had the Nobel prize been in existence then, I'm pretty sure he would have been added to the list of laureates. Such was his reputation that when he died at the age of 58, his family were offered a burial in Westminster Abbey, but chose his local cemetery in Edinburgh. Scotland declared a public holiday and more than 100,000 lined the route for the cortège and 1,700 colleagues and friends joined the procession. His headstone bears the stunningly appropriate inscription 'Victo Dolore' (pain conquered).

Two Scots played key roles in the treatment of one of the world's greatest scourges: malaria. In the 18th century, Dr George Cleghorn (born Cramond, near Edinburgh, 1716–94) was the army surgeon who discovered that quinine extracted from cinchona bark acted as a remedy for malaria, a form of which was then endemic in Britain. More than a century later, Sir Patrick Manson (born Old Meldrum, Aberdeenshire, 1844–1922) established the link between the disease and the mosquito. The importance of these breakthroughs is underlined by the fact that even today malaria hits more than 200 million people a year and kills half a million, most of them children, in sub-Saharan Africa. Quinine, which dramatically improves the condition of the sufferer, was the first effective treatment and it remained the anti-malarial drug of choice until the 1940s. Since then, there have been many effective new drugs but quinine is still used in some critical situations.

George Cleghorn was only three when his farmer father died and his early education at the parish school was somewhat basic. When he was 12, however, all that changed and the ferociously bright young man was sent to Edinburgh to learn Latin,

French, Greek and mathematics. At 15, he moved on to the study of medicine under a mentor who was one of the university's most illustrious figures – Alexander Monro, the professor of anatomy who had founded the Edinburgh Medical School in 1726. Despite the intensity of his studies – botany, chemistry and the theory and practice of medicine – the by now 18-year-old George found time to help create Edinburgh Medical Society in 1734. It continues to flourish today as the Royal Medical Society.

Another of his professors was Andrew St Clair, whose brother was commanding officer of the 22nd Regiment of Foot (later the Cheshires). On his recommendation George Cleghorn – still only 19 – was signed up as the regiment's surgeon and soon found himself comfortably billeted on the Balearic island of Menorca. He served there for 13 years and balanced his time on regimental duties with continuing studies in medicine and researching the island's endemic diseases. When the regiment was posted to Ireland he went with it, but stayed in Dublin for just a year before resigning his commission to move to London. There he pulled all his Mediterranean researches together to produce his first book *Observations on the epidemical diseases in Minorca from the year 1744 to 49*. It was immediately successful and ran to four editions.

With his reputation as a writer assured, he succumbed to the romantic lure of the Emerald Isle and returned to set up practice in Dublin. This too turned out to be highly successful and over the years he established himself as one of the landed gentry with a large estate in County Meath. His passion for medicine, however, remained undiminished and, enthused by the lectures in anatomy he had heard from William Hunter at the Royal Academy in London, he took a teaching post at Dublin University. There he laid the foundations for a new school of anatomy.

Given the serious and global impact of malaria, it seems surprising that it was more than a century later – in 1877 – before Patrick Manson was able to demonstrate the link with the mosquito. As has been so often the case in medicine, he was actually searching for something else – possible treatments for elephantiasis, another tropical parasitic disease – when he made the discovery about the malaria-bearing mosquito. What makes this more remarkable is that he was working at the time in profound isolation, in Amoy (now Xiamen) in south-east China. He was a lone westerner thousands of miles from home, separated by a difficult language from the naturally suspicious and reserved Chinese, without intellectual peers and without the research facilities so readily available to his colleagues back in Aberdeen.

It was one of the most important medical breakthroughs of the time and it led to the introduction of effective preventative measures such as mosquito nets, insect repellents and drainage of stagnant water. Manson's pioneering work triggered the establishment of a whole new field of research and earned him the title 'Father of Tropical Medicine.' His pre-eminence was confirmed in 1899, when he founded the London School of Tropical Medicine.

At 15, Patrick Manson had been apprenticed to a local ironmaster but his delicate health caused a re-think and he went to read medicine at Aberdeen University. When he passed his final exams, he was still only 20 and too young to practise. Possibly frustrated by this hiatus, he accepted an exotic-sounding post as medical officer for the Chinese Imperial Maritime Customs Service in Formosa (now Taiwan). He was 22 by the time he arrived on station and it was there that he developed his lifelong interest in tropical diseases, including beriberi and sleeping sickness. After five years, he was transferred to Amoy. There, in between the routine of running a seaman's hospital, he embarked on more pioneering work after being confronted with elephantiasis on an all too regular basis. It was only after several failed suicide bids that one young despairing patient submitted to a suggested operation to remove a huge elephantoid tumour. Its success led to a string of patients and a dramatic upturn in Patrick Manson's reputation and, at last, an acceptance by the Chinese community. However, he was deeply concerned by his own lack of knowledge of the disease and, in the hope of finding a non-surgical treatment, he made the long trip back to Britain. Tropical diseases were not exactly top of the agenda in London and this fact clearly sowed the seeds in Manson's mind that would eventually lead to the founding of a specialist hospital there.

In the meantime, he returned to China, where demands for his services were to take him regularly to Hong Kong. He became part of an elite group which included the British colonial governor, trying to convince the Chinese that western medicine could, at the very least, complement traditional methods. Out of their combined efforts came the Hong Kong College of Medicine for Chinese and, in 1892, one of Patrick Manson's first graduates was the young Sun Yat-sen, who in 1912 became the first President of the Republic of China after leading the charge to overthrow the Qing dynasty. To have helped educate the man described as 'The Father of Modern China' must be seen as a signal honour but Dr Manson was probably more pleased that, in 1911, his school of medicine grew into the University of Hong Kong.

He, however, had left China before those turbulent days. He returned to Britain in 1889, hoping to resume his researches at home in semi-retirement in Scotland. Sadly, his investments in China had borne little fruit and his savings were not sufficient to fund that lifestyle so instead he set up a general practice in London. The comparatively sedate life in the city's West End clearly didn't suit him and in 1892 he signed up with the Seamen's Hospital Society to run a ward in the new Albert Dock Seaman's Hospital, treating some of the world's most travelled sailors. Manson was in his element. He continued to develop his interest in their diseases and firmly established tropical medicine as a new discipline. When, in 1897, he was appointed medical adviser to the Colonial Office, it was another step towards his dream. He convinced the colonial secretary, Joseph Chamberlain, and Chamberlain convinced the Treasury. In 1899, despite some opposition from the medical profession, the doors opened on his School of Tropical Medicine (now the London School of Hygiene and Tropical Medicine and part of the University of London). As a stimulus to students, he wrote *Tropical diseases: A manual of the diseases of warm climates*. Almost immediately it became a bestseller, and he was formally recognised as the world authority in his field. He was elected to the Royal Society in 1900, knighted in 1903 and the following year he was made an honorary Doctor of Science at Oxford University.

He retired in 1912 to fish in Ireland but returned to London at the beginning of the First World War. Despite crippling attacks of gout he continued to take a lively interest in medical education until his death in 1922.

It was the Edinburgh-born and very dogged naval surgeon James Lind who finally ended the scourge of scurvy, the great seafarer's plague that had wiped out more than half of the 1,955 men who sailed with Lord Anson's seven-ship fleet on his epic circumnavigation of the globe in 1739. The Spanish fleet sent to intercept him suffered even worse. There were only 100 survivors from around 3,000 sailors. The same year, 23-year-old Lind joined the Royal Navy as a lowly surgeon's mate to serve aboard ships sailing to West Africa, the West Indies and the Mediterranean. He was appalled by the unhygienic conditions and the privations the ordinary seamen underwent as we sought to rule the waves. He is quoted as saying that scurvy killed more British sailors than the combined enemy forces of the Spanish and French, and yet it was to take more than half a century for the British government to finally take notice of his exhortations.

As surgeon's mate, he was unable to do more than tend to the poor souls suffering terrible symptoms: 'putrid gums, loose teeth, spots, lassitude with weaknesses of their knees and haemorrhages.' However, in 1747 and with all the confidence of the fully-qualified surgeon that he then was, on board HMS *Salisbury* (a Royal Navy fighting ship of nearly 1000 tons and 50 guns) he carried out an experiment to determine how to deal with scurvy once and for all. He picked what today would be an unacceptably small sample of just 12 sailors suffering from the condition. He kept them all in the same fore-hold and gave them each the same basic diet: 'water gruel sweetened with sugar in the morning; fresh mutton broth often times for dinner; at other times puddings, boiled biscuit with sugar etc; and for supper barley, raisins, rice and currants, sago and wine or the like.' They were divided into six pairs and each given supplements to their basic diet: two were given cider, two vitriol, two seawater, two a mixture of garlic, mustard and horseradish, two had to swallow spoonfuls of vinegar and two ate oranges and lemons.

While there was no understanding of vitamins and their essential role in our diets, James Lind was quick to see the difference that the citrus fruit made. In his notes on the experiment, he wrote: 'The consequence was that the most sudden and visible good effects were perceived from the use of the oranges and lemons; one of those who had taken them being at the end of six days fit for duty. The spots were not... quite off his body, nor his gums sound; but without any other medicine than a gargarism or elixir of vitriol he became quite healthy before we came into Plymouth... The other was the best recovered of any in his condition, and being now deemed pretty well, was appointed nurse to the rest of the sick.' That should have been fairly conclusive evidence of the importance of fresh fruit but unfortunately no one in the Royal Navy establishment seemed to take any heed and James Lind was plaintive in the final line of his 1753 *Treatise of the Scurvy*: 'Perhaps one history more may suffice to put this out of doubt.'

He left the Navy just a year later and returned home to Scotland, not to sulk but to attend the University of Edinburgh in order to gain further medical qualifications and set himself up in private practice. The plight of the sailors never left him, however, and nothing if not tenacious, he rejoined the Royal Navy in 1758 as chief physician at Portsmouth naval hospital, and yet again turned his attention to the health of the crews on Britain's fighting ships.

In another experiment, he discovered that the steam from boiled salt water tasted like fresh rainwater and he proposed using the Sun's energy to distil water aboard ships, but the idea wasn't adopted until more than 60 years later, when someone came up with a new cooking stove that could double as a boiler. He had better luck when, in 1762, he recommended growing salad on wet blankets! That only took 13 years to filter through to her majesty's ships. It was not until the year after he died that James Lind's solution to the problem of scurvy was finally taken up by the Navy, and that was due to another, equally determined Scot, Gilbert Blane (born Ayrshire, 1749–1834).

Blane also studied medicine at Edinburgh University but then moved to London, where he became personal doctor to Admiral Sir George Rodney (later Lord Rodney) and was enlisted to serve as chief physician on his West Indies voyage of 1779. With this connection, he had the ear of both naval and civilian authorities and so he was able to improve the health of sailors by improving their diet and enforcing better hygiene. But even he had to labour for another 15 years before the Navy – in 1795 – finally agreed to include fresh citrus fruit in the shipboard diet. He was knighted in 1812 and made a fellow of the Royal Societies of London, Edinburgh and Göttingen, and of the Imperial Academy of Sciences of St Petersburg and the Royal Academy of Sciences of Paris.

James Lind – still plain mister – retired from the Portsmouth naval hospital in 1873 (to be succeeded by his son) and died 11 years later. He is commemorated by a plaque in the medical school of Edinburgh University. At a major conference in 1953, more than two centuries after his first clinical trial aboard HMS *Salisbury*, the Medical Director General of the Royal Navy, Surgeon Vice-Admiral Sir Alexander Ingleby-Mackenzie, said of him: 'To Lind… even thus far, we owe as much saving of human life as probably to no other man except perhaps the discoverer of vaccination.'

I can't think of the hypodermic needle without flinching, but once my muscles have relaxed, I can just about appreciate the efforts of Alexander Wood (1817–84), the Edinburgh doctor who first experimented with hollow needles in 1853. He was looking for a more effective way of administering morphine when treating neuralgia and to be sure that his syringe did what it said on the label, he gave it a very long label. In the *Edinburgh Medical and Surgical Journal* he described his invention as 'a new method for treating neuralgia by the direct application of opiates to painful points.' What he was aiming at was to develop a needle fine enough to pierce the skin comparatively painlessly (depending on which end of the needle you are looking from, of course) and deliver the morphine subcutaneously.

His success was confirmed by a Cupar GP, Dr Lindsay Bonnar, who wrote in the *British Medical Journal* of August 1857 about his use of the needle in a patient with neuralgia in the ischiatic nerve: 'The instantaneous effects of the first application of the narcotic surprised me much. I confess I should have felt very considerable alarm at the sudden plunge the patient made into the depth of narcotism had not Dr Wood assured me that he had seen the same in other cases and that it had never been followed by any unpleasant result... As soon as the remedy had been applied directly to the diseased point and had proved effectual there, the general system rapidly improved.' Dr Wood, who practised in Edinburgh's New Town, was secretary (1850) and later president of the Royal College of Physicians of Edinburgh.

William McEwan (born Isle of Bute, 1848–1924), who succeeded Joseph Lister as professor of surgery at Glasgow University, was as industrious as he was ingenious. He developed Lister's principles on the use of antiseptics and a sterile surgical environment. He was the first to operate on a brain abscess (1876) and the first to successfully remove a brain tumour (in 1878, while working at the Western Infirmary), laying the grounds for a new discipline: neurosurgery. He then went on to do the first bone graft (1879), the first excision of the lung (1895), and between times he devised the first formal training course for nurses in 1892. He was elected a fellow of the Royal Society in 1895 and knighted in 1902.

More recently, two other Glasgow University men – both English – pushed the boundaries of neurosurgery when they devised a method of measuring the effects of head injuries. Professor Sir Graham Teasdale (born Durham 1940, knighted in 2006) and Professor Bryan Jennett (born Twickenham 1927–2008) devised the Glasgow Coma Scale in 1974, with the aim of providing a reliable and objective way of recording a patient's conscious state. Considering more than a million people in the UK suffer some form of head injury every year, it was a major development and seven years later the pair produced a seminal textbook, *Management of head injuries*. Sir Graham served as chairman of the NHS board for Quality Improvement in Scotland from 2006–2010. He was president of the Royal College of Physicians and Surgeons of Glasgow until 2006 and also chaired the Scottish Academy of Medical Royal Colleges and the Federation of the Royal Colleges of Physicians of the United Kingdom. Always a controversial figure, it was Professor Jennett (with an American colleague) who introduced the term 'persistent vegetative state' for victims of brain damage who show no evidence of awareness.

Glasgow-born virologist Alick Isaacs (1921–1967) had been working at the World Health Organisation Influenza Centre in London for nearly ten years in 1957 when, with a Swiss colleague, he discovered and named interferon, the body's default mechanism against viruses. He had been studying our natural responses to different strains of the flu virus and was trying to find the still-elusive cure but, in one of those accidents of fate, stumbled upon something that was to have therapeutic effects on some cancers. I have long since learned to be cautious when writing about cancer and its treatment. Too many hopes have been raised and too many subsequently dashed and even now, more than half a century later, interferon is still described circumspectly on the *British Medical Journal* website: 'Does it work? We can't be sure. If your doctor thinks your melanoma is likely to come back, there's a good chance that taking high doses of interferon alfa-2b after surgery will give you more time before it does. But it may not help you live any longer and it has serious side effects.' But, clearly Alick Isaacs' work was a major development and he was appointed director of the flu centre (1961–64) and went on to be head of the laboratory for research on interferon at the National Institute for Medical Research from 1964 until his early death in 1967, at the age of 46.

When, in *The Lancet* in 1958, three Glasgow-based pioneers published their joint paper *Investigation of Abdominal Masses by Pulsed Ultrasound* they caused a positive revolution in medical care and especially in the maternity field. They were obstetricians Professor Ian Donald (born Moffat, 1910–1987) and Professor John MacVicar (born Mull of Kintyre, 1927–2011), and engineer Thomas Brown (born Glasgow, 1933) and the 50th anniversary of their pioneering work was celebrated in early 2008 with a day-long symposium at the Royal College of Obstetricians and Gynaecologists in London.

It was Ian Donald's wartime experiences of radar and sonic devices, gained while serving in the Royal Air Force, that triggered the complex research programme which came to fruition with the first ultrasonic image of a baby in the womb: 'From this point there could be no turning back. I think I shall always look back on that article as the most important I ever wrote and what is comforting is that all the conclusions which we reached at that time have since been vindicated by further results.' They have indeed. Today, ultrasound scans are, of course, routine and millions around the world have benefited from the technique.

As is so often the case, the discovery came about through a series of accidents, coincidences and people being in the right place at the right time. The trio came together in the early 1950s when Professor Donald was the regius chair of midwifery at Glasgow University, where, in his own words, he arrived with 'a rudimentary knowledge of radar from my days in the RAF and a continuing childish interest in machines, electronic and otherwise.' That childish interest was clearly shared by the young engineer who had talked his way into working alongside the professor in a remarkable collaboration.

Thomas Brown had a classic engineering background. He had been a pupil at Allan Glen's School in Glasgow and his early hobbies were model-making and building radios. When he was old enough, he became a technical apprentice with a scientific instruments firm, where he found himself using ultrasound for non-destructive testing of materials. His potential was spotted and the company sponsored him to study applied physics at Glasgow University. However, he was more of a hands-on researcher than an academic. He didn't finish the degree course and went back to his old job. But he'd heard about Professor Donald's work and how he was having to use old equipment... so he rang him. 'He sounded rather posh to this young native

Glaswegian but he was friendly and very courteous but told me that he had all the technical help he needed… However, I was welcome to come and see what he was doing.' He did, and was later able to persuade his company to lend the professor more up-to-date equipment. Then he joined the team.

The third element of the triangle was John MacVicar, Professor Donald's obstetrics registrar, and he confesses to having had no idea what impact their work would have. 'It was rather marvellous to see inside the body,' he recalled on the anniversary of the discovery in 2008. 'Of course there were X-rays, but to be able to tell the differences in soft tissue – that was something. We used echoes. It was exactly the same as radar on a submarine screen. We could see the baby moving. It was there and then it shifted.'

Success was not exactly instantaneous and it took time for the new technique to catch on with the cautious clinicians. Then, John MacVicar recalls, 'people suddenly thought "this is something really worthwhile". Then they started measuring the baby's head so you began to see the growth of a baby. That was really something.' The ultimate breakthrough came when Tom Brown developed a new, hand-held scanner that could be moved across the patient's abdomen. This gave more control of the angle at which the ultrasound wave was introduced into the body and produced the sort of detailed images that are now the stuff of so many medical television programmes showing happy mothers-to-be looking at their scans.

Medical imaging was also a passion of John Mallard, Scotland's first professor of medical physics when he took up the post at Aberdeen University in 1965. In his first lecture, he asserted that the then experimental PET (positron emission tomography) technique would become one of the most powerful tools for studying human diseases. He went on to pioneer work in magnetic resonance imaging (MRI). By 1980, he and his team had created the first 'clinically useful MRI image of a patient'. They were one of six research groups working to extend the technique already used in laboratories for chemical identification. They also created the first full-body scanner, which improved diagnosis and revolutionised treatment in hospitals around the world.

John Mallard, who retired in 1992, gave his name to the Scottish PET Centre opened in Aberdeen Royal Infirmary in 1998. He received the freedom of the city of Aberdeen in 2004 and in the same year the Institute of Physics and Engineering in Medicine established a lecture in his honour, to be given annually at the United Kingdom Radiological Congress. He was showered with many other honours by scientific peers around the world, and when he was awarded the medal of the European Federation of Organisations for Medical Physics, the citation said: 'the production of the first clinically valuable magnetic resonance images from patients in 1980 was a major scientific event. The benefits that his discovery have brought to thousands of people since then cannot be underestimated.'

Although Arthur Henderson (born Glasgow, 1863–1935) was the first Labour politician to serve in the British Cabinet, in 1915, and was twice leader of his party, he never made it to Downing Street. Ironically, that was due in no small measure to his integrity and sense of personal loyalty, qualities more fully recognised when he won the Nobel peace prize in 1934.

During his two years as foreign secretary (1929–31), his contribution towards world peace was remarkable. He re-established diplomatic relations with Russia (severed in 1917), achieved acceptance of America's Young Plan for German war reparations, persuaded the French to pull their troops out of the Rhineland earlier than the date stipulated in the Versailles Treaty, set the ball rolling for Egypt's independence (although sadly he didn't live to see it happen in 1936) and, as evidence of his determination and endurance, he attended every session of the Tenth and Eleventh Assemblies of the League of Nations. He was the crucial influence in the League's conciliation efforts. He steered through the controversial plans for a World Disarmament Conference and was unanimously approved as president for the opening session in Geneva in February 1932. But success – and the desperately sought-after peace – eluded him. With most of the world reeling from the economic depression, all his determination, persistence and hard work came to naught. Hitler withdrew from the discussions in October 1933 and, although Henderson managed to keep the other nations onside for a further year, his efforts ultimately failed. Even then, his optimism never wavered: at the Nobel ceremony in Oslo in December 1934 he still insisted that the Conference could be made to work and he remained chairman until his death in 1935.

There was further evidence of astonishing resilience. After first being elected as an MP in 1906, he lost his seat no fewer than four times (1918, 1922, 1923 and 1931) but bounced back on each occasion. In many ways, he was the archetypal Labour politician. His father was a cotton-spinner who faced long periods of unemployment and Arthur was therefore forced by circumstances to leave school at nine. He got a job as a messenger boy in a city photographer's shop and his meagre wage became even more important when his father died in 1874. His mother later re-married and the family moved to Newcastle when Arthur was still only 13. He immediately went to work in Robert Stephenson's locomotive works and despite working ten hours a day enrolled in evening classes, determined to achieve some semblance of an education. He later became a Methodist lay preacher and an active member of the Temperance Society.

After qualifying as a journeyman iron-founder at 17, he became a keen trade unionist and also formed a debating society for his workmates at the Stephenson plant. Within three years, however, he too suffered the anguish of unemployment and was out of work for more than a year. In an early show of his resilience, he put the time to good use: widening his educating and preaching on the north-east of England Methodist circuit. In 1892, he became a paid organiser of the Friendly Society of Iron Founders and was one of the worker representatives on the local conciliation board. He was a moderate and a believed strongly in non-confrontational industrial relations. He favoured arbitration and cooperation with the bosses and even went as far as opposing the formation of an early version of the TUC, because he feared it would increase the frequency of industrial disputes. He was one of the 129 delegates at the 1900 conference of all Britain's socialist groups (the Independent Labour Party, Social Democratic Federation, Fabian Society and trade unions). They agreed to establish 'a distinct Labour group in Parliament' and laid down tenets to 'embrace a readiness to cooperate with any party which for the time being may be engaged in promoting legislation in the direct interests of labour.' To manage the policy, they appointed the Labour Representation Committee (LRC) and charged it with ensuring 'working-class opinion being represented in the House of Commons'. Keir Hardie was the founding chairman and, despite some socialist opposition to his liberal views, Arthur Henderson was elected treasurer in 1903.

Later that year he was elected MP and in 1906 he chaired the conference that effectively created the Labour Party, becoming chairman when Keir Hardie stood down two years later. He took over the leadership when Ramsay MacDonald gave it up in 1914 (because of his opposition to the First World War) and joined Asquith's wartime coalition cabinet as education secretary the following year. In 1916 he became paymaster-general.

He found the coalition an uneasy alliance and within a year, frustration overcame ambition. When he failed to persuade his cabinet colleagues of the merits of an international peace conference, he resigned. Soon afterwards, he gave up the party leadership and in the 1918 general election, the electorate gave him up. He lost his seat. He came back in a by-election months later and was rewarded with the role of chief whip. He again lost his seat in 1922 but bounced back yet again in another by-election in 1924. He refused to challenge Ramsay MacDonald for the leadership and instead became his home secretary.

The latest Scottish Nobel laureate is Professor Sir James Mirrlees (born Kirkcudbrightshire, 1936), who shared the 1996 Nobel Prize for Economics with his colleague William Vickery for 'fundamental contributions to the economic theory of incentives under asymmetric information.'

I have to confess to needing to take a deep breath at this point because an economist I am not. I'm therefore indebted to Google for leading me to this explanation from the Chinese University of Hong Kong of what it describes as one of the key problems in modern economic research: 'Asymmetric information…is where different decision-makers have different information. For example, if the government thinks about raising income tax, it doesn't know if [someone] will then decide to work less hard than [they] do now. If the government doesn't know this, how can it set taxes so as to optimise revenue without stifling [the] incentive to work hard?' His colleagues say that Sir James's solution was so powerful that it has provided the basis for the construction of taxation systems around the world, and for an understanding of other markets and systems including insurance, auctions, wages, and share markets.

The son of a bank clerk, Sir James went to Douglas Ewart High School in Newton Stewart, where his ambition was to be a professor of mathematics. Once at

Edinburgh University, however, he found himself so comfortable with the subject that he was able to develop wider interests in literature, music, art and philosophy. He is reported as saying it was his study of utilitarian moral philosophy that led him to ask fundamental questions including 'what is a good life?' and 'what is truly rewarding?' The ensuing debate with other students took him on to wider questions of welfare economics. At Cambridge, he was deeply concerned with the moral issues of poverty and the distribution of wealth and chose economics as the basis for his PhD thesis. In the swinging 60s he began to work on what he saw as the neglected question of uncertainty and how, for example, it affected the optimal rate of savings in an economy. With his background in mathematics, he produced an original model for showing that 'uncertainty is a reason for saving more, not less.' After five years as a lecturer, he moved to Oxford University to take the chair in economics. It was here he did the work that led to the Nobel prize and which has become a principal constituent of the modern analysis of complex information and incentive problems in economics.

In 1995, he returned to Cambridge as professor of political economy, a post he held until becoming emeritus professor in 2003. He has also held numerous visiting professorships at seats of learning including the Massachusetts Institute of Technology, Berkeley, Yale, Edinburgh, Oxford, Peking and Macau universities. He has published widely and his papers include 'The economics of carrots and sticks' (in Stockholm 1996), 'Optimum taxation' (IIPF Congress 1997), 'The economic consequences of ageing populations' (Royal Society/British Academy Conference on Ageing 1997) and 'The theory of moral hazard and unobservable behaviour' (Review of Economic Studies 1998).

In 1997, he was knighted and awarded an honorary doctorate by Edinburgh University and the following year he was elected an honorary fellow of the Royal Society of Edinburgh. He has also received honorary degrees from many universities, including Warwick, Portsmouth, Brunel, Edinburgh, Oxford, Peking and Macau. In 2002, he was appointed Distinguished Professor-at-Large at the Chinese University of Hong Kong and four years later became master of the university's Morningside College. He also spends several months a year in Melbourne and is a member of Scotland's Council of Economic Advisers.

3

SCOTLAND THE BRAVE

 'Towering in gallant fame'
— Cliff Hanley

When it comes to bravery and military skills, I can't think there are many who would dispute that there's a place in the pantheon of courage for thousands of Scots down the ages. This small nation's military minds are so multifarious that it becomes difficult to assess their proper contribution to the disciplines of warfare. Throughout history, the individual stories of bravery are too many to adequately record and the battle colours of the great regiments speak for themselves. In developing strategies, weapons and even new forces, Scots have a pre-eminence all of their own and, in the Royal Scots, boast the oldest regiment in the British Army and possibly the world. But the real nobility of courage is found among those thousands of individual Scots who would never have seen themselves as anything but ordinary, peace-loving souls… until the call came, until their comrades and their country needed them most.

My notebooks are full of names, dates, events, heroic deeds, tales of self-sacrifice and commendations for brave leadership of the highest quality. This chapter does not purport to be a commentary of war, but rather a series of snapshots of the Scots who played a special part in battle. This will not be a short chapter. I have chosen as my benchmark of bravery the award of the Victoria Cross. The adventures recounted – albeit sometimes all too briefly due to lack of information – are, I think, worthy of a separate book. Each of the three great military services provides countless examples of the grit and guts that it takes to make a fighting man or woman and, to set it in context, it's important to remember the truly awful horror of the battlefield.

One grim day sums it up: 1 July 1916, the first day of the Somme offensive, in the middle of what has been called The Great War (in which more than 70 Scots won the

VC), and the bloodiest day in the history of the British Army. That summer's day in France, 60,000 British soldiers became casualties of the carnage indiscriminately visited upon them; 19,000 died. Many of them were still boys, away from home for the first time, missing their family and friends and totally bewildered by the multiple options of death on offer – artillery fire, raking machine guns, the sniper's rifle, grenades, deadly gas, drowning in mud, or the savage thrust of a bayonet when close combat became too close. It was a day when many young, inexperienced British officers led their troops into battle, armed with nothing more than a pistol in their taut fists and unbelievable courage in their hearts. They were cut down so fast that it was soon left to even younger and less experienced soldiers to try to regroup and rally their comrades.

One of those was who did so – and valiantly – was Drummer Walter Ritchie of the 2nd Battalion, the Seaforth Highlanders. Although he had briefly been an apprentice blacksmith, Walter Ritchie had known little else but army life. He lied about his age so he could enlist at 16. His regiment had been one of the first to be sent to France in 1914 and he had already seen action in several fierce battles. But nothing could have prepared him for that bloody day on the Somme. His regiment was ordered to attack at nine o'clock in the morning. They broke through the Germans' first three lines of defence, but at a price: their ranks were decimated by heavy machine guns. The 25-year-old Glaswegian, who had spent hours ferrying messages between front-line commanders, saw the danger of demoralisation among the troops. He saw, presumably instinctively, that it was up to him to help as best he could. In the face of the Germans' scything machine guns and lacerating shrapnel, he ignored the danger to himself. He stood full-square on the parapet of an enemy trench and continually rattled out the charge while the Germans concentrated their machine guns and rifles in his direction. It was an act of outstanding valour and it won him the Victoria Cross. Of his act of courage, the citation said: 'This served to rally many men of the various units who, having lost their commanders, were wavering and wanting to retire from the fighting. During the day, over ground that was swept by enemy fire, Drummer Ritchie carried messages.' The French also awarded him the *Croix de guerre* and he was later promoted to drum major. He was gassed twice and wounded twice but survived the war. He was in the guard of honour when Queen Elizabeth held a centenary review of VC holders in Hyde Park in 1956. His medal is privately owned after being sold at auction.

It's important not to underplay the gruesome context of these actions. Not only were the soldiers faced with the enemy, but they had to survive the awful conditions on the battlefield. In his book *Twelve Days on the Somme*, Sidney Rogerson, a 22-year-old infantry captain when he served in France, recalled how he was ordered to take his men out of the front line to recover. The only resting place was the site of previous pitched battles. He wrote: 'Men vomited over the task of building new trenches, for bodies were unearthed at every yard. The deepening of the front line turned a German officer out of the mud at our very feet. Further digging led into an overgrown trench full of French skeletons from 1914. Most pitiful, an attempt to straighten a piece of trench broke into an old dug-out where sat three Scottish officers, their faces mercifully shrouded by the grey flannel of the gas masks they had donned before death came upon them.'

Men slept whenever and wherever they could. Often they were only able to slump to the ground, sitting in the cloying mud, held upright by their limited equipment, 'reminiscent of figures in a prehistoric burial ground,' as one officer put it. A former Highland Brigade sergeant I interviewed on the 50th anniversary of the battle recalled: 'I don't know if I ever really slept. My eyes would sometime shut involuntarily but never for very long. The mud was freezing. The air was thick with shell fumes... and worst of all, the stench of death. Bodies lay around in grotesque tableaux. Some were missing limbs. Some were only recognisable as bodies by the scraps of uniform that still clung to blackened bones. But you could not mistake the smell... or get away from it.' On top of that, there was the constant, deadly stutter of heavy machine guns, bullets screaming through the air, shells exploding and planes buzzing angrily overhead. Ironically, these were noises that reassured the men that they were still alive. It was the silence that got to you, said the soldiers.

For the Scots on that grim battlefield, the only heartening sound was the skirl of the pipers and the rattle of the drummers (including Walter Ritchie) defiantly playing their regimental tunes. It somehow gave them the strength to drag their weary bodies through the mud, crawling slowly but ever closer to the enemy. Sometimes they had the shelter and support of a creeping barrage of artillery shells and occasionally they were able to clamber along in the lee of armoured vehicles, but more often than not it was only iron self-discipline and ferocious pride that kept them inching forward.

It was also on the Somme – but sixteen months later – that another Seaforth Highlander, 19-year-old Robert McBeath (born Kinlochbervie, Sutherland, 1898–1922), became the youngest ever Scottish soldier to receive the VC. His was not a single act of great bravery but, according to his CO, 'conduct throughout three days of severe fighting [that] was beyond all praise.' His citation in the *London Gazette* of January 11, 1918, read: 'For most conspicuous bravery west of Cambrai, France, on November 20, 1917, when with his company in attack and approaching the final objective, a nest of enemy machine guns in the western outskirts of a village opened fire both on his own unit and on the unit on his right. The advance was checked and heavy casualties resulted. When a Lewis gun was called for to deal with these machine guns, Lance Corporal McBeath volunteered for the duty and immediately moved off alone with a Lewis gun and revolver. He found however, several other hostile machine guns in action and, with the assistance of a tank, attacked them and drove the gunners to ground in a deep dug-out. Lance Corporal McBeath, regardless of danger, rushed in after them, shot an enemy who opposed him on the steps and drove the remainder of the garrison out of the dug-out, capturing three officers and 30 men. There were in all five machine guns mounted round the dug-out and by putting them out of action, he cleared the way for the advance of both units.'

After the war, in 1920, Robert McBeath emigrated to Canada, where he joined the British Columbia Provincial Police (and later the Vancouver City Police). Two years later, in a tragic irony considering what he had survived on the Somme, McBeath was fatally shot while attempting to make a routine arrest. A police marine vessel was named in his honour and in Kinlochbervie, a small housing development is called McBeath Court.

In an incident on another French battlefield around a year and a half earlier, another young Scot, Lance Corporal William Angus (who had played football for Celtic before the war), performed what was described by his commanding officer as 'the bravest deed in the history of the British Army' and he, too won the VC. The Royal Scots were in a front-line trench on the outskirts of Givenchy in northern France. Only 70 yards lay between them and the Germans, who for many weeks had held a strategic point on top of a small embankment protected by a parapet. It gave them an elevated view over no man's land and that allowed them to hold up the British advance.

During the night of the 11th of June, it was decided that a raiding party led by Lieutenant James Martin would launch yet another attack to try to dislodge the enemy. However, the Germans had mined the area and a huge explosion, which left a crater more than 15 feet wide, forced the Scottish troops to hastily retreat to their own trenches. As they regrouped, Lieutenant Martin was missing. He was a very popular young officer – just 23 – and this hit his men hard. When dawn broke, they could see him lying close to the parapet and the enemy machine guns. They saw him stir, barely conscious but obviously alive. Luckily he was so close to the parapet that the Germans couldn't see him and couldn't bring their guns to bear on him. As the sun became stronger, the young Scottish officer pleaded for water but the German response was to lob a grenade over the parapet.

The Royal Scots were outraged and 28-year-old Lance Corporal Angus immediately volunteered to attempt a rescue. Senior officers said it was too dangerous, but Angus was adamant, explaining that he and Martin both came from Carluke. 'I can't go back home knowing that I'd left him to die,' he said.

His pleas were rejected until the arrival of a brigadier, who reluctantly agreed to let him try, with the warning that he was facing certain death. William Angus is said to have replied that it didn't matter much to him whether death came then or later! A rope was tied around the lance corporal so he could be dragged back if he was killed or seriously wounded. He squirmed inch by inch across the open ground so effectively that he reached the badly wounded officer without being seen by the Germans. He transferred the rope lifeline to the officer, raised him up and gave him a sip of brandy in preparation for the long, hazardous return to his own trench.

As he got Martin to his feet and began to half carry him unsteadily back across the 70 yards of no man's land to the safety of the trench, the Germans spotted them and spewed out a hail of deadly fire.

Angus was hit no fewer than 40 times. Several times he fell to the ground under the force of the bullets, only to somehow get up again to continue guiding his officer towards safety. Luckily, the German guns had created so much smoke and dust that their snipers couldn't get an accurate aim. Eventually, the lance corporal got to the point where he was able to signal his colleagues to use the rope to pull the officer in the rest of the way while he turned off at right angles to draw the enemy fire.

Somehow, he too made it back to the trench, where he collapsed and was rushed to a medical station. His injuries were to cost William Angus his left eye and part of his right foot. In a letter to William's father, his CO wrote: 'Your boy went gladly to what was almost certain death, determined to try and rescue his officer. That he ever returned was a miracle. The General has sent forward his name for the Victoria Cross and that he will get it there is little doubt, as no braver deed has ever been done in all the history of the British Army. Your son has no fewer than 40 wounds, many of them serious, some very slight, but I am glad to say the doctors say there is no fear for him and he will recover from them all. Mr Martin, you will be glad to hear, will also recover. Just in closing may I say how proud we all are to have such a man as your son in our battalion and to have seen such a deed as this has been the privilege of few.'

There were many other tributes paid, not least by the King, but the one that always mattered most to William Angus came from Lieutenant James Martin. At a homecoming ceremony in Carluke, Lieutenant Martin was so emotional he found it difficult to speak: 'I know you will bear with me if I do not make a long speech. My heart is too full for words. When I lay on the German parapet that Saturday in June, my plight seemed hopeless but Angus at the risk of his life came out and saved me. Carluke may well be proud of her hero. For it was an act of bravery second to none in the annals of the British Army. Corporal Angus, I thank you from the bottom of my heart. I hope you will soon be restored to your wanted health and strength and that you may be long spared to wear this watch and chain which please accept as a small memento of that day.' The two men became firm friends. On every anniversary of the amazing rescue, James sent a telegram repeating his deep gratitude to William, and after James's death in 1956, his brother continued the tradition. Despite his serious injuries, William Angus later became Master of Works for the Racecourse Betting Control Board, a local magistrate and president of his beloved Carluke Rovers. He died in 1959 and his headstone in the local cemetery bears the VC insignia. The town has also named a street in his honour.

Four million British soldiers fought in the Great War. Nearly half of them were wounded and more than 670,000 never returned to their loved ones.

The Victoria Cross is, of course, the most important of all Britain's bravery medals. It is awarded 'for valour in the face of the enemy.' When she established it in 1856, Queen Victoria specified the use of the word 'valour' because, she said, everyone who served their country in time of war was brave and courageous. It was also the first medal for which lower ranks had been eligible: previous awards were for officers only; the men received campaign medals to show they had served there! To date, 1,357 VCs have been awarded to members of the British and colonial armed forces. Three men have won it twice, including Captain Noel Chavasse, a medical officer with the Liverpool Scottish

Regiment, and one was symbolically awarded to the American Unknown Soldier. Most of the hard won medals are held and proudly displayed in the National War Museum in London, others in the various regimental headquarters, but many more are still in private ownership and have changed hands for anything up to the £235,250 paid at auction in 2004 for the VC won in 1944 by Sergeant Norman Jackson of the RAF. Such is the price of glory.

All too many of the medals were awarded posthumously and, even worse, many brave men lie in unmarked graves on the former battlefields. The grimness of the wars had serious mental and physical impacts on some of the medal-winners, as it did, of course, on thousands of their comrades. Too many of their post-war stories make very sober reading. It should also be said, of course, that many thousands of servicemen and women who merited the award never received it because their actions went unnoticed by senior figures, or the witnesses were killed, or their self-sacrifice resulted in a lonely death and an unmarked grave. Equally, I should reiterate that I'm looking at the concept of bravery through a prism of narrow self-interest: I'm concentrating only on examples relevant to *my* theory of Scottish Empire. This shouldn't be taken as a suggestion that Scots are in any way braver than other nations, but simply that they played their part.

Most reference books suggest 158 Scots have been awarded the VC but my far-from-academic research suggests slightly more than that. There is, however, some uncertainty over two or three who could be non-Scots serving in Scottish regiments and a number of Scots-born soldiers with colonial forces. I have compiled a list of 169 but make no claim about its comprehensiveness.

CRIMEAN WAR

The award was back-dated to recognise the special service given by those who were served in the Crimean War (1854–56) and at the first investiture, in London's Hyde Park on 26 June 1857, 62 of the first recipients lined up to receive their awards from a grateful Queen. Twelve of them were Scots: Sergeant Major John Grieve, 2nd Dragoons; Corporal John Ross and Sapper John Perie, both Royal Engineers; Brevet Major Robert Lindsay, Sergeant James McKechnie and Private William Reynolds, all of the Scots Fusilier Guards; Lieutenant William Hope, 7th Royal Fusiliers; Private Samuel Evans, 19th Foot; Captain William Cuninghame, Sergeant John Knox, Private Roderick McGregor, all of the Rifle Brigade and Captain Charles Lumley, Queen's Own Royal West Kent Regiment.

As *The Times* reported: 'On parade were a large body of troops under Sir Colin Campbell [the Scottish general who, only six months later, succeeded in breaking the siege of Lucknow during the Indian Mutiny] 'comprised of Life Guards, Dragoons, Hussars, Royal Engineers, Artillery and Line Regiments, together with a detachment of Bluejackets from the Royal Navy. Just before ten o'clock in the morning, following a royal salute from the artillery, her Majesty, the Prince Consort, the Crown Prince of

Prussia, the Prince of Wales and the Queen's son Prince Alfred rode into the park and took places near the dais prepared for them. The Victoria Crosses lay upon a small table covered with scarlet cloth. The 62 recipients stood at ease some distance off and came forward one at a time as Lord Panmure, Secretary for War, read their names. The presentation of the crosses was followed by a military review and the proceedings were finished.'

Such is the dryness of that report that one could be forgiven for not realising the events being commemorated included the disastrous charge of the Light Brigade 'into the Valley of Death' (as Tennyson put it), the famous Battle of Balaclava in which the heroic 'thin red line' of the 93rd Highland Regiment (later to become the Argyll and Sutherland Highlanders) stood firm against the Russian cavalry charge, other ferocious battles at Alma and Inkerman, and the long, savage siege of Sebastapol. This was the Crimean War, fought between the Russia Empire and an alliance of Britain, France, the Kingdom of Sardinia and the Ottoman Empire. It's seen as the first modern conflict and introduced technical changes which affected the future course of warfare. Much of the fighting took place on the Crimean peninsula (now Ukraine) in the Black Sea.

In Scottish terms, the performance of the 'thin red line', the turning point at Balaclava, was the finest hour of the 93rd Highland Regiment during the Crimean campaign. Led by Sir Colin Campbell, commander of the Highland Brigade, the 93rd had already taken part in fierce battles at Alma and Sebastopol but on October 25 1854, together with two other small forces, they faced an enormous challenge: to stop the Russians reaching and destroying the British encampment at Balaclava, a small harbour used by local fishing boats. The fearsome Tsarist cavalry, 2,500 of them with sabres flashing in the early-morning light, rode imperiously down the road to Balaclava. All that lay between them and the clearly vulnerable British supply base was that thin red line.

While the military convention of the day was for the defending infantry to line up four deep, Sir Colin set his troops in just two rows so that the line could be more effectively stretched across a broader front. It looked a classic mismatch, almost suicidal, and Campbell is said to have told his regiment: 'There is no retreat from here, men. You must die where you stand.' To which his aide replied simply and without emotion: 'Aye, Sir Colin. If needs be, we'll do that.' Campbell then ordered that no shot should be fired until the mounted Russians were at close quarters. When a vicious first volley failed to stop the advance, he had his men wait until the charging cavalry was no more than 50 yards away – less than half the length of a football pitch – before he ordered the second hail of fire. This broke the charge and the Tsar's cavalrymen scattered in utter confusion. To capitalise on their success, the Scots instinctively set off in pursuit but Sir Colin stopped them in their tracks with the cry: 'Damn all that eagerness!' In reporting the battle, the *Times* war correspondent, William H. Russell, said he could see nothing between the charging Russians and the British base of operations at Balaclava except 'the thin red streak tipped with a line of steel' that was the 93rd, and that popularly became the thin red line, a phrase that seemed to epitomise British sangfroid in battle.

This might give the impression of a clean and clinical rout of the enemy but, as always, the small print reveals a very diffcrent story. Two members of the regiment were cited for Victoria Crosses that day and their commendations reveal something of the horror, brutality and gore of the battle. Sergeant John Grieve, from Musselburgh and serving with the 2nd Dragoon Guards (Royal Scots Greys), saved the life of an officer who was surrounded by Russian cavalry, 'by his gallant conduct of riding up to his rescue and cutting off the head of one Russian, disabling and dispersing others.' His exploits were well reported in the newspapers of the day and Charles Dickens gave an excellent contemporary commentary on young Sergeant Grieve's brand of courage in an early edition of his journal *All the Year Round*. He wrote: 'It is not a thing that should be suffered to die away. When he cut off a soldier's head at a blow and disabled and dispersed several others, he had no very exciting motives of self-devotion. Pay, promotion or popularity could not well enter his head, for he knew the rules of the Service about rising from the ranks, and he knew, too, that the British public rarely asks the names of the poor privates and non-commissioned officers who fall. What John Grieve did, then, was an act of the purest and most unselfish heroism; but I daresay, when the Queen pinned the Victoria Cross to his breast in Hyde Park that day, he felt he was more than rewarded for what to him was a very ordinary matter-of-fact bit of duty.' Unlikely as Dickens found it, John Grieve did later rise from the ranks to lieutenant and served as adjutant to his regiment. His medal was sold at auction in 1966 for £700.

The other Balaclava VC went to 27-year-old Sergeant Henry Ramage, also of the 2nd Dragoons, from Edinburgh. His citation reveals yet another act of heroism in which he unhesitatingly took on the enemy to save one of his soldiers: 'On October 25 1854 at Balaclava, Sergeant Ramage galloped out to the assistance of a private who was surrounded by seven Russians. The sergeant dispersed them and saved his comrade's life. On the same day, he brought in a prisoner from the Russian line and also, when the Heavy Brigade was covering the retreat of the Light Cavalry, lifted from his horse a private who was badly wounded and carried him safely to the rear under heavy cross-fire.' His Victoria Cross is in the Royal Scots Dragoon Guards Museum in Edinburgh Castle.

The first clash of the war had been a month earlier, at the River Alma on September 20, exactly a week after the British-French forces had landed on the western coast at Calamita Bay (ominously nicknamed 'Calamity Bay'), about 25 miles north of Sebastopol. After weeks at sea, the soldiers were seriously weakened by diseases such as cholera and dysentery. They were also disoriented and, it has to be said, disorganised. They were very lucky their landing was not contested by the Russians and they managed to establish a beach-head four miles inland. That allowed an essential degree of consolidation but, six days later, they headed south towards Sebastopol. It was not an easy journey. A young Scottish soldier wrote in his diary: 'We passed over large tracts of open ground, my water supply failing. I was all but done up and going to lie down, when the colonel gave me a spoonful of brandy. This kept me going until we reached the ground where we had to pass the night. Several of our men died from cholera and were buried before we had fired a shot. Early next morning, we stood to arms and after much delay, the Army moved on and came within sight of the enemy's forces posted on the high ground beyond the Alma.'

The Alma was the second of three rivers the British forces had to cross en route for Sebastopol and it was there that the Russians decided to make their stand. They had greater numbers and were in a strong, natural defensive position on the south bank of the river, where the cliffs rose to 350 feet. They had also established a series of formidable redoubts that gave them wide fields of fire. This did not deter the British generals, as our young Scot reports: 'The division was ordered to advance to support the Light Division, the Russians firing heavily but did little execution.'

The writer was John Knox, a 25-year-old sergeant in the Scots Fusilier Guards, in a letter home, and he went on to describe what happened next: 'At last we crossed the river and on reaching the path on the opposite side running parallel with the river, the battalion, still in line, began to reform their ranks. Repeated and pressing requests came several times from the Light Division asking us to hurry to their support. Before the ranks were properly reformed, Sir Charles Hamilton ordered the battalion to advance and away they went, leaving, to my surprise, many of our men under the shelter of the river bank. I did all I could to clear them out and send them on to glory, before passing over myself and to my surprise found our battalion retiring, mixing up with the men of the Light Division.

'Captain Scarlett [later Major General Sir James Scarlett and Conservative MP for Guildford] was frantic, flourishing his sword and violently exerting himself to stop the retreat, asking me to help. By good fortune an old campaigner, Bill Douglas, was nearby and I called upon him to stand still, face the enemy, and fire. Without any hesitation, the old soldier obeyed. I got others to join him and about the same time order was restored in the ranks, the line reformed and file-firing opened on the enemy. This fire, combined with cross-fire from the left company of the Grenadier Guards, quickly settled the enemy and enabled us without any loss to capture the Russian battery.

'During the time our men were firing, an order was passed down the line for us to retire and some of the companies had actually faced about, when I persuaded Colonel Dalrymple we were making a serious blunder, our interests urgently requiring an advance and not to retreat. Colonel Dalrymple took my view and stopped it. After capturing the battery, there was no more fighting; we remained in possession of the field, the enemy's troops retiring.'

Sergeant Knox, from Glasgow, was overly modest about his role in the battle. His courage throughout the Crimean campaign was of the highest order. When he won the French *Légion d'honneur*, the citation said: 'Sergeant Knox behaved with conspicuous courage in re-forming the ranks of the Guards at a decisive moment of the action.' He was promoted to the rank of lieutenant in the Rifle Brigade and the following year was again commended, this time 'for valour' during the siege of Sebastopol; his VC citation said: 'On June 18, 1855, he volunteered for the ladder party in the attack on the Redan, acting with great gallantry and remaining on the field until twice wounded.' The attack, on this occasion, was unsuccessful. Lieutenant Knox lost his left arm and saw one of his brother officers die alongside him. Despite that, he was promoted to brevet major and saw out the rest of the war. He was personally decorated by Queen Victoria at that first investiture in Hyde Park.

Another Scot who fought at Alma but won his VC in a later battle was Captain Robert Lindsay, also of the Scots Fusilier Guards, and he too is credited with rallying the troops. 'When the form of the line of the regiment was disordered, Captain Lindsay and a group of other officers stood firm with the colours,' said his commanding officer. 'They rallied a party of men about them and held their ground against overwhelming odds until the enemy retired on seeing the remainder of the battalion coming up the hill.' His VC citation describes the second example of his courage: 'On November 5, at a most trying moment, Captain Lindsay, with a few men, charged a superior party of Russians at Inkerman, causing them to retreat and running one of them through the body himself.'

Following his return from the Crimea, Robert Lindsay was the first soldier to receive the VC from Queen Victoria in the Hyde Park ceremony. He retired with the rank of lieutenant-colonel and was appointed equerry to the Prince of Wales. In 1885, he was created Baron Wantage of Lockinge for his role in founding of what was to become the British Red Cross Society. After he died in 1901, a marble cross was erected in his memory and it can still be seen on the Ridgeway in Oxfordshire, about a quarter of a mile east of its junction with the B4494.

The two Scots awarded the VC for their part in the battle at Alma River were 27-year-old Private William Reynolds, from Edinburgh, and 28-year-old Sergeant James McKechnie, from Paisley. Both were with the Scots Fusilier Guards and both are credited with rallying their dispirited comrades at crucial moments in the battle. Private Reynolds' citation reads: 'On 20 September 1854 at the Battle of the Alma, Crimea, when the formation of the line was disordered, Private Reynolds behaved with conspicuous gallantry, in rallying the men round the Colours.' This hint at the importance of the regimental colours in those grim days is underscored in Sergeant McKechnie's citation: 'When the shot and fire from the batteries just in front of the battalion threw it into momentary disorder, it was forced out of its formation, becoming something of a huge triangle, with one corner pointing towards the enemy. A captain was carrying the Queen's Colour which had the pole smashed and 24 bullet holes through the silk. Holding up his rifle, Sergeant McKechnie charged towards the colour, shouting, "By the centre, Scots, by the centre! Look to the Colours and march by them!"' The sergeant was seriously wounded in the leg. Despite that, he also took part in the battles of Balaclava and Sebastopol and later served for three years in Canada. When he retired from the army, at the age of 39 and after 21 years service, he was given a pension of a shilling a year. McKechnie died in Glasgow when he was 60. His Victoria Cross is in the Guards Regimental HQ in London. Private Reynolds was later promoted to corporal. After leaving the army, he became a bank messenger and died in London at the age of 42. He was buried in an unmarked grave but the Scots Guards erected a headstone some 150 years later.

The odds against the British troops at the Battle of Inkerman on November 5 1854 were overwhelming. The Russians had amassed an army of 42,000 men supported by 134 field guns, and moved out of Sebastapol to attack the British Second Division of just 2,700 men and 12 guns. It was the third major engagement of the Crimea and came just a week after Balaclava. Despite the horrendous odds and all too much confusion (in which Sir George Cathcart from Greenock lost his life leading a pointless charge against an impregnable position), history records that the Russians were again routed in an astonishing three-hour battle. One of the British commanders summed it up neatly: 'I tell you, we gave 'em a hell of a towelling.' They had: 24 of the 50 Russian battalions were all but destroyed.

In the thick of it once again there were a number of Scottish units, including the Gordon Highlanders. They were heavily outnumbered but when their CO fell, Private Thomas Beach of Dundee, showed complete disregard for his own safety and ran to help his officer. His action won him the VC, for which the citation read: 'For conspicuous gallantry at the Battle of Inkerman, November 5 1854, when on piquet, in attacking several Russians who were plundering Lieutenant-Colonel Carpenter, 41st Regiment, who was lying wounded on the ground. He killed two of the Russians, and protected Lieutenant-Colonel Carpenter until the arrival of some men of the 41st Regiment.' Thomas Beach left the army in 1863 and returned to Dundee. He died a year later, aged 40, from what is thought to have been alcoholism. He was buried in an unmarked grave in the poor ground of his local cemetery. It was not until 2003 that a small bench was inscribed there in his honour. His Victoria Cross was bought in the 1920s by the Maharaja of Patiala and is one of five VCs included in the Sheesh Mahal Medal Collection in India.

In a similar incident, 22-year-old Private John McDermond (from Glasgow) of the 47th Regiment of Foot also won the VC. His citation reads: 'On 5 November 5 1854 at the Battle of Inkerman, Private McDermond saved the life of Colonel Haly, 17th Foot, who was lying wounded on the ground surrounded by the enemy. Private McDermond rushed to the rescue and killed the Russian who had wounded the colonel and thus saved the officers life.' John McDermond died 14 years after the war (on July 22, 1868). He was just 36 and is buried in an unmarked grave at Woodside Cemetery, Paisley.

The Crimean was effectively a war of attrition. While the battles at Alma, Balaclava and Inkerman were bloody, they were also comparatively brief, while it was the long siege of Sebastapol that wreaked the most terrible havoc (and proved to be a foretaste of the terrible trench warfare of the First World War). From September 1854 through to April 1856, soldiers manned the trenches night after night, while daily the Russians used their specially prepared redoubts to rain down cannon fire, which meant fortifications had to be re-dug and secured before the next day's bombardment. It was a campaign dominated by the engineers and the artillerymen, but there was also constant hand-to-hand fighting and the Russians proved adept at sniping from carefully disguised rifle pits.

The nightmare was at its worst in the first winter, when the British soldiers had little proper winter equipment or uniform and struggled in sub-zero temperatures. One VC awarded for valour shown during that first harsh winter was gained by Lieutenant William Cuninghame. He was 20 and from Maybole, Ayrshire, and, as one of the Rifle Brigade's youngest officers, he showed his raw courage very early in the campaign. His VC citation reads: 'On November 20 1854 at Sebastopol, Lieutenant Cuninghame, with another lieutenant, was with a party detailed to drive the Russians from some rifle pits. Advancing on the pits after dark, they launched a surprise attack and drove the Russian riflemen from their cover but in the fierce fighting which ensued, the officer in command of the party was killed. The two lieutenants, however, maintained their advantage, withstood all attacks from the enemy during the night and held the position until relieved next day.' William Cuninghame went on to become a lieutenant colonel. He inherited the family baronetcy in 1874, retired from the army and became the Conservative MP for Ayr for the six years to 1880.

Henry MacDonald, from Inverness and a 34-year-old colour sergeant in the Royal Engineers, won his medal after taking command of his unit when all the officers were killed or wounded. 'On April 19 1855 at Sebastopol, Colour Sergeant MacDonald acted with great gallantry when engaged in effecting a lodgement in the enemy's rifle-pits in front of the left advance of the Right Attack. Subsequently when the Engineer officers were badly wounded, Colour Sergeant MacDonald took command and he determinedly persisted in carrying on the sap notwithstanding the repeated attacks of the enemy.' After the war, he was commissioned in 1862 and, five years later, was appointed garrison quartermaster in Gibraltar. He remained in that post with the rank of captain until ill-health forced his retirement in 1876.

Another Rifle Brigade VC winner was Inverness-born Private Roderick McGregor, just 23 at the time. 'At the Quarries, in the Crimea, on April 22 1855, whilst fetching water from a well situated in front of the trench, a bandsman was killed. Determined to drive away the Russian riflemen from the pits that they occupied, several men rushed out. Private McGregor and two others were first on the scene and drove the Russians out, killing some.' Private McGregor was mentioned again in dispatches three months later. In July, he was in the advance trenches before Sebastopol and while under heavy fire, he ran across open ground to get a better angle that enabled him to dislodge two Russians snipers. His name is inscribed on the Rifle Brigade Memorial in Winchester Cathedral and his VC is in the museum of the Royal Green Jackets, Winchester.

Throughout the siege, the British defences were constantly threatened and Private Samuel Evans (34 and from Paisley), of the 19th Regiment of Foot, was one of those who showed astonishing and continuing courage in repairing the damage. 'On April 13 1855 at Sebastopol, Crimea, Private Evans volunteered to go into an embrasure to repair a breach. He and another private went into the battery and leapt into the embrasure, where they carried out the necessary repairs under very heavy fire.'

His Victoria Cross is in the Green Howards Museum.

Showing all the courage expected of an officer and gentleman, Captain Thomas Hamilton (27) of the 68th Regiment (later the Durham Light Infantry) had already been commended for bravery at Inkerman, but it was his leadership of a sabre-and-bayonet charge during the siege that won him his VC. Under cover of driving rain and wind, the Russians emerged from Sebastapol to attack the British trenches and the infantrymen found themselves fighting for their lives. For more than an hour, two companies – about 250 men – fought off 2,000 Russians, holding them first with bullets and then with bayonets. Despite the ferocious resistance, 30 Russians fought their way into the trenches and captured a gun. What happened next is outlined in Thomas Hamilton's citation: 'On May 11 1855 at Sebastopol, in a most determined sortie, Captain Hamilton boldly charged great numbers of the enemy with a small force, driving them from a battery of which they had taken possession at the point of the bayonet. He was conspicuous for his gallantry on this occasion and his action saved the works from falling into enemy hands.' Thomas Hamilton, who was a native of Stranraer, went on to become a major general.

Four Scots won their VCs on a single, bloody day – June 18 1855. They were Sergeant John Knox (mentioned earlier), 21-year-old Lieutenant William Hope of the Royal Fusiliers, Colour Sergeant Peter Leitch (35) and Sapper John Perie, both of the Royal Engineers. Lieutenant Hope, from Edinburgh, was commended for saving the life of a senior officer. According to his citation, 'he went to the assistance of the adjutant, who was lying outside the trenches badly wounded. Having found that it was impossible to move him, even with the help of four men, he ran back across the open ground under very heavy fire from the enemy batteries and procured a stretcher to bring the wounded officer in.' He later achieved the rank of colonel. His Victoria Cross is in the Royal Fusiliers' museum in the Tower of London.

Colour Sergeant Leitch, from Kinross, was a career soldier who had already served with the Royal Sappers and Miners in the Baltic campaign. He was posted to the Crimea just before Christmas 1854. His finest hour came during that June assault on Sebastopol: 'Colour Sergeant Leitch, after approaching the redan [a v-shaped protrusion in the siege defences] with the leading ladders, formed a caponnière [a makeshift hide] across the ditch as well as a ramp by fearlessly tearing down gabions [open-ended metal baskets] from the parapet and placing and filling them until he was disabled from wounds.' Peter Leitch's actions also earned him a French *Légion d'honneur*. After the war he served in South Africa, was promoted to sergeant major in 1870 and retired from the army in 1872. His Victoria Cross is in the Royal Engineers Museum at Gillingham in Kent.

His fellow Royal Engineer, Sapper Perie, from Huntly, was also in a ladder party at the redan: 'Sapper Perie showed conspicuous gallantry, with Lieutenant Gerald

Graham, in leading a ladder party at the assault on the redan. He was invaluable on that day when he also volunteered to go with the lieutenant to help bring in a wounded sailor lying in the open, even though he was himself suffering from a musket wound in the side.' John Perie had initially enlisted into the Royal Artillery in 1848 but transferred later in the year to the Royal Sappers and Miners. After the Crimea, he served in China and took part in the capture of Hankow and the attack on the forts of Peiho. He was discharged in 1860 and settled in Aberdeen. Sadly, he and his family fell on hard times and he became seriously ill and died at the age of 43. He also won the French *Médaille militaire*. He was one of those who received his VC from Queen Victoria at the Hyde Park ceremony on June 26 1857. His medal is now in the Royal Engineers Museum.

It was the following month that Royal Engineer Corporal John Ross (33) from Stranraer was cited not for a single act of bravery but for a constant concern for his comrades: 'He showed distinguished conduct on July 21 1855, in connecting the 4th Parallel Right Attack with and an old Russian rifle-pit in front. Extremely creditable conduct on August 23 1855, in charge of the advance from 5th Parallel Right Attack on the Redan, in placing and filling 25 gabions under a very heavy fire whilst annoyed by the presence of light balls. Intrepid and devoted conduct in creeping to the Redan in the night of 8 September 1855, and reporting its evacuation, on which its occupation by the English took place.' John Ross enlisted when he was 21. He had previously been a stone mason. He served 13 years with in the army, six of which were in Gibraltar, before being sent to the Crimea. He left the Royal Engineers as a sergeant in April 1867 and worked at Pentonville Prison, London. He was presented with his VC by Queen Victoria in the Hyde Park ceremony on June 1857.

Another Scot to win the VC at Sebastapol was 30-year-old Colour Sergeant James Craig of the Scots Fusilier Guards and, again, it was a deep concern for his comrades that inspired his gallantry: 'On September 6 1855 at Sebastopol, Crimea, Colour Sergeant Craig volunteered and personally collected other volunteers, to go out under heavy fire to look for a captain of his regiment who was supposed to be wounded. Sergeant Craig brought in the body of that officer, whom he found dead, and while doing so was himself wounded.' James Craig, from Perth, was later promoted to lieutenant. His Victoria Cross is in the Scots Guards' regimental headquarters in London.

The last of the Scots to win the VC at Sebastapol was 31-year-old Captain Charles Lumley from Forres. He was serving with the Queen's Own Royal West Kent Regiment when he distinguished himself on September 8 1855. His citation reads: 'At the assault on the redan, Captain Lumley was among the first inside the work, where he was immediately attacked by three Russian gunners who were reloading a field piece. He shot two of them with his revolver when he was knocked down by a stone which stunned him for a moment, but on recovery, he drew his sword and was in the act of cheering his men on, when he was severely wounded in the mouth.' Charles Lumley received his VC from Queen Victoria at the first investiture in Hyde Park. He was also promoted to major but never recovered from his wounds and died three years after the war ended. He was just 34. His medal is in his regimental museum in Maidstone.

The Crimean War ended on April 1 1856. Of the 112 Victoria Cross recipients, 19 were Scots.

ANGLO-PERSIAN WAR

This war lasted from November 1856 to April 1857, and was caused by Britain's opposition to attempts by Persia to retake the city of Herat, which was at the time an independent emirate under British Indian protection, but had been part of Persia under a previous dynasty. Of the four VCs awarded during the bloody campaign, two were won by Scots serving with units of the Indian Army.

The first went to John Wood, 38, from Fort William, who was a captain in the Bombay Native Infantry on December 9 1856. His citation reads: 'At Bushire, Persia, Captain Wood led a Grenadier Company which formed the head of the assaulting column and was the first man on the parapet of the fort, where he was immediately attacked by a large number of the garrison. A volley was fired at Captain Wood and the head of the storming party at very close range but although the captain was hit by seven musket balls he at once threw himself upon the enemy, killing their leader. He was closely followed by the men of his company and speedily overcame all opposition.' John Wood was later promoted to colonel.

The second VC was won by 21-year-old Lieutenant John Malcolmson from Inverness. He was serving with the Bombay Light Cavalry, which had arrived at Bushire in 1856, and he had already helped capture the fort at Reshire, before distinguishing himself in the most telling action of the campaign, the Battle of Khush-ab on February 7 1857. With fellow officers including the squadron adjutant Lieutenant Arthur Moore, he led a heroic charge on a large force of Persian soldiers, who were well set out in the traditional square-shaped defensive formation. Of their courage, another officer later wrote in a Calcutta newspaper: 'In spite of steel, fire, and bullets, they tore down upon the nearest face of the Persian square. Daunted by the flashes, and the fire, and the noise and crackle of musketry, Moore's horse swerved as they came up. Dropping his sword from his hand and letting it hang by the knot at his wrist, he caught up the reins in both hands, screwed his head straight, and then coolly, as if riding a fence, leapt him at the square. Of course the horse fell stone dead on the Persian bayonets.' The VC citation tells the rest of the story: 'The adjutant speedily extricated himself and attempted with his broken sword to force his way through the press; but he would assuredly have lost his life had not the gallant young Lieutenant Malcolmson, observing his peril, fought his way to his dismounted comrade through a crowd of enemies, to his rescue, and giving him his stirrup, safely carried him through everything out of the throng. The thoughtfulness for others, cool determination, devoted courage and ready activity shown in extreme danger by this young officer,

Lieutenant Malcolmson, appear to have been most admirable, and to be worthy of the highest honour.'

The squadron rode through the defensive square twice and, of 500 Persian soldiers, only 20 escaped. John Malcolmson was later promoted to captain, served throughout the Indian Mutiny and took part in the Central India operations from the siege of Ratghur to the fall of Calpee. He received his VC from Queen Victoria at Windsor Castle in November 1860. The medal is privately owned. In 1870, he was appointed one of the Queen's gentlemen-at-arms.

The war ended when Persia agreed to surrender its claim to Herat.

THE INDIAN MUTINY

We call it the Indian Mutiny. India calls it the First War of Indian Independence. What is beyond question is the monstrous bloodiness of the fighting that raged from the first uprising of sepoys (Indian infantrymen serving in the British Army) in May 1857 through to the spring of 1859. Evidence of that bloodiness are the facts that many field surgeons were among those cited for gallantry awards and that the dreadful fighting saw the largest number of VCs – 24 – ever awarded in a single battle, at Lucknow in November 1857. Fourteen of them were won by Scots, including, famously, 'six before breakfast' for the 93rd Highlanders.

The grim irony is that the full-blooded mutiny broke out because of the introduction of the famous rifle patented by the Scot James Paris Lee, from Hawick. The cartridge of his new Lee-Enfield was greased with animal fat to make its loading easier and the rumour grew among the native soldiers that the fat was a mixture of cow fat (an outrage to Hindus) and pig fat (abhorrent to Muslims). The first sepoys who protested about having to use the rifles were promptly disciplined and some of them clapped in irons. At this stage, the British Empire was the largest and richest in the world and India was being administered imperiously as well as imperially by the East India Company (in a manner I would never countenance for my Scottish Empire). There had been simmering unrest for many years, but the flashpoint came at the garrison town of Meerut, 45 miles north of Delhi. The sepoys broke into open rebellion and marched on the city. Everything escalated from there into a bloody and widespread confrontation.

The Scottish regiments, many of their men still recovering from their efforts in the grimness of the Crimea and redirected to India during a voyage to China, were deployed across a wide front and were involved in many of the vicious clashes clearly charted by the citations for gallantry and the award of Victoria Crosses.

Among the first Scots to win the VC was Thomas Cadell from Cockenzie. He was 21 and a lieutenant in the 2nd European Bengal Fusiliers (later The Royal Munster Fusiliers). He was the first of an astonishing nine former pupils of Edinburgh Academy to win the VC. As with so many young Scots officers, it was an unswerving concern for the men under his command that drove him. His citation reads: 'On June 12 1857 at Delhi during the siege, Lieutenant Cadell brought in a wounded bugler of his own regiment [who was] under most severe fire. Later on the same day, when the Fusiliers were retiring, this officer went back of his own accord and, accompanied by three men, brought in a severely wounded man under heavy fire from the advancing enemy.' He was later promoted to colonel. After leaving the army, he went into the diplomatic service and became governor of the Andaman and Nicobar Islands. He died in 1919 and is buried near Edinburgh. His VC is privately owned.

Twenty-five-year-old Lieutenant William Kerr, from Melrose and a former pupil at Loretto School, was serving with the Bombay Native Infantry at Kolapore on July 10 when his heroic actions won him acclaim as the 'Saviour of Kolapore'... and the Victoria Cross. A large group of well-armed mutineers had set up a strong position just outside the town and Lieutenant Kerr could muster only 17 men armed with swords. The citation completes the picture: 'The attacking party had no guns and the enemy kept up a ceaseless fire but Lieutenant Kerr made a dash at one of the gateways with some dismounted horsemen and forced an entrance. The attack was successful and the defenders were all killed, wounded or captured.' William Kerr was later promoted to captain. His VC is in Lord Ashcroft's collection.

Just eight days later, 31-year-old Lieutenant Richard Wadeson (formerly a sergeant major) of the 75th Regiment (Gordon Highlanders) won his medal. His was a double act of valour in the face of the fearsome Indian Cavalry. His citation read: 'For conspicuous bravery at Delhi on July 18 1857, when the regiment was engaged in the Subjee Mundee, in having saved the life of Private Michael Farrell, when attacked by a sowar [horseman] of the enemy's cavalry and killed the sowar. Also on the same day, for rescuing Private John Barry, of the same regiment, when wounded and helpless, he was attacked by a cavalry sowar, whom Lieutenant Wadeson killed.' Richard Wadeson was later promoted captain (1864), major (1871) and then lieutenant colonel in command of the 75th Regiment. After leaving the army, he became the governor of Chelsea Hospital. His VC is in the Gordon Highlanders Museum.

Lieutenant Andrew Bogle, 28, born one of nine children in Govan, was serving with the 78th Highlanders when he won his VC: 'On July 29, 1857 in the attack on Oonao, Lieutenant Bogle led the way into a loop-holed house which was occupied by the enemy and from which a heavy fire harassed the advance of his regiment. He was severely wounded in this action.' Andrew Bogle was later promoted to captain and, in 1865, was aide de camp to Lieutenant General Sir John Pennefather. He was further promoted to major in 1870. His Victoria Cross is displayed at the Regimental Museum of the Queen's Own Highlanders in Fort George, Inverness-shire. He died in 1890. His brother, Captain Robert Bogle, also serving with the 78th, was killed in action at Lucknow.

James Blair was 29 and hailed from the Scottish Borders but, when he won his VC, was serving as a captain in the 2nd Bombay Light Cavalry of the Indian Army. He was involved in at least two clashes and was wounded on both occasions. 'On August 12

1857 at Neemuch, India, Captain Blair volunteered to apprehend seven or eight armed mutineers who had shut themselves up in a house. He burst open the door and after a fierce encounter during which he was severely wounded, the rebels escaped through the roof. In spite of his wounds he pursued, but was unable to catch them. On October 23, at Jeerum, the captain fought his way through a body of rebels who had surrounded him. In the action he broke his sword and was wounded but nevertheless he led his men in a charge on the rebels and dispersed them.' James Blair later achieved the rank of general. He was the cousin of Robert Blair VC (see later mention). He died and is buried in Melrose. His medal is held privately.

William Rennie, from Elgin, enlisted as a private in the 73rd Perthshire Regiment in 1746 and had been promoted to ensign 'for gallantry in the Crimea' in 1854. He then joined the Perthshire Light Infantry (later the Cameronians) as a lieutenant. He was 34 and adjutant when the regiment went to Lucknow in 1857. He, too, won his VC for two acts of outstanding courage. His citation reads: '[Lieutenant Rennie] charged the enemy's guns in advance of the skirmishers of his regiment, under heavy musketry fire, and prevented them from dragging off one gun, which was subsequently captured. On 25 September he again charged in advance of the 90th column, in the face of heavy grape fire, and forced the enemy to abandon their guns.' William Rennie was promoted to captain in 1863, major in 1873 and lieutenant colonel in 1874. He died, in Elgin, at the age of 75. His VC was auctioned and bought for £1,700 in 1969 by the Museum of The Cameronians (Scottish Rifles).

Surgeon Joseph Jee was one of the field surgeons whose citation for the VC provides a graphic picture of the heroic performances of the Scottish regiments in India. Although born and medically trained in England, he joined the 78th Highlanders (The Seaforths) in 1854 and served with them in the Persian campaign in 1857. In one battle, he had had his horse shot from under him and was already much-decorated for bravery by the time of the Mutiny. At its outbreak, the 78th was one of the regiments rushed to India, and Surgeon Jee was present at the relief and defence of Lucknow, the action at Alambagh, the final capture of Lucknow, the Rohilkand Campaign and the capture of Bareilly. However, it was at Lucknow that he displayed the extraordinary devotion and gallantry which resulted in the award of the Victoria Cross. His citation reads: 'For most conspicuous gallantry and important services on the entry of the late Major General Havelock's relieving force into Lucknow, on September 25 1857, in having, during action (when the 78th Highlanders, then in possession of the Char Bagh, captured two 9-pounders at the point of the bayonet), by great exertion and devoted exposure, attended to the large number of men wounded in the charge, whom he succeeded in getting removed on cots and the backs of their comrades, until he had collected the dhooly bearers who had fled. Subsequently on the same day, in endeavouring to reach the Residency with the wounded men, Surgeon Jee became besieged by an overwhelming force in the Mote Mehal, where he remained during the whole night and the following morning, voluntarily and repeatedly exposing himself to heavy fire in proceeding to dress the wounded men who fell while serving a 24-pounder in a most exposed position. He eventually succeeded in taking many of the wounded through a cross-fire of ordnance and musketry safely into the Residency by the river bank, although repeatedly warned not to make the perilous attempt.' Joseph Jee went on to become the army's assistant surgeon general.

Serving with the 90th Highlanders (later The Cameronians), 30-year-old surgeon Anthony Home from Dunbar, on the same day showed the same selfless courage in tending to the wounded during the height of battle: 'Surgeon Home was in charge of the wounded men left behind when the troops forced their way into the Residency. The escort left with the wounded had been reduced, by further casualties, to a small party, who were forced into a house which they defended until it was set on fire. They then retreated to a shed nearby and defended this for more than 22 hours until relieved. At last only six men, with Surgeon Home in charge, remained to fire and the fact that the wounded were safe and the defence was successful, was mainly attributable to his brave conduct throughout.' Anthony Home later took part in the Ashanti War of 1874. He was knighted and as Sir Anthony, became surgeon general (1880) and then principal medical officer, India (1881–85). He died in 1914. His Victoria Cross is displayed at the Army Medical Services Museum in Aldershot, Hampshire.

Another young medic, 23-year-old Assistant Surgeon Valentine McMaster, serving with the 78th Regiment (later the Seaforth Highlanders), also worked tirelessly during the siege and was not content to minister to the men's wounds but also helped to rescue many of them. 'Assistant Surgeon McMaster showed great bravery in exposing himself to the fire of the enemy when bringing in and attending to the wounded.' He was later promoted to the rank of surgeon. He died on January 22 1872. His VC is in the National War Museum, Edinburgh.

On the day Valentine McMaster won his VC, his adjutant, Lieutenant Herbert Taylor MacPherson (from Ardersier in Inverness-shire) showed the same selfless courage. His citation reads: 'For distinguished conduct at Lucknow on September 25, in setting an example of heroic gallantry to the men of the regiment at the period of the action in which they captured two brass nine-pounders at the point of the bayonet.' Herbert MacPherson became a brigadier general and was later knighted.

Three days later, Lieutenant Robert Blair, 23 years old, from Linlithgow, and serving with the 2nd Dragoon Guards (The Queen's Bays), showed the quality of his leadership when he led a small party of men to try to recover an abandoned wagon of desperately-needed ammunition at Bolandshahr: 'As they approached the wagon, 50 or 60 of the enemy on horseback attacked them but, without hesitation, Lieutenant Blair formed up his men and gallantly led them through the rebels. He made good his retreat without losing a man but leaving nine of the enemy dead on the field. He himself was severely wounded in this action.' After being promoted to captain, Robert Blair was killed in action at Cawnpore (now Kanpur) on March 28 1859. He was 25. His VC is in the Queen's Dragoon Guards Museum in Cardiff Castle. He was the cousin of James Blair VC.

Stewart McPherson, from Culross in Fife, had been an apprentice weaver in Dunfermline but two years into the training he was bored and decided to join the army. The nearest recruiting office was about 25 miles away, in Stirling. However, he was just 17 and unconcerned about having to walk there. He joined the 78th Highlanders in 1839 and saw action in Persia, India and Ireland before returning to Bengal as a colour sergeant. He was 35. In the fighting at Lucknow, on September 26, he showed courage of the highest order and won the VC. His citation says: 'In the Residency at Lucknow, Colour Sergeant McPherson saw Private James Lowther lying badly wounded but alive and he made his way under heavy enemy fire to his injured comrade. Exposed to a continuous bombardment, he tended him and carried him back to safety, but Private Lowther later died from his injuries.' Stewart McPherson received his medal from Queen Victoria at Windsor Castle in December 1880. Three weeks later, he left the army and returned to Scotland, where he became superintendent of Glasgow Industrial Schools. As a reminder of his experience, he named his house Lucknow Villa. In 2000, Fife Council awarded an £1,800 grant from the common good fund to pay for a new Indian granite memorial stone – from a quarry near Lucknow. His Victoria Cross is in the Regimental Museum of the Queen's Own Highlanders.

At home in Glasgow James Miller had been a candle-maker, but when he was 21 he signed on for service with the East India Company. Such is the astonishing paper-trail he left, we know the precise date – 22 June 1841 – and the bounty he initially received – £3 17s 6d. Six months later, in January 1842, he disembarked at Calcutta and launched on a military career that was to bring him the Victoria Cross. First there was the small matter of the march to Agra – more than 1,200 kilometres. It took four months. On arrival, he joined the Bengal Artillery. Two years later he was promoted to bombardier (3 May 1944), then sergeant (12 August 1845) and acting staff sergeant (20 June 1846). At that point, he returned to Calcutta to serve in the arsenal at Fort William. The next important date in his diary was 24 October 1849: he married Agnes Forsyth, a gunner's daughter and a widow. The following year he moved to Fort Dum Dum (also in Calcutta) and on 31 January 1851, he was listed as blacksmith sergeant working for the Select Committee of Artillery Officers. He then held several other posts between Calcutta and Agra and passed his officer examinations in double-quick time (two months instead of the usual six).

When the Mutiny began in May 1857, he was 37 and conductor (the most senior warrant officer rank) at the Bengal Ordnance Depot. In that capacity, he was in action at Fattehpoor Sikri, when he saved the life of an officer and won the VC. His citation is simple, straightforward and brief: 'For having, on October 28, 1857 at great personal risk, gone to the assistance of, and carried out of action, a wounded officer, Lieutenant Glubb of the… Bengal Light Infantry. He was himself was wounded and sent to Agra. Conductor Miller was at the time employed with heavy howitzers and ordnance stores attached to a detachment of troops.' Lieutenant Glubb showed his gratitude in a letter to Miller's CO, saying the VC was well-deserved: 'Soon after we broke into the Serai at Fattehpoor, I was wounded. I was at the bottom of a long passage up which I was trying to force my way as it was the only road we could get at the rebels. No sooner did Miller see me stagger and fall than, regardless of the shower of balls that came down the passage and also of the shots that came from the other three sides of the quadrangle, which they concentrated on this point, he ran to me and as I could not walk he put me on his back and carried me out of danger. Directly this was done, he returned to his duty, that is to the place where they were then fighting and had the bad luck to be wounded himself whilst passing the very same place from whence he had just brought me. I shall be happy at any time to serve Conductor Miller if it is in my power for had it not have been for him, I might not now have been alive [… to give] this testimony to his meritorious conduct.' James Miller was later promoted to honorary lieutenant and appointed to the Gun Carriage Agency at Fattehpoor (1863–79). He was Deputy Commissary from 1879 until his retirement, as an honorary major, in 1882. There is a classroom named in his honour at the Defence Logistic & Supply School of the Royal Logistic Corps, Camberley, Surrey.

One of the most fiercely fought confrontations of the Indian campaign was again at Lucknow, less than a month later. The small British community were still barricaded in the Residency, the series of administrative buildings and family quarters in the highest part of the city. Figures vary but there were somewhere around 1,700 soldiers in the garrison, which had been besieged by more than 6,000 sepoys since the beginning of July 1857. British morale was low following the death, on only the second day of the onslaught, of the provincial chief commissioner, Sir Henry Lawrence. He was killed by a shell burst. For three long months, the garrison hoped for relief, but more realistically the soldiers faced the probability that each day could be their last as thousands of sepoys sought to breach their fragile defences.

As dawn broke on 16 November 1857, the beleaguered British men and women in the Residency prepared themselves for another day of desperate resistance. They had faced constant frustration in seeing each attempt to break through to them foiled as thousands of sepoys also tried to breach their fragile defences. Suddenly, above the usual, awful cacophony of heavy weaponry and explosions, they heard the skirl of the bagpipes and the rattle of military drums. At first, it must have seemed like a dream but soon they could actually see the kilted soldiers of the 93rd Highlanders swaggering towards the residency with battle colours flying and fixed bayonets gleaming in the early morning sunshine. They didn't know it at the time, but at the head of the Highlanders was the battle-scarred veteran from Glasgow, General Sir Colin Campbell.

Campbell (later Field Marshall and elevated to the peerage as Baron Clyde) was lately from the Crimea, where he had helped hold the thin red line at Balaclava, had his horse shot from under him at Alma and achieved an astonishing number of victories over the Russians. At Lucknow, he ordered: 'bring furrit the Tartan' (bring forward the Highlanders) a phrase deeply etched in military history. Salvation, it seemed, was at hand… but not before one of the bloodiest days of an especially bloody war.

The mutineers' stronghold was the Secundra (now Sikandar) Bagh, a fortification garrisoned by 2,000 sepoys. This had to be taken before the siege could be broken. Campbell's relief column had fought its way across what one journalist described as 'a country stained with blood from some of the worst atrocities ever perpetrated against British men, women and children.' The rebels, of course, had been well trained – by the British army – and knew all about the fighting methods of their former masters. The struggle between the two sides was desperate. Most of the fighting was vicious hand-to-hand, swords against bayonets in savagely confined spaces, from which it was impossible to either advance or retreat without clambering over dead bodies. In such a nightmare, men performed deeds of bravery far beyond any reasoned expectation. The 93rd Highlanders fought so valiantly and against such overwhelming numbers that they famously won six VCs before breakfast! By the end of the day, when the Highlanders prevailed and most of the sepoys were dead, 24 VCs had been awarded, 14 of them to Scottish soldiers.

At this distance in time, it might be difficult for many of us to appreciate just how important regimental colours were to the fighting men but Private David MacKay from Lyth in Caithness – just 26 but, like his commanding officer, already a veteran of Alma, Balaklava and Sebastapol – did know, only too well. His target was the colours of the enemy's key unit, the 2nd Loodhiana Indian Sikhs Regiment. Despite seeing many of his mates cut down, he fought through the Sikh ranks to snatch their standard to the cheers of his comrades and the dismay of the enemy. It was exactly the encouragement, the Highlanders needed and they went on to relieve the Lucknow garrison. Private MacKay's fellow soldiers nominated him for the VC, the first of the six achieved 'before breakfast' that morning: 'For great personal gallantry in capturing an enemy colour after a most obstinate resistance, at the Secundra Bagh, Lucknow, on 16 November 1857. He was severely wounded afterwards at the capture of the Shah Nujjif.'

David MacKay's wounds were serious enough that he would have been immediately evacuated… had there been a first aid station. As it was, he was not able to return to Britain until the following spring. He received his VC from Queen Victoria (at the Hyde Park ceremony in 1879) and for his wounds, he was also awarded an annual pension of £10. He became a recruiting sergeant in Aberdeen but was medically discharged from the Army in 1861, when his 10 years was up. He had re-enlisted as a sergeant in the 1st Kincardinshire Volunteers by 1863. He suffered from heart disease, was unable to work and had to sell his medals to buy food for his wife and five children. He died in 1880, aged 48, and was buried in a pauper's grave. His regiment placed a commemorative plaque in Lesmahagow cemetery in 1998. His medal was sold at auction in January 1901 for £75.

His regimental colleague, Colour Sergeant James Munro, from Nigg in the Highlands, was also seriously wounded in the incident that won him the VC, awarded 'for devoted gallantry in having promptly rushed to the rescue of Captain Walsh of the same corps, when wounded and in danger of his life, whom he carried to a place of safety, into which place the sergeant was brought in shortly afterwards badly wounded.'

James Munro, who joined the army when he was 20, had also served in the Crimea. He received his medal personally from Queen Victoria at Windsor Castle in 1860. Sadly, he clearly suffered mentally as well as physically from his wounds and was eventually committed to Inverness District Asylum, where his condition deteriorated, and he died in 1871. He was 45, and it is believed he was buried in the asylum cemetery either because there were no relatives to collect the body or they were too poor to do so. His Victoria Cross is displayed at the Argyll and Sutherland Highlanders Museum in Stirling Castle.

Breaching the sepoy defences was all-important and one of the first to achieve that was 23-year-old Sergeant John Paton from Stirling: 'Sergeant Paton went alone round the Shah Nujjiff and, under extremely heavy fire, discovered a breach in the opposite side. He afterwards led the Regiment to this breach and the important position was taken.' Sergeant Paton was another winner to have been nominated by his comrades-in-arms. His VC is also in the Argyll and Sutherland Highlanders Museum.

Fearing he might be accused of partiality in making these ultimate awards for valour, Sir Colin Campbell decided that only one should be given to an officer and he asked for nominations from the commissioned ranks. The unanimous choice was Captain William Stewart. He was 26, from Grandtully in Perthshire, and yet another veteran of the Crimea, where he had served under Sir Colin, had been part of the thin red line and was wounded in the siege of Sebastapol. His citation reads: 'Captain Stewart led an attack, with a small force, on two of the enemy's guns which were maintaining a heavy flanking fire and which covered the approach to the barracks. Captain Stewart captured the guns and was able to gain possession of the barracks.' The importance of William Stewart's action is underlined by a lengthy mention in Lord Roberts' memoirs, *Forty-one years in India*. It was, he wrote, as serviceable as it was heroic because it silenced the enemy fire that had threatened to destroy the attacking force, and because capturing the building 'greatly facilitated' the ultimate victory: 'Stewart, perceiving the annoyance which these two guns were causing, and the injury that they might still cause, called upon his company and, at the head of it, increased in weight and numbers by a few men of the other companies, and of the 53rd, who had joined our men, dashed forward in the most gallant style, captured the guns at the point of the bayonet, turned the guns on the flying rebels, and then, pushing forward at the double, while Captain Cornwall, with his company and the men of other companies, followed in support, assaulted the large pile of building called the barracks, situated in the left front of the Sikanderbagh, drove the enemy out, and established themselves in it.' William Stewart was promoted to major but left the Army in 1860 and died in a bizarre incident eight years later. He was giving a demonstration of sword-swallowing when the trick went fatally wrong. He died from internal injuries. He was 37.

The fifth and sixth before-breakfast heroes of the 93rd Highlanders were both Irish. Lance Corporal John Dunley, 26 and from Cork, was among the first to get in through one of the breaches in the Secundra Bagh and Private Peter Grant was reported as having killed five of the sepoys with one of their own swords. Peter Grant did not prosper when he left the army. He went to live in Scotland and his local paper, the *Dundee Advertiser* of 11 January 11 1868, records his desperately sad ending: 'On Friday, December 27, Private Peter Grant of the 93rd Regiment, was missed from where he lived in Dundee and was not again seen till yesterday morning, when his body was discovered by Constable Bremner, floating in the river a little to the east of the Craig Harbour. The constable had the body taken out and conveyed to the dead-house. On the breast of Grant's uniform coat were five medals and the Victoria Cross. One medal had two clasps, bearing on them 'Relief of Lucknow' and 'Lucknow', 1857. The others were for Pegu, Sobraon, Sebastopol and the Crimea. The Cross had inscribed on it the name of the deceased and is dated 1857. In the pockets were found a four-penny piece, a penny and a knife. Grant was stationed in Aberdeen and was here on a visit to his friends. It is said that he was last seen in Wheatley's public house, Overgate.' Peter Grant's Victoria Cross has never been sold or auctioned and its whereabouts, after being discovered on his uniform coat following his death in the River Tay, is unknown. Of course, there is a possibility that Grant was buried still wearing his Victoria Cross and other medals.

(The 93rd Highlanders went on fighting the sepoys in a series of battles at Cawnpore, at Serai Ghat on the Ganges, at Kala Nadi and, just days later, at Shamshabad. In March 1858 they finally captured Lucknow after another long and bloody battle in which they suffered 81 casualties, including 15 killed. The regiment remained in India and went on hunting down rebels until 1871, its members continuing to win medals for their exceptional courage.)

Not all Scottish bravery was displayed by Scottish Regiments. Lieutenant Robert Aitken, 29 and from Cupar, was serving with the Bengal Native Infantry during the campaign. His citation does not quote a single act of valour but, astonishingly, shows a consistent record of bravery almost from the moment he set foot in India: 'From June 30 to November 22, 1857 at Lucknow, Lieutenant Aitken performed various acts of gallantry during the defence of the Residency. On one occasion when the enemy had set fire to the Bhoosa Stock in the garden, the lieutenant and other officers cut down all the tents in order to stop the fire spreading to the powder magazine which was there. This was done close to the enemy's loopholes under the bright light of the flames. Other exploits included saving the Baillie Guard Gate, taking enemy guns and capturing the Fureed Buksh Palace.' He was later promoted to colonel. His Victoria Cross is displayed at the National Army Museum.

Two Scots were among those elected by the Bengal Artillery to receive the VC on behalf of the regiment (under the special provision when an entire unit is deemed worthy of the honour) during the relief of Lucknow. One was Gunner Hugh McInnes, a grizzled veteran of 41 from the Anderston district of Glasgow, and the other was 22-year-old Gunner James Park from Inverkeithing, Fife. The citations for the two men are identical and unusually brief, citing 'conspicuous gallantry at the time of the relief of Lucknow' during the whole period of 14–22 November 1857. After leaving the army, Hugh McInnes returned to Glasgow. He married in 1876 but died just three years later. He was buried in an unmarked grave in a local cemetery. It was not until 2004 that an official army headstone was erected and a small rose garden established in his memory. The whereabouts of his VC is unknown. James Park was killed in action at Lucknow seven months later. His VC is privately owned.

Troop Sergeant Major David Spence from Inverkeithing, Fife, was 40 and a veteran of 16 years service with 9 Lancers (The Queen's Royal), when he won the VC at Shunsabad (northern India) on 17 January 1858 for his single-handed rescue of one of his men. Again the citation is brief: 'Troop Sergeant Major Spence went to the assistance of a private who had been wounded and his horse disabled, and rescued him from a large number of rebels.' David Spence was later promoted to regimental sergeant major and when he left the army, in 1862, he became a yeoman of the guard at the Tower of London. He died in 1877. His VC is in the Regimental Museum of the 9th/12th Royal Lancers, Derby.

Lieutenant John Tytler was another old boy of Edinburgh Academy to win the VC during the campaign. He was serving with the 66th Bengal Native Infantry, Indian Army (later 1st Gurkha Rifles) at Choorpoorah on 10 February: 'On the attacking parties approaching the enemy's position under a heavy fire of round shot, grape, and musketry, on the occasion of the Action at Choorpoorah, on the 10th February last, Lieutenant Tytler dashed on horseback ahead of all, and alone, up to the enemy's guns, where he remained engaged hand to hand, until they were carried by us; and where he was shot through the left arm, had a spear wound in his chest, and a ball through the right sleeve of his coat.' John Tytler rose through the ranks to brigadier general and was made a Companion of the Order of Bath. His VC is in the Gurkha Museum.

Yet another former Edinburgh Academy pupil, 28-year-old Lieutenant James Innes, was serving with the Bengal Engineers in Bengal when he was tested in the face of the enemy. His citation reads: 'On February 23 1858 at Sultanpore, Lieutenant Innes, far in advance of the leading skirmishers, was the first to secure a gun which the enemy were abandoning. They then rallied round another gun from which the shot would have ploughed through our advancing columns. Lieutenant Innes rode up, unsupported, shot the gunner and remained at his post keeping the enemy at bay until assistance reached him.' James Innes was later promoted to lieutenant general and was made a Companion of the Order of Bath (CB). His VC is in the Royal Engineers Museum.

Lieutenant Frederick Aikman was another Scot who won his VC while serving with the Bengal Native Army (attached to the Sikh Irregular Cavalry). He was 29 and from Ross, Lanarkshire: 'On March 1 1858 near Amethi, India, Lieutenant Aikman, commanding an advanced picket with 100 of his men, was informed of the proximity of a body of 500 rebel infantry and 200 horse and guns. The lieutenant attacked and utterly routed this large enemy force, cutting up more than 100 of them, capturing two guns and driving the survivors over the River Goomtee. This feat was carried out over broken ground and partly under flanking fire from an adjoining fort. Lieutenant Aikman himself received a severe sabre cut in the face.' He was later promoted to colonel but his wound eventually forced him to retire early from the army. He died in October 1888 after collapsing while attending a ball in Hamilton, Lanarkshire.

Lieutenant William McBean had been a ploughman in Inverness before he signed on as a private in the 93rd Highlanders but had risen to be the regiment's adjutant by the time he won his VC – the regiment's seventh in India – at Lucknow: 'On March 11 1858, Lieutenant McBean killed 11 of the enemy with his own hands in the main breach of the Begum Bagh.' His response when he heard of the citation was typically modest: 'It didn't take me 20 minutes.' William McBean continued to soar through the ranks and was a major general when he retired from the army, fulfilling one of his early prophecies. During his initial training as a private, he was continually harassed by the drill instructors for having an odd, rolling gait. When it was suggested he retaliate by giving the main culprit a hiding, he replied, 'man, that would ne'er do. I intend to be in command of this regiment before I leave it. It would be an ill beginning to be brought before the colonel for thrashing the drill corporal.' Major-General McBean, who also served in the Crimea, died in 1878 at the age of 60.

Glasgow-born Lieutenant Francis Farquharson of the 42nd Regiment (later The Black Watch) was just 20 when he earned his Victoria Cross: 'On March 9 1858 at Lucknow, India, Lieutenant Farquharson led a portion of his company and stormed a bastion mounting two guns and then spiked them. This meant that the advance positions held during the night were rendered secure from artillery fire. Lieutenant Farquharson was severely wounded while holding an advanced position the following morning.' The young lieutenant went on to achieve the rank of major. His VC is in the Black Watch Museum in Perth.

Private James Davis, a 23-year-old from Edinburgh, was also serving with the 42nd Regiment in April 1858 when he won his VC: 'For conspicuous gallantry at the attack on the fort at Ruhya, when, with an advanced party to point out the gate of the fort to the engineer officer, Private Davis offered to carry the body of Lieutenant Bramley, who was killed at this point, to the regiment. He performed the duty of danger and affection under the very walls of the fort.' James Davis died in Edinburgh in 1893. He was 58 and was buried in a grave unmarked until his regiment placed a tombstone on it in 2003.

Lieutenant Hugh Cochrane, from Fort William, was 28 and a lieutenant in the 86th Infantry Regiment of Foot (later The Royal Irish Rifles) when he won his medal on 1 April 1858 at the storming of the fortress city of Jhansi: 'When No. 1 company of the regiment was ordered to take a gun, Lieutenant Cochrane dashed forward at a gallop under heavy musketry and artillery fire, drove the enemy from the gun and kept possession of it until the company came up. He also showed conspicuous gallantry in attacking the rear guard of the enemy when he had three horses in succession shot under him.' Later in the same month, Lieutenant Cochrane was also mentioned in dispatches by Major General Sir Hugh Rose and again in May for his part in several other battles. He went on to become colonel and commanded the Irregular Cavalry under Sir Robert Napier. He served in Ireland briefly before returning to India in 1874. He died, aged 55, in England.

Lieutenant James Leith from Glenkindie, Aberdeenshire, was the son of General Sir Alexander Leith and a cricketing blue at Cambridge before he joined the 14th Hussars. He was 31 and serving at Betwa on 1 April 1858 when he won his VC for the daring rescue of a fellow officer: 'Captain Need had become separated and found himself on difficult, rocky ground, surrounded by a large number of rebel infantry and fighting for his life. Despite his skill with the sword, his saddle, reins and clothing were slashed to ribbons by the enemy's tulwars [swordsmen], and he would certainly have been killed had not Lieutenant James Leith charged alone and rescued him.' James Leith was later invalided out of the army because of his failing health and he died aged 43. His VC is in the Hussars Museum, Preston.

A private and a lance corporal in the 42nd Regiment (later the Black Watch) both won the VC for their part in recovering under fire the body of a fallen comrade during the attack on Fort Ruhya on 15 April 1858. They were 20-year-old Private Edward Spence, from Dumfries, and Lance Corporal Alexander Thompson, 34, a veteran of the battles of Alma and Balaclava and the siege of Sebastopol during the Crimean War. When one of their officers fell during the battle, the two immediately volunteered to recover him. Private Spence's citation says: 'He deliberately placed himself in an exposed position so as to cover the party bearing away the body.' Lance Corporal Thompson's reads: 'He carried the body in a most exposed position and under very heavy fire.' Edward Spence was seriously wounded during the incident and died two days later. He is buried in an unmarked grave in Fort Ruhya Cemetery, Oude, India. He was the first to be awarded the VC posthumously. Alexander Thompson was later promoted to sergeant. Both VCs are in the Black Watch Museum.

The third Black Watch soldier to win the VC on the same day was 32-year-old Quartermaster Sergeant John Simpson, from Edinburgh, and he too was decorated for showing exceptional concern for his comrades. According to his citation, 'he volunteered to go to an exposed point within 40 yards of the parapet of the fort under heavy fire and carried back a lieutenant and a private, both of whom were seriously wounded.' John Simpson was later promoted to major. His VC is in the County Museum of Natural History, Los Angeles.

William Gardner, from Nemphlar, Lanarkshire, also won his VC for saving the life of an officer. He was 37 and a colour sergeant with the 42nd Highland Regiment at Bareilly on 5 May: 'He went to the assistance of the commanding officer, who had been knocked off his horse and set upon by three Ghazis. He bayoneted two of the Ghazis and was in the midst of attacking a third when his opponent was shot down by another soldier.' William Gardner was later promoted to sergeant major. His VC is privately owned.

Brevet Major Charles Fraser, the second son of Sir James Fraser of Leadclune and Moray, was 29 when he won his Victoria Cross for rescuing colleagues from drowning on New Year's Eve 1858: 'An officer and some men of his regiment had pursued mutineers into the river Raptee, Oude, on the borders of Nepal, and were in imminent danger of being drowned. Major Fraser, although at the time partially disabled from a wound received while charging with his squadron in the action at Nawabgunge on June 13, at once volunteered at great personal risk, to jump in and swim to their rescue. Major Fraser succeeded in saving the officer and men while all the time under terrible musketry fire from mutineers on the opposite bank of the river.' Charles Fraser went on to have a glittering career both in the army and in politics. He became CO of the 11th Hussars in 1861, HQ commandant during the Abyssinian Campaign in 1867, colonel of the 8th Hussars in 1868, major general in 1870, inspector general of cavalry in Ireland in 1880, lieutenant general in 1886 and retired from the army in 1890. He was knighted in 1891 and served as Conservative MP for North Lambeth 1885–92. Sir Charles Fraser died in 1895.

On the same day, Private Same (sic) Shaw from Prestonpans, East Lothian, who was serving in the Prince Consort's Own Rifle Brigade won his VC at the battle of Nawabgunge in Lucknow. A *Scotsman* article of 2003 about the plans for a memorial in his home town related the deed that did it: 'He encountered a Ghazee – a veteran Muslim warrior and "slayer of infidels" – who was cut off from his companions. The man stood, sword in hand, facing his pursuers and ready to fight to the death. Private Shaw charged at him. The Ghazee wounded him on the head with his tulwar [curved sword] but Private Shaw, drawing his pioneer's sword, hacked at him with its serrated back and "dispatched him". Many who witnessed the fight, apparently declared it the greatest instance of cool-headed courage they ever saw.' Same Shaw was later promoted to corporal but, a year after the battle, he drowned at sea while returning from India two days after Christmas, 1859. His name is on the war memorial at the Royal Green Jackets Museum, where his VC is also on display.

Private George Rodgers from Glasgow was another veteran of the Crimean War serving in India. He was 29 and with the 71st Highland Regiment at Marar Gwalior when he won the VC on 16 June 1858. His citation read: 'For daring conduct, in attacking by himself a party of seven rebels, one of whom he killed. This was remarked as a valuable service, the party of rebels being well armed and strongly posted in the line of advance of a detachment of the regiment.' George Rodgers died in Glasgow in March 1870, after drinking vitriol poison thinking it was alcohol. He was buried in an unmarked grave in the city's Southern Necropolis but a memorial stone was erected by his regiment in December 2004. His VC is in the Museum of The Royal Highland Fusiliers, Glasgow.

Private Duncan Millar, 34, from Kilmarnock, was serving with the 42nd Regiment at Maylah Ghat when he won his VC on 15 January 1859. His citation read: 'At the time the fight was the severest and the few men of the 42nd Regiment were skirmishing so close to the enemy (who were in great numbers) that some of the men were wounded by sword cuts, and the only officer… was carried to the rear, severely wounded, and the colour sergeant was killed, these soldiers [Millar and another private, Walter Cook] went to the front, took a prominent part in directing the company and displayed a courage, coolness and discipline, which was the admiration of all who witnessed it.' His VC is in the National War Museum of Scotland.

The Mutiny was finally put down in 1859. Of 182 recipients of the VC, 42 were Scots. This signalled the end of the British East India Company's rule in India and led to direct rule by the British government (the British Raj). Sadly, it didn't end hostilities and tension remained high on the subcontinent for many years, with numerous bloody battles in which young soldiers were again called on to show their indefatigable courage. The experience they gained there was to prove invaluable in other parts of the world.

Lieutenant Colonel John McNeill, 33 and from Colonsay, Argyll, had served in the Bengal Infantry but had transferred to the Royal Sussex Regiment to serve in the Waikato-Hauhau campaign during the Maori War in New Zealand. He won his VC on 30 March 1864: 'Lieutenant Colonel McNeill was proceeding to Te Awamutu on duty at the time… having seen a body of the enemy in front, [he] sent Private Gibson back to bring up infantry from Ohanpu, and he and Private Vosper proceeded leisurely to the top of a rise to watch the enemy. Suddenly they were attacked by about 50 natives.… Private Vosper's horse fell and threw him. The natives thereupon rushed forward to seize him, but Lieutenant Colonel McNeill… returned, caught his horse and helped him to mount. The natives were firing sharply at them, and were so near that… it was only by galloping as hard as they could that they escaped.' John McNeill was later promoted to major general, knighted and served as equerry to Queen Victoria for 27 years. He died at St James's Palace in 1904. His VC is privately owned.

The British-French allies had been fighting the second Opium War (1856–60) in China for four long years when a 20-year-old soldier from Edinburgh exhibited the sort of courage that wins VCs. Private John McDougall was serving with the 44th Regiment (later the Essex Regiment) when they were ordered to take the Taku Forts at the mouth of the Pei Ho River, crucial to the Qing dynasty and Peking. They began their assault at 6am on 21 August 1860. They surged across a dry ditch but then had to struggle across two moats before reaching the walls of the fort. Attempts to use scaling ladders were repelled. Private John McDougall was part of a small group led by a young lieutenant and they improvised by sticking their bayonets into the mud walls, creating a makeshift ladder the Chinese could not throw off. John McDougall was immediately on the shoulder of the officer in the scramble and their breach of the fort was the beginning of the end for the Chinese. By the end of the skirmish, 400 out of the 500 defending the fort were dead or wounded. Private McDougall's part is described in his VC citation: 'Private McDougall along with his officer, Lieutenant Rogers and an officer of the 67th Regiment, Lieutenant Lenon, displayed great gallantry by entering the North Taku Fort by a small opening in the parapet, after swimming across the ditches. They were the first of the British to be established on the walls of the fort. Lieutenant Rogers was the first through followed next by Private McDougall, then Lieutenant Lenon.' John McDougall died just nine years later at the age of 29. His Victoria Cross was stolen in 1960 and never recovered. The thief left behind the ribbon and suspension bar, which are in the Essex Regiment Museum. (Twenty-four other VCs have been stolen, lost or destroyed.)

Lieutenant James Dundas, son of a Scottish judge and just 22 years old, was serving in the Himalayas, attached to the Bengal Engineers in the Bhutan War – described as 'a small punitive expedition' – when he won his VC. His handful of soldiers had been fighting for three hours under a blistering sun against about 200 enemy tribesmen. His citation tells the story: 'On April 30 1865 at Dewan-Giri, Bhutan, the enemy had barricaded themselves in the blockhouse, which they continued to defend after the main body was in retreat. The blockhouse, which was loop-holed, was the key to the enemy's position and on the orders of the general in command, Lieutenant Dundas and another officer [William Trevor] had to climb a 14-foot wall and then go head first through an opening only two feet wide. The two officers scaled the wall, followed, after they had set the example, by the Sikh soldiers, but they were both wounded. Dundas continued to fight and eventually killed four combatants and took eight prisoners.' Lieutenant Dundas's injuries included an arrow wound in the side and serious cut on his head. As William Trevor wrote in a letter home: 'Dundas was covered in blood... and glory. Despite his wounds, he borrowed a musket and got five or six. Luckily, the arrow turned on a rib or it might have been disagreeable. After that there was a desperate hand-to-hand struggle as the Bhutans charged with their swords but we were by then strongly established and they were shot down faster than they had calculated.' James Dundas was later promoted to Captain but was killed in action at Sherpur in Afghanistan, on 23 December 1879. He was 36. The Dundas Bridge between Kabul and Bagram was named after him by the Royal Engineers who were involved with reconstruction work in the country in 2002. His VC was auctioned in 1997 for more than £28,000.

In the 1870s, Assam in the east of India was home to many British tea planters, who were far from popular with the local tribes, the Nagas and the Lushais. The simmering unrest boiled over when a Scots couple, the Winchesters from Elgin, were killed and their six-year-old daughter Mary kidnapped by the Lushais. The Gurkha Rifles were part of the expedition force sent to rescue the child. It was not an easy task because of the mountainous terrain and thick jungle. As the Gurkhas approached, the tribesmen set up a bamboo stockade and set fire to buildings to provide a smoke screen but Major Donald Macintyre and a rifleman scaled the nine foot high barricade and fought their way through the fierce tribesmen. Major Macintyre, 40 and from Kingcraig in Ross and Cromarty, was awarded the VC for his gallantry: 'On January 4 1872, Major Macintyre led the assault on the stockaded village of Lalgnoora. He was the first to reach the stockade, at that time about nine feet high, and successfully stormed it under heavy fire from the enemy.' The young girl, who had been in captivity for more than a year, was found alive and unharmed. She had been taught the native language and, despite her age, smoked a pipe. The tribesmen had cut off her hair and kept it as a souvenir. Donald Mcintyre later reached the rank of major general and was knighted. He died in 1903 and his VC is in the Gurkha Museum, Winchester.

Having enlisted in the 42nd Highland Regiment in 1858, 36-year-old Sergeant Samuel McGaw, from Kirkmichael, Ayrshire, was already a veteran of the Indian Mutiny when he went with his regiment to West Africa in 1874. He had been at the infamous Siege of Lucknow and fought in a string of ferocious battles on the sub-continent. But it was in Ashanti, during an attack on the small town of Amoaful (now part of Ghana), on January 21 that Sergeant McGaw won his VC. His citation read: 'Sergeant McGaw, although severely wounded early in the initial attack, led his section through the dense thorny bush and engaged the enemy several times during the day. For his conduct throughout the battle Samuel McGaw was later awarded the Victoria Cross.' Samuel McGaw served in Malta (1874–78) before moving to Cyprus. During the march from the Larnaca docks to his new camp, Sergeant McGaw collapsed and died of heat stroke. He was buried close to where he died and his grave was marked by a small wooden cross. Some time later, a Black Watch officer learned the grave had been ploughed over by a local farmer. He arranged for the remains to be collected and re-buried in the English Cemetery at Kyrenia. The sergeant's VC is in the Lord Ashcroft collection.

There were four Scots awarded VCs in the Afghanistan campaign in which James Dundas (see above) died. This was a comparatively minor skirmish which involved British demands for a military presence in Kabul being resisted by the emir. This inevitably escalated and, in September 1878, the British residency at Kabul was attacked and only a handful of people were able to escape. The military fought their way back, prompting a call among the Afghans for a jihad. That in turn led to an inglorious retreat to Kandahar and a protracted series of actions.

One of the Scots who showed exceptional courage was Captain John Cook, from Edinburgh. He was 35 and serving with the Bengal Staff Corps. He was a career soldier who had been nominated as a cadet for the Bengal Cavalry when he was just 11 and served in India from the age of 17. He saw early action with the 3rd Sikh Regiment and was mentioned in dispatches for 'leading a very effectual bayonet charge.' In 1868, he was promoted to adjutant and then went on to serve with the Gurkhas. He won the VC for his courage in the battle at Peiwar Kotal, not far from Kabul, on 2 December 1878: 'Captain Cook, through heavy fire, charged out of the entrenchments with such impetuosity that the enemy broke and fled. At the close of the melee, seeing that Major Galbraith was in personal conflict with an Afghan soldier, Captain Cook distracted attention to himself and a hand-to-hand encounter ensued, during which both men fell to the ground. The Afghan seized the captain's arm in his teeth until the struggle was ended by the man being shot in the head.' That citation offers a dramatic enough report of the incident but in a letter to a young relative in 1926, John Cook's brother Walter (Lieutenant Colonel Cook, also of the 3rd Sikh Regiment) wrote in more hair-raising detail: 'The official account says "both fell to the ground" but, as a matter of fact, your uncle cross-buttocked the Afghan and, being an immensely powerful man, strangled him with his hands. Some pretty stiff fighting followed but the enemy's position being taken in flank was ultimately vacated and the position occupied. The safety of the Roberts Force and its further advance was thus secured but, while it lasted, the initial scrimmage was touch and go and one moment's hesitation on your uncle's part would have given the enemy, already alarmed, time to man all his breastworks. The saving of Major Galbraith's life was merely the official peg to hang the VC on, so to speak, the real service was the instant and successful onslaught on the breastwork. On this depended the safety of the whole Force and, it is not too much to say, the whole of the future Lord Roberts' career as a great and successful general. Some months later, the general personally decorated your uncle with the VC and never forgot the great service he had rendered.' John Cook was promoted to major but was killed in action a year later at Sharpur.

Lieutenant William Dick-Cunyngham (28) of Edinburgh and the Gordon Highlanders, won the VC but he, too, later died from war wounds received during the 118-day siege of Ladysmith in 1900. But it was at Kandahar that the lieutenant showed extreme courage in the face of the enemy. His citation reads: 'For the conspicuous gallantry and coolness displayed by him on 13 December 1879 at the attack on the Sherpur Pass, in Afghanistan, in having exposed himself to the full fire of the enemy, and by his example and encouragement rallied the men who, having been beaten back, were, at the moment, wavering at the top of the hill.' William Dick-Cunyngham was promoted to captain before being fatally wounded during an attempt to break the stalemate at Ladysmith. He is buried there and his VC is in the Gordon Highlanders Museum.

A day later, 28-year-old Lance Corporal George Sellar from Keith, serving in the Seaforth Highlanders, showed the courage it takes to win the VC. His citation reads: 'On December 14, 1879 at the Asmai Heights, near Kabul, Lance Corporal Sellar led the attack under heavy fire and dashing on in front of the party up a slope, engaged in desperate conflict with one of the enemy who sprang out to meet him. In this encounter Lance Corporal Sellar was severely wounded.' George Sellar recovered from his injuries and was later promoted to sergeant, but died in 1889 when he was just 39. His VC is in the Highlanders Museum at Fort George.

The fourth Scot to win the VC in Afghanistan was Captain William Vousden (34) from Perth. He had trained at Sandhurst and was serving with in the 5th Punjab Cavalry when he won his medal: 'On 14 December 1879 on the Koh Asmai Heights, near Kabul, Captain Vousden charged with a small party into the centre of the line of the retreating Kohistani Force, by whom they were greatly outnumbered. After rapidly charging through the enemy backwards and forwards several times, Captain Vousden and his party swept off round the opposite side of the village and joined the rest of the troops.' He later achieved the rank of major general and served as commandant of the

5th Punjab Cavalry and then as Inspector General of Cavalry in India. Sadly his service in the Indian climate was to cost him his life. He died in Lahore, of dysentery, when he was just 54.

The tension in India continued for many years, the conflict often starting among the region's royal factions and escalating when the British tried to intervene. Such was the case in Manipur on the north-east border with Burma in 1891, and just how bloody it was can be seen in a contemporary report of what happened when the viceroy (then Lord Lansdowne) sent in his officers to remove one of the warring chiefs, Tikendrajit Singh: 'When the British officers moved towards the gate, the infuriated people attacked them and the officers found themselves in the gravest danger. Mr Quinton, the chief commissioner of Assam, Colonel Skene, Mr Cossins, Lieutenant Simpson and the bugler were beheaded by the public executioner just in front of the two dragons by the order of Tikendrajit Singh and General Thangal.' That was on 24 March 1891 and then Manipur troops attacked all the British outposts in the district. Among those trying to retrieve the situation was Lieutenant Charles Grant. He was 29, from Bourtie, Aberdeenshire, serving with the 8th Gurkha Rifles. His bravery throughout the conflict (21 March to 9 April 1891) won him the VC. The citation offers just one example of his heroic deeds: 'Lieutenant Grant volunteered to attempt the relief of the British captives with 80 native soldiers. Inspiring his men with his example of personal daring and resource, the lieutenant captured Thobal, and held it against a large force of the enemy.' Charles Grant was later promoted to brevet colonel. His VC is in the National Army Museum.

One of the last bloody exchanges on the Indian subcontinent was the 1897–98 Tirah Campaign on the North-West Frontier, when the British troops were under the command of the Scottish General Sir William Lockhart (known affectionately by the native troops as 'Amir Sahib'). Lockhart, who was from Lanarkshire, became commander-in-chief of all British forces in India at the end of the campaign.

Three officers serving with the Indian Army's Corps of Guides in the campaign were 41-year-old Major Sir Robert Bellew Adams, whose family was well known in Inverness, 26-year-old Lieutenant Viscount Fincastle, and 27-year-old Lieutenant MacLean, a former student at Fettes College, Edinburgh. They each won the VC for their part in the daring attempted rescue of a wounded fellow officer surrounded by savage tribesmen. Their citation said: 'On 17 August 1897 at Nawa Kili, Upper Swat, Lieutenant Colonel Adams, Lieutenants Hector MacLean and Viscount Fincastle and five men of the Guides, went under a heavy and close fire, to the rescue of a lieutenant of the Lancashire Fusiliers who was lying disabled by a bullet wound and surrounded by enemy swordsmen. While the wounded officer was being brought under cover, he was unfortunately killed by a bullet. One of the officers of the rescue party was also mortally wounded and Colonel Adams' horse and three others were shot.' Second cousin of another VC winner (Lieutenant Edward Bellew Adams at Ypres in April 1915), Sir Robert rose to the rank of major general and served as aide-de-camp to the

King. He was one of the last to receive his medal from Queen Victoria, at Windsor Castle in 1898. Lord Fincastle went on to become aide-de-camp to the Viceroy of India (1894) and then served in the Boer War, during which he commanded Fincastle's Horse (cavalry). The 'mortally wounded' officer was Lieutenant MacLean. His VC was awarded posthumously. He is buried at Mardan on the India-Afghanistan border. The headstone was erected by his brother officers.

The last Scot to be awarded the VC in India was Piper George Findlater from Turriff, Aberdeenshire. He was 25 and serving with the Gordon Highlanders when he won his medal on 20 October 1897 for his outstanding bravery during the attack on the Dargai Heights. Piper Findlater was no stranger to courage in the face of the enemy. Earlier in the year he had taken part in the famous charge up the heights at Malakand and had a narrow escape when a bullet tore away the heel of his boot. He was said to have acquitted himself 'nobly' in other actions. At Darghai, as was the tradition, he and his fellow pipers were in the fore of the attack, playing the regimental march 'Cock o' the North' to spur on the infantrymen. The young piper was struck down in the heavy gunfire with wounds to both his legs. Despite that, he struggled to prop himself up against a boulder and the skirl of his pipes continued to soar above the sound of the grim battle. In his subsequent dispatch to the adjutant general in India, Sir William Lockhart wrote: 'The Gordon Highlanders went straight up the hill without check or hesitation. Headed by their pipers... this splendid battalion marched across the open. It dashed through a murderous fire.' Later, Findlater wrote home: 'I remember the colonel addressing the regiment, telling them what they were expected to do. I remember again the order for the regiment to attack and the order "Pipers to the front". When I got wounded, I remember falling and playing on but I was bleeding profusely and in a few minutes sickened. I am told I played for about five minutes. It never occurred to me that I had done anything to merit reward. What I did I could not help doing.' He later achieved the rank of pipe major, was invalided out of the army and turned down a job at Balmoral because of the poor pay. He instead went on a concert tour. His VC is in the Gordon Highlanders Museum.

Anglo-Sudan War

Before joining the army, Alexander Hore-Ruthven, the younger son of Lord Ruthven, had worked for a Glasgow tea merchant and tried his hand as a tea planter in Assam. Succumbing to malaria, he returned home and joined the Highland Light Infantry in 1892. He held a number of low-key posts until the outbreak of the second Anglo-Sudanese War in 1898. He managed to get himself seconded to the Egyptian Army and was given command of the Slavery Department Camel Corps. On 22 September 1898, he faced the Dervishes in the Battle of Gedaref, in which he showed such courage that he won the VC: 'Captain Hore-Ruthven, seeing an Egyptian officer lying wounded within 50 yards of the advancing Dervishes, who were firing and charging, picked up and carried him towards the 16th Egyptian Battalion. He put down the wounded officer two or three times and fired on the Dervishes, who were following, to check their advance. Had the officer been left where he dropped, he might have been killed.' A year later, Sandy Gore-Ruthven joined the Cameron Highlanders and in 1903 was appointed special services officer in Somaliland. He then went to Dublin as military secretary to the lord lieutenant of Ireland (1904–08). He then held the same post with the governor-general of Australia (1908–10), transferred to the Indian Army (1910–12) and joined the staff at the Quetta Staff and Command College. At the outbreak of the First World War, he went to France and in 1915 became a major in the Welsh Guards. He was seriously wounded during action in Gallipoli and was invalided back to Britain. Once recovered, he returned to France with the Guards Division and in 1918 was appointed brigadier general on the general staff of 7th Army Corps. He was mentioned in dispatches no fewer than five times. He won the DSO and Bar and was made a Companion of the Order of the Bath (CB). After the war, he commanded 29th Infantry Brigade, 28th Highland Brigade, the Welsh Guards and finally 1st Infantry Brigade before retiring in 1928.

This distinguished military service led to his appointment (by Prime Minister Stanley Baldwin) as governor general of South Australia (1928–34) and a knighthood. He is credited with easing the tensions caused by cricket's bodyline bowling row. His popularity in Australia was underlined by the huge crowd – said to be 100,000 – that turned up to say goodbye when he left for Britain. This may have influenced his further appointment as governor of New South Wales (1934–36) and then, as Baron Gowrie of Canberra and Dirleton, governor general of Australia (1936–45). He was due to leave Australia in 1939, when he would have been replaced by the Duke of Kent, but on the declaration of war, he was asked to stay on and completed the longest appointment of a governor general. In 1945, he was created the first Earl of Gowrie and appointed deputy constable and lieutenant governor of Windsor Castle, 1945–53, and was also made president of the MCC in 1948; he died in 1955, aged 82.

MATABELE REBELLION

When Rhodesia was established in 1895 (from the territories previously run by the British South Africa Company), the Matabele refused to accept the subsequent conditions imposed on them and rose in rebellion in March 1896. To counter this, the Bulawayo Field Force was raised, with officers including Robert Baden-Powell.

It was a savage campaign. The Matabele Impis worked in small groups, set up mountain strongholds and carried out raids and ambushes. In the first raid, on Friday 20 March, a native policeman was killed, and that was followed two days later by the death of a British family attacked by assegais. Everything escalated from there, with isolated farmers and small communities under constant threat.

In his book *Sunshine and Storm in Rhodesia*, the leader of the Field Force, Frederick Selous, said the government was able to muster less than 600 rifles and a few machine guns in Bulawayo. Horses and food were in short supply, while the Matebele had more than ten thousand well-armed warriors, including many native policemen who had deserted to the enemy with their rifles.

It was against this grim backdrop that Herbert Henderson from Hillhead, Glasgow, enlisted in the Artillery Troop of the Bulawayo Field Force. He was a former pupil of Kelvinside Academy who, after completing his engineering apprenticeship, had gone to Belfast to work in the Harland and Wolff shipyard. He wasn't happy there so he went to work in the goldmines of South Africa in 1892 and two years later moved to Rhodesia, where he was engineer of the Queen's Mine. As the rebellion grew and his community was threatened, Herbert Henderson volunteered to ride to Bulawayo for help. A contemporary report underlines the chronic shortage of weapons and ammunition: 'For protection on this perilous ride he had been given a revolver and one cartridge, all that was available.' On 30 March, ten days into the rising, Trooper Henderson should have been celebrating his 26th birthday. Instead, he and another man, Trooper Celliers, were in a dangerous game of hide-and-seek with the marauding Matebele. They had been scouting for their 30-strong group, which had been sent from Bulawayo to rescue another beleaguered patrol. They were ambushed and, during a ferocious skirmish with the rebels, the two were isolated. Trooper Celliers was wounded in the knee and his horse was shot from under him. Henderson immediately dismounted, lifted the injured man onto his horse and headed away from the battle. Trooper Celliers, suffering serious loss of blood, bravely asked to be left while his comrade escaped. Herbert Henderson ignored the plea and started the 56-kilometre walk – through thick bush and a countryside still crawling with the rebels – to Bulawayo. For two days and two nights they struggled through the bush, somehow evading the rebels, before eventually staggering to safety. It was an act of courage and endurance that won Herbert Henderson the VC.

Earl Grey (then administrator for Rhodesia) referred to it as 'gallant conduct and a brave feat.' It was the first VC to be won in Rhodesia. After the rebellion, Herbert Henderson returned to the gold mining industry. He received his VC from the governor of the Cape Colony in November 1897. He was unable to enlist for service in the First World War because his was a reserved occupation. Throughout the Second World War, he committed the profits from the Prince Olaf Mine to the War Fund. He died in 1942 and is buried in Bulawayo. The conflict was finally brought to an end when Baden-Powell was able to arrange talks between the Matebele chiefs and Cecil Rhodes.

BOER WAR

The Boer War (1899–1902) was a very different military campaign from those that had gone before. It was fought between two massively unequal protagonists: nearly half a million British and Commonwealth troops massed against 88,000 Afrikaners from the republics of Transvaal and the Orange Free State. Recognising they could never win in full confrontation with such a numerically superior force, the Boers shrewdly developed guerrilla tactics with new-style hit-and-run attacks on British targets. The Afrikaners called them 'kommando' raids and thus introduced the word into military language.

The war started off conventionally and within ten days of arriving in South Africa in October 1899 the Gordon Highlanders were among the first to confront the Boers at the Battle of Elandslaagte (in Natal). Contemporary reports say the battle was a foretaste of two long years of conflict: 'The sky had steadily been growing dark with thunderclouds and, as the British made their assault, the storm burst. In the poor visibility and pouring rain, the infantry had to face a barbed wire farm fence, in which several men were entangled and shot. Nevertheless, they cut the wire or broke it down and occupied the main part of the Boer position.' Although some of the Boers quickly surrendered, others led a counter-attack that initially drove the British infantry back in confusion. The Gordons rallied, inspired by their pipers, and charged again to win what was to be one of the few tactical victories of the war.

With that also came the award of the first VC of the campaign: to Sergeant Major William Robertson from Dumfries. He was 34 and already a veteran of the long conflict in India. As his citation makes clear, his gallantry could not have been more in the face of the enemy: 'During the final advance on the enemy position, this warrant officer led each successive rush, exposing himself fearlessly to the enemy's artillery and rifle fire to encourage the men. After the main position had been captured, he led a small party to seize the Boer camp. Though exposed to a deadly cross-fire from the enemy's rifles he gallantly held the position and continued to encourage the men until he was wounded in two places and sustained a compound fracture of the left arm.' That commendation was endorsed by the Scottish CO, Brigadier General Ian Hamilton, who witnessed the sergeant major's bravery. He wrote: 'No better VC was ever won than William Robertson's. There was no vainglory about it but the danger was incurred in a cool and reasoned spirit for a military end of real importance.' William Robertson received his medal personally from Queen Victoria at Windsor Castle and was given the Freedom of Dumfries on Christmas Day, 1900. He went on to become an honorary lieutenant. In the 1914–18 war, he was promoted to lieutenant colonel and served in the crucial role of recruiting officer in Edinburgh. He also received an OBE. One son, also William, became a captain in the Royal Army Medical Corps. Another, Jon Gordon, followed him into the Gordons and was a second lieutenant when he was killed in action on the Somme in 1916. Lieutenant Colonel Robertson's VC is in the National War Museum of Scotland.

In the same battle, another Gordon Highlander, Captain Matthew Meiklejohn, of St Andrews, also won the VC: 'After the main Boer position had been captured, some of the men of the Gordon Highlanders, when about to advance, were exposed to a heavy crossfire, and, having lost their leaders, commenced to waver. Seeing this, Captain Meiklejohn rushed to the front and called on the Gordons to follow him. By his conspicuous bravery and fearless example he rallied the men and led them against the enemy's position where he fell, desperately wounded in four places.' The wounds were so serious that he lost his right arm, but he was later promoted to major and in 1901 he was garrison adjutant on St Helena. He died in July 1913 after falling from his horse in Hyde Park, London. He was given a military funeral and he is commemorated by a plaque on the wall of the Hyde Park Barracks. His Victoria Cross is in the Gordon Highlanders Museum.

There were 78 VCs awarded during this war. Nine went to Scots. Major William Babtie, from Dumbarton, was 40 and serving in the Royal Army Medical Corps when he won the VC for his bravery in assisting wounded soldiers while under fire in the Battle of Colenso, December 1899: 'Major Babtie rode up under heavy rifle fire to attend to the wounded, who were lying in an advanced donga [gully] close to the rear of the guns. When he arrived at the donga, he attended to all the wounded, going from place to place, exposed to the heavy rifle fire levelled at anyone who showed himself. Later in the day Major Babtie went out with another officer to bring in a lieutenant who was lying wounded on the veldt. This also under very heavy fire.' William Babtie was later given responsibility for medical provision in both the Mesopotamian and the Dardanelles campaigns during the Great War. He achieved the rank of lieutenant general, was knighted and became Inspector of Medical Services. At the end of the war, in 1918, he chaired the Babtie Committee on the reorganisation of army medical services. His VC is in the Army Medical Services Museum, Aldershot.

A month later, Lieutenant Robert James Digby-Jones, 23 and a Royal Engineer from Edinburgh, was posthumously awarded the VC for his crucial part in the defence of Wagon Hill, during the siege of Ladysmith. A subsequent report in the *South African Review* (24 February 1900) said of the young lieutenant: 'So far as can be humanly judged, it was this officer who saved Ladysmith and the British army from the mortification of a defeat and its incalculable consequences.' Lieutenant Digby-Jones and his engineers were responsible for strengthening the defences and preparing gun positions. As they set up the two 12-pounder guns and a 4.7 inch howitzer under cover of darkness, they came under withering rifle fire. It was an onslaught that lasted for more than 12 hours. During those long hours, all the officers of the main British units – the Gordons and the Imperial Light Horse – were killed or seriously wounded, so Digby-Jones took command, rallying the hard-pressed men again and again as they fought to keep control of the crest of the hill. At one point, the exhausted defenders looked likely to be overwhelmed and some retreated in disarray. When Digby-Jones realised how close the enemy was he snatched up a rifle and, breaking cover, shot the Boer commander at almost point-blank range. He was then heard to say: 'What's up? The infantry have gone.' One of his men shouted: 'There's an order to retire, sir.' His simple reply was: 'I have no order to retire.' He told his men to fix bayonets, led them in a charge and succeeded in re-occupying the firing line in front of the emplacement. While later leading his men forward on yet another charge, he was struck in the throat by a bullet and died instantly.

As the *Army and Navy Gazette* reported on 27 January 1900, 'Lieutenant Digby-Jones' name will stand out in the history of the siege of Ladysmith as one who set a brilliant example to all about him, and brought no little credit on the corps of Royal Engineers. He did his duty nobly to the end!' The young lieutenant had previously been mentioned in dispatches for having successfully destroyed the 4.7 inch Boer gun on Surprise Hill, during the sortie from Ladysmith on 10 December 1899. A press witness reported: 'The first fuse inserted into the gun was defective but Lieutenant Digby-Jones went back at the risk of death or mutilation and inserted another, which successfully destroyed the gun, which had been causing much annoyance to the garrison.' Lieutenant Digby-Jones' younger brother, Owen, was commissioned in the Royal Engineers on the very day that his brother was killed; his grand uncle was Major General John Christie, aide-de-camp to Queen Victoria, who raised the 1st Bengal Cavalry in 1838; one cousin, Major General John Graham, served during the Indian Mutiny; and another, Lieutenant Colonel Robert Aitken, won the VC at Lucknow. He is buried in Ladysmith. His medal, which was sent to his parents by post (on the order of the King) is in the Royal Engineers Museum.

Lance Corporal John Mackay was 26, yet another veteran of the North-West Frontier campaign in India, and serving with the Gordon Highlanders just outside Johannesburg when he faced the soldier's ultimate test – the chance to risk his life for his comrades. He didn't hesitate and his gallantry won him the VC: 'On May 20 1900, during the action at Doornkop, near Johannesburg, Mackay repeatedly rushed forward, under a withering fire at short range, to attend to wounded comrades, dressing their wounds while he himself was without shelter and, in one instance, carrying a wounded man from the open under heavy fire to the shelter of a boulder.' Two months later and by then a corporal, John Mackay was again mentioned in dispatches 'for an act of gallantry.' When one of his officers, Captain David Younger (see later entry) 'was lying mortally wounded and exposed to a terrific fire, Corporal MacKay went out alone and carried him to a place of safety.' John Mackay later served in the First World War and achieved the rank of lieutenant colonel in command of the 2/6th Battalion of the Highland Light Infantry. When that was disbanded in 1919, he served with the Argyll and Sutherland Highlanders. His Victoria Cross is displayed at the Gordon Highlanders Museum in Aberdeen.

John Mackenzie, from Contin in Ross-shire, was 29 and a sergeant in the Seaforth Highlanders when he showed his astonishing courage at Dompoase, Ashanti (now Ghana) on 6 June 1900: 'Sergeant Mackenzie, after working two Maxim guns under heavy fire and being wounded while doing so, volunteered to clear the stockade of the enemy. This he did, most gallantly, leading the charge himself and driving the enemy headlong into the bush.' John Mackenzie was later commissioned as second lieutenant in the Black Watch and became a captain in the Royal Scots on 22 January 1904. He was mentioned in dispatches for his work during the Aro Expedition, also in 1906 when he was staff officer of the Munster Field Force, and once more during the Kano-

Sokoto Expedition. He was promoted to major during the First World War and was commanding officer of the 2nd Battalion of the Bedfordshire Regiment. He was killed while leading his men out of the trenches in the Battle of Loos, on 17 May 1915. He is buried in the Guards Cemetery, Windy Corner, Cuinchy, in Northern France. His pipe banner is located in the Museum at Edinburgh Castle and his Victoria Cross is in the Regimental Museum of the Queen's Own Highlanders.

Captain William Gordon, 34, of Bridge of Allan, Stirlingshire, was another veteran of the Tirah Expedition Force in India where he had been adjutant to the Gordons. He had won a series of bravery awards – five clasps to his Queen's Medal, two clasps to his King's Medal, three mentions in dispatches – before the action that brought the Victoria Cross: 'On July 11 1900, during the action at Leehoehoek (near Krugersdorf), a party of men, accompanied by Captains Younger and Allan, having succeeded in dragging an artillery wagon under cover, when its horses were unable to do so by reason of the heavy and accurate fire of the enemy. Captain Gordon called for volunteers to go out with him to try and bring in one of the guns. He went out alone to the nearest gun under a heavy fire and with the greatest coolness, fastened the drag-rope to the gun and then beckoned to the men, who immediately doubled out, to join him, in accordance with his previous instructions. While moving the gun, Captain Younger [see below] and three men were hit. Seeing that further attempts would only result in further casualties, Captain Gordon ordered the remainder of the party under cover of the kopje again and, having seen the wounded safely away, himself retired. Captain Gordon's conduct under a particularly heavy and most accurate fire at only 600 yards' range was most admirable and his manner of handling his men most masterly; his devotion on every occasion that his battalion has been under fire has been remarkable.' He received his medal from Lord Kitchener on Peace Thanksgiving Day in June 1902. He later served as quartermaster general to the Highland Division and in 1913, he was appointed aide-de-camp to the King and promoted to colonel. He was taken prisoner in the Great War but released in an exchange of prisoners. His medal is on display at the Gordon Highlanders Museum, Aberdeen.

The Captain Younger mentioned in William Gordon's citation was David Reginald Younger. Hailing from Moffat, he was just 29 when he was killed in the action that won him the posthumous VC: 'Captain Younger took out a party which successfully dragged an artillery wagon under cover of a small kopje, though exposed to very heavy and accurate enemy fire. He also accompanied a second party who went out to try to bring in the guns but during the afternoon he was mortally wounded, dying shortly afterwards. His cool and gallant conduct was the admiration of all who witnessed it.' Captain Younger, cousin of William Younger MP, was buried in the cemetery at Krugersdorp. A marble cross was erected over his grave by brother officers.

Private Charles Kennedy, from Edinburgh, was serving with the Highland Light Infantry in November 1900, when his company was assigned to the garrison at Dewetsdorp, 40 miles south-east of Bloemfontein, capital of the Orange Free State.

They were attacked by a Boer guerrilla unit and forced off Gibraltar Hill, a crucial vantage point overlooking the town. Private Kennedy and six other men volunteered to retake the position but when one of the group went to get water, he was shot. Charles Kennedy immediately rushed to help him without regard for his own safety. It was a selfless act that won him the VC. The citation said: 'Private Kennedy carried a comrade, dangerously wounded and bleeding to death from Gibraltar Hill to hospital for three-quarters of a mile under very hot fire. Next day, volunteers were called for to take a message across a space over which it was almost certain death to venture and Private Kennedy at once stepped forward. He did not, however, succeed in delivering the message, being severely wounded before he had gone 20 yards.' Private Kennedy received his VC from King Edward VII at St James' Palace in December 1901. His wound was so serious he was discharged from the army the following year and returned to Edinburgh. A few years later, he again showed his courage when a horse pulling a cart bolted in Leith Walk. While trying to stop it, he was run over by the cart. He died on the way to hospital. He was buried in an unmarked grave. The Royal Highland Fusiliers finally arranged a headstone in 2001.

Sergeant Donald Farmer (from Biggar) was just 23 but already a decorated veteran of the Sudan campaign of 1898, when he became the first Cameron Highlander to win the VC. His citation reads: 'On 13 December 1900, during an attack at Nooitgedacht, a lieutenant with 15 men went to the assistance of a piquet which was heavily engaged, most of the men having been killed or wounded. The enemy, who were hidden by trees, immediately opened fire on the relief party, killing two and wounding five, including the lieutenant. Sergeant Farmer at once went to the officer, who was quite helpless, and carried him away under heavy fire to a place of comparative safety, after which he returned to the firing line and was eventually taken prisoner.' The officer whose life Donald Farmer saved later became Major General Sandilands, while he himself served in the Great War as a regimental sergeant major with the Liverpool Scottish and went on to become a lieutenant colonel. At his funeral in Liverpool in 1956, his coffin was carried by six warrant officers while the piper played 'Flowers of the Forest' and the specially composed march 'Colonel DD Farmer VC'. His medal is in the Regimental Museum of the Queen's Own Highlanders, Fort George.

The Boer War was finally concluded with the signing of the Treaty of Vereeniging in May 1902.

FIRST WORLD WAR

The chronology now takes us to the Great or First World War, in which the award of 67 VCs to Scots soldiers indelibly illustrates both the scale and horror of the conflict and the crucial part that Scottish regiments played in it.

On 22 August 1914 the campaign had just entered its fourth week when 33-year-old Lance Corporal Charles Jarvis (born in Fraserburgh but brought up in Carnoustie) was awarded the first Victoria Cross of the grimmest of grim campaigns. He was serving with the 57th Field Company Royal Engineers as part of the British Expeditionary Force, which had moved up to the Mons-Condé canal during the night with the intention of advancing into Belgium in the morning. However, the force found itself seriously outnumbered and the order was given to defend the line of the canal and destroy the bridges. That was a task for the Royal Engineers. Charles Jarvis and a sapper called Neary were given the job of blowing up the Bridge of Jemappes. His VC citation completes the story: 'Working from a small boat held in position by two infantrymen, Jarvis and Neary painstakingly applied demolition charges to the girder supports. All the while they were in full view of the enemy and under intense fire. As their situation worsened, Jarvis sent the infantrymen back into cover. He himself continued to work for over an hour, occasionally dashing back for extra explosives and to run out the leads. As the gunfire intensified, the infantry themselves were forced to fall back, leaving Jarvis dangerously exposed. An electrical exploder was now needed to set away the demolition but there was only one to destroy five bridges spaced three miles apart. Ducking down in the boat, Jarvis pulled himself along the bank to safety. It was nothing short of a miracle that he escaped unhurt. Only one of the eight bridges allocated to 57th Field Company was destroyed, but this in no way detracts from the heroism of those who attempted it.' Two months later, in a further action, Charles Jarvis was wounded and invalided home. He was presented with the medal by King George V at Buckingham Palace on 13 January 1915. He was discharged in January 1917 and claimed in a newspaper interview that this was because the army wanted to avoid paying him the pension then granted for 18 years' service (he had served since 1900). He worked in Portsmouth Dockyard during the Second World War. He died in 1948 and is buried in Cupar, Fife. In Carnoustie, he is commemorated with a bronze plaque in Jarvis Place.

Less than a month later, the Highland Light Infantry went into action in Verneuil in Normandy and within an hour 28-year-old Private George Wilson had embarked on what was described as 'a remarkable deed of heroism and one of the most effective and courageous of the war.' Private Wilson, from Edinburgh, was scouting with an officer when he saw two German snipers, but before they could react, the officer was shot dead. George Wilson returned fire and killed both enemy soldiers.

As he moved forward about a hundred yards, he saw eight more Germans and, again without stopping to consider options, he charged at them, shouting as though he was accompanied by other troops. The Germans immediately surrendered and also handed over two British prisoners they had taken. Shortly afterwards, as his troop was pinned down by the deadly fire of the German Maxim machine gun, the Edinburgh man was shocked to see scores of dead and wounded soldiers who had been part of an earlier attack and had been mown down. He was so angered by the carnage that he determined to destroy the German position. With another volunteer, he inched his way forward, ignoring the withering hail of heavy bullets. After less than a hundred yards, his mate was killed. Undeterred, he took aim and killed the machine-gunner... and then wiped out the gunner's forward support group of six. When he was within yards of the gun, the sole remaining German officer emptied his revolver at him. Somehow, he missed and George Wilson ran him through with his bayonet. Having captured the gun, he immediately turned it on the German lines and is reported to have fired 750 rounds at the enemy, ignoring heavy shellfire. He was eventually forced back to his own lines, where he fainted. After coming round, he found no one had retrieved the Maxim so he set off again to bring it back and then took two more trips to retrieve two and a half cases of ammunition. Even then he wasn't finished: he went back once more to recover the body of his dead comrade. George Wilson received his VC from King George V two days before it was even gazetted. It is in the Royal Highland Fusiliers museum in Glasgow. He died from tuberculosis at the age of 40 and was buried in a grave unmarked until his regiment erected a tombstone in 2003.

Captain Harry Ranken, at 31, was already a veteran of Glasgow Western Infirmary and a fever hospital in London when he joined the Royal Army Medical Corps. Son of a minister in Irvine, he was destined for a glittering career in medicine after taking top place in the entrance exams, winning the Tulloch medal, prizes for military medicine, another for hygiene and coming first in the Order of Merit. He became an MRCP (1910) and passed his captain's exams in 1912, when he was posted to the Sudan as a member of the Sudan Sleeping Sickness Commission. At the outbreak of war, he immediately returned to London, enlisted in the King's Royal Rifle Corps and became part of the British Expeditionary Force in France.

In the fighting at Haute-Avesnes between 21 and 30 August 1914, Captain Ranken showed his gallantry by ignoring heavy enemy action to tend wounded soldiers and was awarded the French *Légion d'honneur* (Chevalier class). The next month his battalion moved to Soupir, where he was to win the VC for again looking after seriously wounded soldiers during a prolonged face-to-face confrontation with the Germans on September 19 and 20. On this occasion, however, he was badly wounded in the leg. He was taken to a military hospital but died of his wounds a few days later. The announcement of his VC the *London Gazette* was simple: 'For tending wounded in the trenches under fire and shrapnel fire and continuing to attend the wounded after his thigh and leg had been shattered (he has since died of his wounds).' *The Times History of War* states: 'No man ever won the Victoria Cross more nobly than did Captain Harry Ranken RAMC.' The administration block at the Queen Elizabeth Military Hospital was named in his honour. Although it is now a civilian hospital, his photograph and a copy of his citation are still displayed in the reception. His Victoria Cross is displayed at the Army Medical Services Museum in Aldershot. Two streets in Irvine also bear his name.

Private Ross Tollerton, from Ayr, was 24 and serving in the Queen's Own Cameron Highlanders when he won the VC at the Battle of the Aisne on September 14: 'Private Tollerton carried a wounded officer, under heavy fire, as far as he was able, into a place of greater safety. Then, although he himself was wounded in the head and hand, he struggled back to the firing line where he remained until his battalion retired. He then returned to the wounded officer and stayed with him for three days until they were both rescued.' When Ross Tollerton returned to civilian life, he became a school janitor in Irvine, but he never fully recovered from his wounds and died at the age of 41. Among the wreaths at his funeral was one from the officer he had saved. His Victoria Cross is in the regimental museum of the Queen's Own Highlanders.

Captain William Johnston was 34 years old, from Leith, and a career soldier first commissioned into the Royal Engineers in 1899. He served in Intelligence in Gibraltar (1900–05) and China (1908–11) and was at the Staff College, Camberley when war broke out. He then joined 59th Field Company Royal Engineers and went to Europe where he fought at Mons, Aisne, the Marne and Neuve Chapelle. He too won his VC on September 14 but at Missy, in an action described in his citation: 'Under heavy fire all day until 7pm, he worked single-handedly using two rafts to bring wounded soldiers and returning with ammunition thus enabling the advance brigade to maintain its position on across the river.' William Johnston received his VC from King George V on a visit to France in December 1914 and was promoted to major. Less than a year later, on 8 June 1915, he was killed by a sniper in the Ypres Salient, just four days after being appointed brigade major of 15th Brigade. He is buried in Perth Cemetery (China Wall), Zillebeke, Belgium. His VC is in the Royal Engineers Museum.

More than 20,000 men from Glasgow were killed in action in some of the bloodiest battles in the history of modern warfare. The first Glaswegian to be awarded the VC in 1914 was 29-year-old Private Henry May of the 1st Battalion Cameronians (Scottish Rifles). He had joined the army when he was just 17. At daybreak on 22 October, his platoon was the covering party ordered to hold the enemy in check while the battalion entrenched its position about 700 yards to the rear, close to the village of La Boutillerie. Although the Germans were only 50 yards to the platoon's front and attacked in numbers, Private May and his mates held out until the trench-digging to the rear had been completed. During the fighting, a lance corporal had been wounded and was lying about a hundred yards away. Ignoring a hail of bullets, Henry May dashed right across the German's firing line to try to help. As he and another NCO tried to assist the wounded man, he was shot dead in their arms. The NCO was also shot and left unconscious. At that moment, Private May saw his platoon commander fall to the ground with a bullet in his leg. He and another private managed to carry the officer towards safety before the other private, too, was shot and wounded. The lieutenant, who had lost a lot of blood, ordered Private May to leave him and look after himself. Henry May, for once, disobeyed. As the citation for his VC said: 'He, by some supreme effort, then dragged the wounded officer to the British trenches and safety. Private May's heroism and utter disregard for the safety of his own life was in the true tradition of the holders of the Victoria Cross.' But at a civic reception when he returned to Glasgow, Henry was the model of modesty. In replying to the toast he said: 'I only did what any other soldier would have done. Plenty of men have equalled what I did.' Henry May left the army when his regular engagement of 13 years expired in 1915. Having recovered from his wounds, he re-enlisted in 1918 – in the Army Service Corps – and reached the rank of lieutenant. After the war, he joined Glasgow Manufacturing, a hosiery company in which he became a partner. He died days before his 51st birthday and his funeral was attended by the Cameronians' CO and four other Scottish VC holders: Sergeant John McAulay, Sergeant Robert Downie, Private David Lauder and Drum Major Walter Ritchie. He is buried and has a family headstone at Riddrie Park Cemetery, Glasgow. His VC is in the Cameronians' Museum, Hamilton.

Aberdeen-born Lieutenant James Brooke was the son of Sir Harry Brooke and had won the 'Sword of Honour' as the best cadet in his year at Sandhurst. He was 30 and serving with the Gordon Highlanders in Belgium when, on 29 October, he noticed the Germans were breaking through part of the line. He immediately gathered his men and led a charge that, according to report, 'saved the situation and a huge number of British lives.' And then he did it all over again… but this time he was killed. His VC was awarded posthumously. The citation reads: 'For most conspicuous bravery and great ability in leading two attacks on the German trenches under heavy rifle and machine-gun fire, regaining a lost trench at a very critical moment. He was killed on that day. By his marked coolness and promptitude on this occasion, Lieutenant Brooke prevented the enemy from breaking through our line at a time when a general counter-attack could not have been organised.' As well as his VC, Lieutenant Brooke was promoted posthumously to the rank of captain. He was buried at Zandvoorde British Cemetery, not far from Ypres. His medal is in the Gordon Highlanders Museum, Aberdeen.

Lieutenant Walter Brodie was 29 and from Edinburgh and a veteran of ten years' service with the Highland Light Infantry when he found himself in what he described as 'a bit of a scrap' in Flanders. When the Germans captured his two machine guns, he grabbed a rifle, shot five of them and then bayoneted another four. He then managed to get one of the machine guns back into action just as reinforcements charged in 'using bayonets, butts, boots and fists.' His citation read: 'For conspicuous gallantry near Becelaere on November 11, 1914 in clearing the enemy out of a portion of our trenches which they had succeeded in occupying. Heading the charge, he bayoneted several of the enemy, and thereby relieved a dangerous situation. As a result of Lieutenant Brodie's promptitude, 80 of the enemy were killed and 51 taken prisoner.' Walter Brodie was later promoted to lieutenant colonel and CO of the 2nd HLI. He won the Military Cross in 1916 but was killed in action leading his men at Moeuvres, France, in August 1918. He is buried in Bienvillers Military Cemetery.

Although a long way from the European theatre of war, Commander Henry Ritchie of the Royal Navy showed astonishing courage in the face of the same enemy – at Dar es Salaam, the Germans' colonial enclave in East Africa – and won the navy's first VC of the war on 28 November 1914. He had signed up in 1890 as a midshipman, two weeks before his fourteenth birthday. At 38, he was second-in-command of HMS *Goliath* and was ordered to the Tanganyikan port to counter German attacks on commercial shipping. With a commando-style crew, he sailed into the harbour in the ship's steam pinnace (a cross between a launch and an admiral's barge) armed only with a machine gun. He and his men caused havoc. They sank several small ships, destroyed the crucial wireless station and set fire to the governor's mansion. However, as they started to make their way back to *Goliath*, the German retribution was savage: they rained shells, machine-gun and rifle fire on the pinnace and Commander Ritchie was wounded no fewer than eight times. He never fully recovered and took early retirement in 1917 with the rank of acting captain. He did not receive his VC until November 1916 because of uncertainty at the Admiralty about what level of medal he should be awarded.

Edinburgh-born Lieutenant William Bruce was 24 and a Sandhurst graduate serving with the 59th Scinde Rifles, Indian Army. During the Battle of Givenchy in France, on 19 December 1914, he ignored his wounds to encourage his men in repelling German attacks on their position. His citation for the Victoria Cross tells the story: 'For most conspicuous bravery and devotion to duty: during a night attack, Lieutenant Bruce was in command of a small party which captured one of the enemy's trenches. In spite of being severely wounded in the neck, he walked up and down the trench, encouraging his men to hold on against several counter-attacks for some hours until killed. The fire from rifles and bombs was very heavy all day and it was due to the skilful disposition made and the example and encouragement shown by Lieutenant Bruce that his men were able to hold out until dusk, when the trench was finally captured by the enemy.' His VC, awarded posthumously, is in Victoria College, Jersey (his old school). There is a Bruce house there and each year his citation is read out on Remembrance Day.

Private James MacKenzie, from West Glen, Kirkcudbrightshire, was 26 and serving with the 2nd Battalion, Scots Guards at Rouges Bancs on 19 December 1914, when he made the ultimate sacrifice: he died trying to save his comrades. His VC citation read: 'A stretcher party had been forced to abandon an attempt to rescue a wounded man and Private McKenzie, under extremely heavy fire, went out and rescued the man from where he lay in front of the German trenches. Later, on the same day while carrying out the same kind of rescue, Private McKenzie was killed.' Private MacKenzie has no known grave but his name is on the Ploegsteert Memorial to the Missing in Belgium. There is also a memorial in Troqueer Parish Church, Dumfries. His Victoria Cross (the first won by the Scots Guards) is in the Guards' regimental headquarters.

Corporal William Anderson, 29 and from Dallas, Moray, was serving in the Yorkshire Regiment at Neuve Chapelle in France when he won his VC on 12 March 1915: 'Corporal Anderson led three men with bombs against a large party of the enemy who had entered the Allied trenches, and by his prompt and determined action saved what might have otherwise become a serious situation. Corporal Anderson first threw his own bombs, then those in the possession of the other men (all of whom had been wounded) amongst the Germans, after which he opened rapid fire upon them with great effect notwithstanding that he was at the time quite alone.' William Anderson was killed in the action and his body was never recovered. Such was the confusion of war that at home his local newspaper, the *Forres Gazette*, reported on 7 July 1915: 'After the engagement at Neuve Chapelle, he was reported missing but as a result of inquiry it was found that he had been wounded and his relatives are still in hopes that he was captured and is now a prisoner in Germany. In addition to his brother James who is in the same regiment drilling troops at Aldwick, another brother – the youngest of the family, is serving at the front with the Highland Light Infantry. Mrs Macleod, Caroline Street, Forres, is a daughter of the family. Her friends here congratulate her on the honour gained by her brother and will cherish with her the hopes that he may ere long be traced and return home in safety.' Corporal Anderson's VC was awarded posthumously and is in the Green Howards Museum.

Seaman George Samson of the Royal Navy Reserve, aged 26 and from Carnoustie, won his VC on the landing beaches at Gallipoli on 25 April 1915. He was serving aboard the SS *River Clyde*, an old coal boat that had been converted into a troop-carrier that could land solders – in this instance, men of the Dublin Fusiliers – via lighters and gangways direct onto the beaches. A contemporary report shows how hazardous it was: 'The open boats and the *River Clyde* touched ground almost at the same moment and no sooner had the first of them grated on the bottom than a terrific fire was opened from the whole of the surrounding hills that dominated the beach. For a considerable distance to seaward the bottom had been strewn with barbed wire and as the Dublin Fusiliers leapt into the water they found themselves entangled in the wire and were shot down where they stood. The open boats were held fast and their naval crews were wiped out.' George Samson's role was to secure the lighters and gangways and, as his citation states, 'he worked all day under very heavy fire, attending wounded and getting out lines. He was eventually dangerously wounded by Maxim fire.' He received his VC from King George V in a ceremony at Buckingham Palace. He was later promoted to petty officer.

Two Black Watch NCOs won their VCs in the same action at Rue de Bois on 9 May 1915. Corporal John Ripley was 47 and from Keith, Banffshire. He was a section leader and set a fine example, as his citation makes clear: 'Corporal Ripley led his section on the right of the platoon in the assault and was the first man of the battalion to climb the enemy's parapet. From there he directed those following him to the gaps in the German wire entanglements. He then led his section through a breach in the parapet to a second line of trench. With seven or eight men he established himself, blocking other flanks, and continued to hold the position until all his men had fallen and he himself was badly wounded in the head.' John Ripley was later promoted to sergeant. He died in St Andrews in 1933. His VC is privately owned.

Lance Corporal David Finlay was 22 and from Guardbridge in Fife. His citation read: 'Lance Corporal Finlay led a bombing party of 12 men in the attack until 10 of them had fallen. He then ordered the two survivors to crawl back and he himself went to the assistance of a wounded man and carried him over a distance of 100 yards of fire-swept ground into cover, quite regardless of his own safety.' David Finlay was also promoted to sergeant but he was killed in action less than a year later in the Persian Gulf (21 January 1916). His Victoria Cross is in the Black Watch Museum.

Private David Lauder, 21 and from Airdrie, was serving with the Royal Scots Fusiliers in Gallipoli, North Africa. On 13 August 1915, he was part of a squad sent to recapture a tunnel that had been occupied by the enemy. His citation reads: 'Private Lauder threw a bomb which failed to clear the parapet and fell amongst the bombing party. There was no time to smother the bomb, and Private Lauder at once put his foot on it, thereby localising the explosion. His foot was blown off, but the remainder of the party through this act of sacrifice escaped unhurt.' He was invalided out of the army and died in 1971. His VC is owned privately.

Piper Daniel Laidlaw, from Little Swinton in the Borders, was 40 and serving in the King's Own Scottish Borderers north of Lens in France, when he did what pipers are best at: inspired his comrades. It was at 6.30 a.m. on Saturday 25 September 1915, in the middle of the Battle of Loos. The battalion was waiting to advance behind the cover of chlorine gas when the wind suddenly changed, blowing it back towards them and all but halting the soldiers in their tracks. To get them moving again, Daniel Laidlaw clambered out the trench and strode along the parapet playing 'Blue Bonnets over the Border'. He later recalled: 'The laddies gave a cheer as they started off for the enemy's lines. As soon as they showed themselves over the trench top they began to fall fast, but they never wavered but dashed straight on. I ran forward with them, piping for all I knew. As we were getting near the German lines, I was wounded by shrapnel in the left ankle and leg but I was too excited to feel the pain just then and scrambled along as best I could. I changed my tune to "The Standard on the Braes o' Mar", a grand tune for charging on. I kept on piping and piping and hobbling after the laddies until I could go no farther.' His citation tells the rest of the story: 'The effect of his splendid example was immediate and the company dashed to the assault. Piper Laidlaw continued playing his pipes even after he was wounded and until the position was won.' He was later promoted to sergeant piper. He died in 1950 and his VC is in Scotland's National War Museum.

Another Scot to win the VC in that same battle was 52-year-old Lieutenant Colonel Angus Douglas-Hamilton of 52nd Reserve of Officers and Commander 6th Battalion of the Queen's Own Cameron Highlanders. The great-grandson of the Duke of Hamilton, he was killed in the battle and his medal was awarded posthumously. The citation read: 'Lieutenant Colonel Douglas-Hamilton, when the battalions on his right and left had retired, rallied his own battalion again and again and led his men forward four times. The last time he led all that remained, about 50 men, in a most gallant manner and was killed at their head. It was due to his bravery and splendid leadership that the line at this point was able to check the enemy's advance.' He is commemorated in Dud Corner Cemetery (so called because of the number of unexploded bombs found there after the war) in France but there is no marked grave. In 2013, there were unconfirmed reports that his remains had been found on the site of the former battlefield. His Victoria Cross is in the Regimental Museum of the Queen's Own Highlanders.

The very same day, 23-year-old Private Robert Dunsire from Methil in Fife, who was serving with the Royal Scots Lothian Regiment, also acted with valour sufficient to win him the VC. His citation reads: 'Private Dunsire went out under very heavy fire and rescued a wounded man from between the firing lines. Later another man, considerably nearer the German lines, was heard shouting for help and Private Dunsire crawled out again, with complete disregard for the enemy, and carried the wounded man in. Shortly afterwards the Germans attacked over this ground.' Robert Dunsire was promoted to corporal but was killed in action four months later (in January 1916) at Mazingarbe, France. Like so many of his comrades, he left a very simple will: 'In the event of my death, I leave the whole of my property and effects to my wife.' His Victoria Cross is in the Royal Scots Museum, Edinburgh Castle.

On 27 September 1915, 25-year-old Corporal James Pollock from Tillicoultry was serving near the Hohenzollern Redoubt on the Western Front, a key German defensive position, when he won his VC. He had been working in the Paris branch of his firm when the war broke out in 1914. He immediately returned to Britain and tried to enlist in his local unit of the Scottish Rifles but they already had a full complement so he joined Lochiel's Battalion of the Queen's Own Cameron Highlanders. He went to France as part of Haig's First Army and was soon in action at Loos and then at Hohenzollern, where casualties were high. At noon, the enemy's grenade bombers were causing serious problems. Corporal Pollock was one of a group of Black Watch and Cameron Highlanders sent to deal with the situation. His citation reads: 'This party rallied the defenders and checked the German advance after several prolonged bombing fights. Corporal James Pollock, after obtaining permission, got out of the British trench alone and walked along the top edge of the enemy parapet with the utmost coolness, complete disregard to danger and compelled the enemy bombers to retire by bombing them from above. He carried his grenades across the trench under heavy fire and worked his way along it hurling bombs at the enemy. The Germans were taken completely by surprise and were held at bay for an hour by Pollock who, although under heavy machine gun fire, remained unscathed until he jumped down into his own trench, when he was wounded in the arm.' James Pollock received his VC from King George V on 4 December 1915. While still recovering from his wound, he attended the first officer cadet school at Gailes, Ayrshire. In July 1916 he was commissioned and then served as a captain on the Somme. He was again wounded – at the Battle of Arras in 1917 – and lost the sight of his left eye. He was invalided out of the army. He was on parade for the VC centenary celebrations in June 1956. He died in 1958, three weeks after returning from a business trip to Canada. He was 67. He is buried in the family grave in Ayr Cemetery. His Victoria Cross is in the Highlanders Museum in Fort George.

In an astonishing coincidence (which had me checking and rechecking my notes), just 16 days later and in the same place, James Pollock's 23-year-old cousin, Corporal James Dawson, also won the VC.

He, too, was born in Tillicoultry and had moved to Glasgow to work as a science teacher. When he volunteered for war service in 1914, he *was* in time to join the Scottish Rifles. However, when he went to France in March of the following year, he was posted to the Royal Engineers. Then on 13 October 1915, at the Hohenzollern Redoubt, his courage was tested and he won the family's second VC: 'During a gas attack, he fearlessly put himself into enemy fire to give directions to his sappers and to clear the infantry out of sections of the trench which were full of gas. Finding three leaking cylinders, he rolled them well away from the trench, again under heavy fire, and then fired rifle bullets into them to let the gas escape. His gallantry undoubtedly saved many men from being gassed.' James Dawson later returned to teaching in Glasgow (1921–27) but took up military service again in 1928, as a captain at the Army School of Education. He rose to the rank of colonel before retiring in 1951. He died in 1967. His VC and other medals are in Glasgow University's Hunterian Museum.

It was Private William Young's concern for a comrade that won him the VC. The 39-year-old was serving with the East Lancashire Regiment near Foncquevillers, France, just a few days before Christmas 1915, when his battalion ran into stiff resistance from the Germans. 'Private Young saw from his trench that one of his company's NCOs was lying wounded in front of the wire. Acting without orders and heedless of his exposure to enemy fire, he climbed over the parapet and went to the rescue of his sergeant. He was hit by two bullets, one shattered his jaw and the other entered his chest. Undeterred, he went on and, with another soldier who came to assist, brought the wounded sergeant back to safety. Later Private Young walked back to the village dressing station to have his injuries attended to.' His Victoria Cross is displayed at the the Queen's Lancashire Regiment Museum.

Sergeant John Erskine, 22 and from Dunfermline, was another Scot who showed selflessness in the height of battle, at Givenchy, where a couple of weeks later, William Angus (see start of chapter) won his VC. The young sergeant was serving with the Scottish Rifles and, on 22 June 1916, was helping to repair damage caused by a mine explosion. He had already carried two wounded comrades to safety when he saw his officer, who he had thought dead, showing faint signs of movement. He didn't hesitate: 'Sergeant Erskine rushed out under continuous fire and rescued a wounded sergeant and a private. Later, seeing his officer, who was believed to be dead, showing signs of movement, he ran to him, bandaged his head and remained with him for fully an hour, being repeatedly fired on. When assistance arrived, he helped to bring in the officer, shielding him with his own body to lessen the chance of his being hit again.' Less than a year later, in April 1917, John Erskine, by now promoted to company sergeant major, was killed in action at Arras. He has no known grave but his name is inscribed on the war memorial at Arras. His VC is in the Cameronians Regimental Museum, Hamilton.

The second Scot – the other was Drummer Walter Ritchie – to win a VC on the first day of the Somme (1 July 1916) was also a Glaswegian, 32-year-old Sergeant James Turnbull of the Highland Light Infantry. The night before, the battalion gathered in assembly trenches close to the Leipzig Redoubt, the German strongpoint. In the morning, around 7.30 a.m. and under cover of artillery fire, Sergeant Turnbull's company pressed forward to within yards of the German line. When the artillery stopped, he led his men and rushed forward to take advantage of gaps that had been created. Unfortunately, they found themselves exposed and caught in crossfire. Sergeant Turnbull quickly established a position which they were able to defend. They held out for most of the long day although several of his men were killed or badly wounded. Reports of the day say the sergeant never wavered in his determination to hold the position, even when he was sometimes left fighting nearly alone. His VC citation tells the story: 'Sergeant Turnbull's party captured a post of apparent importance to the enemy who immediately began heavy counter-attacks which were continued throughout the day. Although his party was wiped out and replaced several times, Sergeant Turnbull never wavered in his determination to hold the post, the loss of which would have been very serious. Almost single-handed he maintained his position, displaying the highest degree of valour and skill in the performance of his duty.' James Turnbull was killed later in the day while launching yet another counter-attack. His VC was presented to his father and sister by King George V at Buckingham Palace and it is still owned by the family. His name is on a war memorial at his old rugby club in Glasgow.

Captain William Bloomfield, 43 years old and from Edinburgh, was serving with the Scout Corps of the South African Mounted Brigade in German East Africa on 24 August 1916 when he too showed outstanding bravery in rescuing one of his men without regard for his own safety. He was awarded the VC after a citation that read: 'At Mlali, Tanganyika [now Tanzania], when consolidating his new position after being heavily attacked and being forced to retire, Captain Bloomfield found that one of the wounded – a corporal – had not been evacuated with the rest. At considerable personal risk, the captain went back over 400 yards of ground swept by machine-gun and rifle fire and managed to reach the wounded man and bring him back to safety.' He was later promoted to major. He died in 1954 in South Africa. His VC is family owned.

James Richardson was born in Bellshill and went to school in Glasgow. In 1912, when he was 17, the family emigrated to Canada and his father became the police chief in Chilliwack, a small city not too far from Vancouver, where James signed up as a cadet in the Seaforth Highlanders, mainly because the regiment had a renowned pipe band and he was keen to learn to play. When the war broke out, he was already good enough to enlist as a piper with the Canadian Scottish Regiment and he became part of the Canadian Expeditionary Force arriving in France in February 1915, later taking part in several battles in the Somme offensive. On 8 October 1916, 20-year-old Jimmy Richardson piped his way into history and won the VC at the Regina Trench at Courcelette. He wasn't actually rostered for duty and he is reported as having pleaded with his CO to allow him to pipe his regiment over the top. As they got to the enemy wire, they were hit by artillery fire and lost momentum and morale. At this critical point, with their officer among the dead and casualties mounting, the piper asked his sergeant major in his broad accent: 'Wull I gie them wund?' The answer was 'yes' and his citation revealed what happened then: 'Piper Richardson strode up and down outside the wire playing his pipes with the greatest coolness. The effect was instantaneous. Inspired by his splendid example, the company rushed the wire with such fury and determination that the obstacle was overcome and the position captured.' Later, the young piper recovered a wounded comrade and carried him more than 200 yards to safety... and then insisted on going back for his pipes. Sadly, he was not seen again and was listed as killed in action. His remains, years later, were buried in the Adanac Military Cemetery, France. His pipes were found, broken and mud-encrusted, 90 years later in 2006, and were returned to be housed in the government building in Vancouver after a ceremony presided over by the prime minister of British Columbia. A commemorative statue to him was unveiled outside Chilliwack City Hall in October 2003.

Yet another Glaswegian, 22-year-old Sergeant Robert Downie of the Dublin Fusiliers, won his VC on the Somme – at Lesbouefs on 23 October 1916. His citation reads: 'When most of the officers had become casualties, Sergeant Downie, utterly regardless of personal danger and under very heavy fire, organised the attack which had been temporarily checked. At the critical moment he rushed forward shouting 'come on the Dubs!' which had an immediate response and the line rushed forward at this call. Sergeant Downie accounted for several of the enemy and in addition captured a machine gun, killing the team. Although wounded early in the fight, he remained with his company, giving valuable assistance while the position was being consolidated.' Robert Downie later won the Military Medal and when he eventually got home to Glasgow, he was met by a huge crowd and was carried shoulder-high through the streets. A modest man, he would say he won his medals 'for shooting the cook.' His VC was donated to Celtic Football Club and is on display at Parkhead, where he worked on the turnstiles in his later years. He died in 1968.

Captain Archibald Smith, 39 and from Cults in Aberdeenshire, was the master of the merchant ship SS *Otaki*, sailing from London to New York when it was intercepted in the Atlantic on 10 March 1917, by the heavily-armed German ship SMS *Möwe*, which had already sunk more than 30 British vessels. Captain Smith ignored orders to stop and so began what the Germans later described as 'a duel as gallant as naval history can relate.' The *Otaki* had a single 4.7-inch gun but in the 20-minute ferocious exchange with the enemy, Captain Smith scored several direct hits and caused a fire that was to blaze for three days. The citation for his VC gives a vivid account of the action: 'The SS *Otaki*, whose armament consisted of one 4.7-inch gun, commanded by Captain Smith, sighted the German raider SMS *Möwe* who was armed with four 5.9-inch, one 4.1-inch and two 22-pounder guns. The raider called on *Otaki* to stop but on Captain Smith refusing to do so, a duel ensued, during which *Otaki* secured a number of hits and caused considerable damage but she herself sustained much damage and was on fire. Captain Smith therefore ordered his crew to abandon ship but he himself stayed on board and went down with his ship.' As a merchant seaman, Archibald Smith was not technically eligible for the award of the VC. However, in a unique act, the Royal Navy promoted him posthumously to the rank of lieutenant in the Royal Navy Reserve so that he could receive the award. In 1936, his family presented the Otaki Shield to his old school, Robert Gordon's College, Aberdeen. It is awarded annually to the scholar judged pre-eminent in character and leadership.

Private William Milne was 24 and a Lanarkshire man who had emigrated to Canada before the war. Like so many fellow countryman, he enlisted in the Canadian Scottish Regiment (at Moose Jaw, Saskatchewan, in September 1915) and was serving at Thelus in France when he won the VC on 9 April 1917. His citation read: 'On approaching the first objective, Private Milne observed an enemy machine gun firing on our advancing troops. Crawling on hands and knees, he succeeded in reaching the gun, killing the crew with bombs and capturing the gun. On the line reforming, he again located a machine gun in the support line, and stalking this second gun as he had done the first, he succeeded in putting the crew out of action and capturing the gun. His wonderful bravery and resource on these two occasions undoubtedly saved the lives of many of his comrades.' Private Milne then captured a second gun but was killed during the action. He has no known grave but his name is on the Vimy Memorial at Pas de Calais and in the National Archives of Canada. His VC is in the Canadian War Museum in Ottawa.

Lieutenant Donald Mackintosh, from Glasgow, was 21 years old and serving with the Seaforth Highlanders just north of Fampoux in France. His courage is evident in the citation for the VC awarded for his actions on 11 April 1917: 'During the initial advance, Lieutenant Mackintosh was shot through the right leg but although crippled, continued to lead his men and captured the trench. He then collected men of another company who had lost their leader and drove back a counter-attack. He was again wounded and although unable to stand, nevertheless continued to control the situation. With only 15 men left, he ordered them to be ready to advance to the final objective and with great difficulty got out of the trench, encouraging them to advance. He was wounded yet again and fell.'

Donald Mackintosh's VC, awarded posthumously, is in the Regimental Museum of the Queen's Own Highlanders.

Black Watch Private Charles Melvin, 31, was from a military family in Kirriemuir, Angus. One brother, James, was also a private in the Black Watch and another, David was with the Scottish Horse Regiment. He was a veteran of nine years when he went to Mesopotamia (now mostly in modern-day Iraq) in 1917. He won the VC for conspicuous bravery, coolness and resource in action on 21 April: 'Private Melvin's company had advanced to within 50 yards of the front-line trench of a redoubt, where, owing to the intensity of the enemy's fire, the men were obliged to lie down and wait for reinforcements. Private Melvin, however, rushed on by himself, over ground swept from end to end by rifle and machine-gun fire. On reaching the enemy trench, he halted and fired two or three shots into it, killing one or two enemy but as the others in the trench continued to fire at him, he jumped into it and attacked them with his bayonet in his hand as, owing to his rifle being damaged, it was not fixed. On being attacked in this resolute manner most of the enemy fled to their second line, but not before Private Melvin had killed two more and succeeded in disarming eight unwounded and one wounded. Private Melvin bound up the wounds of the wounded man, and then driving his eight unwounded prisoners before him, and supporting the wounded one, he hustled them out of the trench, marched them in and delivered them over to an officer. He then provided himself with a load of ammunition and returned to the firing line where he reported himself to his platoon sergeant. All this was done, not only under intense rifle and machine-gun fire, but the whole way back Private Melvin and his party were exposed to a very heavy artillery barrage fire. Throughout the day Private Melvin greatly inspired those near him with confidence and courage.' Private Melvin left the army in 1919. He shares a memorial at Kirriemuir with two other local VC winners, Lord Lyell and Corporal Richard Burton. His Victoria Cross is in the Black Watch Museum.

John Graham was 24 years old and a lieutenant in the Argyll and Sutherland Highlanders attached to the Machine Gun Corps when he won the VC on 22 April, also at Istabulat in Mesopotamia: 'Lieutenant Graham was in command of a machine-gun section which came under very heavy fire. When his men became casualties he insisted on carrying the ammunition and although twice wounded, he continued in control and with one gun opened accurate fire on the enemy. This gun was put out of action and he was again wounded and forced to retire, but before doing so he disabled his gun and then brought a Lewis gun into action with excellent effect until all the ammunition was expended. He was wounded yet again and was again forced to retire.' John Graham was later promoted to lieutenant colonel. He succeeded his father to a baronetcy in 1936 and as Sir John was Usher of the Green Rod to the Order of the Thistle, 1959–79.

Captain Arthur Henderson, 24 and from Paisley, had already won the Military Cross when he was with 2nd Battalion, The Argyll and Sutherland Highlanders and won the VC on 23 April 1917 at Fontaine-lès-Croisilles in France: 'During an attack on enemy trenches, Captain Henderson, although almost immediately wounded in the left arm, led his company through the enemy's front line until he gained his final objective. He then proceeded to consolidate his position which, owing to heavy gun and machine-gun fire and bombing [grenade] attacks, was in danger of becoming isolated. By his cheerful courage and coolness he was able to maintain the spirit of his men under most trying circumstances. Captain Henderson was killed after he had successfully accomplished his task.' He was buried at Cojeul War Cemetery, Pas-de-Calais. His name is on the war memorial at Gordon in the Scottish Borders. His VC is in the collection owned by Lord Ashcroft, former chairman of the Conservative party.

Lieutenant Robert Combe was born Aberdeen in 1880 but emigrated to Canada in 1906 and first worked as a pharmacist and then owned his own pharmacy in Saskatchewan before joining the Manitoba Regiment of the Canadian Infantry soon after war was declared. In a letter that appeared in his old school magazine on 2 January

1915, he wrote about his new life as a soldier and his hankering for a return visit to Scotland: 'Training conditions here are sublime. I had 50 recruits out the other morning for a route march with the thermometer at 18 degrees below zero. I froze my chin and one cheek. Several of the men had frozen noses and cheeks. We all feel very fit, however, and the cold is most invigorating. We are all very anxious to get over [to France]. We expect to concentrate at Regina or Winnipeg any day now, and after a short course there, hope to embark. I have a lieutenancy in the 95th Saskatchewan Rifles. I have been trying to get back for a visit to the old country for two or three years but being a married man now, it is not so easy to pick up one's traps and march. My wife has never been in Scotland and one of the things she is most anxious to see is the old school. I hope it will come up to my boastful accounts.'

Once he had embarked, Robert Combe was promoted to major and assigned to a training role. He didn't take to that, however, and opted to go back to the role of combat lieutenant. In the early hours of 3 May 1917, his battalion launched an assault on the German trenches at Acheville, near Vimy, where he won his VC. The ferocious enemy artillery barrage caused heavy and sustained casualties. His company was reduced to himself and just five men... and they were still 500 yards short of the objective. As his citation makes clear, he pressed on: 'He steadied his company under intense fire and led them through the enemy barrage, reaching the objective. With great coolness and courage Lieutenant Combe proceeded to bomb the enemy and inflicted heavy casualties. He collected small groups of men and succeeded in capturing the company objective, together with 80 prisoners. He repeatedly charged the enemy, driving them before him, and whilst personally leading his bombers was killed by an enemy sniper. His conduct inspired all ranks, and it was entirely due to his magnificent courage that the position was carried, secured and held.' Lieutenant Combe's tiny force captured more than 250 yards of trench and took 80 prisoners. Minutes later, he was shot and killed by a German sniper. A fellow officer wrote to his wife: 'Would that we had more Bob Combes! He was a splendid comrade, a first-class officer of infinite charm, whose cheery outlook on life enriched every topic he touched.' Robert Combe has no known grave but his name is inscribed on the Vimy War Memorial and his VC is in the Saskatchewan Archives, Regina, Canada.

Skipper Joseph Watt of the Royal Navy Reserve was 31 and from Gardenstown on the Banffshire coast. The sea was in his blood. His father ran a fishing boat until he was lost in the North Sea in 1897. Joe was only ten, but not long afterwards he joined the crew of *The White Daisy* working out of Fraserburgh. As soon as he could afford it, he bought a stake in the drifter *Annie* and became a popular figure in the tight fishing circle. When the war started in 1914, Joe volunteered his services to the Royal Navy and joined the special patrol service keeping a watch for enemy ships and submarines.

In 1915, he was posted to Italy as skipper of the drifter HMS *Gowanlea* on patrol in the Strait of Otranto. It was a strategic stretch of water where the Allies had set up a blockade to stop the Austro-Hungarian Navy getting into the Mediterranean. In January

1916, the *Gowanlea* was one of the ships that rushed to the aid of the remnants of the Serbian Army as they were forced to retreat to Albania. For his help in the brave rescue effort, Joe was awarded the Serbian Gold Medal. Later in the year, just before Christmas, his ship was attacked by an Austrian destroyer trying to break through the blockade. It was hit several times but wasn't seriously damaged and none of the crew was injured. It was, however, a foretaste of much worse to come. On 15 May 1917 the Austrians launched a determined attack on the blockade, with five battleships and two submarines. The odds against the Allied drifters were overwhelming. The Austrians created havoc and sank 14 trawlers and drifters.

Joe Watt and his eight-man crew on their tiny ship faced the heavily-armed cruiser *Novaro* and demands from its captain to surrender and abandon ship. Skipper Watt's response is vividly revealed in the citation for his VC: 'When hailed by an Austrian cruiser at about 100 yards range and ordered to stop and abandon his drifter *Gowanlea*, he ordered full speed ahead and called upon his crew to give three cheers and fight to the finish. The cruiser was then engaged but after one round had been fired, a shot from the enemy disabled the breech of the drifter's gun. The crew, however, stuck to the gun, endeavouring to make it work, being under heavy fire all the time. After the cruiser had passed on Skipper Watt took the *Gowanlea* alongside the badly damaged drifter *Floandi* and helped to remove the dead and wounded.' Joe Watt also received the French *Croix de guerre* and the Italian Medal of Military Valour and was promoted to Chief Skipper. He returned to Fraserburgh after the war and refused to speak of his war experience, even to his wife. While he was away, his boat *Annie* had been destroyed after hitting a mine and he bought the *Benachie* as a replacement. He served on several other fishing vessels over the next 20 years before joining the Royal Navy again (1940–45) as a drifter captain to serve in the Second World War in home waters. He complained about having been refused foreign service because of his age. He died of cancer in 1955.

Second Lieutenant John Craig, from Comrie, Perthshire, was just 21 and serving with the Royal Scots Fusiliers in Egypt when he won his VC. As his citation says, he had already been mentioned for 'conspicuous bravery' on three previous occasions. On 5 June 1917, one of the regiment's advanced posts had been rushed and overwhelmed by the enemy. Second Lieutenant Craig immediately mustered a rescue party: 'During the course of this operation his men came under heavy rifle and machine-gun fire, an NCO was wounded and the medical officer who went out to his aid was also severely wounded. Second Lieutenant Craig at once went to their assistance and succeeded in taking the NCO under cover. He then returned for the medical officer, and whilst taking him to shelter was himself wounded. Nevertheless, by great perseverance, he succeeded in rescuing him also. As the enemy continued a heavy fire and in addition turned on shrapnel and high explosives, Second Lieutenant Craig scooped cover for the wounded and thus was the means of saving their lives. These latter acts of bravery occurred in broad daylight, under full observation of the enemy and within close range.' John Craig later joined the RAF and became a wing commander. His VC is in the Guards Museum, London.

Born in Slamannan, Stirlingshire, Sam Frickleton emigrated to New Zealand where he worked as a miner before the war. In 1915, he enlisted in the New Zealand Rifles but was then discharged as medically unfit because of tuberculosis. Somehow he managed to re-enlist the following year and went to Europe as part of the New Zealand Expeditionary Force. A year later and then a lance corporal, he was cited for the VC for his part in action at Messines, Belgium, on 7 June 1917. The citation read: 'Lance Corporal Frickleton, although slightly wounded, dashed forward at the head of his section, pushed into our barrage and personally destroyed with bombs [grenades] an enemy machine gun and crew which was causing heavy casualties. He then attacked a second gun, killing all the crew of 12. By the destruction of these two guns he undoubtedly saved his own and other units from very severe casualties. During the consolidation of this position he received a second severe wound.' Sam Frickleton was later promoted to second lieutenant and, when he joined the TA in 1934, he was made captain. His VC is in the QEII Army Memorial Museum, Waiouru, New Zealand.

Private George McIntosh from Rathven in Banffshire was just 20 when he won his VC serving with the Gordon Highlanders in Ypres on 31 July 1917: 'During the consolidation of a position, the company came under machine-gun fire at close range and Private McIntosh immediately rushed forward under heavy fire and reaching the emplacement, threw a Mills grenade into it, killing two of the enemy and wounding a third. Subsequently entering the dug-out, he found two light machine guns, which he carried back with him. His quick grasp of the situation and the rapidity with which he acted undoubtedly saved many of his comrades and enabled the consolidation to proceed unhindered by machine-gun fire. Throughout the day the cheerfulness and courage of Private McIntosh was indomitable and to his fine example in a great measure was due the success which attended his company.' Private McIntosh also went on to join the Royal Air Force and served in the Second World War, during which he achieved the rank of flight sergeant.

The army records list him as Company Sergeant Major John Skinner but his friends knew him as Jock. He was 35, a Glaswegian and had joined the army to fight the Boers (in 1900). He had already seen action with the King's Own Scottish Borderers at Mons, Gallipoli and on the Somme. He had won the Distinguished Conduct Medal and the *Croix de guerre*… and had been wounded five times! No one, therefore, would have been surprised at his outstanding courage at Passchendaele on 18 August 1917: 'When his company was held up by machine-gun fire, Company Sergeant Major Skinner, although wounded in the head, collected six men and with great courage and determination worked round the left flank of three blockhouses from which the machine-gun fire was coming, and succeeded in bombing and taking the first blockhouse single-handed. Then leading his six men towards the other two blockhouses he cleared them, taking 60 prisoners, three machine-guns and two trench mortars.' Jock Skinner was sent home and assigned to a training battalion in Edinburgh. He didn't stay long and, against orders, found his way back to Belgium and the frontline. On 17 March 1918 he is reported as having ignored orders again and crawled out on several occasions into no man's land to recover the bodies of comrades, before he himself was killed. His body was carried the 16 miles to a war cemetery by six other VC holders. His medal is in the regimental museum of The King's Own Scottish Borderers.

Sergeant John Carmichael, from Glenmavis, Lanarkshire, was 24 and serving with the North Staffordshire Regiment when he won the VC. It was 8 September 1917 and he was digging out a trench near Hill 60, close to Ypres, when he saw a grenade had been exposed and had started to burn. His citation completes the story: 'He immediately ordered his men to get clear, put his helmet over the grenade and then stood on the helmet. The grenade exploded and blew him out of the trench. He could have thrown the bomb out of the trench but realised that by doing so he would have endangered the lives of the men working on top. He was seriously injured.' In her book, *They Called it Passchendaele*, Lyn Macdonald details just how serious were his injuries: 'Both his legs were shattered and his right arm was injured and he remembered nothing about the journey to No 53 Casualty Station at Bailleul nor of the first few days he spent there. As soon as he was able, John Carmichael wrote to his anxious mother in Airdrie to tell her he was recovering well. He didn't think it worth mentioning that he had won the Victoria Cross!' The modest Sergeant Carmichael received his VC from King George V at Buckingham Palace. He died in 1977. His medal is in the museum of the Staffordshire Regiment, Lichfield.

It was also at Ypres that 32-year-old Sergeant Alexander Edwards from Drainie, Moray, won his VC. The son of a fisherman, he had joined the Seaforth Highlanders at Elgin just after the outbreak of the war in 1914. He was on the Pilckem Ridge on the first day of the third Battle of Ypres, on 14 September 1917: 'Having located a hostile machine gun in a wood, he, with great dash and courage, led some men against it, killed all the team and captured the gun. Later, when a sniper was causing casualties, he crawled out to stalk him, and although badly wounded in the arm, went on and killed him. One officer only was now left with the company, and, realising that the success of the operation depended on the capture of the furthest objective, Sergeant Edwards, regardless of his wound, led his men on till this objective was captured. He subsequently showed great skill in consolidating his position, and very great daring in personal reconnaissance. Although again twice wounded on the following day, this very gallant NCO maintained throughout a complete disregard for personal safety, and his high example of coolness and determination engendered a fine fighting spirit in his men.' Seven months later, he was killed in action near Arras (4 March 1918). He has no known grave but his name is on the Arras War Memorial.

Lance Corporal John Hamilton from Dumbarton was 21 years old and serving with the Highland Light Infantry when he won his VC during the battle of Passchendaele on 26 September, north of the Ypres-Menin Road. His citation read: 'Great difficulty was experienced in keeping the front and support line supplied with small arms ammunition, owing to the intense artillery fire. At a time when this supply had reached a seriously low level, Lance Corporal Hamilton on several occasions, on his own initiative, carried bandoliers of ammunition through the enemy's belts of fire and then, in full view of their snipers and machine guns, which were lying out in the front of our line at close range, he distributed the ammunition.' John Hamilton was later promoted to sergeant. After the war, he remained an active reserve in the Territorial Army. He was in hospital at the outbreak of the Second World War and missed the mobilisation of his unit (which was captured at the defence of Dunkirk). He rose through the ranks and finished the war as colonel in charge of an Italian prisoner-of-war camp in England. His VC is in the National War Museum of Scotland.

Although still only 25 when he won his VC at Passchendaele, Corporal William Clamp from Motherwell was already veteran of heavy fighting in France. He had enlisted with the Cameronians in 1914 and had twice been seriously wounded, but after leaving hospital he transferred to the Green Howards and was with them on 9 October 1917: 'When an advance was checked by intense machine-gun fire from concrete blockhouses and by snipers in ruined buildings, Corporal Clamp dashed forward with two men and attempted to rush the largest blockhouse. His first attempt failed owing to the two men with him being knocked out but he at once collected some bombs [grenades] and, calling two men to follow him, again dashed forward. He was first to reach the blockhouse and hurled his bombs, killing many of the occupants. He then entered and brought out a machine-gun and about 20 prisoners whom he brought back under heavy fire from neighbouring snipers. The corporal then again went forward encouraging and cheering the men and succeeded in rushing several snipers' posts. He continued to display the greatest heroism until he was killed by a sniper. His magnificent courage and self-sacrifice was of the greatest value and relieved what was undoubtedly a critical situation.' Corporal Clamp's body was never recovered. His name appears on the Tyne Cot Memorial near Passchendaele. A street in Motherwell is named after him and a gold medal is awarded annually in his name at his old school. His VC was presented to his parents at Buckingham Palace and is now in the Green Howards Museum, Richmond, Yorkshire.

Another Scottish VC winner at Passchendaele was 24-year-old Colin Barron. He was born in Boyndie, Banffshire but emigrated to Canada in 1910, where he enlisted in 3rd (Toronto) Battalion when war broke out. His citation reads: 'On November 6 1917, when his unit was held up by three machine guns, Corporal Barron opened fire on them at point-blank range, rushed the guns, killed four of the crew and captured the remainder. He then turned one of the captured guns on the retiring enemy, causing severe casualties. This action produced far-reaching results and enabled the advance to continue.' Colin Barron was later promoted to sergeant. He died in 1959.

Another Canadian immigrant and former pupil of Edinburgh's Royal High School, Harcus Strachan from Bo'ness was 33 and serving with the Canadian Expeditionary Force when he won his VC. He was a lieutenant in the Fort Garry Horse during the Battle of Cambrai on 20 November 1917. He immediately took over when his squadron leader was cut down while charging the German front line at a gallop. His citation reads: 'Lieutenant Strachan led the squadron through the enemy line of machine-gun posts and then, with the surviving men, led the charge on the German battery, killing seven of the gunners with his sword. When all the gunners were killed and the battery silenced, he rallied his men and fought his way back at night on foot through the enemy's lines, bringing all unwounded men safely in, together with 15 prisoners.' Harcus Strachan had already been promoted to captain when he received his VC from King George V and he later received a major's crown. After the war, he returned to Canada and went into banking. At the outbreak of the Second World War, he re-enlisted as a major in the 15th Alberta Horse and a few months later was made lieutenant colonel and commanding officer of the Edmonton Fusiliers.

Lieutenant Samuel Wallace, from Thornhill, Dumfries, was serving with the Royal Field Artillery in France when he won his VC. The 25-year-old gunnery officer was leading his men at Gonnelieu on 20 November: 'When the personnel of Lieutenant Wallace's battery were reduced to five, having lost their commander and five sergeants, and were surrounded by enemy infantry, he maintained the firing of the guns by swinging the trails close together, the men running and loading from gun to gun. He was in action for eight hours, firing the whole time and inflicting severe casualties on the enemy. Then, owing to the exhausted state of his men, he withdrew when the infantry supports arrived, taking with him all essential gun parts and all the wounded.' Samuel Wallace was later promoted to captain. His VC is in the Royal Artillery Museum, Woolwich.

Like so many of his colleagues, John McAulay made the transition from the Glasgow Constabulary to the Scots Guards at the outbreak of the war in 1914. When his battalion was sent to France, he and his mates experienced some of the fiercest battles of the war. In July 1916, by then a sergeant, he took part in the Battle of Ypres, and received his first commendation for bravery. When a sniper shot and killed his young officer, he took command and counter-attacked and killed several hidden riflemen. For his actions, he won the Distinguished Conduct Medal. Eighteen months later and then 28, Sergeant McAulay was with his platoon at Fontaine-Notre-Dame when an officer was hit by machine-gun fire. Without hesitating, the sergeant rushed to his rescue. Twice, he was knocked down by exploding shells and then two German soldiers tried to cut him off. He killed both of them and struggled back with the wounded officer on his shoulders. His CO was rightly proud. He later wrote: 'Sergeant McAulay took command of the company after all his officers had been hit, cheered and encouraged them, brought back Lieutenant Kinnaird and many wounded men from positions of danger, beat back a counter-attack, killed several Germans and was altogether splendid. I am recommending him for a VC but they are hard to get.' As we now know, the recommendation was successful and the citation told the rest of the story of valiant action: 'Sergeant McAulay assumed command of the company and under shell and machine-gun fire successfully held and consolidated the objectives gained.

He reorganised the company and noticing a counter-attack developing, repulsed it by the skilful and bold use of machine-guns, causing heavy enemy casualties.' Sergeant McAulay was demobbed in 1919 and returned to his role as a policeman in Glasgow. Within weeks, he was promoted to police sergeant and in 1926 to inspector. His Victoria Cross is in the Guards' regimental headquarters.

Second Lieutenant Stanley Boughey, born in Ayrshire, joined the Royal Scots Fusiliers at the outbreak of war, when he was just 18. He went to France, was wounded seriously enough to be invalided home and there was discharged from the army. Undeterred, he later rejoined and in 1917 went with his battalion to Palestine. It was for his heroism in the final advance on Jerusalem on 1 December 1917 that he won his VC, sadly awarded posthumously as he died three days later from the injuries sustained. His citation said: 'When Turkish soldiers in large numbers had managed to crawl up to within 30 yards of the British firing line and, with bombs and automatic rifles, were keeping down the fire of the British machine-guns, Second Lieutenant Boughey rushed forward alone with bombs right up to the Turks, killing many and causing the surrender of a party of 30. As he turned to go back for more bombs, he was mortally wounded at the moment when the Turks were surrendering.' Stanley Boughey is buried in Gaza War Cemetery. His VC is privately owned.

On the day Stanley Boughey won his VC in Palestine, another young Scot showed valour in the face of the enemy at Gonnelieu in France. Captain George Paton, from Innellan, Argyllshire, was just 22 and serving with the Grenadier Guards. He had already been tested in battle and had the Military Cross as evidence of his bravery. Sadly, he too died in the action that won him the VC. His citation reads: 'When a unit on Captain Paton's left was driven back, thus leaving his flank in the air and his company practically surrounded, he walked up and down adjusting the line, within 50 yards of the enemy, under a withering fire. He personally removed several wounded men and was the last to leave the village. Later he again adjusted the line and when the enemy counter-attacked four times, each time sprang on to the parapet, deliberately risking his life, in order to stimulate his men. He was eventually mortally wounded.' Captain Paton is buried in Metz-en-Couture Communal Cemetery. His Victoria Cross is in the Guards' regimental headquarters.

Lieutenant Allan Ker, 35 and from Edinburgh, was a Gordon Highlander on attachment to the Machine Gun Corps when he won his VC on 21 March 1918 at the Battle of St Quentin in France. His citation reveals a story of astonishing and enduring courage in the face of the enemy: 'After a heavy bombardment, the enemy penetrated our line, and the flank of the 61st Division became exposed. Lieutenant Ker, with one Vickers gun, succeeded in engaging the enemy's infantry, approaching under cover of dead ground, and held up the attack, inflicting many casualties. He then sent back word to his battalion headquarters that he had determined to stop with his sergeant and several men who had been badly wounded and fight until a counter-attack could be launched to relieve him. Just as ammunition failed, his party was attacked from behind with bombs, machine guns and the bayonet. Several bayonet attacks were delivered but each time they were repulsed by Lieutenant Ker and his companions with their revolvers, the Vickers gun having by this time been destroyed. The wounded were collected into a small shelter and it was decided to defend them to the last and to hold the enemy as long as possible. In one of the many hand-to-hand encounters, a German rifle and bayonet and a small supply of ammunition was secured and subsequently used with good effect against the enemy. Although Lieutenant Ker was very exhausted from want of food and gas poisoning and from the supreme exertions he had made during ten hours of the most severe bombardment, fighting and attending to the wounded, he refused to surrender until all his ammunition was exhausted and his position was rushed by a large number of the enemy. His behaviour throughout the day was absolutely cool and fearless, and by his determination he was materially instrumental in engaging and holding up for three hours more than 500 of the enemy.' Allan Ker was later promoted to major and during the Second World War served in Military Intelligence where, as second-in-command of Allied Liaison, he worked alongside Anthony Powell. He is said to have been the writer's inspiration for Lieutenant Colonel Lysander Finn in his epic cycles of novels *Dance to the Music of Time*.

Another Scot who defied overwhelming odds to protect his men was 25-year-old Lieutenant John Buchan of the Argyll and Sutherland Highlanders. He won his VC, sadly posthumously, at Marteville on March 21: 'Although wounded early in the day, he insisted on remaining with his platoon which was suffering heavy casualties from most severe shell fire. He continually visited all his posts, encouraging his men in the face of the approaching enemy and heavy machine-gun fire. When called on to surrender, he fought his way back to the support line where he held out until dusk. He then withdrew as ordered but refused to have his injuries attended to. He was eventually completely cut off and was last seen fighting valiantly against overwhelming odds.' The location of Lieutenant Buchan's grave is unknown.

The men of the 12th Highland Light Infantry spent two long days on a train and then marched for 17 miles to join the 35th Division on the Somme on 24 March 1918. Their CO was 36-year-old Lieutenant Colonel William Anderson from Largo, a former pupil at Fettes College in Edinburgh.

In its confrontation with the Germans the next day, the HLI was outnumbered by five to one. That didn't deter William Anderson. He personally led the bayonet charge that pushed the Germans back more than a mile. His gallantry won him the VC – again, sadly posthumously – and his citation makes astonishing reading: 'The enemy attacked on the right of the battalion frontage and succeeded in penetrating the wood held by our men. Owing to successive lines of the enemy following on closely there was the greatest danger that the flank of the whole position would be turned. Grasping the seriousness of the situation, Colonel Anderson made his way across the open in full view of the enemy now holding the wood on the right, and after much effort succeeded in gathering the remainder of the two right companies. He personally led the counter-attack and drove the enemy from the wood, capturing 12 machine guns and 70 prisoners, and restoring the original line. His conduct in leading the charge was quite fearless and his most splendid example was the means of rallying and inspiring the men during the most critical hour. Later on the same day, in another position, the enemy had penetrated to within three hundred yards of the village and were holding a timber yard in force. Colonel Anderson reorganised his men after they had been driven in and brought them forward to a position of readiness for a counterattack. He led the attack in person and throughout showed the utmost disregard for his own safety. The counter-attack drove the enemy from his position, but resulted in this very gallant officer losing his life. He died fighting within the enemy's lines, setting a magnificent example to all who were privileged to serve under him.' Lieutenant Colonel Anderson was buried at Maricourt Military Cemetery on the Somme. His VC is privately owned.

Although he was still only 19, Sergeant John Meikle, from Kirkintilloch, was already a decorated veteran when he won the VC (again posthumously). He was a former railway booking clerk who had enlisted at 16 and was already the holder of the Military Medal when his battalion of the Seaforth Highlanders went into action at Marfaux in France on 20 July 1918. His citation reads: 'Sergeant Meikle, single-handed and armed only with a revolver and a stick, rushed and put out of action a machine gun which was delaying his company's advance. Shortly afterwards, seizing a rifle and bayonet from a fallen comrade, he charged another machine-gun post, but was killed almost on the gun position. His bravery enabled two other men who followed him to put this gun out of action.' Sergeant Meikle is buried at Marfaux British Cemetery. A memorial to him was erected at Nitshill Station in Renfrewshire, where he had been the booking clerk. His VC is in the Dingwall Museum.

James Tait was born in Dumfries and emigrated to Canada to work for a government survey company in the North West Territories. Already the holder of the Military Cross, he was a lieutenant in 78 Battalion when he won his VC at the Battle of Vimy Ridge over the three-day period 8–11 August 1918. His citation read: 'When the advance had been checked by intense machine-gun fire, Lieutenant Tait rallied his company and led them forward with consummate skill under a hail of bullets. He then went forward alone to a machine gun which was causing many casualties and killed the gunner. This so inspired his men that they rushed the position, capturing 12 machine guns and 20 prisoners. Later, when the enemy counter-attacked Tait's position under intense artillery bombardment, this officer displayed outstanding courage.' Lieutenant Tait was mortally wounded but continued to direct his men until he died. He is buried in Fouquescourt British Cemetery, France. His VC is in the Glenbow Museum, Calgary, Canada.

Private Hugh McIver, 28 and from Linwood in Renfrewshire, had also won the Military Medal, not once but twice (in 1916 and 1917), serving with the Royal Scots before the action that won him the VC. On 23 August 1918, he single-handedly captured a German machine-gun post at Courcelles in northern France: 'He was acting as a company runner, carrying messages under heavy artillery and machine-gun fire. Single-handed, he chased a German scout into a machine-gun post. He killed six enemy soldiers then captured 20 more and two machine guns.' In a later incident, Hugh McIver risked his life in stopping a British tank which had mistakenly opened fire on British soldiers. He was killed in action just ten days later while charging yet another machine-gun post. He is buried in Vraucourt Copse Cemetery and his Victoria Cross is in the Royal Scots Museum, Edinburgh Castle.

Lieutenant David McIntyre was 23, from Portnahaven on the isle of Islay. He had joined the Argyll and Sutherland Highlanders at the beginning of the war but was attached to the Glasgow battalion of the Highland Light Infantry when he won his VC for sustained valour over the three-day period 24–27 August 1918 at Hénin and Fontaine-lès-Croisilles. His citation reads: 'Lieutenant MacIntyre showed conspicuous bravery when, acting as adjutant of his battalion, he was constantly in evidence in the firing line, and by his coolness under the most heavy shell and machine-gun fire inspired the confidence of all ranks. Three days later… when strong barbed wire was encountered… he organised and took forward a party of men, and under heavy machine-gun fire, supervised the making of gaps. Later… after he had been relieved of command of the firing line… an enemy machine gun opened fire close to him. Without any hesitation he rushed it single-handed, put the team to flight and brought in the gun.' After the war, David McIntyre joined the Civil Service and rose to under secretary at the Ministry of Works (Scotland) when he retired in 1959. His VC is in the National War Museum of Scotland at Edinburgh Castle.

After graduating from college, William Clark-Kennedy went to work in the Edinburgh office of the Scottish Life Insurance Company but promptly signed up to serve with the Imperial Yeomanry and Rhodesian Horse at the outbreak of the Boer War (1899–1902). He was just 20. He returned to Scotland after the war and within a year was promoted to work in the company's Montreal office. He had obviously enjoyed his military experience because, at the start of the Great War, he again took up a commission, initially with 13th Battalion and later, when he went to France, the Victoria Rifles. By the time he was lieutenant colonel and CO of 24th Battalion, he was a much-decorated hero, having won the DSO (and Bar) and the *Croix de guerre* (with Palm), been admitted to the Order of St Michael and St George, and been mentioned in dispatches four times.

On the second day of the Arras Front offensive, 27 August 1918, he added the VC to his highly distinguished record. A contemporary report says: 'Lieutenant Colonel William Clark-Kennedy led his battalion in the central position of the attack. It became the focal point of German shelling and machine-gun fire and would have broken down completely if it were not for his example of personally leading assaults on enemy machine-gun nests and putting them out of action. By mid-afternoon, his unprecedented leadership and skill had so strengthened the line of advance that it enabled the brigade to reach and occupy the Occident trench in front of the barbed wire fences protecting the Fresnes-Rouvroy line. Next day, he again demonstrated his leadership and gallantry in the attack on the Line and the Uptown Wood. Bleeding profusely and in intense pain from a serious leg wound, he refused to be evacuated. Using a shell hole as his command post, he continued to direct his battalion. Realising that further advance was impossible he established a firm defence line. After five hours he allowed stretcher-bearers to carry him to a dressing station to have his wounds tended.' After the war, William Clark-Kennedy returned to the insurance business in Montreal. In 1940 he was appointed honorary lieutenant colonel of 3rd Battalion, the Black Watch. He died at 81.

James Huffam, from Dunblane, was just 21 and a second lieutenant in the Duke of Wellington's Regiment at St Servin's Farm when he won his VC on 31 August: 'Second Lieutenant Huffam with three men rushed an enemy machine-gun post and put it out of action. His position was then heavily attacked and he withdrew, carrying back a wounded comrade. Again in the night, accompanied by two men only, he rushed an enemy machine gun, capturing eight prisoners and enabling the advance to continue.' James Huffman also served in the Second World War and was promoted to major. After the war, he was seconded to the RAF as a flying officer. His VC is privately owned.

David Hunter, 26 and from Dunfermline, had been a miner before he joined the army. He enlisted with the Highland Light Infantry and was serving as a corporal when he won his VC at Moeuvres, west of Cambrai, on 17 September 1918. He was in charge of a machine-gun post: 'Corporal Hunter was detailed to take on an advanced post close to the enemy, who drove back the posts on Corporal Hunter's flanks and established posts in close proximity to and around him, thus completely isolating his command. Nevertheless, he maintained his position and repelled frequent attacks until the evening of the third day, when a counter-attack relieved them. Without food and water he had held on to his post for over 48 hours. The outstanding bravery, coupled with the determination, fortitude and endurance displayed by Corporal Hunter is beyond all praise and is a magnificent example to all.' He was later promoted to sergeant. After the war, he returned to his old job as a miner at Dean Colliery, Kingseat. In 1920 he attended the Buckingham Palace garden party for VC holders and the same year sat for a bust by Jacob Epstein, commissioned by the Imperial War Museum. When he died, his grave was unmarked until 2004, when the Royal Highland Fusiliers erected a memorial stone. His Victoria Cross is in his regiment's museum.

Louis McGuffie, 24 and from Wigtown, was just getting used to his sergeant's stripes serving with the 1st Battalion King's Own Scottish Borderers when they went into action at Wyteschaete in Flanders. He showed extraordinary courage and leadership that was to win him the VC on 28 September: 'During an advance, Sergeant McGuffie single-handed, searched many dug-outs and took several prisoners. In the operations that followed he dealt similarly with many more dug-outs, resulting in one officer and 25 other ranks surrendering to him. Whilst consolidating the first objective, he pursued and returned with several of the enemy who had slipped away. Some British troops were being led away as prisoners by the enemy and Private McGuffie was significant in their rescue. Later in the day, whilst in command of a platoon, he took many more prisoners.' Sergeant McGuffie was killed in action six days later. He is buried in the Zandvoorde British Cemetery in Flanders. His VC is in the museum of the King's Own Scottish Borderers in Berwick upon Tweed.

Sergeant John O'Neill from Airdrie was also in Flanders, serving with the Prince of Wales Leinster Regiment, when he won his VC on 14 October. He was just 21, frustrated at his unit being pinned down by two enemy machine guns and a field battery, and saw only one course of action: 'Leading a charge consisting of himself and 11 men against the battery, they captured four field guns, two machine guns and took 16 prisoners. On October 20, Sergeant O'Neill and one other man charged an enemy machine-gun position, routing approximately 100 of the enemy and causing many casualties. Throughout these operations he showed the most outstanding courage and powers of leadership.' John O'Neill later won the Military Medal and rose through the ranks to lieutenant. His Victoria Cross was stolen on 13 February 1962 during a burglary at a London medal dealer. It has never been recovered.

Royal Engineer Corporal James McPhie from Edinburgh was 24 years old when he won the VC and sadly his was to be another posthumous award. He was working on trying to establish portable bridges across the Canal de la Sensée, near Aubencheul-au-Bac in northern France on 14 October 1918. His citation reads: 'Corporal McPhie was with a party of sappers maintaining a cork float bridge which, when our infantry started to cross it just before dawn, began to break away and sink. Corporal McPhie jumped into the water and tried to hold the cork and timbers together, although he kept the bridge together, the effort killed him.' James McPhie is buried in the Naves Communal Cemetery near Cambrai, in northern France. His Victoria Cross is in the Imperial War Museum.

Sergeant John Daykins, 35, from Hawick in the Borders and already a holder of the Military Medal, was serving with the York and Lancaster Regiment at Solesmes, north-west France, when he won his VC on 20 October. His citation read: 'Sergeant Daykins, with 12 remaining men of his platoon, rushed a machine gun and during subsequent severe hand-to-hand fighting he himself disposed of many of the enemy and secured his objective. He then located another machine gun which was holding up an operation of his company. Under heavy fire he worked his way alone to the post and shortly afterwards returned with 25 prisoners and an enemy machine gun, which he mounted at his post. His magnificent fighting spirit and example inspired his men, saved many casualties and contributed largely to the success of the attack.' John Daykins' VC is in the York & Lancaster Regiment Museum, Rotherham.

David McGregor, 23 and from Edinburgh, was a lieutenant in the Royal Scots but attached to the Machine Gun Corps when 'his great gallantry and supreme devotion to duty were the admiration of all ranks.' He won his VC in Flanders on 22 October, sadly posthumously because he was killed in action. His citation read: 'Lieutenant

McGregor was in command of a section of machine guns attached to the right flank of the assaulting battalion. He concealed his guns, on a limber, under the bank of a sunken road but immediately the troops advanced, they were subjected to enfilade fire from enemy machine guns. He realised that he could not get the guns carried forward without some delay. He ordered the teams to take a safer route, whilst he lay flat on the limber. The driver then galloped forward for about 600 yards under extremely heavy machine-gun fire. The driver, the horses and the limber were all hit. Lieutenant McGregor succeeded, after getting the guns into action, in effectively subduing the enemy fire, allowing the advance to continue. In order to direct the fire of his guns, he continually exposed himself to the enemy. He worked like this for about an hour, until he was killed.'

David McGregor is buried in Stasegem Communal Cemetery, Flanders. His VC is in the Royal Scots Museum, Edinburgh Castle.

Lieutenant William Bissett (25), from St Martins, Perthshire, was with the Argyll and Sutherland Highlanders at Maing, France, when he won his VC on 25 October 1918. His citation read: 'Lieutenant Bissett was commanding a platoon, but owing to casualties took command of the company and handled it with great skill when an enemy counter-attack turned his left flank. Realising the danger, he withdrew to the railway but the enemy continued to advance and when the ammunition was exhausted Lieutenant Bissett mounted the railway embankment under heavy fire. Calling for a bayonet charge, he drove back the enemy inflicting heavy losses and again charged forward, establishing the line and saving a critical situation.' William Bissett was later promoted to major and was also awarded the French *Croix de guerre avec Palme* (the *Palme* being the equivalent of a bar). In the Second World War, he served with Royal Army Ordnance Corps and Royal Pioneer Corps. His VC is in the Argyll & Sutherland Highlanders Museum, Stirling.

John MacGregor, 30, was another one of the Scots serving with a colonial regiment when he won the VC. He was born in Cawdor, near Nairn, but had gone to Canada in 1909. After the outbreak of war, he walked 120 miles cross-country on snowshoes to enlist as a private the Canadian Mounted Rifles. He was given a battlefield commission, won the Military Cross and the Distinguished Conduct Medal and was a captain when he won the highest honour at Cambrai for his actions between 29 September and 3 October, as his citation details: 'Captain MacGregor led his company under continuous heavy fire. Although he was wounded, he located and terminated the action of the enemy machine guns which were preventing Allied progress. He killed four men and took eight prisoners. He reorganised his company and continued the advance under heavy fire and against stubborn resistance. Later, after personally making a daylight reconnaissance under extremely heavy fire, he consolidated his company in Neuville-Saint-Rémy, thus assisting the advance forward and into Tilloy.' John MacGregor was promoted to lieutenant colonel. After the war, he returned to Canada and worked as a carpenter. He stood unsuccessfully for the British Columbia Legislature in 1933. In

1940, he re-enlisted as a private and again rose through the ranks, this time to full colonel and CO of the 2nd Canadian Scottish Regiment. He has been described in the press as Canada's most-decorated soldier.

Thomas Caldwell was a farmhand and carter in Carluke before he enlisted with the Lanarkshire Yeomanry. He had transferred to Royal Scots Fusiliers and was a sergeant by the time he won his VC. His citation read: 'For most conspicuous bravery and initiative in attacking near Audenarde on 31 October 1918, when in command of a Lewis gun section engaged in clearing a farmhouse. When his section came under intense fire at close range from another farm, Sergeant Caldwell rushed forward towards the farm, and, in spite of very heavy fire, reached the enemy position which he captured single-handed, together with 18 prisoners. This gallant and determined exploit removed a serious obstacle from the line of advance, saved many casualties, and led to the capture by his section of about 70 prisoners, eight machine guns and a trench mortar.' Thomas Caldwell was later promoted to company sergeant major. He received his VC from King George at Buckingham Palace. He emigrated to Australia, where he died in 1969. His VC is in the Royal Highland Fusiliers Museum in Glasgow.

Underlining the key role played by the Royal Engineers, two Scots sappers won VCs in the Battle of Sambre, the very last offensive of the war, both on the same day – November 4 – with Armistice just a week away. Sapper Adam Archibald, from Leith, had enlisted two years earlier and was with 218 Field Company. Major George Findlay, from Boturich and a career soldier with more than eight years' service, was with 409 Field Company. Both were 39 and both were in action at different points on the Sambre-Oise Canal near Ors. Sapper Archibald's company faced a scene of death and destruction as they struggled to bridge the canal. It must have been hard to believe that the end of the war was imminent. The Germans constantly swept the area with devastating artillery shelling and machine-gun fire and all too many sappers were wounded or killed. In the end, it was left to Adam Archibald and a single officer to provide a floating bridge for the infantry. Even as they worked, bullets ripped into the wooden structure and sparks flew off the wire supports. Only two platoons were able to cross before the bridge was destroyed. For 'most conspicuous bravery and self-sacrifice', Sapper Archibald was given this VC citation: 'He was foremost in the work under heavy artillery barrage and machine-gun fire. The supreme devotion to his duty of this gallant sapper, who collapsed from gas poisoning on completion of his work, was beyond all praise.' He died in Leith aged 76. His VC is in the Royal Engineers Museum, Chatham.

Further along the canal, Major George Findlay faced the same brutal conditions and the same horrific casualty rate. He had already proved his courage in the mud at Passchendaele the year before, when he was awarded the Military Cross. On this occasion he too was wounded but, with a small number of men, was still able to repair the bridge and get it into place across the canal lock. He was the first man across and stayed at the front until the objective was achieved. His citation read: 'Major Findlay's cool and gallant behaviour inspired volunteers from different units at a critical time when men became casualties almost as soon as they joined him in the fire-swept zone and it was due to his gallantry and devotion to duty that this most important crossing was effected.' George Findlay was later promoted to colonel and served in the Second World War. He was appointed deputy lieutenant (the Queen's local representative) of Dunbartonshire in 1957. He received his VC from King George V at Buckingham Palace and it is now in the Royal Engineers Museum.

The 'war to end all wars' ended on 11 November 1918. Scots had won 70 VCs.

THE ARAB REVOLT

This conflict began in May 1920, when it was announced (after the San Remo Conference) that Arab lands of the Ottoman Empire were to be divided between Britain and France. Britain was to take Iraq and Palestine, which was also named as the site for a new Jewish state. It was, and still is, a highly complex situation that has no real part in this commentary other than it was the theatre of war in which a young Scot won a posthumous Victoria Cross. It was a ferocious dispute into which 26-year-old Captain George Henderson, from East Gordon, Berwickshire, found himself catapulted when he was posted to Mesopotamia with 2nd Battalion, the Manchester Regiment. It was at Hillah on 24 July 1920 that he was cited for the VC: 'Captain Henderson led his company in three charges against the enemy, who had opened fire from the flank. At one time when the situation was extremely critical, the captain, by sheer pluck and coolness, steadied his command and prevented his company from being cut up. During the second charge he fell wounded but refused to leave his command and just as the company reached the trench, he was again wounded, this time mortally.' Captain Henderson has no known grave but his name is on the war memorial at Basra. There is also a plaque in the Gordon churchyard that includes the inscription: 'All that he had he gave.' His VC is in the Museum of the King's Regiment Liverpool.

SECOND WORLD WAR

The peace in Europe lasted, often uneasily, until 1939. Despite repeated attempts at brokering some sort of agreement and Neville Chamberlain's optimistic 'peace for our time' speech in 1938, war was declared again the following year and the world was riven into the Allies and the Axis. Almost half of mankind was embroiled in what was to be the deadliest conflict in human history. There is little that has not already been written about the war (and that is not the purpose of this commentary) but it is worth reminding ourselves that it resulted in the deaths of 60 million people. That serves to underscore the courage of the soldiers, sailors and airman who fought for their country between 1939 and 1945.

An example was John Hannah from Glasgow. At 18, he was an RAF flight sergeant and became the youngest airman to win the VC – one of four Scots among Bomber

Command's 19 awards. He was a wireless operator and air gunner in a Handley Page bomber (known to the airmen as 'the suitcase' because of its cramped space) in 83 Squadron RAF on 15 September 1940. The squadron was attacking German barges, thought to be part of the build-up to the invasion of Britain, at Antwerp. His plane was on its second run and flying at 2,000 feet when it was hit by anti-aircraft guns and burst into flames. The bomb bay and the wing petrol tanks were badly damaged and the heat was so intense that the floor of the plane melted and the navigator and the tail gunner had no option but to bale out. With his own ammunition exploding around him, Hannah used fire extinguishers and then his bare hands to smother the flames. Ten minutes after the first hit, he reported that the fire was out. His flying suit was charred beyond recognition, his face was burned black, his eyes were badly swollen and both his hands were seriously burned. Despite that, he was able to retrieve the navigator's maps and struggle to the cabin, where he helped the pilot navigate a safe return to base and landing. His citation read: 'He was almost blinded by the intense heat and fumes but had the presence of mind to obtain relief by turning on his oxygen supply. This airman displayed courage, coolness and devotion to duty of the highest order and by his action in remaining and successfully extinguishing the fire under conditions of the greatest danger and difficulty, enabled the pilot to bring the aircraft to its base.' John Hannah received his VC at Buckingham Palace in October 1940. In December 1941, suffering from tuberculosis thought to have been caused by the severe burns, he was invalided out of the RAF. He couldn't take a full-time job and became a taxi driver. His health continued to deteriorate and he died in a sanatorium in June 1947. He was 25. His VC is in the Royal Air Force Museum, Hendon.

In March 1941 the French Resistance told London that two of Germany's newest battleships and symbols of Nazi power, *Gneisenau* and *Scharnhorst,* had arrived in Brest. An RAF reconnaissance Spitfire confirmed the report and plans were immediately made to attack them. On the night of 4/5 April, the RAF scored a direct hit that damaged the *Scharnhorst*. With the prospect of further attack, the captain of the *Gneisenau* decided to move to a mooring in the outer harbour. Because of bad weather, a second British attack was aborted without damage to the ships. Three Bristol Beauforts were then sent in but again the weather created problems and only one plane found the target. The pilot was Flying Officer Kenneth Campbell from Saltcoats. He was just 23 and had joined the RAF Volunteer Reserve straight from Cambridge University. Reports say he went in 'almost at sea level and passing the German flak ships at less than mast height.' His action that morning won him the VC – sadly posthumously – for which the citation read: 'This officer was the pilot of a Beaufort aircraft of Coastal Command which was detailed to attack an enemy battle cruiser in Brest Harbour at first light on the morning of April 6 1941. The aircraft did not return but it is known that a torpedo attack was carried out with the utmost daring. The battle cruiser was secured alongside the wall on the north shore of the harbour, protected by a stone mole bending around it from the west. On rising ground behind the ship stood protective batteries of guns. Other batteries were clustered thickly round the two arms of land which encircle the outer harbour. In this outer harbour near the mole were moored three heavily-armed anti-aircraft ships, guarding the battle cruiser. Even if an aircraft succeeded in penetrating these formidable defences, it would be almost impossible, after delivering a low-level attack, to avoid crashing into the rising ground beyond. This was well known to Flying Officer Campbell who, despising the heavy odds, went cheerfully and resolutely to the task. He ran the gauntlet of the defences. Coming in at almost sea level, he passed the anti-aircraft ships at less than mast-height in the very mouths of their guns and skimming over the mole launched a torpedo at point-blank range. The battle cruiser was severely damaged below the water-line and was obliged to return to the dock whence she had come only the day before. By pressing home his attack at close quarters in the face of withering fire on a course fraught with extreme peril, Flying Officer Campbell displayed valour of the highest order.' The Beaufort, which had crashed into the harbour, was recovered by the Germans. They buried Kenneth Campbell and his other three crew members with full military honours in Brest cemetery. Reports said that, had the two ships linked up with the *Bismarck* in the Atlantic, the impact on British supply convoys would have been disastrous. There is a memorial plaque and bench dedicated to Campbell in Saltcoats and a further memorial in his old school at Sedbergh. His VC is in the museum of 22 Squadron RAF.

Major General Jock Campbell from Thurso was one of the great personalities of the war. Probably the most famous of the famous Desert Rats, he was already a veteran of action in North Africa and had won the Military Cross and the Distinguished Service Order (and bar) before he was further decorated with the VC in 1941. He was 47 at the time. He had started the war as a lieutenant colonel and commander in the Royal Horse Artillery, part of the 7th Armoured Division Support Group, and created the highly effective 'Jock columns'. These were small multi-disciplined units (made up of armoured cars, artillery and motorised infantry) used to harass Italian forces. There have been dozens of books and articles about his exploits, allowing me to be brief. Quoting the citation for the award won on 22 November is surely enough: '[He] was commanding the troops, including one regiment of tanks, in the area of Sidi Rezegh ridge [now part of Libya]… His small force holding this important ground was repeatedly attacked by large numbers of tanks and infantry. Wherever the situation was most difficult and the fighting hardest, he was to be seen with his forward troops, either on his feet or in his open car. In this car, he carried out several reconnaissances for counter-attacks by his tanks, whose senior officers had all become casualties earlier in the day. Standing in his car with a blue flag, this officer personally formed up tanks under close and intense fire from all natures of enemy weapons. On the following day the enemy attacks were intensified and again Brigadier Campbell was in the forefront of the heaviest fighting, encouraging his troops, staging counter-attacks with his remaining tanks and personally controlling the fire of his guns. On two occasions he himself manned a gun to replace casualties.

During the final enemy attack on 22 November he was wounded but continued most actively in the foremost positions, controlling the fire of batteries which inflicted heavy losses on enemy tanks at point-blank range, and finally acted as loader to one of the guns himself.... He refused to be evacuated and remained with his command where his outstanding bravery and consistent determination had a marked effect in maintaining the splendid fighting spirit of those under him.'

When he heard of Jock Campbell's award, his German Afrika Corps adversary, General Johann von Ravenstein (second in command to Rommel), wrote to congratulate him: 'It was my 21st Panzer Division that has fought in these hot days with the 7th Armoured Division, for whom I have the greatest admiration. Your Support Group of Royal Artillery, too, has made the fighting very hard for us and I remember all the many iron that flew near the aerodrome around our ears. The German comrades congratulate you with warm heart on the award of the Victoria Cross. During the war your enemy – but with high respect, Von Ravenstein.' Jock Campbell was promoted to major general and given command of the 7th Armoured Division – the Desert Rats – in February 1942, but he and his driver were killed three weeks later when their jeep overturned on soft sand in Libya. He was 48 when he died and is buried at Cairo War Memorial Cemetery. His Victoria Cross is displayed at the Royal Artillery Museum, Woolwich. A seaside walk in Thurso was named the Victoria Walk in his honour. There is also a memorial to him in his old school, Sedbergh. The Royal Artillery bestowed the name Campbell on one of the batteries of its Junior Leaders Regiment at Bramcote.

Commander Anthony Miers, from Inverness, was a career sailor who had joined the Royal Navy in 1924 as an 18-year-old cadet. He later served on battleships of the Home Fleet before transferring to submarines in 1929. In the early part of the war, he was commander of the *Torbay* operating out of Alexandria, won the DSO (and bar) and was regarded as one the most successful submarine aces in the Mediterranean. He won his VC at Corfu on 4 March 1942. The citation read: 'Commander Miers, having followed an enemy convoy into the harbour the previous day, fired torpedoes at a destroyer and two 5,000-ton transports, scoring hits on the two supply ships, which almost certainly sank. *Torbay* then had a very hazardous withdrawal to the open sea, enduring 40 depth-charges. The submarine had been in closely-patrolled enemy waters for 17 hours.' Anthony Miers was appointed submarine staff liaison officer to the commander in chief of the United States Pacific Fleet (1943–44) and commanded 8th Submarine Flotilla (1944–45); he was promoted to captain in 1946 and commanded the aircraft carrier HMS *Theseus*, 1954–5; in 1956 he achieved the rank of rear admiral, and was a flag officer in the Middle East, 1956–9. He was made a companion of the Order of Bath in 1958, knighted in 1959 and retired from the Royal Navy in 1962. His VC is in the Imperial War Museum.

Although still only 25, Wing Commander Hugh Malcolm, from Broughty Ferry in Dundee, was in command of a squadron of light bombers (Bristol Blenheim IVs) in North Africa in November 1942. He took advantage of low cloud to lead an attack on a German air base at Bizerta. As they neared the target, the sky cleared and the squadron had to run the gauntlet of anti-aircraft fire and enemy fighters but managed to unload all their bombs on the airfield. Three British planes were lost. The operation was repeated days later and this time it was rounded off by the wing commander leading his men in raking the airfield with machine-gun fire. All the planes returned safely to base. On 4 December, the squadron was detailed to give urgent support to the First Army. Again there was no fighter escort but this time the squadron met with overwhelming odds. For his outstanding bravery, Hugh Malcolm was cited for the VC which, sadly, was awarded posthumously: 'He led an attack on an enemy fighter airfield near Chougui, Tunisia. On reaching the target, however, and starting the attack, the squadron was intercepted by an overwhelming force of enemy fighters. One by one his bombers were shot down until he himself was shot down in flames.' Hugh Malcolm is buried in Beja War Cemetery. The social centres established by Lord Tedder for off-duty airmen serving around the Mediterranean (and later throughout the RAF) were named the Malcolm Clubs in his honour.

Lorne Campbell of Airds, Argyllshire, took a commission with the Argyll and Sutherland Highlanders (TA) while he was still at Oxford University. At the outbreak of war he went to France, where his bravery won him the DSO in 1940. In 1942 (then 29 years old), he was promoted to lieutenant colonel and given command of the Argylls' 7th Battalion and fought at El Alamein, where he was awarded a bar to his DSO. It was in the attack on Wadi Akarit (Tunisia) that he won the VC on 6 April 1943. The citation reads: 'The battalion commanded by Lieutenant Colonel Campbell had to break through an enemy minefield and anti-tank ditch in order to form a bridgehead. The battalion formed up in darkness and then attacked at an angle. This difficult operation was successfully completed and at least 600 prisoners taken. Next day the position was subjected to heavy and continuous bombardment and although the colonel was wounded, his personality dominated the battlefield. Under his inspiring leadership the attacks were repulsed and the bridgehead held.' Lorne Campbell was wounded in the neck during the fighting but refused to have medical attention until the action was successfully completed. He was later promoted to brigadier in 13th Infantry Brigade (8th Army Division) in the Sicilian and Italian campaigns. He was a staff officer in Washington (1944–45) where he was awarded the US Legion of Merit and a military OBE. His VC is in the Argyll & Sutherland Highlanders Museum, Stirling.

Charles Lyell, from Forfar, was 29 and a captain in the Scots Guards. He was also the second Baron Lyell, after inheriting the title from his grandfather in 1926. In April 1943, he was company commander of a unit serving alongside the Grenadier Guards in Tunisia. For four days, he led his men 'with great gallantry, ability and cheerfulness' in a series of attacks under heavy enemy fire and consistently repelled counter-attacks. At times, he acted as wireless operator in particularly exposed positions. His action (said to be 'one of the greatest personal feats of the war') on the fourth day was to win him a posthumous VC. The citation reads: 'Captain Lord Lyell's outstanding leadership and gallantry enabled his company to take its objective. On 27 April, accompanied by a sergeant, a lance corporal and two guardsmen, he led an attack on an enemy post consisting of an 88 mm gun and a heavy machine gun in two separate pits. He destroyed the crew of the machine gun with a hand grenade and then, three of the party having become casualties, and with the lance corporal to give covering fire, he leapt into the second pit, bayoneting and killing several of the crew before being overwhelmed and killed. Both the guns had been silenced. The company was then able to advance and take its objective. There is no doubt that Lord Lyell's outstanding leadership, gallantry and self-sacrifice enabled his company to carry out its task, which had an important bearing on the success of the battalion and of the brigade.' Lord Lyell is buried in Massicault Cemetery, northern Tunisia. His VC is privately owned.

On 22 September 1942 Donald Cameron, from Carluke, was a 27-year-old Royal Naval Reserve lieutenant commanding the midget submarine prototype *X6*. Together with five others of its kind (each with a crew of four), it was towed by conventional submarine from Scotland to north Norway to make an attack on the Germans' biggest battleship, *Tirpitz,* sitting in a well-protected fjord anchorage. The 1000-mile voyage meant running the gauntlet of minefields, boom defence nets, coastal listening posts and then heavy shelling from the battleship. One X-sub lost its towline, two had to pull out because of technical problems and a fourth was sunk after being hit by the *Tirpitz* guns. Only *X6* and *X7* (commanded by Lieutenant Godfrey Place) managed to lay charges under the *Tirpitz*. For their outstanding courage, the two young officers were both cited for the VC. The citation read: 'In the course of the operation these very small craft pressed home their attack to the full, in doing so accepting all the dangers inherent in such vessels and facing every possible hazard which ingenuity could devise for the protection in harbour of vitally important capital ships. The courage, endurance and utter contempt for danger in the immediate face of the enemy shown by Lieutenants Place and Cameron during this determined and successful attack were supreme.' At the end of the action, both the midget subs had to be scuttled and abandoned and two more men drowned. Lieutenant Cameron and the others were captured and were aboard *Tirpitz* when their time-delayed charges exploded, severely damaging the battleship and knocking her out of action for months. The lieutenant was transferred to a German prison camp for naval officers, where he remained for the rest of the war. Later, he was promoted to commander. He acted as a technical adviser on a 1955 film about the action, *Above us the waves*. His part was played by John Gregson. He died in 1961 at the age of 45 at the Royal Navy Hospital Haslar, Portsmouth. His VC is privately owned.

When Glaswegian Bill Reid, the son of a blacksmith, was 18, he had decided on going to university to study metallurgy but when the war started he quickly changed his mind. He applied to join the RAF and after training in Canada came back with a commission and his wings. Instead of sending him to war, however, the RAF decided to use his skills as a training instructor and he found himself flying obsolete bombers preparing other young men for combat. It wasn't until July 1943 that he flew on his first operational mission – a raid on Mönchengladbach. A few months later, he transferred to 61 Squadron and flew a Lancaster on various sorties. Then on the night of 3 November, flying Lancaster 'O for Oboe', the young flight lieutenant's target was the industrial city of Düsseldorf. Two hundred miles out, he hit trouble in the deadly shape of a Messerschmitt 110 night-fighter. He managed to shake that off but then was attacked by a Focker-Wulf 190. In the hail of bullets that raked the full length of the Lancaster, his navigator was killed, the wireless operator badly wounded, the flight engineer hit in the arm and Reid himself took four wounds in the head and chest. The cockpit window was shattered. The intercom, the oxygen supply, one of the gun turrets and his compasses were all knocked out of action. For his courage in maintaining the mission, Flight Lieutenant William Reid became the eleventh member of Bomber Command to win the Victoria Cross. The citation tells the rest of the story: 'Despite all this, Reid pressed on, bombed the target accurately and then, steering by the Pole Star and the moon, set about bringing the aircraft home. At one point he lost consciousness and the wounded flight engineer had to operate the controls. Recovering, Reid then took over again. Despite mist, a partial collapse of the undercarriage and blood running into his eyes from his head wound, he put down successfully at an airfield in Norfolk. His tenacity and devotion to duty are beyond praise.' When asked by the Bomber Group commander why he hadn't turned back after being wounded, William Reid replied: 'The idea never occurred to me.' After recovering from his injuries, he returned to active duty in January 1944, with the 617 (Dambuster) Squadron led by Leonard Cheshire and flew sorties to various targets in France. Six months later, he flew a Lancaster carrying a 'Tallboy', the 12,000 lb deep-penetration bomb devised by Barnes Wallis, in an attack on a V-bomb storage depot near Reims. He managed to get the bomb away successfully but his plane was hit and he and the crew were forced to bale out. He broke his arm in the jump, was captured by a German patrol and spent the rest of the war in a PoW camp near Berlin. William Reid received his Victoria Cross from King George VI at Buckingham Palace. He left the RAF in 1946 and went back to study at Glasgow University and then the West of Scotland Agricultural College. He became an adviser to an animal-feed company.

Frank Blaker was just 24 but already a major in the City of Glasgow Regiment of the Highland Light Infantry and the holder of the Military Cross for bravery when he was attached to the Gurkha Rifles (part of the Chindits special force) in Burma. Another symbol of his courage was the Japanese flag he captured in 1943. During the second Chindit campaign, on 9 July 1944, he was commanding a company held up during an important advance by close-range firing from medium and light machine guns. His response won him the VC, sadly posthumously. The citation reads: 'The major went ahead of his men through very heavy fire and despite being severely wounded in the arm, located the machine guns and charged the position alone. Even when mortally wounded he continued to cheer on his men whilst lying on the ground. His fearless leadership and outstanding courage so inspired his company that they stormed the hill and captured the objective, while the enemy fled in terror into the jungle.'

Dr U Maung Gyi, one of the Gurkhas serving with Major Blaker, later wrote a vivid eyewitness account of the incident: 'After five hours of strenuous climbing, we reached the edge of the second plateau, followed by 2nd and 3rd Platoons. We discovered eight men were missing from our company. No one could say if they had been bitten by snakes or fell and died for some other reason or simply lost their way in the thick and tangled bushes. A Gurkha scout crawled silently to Captain Blaker and told him there was another ridge to climb. He had spotted two machine-gun nests, well hidden behind thick brush between the trees. There were also two large bunkers near the top. The enemy was well dug in. Captain Blaker radioed for a mortar barrage to weaken the Japanese defence and cover our movement. According to Blaker, our C Company was to coordinate its assault with B Company, which was approaching from the other side of the hill. There was still a considerable distance for us to cover before we would reach our target. The captain therefore signalled us to move onto a narrow but well-trod path made earlier by the Japanese. It was the only direct route to the objective. Our mortar bombardment stopped, and soon we heard gunfire and loud yells coming from the other side of the hill. B Company had begun its assault. Realising our company was behind schedule, Captain Blaker rushed up the ridge along the path, leading the column. The Japanese opened fire, and several Gurkhas from 1st Platoon fell. The rest of the men dove behind trees, rocks and bushes to find cover. Some crawled through the underbrush to try to silence the machine guns, but they were stopped by Japanese grenades. We were caught in a crossfire. When the firing stopped we could hear the wounded men groaning. I crawled toward several wounded and administered field dressings. The men lay low and waited for orders. The Japanese machine gunners were also waiting for us to rise. To our horror, Captain Blaker suddenly sprang up and charged at the concealed enemy position up the path, firing his carbine as he advanced. A blast from a Japanese machine gun hit him. He fell sideways. But then stood up and charged again, firing wildly and yelling "Charge! Charge, men! Charge!" Another blast threw him against a tree. He dropped his weapon, clutched his chest and shouted: "I'm dying! Come on C Company! Take this hill!" Then he collapsed, his body riddled with bullets. Inspired by the daring of this British officer, the Gurkhas sprang up, yelling: "Gorkhali Ayo! The Gurkhas are coming!" With drawn kukris and fixed bayonets they charged. The Japanese continued to fire and more Gurkhas fell but they fanned out and rushed through the dense trees and tangled thickets. When they reached the enemy positions, they cut down the Japanese in their foxholes and trenches. They succeeded in securing the second plateau.' Frank Blaker died from his wounds while being carried away from the battlefield. There is a memorial to him in the Taukkyan War Cemetery, north of Rangoon (now Yangon).

Aberdonian John Cruickshank was 19 when he enlisted in the Royal Artillery in May 1939. After two years, he transferred to the RAF and after earnings his wings joined 210 Squadron (RAF Volunteer Reserve) as a flying officer in March 1943. He was piloting a Catalina flying boat on anti-submarine patrol in the North Atlantic on the night of 17 July when he became one of only four Coastal Command pilots to win the VC. His citation read: 'He was attacking a U-boat in a hail of flak shells when one burst inside the aircraft, causing a great deal of damage. One member of the crew was killed and two wounded and, although he too had been hit, Flying Officer Cruickshank went in again, releasing his depth charges, which straddled the U-boat perfectly and it sank. On the hazardous five-and-a-half-hour return journey, the flying officer several times lost consciousness but insisted on helping to land the Catalina.' When he returned to base, John Cruickshank had 12 wounds: two to his lungs and ten penetrating wounds to both legs. He recovered sufficiently to return to administrative duties, was promoted to flight lieutenant but did not return to flying. He left the RAF in 1946 to return to banking.

Richard Burton was 21 years old and a private in The Duke of Wellington's Regiment serving in Italy when he won the VC. It was at Monte Ceco on 8 October 1944. Two companies of the regiment were trying to take a crucial hill position but when they were just 20 yards from the crest of the hill they came under withering fire from the German machine guns. Without hesitation, Private Burton ran forward and, with his Tommy gun, killed all three gunners. His citation completes the story: 'When the assault was again held up by murderous fire from more machine guns, Private Burton, again showing complete disregard for his own safety, dashed forward toward the first machine gun, using his Tommy gun until his ammunition was exhausted. He then picked up a Bren gun and, firing from the hip, succeeded in killing or wounding the crews of the two machine guns. Afterwards, in spite of the fact that most of his comrades were either dead or wounded, he repelled two counter-attacks, directing such accurate fire that the enemy retired. Thanks to his outstanding courage the company was then able to consolidate on the forward slope of the feature. Private Burton's magnificent gallantry and total disregard of his own safety during many hours of fierce fighting in mud and continuous rain were an inspiration to all his comrades.' Richard Burton was later promoted to corporal. He shares a monument at Kirriemuir with two other local VC winners, Lord Lyell and Private Charles Melvin. His VC is in private hands.

George Thomson was just 18 and an apprentice grocer in Kinross when the war broke out, but he immediately joined the Local Defence Volunteers (later Home Guard). Two years later, he became a ground-crew wireless operator in the RAF and served in the Middle East. Then he volunteered for aircrew and joined Bomber Command as a flight sergeant in 9 Squadron, RAF Volunteer Reserve. On New Year's Day 1945 he was the wireless operator in a daylight mission on the Dortmund-Ems Canal. It's yet another example of the indomitable spirit of the young airmen and won George Thomson a posthumous VC for 'superb gallantry and self-sacrifice.' The citation reads: 'Just after his aircraft had bombed, flak tore holes in the fuselage and started several fires. Thomson saw that the mid-upper turret was ablaze, and that the gunner inside was unconscious. At the cost of severe burns to his hands and face, he managed to reach the gunner and carry him clear. By this time he was aware that the rear turret too was on fire, and that the gunner there was likewise overcome by fumes. With his already-burnt hands Thomson beat out the flames on the rear-gunner's clothing and pulled him clear. Then he made his way forward, edging round a hole in the flooring, to tell his captain what was happening. Despite much damage to the aircraft and a fire in one engine, the pilot managed to reach Belgium and successfully crash-land.' George Thomson died from his wounds three weeks later. His Victoria Cross is in the National War Museum of Scotland.

It was on 1 March 1945 that Jimmy Stokes, from the Gorbals area of Glasgow, won his VC. He was five foot two and as tough as they come in those city streets. He had worked as a labourer and then tried his hand as a waiter in London, but at the outbreak of the war he immediately enlisted in the Royal Artillery. Then when he heard more infantrymen were needed, he transferred, improbably, to the King's Shropshire Light Infantry. Just three weeks after his thirtieth birthday, his platoon was pinned down during an attack on the village of Kervenheim on the Dutch-German border. Heavy rifle and machine-gun fire was coming from a nearby farm building. In what was later described as 'an incredible act of selfless bravery', Private Stokes rushed the building and, despite being wounded in the neck, emerged with 12 German soldiers he had captured single-handedly. He was bleeding heavily and his officer told him to retire to the field hospital for urgent treatment. However, a short distance on the platoon came under fire from another machine gun in a farmhouse. Still bleeding, Jimmy Stokes repeated his previous exploit... and brought out five more prisoners. His VC citation reads: 'His gallantry enabled his platoon to continue the advance. In the final assault, Private Stokes, now severely wounded, once more dashed to the objective through intense fire. He finally fell, firing his rifle to the last. It was found that he had been wounded eight times in the upper part of the body. Private Stokes' one object throughout this action was to kill the enemy, at whatever personal risk. His magnificent courage, devotion to duty, and splendid example inspired all around him, and ensured the success of the attack at a critical moment; moreover, his self-sacrifice saved his platoon and company heavy casualties.' Still he insisted on joining the advance but his wounds were too serious and he finally fell and died 20 yards from the enemy lines. He is buried in the military cemetery at Reichswald, Germany. Twenty years later, Jimmy Stokes was featured on the front page of *The Victor* (the boys' comic published in Dundee by DC Thomson 1961–92). It headlined his story: 'Stokes VC: the soldier who would not give up.' Sixty years after his death, a memorial was unveiled in the Gorbals garden where he played as a boy.

Tom Hunter was also hewn from exceptionally tough material. He was 21, raised in Stenhouse, Edinburgh, and already a corporal in the Royal Marine Commandos when he became the youngest in the corps to win the VC. He was part of Operation Roast, the Allies' major spring offensive to push the Germans back across the River Po and out of Italy. On 2 April 1945 at Lake Comacchio, Tom Hunter, in charge of a Bren gun section, showed selfless courage in the action that brought him the posthumous award of the country's highest award for valour – the last awarded to a Scot in the Second World War. His citation read: 'Armed with a Bren gun, Corporal Hunter led his troop to within four hundred yards of the canal when he realised the enemy held the ruined houses ahead and would soon engage his troop out in the open. Charging alone over two hundred yards, he cleared the defences and attracted the fire of enemy positions on the north bank of the canal whilst his troop advanced for cover before he was hit by bullets. There was no doubt that Corporal Hunter offered himself as a target in order to save his troop and only the speed of his movement prevented him being hit earlier. Throughout the operation, his magnificent courage, leadership and cheerfulness had been an inspiration to his comrades.' Tom Hunter was still firing his Bren when he was mortally wounded. He is buried in the Argenta Gap War Cemetery in Italy. King George VI presented his parents with his posthumous Victoria Cross, which is now in the Royal Marines Museum.

A little more than a month later, the Allies formally accepted Germany's unconditional surrender. The war in Europe ended on 8 May 1945. The Japanese finally surrendered on 15 August.

4

LEADING THE WAY

 'Whoever is providing leadership needs to be as fresh, thoughtful and reflective as possible to make the very best fight.'

— *Faye Wattleton*

Just as Scotland has produced a long line of brave soldiers so it has spawned a brand of military geniuses of which any empire would be proud. They provide a heady mix of courage, leadership, training skills, strategy and original thinking in a tradition as long as the history of human conflict.

Perhaps it comes from the background of almost continual internecine conflict between the clans and the constant need to fend off Big Brother England, but the Scottish character clearly has an aggressive gene and, in any case, such a positive attitude would seem an essential element in even imaginary empire building.

We have fought for our cause in many foreign fields and on inhospitable oceans and we've been more than ready to lend – and quite often sell – a helping hand to others' causes, wherever that may take us. At one time or another, Scots have ruled the waves around much of the world, creating or helping to develop the navies of the United States, Russia, Japan, Australia, Chile, even Hawaii, and we have also provided admirals for Peru, Brazil and Greece. Scots have served as generals and field marshals for foreign armies all across Europe including Holland (as early as the 1570s), France, Prussia, Sweden, Poland and Russia and, of course, in the Americas, where they happily took commissions on both sides. Closer to home and more recently, distinguished Scots were primarily responsible for setting up the British Army's first sniper unit, the Royal Flying Corps, the Women's Auxiliary Air Force, the Special Operations Executive, the SAS, the Lovat Scouts, the Commandos, the first paratroops, the first full-time military intelligence service and, mindful of the need to look after people when their war service was over, the British Legion.

Scots have also had a hand in the creation of the weapons of war from Thomas Cochrane's fire ships, used against Napoleon, to the British Army's favourite rifle. James Paris Lee (born Hawick, 1831–1904) was the Lee in Lee-Enfield rifle, one of the most famous rifles used by the British armed forces in both world wars. The Enfield comes from the Essex town where the .303 guns were first produced in 1895. They were still standard issue when I did my National Service in the late 1950s. Around 17 million were made for the British and Commonwealth armies. Lee left the Borders with his family to emigrate to Canada and he became an apprentice in his father's jewellery and watch-making business. He had developed a fascination for guns – having tried to make one when he was 12 – and as soon as he had the capital, he set up his own small business in the United States, where he found gun-making a more lucrative business. His first contract was for 1,000 rifles from the US Army in 1861, the beginning of the Civil War.

The oldest regiment in the British Army is the Royal Scots, raised by Sir John Hepburn in 1633. But a readiness to take up the challenge wherever and whenever it's presented is evidenced in the fact that Louis IX of France hired as his personal bodyguard 'le Guarde Ecossaise' – described simply as 'a group of Scottish gentlemen' – even before the Auld Alliance was signed in 1295.

For Hugh Mackay (1640–92), of Scourie in Sutherland, it was the Dutch who offered the biggest challenge, or perhaps made the best offer of the day. He had served in the French army that invaded the Netherlands in 1672 but, not long after marrying a Dutch lady, he switched sides and became a general in command of the Scottish Regiment of William of Orange. He acted as King Billy's aide-de-camp during the Bloodless Revolution, in which he acquired the thrones of England, Scotland and Ireland. As a reward, the general (whose second in command was Bonnie Dundee) was made commander-in-chief of the army in Scotland in 1688. He took his responsibilities very seriously and found time to design the ring bayonet that allowed a rifle to be fired through fixed bayonets. He was killed at the Battle of Steenkerke (Flanders) in 1692 during the Nine Years War against France.

The first half of the eighteenth century seems to have been mainly peaceful, at least as far as Scots armies were concerned, although it's pretty certain that individuals did turn out for the Swedes in the Great Northern War (against Peter the Great's Russia) in 1700, for the Holy Roman Empire in the War of Spanish Succession, 1701–13, on both sides in the civil War of the Polish Succession 1730–38, and for the Austrians in the War of the Austrian Succession (against the other half of Europe), 1740–48. There were certainly Scots on both sides in the American Revolutionary War, or War of Independence (1775–83), too: John Paul Jones and a number of fellow Scots fought for the 13 rebellious colonies, while there were also plenty of Scots still flying the flag for King George III. (See Chapter 8: Scotland and the Stars and Stripes.)

If Admiral Thomas Cochrane had had anything to do with it, 'Rule Britannia' could so easily have been rewritten as 'Rule Scotia'. He was described by some of his Royal

Navy superiors, who clearly had difficulty keeping up with him, as a supreme egotist. They obviously found it hard to grasp the full extent of the admiral's considerable abilities as he threw out streams of bright ideas, spouted strong political beliefs and then successively took command of the navies of Chile, Peru, Brazil and Greece and, in various ways, helped each of them towards independence. Destined to be the 10th Earl of Dundonald, he was one of the most daring and successful naval captains of the Napoleonic Wars (1803–19). The French gave him the nom de guerre 'the Sea Wolf' and C.S. Forester found him an irresistible inspiration for no fewer than eleven Horatio Hornblower novels. Cochrane also found time to introduce and improve steam propulsion in fighting vessels and to have His Majesty's Ships fitted with gas lighting, tubular boilers, smoke screen equipment and chemical weapons.

The aristocrat was born at Annsfield, Lanarkshire, and if naval records are to be believed, he was precocious enough to have served aboard at least four ships of the Royal Navy when he was just five! In truth, he signed up in 1793, when he was 17 and had simply been the intended beneficiary of a doting uncle's ploy, common at the time, to earn him an early commission based on length of service. The uncle's devotion nevertheless helped out: as captain of the HMS *Hind* serving in the Baltic, he ensured his young nephew was able to join the ship and then, at the earliest opportunity, arranged for his promotion to acting lieutenant on HMS *Thetis* in 1795. Long live nepotism. The young Hornblower (it's not easy separating fact from fiction in this case) duly passed his exams and was firmly and justifiably on the promotional ladder. By 1798, he was a lieutenant on Admiral Keith's flagship in the Mediterranean and distinguished himself when taking temporary command of a captured French ship. As he headed for Mahon in Minorca, he hit a storm that left most of the crew poleaxed by seasickness. Undeterred, he climbed the mast himself and guided the ship to safety. On another occasion, he took advantage of nightfall to send a pursuing Spanish frigate in the wrong direction. He launched a barrel mounted with a candle lantern and watched it float west as he sped off to the east. One of his most talked-about exploits was the 1801 capture of the formidable frigate *El Gamo*. The Spanish warship carried 32 guns and had a crew of more than 300. He was commanding HMS *Speedy*, with 14 guns and just 54 sailors. It was a classic mismatch. However, he fooled the enemy by flying an American flag and getting so close to *El Gamo* that the captain couldn't depress his mighty guns enough to score a hit, and the Royal Navy boarding party took advantage of the resulting confusion. He went on to capture or destroy more than 50 ships in a 15-month tour of duty and was rewarded with promotion to post captain.

In 1809, during the Battle of the Basque Roads, he led a flotilla of fire ships in an attack on a French squadron that was anchored offshore waiting for orders from Napoleon to set sail for Martinique. The fire ships were old vessels stuffed with highly flammable materials that were set alight and allowed to drift unmanned into the enemy ships. The ever-inventive Cochrane went one better and included fused barrels of gunpowder to cause much more damage. He was successful in driving all but two of the French ships to retreat to their home ports but was angered by the failure of his admiral to press home the advantage. He ignored orders and took his ship into a dangerous position while managing to destroy several of the French warships. Although he returned to Britain as a popular hero with a much-acclaimed knighthood, the Admiralty was not amused. They refused to give him another command and that appeared to be the effective end of a glorious but controversial naval career. Unbowed, he turned to politics, in which he had previously dabbled, and was elected MP for Honiton. He proved to be as much a thorn in the side of the political establishment as he had been to the Royal Navy. When he became embroiled in the stock market scandal of 1814, it looked like an even more ignominious end: shadowy figures put around a rumour that Napoleon had been killed and the war was therefore at an end, stock prices soared and shrewd investors made fortunes. In the inevitable witch hunt, his enemies were happy to let the blame fall on Cochrane. Despite his protestations, he was found guilty of trying to manipulate share prices and sentenced not only to a year in jail but also a spell in the public pillory! The establishment must have thought it a fitting end as he was ejected from Parliament and stripped of his naval rank and knighthood.

But they underestimated the great British public. The outrage was such that, fearful of a riot, the authorities cancelled the pillory punishment and the wretched equipment was put away, never to be used again. Historians appear to accept his innocence as readily as did his supporters, but Cochrane did not receive a royal pardon until 1832 (the year he inherited his title of Earl of Dundonald) and he had to wait until Queen Victoria was secure on her throne before his knighthood would be restored, in 1842.

Admiral Cochrane, however, had not sat around twiddling his thumbs while he tried to make the British authorities see sense and look for the real culprit (who was never found). He shouldered the burden of official disgrace and took up the offer of the improbably named Chilean leader, Bernardo O'Higgins, to take command of his navy during the struggle for independence from Spain. He reached Valparaiso in November 1818, donned the uniform of a Chilean vice admiral and promptly reorganised his new navy by introducing British practices and customs. In his flagship, the *O'Higgins*, he caused havoc among the enemy along the coasts of Chile and Peru. He captured Spain's most important base in Chile and then, in 1820, he captured the most powerful ship in its South American fleet. Señor O'Higgins was so pleased that he asked his new saviour to pull off the same trick for Peru's independence bid – with a little bit of help from the Chilean Navy, of course. With his reputation running high, it was only a matter of time before Brazil asked him to help them take on Portugal. He did, and ran rings round the Portuguese in a series of bluffs and cunning ploys. A grateful Emperor Pedro dubbed him Marquês do Maranhão and made him a provincial governor.

However, the lure of the open sea was too much for the Sea Wolf and at the earliest opportunity he jumped land and took passage on a boat for Britain. In what was little more than a brief detour, he went to help the Greeks in their rebellion against a heavy-handed Ottoman Empire force, but before he could claim any major achievement the superpowers of Britain, France and Russia intervened and brought a troubled chapter to a close with talks around a conference table rather than through heroic naval action.

Back home, Cochrane resumed his other battle: getting his name cleared. The royal pardon restored his standing in the Royal Navy and he was now the Earl of Dundonald, but there was still the matter of the knighthood. The Earl was resolute. He would not accept a naval command or position until he was again 'Sir' rather than 'Aye, aye, sir.' After Queen Victoria's personal intervention had restored the knighthood in 1847 and with his honour once more intact, the following year he graciously – at the grand old age of 73 – accepted the role of commander-in-chief of the North American and West Indies station and served there until 1851. Despite all his travails, his ego was still such that he expressed great disappointment when, in 1854, he was not given a command in the Crimea. He failed to see what being 80 had to do with anything. He had to settle for the honorary appointment of rear admiral. He died in 1860 and was buried with full ceremony at Westminster Abbey.

Acting as aide-de-camp to the Duke of Wellington at the Battle of Waterloo would have been enough to secure George Cathcart a footnote in history. But the young aristocrat – third son of the Earl of Cathcart – nevertheless went on to distinguish himself further, not least by his heroic death at the head of his men in a cavalry charge at Inkerman in the Crimea.

Born in Greenock in 1794, he joined the army as a cornet in the Life Guards when he was 16, rose to lieutenant in the Dragoon Guards within the year and then went to Russia, where he replaced his elder brother as aide-de-camp to his father, who was both ambassador to Tsar Alexander and military commissioner with the Russian Army. He was effectively a messenger between the Earl and the British officers attached to various Russian battalions, but it meant that he was present at most of the major battles against the French and was with the allies when they entered Paris on 31 March 1814. After Waterloo in 1815 he returned to Paris, where he served with Wellington until 1818. In return for services rendered, he was given command of the 1st West Indian Regiment but swiftly moved on to the 7th Hussars and assiduously gained promotion until he was a lieutenant colonel in 1828 and colonel of the 1st Dragoons in 1841. He resigned that command to become deputy governor of the Tower of London and remained in that post until the Iron Duke's patronage saw him appointed governor and commander-in-chief of the Cape Colony in what is now South Africa, with the rank of major general. He granted the colony its first constitution, ended the eighth Xhosa War, and quelled a rising among the Basutos. He was knighted and appointed adjutant general of the Horse Guards, but on his arrival back in London he found that several units of the army had already left for the Crimea.

Pausing only to accept appointment as commander of the 4th Division and to receive instructions that he should take over as commander-in-chief if anything happened to Lord Raglan, he rushed off to the new theatre of war in the Ukraine. He played little part at Alma and when leading his troops at Inkerman he found scenes of confusion and was pressed into trying to rush men into the line wherever gaps appeared. At one point, he led 50 men of the 20th Regiment in a cavalry charge against the Russians and appeared to have succeeded in pushing them back when he was shot through the heart and died instantly. Many tributes were paid to him after his death and back home in Britain a memorial stone was erected in St Paul's Cathedral. He was buried in the Crimea.

Another key Scottish figure on Wellington's staff during the Peninsular War (1808–14) was Lieutenant Colonel Colquhoun Grant from Moray. He served as the most trusted of intelligence officers and his courage and tenacity earned him a remarkable personal tribute from the Duke: 'No army in the world ever produced the like.' His official designation was 'exploring officer' because in those more genteel days of the nineteenth century, officers and gentlemen didn't do anything as underhand as spying and, in any case, Major Grant (as he then was) always wore the scarlet uniform of his 11th Devonshire Regiment and thus could never be accused of deception. Whatever the title, his job was, well, to spy on the enemy from behind their own lines. During his explorations, accompanied only by a native guide who knew the terrain, he collected first-hand information about the French Army's disposition and produced detailed sketches for Wellington and his strategists. He earned a reputation for being fearless and getting close enough to know what vintage of wine the generals were drinking! Inevitably, he overstepped the mark and in Portugal on 16 April 1812 he was captured by the French Dragoons. As a career soldier of considerable experience, he was the perfect, well-rounded officer who could be relied upon in tight scrapes and this was the tightest of tight scrapes. Undaunted to find himself prisoner, he used his excellent command of French to charm his captors so much that he ended up as the supper guest of no less a figure than Marshal Marmont, Duke of Ragusa and commander-in-chief of Napoleon's army in Portugal. On the surface at least, this was chivalry of the highest order but, of course, the Marshal was undoubtedly eager to learn more about the great Wellington and his plans. He seems to have been frustrated in his surreptitious interrogation, decided the major *was* a spy after all and therefore beneath the dignity of the army. He ordered his transfer to France and his handing over to the police. Major Grant, however, had other ideas and once inside France he escaped, passed himself off as an American and somehow made it to Paris, from where he was able to pass messages to Wellington before eventually fleeing to Britain. From there, he rejoined his regiment in Spain and continued to serve as an 'exploring officer.'

After the war, he was promoted and, in 1821, took command 54th Regiment of Foot (later 2nd Dorsets) in India and then served with distinction in the first Burmese War (1823–26), for which he was awarded the CB (Companion of the Order of the Bath). But the steamy conditions in Burma took their toll on his health – he was forced to retire from the army in 1929 and died soon afterwards. He was 49.

The role of commanders, such as Sir Colin Campbell, in the Crimea (1854–56) and during the Indian Mutiny (1857–59) is documented in chapter 3: Scotland the Brave.

If you're going to take sides in someone else's war, it's pretty important to pick the winning side. Thomas Glover got it spectacularly right when, in 1867 and far from his native Fraserburgh, he joined Japan's noble samurai in their successful opposition to the repression of the shoguns. He was no military tactician but rather a very shrewd businessman, and he made his decision in traditional samurai style: 'within the space of seven breaths', that is, quickly. He agreed to factor the arms deals that gave the samurai superiority and, after that initial haste, he went on to prosper at leisure as Japan emerged from its isolation. He has gone down in many a history book as the Father of Modern Japan.

Glover arrived in Nagasaki when he was just 21 and a very green representative of the flourishing Scottish trading company, Jardine Matheson. However, in good empire-building style, he was bursting with the pioneering spirit and imbued with the idea of adding value to his host country's commerce. After just two years, he set up his own company and within another couple of years had established himself as one of the province's most successful and influential businessmen. He was clearly impressed by the samurai's struggle and by their determination to make Japan a serious player in world trade. While the French, who had a military mission in Japan, were already involved in re-training the Samurai army, he turned his attention to the navy.

He arranged to send cadets from the Nagasaki naval school to study in Britain. One of them was the young Itō Hirobumi, who was later to become the samurai prime minister of Japan for a record four terms. (It was Hirobumi who, in 1908, made Glover the first foreigner to be honoured with the award of the Order of the Rising Sun.) Much of the shogun domination had been sustained through their fleet of eight steam battleships. So, more importantly, Glover also commissioned three warships for the samurai and, mindful of his Scottish roots, had them built in Aberdeen. Once all that was in train, he set up his own shipyard in Nagasaki and that was later merged into what is today the huge Mitsubishi conglomerate. He gave the samurai a modern military might that allowed them to restore Emperor Meiji to the throne in 1867. He also introduced Japan's first railway locomotive and mechanised coal mine and helped found the Japan Brewing Company, makers of Kirin beer.

But it certainly wasn't a case of all work and no play. He had clearly adapted the old sailor's adage of a girl in every port into having numerous girls in the one port: Nagasaki. He did marry the daughter of a samurai but is also reported to have had children by at least four other women, and some say he was the inspiration for the libidinous Lieutenant Pinkerton in Puccini's *Madam Butterfly*.

He was 73 when he died in 1911. His home – Glover House, overlooking the harbour – somehow survived the atom bomb attack on Nagasaki. It's the oldest western-style building in the country and one of Japan's top tourist attractions with more than two million visitors a year.

For details of Scottish involvement in the American Civil War (1861–65) see chapter 8: Scotland and the Stars and Stripes.

The unique skills of the Highland ghillie were very shrewdly adapted to military use in the Boer War by the 14th Lord Lovat and 23rd Chief of the Fraser Clan, Simon Fraser. When he was raising the famous Lovat Scouts, Fraser recruited in the area he knew best and his key targets were the men he knew best: the beaters and stalkers and gamekeepers who had ensured the lairds of good sport in their hunting, shooting and fishing. His lordship, who had served in the Queen's Own Cameron Highlanders and the Life Guards, designed the Scouts' stag's head cap badge and gave them the motto 'Je suis prest' – I am ready.

When he transported them from the Scottish grouse moors to the veldts of South Africa, he reduced the shock by eschewing the British Army khaki battledress, retaining their ghillie suits and simply adapting their bracken camouflage to the requirements of the new landscape. The 1st Company was a cavalry unit... of sorts: they were mounted on Highland ponies. The 2nd Company were on foot. Their combined tactics 'considerably increased the army's intelligence capability' and made them, according to reports, 'an unseen and deadly foe.' Initially, their job was to stalk the enemy and provide invaluable intelligence to field commanders. They were attached to the Black Watch and the campaign commander-in-chief, Field Marshal Lord Roberts, was mightily impressed with their contribution to the war. In praising them, he described them as 'half wolf and half jack rabbit.' For his brilliant leadership and bravery, Simon Fraser won the Distinguished Service Order. Although the Scouts were formally disbanded at the end of the war, their value was recognised: two companies were established within the volunteer cavalry regiment, the Imperial Yeomanry, and the following year, 1903, they were reformed as two full regiments. At the outbreak of the Great War in 1914, Lord Lovat was promoted to brigadier general and commanded the Highland Mounted Brigade. His distinguished service was again recognised and, in 1915, he was created a Knight of the Thistle. The next year, the Lovat Scouts were given additional duties – as 'sharpshooters', the British Army's first snipers, and served on the Western Front. After the war, Lord Lovat was made the first chairman of the Forestry Commission (1919– 27) and was Stanley Baldwin's under-secretary of state for dominion affairs (1926–27). When he died in 1933, he was succeeded by his eldest son, also Simon, who helped develop the British Commandos and distinguished himself during the D-Day landings at Normandy in June 1944 (see later in chapter). His younger son was the Conservative MP, Sir Hugh Fraser.

As the commander-in-chief of the British Expeditionary Force in France and Flanders, Douglas Haig was one of the most influential and controversial figures of the Great War. He was a member of an Edinburgh whisky family, but rather than going into the business he opted to become a career soldier. After studying at Brasenose College, Oxford, he went to Sandhurst, joined the Hussars in 1885 and, as a young subaltern, fought at the Battle of Omdurman in the Sudan. He then served with distinction throughout the Boer War. He was mentioned in dispatches four times and was said to have been marked out for a key role by his senior officers, including Kitchener.

While still commanding 17th Lancers, he served for two years as aide-de-camp to King Edward VII, and in 1904 he joined Kitchener in India as inspector general of cavalry, becoming the youngest serving general in the British Army. On his return to Britain, he was appointed to a senior staff post in the War Office, where he helped fellow Scot Richard (later Viscount) Haldane, the Liberal secretary of state for war, in reforming the army, including the setting up of the Territorial Force by combining the Volunteer Force, the militia and the yeomanry. With remarkable foresight, he also laid the plans for the creation of the expeditionary force for 'any future war in Europe.' He then became director of staff duties for a couple of years, before going to India in 1909 as chief of the Indian general staff. Three years later, he was back in Britain and general officer commanding at Aldershot, until early in 1914 when he returned to royal duties as aide-de-camp to King George V.

At the outbreak of the war for which he laid such meticulous plans, he led the 1st Corps in northern France, but within months he had become commander of the 1st Army before rapidly succeeding Sir John French as commander in chief of the British Expeditionary Force. It was in that role that he controversially found himself at loggerheads with Lloyd George (first as war secretary and then prime minister from 1916) and also at some variance with the French military about the war strategy and the direction of attacks. The arguments have raged on down the ages without resolution but there is no doubt that British public were shocked by the horrific scale of casualties, especially on the Somme in 1916 and at Passchendaele and Ypres the following year (see chapter 3, Scotland the brave). For many, it was a sacrifice too far. For others, he was the colossal figure who won the war. Promoted to field marshal and given a viscountcy in 1919, Earl Haig showed tremendous commitment to the men who had served Britain so well and to the families of the thousands who perished. He founded the British Legion in Edinburgh in 1921, launched the now famous Poppy Appeal and travelled the world raising funds for his ex-servicemen. When he died in 1928, former soldiers lined the whole of the Royal Mile in Edinburgh for his funeral procession.

Haig's replacement as Commander of 1st Corps in 1914 was fellow Scot and then lieutenant general, Charles Monro. He, too, was a veteran of India and the Boer War and he led the Corps successfully in France at Aubers Ridge, Festubert and Givenchy. The following year, he took charge of the new Third Army and was sent to the Gallipoli peninsula. He quickly realised the difficulty of the position and recommended an evacuation. That evoked the wrath of Winston Churchill, who had initially advocated the Dardanelles expedition, and it needed a personal visit and a second opinion from Kitchener before the withdrawal took place. Monro's decision was vindicated and thousands of lives were saved. He returned to France and command of the First Army in early 1916 and suffered serious setbacks at Vimy Ridge and then at Fromelles. In January of the following year, he was sent to India as regional commander-in-chief and was responsible there for bringing a new efficiency to the Indian Army. After the Boer War, Monro had been chief instructor (in 1901) and then commandant (1903) of the

School of Musketry, Hythe, where he introduced a new concept of fire and movement and rapid aimed fire. This proved so effective in the early stages of the Great War that the Germans thought they were being met with machine-gun fire and it stopped them in their tracks. Charles Monro was knighted in 1921 and served first as governor, then commander of Gibraltar, 1923–28. In 1928, he was again a replacement for Haig – as a trustee of the Imperial War Museum. He died in 1929.

In the days preceding the Great War, it was clear that the aeroplane would have a key role to play in any conflict and the Royal Flying Corps was established to provide support for the army in the form of spotting for the artillery regiments and general reconnaissance. The Corps' first commander was Glaswegian David Henderson (1862–1921), who later went on to play a major part in establishing the RAF. He was a career soldier and decorated veteran of the Boer War, in which he served at Ladysmith and in the advance into the Transvaal. More importantly, he was the army's senior intelligence officer. After the war, he was appointed director of military intelligence and his manuals *Field Intelligence: Its Principles and Practice* (1904) and *The Art of Reconnaissance* (1907) did much to establish his reputation as a military strategist. Recognising the growing importance of the aeroplane in reconnaissance, he trained as a pilot. When he won his wings in 1911, he was already 49 and the world's oldest pilot. At the outbreak of the Great War in 1914 he was given command of the RFC in France but there was then a month-long hiatus when the War Office transferred him to GOC the 1st Infantry Division. Lord Kitchener had not approved that move and he asked General Henderson to resume command of the fliers, who were then engaging the Germans in air dogfights. He returned to the War Office in London the following year as director general of military aeronautics. The RFC had been expanding its role into strafing the German front-line troops and it was becoming clear that it would be much more important than previously thought.

When General Jan Smuts was asked to write a review of the development of air services, he relied heavily on David Henderson's personal experience and recommended amalgamation of the RFC and the Royal Navy Air Service, creating the Royal Air Force in April 1918. (Another key figure in the amalgamation was also a Scot, Sir William Weir: he was secretary of state for air in the Lloyd George government.) David Henderson's reward was to be made vice-president of the Air Council but, having been bypassed for the much more important role of chief of the air staff, he quietly stepped down from the political arena and asked to return to active duty in France for the last few months of the war. When the war ended, the general – now also a knight – became the honorary colonel of the Highland Light Infantry and served as a military representative at the Paris Peace Conference, which drew up the Versailles Treaty in 1919. When the ink was dry on the treaty, he turned his driving energies towards securing long-term peace and then took on the job of director general of the Red Cross in Geneva. He served there, showing as much distinction as he had when wearing his army uniform, until his early death at the age of 59.

One of the central figures in establishing the formidable reputation of the Anzac forces was Colonel Ewen Sinclair MacLagan, an Edinburgh banker's son. He was commanding the men of the Third Infantry Brigade of the Australian and New Zealand Army Corps when they first entered the Great War at Gallipoli in 1915 and again three years later in a decisive battle on the Somme. He became a soldier after his father died and his mother remarried to an army officer. He served in the militia before being commissioned, at 21, as a second lieutenant in the Border Regiment in 1889. While serving in India in 1898 he rose to captain, and during the Boer War to adjutant of 1st Battalion. He was mentioned in dispatches (the first of five such honours), awarded the Distinguished Service Order, and wounded in action. After the war and recovered from his wounds, he was seconded to Australia as adjutant of the New South Wales Scottish Rifles and deputy adjutant general of 1st Military District. In 1904, he returned to Britain and the Border Regiment and four years later was promoted to major and transferred to the Yorkshire Regiment. MacLagan had clearly left a good impression in Australia, because when Greenock-born William Bridges became the first commandant of the new Royal Military College in Canberra in 1910, he invited him back as his drill director with the rank of lieutenant colonel.

He was there when the war broke out and he was appointed to the Australian Imperial Force as colonel and commanding officer the Third Infantry Brigade. He took them to Egypt for desert training and then through the Dardanelles and into action on the beaches at Gallipoli in the spring of 1915. The stated objective was to take some of the pressure off the allied Russian forces and to open up a supply route through the Black Sea. But that first Anzac day – as April 25 was to become forever known – got off to a horrendous start. When the 16,000 men landed on the designated beachhead, there was such chaos that it was sometime impossible to distinguish enemy from friendly troops. The Turkish resistance had been grossly underestimated and they had the added advantage of being supported by heavy artillery fire as they poured down from the steep hills behind the beach. Carefully-laid plans had to be abandoned and Colonel MacLagan took the hardest of all military decisions. He ordered the men to fall back. It was as crucial as it was hard and it saved his troops from being decimated or driven back into the sea. An Australian historian later wrote: 'On that very first day, he became a central figure in establishing the whole legend of the Anzac forces.' He was also mentioned in dispatches for his tenacity. Through the six long months of constant barrage from the Turkish artillery, the Anzac soldiers fought valiantly against both the enemy and the appalling conditions. Fresh water was in short supply and hygiene was virtually non-existent. Ewen MacLagan suffered the personal indignity of such severe dysentery that he had to be taken to a field hospital. The gruelling campaign could not be called a victory but the *Sydney Morning Herald* reported the comment of one of the soldiers: 'There is no doubt the sturdy Third under Colonel MacLagan fought like Trojans and covered themselves with glory.' In those six months, they had lost nine thousand men and thousands more were wounded. They were then posted to the Somme.

Colonel MacLagan was the only British officer retained by the Australian High Command and he stayed with them for the rest of the war. He was promoted to major general in 1917 and took command of the Fourth Division in Flanders. At Passchendaele, where the fighting was at its most ferocious, the division again suffered massive casualties and he was once more mentioned in dispatches and this time awarded the CB. On the Somme in March 1918, in what has been described as the turning point in the war, he poured his Anzac troops in to secure breaches and repel the German offensive that had broken through Allied lines at Hébuterne, Dernancourt and Villers-Bretonneux. Four months later, this time with support from the Americans, the Fourth Division were again successful at Hamel. In the attack on the Hindenburg Line in September, again fighting alongside American troops, they were stopped short of their objective but MacLagan simply rested his men, sent forward a hot meal and then resumed the attack successfully! During this prolonged action, Ewen MacLagan was again mentioned in dispatches on three separate occasions. When the war ended, he returned to the British Army and was promoted to major general and made a Companion of St Michael and St George. He commanded 51 Highland Division, 1919–23. He retired in 1925 and died in 1948.

Certainly one of the most distinguished women of the Great War was Helen Gwynne-Vaughan, daughter of the aristocratic Fraser family from Aberdeenshire. She was overseas commander of the Women's Auxiliary Army Corps (1917) before becoming commander-in-chief of the Women's Royal Air Force (1918–19). After her appointment by Air Minister Sir William Weir, she immediately recruited 9,000 women to work as clerks, fitters, drivers, cooks and storekeepers. Air Vice Marshal Sir Sefton Brancker later said that, under her, 'the WRAF was the best disciplined and best turned-out women's organisation in the country.' She was the first woman to win a military CBE (1918). After the war she was made a dame and returned to her civilian role as a botanist at Birkbeck College, London, where she had been the first woman professor appointed, in 1909. At the outbreak of Second World War in 1939, when she was 60, she declined the invitation to lead the new Women's Auxiliary Air Force (WAAF) but instead agreed to serve as the first chief controller and major general in the newly-formed Auxiliary Territorial Services (ATS), 1939–41.

Another veteran of both the Boer and First World Wars was George Milne, a career soldier from Aberdeen. He had the classic military background: after the Royal Military Academy, he joined the Royal Artillery, served in the Nile Expedition (1898) and then went to South Africa (1899–1902), where he won the Distinguished Service Order. In the Great War, he was brigadier general of the Royal Artillery, with 4th Division of the British Expeditionary Force in France (1914–15) and held a series of commands. Later he was made commander-in-chief of what became known as the Salonika Army, which pushed back the pro-German Bulgarians and helped establish a new, temporary government that controlled northern Greece and the Aegean against the official government of the king in Athens. It was an arduous campaign and he reported local conditions in detail in his official dispatches: 'The area was found to be highly malarious, the heat intense and damp and the single road from the base was long, hilly and of uneven surface.' The Bulgarians were also proving to be a formidable enemy: 'The Gloucesters and the Cameron Highlanders advanced under cover of an artillery bombardment and by 8 a.m. had seized the village of Karadzakoj Bala. Shortly after the occupation of the village, the enemy opened a heavy and accurate artillery fire but the remaining two battalions of the brigade, the Royal Scots and Argyll and Sutherland Highlanders, though suffering severely from enfilade fire, pushed on against Karadzakoj Zir. By 5.30 p.m. that village also was occupied, in spite of the stubborn resistance of the enemy. Attempts to bring forward hostile reinforcements were frustrated during the day by our artillery but during the night the Bulgarians launched several strong counter-attacks, which were repulsed with heavy loss. During the following night determined counter-attacks of the enemy were again repulsed, and by the evening of 2 October, the position had been fully consolidated.' Towards the end of the war, Milne took on the additional duties of commander-in-chief of the British Army of the Black Sea (1916) and was knighted in 1918, when he also became colonel commandant of Royal Artillery (a role he held until his death in 1948). From 1922, he was general officer commanding at Eastern Command, before becoming chief of the imperial general staff in 1926 and finally field marshal in 1928. When he left the High Command, he was given a peerage and appointed to the honorary post of constable of the Tower of London (1933–38). In the Second World War, he served in the Home Guard and Civil Defence and was colonel commandant of the Pioneer Corps. He also worked as a military correspondent for the *Sunday Chronicle* between 1941 and 1944.

In between flying airships, being mentioned in dispatches in the Great War, and planning Operation Chastise (the famous 617 Squadron Dambuster raids in the Second World War), Fife-born Ralph Cochrane helped set up and was first commander of the Royal New Zealand Air Force, founded in 1936. The son of Lord Cochrane of Cults, he was just 14 when he went to the Royal Navy College and 17 when he joined HMS *Colossus* as a midshipman in 1912. When the war started, he joined the RN Air Service, qualified as an airship pilot and played his part in the coastal defence. He also served as a staff officer in the Admiralty airship department. He transferred to the RAF as a flight lieutenant in 1919, was awarded the Air Force Cross and could well have served the rest of his career in airships, were it not for a chance meeting in 1921 with Air Marshal Lord Trenchard. The older man told Cochrane he was wasting his time with airships and urged him to learn to fly an aeroplane. He did and within months was a flight commander in 45 Squadron. After attending RAF Staff College, he served in a number of posts in the UK and the Middle East and was with Training Command when he was seconded to the New Zealand Government in 1936. His task was to help establish the RNZAF as an independent service (it had previously been part of the army command structure) and when he achieved that, he became the Kiwis' chief of air staff. When he returned to Britain at the start of the war, he commanded 7 Group, 3 Group and, from 1943 to 1945, 5 Group, which included the Dambusters. He was knighted in 1945 and acted as commander-in-chief at Transport Command, 1945–47, and at Training Command, 1947–50. He managed the RAF's role in the Berlin Airlift (June 1948 to May 1949) and, in 1950, he was appointed vice chief of the air staff. He retired in 1952 and became a director of Rolls Royce.

Ironside is a great name for a warrior and Field Marshal Lord William Ironside, chief of the imperial general staff at the outbreak of the Second World War in 1939, lived up to expectations in such style that he is said to have been John Buchan's model for Richard Hannay in the series of novels that began with *The Thirty-Nine Steps*. He had just the right pedigree: son of an Edinburgh army surgeon, Royal Military Academy, commission in the Royal Artillery, a hero with a mention in dispatches in the Boer War (in which he was a spy), fought in the Great War with 4th Canadian Army at Vimy Ridge and Passchendaele and won the DSO. At the end of that war, he was briefly commandant of the army's Small Arms School, but later in 1918 he was sent to Archangel to command the seriously-outnumbered Allied army – including Canadians, French, Italian and Americans – fighting the Bolsheviks in a grim war of attrition on permafrost terrain. The Red Army, more acclimatised to the conditions, managed to gain superiority in 1919 and William Ironside was forced to withdraw, an experience that was to have a sobering effect on him.

When, in 1920, he took command of the British troops in Persia, one of his first acts was to sack the hundred or so Russian officers and NCOs of the Cossack Division. His justification, which he had not discussed with his superiors in London, was that he wanted to save Tehran from possible Bolshevik occupation. He replaced the hapless men with Persians under the command of Reza Khan, the general who later led a British-supported coup to become first prime minister of the new regime in 1923 and then the self-proclaimed Shah in 1925. On his return to Britain, his efforts were rewarded with a knighthood and promotion to major general and appointment, in 1924, as commandant of the army's Staff College. He then had a three-year stint in India (1928–31) and two years as lieutenant of the Tower of London (1931–33) before returning to India as quartermaster general (1933–36). Serving as governor and commander-in-chief of Gibraltar when war broke out in 1939, he was quickly recalled to Britain, where he was he was promoted to Field Marshal and chief of the imperial general staff. In November of that year, when he was nearly 60, he was appointed to the Army Council and went to France in May 1940 to liaise with the British Expeditionary Force and the French. He had a lucky escape when his Calais hotel suffered a direct hit from a German bomb and he was blown out of bed. On his return to Britain, with a German invasion looking imminent, he was appointed commander-in-chief of the Home Forces. In 1941, he was made a peer and retired from active service. He died in 1959.

The architect of the RAF's finest hour was Hugh Dowding, from the small border town of Moffat. He was commander-in-chief of Fighter Command and designed what became known as the 'Dowding System', the complex, integrated defence involving radar, raid-plotting and radio control of aircraft that allowed the RAF's few to resist the might of the Luftwaffe in the pivotal Battle of Britain in 1940. Little more needs to be said about the famous Battle: not surprisingly, it has been the theme for countless books and films, including the 1969 epic *Battle of Britain,* in which the man nicknamed 'Stuffy' by his men was played by Laurence Olivier.

Air Chief Marshal Lord Dowding, as he became, was just 17 in 1899 when he went to the Royal Military Academy. He was commissioned into the Royal Garrison Artillery and served in Gibraltar, Ceylon, Hong Kong and on India's North-West Frontier. Like Glaswegian David Henderson, he too recognised the growing importance of the aeroplane and decided to go to flying school in 1929. He won his wings after less than two hours flying time. He was added to the Royal Flying Corps reserve list but returned to duty with his regiment. In early 1914 he joined the RFC full-time and at the outbreak of war he was flying with 6 Squadron. He was promoted to flight commander the following year and went on to command the Wireless Experimental Establishment, 7 Wing (Farnborough), 9 Wing (HQ) and Southern Group before becoming brigadier general in charge of Southern Training Brigade. When the RAF was established in April 1918 he was responsible for setting up the new administrative structures. The next year, he was promoted to major general and was appointed general officer commanding HQ Northern Area. He was the chief staff officer at Iraq Command, 1924–26, and then spent three years as the RAF's director of training. In 1929, with the escalation of trouble in the Middle East, he went to Palestine to lead an inquiry and report on the critical need for and form of reinforcements. After completing that mission, he was next responsible for shaping Britain's air defences and especially for supply and research. He was knighted in 1933 and was one of three senior officers at the funeral of King George V in 1936. He was appointed commander-in-chief of Fighter Command and made principal air aide-de-camp to King George VI the following year.

He was due to retire – after 30 years' service – in 1939, but due to the tense international situation, his service was extended by nine months and thus he was, almost by accident, in charge of Fighter Command at the crucial time. After his success in leading the RAF in the Battle of Britain, he was appointed head of the British Air Commission in Washington and was then asked to do a major review of the RAF. He finally retired and was made a peer in 1943, and died in 1970. There is a statue to his memory at London's St Clement Danes in the Strand. The inscription reflects his toughness in the face of political pressure from the likes of Winston Churchill: 'With remarkable foresight, he ensured the equipment of his command with monoplane fighters, the Hurricane and the Spitfire. He was among the first to appreciate the vital importance of radar and an effective command and control system for his squadrons. They were ready when war came. His wise and prudent judgement and leadership helped to ensure victory against overwhelming odds and thus prevented the loss of the Battle of Britain and probably the whole war. To him, the people of Britain and of the Free World owe largely the way of life and the liberties they enjoy today.'

When, in 1940, Marshal Pétain signed the Vichy armistice with Nazi Germany, Winston Churchill was unequivocal about how he wanted Britain to respond to the plight of occupied France. 'Now set Europe ablaze,' he declared, in approving the creation of the Special Operations Executive. War Minister Hugh Dalton had proposed this new organisation 'to coordinate, inspire, control and assist the nationals of the oppressed countries who must themselves be the direct participants.' The SOE had an inauspicious start. Its HQ was an unprepossessing London office at 64 Baker Street (not far from where Arthur Conan Doyle had quartered Sherlock Holmes), but then, in a stroke of British genius, the War Office made exactly the right appointment. Brigadier Colin Gubbins, from Mull, was a veteran of the Great War, in which he had won the Military Cross, and had served as an intelligence officer with William Ironside in Russia and in the Anglo-Irish war.

With his experience and insights into the nature of guerrilla warfare, he was the perfect choice for director of operations and training. He saw the twin needs for success as 'daring leadership and a sympathetic population' and he saw his job as providing practical information on how the two could work together: for example, how to organise a road ambush, how to cripple a railway engine and how to kill the enemy. He chose his recruits carefully – usually people with extensive experience of the area where they were to be sent to help the local resistance. Initial training was in a country house in Surrey, all the lessons were in French and participants only knew each other by their codenames. They learned coding and decoding, radio operations and repairs and other basic skills. After that, they went on a very tough commando course in the Highlands where they were taught how to use guns and explosives and schooled in the black arts of sabotage, unarmed combat, silent killing and how to survive in occupied territories. To underpin this training, Brigadier Gubbins produced a series of expert guides including *The Art of Guerrilla Warfare*, *Partisan Leader's Handbook* and *How to Use High Explosives*. Not everyone was happy about the development of the SOE. The chief of the air staff, Air Chief Marshal Charles Portal, wrote to a fellow officer: 'The dropping of men dressed in civilian clothes for the purpose of attempting to kill members of the opposing forces is not an operation with which the Royal Air Force should be associated. I think you will agree that there is a vast difference, in ethics, between the time-honoured operation of the dropping of a spy from the air and this entirely new scheme for dropping what one can only call assassins.' Despite these misgivings, Colin Gubbins sent more than 470 agents, including 39 women, into France. They are said to have had an average survival time of just three months. Many of the 200 who never returned were said to have been executed on the direct orders of Hitler. After the war Brigadier Gubbins was knighted and published *Resistance Movements in the War* (1948).

At this point, I feel almost if I'm straying into fiction... into *Boy's Own* territory with tales of extraordinary derring-do, of unlikely deeds and improbable heroes. Colin Gubbins and his SOE exploits are one thing, but then there was the polo-playing general who cocked a snook at Rommel, the Scots Guards officer who became known as the

'Phantom Major', the handsome Highlander who went into battle with his personal piper, and the dashing ex-diplomat who put the sangfroid into James Bond. As the cliché says: you couldn't make it up!

Rommel's bête noir was Jock Campbell and his particular heroics in winning the VC are detailed in the previous chapter, Scotland the brave. When the Italians entered the war, he showed he had as much guile as he had courage. In 1940, Lieutenant Colonel Campbell was artillery commander of 7th Armoured Division and when it was realised they were heavily outnumbered by the Italians, he was detailed to harass the enemy by using swift-moving hit-and-run tactics. It remains unclear whether or not it was he who devised the technique of combining tight-knit groups of armoured cars, artillery and infantry, but he was so expert in the operation that they became known as Jock Columns. During Operation Compass, the first major offensive in the Western Desert Campaign, Campbell's artillery played a crucial part in pushing across Libya and forcing the surrender of more than 100,000 men of the Italian Tenth Army. In Operation Crusader in 1941, his 7th Support Group helped foil the Afrika Corps' attempts to take the crucial airfield at Sidi Rezegh, south of Tobruk. It was a bloody battle in which he won the VC for his courage and his leadership. Although wounded, he refused to be evacuated. He died in a tragic accident when his car overturned on a newly-built road not far from Tobruk.

The Phantom Major was David Stirling, founder of Britain's most famous military outfit: the SAS. He earned his nom de guerre for the efficiency with which he was consistently able to strike at the heart of the enemy without detection. He was the son of a general, born in 1915 at Doune, the ancestral family home in Stirlingshire. He grew up to be a keen sportsman and mountaineer. Upon the outbreak of war, he joined the Scots Guards but his blood quickened when he heard about the formation of the Commandos and so he was first to volunteer. He was given command of 8 Commando (one of three battalions, each of about 250 men) and sent to Egypt, under the banner of what the generals called 'Layforce'. Just as some RAF bigwigs had been sniffy about the SOE, so the army brass was sceptical about the development of commando units. *Not very British*, was the reaction. The lack of any immediate success in Egypt gave the doubters the excuse they were looking for, and the commando battalions were disbanded.

That would have been the end of the idea but for the determination of David Stirling. Rather than return to his old unit, he signed up for parachute training. His inordinate exuberance, combined with his height and bulk led, almost inevitably, to a jumping accident that left him in hospital. Forced into physical inactivity, his mind made numerous leaps of imagination and he devised a new special unit that would operate with small groups of highly-trained men making hit-and-run attacks behind enemy lines on sensitive targets such as airfields, fuel depots and ammunition dumps. He scribbled his scheme on a scrap of paper but had difficulty in getting access to the appropriate senior officer. In frustration, he limped out of hospital on crutches and made his way unsteadily to the HQ in Cairo. He somehow evaded the sentries, clambered over the high wire fence and blagged his way into the general's office. The general in question was Neil Ritchie, destined to be commander of the Eighth Army, and he looked on the escapade with wry amusement and some admiration for the young David Stirling. He talked to his boss, General Claude Auchinleck, and the SAS was born.

Stirling led in the only way he knew, from the front, and again there was a kind of inevitability when, in 1943, he was caught by the Nazis and ended up in Colditz until the end of the war. He was awarded the Distinguished Service Order and a military OBE for his services and was eventually knighted, in 1990, shortly before he died. The SAS is based at Stirling Lines in Hereford. Appropriately, a larger-than-life statue of David Stirling – it stands nine feet tall – was unveiled near his home in 2002.

The man who paid the piper was David Stirling's cousin and another swashbuckler. In 1941, Simon Fraser, the 15th Lord Lovat and the 24th Clan Chief, formed and was the first commander of the famous Special Services Brigade. Shimi (his Gaelic name) Fraser had served in the Scots Guards since 1932 (not long after inheriting his title from his father) but he resigned in early 1939 intent on managing the family estate. At the outbreak of the war, however he immediately followed in his father's footsteps by joining up as a captain in the Lovat Scouts. Hearing tales of the newly-formed commandos, he quickly transferred to one of the all-action units in 1940 and led 4 Commando on a series of spectacular hit-and-run attacks behind enemy lines. The following year, he led a raid on the German-occupied Lofoten Islands, off the northern coast of Norway. The commandos destroyed factories, petrol dumps and no fewer than 11 ships, captured more than 200 German troops, and freed more than 300 Norwegians. They also seized encryption equipment and codebooks that proved invaluable to the cipher experts at Bletchley Park. That proved to be the pattern of events for the next three years, with the commando raids becoming ever more daring. When the Normandy invasion drew near, the need was recognised for all the commando forces to come under a single leadership. Shimi Fraser was promoted to brigadier and given charge of the new 1st Special Service Brigade (not to be confused with Stirling's SAS). He is reported to have landed on Sword Beach armed with an old Winchester rifle and his brolly, as portrayed in the 1962 film *The Longest Day*. He is also said to have defied specific orders and had his piper play the men ashore.

A week later, his war ended abruptly. He was seriously wounded when a stray shell landed among a group of senior officers. Although he eventually recovered, he was unable to return to service. He was decorated for his bravery by the British (Distinguished Service Order and Military Cross), the French (*Légion d'honneur* and *Croix de guerre*) and Russians (Order of Subarov). In a magazine article in 1945, journalist John Rennie wrote: 'It is sometimes a little difficult to determine whether Lord Lovat was designed for the Commando Service or the Service was designed for him. What is certain is that here is an amazing case of a man and an hour coming together.' After the war, Churchill asked him to be captain of the gentlemen-at-arms in the House of Lords. He declined but did accept the post of junior minister in the Foreign Office in 1945 and later became minister for economic warfare. He was part of the parliamentary delegation sent to Moscow to ease strained relations with Stalin. In his note to the Russian leader, Churchill described Lord Lovat as 'the mildest-mannered man that ever scuttled a ship or cut a throat.'

Bond creator Ian Fleming got his inspiration for his improbable hero from his close friend Fitzroy MacLean and it's easy to see why. The Hebridean was a diplomat-turned-soldier, a founder member of David Stirling's SAS, a politician and a writer. As a young man in the Diplomatic Corps, he got bored in Paris and asked to be transferred to Moscow, where, in the 1930s, he witnessed the Stalinist purges and the gory demise of Bukharin, Zinoviev, Smirnov and other revolutionaries (later the basis of his book *Eastern Approaches*). Eager to learn more about the Soviet Union and not being in the classic mould of establishment figures, he ventured far beyond permitted limits and travelled by train and often foot into remote regions, aware that his every move was being watched by Stalin's secret police, the NKVD.

When the war started, he was prevented from joining the army because of his diplomatic status. The only get-out from the Corps then was if he could somehow become an MP. That proved not to be a problem for the Old Etonian. He threw his hat into the ring at a by-election in 1941 and became the Tory MP for Lancaster (as which he served until 1959, before switching to the constituency of Bute and North Ayrshire) and, under the traditions of the day, was then able to enlist as a private in the Queen's Own Cameron Highlanders. He distinguished himself – often behind enemy lines – in North Africa, rose steadily through the ranks and had become an officer by the time the SAS was launched. He developed a brand of guerrilla tactics (similar to T.E. Lawrence in the Great War) and perfected the art of driving across the near-impossible desert terrain. In one famous escapade, he snatched the German consul from Axis-controlled Baghdad – an event that was said to have led to Hitler withdrawing his support for the Iraqi military junta. During this period, he was reporting directly to Churchill, who hand-picked him to head a mission to Belgrade because of his acquaintance with Tito, dating from the time that the Yugoslavian leader was working in the Balkan section of Communist International in Moscow. His mission was, as he said, quite simple: 'To find out who was killing the most Germans and suggest means by which we could help them to kill more.' On the face of it, an Old Etonian and a Communist leader are not natural bedfellows and his initial relationship with the partisans was uneasy, but in the end he developed strong links that were useful in the post-war years. He also received a fistful of decorations including Yugoslavia's Order of the Partisan Star and retired from the army as a major general in 1947. His wilder excesses spent, he resumed civilian life as an MP and served briefly as a junior war minister in Churchill's government between 1954 and 1957, when he was knighted. He also became the chief scout of the Commonwealth and the Empire in 1959. Later, he was a member of the Parliamentary

Assembly of the Council of Europe and Western European Union for two years, before retiring from the Commons in 1974. He sharpened his writing skills and, as well as his autobiography, he published novels, works on Scottish history, a biography of Tito, books about Russia, and *Take Nine Spies* – a collection of true stories about Mata Hari, Kim Philby, Gordon Lonsdale, Guy Burgess, Donald MacLean (no relation) and others. His appointment as lord chamberlain (1971–84), the senior official of the Royal Household, took him to the very heart of the establishment. In that role, he organised Princess Anne's wedding in 1973, the Queen's Silver Jubilee celebrations in 1977, Lord Mountbatten's funeral in 1979 and Prince Charles' wedding to Princess Diana in 1983. When he retired, he became a full-time writer. He was made a Knight of the Thistle in 1994 and died two years later.

After the war, Scots continued to play important roles in the armed forces. Major General Robert Arbuthnott, from Edinburgh, became chief of the British Military Mission with the Egyptian Army in 1946. A decorated veteran of both wars (CB, CBE, DSO, MC and Commander of the American Legion of Merit), he served in Palestine (1939–42) before commanding 11th Infantry Brigade (1942–44) and then 78th Infantry Division (1944–46) in Italy. He retired in 1952 and was appointed colonel of the Black Watch (1960–64).

Air Marshal Sir Andrew Humphrey, from Edinburgh, was appointed Chief of the Defence Staff in 1976 but died, at the age of 56, after only three months in office. He was 17 when he joined the RAF College, Cranwell, and had won the DFC before he was 21. His citation for the medal read: 'This officer has performed splendid work as a night-fighter pilot. One night in May 1941 he pursued an enemy bomber at a height of 20,000 feet and finally shot it down in the vicinity of an aerodrome off the Dutch coast. Shortly afterwards, he observed another enemy aircraft taking off from the aerodrome and diving down to 50 feet, he destroyed it. Although heavily attacked by the ground defences, he succeeded in flying clear and later attacked another enemy fighter. He was compelled to break off this engagement after one attack as his ammunition was expended. Two nights previously, he destroyed an enemy bomber from close range.' He joined 175 Squadron in early 1942 to fly Hurricanes and was promoted to flight commander with 6 Squadron. By the end of his operational flying he had scored seven confirmed enemy planes destroyed with two probable. He spent the rest of the war in staff posts in the Middle East and India. Returning to Britain in 1946, he served in photo-reconnaissance with Coastal Command and took part in an extensive aerial survey of Africa before becoming an instructor at the RAF Flying College. In 1953, he piloted *Aries IV*, a Canberra B2 from Cape Town to London in a record 13 hours 16 minutes and 25 seconds. He entered the record books again the following year when he made the first RAF jet flight to the North Pole, again in *Aries IV*. While deputy director of operational requirements, he introduced the Lightning, the RAF's first supersonic interceptor, and was awarded the CB, an exceptional honour for a group captain. After a spell in command of RAF Akrotiri in Cyprus, he moved to the Air Ministry and held a number of senior posts including director of defence plans (air). Posted to Aden as AOC, Air Forces Middle East, he oversaw the RAF withdrawal from the region in 1968, after which he returned to Britain and joined the Air Council as air member for personnel. He returned to operational command in 1971, when he was appointed commander-in-chief of Strike Command. He became chief of the air staff (and air aide-de-camp to the Queen) in 1974. He introduced the graduate-entry scheme to the RAF. In 1978, the Andrew Humphrey School (for the children of personnel at RAF Gütersloh) was opened in the village of Blankenhagen, Germany. He died in 1977.

Neil Cameron of Balhousie (born Perth, 1920–85) was a marshal of the Royal Air Force, chief of the air staff, 1976–7, and chief of the defence staff, 1977–79. His was an extraordinary career that began when he went to work as a bank clerk in Newburgh, Fife, in 1937. He joined the RAF in 1939 and was a Hurricane sergeant pilot in 1 Squadron before moving to 17 Squadron during the final stages of the Battle of Britain. After being commissioned, he flew in northern Russia in 1941 and later flew with the Desert Air Force, where he rose to squadron leader of 258 Squadron, and in Burma. He won the Distinguished Flying Cross and the Distinguished Service Order for his outstanding leadership. Returning to civilian life, he was principal of King's College, London and was given a peerage in 1983.

Charles Guthrie of Craigiebank was chief of the defence staff, 1997–2001. He was born in Dundee in 1938. After Sandhurst, he was commissioned into the Welsh Guards in 1959. He served at home and in Libya, Germany and Aden. In 1966, he joined the SAS (of which he is now Commandant) and served in the Middle East, Malaysia and East Africa. He rejoined the Welsh Guards in 1970, when he commanded an armoured infantry company in Germany. He served in the Ministry of Defence and was brigade major of the Household Division from 1975 until 1977, when he commanded the regiment in Berlin and Northern Ireland. In 1981, he commanded 4th Armoured Brigade in West Germany and was then chief of staff at HQ 1st British Corps in Bielefeld. He was general officer commanding 2nd Infantry Division and North East District in 1985 and the following year became colonel commandant of the Intelligence Corps. He was also commander of 1st British Corps, Northern Army Group, and the British Army of the Rhine before becoming the chief of the general staff. He is colonel of the Life Guards, Gold Stick to the Queen and colonel commandant of the SAS.

Guthrie was followed as chief of the defence staff in 2001 by Admiral Lord Boyce, a submariner and antisubmarine warfare specialist, who joined the Royal Navy in 1961. During his service, he commanded two conventional submarines, a nuclear attack submarine and the Submarine Training Squadron. He also commanded the frigate HMS *Brilliant*, was director of the naval staff and had the role of senior naval officer for the Middle East. He was promoted to the Flag List in 1991 and was subsequently flag officer sea training, flag officer surface flotilla; commander-in-chief naval home command and second sea lord, and commander-in-chief fleet. He was knighted and held a number of senior NATO posts before his appointment as first sea lord in 1998. He retired as chief of defence staff in May 2003, when he was given a peerage and appointed lord warden and admiral of the Cinque Ports and constable of Dover Castle in 2004. He is colonel commandant of the Special Boat Service. Like Lord Boyce, Admiral Sir Jock Slater also served as first sea lord and chief of the naval staff, until his retirement in 1998. He joined the Royal Navy in 1956, when he was 18. Among his many appointments, he was equerry to the Queen, 1968–71. He is chairman of the executive committee of the RNLI, vice chairman of the British Forces Foundation, chairman of the White Ensign Association and chairman of Trustees and of the Remuneration Committee of the Imperial War Museum. He is also president of the American Air Museum in Britain and a member of the Churchill Museum Appeal Committee.

Air Chief Marshal Sir Jock Stirrup was appointed chief of defence staff in 2006 and served until his retirement in 2010. He was commissioned at RAF Cranwell in 1970 and while serving with the Sultan of Oman's Air Force in the early 1970s he flew Strikemasters (light bombers) in the Dhofar War. He was appointed air officer commanding 1 Group in 1997, assistant chief of the air staff in 1998 and deputy commander-in-chief, Strike Command in 2000. From September 2001 to January 2002, he was UK National Contingent commander for operations against the Taliban in Afghanistan, and served as chief of the air staff, 2003–06.

5

THE POWER ...

 'All politicians have vanity. Some wear it more gently than others.'
— *Lord Steel, first presiding officer of the Scottish Parliament*

Politicians don't rate too highly with today's electorate and it has to be said that a fair few Scots must take some responsibility for that. But in days gone by there were many who made the transition to statesman, admired and revered for the leadership they offered their country. In this area, it's beyond question that Scotland has provided more than its fair share of leaders of the three main UK parties and representatives serving in governments across what was once the British Empire.

The Scottish contribution to global politics and matters of state has been strong in both quality and quantity. Few corners of the globe have escaped our political influence. Such was the tenacity of those who joined the exodus to the colonies that four ended up as prime minister in New Zealand, two in Australia and two in Canada, and many more served in senior offices. In America, where they have always done things differently, Scots found their way into dozens of key political roles in the founding days of the new republic (see chapter 7: Scotland and the Stars and Stripes). We've also provided senior administrators in India, Africa and even in Russia (see chapter 8: Reaching for the Tsars), Japan and China.

To date, 52 men and a single woman (Margaret Thatcher) have held the post of British prime minister (or first lord of the treasury as it was before 1905). Ten – that's just less than 20 per cent – have been Scots and the biggest name of the twentieth century – Winston Churchill – sharpened his political teeth as MP for Dundee; William Gladstone, the great 19th-century Liberal prime minister took his name from the family seat of Gladstone in Lanarkshire, although he was brought up in Liverpool; and Harold Macmillan, born in London, was the grandson of the famous Scottish publisher, Daniel Macmillan.

All have, of course, been the subject of learned and lengthy tomes down the years so I will pass along swiftly.

The first Scot – and the first Tory – to become Prime Minister was John Stuart, Earl of Bute, in 1762. He replaced the Duke of Devonshire and, like him, he lasted barely a year. His main qualification for the job was that he had been a friend of Frederick, Prince of Wales and tutor to his son, the young Prince George, who on his accession to the throne in 1760 had appointed him Secretary of State. It didn't help matters that the English were still smarting from the 1745 Jacobite uprising and were seriously suspicious and distrustful of the Scots. Nor were they impressed that the tall and handsome aristocrat – cruelly nicknamed Jack Boot – was an amateur actor whose favourite role was Lothario! On the plus side, it was Bute who negotiated the end of the Seven Years War with France, but even that still didn't endear him to the English, who found the 1763 Treaty of Paris a bitter pill to swallow. The final straw came when Bute introduced a cider tax later in the same year. It caused widespread outrage, led to various verbal and physical threats and forced him to resign after only 11 months in office. In that short period, however, he had ended the predominance of the Whigs. Despite the name coming from the Erse for bandit, he made the Tory Party into a political force to be reckoned with. It proudly maintained the name until more sensitive souls founded the Conservative Party in the mid 18th century.

It was almost 90 years before the second Scot made it to the top of the political pile. This time it was the belted Earl of Aberdeen, another Tory, who lasted a full three years. He, too, was rich in patronage. Orphaned when he was just 11, he was brought up under the guidance of two very powerful guardians: Viscount Dundas and William Pitt, the Younger. He inherited his title from his grandfather in 1801, when he was 17. He became Prime Minister in 1852 at the head of a coalition government positively packed with political talent. Lord Russell was foreign secretary, the home secretary was Lord Palmerston and William Gladstone was his chancellor of the exchequer. He'd had some personal experience of government, serving briefly as chancellor of the Duchy of Lancaster in the Duke of Wellington's cabinet. He was then secretary for war and the colonies and had two periods as Pitt's foreign secretary. During the second term, he had settled the long-running boundary dispute between America and Canada. As prime minister, he showed his ability to reform and passed important legislation on taxation, the civil service and legal issues. Within the year, however, he had taken Britain into the Crimean War with Russia, and that was to be his undoing. He was accused of conducting the war badly and attempts were made to set up an official enquiry. He resigned in 1855. In what I am reluctant to call a footnote to his career, he is said to have bought the foot of Hercules, which had been in the Parthenon in Athens for thousands of years! He is reported to have had it shipped to his home (images of a certain Lord Elgin and his marbles come to mind...) but it has since disappeared.

It was early in the twentieth century that we saw the next Scot as prime minister. The nephew of Lord Salisbury (whom he succeeded in office), East Lothian-born Arthur

Balfour had a distinguished political career both before his premiership in 1902 and, more unusually, after he left the post three years later. Having inherited more than a million pounds when he was 21, he was one of the wealthiest men in the country when he was elected Conservative MP for Hertford in 1874. With his uncle as mentor, he became Disraeli's foreign secretary after only four years in the Commons. However, it was when Lord Salisbury (Robert Cecil) became prime minister in 1885 that he began to fully enjoy the fruits of patronage. In the first Salisbury cabinet (1985–86), he was secretary for Scotland. In the second (1986–92), he was controversially given one of the toughest jobs, secretary for Ireland, and earned the nickname 'Bloody Balfour' because of the tough way he restored law and order to the province. In Salisbury's third term (1895–1902) he was first lord of the treasury and leader of the Commons. In a sarcastic reference to the patronage, the press coined the phrase: 'Bob's Your Uncle'!

When his Uncle Bob retired, Balfour emerged as prime minister but soon found the job more difficult than he ever imagined. His cabinet split over the Free Trade issue, his relations with King Edward VII were poor and defeats in the Commons were followed by defeats at by-elections. He resigned in 1905 but that was not the end of his woes. In the subsequent general election, the Liberals won a landslide victory and he lost his seat. He returned to Parliament swiftly in a by-election and continued to lead the Tories until 1911. In the wartime coalition of 1914, he became first lord of the Admiralty and then, as foreign secretary, produced perhaps his most significant policy: the Balfour Declaration was a recognition of the right to a Jewish state in Palestine and paved the way for the later creation of Israel. He remained in Baldwin's government until it fell in 1929. He died the following year.

When he succeeded Balfour in 1905, Glaswegian Sir Henry Campbell-Bannerman was the first man to be given official use of the title prime minister. Previously, the formal office was that of first lord of the Treasury. One of the great Liberal statesmen, he was only months shy of his seventieth birthday when he took office but Asquith later said of him: 'He was not ashamed, even on the verge of old age, to see visions and to dream dreams. He met both good and evil fortune with the same unclouded brow, the same unruffled temper, the same unshakeable confidence in the justice and righteousness of his cause.' His vision led to the introduction of the old-age pension and what we now call sick pay, entente with Russia and autonomy for Transvaal and the Orange Free State. He earned a reputation for being strong and efficient and was unusually successful in embracing the various wings of his party, which had split over the Boer War. In the 1906 general election, he secured a truly landslide victory, winning more than 200 seats from the Conservatives.

The irony is that when he had been elected leader of the Liberal party in 1898, he had been seen as little more than 'a safe pair of hands.' Other possibilities had included Herbert Asquith, David Lloyd George and Winston Churchill, who were all to become ministers in his cabinet. For the first 35 years of his life, he was plain Henry Campbell (son of the Glasgow Lord Provost Sir James Campbell) and only added the Bannerman in 1871 to comply with the will of his maternal uncle, who had no other male heir and wanted to perpetuate the name. In doing so, he inherited a 150-acre estate in Kent. He clearly found life there to be of inestimable comfort when he used it as his country home after becoming Prime Minster. In shades of the current Prince of Wales, he developed the mild eccentricity of talking to his trees. 'He would bow to his favourite specimen and wish them Good Morning,' says one contemporary report.

After graduating from Glasgow University and Trinity College, Cambridge, he worked in the family drapery business before being elected MP for Stirling Burghs in 1868 (and he held the seat until his death in 1908). His first government job came after just three years, when he was appointed financial secretary to the War Office in 1871. It took somewhat longer to get into the cabinet. That came in 1884, when Gladstone (in his second cabinet) made him chief secretary for Ireland and then war secretary in 1886. He held that job through the rest of Gladstone's term and for a year under the Earl of Rosebery, until the Liberals lost to Salisbury's Tories in 1895. One of his last and possibly most signal victories in that post was to persuade Prince George, the cousin of no less a personage than Queen Victoria, to step down from his role of commander-in-chief of the British Army. He had held the post for nearly 40 years and had been the subject of criticism for refusing to accept reforms proposed by a Royal Commission. Clearly the Queen was not unamused because she promptly conferred a knighthood on her secretary of state. In addition to his other achievements, he was also the first prime minister to become the 'Father of the House' (its longest-serving member) in 1907. Early the next year, he became seriously ill, resigned from office on April 3 and died on April 22. In his tribute, Lloyd George said: 'He was not merely admired and respected; he was absolutely loved by us all. The masses of the people of the country, especially the more unfortunate of them, have lost the best friend they have ever had in the high place of the land. He was a truly great man. A great head and a great heart. He was absolutely the bravest man I ever met in politics.'

The shortest-serving prime minister of the twentieth century was Andrew Bonar Law, a former pupil of Glasgow High School and, for six years, Conservative MP for Glasgow Blackfriars. His health was already deteriorating when he took office in October 1922 and he resigned after just 209 days, when he was diagnosed with throat cancer. He died six months later. He is often referred to as 'the unknown Prime Minister' (the title of his biography written by historian Robert, later Lord, Blake in 1955). He was born in Canada, the son of a Scottish clergyman, but his mother died in childbirth and when he was 12 he was sent to Glasgow to live with her family of wealthy merchant bankers. While working in the bank, he also attended night classes at Glasgow University and there developed his interest in politics. However, when he finally left the bank it was to become a steel merchant and he had made his fortune by the time he was 27. This plus an inheritance gave him the independence he wanted to pursue a political career, and he was elected to the Glasgow Blackfriars seat in 1900. He quickly established himself as a man of integrity and fearlessness and within a couple of years he was on the ministerial ladder with a job at the Board of Trade. Like so many of his party colleagues, he was swept out of office in 1906 but returned at an early by-election as the MP for Dulwich. When Balfour resigned as Tory leader in 1911, the party appeared deadlocked in the choice between Austen Chamberlain and Walter Long, so Bonar Law emerged and was elected as a compromise candidate. One of his closest associates at the time was Max Aitken (later Lord Beaverbrook). Following the outbreak of war, he joined the coalition as colonial secretary and when Asquith resigned as prime minister, King George V asked him to form a new government. Surprisingly, he declined in favour of the Liberal Lloyd George and then took on the roles of chancellor of the exchequer and leader of the Commons. Despite his obvious rapport with the Welsh Wizard, however, it was Bonar Law's speech at the Carlton Club that dissuaded many of his colleagues from deserting the Tories in favour of the new party proposed by Lloyd George. It was a rousing, emotional address that is said to have saved the Conservative party from crumbling. This time Bonar Law did step forward and went into the ensuing general election on what was described as the Tranquillity Manifesto.

In it, he said he had identified the crying need of the nation: 'A need which in my judgement far exceeds any other, is that we should have tranquillity and stability both at home and abroad so that free scope should be given to the initiative and enterprise of our citizens, for it is in that way far more than by any action of the Government that we can hope to recover from the economic and social results of the war.'

The voters reacted by giving the Conservatives a comfortable majority. Within weeks, his colleagues were shocked when he was diagnosed with throat cancer which left him unable to speak in Parliament. After just 211 days as Prime Minister, he died on 30 October 1923.

Whatever else he achieved, Scotsman James Ramsay MacDonald, the illegitimate son of a farmhand and a housemaid, certainly broke the political mould when he became Britain's first Labour prime minister in 1924. He overcame snobbery, the outrage of a wholly-hostile press (including early examples of spiteful dirty-tricks campaigning) and even the open opposition of the Metropolitan Police Commissioner. His collected opponents won the early skirmishes of social warfare and his minority government lasted only nine months before being unceremoniously turfed out by an ungrateful electorate. But he rose above it all, returned in 1929 for a second and then a third term and changed the face of politics forever. He ensured that high office was no longer the preserve of the moneyed classes, rightfully acknowledged the role of women in government by appointing Britain's first female cabinet minister, and persuaded the more powerful Liberal party to enter an electoral pact. Few could have expected so much from a man with limited formal education. He went to the Free Church of Scotland infants' school in Lossiemouth and then a nearby parish school. It says much for his intelligence that when he was 15 the headmaster took him on as a pupil-teacher and he taught for four years. He then somehow managed to find his way to Bristol, where he became an assistant to a local clergyman and, to ease his loneliness in being so far from home, he joined a radical group that months later became the Social Democratic Federation.

No one seems to know why, but he returned to Lossiemouth before the year was up. However, he had clearly become a restless soul and he soon headed off to find his fortune in London. There, his political interests stood him in good stead and he got a job as general factotum to a Liberal parliamentary candidate (and later MP). As well as giving him an adequate living wage that employment also allowed him to sharpen his political teeth and learn about serious electioneering. The good man's ideology clearly didn't rub off on him and he continued to attend SDF meetings, although initially more for social reasons than anything else. Any ideas he might have had about a full-time career in politics were sharply brought into focus in November 1887. The events of what was the first day to become known as Bloody Sunday (during which mounted police charged into demonstrators in Trafalgar Square) turned him into a committed and determined socialist. He was a callow 21-year-old and so angered by what he witnessed that day that he produced a condemnatory pamphlet that was published by the *Pall Mall Gazette* (the London evening paper then in a short-lived Liberal phase). He was particularly shocked by the attitude of the Metropolitan Police Commissioner Sir Charles Warren. In a letter asking the Home Secretary's permission to appoint 20,000 special constables to police the demonstration, the Commissioner was outrageously condemning of the working-class demonstrators. He wrote: 'We have in the last month been in greater danger from the disorganised attacks on property by the rough and criminal elements than we have been in London for many years past. The language used by speakers at the various meetings has been more frank and open in recommending the poorer classes to help themselves from the wealth of the affluent.' Imagine the reaction if today's commissioner produced such comments! If Ramsay MacDonald had needed any further stiffening of his socialist sinews, it came in a thundering and shocking leader in *The Times* (14 November 1887) on behalf of the ruling classes: 'It was no enthusiasm for free speech, no serious conviction of any kind, and no honest purpose that animated these howling toughs. It was simple love of disorder, hope of plunder and it may be hoped that the magistrates will not fail to pass exemplary sentences upon those now in custody who have laboured to the best of their ability to convert an English Sunday into a carnival of blood.'

Luckily there were still a few liberal newspapers and Ramsay MacDonald again earned a living wage as a journalist while he became more active in politics. He was one of the first to join the new Independent Labour party when it was launched in 1893 (by fellow Scot James Keir Hardie) and made his first – unsuccessful – attempt to get into Parliament in 1895. Undaunted, he patiently rose through party ranks and got his reward when he finally became the MP for Leicester in 1906. He developed a reputation as a deep thinker and in 1911 was elected chairman of the Parliamentary Labour party. Not all his colleagues were supportive and many criticised him for being too moderate, the ultimate insult to a red-blooded socialist. At the outbreak of the Great War, he was quoted as saying: 'We hear war called murder. It is not. It is suicide.' The press joined the chorus of his critics and he was ruthlessly attacked in almost every newspaper with his anti-war stance being described as 'treason' and 'cowardice.' As it appeared that the majority of Labour MPs did not share his views, he stepped down as leader and then lost his seat in the 1918 'khaki election' which saw Lloyd George's coalition win a hefty majority.

He did not return to the Commons until 1922, when he won the Welsh seat of Aberavon and Labour gained 85 seats to replace the Liberals as the main opposition to Stanley Baldwin's Tories. Buoyed with this success, the party re-united and Ramsay MacDonald emerged once more as leader. Less than a year later, the Tories lost 86 seats and, with the support of the Liberals (led by Asquith), Labour formed its historic first government. James Ramsay MacDonald was the first Labour prime minister and, for good measure, he also filled the role of foreign secretary. The arithmetic of the composition of the House of Commons was of little help, however. He was dependent on the goodwill of the Liberals and struggled to achieve and then maintain a semblance of authority. It was not to be, and the electorate were asked to vote for the third time in less than two years. On 25 October 1924 – just four days before the election – the *Daily Mail* carried details of the notorious Zinoviev Letter. Purporting to be from the president of Communist International to a leading British Communist, the letter, said the *Daily Mail*, was a message urging the intensification of Communist agitation in Britain and especially within the armed forces. It was later recognised as a dirty-tricks operation but it had the short-term effect of alarming the great British public. Despite his core vote remaining stable, the vagaries of the first-past-the-post system meant Ramsay MacDonald and his government were swept aside and the Tories regained a massive overall majority of more than 200. The see-saw of public opinion shifted in his favour at the 1929 election. His share of the vote went up by just 3.8 per cent but that brought him 136 extra seats and a return to power, with the cooperation of the much-diminished Liberal party. It was then that he was able to appoint Margaret Bondfield, MP for Northampton, as minister for labour, the first woman in cabinet.

Two years later, in the midst of the Great Depression and with his party split over how to tackle the crisis, he formed an all-party National Government. The Tories agreed to take part but suggested a mandate was needed for such a development and yet another general election was called in 1931. The volatile electorate once more swung behind the Tories. They took 55 per cent of the vote and won a massive majority but as the mandate had been sought for a *National* Government, they honourably confirmed Ramsay MacDonald as prime minister. The Labour party, however, was far from sanguine and he was expelled and replaced as party leader (by yet another Scot, Arthur Henderson). He soldiered on as prime minister for a further four years before resigning and, yet again, losing his seat at the 1935 general election. He did win a subsequent by-election but the stress clearly affected his health and he died at the age of 61 on board a transatlantic holiday liner. His son Malcolm was also a successful politician and diplomat, serving twice as a UK member of parliament (1929–35 and 1936–45) and holding a series of senior diplomatic roles, including high commissioner to Canada (1941–46).

The next Scot to make it to 10 Downing Street was from the opposite end of the social spectrum and, ironically, had to endure almost as much inverted snobbery as Ramsay MacDonald had suffered the straightforward variety. He was the belted 14th Earl of Home, Sir Alec Douglas-Home (pronounced 'Hume'), and he succeeded Harold Macmillan in 1963 – but not without considerable controversy and for just a year. He was the first peer to become prime minister since Salisbury (1902), the first to renounce his peerage, first to have been born in the twentieth century and the only premier to have played first-class cricket (Oxford University, Middlesex and the MCC). In the Swinging Sixties, all that made him something of an anachronism and the cartoonists and satirists had a field day. That he not only survived but rose above it all had much to do with the very background that was mocked: Eton (where his contemporaries included George Orwell and Cyril Connolly) and Christ Church, Oxford. Connolly described him as 'the kind of graceful, tolerant, sleepy boy who is showered with all the laurels, who is liked by the masters and admired by the boys without any apparent exertion on his part. In the eighteenth century, he would have become prime minister before he was 30: as it was, he appeared honourably ineligible for the struggle of life.' His cricketing prowess also proved useful: when an egg was thrown at him during a rowdy public meeting, he was able to make a one-handed catch without breaking the shell!

He was elected Conservative MP for Lanark in 1931 but supported Ramsay MacDonald's National Government. He was parliamentary private secretary to Neville Chamberlain in 1935, was with him at the 1938 meeting with Hitler in Munich and stood alongside him during the infamous 'Peace in our Time' speech on his return to Britain. Any further frontline involvement in politics or the war effort was seriously curtailed when he contracted spinal TB and had to have a major operation that left him in a full plaster cast for two years. He returned to serve briefly in Churchill's caretaker post-war government and then lost his seat in the 1945 Labour landslide. He won it back in 1950 but had to leave the Commons just a year later when he succeeded his father to become the 14th Earl of Home. He was able, however, to serve as the junior minister in the Scotland Office. In 1955, he was promoted to the cabinet and was secretary of state for Commonwealth relations throughout the Suez crisis. He was later also made lord president of the council and leader of the House of Lords. He effectively traded in all three posts for the plum job as foreign secretary in 1960… and had to suffer the indignity of watching Macmillan endure (successfully) a censure vote for having made the appointment which, critics claimed, denied the Commons the right to hold him directly responsible to Members.

The arguments started all over again three years later, when Macmillan resigned suddenly because of prostate trouble. The Tories had no formal procedure for electing a new leader but courtesy of men in grey suits and a bizarre kind of beauty parade at the annual conference, the frail-looking patrician figure of Lord Home emerged triumphant, having seen off the challenge of the bell-ringing, bicycle-riding Quintin Hogg and the unofficial deputy prime minister and nearly-man, Rab Butler. Coincidentally, the new Peerage Act of 1963 (instigated by Viscount Stansgate's desire to become plain Mr Anthony Wedgwood Benn and later even plainer Tony Benn) allowed him to renounce the peerage and he was able to secure political respectability via a by-election and become the MP for Kinross and West Perthshire. The party was still reeling from the shock waves of the Profumo Affair and with little time to establish himself, the now plain Sir Alec Douglas-Home inevitably lost the 1964 election but by the slimmest of margins: Harold Wilson – 'the 14th Mr Wilson' as the wags put it – was left with a wafer-thin majority of four! Sir Alec remained as leader of the Opposition for ten months before handing over to Edward Heath. When Heath won the 1970 election, he promptly brought Home back into government as foreign secretary and he served for four years before retiring at the age of 71. He became Lord Home again in 1974, after being given a life peerage.

Despite the lacerating commentaries of most political journalists, it's still too early for reasoned judgements of the prime-ministerial performances of Edinburgh-born Tony Blair and Glaswegian Gordon Brown, the two most recent Labour politicians to hold the highest office. The Labour party owes much to its Scottish progenitors, and continues to be dominated in the early part of the 21st century by politicians who cut their democratic teeth north of the border. While the jury may be still out on the quality of his leadership (especially over the war in Iraq and the British Army's role in Afghanistan), there is no doubt that Anthony Charles Lynton Blair will have a substantial entry in the history books. He succeeded to the leadership of the Labour party following the untimely death – at just 56 – of fellow Scot, John Smith, in the middle of the 1994 Euro elections. Smith, a somewhat cautious lawyer (born in Argyll), had begun the reform of the party by winning the one-man-one-vote argument with the trade unions, but it was Tony Blair who finished the task of modernising the organisation and transformed its election-winning prospects. In 1997, after more than 18 years of Conservative rule and under the banner of *New* Labour, Blair stormed into No 10 Downing Street with a massive majority that left the Tories without a single MP from a Scottish constituency. With him came a truly astonishing line-up of other Scots: Gordon Brown, of course, as chancellor, Robin Cook as foreign secretary, Helen Liddell as Scottish secretary, Lord Irvine as lord chancellor, Donald Dewar and George Robertson all in the cabinet, and Lord MacDonald, Lord Falconer, Dr John Reid, Alistair Darling and Brian Wilson coming in as ministers of state.

Of that group, Donald Dewar, a junior minister in the Wilson government of the 1960s, chief whip and Scottish secretary under Tony Blair, became the very first first minister in the new Scottish Parliament in 1999, and served until his early death in 2001. Lord Irvine retired and was replaced by Lord Falconer. After serving as defence secretary, George Robertson was given a peerage and went to Brussels as secretary general of NATO, a post he filled with distinction and to universal acclaim. Alistair Darling was promoted into the cabinet as secretary of state for transport and, in 2006, to the department of trade and industry (becoming Gordon Brown's chancellor of the exchequer in 2007). Helen Liddell was also given a peerage and moved on to be high commissioner to Australia. Brian Wilson, formerly editor of the *Free Highland Press*, left parliament.

When the late Robin Cook (who had been demoted from foreign secretary to leader of the Commons) left the cabinet in 2003, after refusing to toe the Blair line on the Iraq war, he was replaced by not one but two fellow Scots: John Reid and Ian McCartney. John Reid joined the cabinet as Scottish secretary in 1999, became the first Catholic to be Northern Ireland secretary in 2001, took over leadership of the Commons, moved swiftly on to become secretary of state for health and then defence secretary and, in 2006, home secretary. As he had also spent a short time as the Labour parliamentary chairman (in 2002), that meant the tough-talking Glaswegian had held seven Cabinet posts in just six years. He made a surprise exit from front-line politics in 2007 at the same time Tony Blair stepped down as prime minister. Ian McCartney was appointed chair of the parliamentary party and a minister without portfolio but became the minister for the department of trade and industry in the 2006 re-shuffle. Dr Reid's defence job went to another Scot, Des Browne; Douglas Alexander got the senior transport portfolio and Alistair Darling stepped up to the department of trade and industry, combining responsibility as secretary of state for Scotland.

Other than recording that he was prime minister from 1997 to 2007, there is little that needs to be said of Tony Blair (born Edinburgh, 1953, and educated at Fettes College). After creating New Labour, he is the most written-about politician of his generation and has garnered praise and generated animosity in almost equal proportions. After a ten-year wait (during which he is said to have had an understanding with Tony Blair about the accession), Gordon Brown finally emerged as prime minister in July 2007. He had been, said many of the pundits, the UK's most successful chancellor of the exchequer. In his first cabinet, there were four Scots: himself, Alistair Darling (chancellor), Des Browne (secretary of state for defence and Scottish secretary) and Douglas Alexander (secretary of state for international development). He got off to a flying start, confounded his critics, won excellent ratings in the opinion polls and brought into his government of all the talents key figures from the other parties, industry and the armed forces. But alas, his honeymoon was not to last long, and within months he was perhaps the most vilified politician of modern times and his poll ratings slumped to an all-time low. When he finally went to the country in 2010, he succumbed to what became the Conservative-Liberal Democrat coalition.

As well filling the No 10 spot on ten occasions, Scots have also played an important role in the historical development of the main political parties, most notably of course in the creation of the Labour party. It was the cloth-capped James Keir Hardie who formed the Scottish Labour party in 1888 and the Independent Labour party in 1893 (which led to the formal founding of the Labour party in 1900). He was the first to be elected MP for West Ham in 1892 and was leader of the party in parliament in 1908. He was born in 1856 in a Lanarkshire village, the illegitimate son of Mary Keir who was in service as a maid. When she later married an unemployed carpenter, David Hardie, they moved to Glasgow. Because of the family's straitened circumstances, James didn't go to school but – at the age of eight – became a messenger boy, working more than 12 hours a day for 3s. 6d. a week. Two years later, he was sacked and denied his last week's wages for being late. His far-from-kindly employer refused to be swayed by the reason: he had been up all night tending to his dying younger brother. With work almost impossible to find in the city, the family moved back to the Lanarkshire coalfields and, still not quite 11, James became a miner and again faced 12-hour days. Unable to read or write, he found time to learn from his mother despite long hours at the coalface, although he was 17 before he could finally write.

Moved by the social injustice of the day, he helped form a trade union at the colliery, led the first strike in 1880 and was immediately sacked. Astonishingly, given his limited educational background, he got a job as a journalist on an Ayrshire local paper in 1881. Five years later, he was secretary of the Ayrshire Miners' Union and was quickly promoted to the Scottish Miners' Federation. There, he combined his unionism and journalism and published *The Miner* to get across the union's message. At that stage, he was a Liberal supporter but he was disillusioned by the performance of Gladstone's government and decided that the working classes ought to have their own party. His first attempt to get elected as an MP in 1888 was a dismal failure. He finished bottom of the poll. He then concentrated on union matters nationally and internationally and travelled extensively throughout Europe.

When he was elected to parliament at the 1892 general election, he changed the face of British politics forever. He shocked the Westminster toffs – who still wore top hats and tails – by turning up in his tweed suit and flat cap. More importantly, he campaigned for higher tax rates for the wealthy to provide old-age pensions and free education for the working classes, women's suffrage and reform of parliament, including the abolition of the House of Lords! He continued to rattle cages and in 1894, he caused further apoplexy in the Commons when he tried to use a motion congratulating the King on the birth of an heir to send a message of condolence to the families of the 251 miners who died in a Welsh colliery disaster. When he was unbelievably ruled out of order, he questioned the privilege of the monarchy. As colleague J.R. Clynes later wrote: 'The House rose at him like a pack of wild dogs. His voice was drowned in a din of insults and the drumming of feet on the floor. But he stood there, white-faced, blazing-eyed, his lips moving, though the words were swept away.' It was clear the establishment was deeply worried and the press barons were equally savage. Keir Hardie was unconcerned. He was reported as saying: 'The life of one Welsh miner is of greater commercial and moral value to the British nation than the whole Royal crowd put together.' The next year, he lost his seat but that just made him the more determined and he spent the next few years working on the party organisation. As well as effectively training members in how to arrange and conduct meetings and campaign, he made the connection between socialism and Christianity. The result was the growth of socialist church groups.

One of the party's stalwarts was Emmeline Pankhurst and Hardie spoke at one of her open-air meetings in Manchester, despite the fact that it had been declared illegal by the city council. More than 50,000 turned out to listen to him but he was arrested and carted off to jail. The public outrage was such that the home secretary had to intervene and used his powers to have him freed. Hardie was elected again in 1900 but, with only one other Labour colleague, he was forced to start thinking about cooperative politics and he somehow persuaded the Liberals into a pact not to oppose Labour candidates in 30 seats. The outcome was that while the Liberals were returned to government in 1906, the new Labour party secured 29 seats. Keir Hardie was elected leader but soon found he didn't have the stomach for internal squabbles and fighting among party colleagues. He resigned in 1908.

He continued to be a serious thorn in the side of the establishment and something of a bête noire for the press. He made speeches calling for India's independence and for equal rights in South Africa and his pacifism also caused him problems at the outbreak of the war in 1914. In a speech calling for a general strike in public protest, he said: 'You have never been consulted about this war. The workers of all countries must strain every nerve to prevent their governments from committing them to war. Hold vast demonstrations against war, in London and in every industrial centre. There is no time to lose. Down with the rule of brute force! Down with war! Up with the peaceful rule of the people!' His views were not shared by many of his party colleagues, however, and he was denounced by some as a traitor. This all took a serious toll on his health, and he died in 1915. One tribute – clearly not from the establishment side – described him as the greatest human being of the time and added: 'when the dust raised by opposition to the pioneer has settled down, this will be known by all.'

Of the other founding fathers of the Labour party, none could have been so dramatically different in background to Keir Hardie than Robert Cunninghame Graham. He was an estate-owning great-grandson of an earl and revelled in the nickname of 'The Gaucho Laird' because of his time as a rancher in Argentina. He was elected as the Liberal MP for North West Lanarkshire in 1886 but, like Keir Hardie, he didn't comfortably fit the Westminster scene. He infuriated colleagues when he described Parliament as the 'National Gasworks', upset peers and was suspended for a 'disrespectful reference' to the House of Lords, and he was the first MP suspended for swearing during a Commons debate. The offending curse was 'damn'! When he joined a demonstration in Trafalgar Square – on Bloody Sunday, 1887 – in protest at the Tory Prime Minister's handling of demands for Irish Home Rule, he was first badly beaten and then arrested. He was defended in court by Herbert Asquith but that didn't prevent him from being sent to Pentonville Prison for six weeks.

Back in the Commons, he continued to champion the rights of the workers and rail against their exploitation. The Establishment thought he overstepped the mark when he protested about the working conditions of chain-makers, and he was once again suspended. It was clear by now that he was seriously out of sorts with his own party and he resigned from the Liberals to join Keir Hardie's group. So infectious was his energy and enthusiasm, he was elected president when the new Scottish Labour party was launched in 1888 and he worked tirelessly in the early stages of the Independent Labour party. He put nationalisation of land, coal mines and other key industries on the political agenda and then added demands for an eight-hour working day, free school meals, the disestablishment of the Church of England and Home Rule for Scotland. He irked almost everyone by saying he wanted a national parliament for Scotland so that he could have 'the pleasure of knowing the taxes were wasted in Edinburgh instead of London.'

Robert Cunninghame Graham's early life on the family estate in Renfrewshire was strongly influenced by his maternal grandmother, who came from an aristocratic Spanish family. He was bilingual by the time he went to Harrow and then extended his languages by finishing his education in Brussels. When he was 17, he decided to go to South America and it is here his story bursts into glorious technicolour. He works as a gaucho near Buenos Aries and gets kidnapped by a bunch of outlaws. He charms them into letting him go. They call him Don Roberto. They all become good friends and he goes on to prosper as a rancher. On a trip to Morocco, he again avoids serious trouble by disguising himself as a smooth-talking sheikh and then goes prospecting for gold in Spain. Romance takes him back to Argentina, where he marries a young beauty he describes as a 'half-French, half-Chilean poet' and persuades her to join him on a wagon train bound for Mexico. In Mexico City, he becomes a fencing instructor. Well, why not?

Roaming the wide open spaces of Texas, a long way from the green fields of Renfrewshire, he befriends William Cody... better-known as Buffalo Bill! Who knows where his adventures may have led if his father hadn't died and he had to return to Scotland in 1883? However, estate management was never going to be enough for him and so began his interest in politics. Having eschewed the high politics of the landed gentry, he found himself more in tune with the likes of William Morris and George Bernard Shaw and, of course, James Keir Hardie.

He also found time to publish several books about his travels and it was he who introduced Joseph Conrad to his publisher, and then helped him with his research for the South American-set *Nostromo* (published in 1904). Shaw also acknowledged his help in writing the 1900 play *Captain Brassbound's Conversion* and his other literary friends included Ford Madox Ford (editor of the *English Review* and the *Transatlantic Review*), John Galsworthy (of *Forsyte Saga* fame) and G.K. Chesterton. Around the time he became a Liberal MP, he also helped found the Scottish Home Rule Association, and it was his abiding passion for independence that finally took him out of the Labour party in 1928 to form the National Party of Scotland. Two years later, he was voted the most popular Scot in a newspaper poll and in 1934 he became the first president of what had become the Scottish National Party. When he died, in Buenos Aries in 1936, the Argentinian president led a national tribute before sending his body back to Scotland, to be buried amid the ruins of the Augustine priory in Stirling. In his own autobiography G.K. Chesterton said he had 'achieved the adventure of being Cunninghame Graham.'

Dundee-born George Barnes was one the key links between the trade unions and the launch of the Independent Labour party. He was assistant general secretary (and later general secretary) of the powerful Amalgamated Society of Engineers and he was instrumental in persuading the ILP not to restrict parliamentary candidature to working-class men. His resolution, at the founding conference in 1893, was passed by 102 votes to 3 and did much to widen the appeal of the fledgling party, of which he briefly became leader in 1910 (in between Henderson and Ramsay MacDonald).

His commitment to trade unionism stemmed from his personal experience of starting work at 11, long spells of unemployment and low wages when he did find work. He had to go south, to Barrow-in-Furness, to finish his engineering apprenticeship in the shipbuilding industry. He then went further south, to London, where he suffered a ten-week spell without work before getting a job in the construction of the Albert Dock. He joined the ASE in 1882 and worked his way up from shop steward to the national executive, where he served alongside Tom Mann, one of the country's most influential trade unionists. He too attended the Trafalgar Square demonstration on Bloody Sunday and was seriously hurt when he was trampled by a police horse. When he became the full-time general secretary of the ASE in 1896, it was Britain's third-largest union and he was one of the country's most powerful labour leaders. The following year, he led a strike in favour of an eight-hour working day. It lasted for six long and grim months. While he failed in his main objective, he did wring a promise from the Employers Federation that it would thereafter be willing to negotiate wages and conditions. After an 1898 fact-finding mission on the continent, during which he found that Britain was falling behind other industrial nations in wage levels and working conditions, Barnes decided the only answer was to ensure more trade unionists were elected to parliament.

He led the way himself and was one of the 29 Labour MPs elected in 1906, enjoying the added pleasure of taking the Glasgow Blackfriars seat from Bonar Law, then the trade secretary. He supported Lloyd George's 1908 Old Age Pensions Act (which was aimed at 'lifting the shadow of the workhouse from the homes of the poor') but protested about the means testing and the rate of benefits: between one and five shillings a week. In 1914, he was a strong advocate of Britain's role in the war and helped by making recruitment speeches around the country and went to Canada to persuade trained mechanics to come to work in Britain. Even when his son was killed on the Western Front, he still supported conscription. In 1916 he backed Lloyd George (against Asquith) and was rewarded with the newly-created post of minister of pensions. At the end of the war, when Labour withdrew from the coalition government, he resigned from the party to remain a minister and held on to the job until ill health forced him to stand down in 1920. He didn't seek re-election at the 1922 general election.

One of the most influential women in the Labour party was Fife-born Jennie Lee. At just 24 she became Britain's youngest MP when she won a by-election in North Lanark in 1928. She married the charismatic progenitor of the NHS, Aneurin Bevan, in 1934 and is best known as the architect of the Open University. She made her mark in the Commons with a maiden speech in which she denounced Churchill's budget proposals. He was impressed enough to congratulate her, but in typical Churchillian style: he said that he, too, wanted to help the poor but she had to understand that 'the richer the rich became, the more able they would be to help the poor.' She lost her seat in the 1931 and because she got caught up in the squabbles between the ILP and the Labour party, she didn't return to Parliament until 1945. In the interim, she lectured in Europe, America and Canada and at one point acted as parliamentary correspondent for the *Daily Mirror*. She also wrote for the left-wing *Tribune*, which had been co-founded by Aneurin Bevan. When they married, she decided to take a back seat and was of enormous support to him as he faced the huge task of muscling the NHS proposals through the Commons in the face of ferocious opposition from the country's doctors.

It was not until after Bevan's death in 1960 that she re-emerged as a political force. When Harold Wilson became prime minister in 1964, he made her minister for the arts and gave her the job of developing his idea for a 'University of the Air.' In its archives, the Open University says: 'Without Jennie Lee, it seems likely that Harold Wilson's idea would have failed. Her total commitment and tenacity gradually wore down the mountains of hostility and indifference that she faced.' Although she was a junior minister, she effectively worked directly for the Treasury and the prime minister. She said later: 'The civil servants hated it: all very irregular. But it was the only way you could get a new job done.' She didn't like the 'University of the Air' terminology 'because of all the nonsense in the press about sitting in front of the telly to get a degree.' Instead she had a strong vision of what she called an open university: 'I knew it had to be a university with no concessions, right from the very beginning. I knew the conservatism and vested interests of the academic world. I didn't believe we could get it through if we lowered our standards.' The proposal became a Labour party manifesto commitment at the 1966 general election and the Open University was launched in 1970. Harold Wilson later described it as the greatest achievement of his government. Jennie Lee gave her name to the university's first library, which now houses her political archive.

As well as the first Conservative prime minister (the Earl of Bute) and another four after that (the Earl of Aberdeen, Balfour, Bonar Law and Douglas-Home), many other Scots reached the upper echelons of that party and made significant contributions to British politics. One of the most distinguished of the post-war Conservatives was David Maxwell Fyfe. Churchill made him solicitor general in 1942, attorney general just before the 1945 election, home secretary in 1951 and lord chancellor in 1954. He kept that job under the premierships of Anthony Eden and Harold Macmillan… until he became a victim of the night of the long knives that occurred in June 1962 when Macmillan sacked a third of his cabinet.

Just as Ramsay MacDonald had changed the face of British politics, so did Maxwell Fyfe change the face of the Conservative party. In 1943, he chaired a committee looking into the reorganisation of his party and the resulting report opened up candidature to people without personal fortunes! Born in Edinburgh, where he went to George Watson's College, he graduated from Oxford with a third-class degree… because he had spent so much time on politics. Although he had initially studied law in his spare time, he developed a glittering legal career. He was called to the bar in 1922 and in 1934 he became the youngest King's Counsel for more than 250 years. He served as a judge from 1936 to 1942, when he was knighted and appointed solicitor general. He was British deputy chief prosecutor at Nuremburg and his cross-examination of Hermann Göring was said to be one of the most effective of the war crimes trials.

He was elected MP for Liverpool West Derby at a 1935 by-election but was very much a part-time parliamentarian as he pursued his legal career. He was a member of the Parliamentary Assembly of the Council of Europe from 1949 to 1952, chairman of its legal and administrative council and rapporteur for the committee drafting the European Convention on Human Rights. Whilst home secretary, he was the centre of controversy over the hanging of Derek Bentley. Despite petitions, including those from 200 MPs, he refused to grant a reprieve to the young man said to have the mental age of 11. The incident is said to have been a major factor in the subsequent abolition of the death penalty. He heard the news of his sacking by Macmillan on the radio. The shock was only partly cushioned when he was made and earl and quietly retired from politics.

Another Scots big beast in the political jungle was Willie Whitelaw. Despite his challenge for the Conservative party leadership against her in 1975, Margaret Thatcher made him her deputy prime minister when she won 1979 general election, and later famously said of him: 'Every prime minister needs a Willie.'

The former Scots Guards major was born in Nairn in 1918 and educated at Winchester and Trinity College, Cambridge, where he won a blue for golf. During the Second World War he won the Military Cross in France, leaving the army after the war in order to look after the family estate. When he first became interested in politics he failed to win a seat in Scotland, but then, at the 1955 general election, he won Penrith and the Borders, the seat he held for 28 years. With his tough and disciplined military background, he was well suited to his first job – as opposition chief whip after the 1964 election that left Harold Wilson and Labour with an overall majority of just four!

His skills in ensuring effective harassing of the prime minister were rewarded when Heath won in 1970 and made him leader of the Commons. His first ministerial job was as secretary of state for Northern Ireland in 1972, when he introduced special category status for paramilitary prisoners. The following year, he moved to the department of

Employment and ran into the bruising conflict with Britain's miners that is regarded as being the cause of the Conservative defeat in the first of the two general elections in 1974.

That election was decidedly inconclusive. While Labour ended up as the biggest single party (with just four seats more than the Conservatives), an increase in support for the smaller parties meant it didn't have an overall majority. Heath made Whitelaw deputy leader of the Opposition and in the second election, in October 1974, he caught the media's attention by accusing Wilson of 'stirring up apathy.' The second defeat (during which the SNP had its best ever showing in a UK election and took its tally of seats to 11), left Heath's position in question and he was forced to call a leadership election the following year. With commendable loyalty, Willie Whitelaw refused to stand against him... until the one-time prime minister was knocked out in the first ballot. He then stood against Margaret Thatcher and won nearly 30 per cent of the MPs' votes, but ultimately lost out to the Iron Lady. She kept him as her deputy and, when she won the 1979 election, made him not just deputy prime minister but also home secretary.

In his four years in the job, he improved police pay and began a programme of prison building. Less successful was his 'short, sharp shock' policy to deal with young offenders; it did little to stem growing crime rates. Then, heavy-handed policing of ethnic minorities caused a serious backlash which was compounded by more IRA terrorist incidents. His most difficult moment, and certainly his most embarrassing, was when a man managed to breach Buckingham Palace security to confront the Queen in her bedchamber! Immediately after the 1984 election, he was given a hereditary peerage (the first created for nearly 20 years) and appointed leader of the House of Lords, while retaining the role of deputy prime minister. Despite one or two defeats in the Lords, he was so generally helpful and supportive of Mrs Thatcher that she gave us her Willie remark! He retired from politics after a suffering a stroke in 1987, and died in 1999.

Mrs Thatcher's other significant Scot was James Mackay from Edinburgh. He was regarded as one of the outstanding lawyers of the twentieth century and she had little hesitation in accepting advice to make him lord advocate, Scotland's senior law officer, when she won her famous victory in 1979. She then made him lord chancellor in 1987. His initial appointment – and elevation as Lord Mackay of Clashfern – was the more remarkable because he was not a member of the Conservative party at the time, as tradition decreed he should be. The son of a railway signalman, he went to George Heriot's School, Edinburgh University and Trinity College, Cambridge, where he took a postgraduate degree in mathematics. He was a lecturer at St Andrews during the 1950s before switching to read law at Edinburgh. He was elected to the Faculty of Advocates 1955 and took silk in 1965. He was later dean of the Faculty of Advocates, the leader of the Scots bar.

He became lord advocate, Scotland's senior law officer, in 1979, a judge of the Court of Session in 1984, and a lord of appeal in ordinary (law lord) the following year.

When Mrs Thatcher resigned, it was Lord Mackay who paid tribute at her final cabinet meeting. He continued to serve in John Major's government and when he retired in 1997 he was the longest-serving lord chancellor. He was made a Knight of the Thistle in 1999 and was lord high commissioner to the General Assembly of the Church of Scotland in 2005 and 2006. In 2007, he was appointed lord clerk register and keeper of the signet, one of the great offices of state of Scotland. It's a mainly ceremonial role but as a commissioner of the regalia he shares responsibility for the safekeeping of the Scottish Crown Jewels and the Stone of Destiny. He is editor-in-chief of *Halsbury's Laws of England* (the legal bible first published in 1907) and continues to attend and take part in debates of the House of Lords. There is a James Mackay Hall, named in his honour, in the King's College Conference Centre, Aberdeen University.

George Younger endeared himself to the Conservative party in 1963 when he nobly stepped down as candidate in the Perth and Kinross by-election to make way for Alec Douglas-Home. Not surprisingly, he was known to his colleagues as 'Gentleman George.' He was elected MP for Ayr in 1964 and went on to be Mrs Thatcher's Scottish secretary (1979–86) and defence secretary (1986–89). He was also chairman of the Scottish Conservatives (1974–76) and president of the UK party (1987–88). He left politics in 1992 when he became chairman of the Royal Bank of Scotland, and was given a life peerage. He inherited the family viscountcy in 1997 and died in 2003 after a battle with cancer.

One of the bleakest days for John Major's dispirited Conservative government was Black Wednesday – 16 September 1992 – and Shetlander Norman Lamont had the misfortune to be chancellor of the exchequer at the time. That was when the pound crashed out of the European Exchange Rate Mechanism, and he spent the day desperately trying to stop the inevitable. He pushed the interest rate up from 10 per cent to 12 and then 15 per cent within the space of a few hours. It was to no avail: sterling had to be taken out of the ERM, the pound was devalued and the UK lost reserves of £4 billion to the currency speculators. He immediately offered his resignation and though John Major would not accept it, his political career nevertheless crumbled. Within months, he was sacked as chancellor, refused a demotion and left the government. In his resignation speech in the Commons in May 1993, he made clear his feeling that he had been unfairly treated, saying that 'the government gives the impression of being in office but not in power.' The party chairman, however, dismissed the speech as 'dud, nasty, ludicrous and silly.' He later said he threw the Prime Minister's 'letter of regret' at his departure into the wastepaper basket, unopened.

Norman Lamont was educated at the Loretto School and Cambridge, where he was a contemporary of Michael Howard, Kenneth Clarke and Leon Brittan. He worked for Rothschild and became a director of their asset-management group. In his first attempt to become an MP, in 1970, he lost to John Prescott but was elected for Kingston upon Thames in a 1972 by-election. He served under Margaret Thatcher and John Major for a total of 14 years in the departments of energy, industry and defence before moving to the treasury. While he was chief secretary to the treasury and John Major was chancellor, he endorsed the decision to join the ERM and then appeared to cement a strong relationship when he ran Major's successful campaign to replace Margaret Thatcher as party leader. However, he was not offered the traditional peerage when he lost his seat in the 1997 election and had to wait until the following year to become Baron Lamont of Lerwick. He is a vice president of the Eurosceptic Bruges Group and chairman of the British-Iranian Chamber of Commerce.

A junior minister under Mrs Thatcher, Edinburgh-born Sir Malcolm Rifkind served as foreign secretary in John Major's cabinet and was initially a contender for the leadership of the Conservative party in 2005. He became MP for Edinburgh Pentlands in 1974 and Mrs Thatcher made him a junior minister in the Scotland Office in her first government and then promoted him to the Foreign Office as a minister of state in 1983. He joined the cabinet as Scottish secretary in 1986 and it was reported that his moderate views on social and economic issues led to occasional clashes with the prime minister. John Major moved him from the Scotland Office to Transport (1990), then Defence (1992) and finally, for the last years of his government, to the Foreign Office in 1994. He was knighted in 1997 but like the other ten Scottish Conservative MPs, lost his seat in that year's general election. Unlike them, he tried to recapture it in 2001. He was unsuccessful and only returned to parliament in 2005, succeeding Michael Portillo as MP for Kensington and Chelsea and the appointment as shadow work and pensions secretary. When Michael Howard stood down as party leader later in the year, he initially threw his hat into the ring but later withdrew to support of Kenneth Clarke. When David Cameron named William Hague as shadow foreign secretary, he said he didn't want any other post but declared his loyalty to the new leader. He sits on the backbenches and has a number of business directorships.

Opposition clearly doesn't suit the Conservatives and within months of their defeat in 1997 and the election of William Hague as the new leader, there was a series of internal dogfights, one of which led to the sacking of the party's leader in the House of Lords. He was replaced by Glasgow peer Lord Strathclyde, who had previously been chief whip. He was 28 and a City insurance broker when he entered the Lords in 1986 on the death of his father, Tom Galbraith, the former MP for Glasgow Hillhead. Within two years he was a government whip and a year after that became minister for tourism. He later held ministerial jobs in Agriculture and Fisheries, the Scotland Office, Environment and the Department of Trade and Industry before joining the cabinet as government chief whip in the Lords in 1994. In the reforms under the 1999 House of Lords Act, he was elected second in the list of 75 hereditary peers to remain in the Lords. He was the Channel 4 Peer of the Year in 2000 and *Spectator* magazine Peer of the Year in 2004.

Two Scots were involved in the drawn-out battle for the Tory leadership, which followed William Hague's speedy exit after his party's disastrous repeat performance in the 2001 general election. While big-hitters Kenneth Clarke and Michael Portillo made the early running, the more genteel Michael Ancram (a belted earl who preferred to play down his aristocratic pedigree) and former Scots Guards officer Iain Duncan Smith (who chose to play down his real first name of George), quietly made their marks in the constituencies. When Michael Ancram was eliminated in the first ballot, he immediately put his weight behind IDS and helped him beat off the final challenge of Kenneth Clarke. When Mr Duncan Smith won, he rewarded his loyal supporter with the party's deputy leadership. Two more Scots were part of the party's inner circle: Dr Liam Fox continued as shadow health secretary and David McLean was appointed Tory chief whip. Unfortunately for IDS, his reign was short-lived and he was ignominiously dispatched by a vote of no confidence from his parliamentarians. Rather than face another unseemly scramble for the leadership, the Tories then appointed Michael Howard as leader and he in turn reappointed Michael Ancram as deputy. That leadership lasted only until after the 2005 election (in which the Tories were again defeated). There were no Scots in the contest this time but the winner, David Cameron, has a decidedly Scottish name and, according to some commentators, Scottish roots.

As a committed Liberal Democrat, I can say it when others might be nervous: the Scots have done the party proud both in the pre-history days of the Liberal party and, more recently, in its emergence as the strongest third party since the early days of the twentieth century. While none of them have been successful in taking the party anywhere near government, they each provided commendable leadership.

The wartime leader of the Liberal party was the distinguished former soldier Sir Archibald Sinclair, MP for Caithness and Sutherland from 1922 to 1945. He was commissioned into the Life Guards in 1910, served on the Western Front in the Great War and rose to the rank of major in the Guards Machine Gun Regiment. At one time, he was second in command to Winston Churchill (then of the 6th Battalion of the Royal Scots Fusiliers) and they formed a lasting friendship. Churchill was then a Liberal and the friendship become a significant political alliance. He served as his military secretary when Churchill was secretary of state for war (1919–21) and went with him as his private secretary at the Colonial Office in 1921 until he became MP for Caithness and Sutherland the following year. He was the party's chief whip in 1930 and was secretary of state for Scotland in the National Government of Ramsay MacDonald in 1931. He became leader of a much-reduced Liberal party of just 20 MPs when his predecessor, Sir Herbert Samuel, lost his seat in 1935. When Churchill returned to head the coalition government in 1940, he was appointed secretary of state for air and played a key role in planning the bombing of Dresden. He was the last Liberal to serve in cabinet. In the 1945 election, he lost his seat by 59 votes and was later given a viscountcy and went into the Lords in 1952. His grandson is John Thurso, the current Liberal Democrat MP for the expanded Caithness, Sutherland and Easter Ross seat and his granddaughter sits in the Lords as Baroness Linklater of Buttermere.

It was the patrician Jo Grimond (born in St Andrews but MP for Orkney and Shetland) who pulled the party up by its bootstraps when he became leader in 1956.

He is credited as 'the man who saved the Liberals.' The party had gone into the 1955 general election contesting less than a fifth of the seats and returned just five MPs. It was a political joke and, not surprisingly, the commentators were ready to write the party's obituary. Jo Grimond had other ideas, though, and he pugnaciously refused to accept the deathbed scenario. He was unfazed by his meagre inheritance of a vote share – somewhere around two and a half per cent, less than three-quarters of a million votes – and within the year he managed to rattle the Conservatives with a stunning by-election victory in Torrington. The party's stock was high, particularly in the press. Lest that should sound as if it was plain-sailing from then on, it wasn't. The main battle in 1959 was to avoid losing deposits and the election was hailed as a success when the party lost only 56 deposits, the lowest number since 1935! When by-election success was repeated in Orpington in 1962 and again in the Scottish Borders in 1965 (when the winning candidate was one David Steel), it set a pattern that continues to make the party a formidable force in these skirmishes. At the 1964 election, the Liberal membership doubled, the number of paid staff doubled and its income trebled. It fielded 365 candidates and won 11.2% of the vote but, frustratingly, just nine MPs. In 1966, Jo's leadership attracted three million votes (that elected just 12 MPs). More importantly, his radicalism, enthusiasm and personal standing attracted to the party the likes of Menzies Campbell and David Steel, who would later play key roles in reviving its fortunes.

After being educated at Eton and Balliol College, Oxford, Jo Grimond became a barrister and publisher. In 1938, he married Laura Bonham Carter, granddaughter of the former Liberal prime minister, Herbert Henry Asquith. He served as a major during the Second World War and afterwards was secretary of the National Trust for Scotland (1947–49). He was elected to the House of Commons in 1950. Having met him in my early days as a party activist, I can safely assert that he had an abundance of personal charm and charisma. He was highly respected across the political spectrum and I have to confess that I was always amazed at his single-minded commitment to Liberalism and the stifling of what is the normal ambition of the politician. He offered his reasoning in his autobiography *Jo Grimond: Memoirs* published in 1977: 'Most politicians want to be prime minister but every politician who feels there is any gravity in the business cannot be out merely for office. It is treating politics with disdain to opt for a party in which you guess promotion will come quickest. Politics are about much else besides being a minister in government. Nor do I concede that to toil as a Liberal is futile weaving in the sands, an abject acceptance of exclusion, leaving one at best with one's nose pressed against the glass watching the world go by. On the contrary, Keynes and Beveridge were two of the most politically influential men in the last 50 years and both were Liberals to their dying day.' He stepped down as leader in 1967 but remained the MP for Orkney and Shetland until 1983, when he retired from the Commons and was given a life peerage. He died in 1993 and is buried in Orkney.

When, in the mid-70s, the party was rocked by revelations of Jeremy Thorpe's homosexuality and his subsequent trial for attempted murder (of Norman Scott, of which, it must be stressed, he was acquitted), it was David Steel who picked up the pieces. After his 1965 by-election win, he had distinguished himself at Westminster by steering the controversial Abortion Act through Parliament in 1967 and he was Thorpe's natural successor to the leadership in 1976. As leader of a still perilously-small group of MPs and peers, he turned to the party's grassroots activists and launched the highly successful era of community politics. He also caused considerable controversy by sustaining Harold Wilson's paper-thin parliamentary majority through the Lib-Lab pact. That wasn't enough to avoid Margaret Thatcher's 1979 advance on Downing Street nor the subsequent fragmentation of the Labour party. Out of that confused period for Labour emerged the 'gang of four' – Roy Jenkins, Shirley Williams, David Owen and Bill Rodgers – and the launch of the Social Democratic party. Steel negotiated an alliance with them but found himself painfully satirised by ITV's *Spitting Image* as the Boy David to David Owen's allegedly grown-up politics. Despite that, the Alliance won a quarter of the vote in the 1983 general election, but was rewarded with a meagre 23 seats. For their 27 per cent of the popular vote, the Labour party returned 209 MPs. Convinced that the only way forward was to create a single party with a single leader, David Steel was the chief proponent of the 1988 merger between the Liberals and the SDP. He did not stand for election as leader of the new party but acted in an interim capacity until Paddy Ashdown emerged, and then took up the Foreign Affairs portfolio. He was knighted in 1990 and retired from the Commons in 1997 and, as a long-time advocate of devolution, he successfully sought election to the new Scottish Parliament in 1999 and became the first presiding officer (speaker), serving until 2003. He was lord high commissioner to the General Assembly of the Church of Scotland in 2003 and 2004.

Paddy Ashdown led the new party with continuing success until 1999, when he stepped down. In the ensuing election for the leadership, the comfortable winner was another charismatic Scot, Charles Kennedy, who led the party through two general elections in which the Lib Dems grew from strength to strength. In his first election as leader in 2001, they won more than 18 per cent of the vote and returned 52 MPs, and in 2005 they had their best result yet and emerged as the strongest third party since the 1920s. They won nearly 23 per cent of votes and 62 MPs. Charles was a graduate of Glasgow University, where he was president of the union and won the *Observer* Mace for debating but still managed an honours degree in politics and philosophy. He also won a Fulbright scholarship to Indiana University, where he taught public speaking while doing his postgraduate research in political rhetoric. He had a job as a journalist and broadcaster with the BBC waiting for him when he finished the PhD programme, but he never made it. The 1983 election intervened. Although still only 23, he applied to be the SDP candidate in the Ross, Cromarty and Skye constituency in the 1983 general election and had to fly back from the US to join five others in the selection hustings. He won the candidature and then, to most people's surprise, including his own, he emerged as the youngest MP in the Commons. He was one of six SDP victors including Roy Jenkins (Glasgow Hillhead), David Owen (Plymouth Devonport) and fellow Scot

Robert Maclennan (Caithness and Sutherland), who was briefly leader of the party during merger talks in 1987. He became the Alliance spokesman on a range of welfare issues and quickly earned a reputation as a future leader. He was the first SDP MP to declare his support for the 1988 merger of the two Alliance parties. The following year, he was named by the *Spectator* as 'The Member to Watch.' His popularity with activists won him the party presidency in 1990 and the leadership in 1999. As leader, he always gave the impression of being laidback – some said he was too laidback – and he was a great favourite of the television producers, to the point that the press gave him the nickname of 'Chat-Show Charlie.' He enhanced his reputation in 2003 by being the only one of the three party leaders to oppose the war in Iraq, and he warned of the steady infringement of civil liberties perpetuated by Tony Blair and New Labour in the name of the war on terror. The party's stock with the public was never higher and it won by-elections in Brent East (2003) and Leicester South (2004) and beat Labour into third place in the 2004 local elections. Despite his popularity and success at the ballot box, however, some within the parliamentary party became concerned about his alcohol consumption and that came to a head at the end of 2005, when there were calls for his resignation from some MPs. Initially he denied having a problem but then in a dramatic speech on 5 January 2006, he admitted it, called a leadership election and insisted he would be a candidate. Two traumatic days later, he changed his mind and – to the great sadness of many Liberal Democrats and most of the public – resigned.

His deputy and fellow Scot Sir Menzies Campbell took temporary charge of the party while a leadership ballot was organised. Ming, a one-time Olympic sprinter once described as 'the fastest white man on the planet,' won comfortably and, at 64, became the oldest leader of the three main parties. More in the mould of Jo Grimond, Sir Menzies cut an elegant, eloquent figure with an impeccable reputation as a highly-successful QC and as an experienced and distinguished expert in foreign affairs. He was the architect of the party's opposition to the Iraq war and consistently demanded that the government should publish the Attorney General's secret advice on the war's legality. He was also highly critical of Tony Blair's unconditional support for President Bush. While he had no time for what he described as the 'visceral anti-Americanism' of some in the anti-war movement, he insisted that 'our two countries are bound together historically by common values and experience but our relationship should be one of mature partnership, not one of undue deference.' As leader, he quickly reassembled a new shadow cabinet which included the Scot Michael Moore (MP for Tweeddale, Ettrick and Lauderdale) as the shadow foreign secretary; Alistair Carmichael (Orkney and Shetland) as shadow transport secretary and, perhaps most surprisingly, 26-year-old Jo Swinson (elected MP for East Dunbartonshire only in 2005) as his new shadow Scottish secretary.

But it was *his* age that was to be Ming Campbell's undoing. When Gordon Brown intimated that there would be no general election before 2010, there were mutterings that Ming would then be 68 and therefore too old to be an effective leader. Perhaps it was time for him to step down to make way for a younger figure? To his obvious frustration, the mutterings grew louder and gave the media the opportunity for negative coverage. While there was still considerable support for him, he had had enough and stepped down in October 2007. In his letter of resignation, he wrote: 'It has become clear that following the prime minister's decision not to hold an election, questions about leadership are getting in the way of further progress by the party.'

One of the great offices of state is, of course, that of speaker of the House of Commons. Only three Scots have held the position and, as it happens, one came from each of the three main parties. The first was the Whig, James Abercromby, in 1835; the second was Conservative MP William Morrison from Argyllshire (1951–59); and the third was Glasgow Labour MP Michael Martin, who served 2000–2009.

The son of the distinguished general who died in the Battle of Alexandria in 1801, James Abercromby was a pupil at Edinburgh's Royal High School before reading law and becoming a barrister in 1800. The following year, he was made a commissioner of bankruptcy and subsequently was appointed auditor to the estates of the Duke of Devonshire. He earned a strong legal reputation before entering politics as the MP for Midhurst in 1807, Calne in 1812 and then, after the Reform Act – which put an end to rotten boroughs and created new city constituencies – he was chosen to represent Edinburgh, 1832–39. He was made a member of the Privy Council and appointed judge advocate general in 1830 by the Whig prime minister Earl Grey. He was then chief baron of the court of exchequer (effectively head of Scotland's treasury) in 1830 and master of the Mint (another treasury post), 1834-35, before becoming speaker. After retiring in 1839, he was elevated to the peerage as 1st Baron Dunfermline and returned to Scotland, where he was elected dean of faculty at Glasgow University (1841–43).

William Morrison was the first speaker in the twentieth century to take office after a contested election. It had been the custom for the parties to take turns in providing the speaker, but when the Conservatives won the 1951 general election, they decided to oppose the Labour nominee and ensured their success by voting on party lines. Educated at George Watson's College and Edinburgh University, Morrison had joined the army during the Great War and served as a captain in the Royal Artillery in France, where he won the Military Cross. He was elected MP for Cirencester and Tewkesbury in 1929 and acquired the nickname 'Shakes' in parliament, from his habit of quoting Shakespeare! He enjoyed a long ministerial career and served under four prime ministers (Ramsay MacDonald, Stanley Baldwin, Neville Chamberlain and Winston Churchill). As minister of food in 1939 he introduced rationing and ration books, but after the war he attacked the continued use of identity cards. He said they were a nuisance to law-abiding people and were largely ineffective. In 1959, he decided to step down as speaker and leave parliament due to his failing health and was made a peer, taking the title Viscount Dunrossil of Vallaquie. It surprised most of his colleagues when, the following year, he was chosen to succeed former Field Marshal Sir William Slim as governor general of Australia. The reason, it was said, was that Prime Minister

Robert Menzies had asked for an appointment that would maintain a Scottish link with Australia. He arrived in Canberra in February 1960 but died a year and one day later, the first governor general to die in office.

When the popular Betty Boothroyd retired as speaker of the Commons in 2000, tradition was once more set aside and there was something of an unseemly scramble for the job. There were multiple candidates (including several Scots) from the three main parties. Inevitably, given their hefty majority, it was Labour's Michael Martin, MP for Glasgow Springburn, who in traditional style was dragged to the speaker's chair. He was the first Roman Catholic to hold the post since the Reformation and elements of the press had a field day with his strong Glaswegian accent. Ignoring the fact that he came from the city's Anderston district, the *Daily Mail* immediately gave him the cruel and unhappy soubriquet of 'Gorbals Mick'.

Mr Martin left school at 15 to work as an apprentice sheet-metal worker and later became a strong trade unionist. He was an Amalgamated Union of Engineering Workers shop steward (1970–74) and a paid official of the National Union of Public Employees (1976–79). He joined the Labour party when he was 21 and was a city councillor from 1973 until becoming an MP in 1979. At Westminster he was parliamentary private secretary to Denis Healey while he was deputy leader of the Labour party (1980–83). However, he saw himself very much as a House of Commons man, and served as chairman of the Scottish Grand Committee (1987–97) and a member of the Speaker's Panel of Chairmen. He served as first deputy chairman of ways and means (deputy speaker) for three years before taking the chair in 2000. He suffered the ignominy of being the first speaker ever to be sacked when he was removed from office in 2009.

6

… AND THE GLORY

'I can't remember a time when I wasn't enthralled by the feats of skill and endurance of the heroes who dominated my schooldays.'
— *Writer*

To launch into an honest assessment of Scotland's sporting history is tantamount to clambering aboard an emotional roller coaster. We have had our share of triumphs and disasters. As this is essentially a commentary on *great* Scots, I hope I will be forgiven, therefore, for concentrating on the high points, of which, it can be said, there are more than enough.

It may well be that we perform better when we suffer underdog status. Battling against the odds seems to be inherent in our character. Giants, it would seem, are there to be toppled. Minnows? Well, let's not go there! As an element of our empire-building, we have spawned world-beaters in all the major team and individual sporting events and in not a few of the lesser sports. If we use the Olympics as a bench mark, Scotland's sporting heroes have acquitted themselves with grit and determination, a lot of glory… and brought home a more-than-reasonable haul of medals. Since the modern Games began in Athens in 1896, Scots have won medals at every meeting and amassed a creditable total of 58 gold, 42 silver and 33 bronze medals.

By any standards, the top-Scot place must go to Beijing 2008 triple gold and London 2012 double gold winner Chris Hoy, from Edinburgh – now, of course, Sir Chris. In just five days in Beijing and 15 races (12 of them knock-out heats), at the age of 32, Chris rode gloriously into the history books as the first Briton to win three gold medals at one games (adding to the one he already had from Athens in 2004) and earned the title of the world's greatest cyclist. The commentators ran out of superlatives in 2012, when he added to the glitter of the London Games by winning another two gold medals, and so became Britain's most successful Olympian of all time. There is not a shadow of doubt that his achievements will stand the test of time and I am totally confident in breaking my own rule about including contemporary figures in this part of the commentary. Medals and titles make the selection so much easier.

Having produced the television coverage of the last Milk Race in 1993, I've seen at close quarters the terrible agony that race cyclists go through. The two-week event covered more than a thousand miles up hill and down dale around Britain. It meant cycling more than a hundred miles a day at an average speed of more than 25 mph. At the end of each stage, when we camp-followers collapsed in a heap after just tracking them in a car, the riders turned their hotel rooms into mini-gyms, put their bikes on rollers, saddled up again and tried to unwind their tortured muscles and stretched sinews. Their groans and occasional howls of pain as they 'cycled down' said it all. That puts Chris Hoy's achievement into perspective for me and I can only fall into sports-journalist jargon and describe it as 'awesome.' The media has given him wall-to-wall coverage so there is little need for me to repeat his story. But record his record, I must: in addition to his six Olympic golds, he won the silver with the sprint team at Sydney in 2000. He has also won ten golds and thirteen other medals in the world championships and two Commonwealth golds. He was voted BBC Sports Personality of 2008. Of his knighthood in the 2009 New Year's Honours List, he said with endearing modesty: 'To become a knight from riding your bike? It's mad! It feels a bit strange and I still can't take it in.' See chapter 11 – Waiting in the wings for further details of those who triumphed in the 2012 London Games.

The first British Olympic medal-winner was Launceston Elliot, who took the gold in the one-handed weightlifting and the silver in the two-handed class in the first of the modern Olympics in Athens in 1896. He was born in Delhi while his Scottish father was serving as a magistrate in the Indian Civil Service. His uncle was the Earl of Minto, viceroy of India from 1905 to 1910 (see chapter 7, The colonials). He also ran in the 100 metres and competed in the wrestling and gymnastic rope-climbing events, but was eliminated in the heats. In the 1900 Games, he represented Britain in the discus (because there was no weightlifting) but again failed to reach the final. He began weightlifting in his early teens, took part in the first British championships in 1890, when he was only 16, and won the title three years later. He was just 21 when he went to Athens. There, he missed out on the two-handed gold although in the final he lifted the same weight as the declared winner. The judge preferred the 'style' of the Danish lifter. In the single-handed lift, he beat the same Dane by a massive margin of 34 kilograms.

A burly six-footer, George Cornet was born in Inverness in 1877 and was already 31 when he won his first gold medal at the 1908 London Olympics. He was the oldest swimmer in the British water polo team then and again when he picked up his second gold, four years later in Stockholm. His medals were especially appropriate because water polo had its origins in Scotland. In the early 1870s, Aberdeen's Bon Accord Swimming Club started to play what they called 'aquatic football.' It was played in the chilly waters of the River Dee and 'players had to sit in the water and kick the ball with their feet when passing or shooting for goal.' It was devised simply to be an entertainment for spectators at major swimming events but it caught on as a sport in its own right. That might have been partly because it required little equipment and was therefore open to everyone, unlike so many other sports at the time.

In common with many sportsmen of the day, George Cornet was an all-rounder. In between winning Olympic medals in the swimming pool, he played as a full-back for the Inverness Amateurs football team that won the Scottish Cup in 1909 and were runners-up on four other occasions. He was capped and played 17 games for the national side between 1897 and 1912. He also played cricket and whenever he had a Saturday spare he took part in the track and field events at Highland Games across the country.

Nowhere was the Olympic spirit more personified than in London in 1908, when Wyndham Halswelle had a walkover in the re-run of the 400 metres final to become Scotland's first track gold medallist. The Highland Light Infantry captain and Boer War veteran was the Scottish champion at 100, 200, 400 and 800 yards (sic) and had won silver (400 metres) and bronze (800 metres) at the interim Games in Paris two years earlier. In the 1908 final in London, however, two American runners were judged to have deliberately blocked him. Officials declared the race void and ordered a re-run but all the other finalists declined to race against him because they didn't want to deny him the medal.

Before London 2012, Scotland's best medal haul was at the Stockholm Games in 1912, with a total of seven (of Britain's ten) gold, plus a silver and a bronze. That was the year George Cornet and Angus Gillan each picked up their second gold (in the water polo and coxless fours respectively); Henry Macintosh, from Kelso, won his medal in the 4 × 100-metre sprint relay; Philip Fleming was stroke of the successful GB rowing eight; William Kinnear from Aberdeenshire won the single sculls; Robert Murray was the best in the small-bore rifle and Glasgow's Isabella Moore was in the winning 4 × 110-metre freestyle swimming team. John Sewell took his silver as a member of the British tug of war team and James Soutter got his bronze with the 4 × 400-metre relay team.

The drama of the 1924 Paris Olympics was replayed in the brilliant film *Chariots of Fire* (starring Ian Charleston), about one of Scotland's great sporting heroes, Eric Liddell. A devout Christian, Liddell refused to run in his favoured 100-metre sprint when the heats were scheduled for a Sunday, but then went on to take the gold in the 400 metres. Born in China, where his parents were missionaries, he became a keen sportsman when he and his brother were sent home to study at Edinburgh University. While reading science he initially began playing rugby, and was capped as wing threequarters seven times for Scotland. He also established himself as a sprinter and won the 100-metre titles at the Triangular (Scotland, England and Ireland) Championships in three successive years, 1921–23. He was, therefore, a hot favourite to take the Olympic gold at that distance. However, instead of running in the heats on the first Sunday of the Games, he was the preacher in the Scots Church in Paris. He opted to run in the 400 metres, for which he hadn't prepared. The rest, of course, is history.

When Dundee's Dick McTaggart took on the world's best boxers, he did it in style. He not only won the lightweight gold medal in the 1956 Olympics in Melbourne, but also picked up the Val Barker Trophy as the Olympic boxer with the best style! His success was my first conscious recognition of the Olympics and the Olympic spirit. I'd had a vague awareness of a Scottish toff on a horse winning something some time before that, but Dick was different and I was able to identify with him. He was from Dundee and was just five foot nine and under ten stone, well within my aspiration as a gangly teenager. I'd also been playing at boxing. I went regularly to my local club and vaingloriously waved my oversize gloves, with enough power to threaten my sparring partners about as effectively as a powder puff. As it happened, I didn't need to endanger my delicate features because Dick McTaggart and his precious gold medal gave me enough to swagger about. In a later era he would undoubtedly have become a fashion icon with his blonde crew cut and flashy white boxing boots.

He was from a family of fighters. One of his brothers boxed for the Army (and was Middle East Forces champion) and another was the Royal Navy champion, so when he was called up to do his National Service, almost inevitably, Dick made it a full house by joining the RAF. As well as becoming the Brylcreem Boys' lightweight champion, he won promotion from cook to corporal. But it's not just his gold medal that earns him a place here: his career record is astonishing. He won 610 of his 634 bouts and won more than 30 cups, nearly 60 plaques and a total of 50 medals. He was Commonwealth champion in 1958, a bronze medallist at the Rome Olympics in 1960, European champion in 1961 and won silver at the 1962 Commonwealth Games, on top of his three ABA lightweight and two light welterweight titles. In 1964 he became the first boxer to have fought in three successive Olympics, although he failed to secure another medal. He never turned professional, but when he retired from the ring he became the honorary director of coaching to Commonwealth Games boxers. BBC boxing commentator Harry Carpenter described him as 'the greatest amateur I ever saw.'

FOOTBALL

Like most of my generation of Scotsmen, I suspect, sport – and especially football – came to me through my mother's milk. I can't remember a time when I wasn't enthralled by the feats of skill and endurance of the heroes who dominated my schooldays or when I could resist the temptation to have a punt at any ball that bounced my way. While any recall of the nation's performance on the world's soccer pitches may bring on all too many groans from Scots and guffaws from Sassenachs, we have had our moments, and individual Scots have stamped themselves indelibly on the 'beautiful game', as the more romantic scribes have come to term it.

Although the game has an honourable history stretching back a couple of hundred years or more, its development as a global spectacle and a major business operation is very much of the twentieth century and that period, inevitably, will be the main thrust of this section, although I will try to keep a sensible perspective. Because I am so steeped in football, especially from the 1950s, I readily confess that my journalistic objectivity tends to go out the window at this point. In selecting players and personalities for a mention, I have tended to let my heart rule my head!

One of my earliest heroes was Hughie Gallacher. He was reckoned, certainly by me, to have been the best centre forward in Europe in the late 1920s. Tempting as it was in my soccer-crazed milieu, I never actually claimed him as a relative but neither did I put right those people who, because of my adulation and despite the 'c' rather than a 'g' in the middle of his surname, assumed he was! I also have to remind myself he had long since stopped playing by the time I was old enough to go to matches, so vivid were the pictures painted for me by my older brother and uncles. Even now I sometimes think I *was* there when he scored both the goals that sent England packing from Hampden in 1925 and when he laid on all five on that glorious day when the Wizards thrashed England 5-1, at Wembley in 1928. But these triumphs, great as they are in my mind, are not all that qualifies him for inclusion in a story of empire. He also showed a readiness to venture beyond his native heath in search of fame and, in comparative terms, fortune.

Hughie was born in Bellshill (in 1903) and played for his local side before joining Queen of the South when he was 17, and then Airdrieonians (now simply Airdrie). He qualified for inclusion in this book when he transferred, in 1925, to Newcastle, for £6,500. By the time he moved on to Chelsea, his value had gone up to £10,000. He played the last of his 19 games for Scotland in 1935, when they beat England 2-0. He was a tenacious player who seemed to view it as an insult when anyone tried to take the ball from him and unfortunately his temper often boiled over. As he had once trained with a couple of champion boxers, his pugnacity didn't endear him to opponents or referees and he was sent off on all too many occasions. Off the pitch, he also lived a tough existence and when all the glamour of his football stardom had sadly faded, he killed himself by walking in front of an express train in 1957, at a place called Dead Man's Crossing near his Gateshead home.

Hughie and his like became heroes through word of mouth. There was no wall-to-wall television sports coverage. My heroes were only as heroic as the language my family and friends were able to muster. If you think today's pundits are cliché-ridden, extravagant exaggerators, you should have heard me and my schoolmates discuss the Saturday afternoon soccer games at Cappielow Park in Greenock. After we had finished our own dour struggles on the local cinder pitch or in the street, we fantasised over the torn-out newspaper pictures, the nearest thing we had to action replays. We raved outrageously about the mesmerising dribbling skills of wingers, the defensive ruthlessness of centre halves and the miraculous stopping abilities of goalies. Although they turned out as a team we saw them very much as individuals, and every one of them was even better than the greats of the seasons before. I lived for the thrill of seeing Greenock Morton run out onto the pitch in their blue-and-white hoops and baggy shorts.

The record books might indicate otherwise but, to me, Morton was a team of giants and first among them was Billy Steel (all five feet six inches of him), inside left and dribbler extraordinaire. At least a little bit of the world seemed to share my view of the great man because he was twice sold for record fees – £15,500 when he left Morton for Derby County and £23,500 when he moved on to Dundee. He played 30 times for Scotland and scored one of the goals that gave the Great Britain team a 6-1 victory over the Rest of Europe in a post-war special match at Hampden in 1947. Steel was a really hard man with a ferocious shot and the pundits have come to count him among the greatest inside forwards of all time. He was not the only one from that small club (even today its ground capacity is only 15,000) to win international acclaim.

Jimmy Cowan, who wore the goalkeeper's yellow jersey, was fearless in diving among those hard toe-capped boots that wreaked such terrible havoc in contact with an unprotected shin and could be nearly lethal to a man on the ground. He won his first international cap in 1949 when Scotland beat England 3-1 at Wembley. He put on such a dazzling display of goalkeeping – it was truly heroic – that it became known as 'Cowan's Match.' He was the first to make goalkeeping into a science. He used to scratch a line with the heel of the boot from the penalty spot to his goal line and from that reckoned he was better able to cover all the angles. He went on to win 25 caps and earned the soubriquet 'Prince of Goalkeepers' in the Scottish papers.

And then there was Billy Campbell and Bobbie Kelly and Tommy Orr, all capped in the late 1940s. In more recent years, the fearsome Joe Jordan played his early games in Morton's blue-and-white hoops. But while my small local team has made a fair contribution to the soccer world and thus to my Scottish Empire, this is but tinkering at the edges of Scottish football. Most of the glamour and success of the domestic game is very much that of the Glasgow giants: Rangers and Celtic. These two – the 'Old Firm' – have staged titanic battles over the years and provided us with streams of world-class players. Having witnessed so many ugly clashes in the aftermath of Old Firm games down the years, I was delighted when Celtic fans won the fair play award from UEFA in the 2002–03 season. The Glasgow teams have found and developed so much world-class talent that it is impossible to offer here anything more than a strictly personal and idiosyncratic selection, and I have again limited myself to those who made it in the wider international arena. The same goes for the other big city clubs from Edinburgh, Aberdeen and Dundee. As it happens, they all have high profiles in the media and countless sports history books and I need do little more than reflect on just how strong has been the Scottish contribution to the game.

The most significant contribution to soccer empire-building must, however, be attributed to one William McGregor, a draper from Perthshire. It was football-mad Mr McGregor who was the driving force behind the creation of England's Football League, arguably now the greatest club competition in the world. In the early 1880s, he had moved to Birmingham, where he opened a linen shop not far from the ground where

Aston Villa regularly fielded three Scottish players. That was a major bonus for him and he jumped at the chance of becoming a Villa director.

The game, at that point, was far from beautiful in the business sense. With professionalism creeping in, fixtures were chaotic and matches were all too often cancelled because one or other of the sides had had a better offer from elsewhere. This offended William's sense of fair play; he thought the game needed to be more organised and, in the absence of anyone else prepared to do something about it, he did. He wrote to the leading clubs suggesting a formal league structure and, at a meeting in a hotel in London's Fleet Street on 22 March 1888, the Football League was born. Twelve clubs signed up and the first season kicked off on 8 September that year. Inevitably, among the stars that Saturday afternoon were a number of Scottish players, including four who turned out for Preston North End, the team that went on to win the first championship without losing a single match. George Drummond (born Edinburgh, 1865–1914), played on the left wing, John Gordon (born Port Glasgow, 1863) played on the right, David Russell (born Beith, 1862–1918) was the no-nonsense centre half and Jimmy Ross (Edinburgh, 1866–1902) was the equally no-nonsense inside forward. John Gordon scored the new league's first goal after just three minutes. He also scored five goals in the team's first round game in that season's FA Cup. Jimmy Ross (whose elder brother Nick also played for Preston but not in the 1888 season) earned his nickname of 'The Little Demon' by scoring 21 goals (13 in just two games) in that first season and repeated the feat the following year, when Preston retained the title. All four were also in the side that won the FA Cup in 1889 without conceding a single goal, earning the terrace accolade of 'The Invincibles'. The Scots had certainly given the new English League a terrific start!

There have been many great Scottish football managers who merit a mention, although, like Jock Stein, they seldom ventured outside Scotland. But their contribution to the beautiful game is evidenced by the fact that in the pre-war years, when the Scots were *fitba mad,* there were attendances of 150,000 at Scotland's home games at Hampden Park.

Bill Struth (born Kinross, 1875–1956) was only the second and also the most successful manager of Rangers. In his 34 years as boss (1920–54), the club won 18 league championships, ten Scottish Cups, two League Cups and seven wartime championships. He was a noted disciplinarian and he insisted that players wore collar and tie when turning up for training. He also made bowler hats compulsory on official occasions!

Willie McCartney (born Edinburgh, 1890–1948) uniquely managed both Edinburgh clubs. He was, unusually, a former referee, who replaced his father to serve as manager of Hearts for 13 years (1923–35). He then moved to Hibernian (1936–48), where he welcomed a young Matt Busby as a wartime guest player and developed a string of stars including Gordon Smith (who scored 364 goals for the club), Lawrie Reilly, Eddie Turnbull and Willie Ormond.

Hugh Shaw (born Edinburgh) replaced Willie McCartney as Hibs manager in 1948 and served for 14 years. During that time, the club won the league title in 1950 and 1953 and were runners-up in the League Cup in 1950 and the Scottish Cup in 1958. He also worked wonders with the supporters and attracted a record attendance of more than 65,000 for a home match against Hearts in the New Year Derby in 1950. The average home gate during the following season was more than 30,000.

If Bill Shankly thought he had everything, then you can take it for granted that Billy Liddell (born Townhill, Fife, 1922–2001) really was the complete footballer. He was another one-club man and that club was Liverpool, which he served from 1938 to 1961. As always, Shanks was on hand to deliver a colourful tribute: 'He was fast, powerful, shot with either foot and his headers were like blasts from a gun. On top of all that he was as hard as granite. What a player! He was so strong… and he took a 19-inch collar shirt!' That chimes with my memory of the almost unstoppable winger, whose popularity was such that at one time the city was known to many as 'Liddellpool'! He was sixth in the 2006 Kop poll of all-time club greats. He made more than 500 appearances and scored more than 200 goals. His haul of medals was awesome. Son of a Fife miner, he became hooked on football after getting his first pair of boots as a Christmas present when he just seven. Within the year, he was in the school team. At high school he got sidetracked into rugby, but soon got that out of his system and was selected for Scotland Schoolboys football team. Matt Busby, then playing for Liverpool, spotted him and he was persuaded to move to Anfield for the then-traditional £3 a week, with a parental proviso that he was allowed to continue studying to be an accountant. When he stopped playing 23 years later, he used that accountancy background to become the assistant bursar at the University of Liverpool and served as a city magistrate.

The elegant and stylish Slim Jim Baxter was a glorious product of the Swinging Sixties and sported a Beatles haircut when he strutted his stuff at Ibrox Park (1960–65), before succumbing to richer rewards in England. He displayed his talent with just the right degree of arrogance and continually frustrated his opponents. For me, he represented the very best of Scottish football and had a background out of the best adventure comics. My best memory of him (and I hope my friends south of the border will forgive me) was when he taunted the English by doing 'keepie-uppies' in the 1967 international, when he captained Scotland to a famous victory over the previous season's World Cup winners at Wembley. He went on to win 34 caps.

He was born in Hill O' Beath in Fife and as soon as he was old enough, he joined his father in the grime of Fordell Colliery, where he spent eight hours a day carrying pit props to the coalface for about £6 a week. He escaped from that by signing for his local team, Raith Rovers, in 1957 and moving on to Dundee in the early 1960s (when the manager was Bill Shankly's brother, Bob). He went to Rangers in 1960 and won three championship medals and four League Cup medals in his first four seasons. He suffered a serious setback in 1964 when he broke a leg in a European Cup game. He recovered well but clearly lost his edge, although that didn't stop former Scotland manager Ian

McColl signing him for Sunderland in May 1965. Two years later, Nottingham Forest paid a club record of £100,000 to secure his services, but his career was in the doldrums; Rangers sought to rescue him and he returned to Glasgow in 1969. Sadly it was in vain. He could not recapture his old bravado. He retired from the game after just one season at Ibrox and bought a pub in the city. He ran that happily for more than 20 years until his health gave out in 1994 and he had to have a liver transplant. In 2001, he was diagnosed with cancer and died at home with his family around him.

Although he spent his entire career at Ibrox, John Greig (born Edinburgh, 1942) more than graces any story of empire – and he has the MBE to prove it! He was captain when Rangers beat Dynamo Moscow in the 1972 European Cup Winners Cup, scored the single goal when Scotland beat Italy in 1965 and was skipper in that 1967 defeat of England. He made 44 appearances for his country and more than 750 for Rangers. He scored 120 goals and led the team to no fewer than three trebles – the Scottish First Division title, the Scottish Cup and the FA Cup.

When he stopped playing in 1978, he became the Rangers manager. Although he took them to the quarter-finals of the European Cup and two wins in both the Scottish Cup and the League Cup, that wasn't enough to satisfy the success-hungry Ibrox crowd and he resigned in 1983. He was awarded his MBE in 1977 and voted the 'Greatest Ever Ranger' in 1999. In 2008, he and Celtic's Billy McNeill were awarded honorary doctorates from Glasgow University. He later sat on the Rangers board (2003–11) and contributed to the club's youth development programme.

While I was tempted to include Billy McNeill (born Glasgow, 1940) in the management section, his phenomenal record – more than 800 games for Celtic and captain of the 1967 Lisbon Lions – puts him more appropriately in the fantastic player category. Celtic fans voted him their greatest ever captain in a 2002 poll and they don't dish out such accolades lightly. Billy McNeill more than earned it: while he was captain, the team won nine League Championships, seven Scottish Cups and six Scottish League Cups. Plus, of course, there was the unforgettable night in Lisbon when he led the team to victory over Inter Milan and became the first Briton to lay hands on the European Cup. Never did his nickname of Caesar seem more appropriate!

He retired from playing in 1975 and the following year he was awarded the MBE. It was then that he became a manager of several clubs but mainly Celtic, who he managed for two spells: 1978–83, when he won three League Championships and both the Scottish Cup and the League Cup, and 1987–91, when he celebrated Celtic's centenary season (1987–88) by winning the double of League Championship and Scottish Cup. They retained the cup the following season. In 2003, he tried his hand at politics when he stood – unsuccessfully – as a Senior Citizens Unity party candidate in the Scottish Parliament elections. In 2008, his honorary degree from the University of Glasgow was awarded for his 'distinguished role as an ambassador for the national sport.'

Burly and barrel-chested, Dave Mackay (born Edinburgh, 1934) was one of the bravest footballers I ever saw. He stood all of five feet seven and a half inches tall, looked almost as wide and was totally fearless. During his career he suffered two broken legs and one of his contemporaries said of him: 'When you were tackled by Dave, you stayed tackled!' In his nine years as a left half with Tottenham Hotspur (1959–68), he was a major player in the team that won the League and FA Cup double (1961), further FA Cup finals (1962, 1967) and the UEFA Cup Winners Cup (1963). In all, he played 318 games for Spurs and as evidence of his ability to turn defence into attack, he scored more than 50 goals. He played 22 games for Scotland. In 1968, aged 34, he was signed for Derby County for a nominal £5,000 by Brian Clough, who later described him as Spurs' greatest ever player. He returned the compliment by playing his heart out to help clinch promotion to the First Division at the end of his first season. He was named 1969 Footballer of the Year.

Mackay had started his career at Hearts, home of his boyhood idols. In his 135 appearances he helped win the Scottish League Cup twice (1955 and 1959), the Scottish Cup (1956) and the Scottish First Division championship (1957–58). He was captain of the league-winning team that notched up the British league record of scoring 132 goals and conceding only 29. He dipped his toe into management in 1971 when he became player-manager of Swindon Town but that didn't last and he moved, again briefly, to Nottingham Forest and then in 1973 to Derby, where he replaced the irreplaceable Brian Clough! And didn't he do well at the Baseball Ground: in his first season, the team finished third in the league. In 1975 he took them to the League Championship. They finished fourth the following season when they also got as far as the semi-finals of the FA Cup, but suffered an early defeat by Real Madrid in the European Cup. Despite that, the vagaries of football saw him sacked after a poor start to the 1976–77 season. He then spent a couple of years at Walsall before departing to the warmer climes of Kuwait, where he spent nine years coaching and managing. He returned to Britain to manage Doncaster Rovers (1987–89) and Birmingham City (1989–91) and then went back to the Middle East before retiring from the game in 1997. He published his autobiography, *The Real Mackay*, in 2004.

One of the most elegant footballers of his era was John White (born Alloa, 1937–64), one of the stars of Tottenham Hotspur's famous 1960s team. He died after being struck by lightning while playing golf when he was just 27. His slight stature, which later earned him the nickname 'the Ghost', misled several English managers, but Bill Nicholson had the benefit of inside information from Dave Mackay, who had played alongside him in the Scottish squad, and he brought him to White Hart Lane in 1959. He was a classic inside forward, able to play on either side, quickly fitted into the Spurs side and was a regular goal-scorer (he scored 18 in his first season). He played in every game of Spurs' 1960–61 season, in which they won the FA Cup and the first division championship. He was also one of the scorers when they beat Atlético Madrid 5-1 to become the first English side to win the European Cup Winners Cup in 1963. He was as skilled off the ball as he was when he had it at his feet. He always seemed to be in the right place and many defenders swore blind they hadn't seen him arrive in their penalty box. That's what earned him his affectionate nickname. There's a John White Lounge at the ground of Alloa Athletic (his first team) and his portrait hangs in the entrance to the Scottish Football Association's Hall of Fame.

RUGBY

Scotland's record on the rugby field is distinctly chequered but there is an abundance of great players to counter the uncertain team performance and to dull the pain of the slide down the world rankings. It's at times like this I am grateful for my self-imposed brief of reporting on the upside. The oldest international fixture is the annual clash for the Calcutta Cup between Scotland and England. It was launched in Edinburgh in 1879, when the first game was drawn 3-3, and has been played every year since (except during the years of the two world wars). Scotland has won about 35 per cent and drawn another 12 per cent of the encounters, which have more recently become part of the Six Nations championship. The English are comfortably ahead. In the Five Nations (England, France, Ireland, Scotland and Wales) Championship, Scotland had three Grand Slams, winning all their fixtures in 1925 (when they beat France 25-4, Wales 24-14, Ireland 14-8 and England 14-11), 1984 (Wales 15-9, England 18-6, Ireland 32-9 and France 21-12, and 1990 (Ireland 13-10, France 20-0, Wales 13-9 and England 13-7) and were points winners in 1964, 1973 and 1986.

Youth was a feature of Scotland's early international game: Robert Irvine (born Blair Atholl, 1853–97) was a month short of his 18th birthday when he won his first cap in the pack against England in 1871. Revelling in the nickname 'Bulldog', he stormed through every international Scotland played over the ten years 1871–80. James Finlay (1852–1930), was just 19 when he won his first cap as a forward. On his debut, he helped beat England by a single goal. He was an ever-present player for Scotland until 1875. Youngest of all was yet another Edinburgh Academical, Ninian Finlay (born Edinburgh, 1858–1936). He was 17 when he was capped in 1875 and went on to play internationally for more than 20 years.

It was Scotland's long-serving captain, stockbroker Bill Maclagan (born Edinburgh, 1858–1905), who was chosen to lead the first official British team to tour South Africa in 1891. It was initially called the England team because it was arranged by the RFU but there were four Scots in the party and the name was soon changed to the British Isles XV. He was educated at the Edinburgh Academy (1869–75) and, inevitably, joined Edinburgh Academicals (often described as 'the cradle of Scottish rugby'), emerging as Scottish full-back in 1878. The following year, he was in the side that drew 3-3 with England in the first Calcutta Cup match. In 1880, he switched to the three-quarter position and, together with fellow Edinburgh Academicals Ninian Finlay and John Campbell, made up the first three-quarter line in international rugby. He was captain of Scotland for the 1884 Home Nations Championship, which saw wins over Wales and Ireland but defeat to England. He stepped down for a couple of years and the captain's role was taken by the Edinburgh University three-quarter, Reginald Morrison (1863–1942), and Scotland won the championship for the first time.

In 1887, Bill Maclagan returned and helped the side retain the championship, during which he scored tries against Ireland and Wales. After winning a record 25th cap, he became the longest-serving international (13 seasons) and resumed the captaincy before retiring in 1889. Despite that, the RFU invited him to captain the tour to South Africa and he played in all three internationals as well as 15 of the other 16 matches. In the final game, he scored one of the team's two tries and brought the team back undefeated. He also played cricket for Scotland, became president of the Scottish Football Union (1894–96) and sat on the International Rugby Board Council (1894–97).

Joining Maclagan on that 1891 tour was William Wotherspoon (born Aberdour, 1868–1942). A former pupil of Fettes College, he had only played one game as half back for Scotland and the ink was hardly dry on his BA from Clare College, Cambridge, when he got the invitation. Three tries in that first game – a 14-0 drubbing of Ireland – to give Scotland the Triple Crown might just have helped his selection! He more than justified his selection by scoring four tries in the first two matches against provincial teams and playing a key part in defeating the national XV in the three test matches. On his return to Britain, he played for West of Scotland and was again selected regularly for the national team but switched from half back to centre. Between rugby fixtures he was a schoolmaster, before becoming a barrister in Alfred Nobel's explosives company in London.

Although he was born and brought up in Greenock and graduated from St Andrews University, James Bridie (1857–93) had the rare distinction of playing for Wales in 1891. It was only a single cap (against Ireland, when he scored a try) because when the Welsh tried to field him for their following away match against Scotland, the home team objected and he faded from the international scene rather rapidly.

Public schoolboy, varsity blue and champion heavyweight boxer David Bedell-Sivright (born Edinburgh, 1880–1915) was a giant personality of Scottish rugby at the turn of the century. In the boisterous aftermath of one international match in 1907, he is said to have rugby-tackled a runaway carthorse in Edinburgh's Princes Street. Scotland won the first encounter. The horse won the second. After Fettes College (where he captained the First XV) and Edinburgh University (where he captained the First XV), he went to Trinity College, Cambridge (where he won four blues and captained the side in the annual Varsity Match) and caught the eye of the Scottish selectors. He won the first of 25 caps in 1900, toured South Africa with the British Isles XV in 1903 (under the captaincy of fellow Scot Mark Morrison) and, in 1904, he skippered the tour to Australia. He broke a leg after the first test and thereafter captained the side from his wheelchair. He was obviously well looked after there and so he decided to settle Down Under. Within the year, however, he was bored. He returned to Britain to read medicine at Edinburgh... and play some more rugby, of course; he was captain of the university team, 1907–09.

In between, he found time to win the Scottish Amateur Heavyweight Boxing title in 1909, which made him all the more intimidating as a rugby forward. At the outbreak of the war, he became a Royal Navy surgeon and was posted to Gallipoli for the Dardanelles Campaign. While he was serving an advanced medical unit in the frontline trenches, he received an insect bite. Unusually for him, he complained of excessive tiredness. He had contracted septicaemia and was taken to the nearby hospital ship, where he died two days later and was buried at sea. He was 35.

It was another Scot who led the British Isles XV tour of South Africa in 1903, only a year after the turmoil and bloodshed of the bitter Second Boer War. Mark Morrison (born Dalmeny, 1877–1945), an East Lothian farmer and former pupil of the Royal High School, had already captained Scotland on nine occasions when he was asked to take the lead in proving that rugby could help mend fractured international relations. He had led Scotland to a second Triple Crown in 1901 so he was perhaps best placed of the home countries' skippers, but there was still plenty of competition. His team, drawn from all four home countries for the first time, included the current captain of Ireland, a future captain of England and two future captains of Scotland (David Bedell-Sivright and Louis Greig). Despite all that power, it was the fired-up South Africans who made most of the running. They drew the first two tests and won the third to take the test series for the first time. On his return to Britain, Mark Morrison assured the RFU that the South Africans 'were ready to come to the Mother Country to measure up against the might of the four Home Unions.' He went on to win a total of 23 Scottish caps and was elected President of the SRU for the 1934–35 season.

Louis Greig (born Glasgow, 1880–1953) was another larger-than-life player. After his glittering rugby career, he went on to become Group Captain Sir Louis Greig KBE, CVO, friend, equerry, mentor and tennis partner of King George V. After the 1903 tour he captained Scotland and, in 1906, he claimed revenge for the 1903 games when his formidable Scottish XV became the only home side to beat the touring Springboks. The son of a city merchant, he read medicine at Glasgow University and after qualifying spent his early professional years as a doctor in the Gorbals. He joined the Royal Navy in 1906 and played rugby for the Combined Services. It was at the RN College that he met and befriended Prince Albert. They were shipmates on HMS *Cumberland*, when he was the ship's surgeon. At the outbreak of war in 1914, he transferred to the Royal Marines and was captured during the fall of Antwerp. He was held by the Germans for eight months before being released in a prisoner exchange. When he joined HMS *Malaya* in 1917, he helped cure Prince Albert's ulcers. He was formally appointed equerry and the two joined the RAF in 1919, the same year he partnered the prince in a doubles match at Wimbledon. He is said to have encouraged the prince, then Duke of York, in his romance with Lady Elizabeth Bowes-Lyon. He later became a friend of fellow Scot Ramsay McDonald (see chapter 5, The power) and gave him advice during the formation of the National Government. He was knighted in 1932. Four years later he was elected chairman of the All England Tennis Club at Wimbledon.

Another former pupil of Fettes College, Herbert Waddell (born Erskine, 1902–88) was capped as fly half in 1924 and toured with the Barbarians and the Lions. He went to Glasgow Academy before switching to Fettes (where he captained the first XV) and later completed his education in France. During the Second World War, he was commanding officer of the 11th Highland Light Infantry and was mentioned in dispatches. Unusually for a player, Waddell was elected to the Barbarians' committee in 1926, became vice president in 1956 and president in 1973. He played in Scotland's first Grand Slam winning team in 1925.

The captain of that side was farmer George MacPherson (born Newtonmore, 1903–81), always shown as *GPS MacPherson* on team sheets. He had first distinguished himself on the playing fields of Fettes College and Oxford University, where he won a blue, before earning his first cap in 1922. He played 26 internationals between then and 1932 but none can have been more satisfying than the final game of the 1925 season. Scotland had already beaten France, Ireland and Wales when they faced England at the newly opened Murrayfield before a 70,000-strong home crowd. As always, the team had the spectators on an emotional roller coaster. At the interval, they trailed 5-11. Then, after a piece of beautiful open play engineered by GPS, they scored a try to reduce the deficit to 10-11. After a dramatic drop goal gave them a 14-11 lead, they had to dig deep to resist the English pack for the final ten minutes. The following year, he took Scotland to a share the Five Nations Championship with Ireland in 1926 and again in 1927, and to an outright win in 1929. He later became vice president of merchant bank Kleinwort Benson (1961–69). In a 2001 poll, he was named in Scotland's all-time greatest XV (see later in chapter) and voted Scotland's greatest ever attacking player.

Another member of the 1925 Grand Slam team was John Bannerman (born Glasgow, 1901–1969), who won a record 37 caps and played in every international between 1921 and 1929, including championship wins in 1926, 1927 and 1929. He was a farmer and later a Forestry Commissioner (1942–57). He was also a Liberal politician who narrowly missed election on several occasions, but was made a life peer in 1967 and took the title Lord Bannerman of Kildonan. The son of a Hebridean post office worker, he was educated at Shawlands Academy and Glasgow High School, the University of Glasgow (where he took his BSc), Balliol College, Oxford (where he won a rugby blue) and Cornell University in America. He was president of the Scottish Rugby Union, 1954–55.

Few are given the accolade of having the match named after them but Robert Wilson Shaw (born Glasgow, 1913–79) earned that for the part he played in Scotland's famous Triple Crown win against England in 1938. After his commanding performance in 'Wilson Shaw's Match' at Twickenham, his team-mates carried him off the pitch on their shoulders. He was a former pupil of Glasgow High School and after scoring a try to help win the 1934 Calcutta Cup, he played wing, centre and half back in his 19 internationals.

One of the outstanding players of the post-war years was Douglas Elliot (born Stow-of-Wedale, Borders, 1923–2005), another farmer, who played for Edinburgh Academicals. He won the first of 29 caps in 1947 and captained the side in seven matches. He was selected for the Lions but had to withdraw because of his farming commitments. In a 1999 poll in *Scottish Rugby*, he was voted the second-best Scots player of all time (behind only Andy Irvine). When he died in 2005, the *Scotsman* carried a tribute from BBC commentator Bill McLaren: 'Douglas was the kind of player who made you proud to be Scottish and brought great respect for Scottish rugby. I remember playing against him once in a Scottish trial and I'd taken the ball at a lineout and felt these great big arms of steel wrap around me. I honestly felt paralysed and it was a moment when I realised how strong you had to be to play rugby at that level. I am often asked about players from different times and it is very difficult to know how players might have performed with different teams and in different styles of rugby but with Douglas there was no doubt. He was a player who would have graced any Scotland team of any period and would have stood out in it.'

Ewen Fergusson (born 1932) won his blue at Oxford and played five games for Scotland in the 1950s before moving on to a highly successful career in the diplomatic service, which culminated in his service as British ambassador to Paris, 1987–92. Known more formally as Sir Ewen Fergusson, GCMG, GCVO, he was also ambassador to South Africa (1982–84) and a senior mandarin at the Foreign Office (1984–87). He was Chairman of Coutts private bank (1993–99) and the Savoy Hotel Group (1994–98), chairman of the governors of Rugby School (1995–2002) and a trustee of the National Gallery (1995–2002).

There were just four Scots on the Lions 1950 tour to New Zealand and Australia: Gus Black, Ranald Macdonald, Grahame Budge and Peter Kininmonth. Gus Black (born Dunfermline, 1925), who played at scrum half for Edinburgh University, won only six caps between 1947 and 1950. During that time, he had four different partners and didn't seem to click in the international squad and, despite being called up by the Lions, he won no further caps. Ranald Macdonald (1928–99), centre for Edinburgh University, won only four caps and scored a winning try in the single test match he played on the tour. Grahame Budge (1920–79), a prop with Edinburgh Wanderers, also played in only a single tour match. He won four Scottish caps.

Peter Kininmonth (1924–2007) only managed to play for the third XV when he was at Sedbergh School but went on to captain Scotland as well as play for the Lions. When he left Sedbergh at 18, halfway through the Second World War, he joined the Indian Army and served with 3rd Gurkhas in Bangalore. Two years later he went to Italy and fought in Assisi and the Arno Valley and returned to the North-West Frontier in 1947, where he saw action against Afghan tribesmen. It was only after all that that he finally returned to the UK to read history at Oxford at the ripe old age of 23. He also took up rugby again and won two blues. He toured Argentina with the varsity team and was said to have met Eva Peron! When he left Oxford, he opted to join the less-glamorous Richmond club and did well enough to win his cap in 1949 and scored a try in the memorable 6-0 win – their first in 21 years – over France at Colombes. During the Lions tour, he played in more than half of the matches, including three of the four New Zealand tests. When he retired from rugby, he went into the City as an insurance broker. He was High Sheriff of Greater London in 1979/80, a patron of the Glyndebourne Opera Festival and chair of the 1992 British Olympic Appeal.

Scotland had a miserable patch in the early 1950s and I hope I'll be forgiven for quickly glossing over 17 defeats in a row between 1951 and 1955. Things picked up in time for six Scots to be included in the party for the Lions 1955 tour (the first by air) to South Africa and Rhodesia: Arthur Smith, Allan Cameron, Tom Elliot, Hughie McLeod, Ernest Michie and Jim Greenwood.

Arthur Smith (born Castle Douglas, 1933–75), who also captained the Lions on a second tour of South Africa in 1962, was a wing of extraordinary talent. While he won his blue at Cambridge and played in four of the annual Varsity matches (1954–57), he also found time to first take a first class degree in mathematics and then a PhD at Gonville and Caius College. He won 33 caps for Scotland. When he captained the Lions in 1962, he played in the first three test matches but injury forced him to miss the last game. He also played for the Welsh club Ebbw Vale and it was said that on one occasion he played for them under a different name because those selected for the Lions were banned from playing after Easter. Would a gentleman be so deceitful?

Allan Cameron (born Glasgow, 1924–2009), who played his club rugby with Hillhead High School FPs, won just three Scottish caps before being invited to join the Lions tour. He captained Scotland in their 14-8 defeat of the Welsh at Murrayfield before a crowd of 60,000. Tom Elliot (born Galashiels, 1926–98) also made his debut in that game. He was a Gala prop and won 14 caps. Hughie McLeod (born Hawick, 1932), who played his club rugby for his home-town team, made his debut as a Scottish lock in 1954 against France at Murrayfield and went on to win a record 40 caps as the cornerstone of the scrum, before retiring from international rugby in 1957. Lock Ernest Michie (born 1933), who played for Aberdeen University , also made his debut in that Paris match and went on to win 15 caps.

Jim Greenwood (born Dunfermline, 1928–2010) won 20 caps (1952–59) and captained Scotland in 1957, when they beat France 6-0 and Wales 9-6. He was a towering six foot two in the back row. He won his first cap in 1952 when he was still at university and playing for his local club team but his somewhat stuttering rugby career illustrates the essential difference between the amateur and professional game. He was a master at Trinity College, Glenalmond and he wasn't able to play club rugby after his return from South Africa. Despite that and although seldom managing more than a dozen games a year, he continued to captain Scotland and led them to a famous victory over the Wallabies in 1958. Sadly, his international career was brought to an abrupt end the following year after a serious injury in the match against Ireland. He took up coaching and was regarded by many as the most influential rugby thinker of the time. His book, *Total Rugby* (first published 1978), is still a much-read manual. Former All Blacks coach Wayne Smith is quoted as saying: 'It took maybe 20 minutes to recognise that Jim's way of coaching was the most effective I'd come across. When I became the All Blacks coach I was into his methods, helped by his books.'

When he wasn't playing rugby for Kelso and Scotland, Ian Hastie (born Kelso, 1930–2009) was boxing for the Army or playing international darts for New Zealand! Educated at Kelso High School, where he played for the 1st XV, the Harlequins and the senior club, he then went on active service with the Cameronians in Malaya. While there, he took up boxing and became the Army's Far East light heavyweight champion. When he was demobbed, he returned to become a stalwart of the Kelso team in the 1950s and early 1960s. He was captain 1954–56 (and played alongside his brother Arthur) and the Kelso RFC Centenary book described him as 'the ideal build for a prop and, apart from being a scrummager, was most useful in the loose.' He won his first cap as prop and occasional hooker in 1955 when he helped Scotland end an unhappy period of defeats with wins against both Ireland and Wales. He didn't play again until 1958, when he scored a try in an 11-9 victory over France. He emigrated in the 1960s to work as a carpenter with New Zealand railways. There he took up darts and was good enough to be selected for the international side.

Only five Scots made it onto the Lions party for the 1959 tour of Australia, New Zealand and Canada: Hugh McLeod, Ken Scotland, Gordon Waddell, Ken Smith and Stan Coughtrie.

A pioneer attacking full-back, Ken Scotland (born Edinburgh, 1936) roared across the firmament for me in 1959 when he was a 23-year-old slip of a lad, weighing a mere 11 stone, I seem to remember. He scored a hat-trick of tries in his first game against the formidable Hawke's Bay (the oldest club outside the UK) and then went on to score another nine. A New Zealand sports magazine described him the player 'most likely to win a match for his side'. Another said he was 'the supreme counter-attacker of his age' and Sir Terry McLean wrote that he 'floated like summer down through the New Zealand defence.' Colleague Arthur Smith said he was 'the best passer of a ball I have played with' and when Irish full back and Lions captain Tom Kiernan was asked to name the greatest player of his time, he replied instantly: 'Ken Scotland. It was a privilege to be on the same field as he was.' He played 27 games for Scotland (until 1965) and also played for the Barbarians. He gave up international rugby when 29 because his job took him to Aberdeen.

Gordon Waddell (born Glasgow, 1937–2012) was a Cambridge University fly half with a reputation for being cool under pressure, but the demands of his business cut short his burgeoning rugby career in his mid-20s. He made his first of 18 appearances for Scotland in the cauldron of Twickenham in front of a crowd of 70,000 in 1957. He trooped off in the side that lost 16-3 to England. Ken Smith (born Edinburgh, 1931) also made his Scotland debut in 1957, but his was in a very tight match at Murrayfield, with Ireland winning 5-3. He played at an international level until 1961 and won 18 caps. He was president of the SRU, 1994–95.

At six feet one and a half inches, Stan Coughtrie (born Hamilton, 1935) was

Scotland's tallest scrum half. He first played for Scotland in the winter before the Lions tour and went on to win ten more caps.

As deft with the artist's brush as he was on the rugby field, Adam Robson (born Hawick, 1928–2007) played 22 games for Scotland (1954–60). He painted delicate watercolours as well as playing as a bruising blindside flanker. He was one of six debutantes in the 1954 team that at last brought Scotland out of the shadows. They lost 3-0 to France at Murrayfield but put on such a spirited performance that they were applauded off the pitch by the French. He quickly became a key figure in those transformative years for Scotland and, in 1957, he was invited to join the Barbarians on their first overseas tour, to Canada. They won all six games and he went on to play a dozen more matches, became a committee member of the club and served for 20 years. He was 57 when he played his last game for the Edinburgh Borderers. He was the first president of the Scottish Schools Rugby Union in 1967, vice president of the SRU (1981–83) and president in the 1983–84 Grand Slam season. In his other life as an artist he exhibited at the Royal Scottish Academy and the Royal Scottish Watercolourists, and was a member of the Society of Scottish Artists. He moved to Dollar Academy in 1956, where he was a boarding housemaster (1963–69) and head of art (1968–88).

When the Lions toured South Africa in 1962, again six Scots won their place in the travelling party, perhaps because of the influence of the captain Arthur Smith. The others were Gordon Waddell and first-timers Ron Cowan, Mike Campbell-Lamerton, John Douglas and David Rollo. Cowan, Campbell-Lamerton and Douglas all made their Scotland debut in the 1961 game against France (when they lost 11-0). Ron Cowan (born Selkirk, 1941) scored one of the Lions' three tries in the final test match of the tour but it wasn't enough to stop the Springboks winning 34-13. He won five Scottish caps before switching to play rugby league for Leeds in 1962. He played in the Rugby League Cup Final.

Mike Campbell-Lamerton (1933–2005) was a giant of a man with the personality to match. Standing at six feet and five inches and weighing somewhere around 17 stone, he had a distinguished rugby career playing in the second row or at No 8 for Halifax, Blackheath, London Scottish, the Army, the Combined Services and the Barbarians as well as the Lions, who he captained in the 1966 tour to Australia and New Zealand. He joined the army in 1952, initially for National Service, but stayed on to become a colonel in the Duke of Wellington's Regiment. He served in Korea, where he narrowly escaped death after stepping on a mine during the Battle of the Hook in 1952. Three years later he was in Cyprus during the EOKA campaign when he suffered serious back and leg injuries after falling 60 feet out of a combat helicopter. Further evidence of his astonishing resilience is in his recovery from having a javelin in his chest when he was a 15-year-old schoolboy.

He played rugby at every opportunity and his selection for Scotland in 1961 was almost inevitable, as was his captaincy in 1965. He retired from rugby after the Lions'

1966 tour to concentrate on his army career. He commanded a battalion in Northern Ireland and then became commander of Victory College at Sandhurst. When he left the army in 1985, he was bursar at Balliol College, Oxford. He died of cancer in 2005.

John Douglas (born 1934), who played No 8 for Stewart's Melville FP, won 12 caps, with his final match being the 3-0 home victory over Ireland in 1963. Considering he didn't take up rugby until he was 20, David Rollo (born Cupar, Fife, 1934), proved a formidable front-row forward glorying in the nickname of 'Prince'. While attending Bell Baxter High School his preference was for football, but he went on to win 40 caps, equalling Hugh McLeod's record. He missed only two games in the nine years 1959-68. The Fife farmer also captained the Barbarians and joined Scotland's tours of South Africa in 1960 and Canada in 1964.

The 1964 season marked another much-needed turning point for Scottish rugby as the national side had its best results since a distant 1938! The Calcutta Cup was snatched from the glue-like grasp of England (for the first time in four years), the French were beaten 10-0, the Five Nations Championship was shared with Wales and the mighty All Blacks were held to a 0-0 draw at Murrayfield (the last international game in which no points were scored).

One of the key figures in each of those games was full back Jim Telfer (born Melrose, 1940). He made his debut against France, scored a try in the England match and was outstanding against the All Blacks, the Irish in Dublin and Wales in Cardiff to become one of the most influential personalities in Scottish rugby over the next 40 years. He has been quoted as saying he became a rugby player because of geography: he grew up in a small village in the Scottish Borders between Melrose and Galashiels: 'If I'd been brought up even 20 miles away, I probably wouldn't have played rugby.' He did play rugby, of course, in some style and with great success, but it may be that Jim Telfer's major contribution has been in his coaching talents. He played his club rugby for South of Scotland and Melrose, won 25 caps between 1964 and 1970 and joined two Lions tours – to Australia and New Zealand in 1966 and South Africa in 1968, when he captained the party. He later said playing in New Zealand was a key influence in his rugby life. It convinced him that the Scottish team could not hope for consistent success unless it developed a distinctive style as recognisable as that of the All Blacks. He spent most of the next 40 years trying to ensure that that was what happened.

His record of outstanding success is well chronicled and needs no repeating here, but I can't resist recording a little from his most famous pep talk (as reported in the *Times*) to the Lions pack just before they faced South Africa on their 1997 tour. He had been the forwards' coach and he urged them: 'This is your Everest, boys. Very few ever get a chance in rugby terms to get to the top of Everest. You have the chance today. To win for the Lions in a test match is the ultimate but you'll not do it unless you put your bodies on the line... every man jack of you for 80 minutes. Defeat doesn't worry me... it's performance that matters. If you put in the performance, you'll get what you deserve... no luck attached to it. They don't rate you. The only way to be rated is to stick one on them... to get right in their faces... turn them back... knock them back. Outdo what they do. Out-jump them, out-scrum them, out-ruck them, out-drive them, out-tackle them until they're sick of you. It's an awesome task you have and it will only be done if everybody commits themselves now. You have to find your own solace, your own drive, your own ambition, your own inner strength because the moment's arrived for the greatest game of your f***ing life.'

The Lions won that game 25-16 and the test series 2-1 and the newspaper added its own comment: 'Jim Telfer epitomised the true Lions spirit, whether he was commanding troops on the field or bellowing instructions off it.'

Three players from London Scottish and three from The Borders were in the 1966 Lions tour to Australia and New Zealand. Mike Campbell-Lamerton was captain of the squad which included his London Scottish teammates Stewart Wilson and Sandy Hinshelwood, Hawick player Derrick Grant, and the Melrose pair, Jim Telfer and Frank Laidlaw.

Stewart Wilson (born 1942) won his 22 caps as full back between 1964 and 1968 and captained Scotland on four occasions. He also played for Oxford in the 1963 and 1964 Varsity matches. On the tour, he played in the second international against Australia and in all four against the All Blacks, scoring a record-breaking 30 points.

Sandy Hinshelwood (born 1942) played 21 games for Scotland as a wing between 1966 and 1970 and scored five tries. He scored a try in his second test against the All Blacks. He also went on the Lions 1968 tour to South Africa but didn't play in the tests.

Derrick Grant (born Hawick, 1938) was a flanker who won 14 caps between 1965 and 1968. He was Hawick's most successful ever coach and, in the 1970s and 80s, led the club to five consecutive first division championships. He also coached Scotland during the 1980s.

Frank Laidlaw (born Hawick, 1940) was Scotland's hooker in 32 games (1964–71) and twice captained the side. As well as the Lions tour to Australia and New Zealand in 1966, he toured South Africa with the Barbarians in 1969. His elder brother, Peter, also captained Scotland and his father, John, played goalkeeper for the Scottish soccer team.

Six Scots joined the 1968 Lions tour to South Africa (and Rhodesia and South West Africa), two veterans – Jim Telfer and Sandy Hinshelwood – and four debutants – Rodger Arneil, Gordon Cornell, Jock Turner and Peter Stagg.

Rodger Arneil (born Edinburgh, 1944) won 22 Scottish caps and was called up as a replacement for both the 1968 series and the 1971 tour to New Zealand. In South Africa, he had an outstanding run and played in all four test matches. In 1971, he played in five matches. He is yet another product of Edinburgh Academy.

Gordon Connell (born Edinburgh, 1944) was also a late replacement scrum half after having earlier made his debut and scored a spectacular drop goal for Scotland in a tight 6-8 defeat by England at Murrayfield. He played his club rugby with London Scottish and won four more caps. He has a special, if small, part in rugby history: his injury in Paris in 1969 was followed by the game's first substitution!

Jock Turner (born Hawick, 1943–1992) played his club rugby with Gala and won 20 caps between 1966 and 1971. His debut was in a tough, tight match in Cardiff, when Wales won 8-3. He played at fly half, centre and full back.

Peter Stagg (who was actually born in Twickenham, 1941) was the world's tallest international at a towering six foot ten. When he made his Scottish debut in 1965 he dwarfed even the mighty Mike Campbell-Lammerton (six foot four)! He played club rugby with the English side Sale.

GOLF

Hard by, in the fields called the Leith Links, the citizens of Edinburgh divert themselves at a game called golf, in which they use a curious kind of bat, tipt with horn, and small elastic balls of leather, stuffed with feathers, rather less than tennis balls but of a much harder consistence. These they strike with such force and dexterity from one hole to another that they will fly to an incredible distance. Of this diversion, the Scots are so fond, that when the weather will permit, you may see a multitude of all ranks, from the senator of justice to the lowest tradesman, mingled together in their shirts, and following the balls with utmost eagerness.

— *Tobias Smollett, writing in 1771*

Down the centuries people all over the world have played games of sorts with a stick and a ball of sorts. It would therefore be daft to enter into an argument about who created golf and when. The earliest Scottish reference to a set of what are recognised as specially made clubs is when James IV commissioned a Perth bow-maker in 1582. When he later took the unified British crown in 1603, one of his early appointments was William Mayne, of Edinburgh, as royal club-maker with an exclusive licence 'throughout the Kingdom.' Mayne hand-carved the club heads from beech or fruit wood and spliced them into ash or hazel shafts to achieve a kind of whip effect. He then began adding lead at the back of the head and thin sections of leather or horn on the club face. His balls were hand-stitched leather usually filled with wet feathers. He was able to produce only four a day and it was estimated that each ball – costing five shillings each – would last two rounds. Good business although that was, he wasn't as lucky as a later holder of the royal warrant. James Melville of St Andrews was given a licence for 21 years and he was allowed to stamp his name on every ball so that any other ball used 'anywhere in the Kingdom' would be confiscated! Mary, Queen of Scots, continued the royal patronage and is said to have been the first woman golfer, around the middle of the sixteenth century. Suffice to say, therefore, the game has been played on the links of eastern Scotland and nurtured for a very long time (as confirmed above by Tobias Smollett, the surgeon turned writer) and it's from there it has been raised to the great game played and loved (and sometimes hated) by millions around the globe, often on courses designed by Scots.

The rules of today's international sport still have their roots in the Royal and Ancient Golf Club of St Andrews (founded in 1754) and much of the game's structure and style was established in the mid-nineteenth century by an extraordinarily large number of singular players from the Fife town. When you see their names on all the early trophies, you can see that St Andrews has truly earned its title as 'the home of golf.' One of the best players, certainly the best known, was Allan Robertson (born St Andrews, 1815–59). Although he was the first to break 80 on the St Andrews course, he doesn't appear to have competed in – let alone won – any of the major championships. Instead, he contented himself playing in individual challenge matches and exhibitions games – for money! He was effectively the first professional at a time when golf was then largely a game for the well-heeled amateur. Clubs were still handmade and very expensive, and access to playing courses was limited. Apart from matches in which he bet on his prowess – and never lost – Robertson also acted as a caddie and developed a reputation as an expert maker of clubs and balls (in the company set up by his grandfather). He was so highly regarded that when he died in 1859 – after an attack of jaundice and aged just 44 – the R&A took the unprecedented step of issuing a statement commending his contribution to golf (and raising a collection for his widow). His fellow players had regarded him as the country's champion golfer and they decided that the only way to determine his replacement was to have a competition. So, the year after his death, they established the Open Championship. The first venue in 1860 was Prestwick, and the Ayrshire course (the first to be purpose-built, in 1850) played host for ten years. Scots – mainly from St Andrews and Musselburgh – dominated the event for most of the first 40 years.

Initially, just eight professionals took part and the first winner was another pioneer player, Willie Park of Musselburgh (1833–1903). He won again in 1863, 1866 and 1875. His fascination with the game began when he was still a toddler and he became a caddie as soon as he was able to carry a full bag – which was when he was ten! He too later combined club-making with challenge matches. His brother Mungo Park (1834–1904) took the title in 1874 and then his son, Willie Park Junior, won in 1887 and 1889. Mungo had played golf as a lad but went to sea for 20 years and didn't start playing seriously until 1872, two years before he became Open champion on his local course in Musselburgh at the ripe old age of 43. After his win, he contented himself with teaching, club-making and then designing courses. Willie Park Junior (born Musselburgh, 1864–1925) was born to the first Open champion and born to be a double Open champion himself. More importantly, perhaps, he followed in his father's footsteps in taking on all comers in regular challenge matches. One of the most remarkable of these was in 1899 when he played Henry Vardon, then three-time winner of the Open, on the North Berwick course. Extra trains had to be laid on for what turned out to be a crowd of more than 10,000!

He also wrote *The Game of Golf*, the first book by a professional. He then turned his hand to course design and produced around 170, including Sunningdale in Berkshire.

When the Parks of Musselburgh weren't winning the Open, it was the Morrises of St Andrews. Father Tom – forever known as Old Tom Morris – won in 1861, 1862, 1864 and 1867. In the following four tournaments, the winner was his son – inevitably, Young Tom Morris. Old Tom (1821–1908), had been an apprentice to Allan Robertson before becoming green-keeper at the R&A. He was runner-up in the first Open and the oldest winner – at 46 – when he took his fourth title in 1867. To this day he is still the oldest winner of the championship. In 1862, he won the Open by 13 strokes and held the record for the biggest margin of victory in a major championship right up until 2000, when Tiger Woods won the US Open by 15 strokes. In addition to his playing skills, he was regarded as the finest green-keeper in the world. It was he who recognised the full importance of the putting surface and he turned green preparation into a fine art. When he turned to course design, he did it in grand style. He standardised the length of the course at 18 holes – nine out and nine back to the clubhouse. Before that, some courses had up to 23 holes and the last could be anywhere! Perhaps less popularly, he was the first to devise bunkers as deliberate obstacles. His work as a course designer includes Prestwick, Carnoustie and Muirfield. The 18th hole at St Andrews Old Course is named in his honour and he is buried in the city's cathedral grounds.

When his son, Young Tom (1851–75), won the Open in 1868, with a round that included the first hole-in-one in a major tournament, he really was young: just 17! This, too, is a record that still stands at the time of writing. To prove it wasn't a fluke, he went on to win it three more times (including in 1869, when his father was the runner-up). In the 1870 Open, he scored the first recorded albatross (and there's a monument on the Prestwick course to commemorate it). So prodigious was his performance that he was allowed to keep the original Championship Belt after his hat-trick. The replacement trophy was the famous Claret Jug, and after his fourth win in 1872, his was the first name to be inscribed on it. When he and his father teamed up to take on all comers in a series of challenge matches for side bets, they were unbeatable. There is no telling what the young man might have achieved in golf. During a game against Willie and Mungo Park, he received a telegram saying that his pregnant wife was ill. By the time he got home, she and their newborn baby were dead. He never recovered: on Christmas Day, 1875, he died of a broken heart. He was just 24.

The man who broke up the family affair that the Open had become was Andrew Strath (born St Andrews, 1836–1868), although he had learned the finer points of golf under the eagle eye of Old Tom Morris. After being frustratingly close in the preceding years (when he came third, fourth and second), he finally won the Open in 1865, and succeeded his mentor as green-keeper at Prestwick in the same year. When the championship was played at St Andrews in 1873, it was won by Tom Kidd (1848–84), a local man and former caddie at the R&A. His cash prize was £11. He too died young – of heart failure when he was 36. Bob Martin (born St Andrews, 1848–1917) was runner-up in the 1875 Open at Prestwick and then won it the following year by default. In 1876, he and Davie Strath were tied after 72 holes but Strath didn't appear when the play-off was called and the title was handed to Martin. Just to prove that he had been a worthy winner, he went on to take the title for a second time at St Andrews in 1885.

Another hat-trick winner (one of only four) was Jamie Anderson (born St Andrews, 1842–1905). He won the Open at Musselburgh in 1877, Prestwick in 1878 and St Andrews in 1879. Anything Jamie Anderson could do, so could Musselburgh-born Bob Ferguson (1848–1915), and he notched up three Open victories in 1880, 1881 and 1882. He picked up a prize of £7 for his first win! Having started caddying when he was eight, he won his first prize when he was 18. His career was cut short when he was struck down by typhoid fever but he recovered well enough to become the Custodian of the Links at Musselburgh.

Willie Fernie (born St Andrews, 1857–1924) had one hand on the Claret Jug in 1882 but was fended off by Bob Ferguson and had to wait until the following year. Even then, he had to suffer the agonies of a play-off with Ferguson before he could call himself champion. He found himself in that frustrating second place again in 1884, 1890 and 1891. He was the club professional at Royal Troon for 37 years and was also a successful course designer. He made significant alterations to his local course, St Andrews Old Course, and created Turnberry's Ailsa and Isle of Arran courses.

Jack Simpson (born Earlsferry, 1858–95) was one of six golfing brothers. He was a one-off Open winner at Prestwick in 1884 and didn't have another high finish in any tournament. His card, however, was notable for the nine on the par four second hole!

David Brown (born Musselburgh, 1865–1930) was the accidental winner of the 1886 Open. Although he was an enthusiastic golfer, he didn't take the game too seriously. He was a slater by trade and was actually working on the Musselburgh clubhouse roof just before the club hosted the championship.

For some reason, the club secretary not only invited him to play but also kitted him out to look the part! In fairy-tale style, he confounded the professionals… and won. He promptly decided to abandon his trade and moved to England to be a club professional. He continued to play and do reasonably well in the Open – well enough to move to America at the turn of the century. In the 1903 US Open, he tied with Willie Anderson after 36 holes but then lost the play-off. He had the same bad luck on the stock market. He was a keen investor and lost all his money in the Wall Street Crash of 1929.

Jack Burns (born St Andrews) was the club professional and green-keeper at Warwick GC when he won the 1888 Open at St Andrews, but that wasn't enough to stimulate his career and the next time he returned to his native town, it was to work on the railways. Hugh Kirkaldy (born St Andrews, 1865–1894) won the 1891 championship played over the Old Course in particularly rough weather. He had an unusually high winning score of 166 for 36 holes, beating off his brother Andrew and Willie Fernie by two shots. He died three years later from lung disease. He was 29.

After Young Tom Morris, the next youngest Open winner was Willie Auchterlonie (born St Andrews, 1872–1963), who took the 1893 title, just 24 days after his twenty first birthday. Having begun his career as an apprentice club-maker, he became honorary professional to the R&A for more than 20 years. Sadly, that was his only major win, but his brother Laurie won the 1902 US Open. St Andrews still boasts an Auchterlonie golf shop.

It was the remarkable James Braid (born Earlsferry, Fife, 1870–1950), who made the running in the early part of the twentieth century. He won the Open five times – in 1901, 1905, 1906, 1908 and 1910 – and was one of the founders and first captain of the Professional Golfers' Association in 1901. He was captain for five years between 1901 and 1910, won the PGA Matchplay title four times and the French Open in 1910. He had been involved in golf since he left school and was a club-maker before becoming a full-time professional player in 1896. When he retired from tournament golf, he became the club professional at Walton Heath GC in Surrey and also established himself as one of the world's great course designers, credited with creating the dog-leg fairway. His masterpieces include the King's and Queen's courses at Gleneagles and the 1926 remodelling of Carnoustie. There is a James Braid Golfing Society based at Brora in the Highlands, near Dornoch.

Breaking up the Braid sequence was Sandy Herd (St Andrews 1868–1944), the club professional at Huddersfield Golf Club (1892–1911). He won the 1902 Open at Hoylake after a particularly tense final round. He had a three-shot lead but posted what seemed an ignominious 81 for the final 18. Hot on his heels were Harry Vardon and James Braid. They both had puttable chances on the last green to force a play-off. They both missed. Herd's Open appearances spanned 50 years, from when he was 21 to his last match at St Andrews in 1939, when he was 71. His brother, Fred, won the 1898 US Open.

Jack White (born Pefferside, East Lothian, 1873–1949) also rained on James Braid's parade, by winning the Open in 1904 at Royal St George's, Sandwich. He was a farm worker's son who had begun working as a caddie when he was ten. From his late teens he was the professional at the North Berwick Golf Club in the summer and at York Golf Club in England in the winter. He moved to Sunningdale, Berkshire in 1902 and stayed there for 25 years.

After James Braid's fifth win in 1910 there was something of a barren period for Scottish golfers until 1920 and the first Open to be staged since the outbreak of war in 1914. It was played at Deal in Kent and it was won by George Duncan (born Methlick, Aberdeenshire, 1883–1945). He was a former carpenter who had turned down an offer to play professional football for Aberdeen to pursue his golfing career as the pro at the Stonehaven Club. He had established himself before the war by winning the Belgian Open in 1912 and the French Open and the PGA Matchplay title the following year. He went on to win the French Open again in 1927 and added the Irish title the same year. In 1920, he and James Braid represented Scotland in an unofficial needle match with England's JH Taylor and Abe Mitchell at the Bedford and County club. It was a dour struggle with the lead changing hands three times. On the final hole, the Scots were ahead by a single stroke but victory was snatched from them when Mitchell put his tee shot two feet from the pin and sunk the birdie putt to halve the match. The following year, Duncan and Abe Mitchell – described by *Vanity Fair* as the New Mandarins of Golf – toured America in a series of exhibition matches that attracted crowds reportedly totalling 250,000. When he got back home – as the current champion golfer of Britain – he took part in the first international match with the United States at Gleneagles in 1921. It shows the imbalance between British and the American golf at the time that the British team won 9-3!

Despite their loss, the Americans – including twice US Open champion Walter Hagen – clearly enjoyed the occasion, although it took until 1926 before another match was staged at Wentworth. This time the British won even more decisively, 13-and-a-half to one-and-a-half, with the single US win coming from Scot-turned-American Tommy Armour. Among the guests in the clubhouse after the match was the seed merchant and golfing enthusiast Samuel Ryder. Over tea, George Duncan said it was a pity the match wasn't an official event and suggested to Ryder that he provide a trophy and persuade the establishment to make the match official and regular. The Ryder Cup was born.

James Braid was one of three selectors for the Great Britain team and George Duncan played in the first match at Worcester Country Club, Massachusetts in 1927. The Americans, now playing with intense seriousness, won by nine-and-a-half to two-and-a-half. George Duncan captained the team for the home match (in Leeds) in 1929 and became the first Briton to claim the trophy after a hard-fought 7-5 win, in which he won his match against Walter Hagen.

The last of the St Andrews-born players to win the Open (until Paul Lawrie in 1999) was Jock Hutchison (1884–1977) but he had arrived at the tournament – ironically held on his native heath at St Andrews – via America, where, like several other leading golfers, he had taken US citizenship, and thus lifted the trophy while wearing the stars and stripes on his shirt and cap. Having won the PGA Championship the previous year, he succeeded George Duncan to the title in 1921. On his return to America, he was given a hero's welcome. The *New York Times* of 9 July 1921 carried the headline 'Famous golf pro comes laden with laurels' and a breathless commentary on the victory which, the paper said, 'was achieved in spectacular fashion.' It was. Until the final round, the Scottish-American was trailing another émigré, Cornish-American Jim Barnes (who later in the year won the US Open) 'but at the close, Jock started a streak of brilliancy that carried him through. A hole-in-one, one of the few times that such a thing has happened in the championship, was the feature of his play.' With one bound, our hero – or rather *their* hero – was level with Barnes at the end of the 72 holes. Initially, he faced a three-way play-off but there was more drama. The third player should have been British amateur Roger Wethered, until he was penalised after stepping on his ball at the last hole. The *Times* reported, 'in the play-off with Barnes, Hutchinson was an easy winner.'

With prescience, the *New York Times* reported in another article about the growing strength of US golf as represented by Jock Hutchinson, now a fully-fledged American in their eyes: 'It is expected that American golf affairs, which have been struggling along as best they could without our leading stars, will proceed to boom and the scene of activity shift from the land over which John Bull holds domain to the one over which Uncle Sam presides.' As for Jock Hutchinson, he went on to win the first PGA Seniors Championship in 1937 and again in 1947 (when he was 63). After that, he suffered the heartbreak of play-off defeats on three further occasions. The last of these was in 1951, just before his seventieth birthday. He shot a three-under-par final round to level with Al Watrous, the defending champion, but sadly he tired during the nine-hole play-off and lost by six shots.

The last Scottish player to win the Open was the dashing Edinburgh-born Tommy Armour, who added the 1931 title to his long list of major wins, including the US Open, won four years earlier. The golf writer, Charles Price, described him as having 'a dash of indifference, a touch of class and a bit of majesty.' More correctly Major Tommy Armour, late of the Black Watch and the Tank Corps and veteran of The Great War, he was of the stuff of heroes. With his prematurely-grey hair, he was dubbed the 'Silver Scot' and showed as much grit on the golf course as he had done on the battlefields of France. He had enlisted as a 20-year-old private in the Black Watch soon after the war started in 1914. His public school background (Fettes College), his Edinburgh University degree and his natural leadership qualities saw him rise quickly through the ranks. En route, his bravery was recognised in several mentions in dispatches. In June 1918, he transferred to the Tank Corps, which was then playing a crucial front-line role in the Allied attack. He escaped death narrowly when his tank took a direct hit. He was one of only two survivors. Not long afterwards, he was caught in a mustard-gas attack and was blinded, suffered skull damage and a seriously wounded left arm. Perhaps Armour's most heroic effort was his fight to recover. He got the sight back in one eye but remained permanently blinded in the other. A small metal plate covered the head injury and his arm was partly repaired with the insertion of another plate, but nonetheless left much weakened. On the face of it, he must have seemed an unlikely champion golfer.

However, he was back on the golf course soon after he left hospital and by 1919, he was again competing in international amateur events. He won three competitions, including the 1920 French Amateur Championship. Later in the year he decided to take his new wife (they had been married less than a year) to America, where he took a job as a travelling salesman, but still found time to enter and win a Pro-Am tournament at Pinehurst Fall. In 1921, he played for the winning British team in the match with US amateurs that proved to be a precursor for the Walker Cup event that took off the following year. The next year, he became an American citizen.

In 1925, Armour turned pro and joined the lucrative US professional golf tour, from his berth as the pro at the Congressional Country Club in Washington. His first couple of years can't have been especially lucrative because his only serious wins were the 1925 Florida West Coast Open and the 1926 Winter Pro Championship. All that changed in 1927. He stormed through an astonishing season in which he seemed to conquer all before him. In a few short months he broke the single-season record by winning the Opens at Long Beach, El Paso and Oregon as well as the Canadian Open and, of course, the US Open. Anyone suspecting that all that might have been a fluke was proved wrong when he again swept the board in 1928, adding the Metropolitan Open, Philadelphia Open, Pennsylvania Open and the Sacramento Open to his astonishing tally. In 1930, he took the PGA title after beating Gene Sarazen (who had won the US Open when he was just 22) at Flushing, New York. He had to wait until 1931, however, for what he regarded as the Big One: *the* Open Championship, held for the first time at Carnoustie, where the official starter was no less a figure than the Prince of Wales.

The Silver Scot didn't get the best of starts. He struggled to keep pace with the field and at the end of the third round he was trailing the leader by five strokes – but then, he was no stranger to heroic fight-backs. Encouraged by the Scottish onlookers, who still regarded him as one of their own, he put together a string of birdies that saw him overtake the flamboyant Henry Cotton and draw level with Argentina's José Jurado on the seventeenth. He won the final hole and the championship by a single stroke. It was a dramatic and fitting end to what proved to be his last major tournament. In *The Story of American Golf*, Herbert Warren Wind wrote of his competitiveness and staying power: 'Whenever the Silver Scot played himself into a contending position, he always seemed to have that extra something that was the difference between barely losing and barely winning. He was singularly unaffected by the pressure of the last stretch. His hands were hot but his head was cool.' When Armour's head finally told him it was time to give up the competitive game in 1935, he turned his hand to teaching golf at a club in Florida, writing instruction manuals and designing clubs.

Tommy Armour was not the first Scot to think the courses were greener on the other side of the Atlantic, as a browse through the early winners of the US Open shows. Right from the time the competition was launched in 1895, there was, almost inevitably, a man from St Andrews among the initial 11 competitors: Jim Foulis (1870–1928).

When you set out to record Jim Foulis's performance, the first thing you find is that you have to use the word 'first' a remarkable number of times. He was certainly a golfing pioneer. He emigrated in 1895 to become America's first club professional, in charge of America's first 18-hole course, at Chicago Golf Club. Possibly because he had only just arrived after a long sea voyage, he only managed to finish third in that first US Open but he entered the record books the following year after claiming first place. This time there was a field of 35 and he finished three strokes ahead of the previous year's winner. He was third in 1897 but didn't manage another top-ten finish and turned his attention to developing the sport in America. He ran Chicago's golf shop with his brother, Dave, and played a pioneering role in the development of equipment. He invented a superior surface pattern for the new rubber-core ball, produced the first mashie-niblick (today's 7 iron) and designed the first courses in the midwest. He had, of course, served the perfect apprenticeship under the eagle eye of his father, the foreman in Old Tom Morris's golf shop and club-making business.

Much as they were keen to learn at the hands of the Scots, the Americans were not always their usual hospitable selves towards them. When Fred Herd (born St Andrews, 1874–1954) became the second Scot to win the US Open – the fourth tournament, at Myopia Hunt Club, Massachussetts in 1898 – he had to pay a deposit before he was allowed to take away the trophy! A club professional in Chicago, Herd had a reputation for heavy drinking and the organisers were afraid he might pawn the silverware to buy booze so they held onto his $150 prize money until it was returned. He did return it the following year and got his deposit back, but he was unsuccessful in three further appearances in the tournament. He was the brother of Sandy, who won the British Open in 1902.

Having thus established a grip on the coveted trophy, the Scots were clearly determined to hold on to their premier place in world golf and proceeded to dominate the US Open for most of the following ten years. In 1899, Willie Smith (born Carnoustie, 1865–1916) won it in grand style. He finished 11 strokes ahead of the field, a record margin that was only beaten by Tiger Woods in 2000. His prize money was $150. In the same year and after a play-off with fellow Scot Laurie Auchterlonie, he won the first Western Open.

Smith had emigrated to take up the professional's job at the Midlothian Country Club just outside Chicago. He played in eight more Opens and although he was in the top ten finishers in seven of them, he never managed another win. He moved south of the border in 1904 to become the pro at the Mexico City Golf Club. Ten years later, he was caught up in the Mexican Revolution of Emil Zapata and was wounded during an attack on the club, which was seen as a symbol of the corrupt ruling class. His wound led to pneumonia and he died in 1916. His body was sent back to Scotland for burial in Carnoustie.

Having been runner-up to Willie Smith in 1899, Laurie Auchterlonie (born St Andrews, 1868–1948) came back to win the US Open at Garden City, New York, in 1902 with a record four-round total of 307. It was the first time 80 had been broken in each round and that was partially attributed to the use of the new rubber-core ball. Having previously won the 1901 Western Open, he went on to have seven top-ten finishes in 11 further US Opens.

Willie Anderson (born North Berwick, 1879–1910) won the 1901 US Open but I've inserted him a little out of sequence because of his subsequent astonishing record of taking the title three times in a row: in 1903, 1904 and 1905. It's a record that still hasn't been bettered. Hailed as the greatest golfer of his generation, he also finished in the top five seven times (from just nine more US Open appearances) and that has been equalled only by Jack Nicklaus. He also won the second US major, the Western Open, four times in 1902, 1904, 1908 and 1909. In the 1902 event, he broke the US record when he was the first to score less than 300 in a 72-hole competition). After his 1904 win, he became the only one ever to hold the two major titles simultaneously. When he wasn't creating records and destroying the opposition in the majors, he earned his living as a club pro (and was said to be the highest paid in the sport), playing exhibition matches (in which he invariably won a lucrative pot), designing clubs (his woods were the first example of an autograph-brand) and giving lessons (for handsome fees).

Educated at the local school in North Berwick, he became a licensed caddie on the West Links when he was 11. When he left school he was apprenticed as a club maker in Gullane. Then, when he was still only 16, he emigrated to America to become the pro at a Rhode Island club. Within a year, he was able to oversee the extension of the local course to 18 holes (fellow Scot, Willie Park Junior, had laid out the first nine the previous year). Then he moved to New York, from where he played in his first US Open, in 1897, and finished just one stroke behind the winner. He changed his club jobs regularly, sometimes going to work in Florida in the winter months, and was known to have worked as a green-keeper in California. In June 1910, he returned from his winter in Florida to take up the position of head golf pro at the inappropriately-named Philadelphia Cricket Club and helped prepare it as the venue for that year's US Open. In October, he played a series of exhibition matches in Pittsburgh.

The day after the final round, he had an epileptic fit and died. He was 30.

The Smiths of Carnoustie made the US Open something of a family affair in its early days. Big brother Willie won in 1889 and Alex (1872–1930) took the title in 1906 and then held off his brother Macdonald to repeat the feat in 1910. Alex Smith first came close to winning the Open in 1906, when he ended the final round tied with the redoubtable Willie Anderson. He lost in the play-off. He had much better luck at Lake Forest, Illinois, in 1906. He rattled off a 72-hole record total of 295, the best at any major to that date. When he won it again in 1910 (on the Philadelphia course so carefully prepared by Willie Anderson and his staff), it was only after a three-way play-off yet another golfing Smith brother, Macdonald, and the teenage American John McDermott. Alex played in a total of 18 US Opens, had 11 top-ten placings, won the Western Open twice and the Metropolitan Open four times.

The Scottish grip on the trophy remained firm when Alec Ross (born Dornoch, 1881–1952) won the 1907 Open, held again on the Philadelphia Cricket Club course. He had emigrated to become the professional at the Brae Burn Country Club near Boston, before moving to the Detroit Country Club, where he stayed for 31 years. He certainly gave the members there terrific value for his wages. He competed in 17 US Opens (and had five top-ten finishes) and his long run of other tournament wins included the North and South Open six times (1902, 1904, 1907, 1908, 1910 and 1915), the Massachusetts Open six times (1906, 1907, 1908, 1909, 1910, 1912) and the Swiss Open three times (1923, 1925, 1926). His brother, Donald, was one America's most successful course designers.

At all of five feet four inches, Fred McLeod (born North Berwick, 1882–1976) holds the unofficial title of the US Open's smallest ever winner. He weighed in at less than eight stone when he won the Open at South Hamilton, Massachusetts in 1908, after fending off the redoubtable Willie Smith in a tense play-off. Fred became a postman when he was 14 and when he was old enough joined the local golf club, whose members played on the public links. Although he hadn't won anything of note by the time he was 21, he did feel confident enough in his game to follow in the footsteps of so many other Scots golfers. He emigrated to America in search of a professional's job. Within weeks of arriving, he was a club pro in Illinois and took part in his first US Open. He wasn't placed but clearly enjoyed the experience and was a regular over the next 22 years, during which he had five top-ten finishes and that 1908 win. Although a further Open title continued to elude him, he chalked up significant successes: the 1909 and 1920 North and South Opens, the 1912 Shawnee Open, the 1924 St Petersburg Open, the 1927 Maryland Open. He played in both the 1921 and 1926 US-Britain challenge matches that led to the annual Ryder Cup competition. He also played in the first four Masters (1934–37) and such was the affection in which he was held by fellow professionals, he was later the honorary starter at the Augusta event from 1963–76. In 1937, he helped form the senior division of the PGA and won the second PGA Seniors' Championship in 1938. When he died at 94, he was given the unique honour of being buried at the Columbia Country Club, the last club at which he had worked as a professional.

After the Smith family struggle of 1910, it was another 15 years before the Scots were able to re-impose themselves and to win the 1925 Open. In that year Willie Macfarlane (born Aberdeen, 1890–1961) had to play an epic 108-hole match against Bobby Jones, a previous winner and one of America's early greats. He looked to have it sewn up when he produced a championship record of 67 in the second round, but he was caught on the last green and went into an 18-hole play-off. They both shot 75 and they then had to go round another 18 holes. Willie squeaked it by a single shot after the longest game in the Open's history. He was clearly hooked on the competition and made a total of 17 appearances but managed only one other top-ten placing. He made up for it in other competitions, however, winning 21 titles on the PGA circuit.

The thirteenth and last Scottish winner of the US Open was Tommy Armour in 1927, although it must be said the Americans regard that as a US victory because of his citizenship. In my book, however, he was still an Edinburgh man. His capture of the trophy came at the end of his best season to date and was achieved at the Oakmont Country Club in Pennsylvania. Yet again he did it the hard way – from behind. He was a stroke adrift of Harry Cooper (an Englishman who had also taken US citizenship) at the end of the third round but drew level in the final round to force a play-off. That went to 18 holes before he won by three strokes. A week later, he discovered just how cruel golf can be to even the best players. In the Shawnee Open, he shot the highest-ever score for a single hole. On a par five, he took 23 strokes, 18 over par! The scorers had to dig deep to find the name for it and settled on 'archaeopteryx' (the first bird known to man), cruelly used for scores of 15 or more over par. He must have been sorely tested by his oft-quoted philosophy: 'It is not solely the capacity to make great shots that makes champions but the essential quality of making very few bad shots.'

It is not recorded what he did with his clubs. Despite that, his book – co-written with Herb Graffis in 1952 – *How to Play Your Best Golf All the Time* is the best-selling playing guide in history.

In all, Scots won 13 of the early US Opens, with Willie Anderson clearly the most outstanding player. His four wins rank him alongside Bobby Jones, Ben Hogan and Jack Nicklaus and he is the only one among them to have won three in a row as previously recorded. In the league table of successes, Scotland (with 13 wins) is second only to the United States (with 80). Since those halcyon days, there have been a fair number of excellent Scottish golfers – from John Panton (who died in 2009) to Colin Montgomerie – but they are fewer and farther apart and their exploits will have to feature in the next edition of the Scottish Empire.

Boxing

For a small country like Scotland to produce seven world champion boxers is truly remarkable but considering the physique of the average Scot, it's more surprising that all of them fought at less than ten stone. In fact, five of them fought as flyweights (eight stone) and the other two at lightweight (nine stone nine pounds). Don't be fooled by the size or their weight, however. While they don't have the clout of the heavyweight, these are some of the toughest men ever to have clambered into the ring. Scotland's first world champion – in 1928 – was Edinburgh-born Johnny Hill, who powered his way to the British, European and World titles in just 18 months. Benny Lynch slugged his way out of the Gorbals and the fairground booths before becoming world champion in 1935. Jackie Paterson from Ayrshire claimed his title in 1943, after less than a minute in the ring. Soon after Walter McGowan from Hamilton won his title in 1966, he was uniquely awarded a Lonsdale belt after a single defence because there wasn't anyone in the world strong enough to take him on. Ken Buchanan took his title in 1970, after 15 gruelling rounds in the searing heat of Puerto Rico. Jim Watt, the Glasgow southpaw, defended the title he won in 1979 a record four times and beat more than half his opponents by a knock-out. Pat Clinton snatched the title from the defending champion, Mexican Isadore Perez, in a 1992 bout that was so torrid his manager refused a rematch with the retort: 'The Mexicans didn't offer a re-match at The Alamo!'

Johnny Hill's story is tragically short. Only months after winning his 1928 world title, he died from a blood clot after a bout of pneumonia. He was 23. One of the few middle-class fighters of the day, he had a sparkling career as an amateur. His father was a former boxer and so he was brought up on a tough training schedule that totally excluded smoking and drinking. He joined the Leith Victoria Club stable of Tancy Lee (the first Scot to win a British flyweight title when he stopped the great Jimmy Wilde inside the distance in 1915) and had almost instant success, winning both the Scottish flyweight and bantamweight titles by the time he was 19. Two years later, in 1926, he won the British flyweight title at the ABA Championships in London's Albert

Hall and was awarded the Best Boxer of the Championship trophy. Soon afterwards, he turned professional and thrilled the upmarket crowds at the National Sporting Club in London. One of his keenest fans was the then Prince of Wales (later Edward VIII and then Duke of Windsor), who visited his dressing room. In less than a year, he was the British champion, months after that European champion, and completed the set with the world title in 1928. He won a points decision after 15 tough rounds with the American Newsboy Brown on 29 August 1928. Less than a year later, he caught a chill while out on a training run. It rapidly developed into pneumonia, which caused the clot that killed him. His funeral was held on the day he should have been defending the title, in June 1929.

On its website, the BBC rates Benny Lynch (born Glasgow, 1913–46) alongside earlier champion, 'Mighty Atom' Jimmy Wilde, as the 'Best of British' flyweight boxers. Sadly, like Jimmy Hill, he too died young and from pneumonia, but his illness was brought on by alcoholism. He learned his drinking where he learned his ring-craft: in the rough, tough boxing-booth circuit, where he slugged it out with all comers often regardless of their weight. Mercifully and before he suffered too much damage, with the country still in the grip of the great recession, he turned professional when he was 18. He celebrated his graduation by winning the Scottish title in 1934. In March 1935, he fought Englishman Jackie Brown, the reigning British, European and world champion, to a 12-round draw that ensured an early rematch for the titles. Watching the film of that fight in September 1935 is a harrowing experience. Despite being stick thin and all of five foot five, he was on the attack from the bell and within seconds he knocked Brown to the canvas, then floored him again with a ferocious left hook less than a minute later. In today's boxing, the referee would almost certainly have declared the bout over then, but on that occasion he didn't, and in the first two minutes of the second round, Brown was hit so hard and so often that he was down for no fewer than six counts before the referee finally stepped in to declare Benny Lynch the world champion. He was still only 22.

As was the bewildering custom of the day, the Americans were not exactly quick to acknowledge his new status and despite 100,000 Glasgow fans giving him a tumultuous reception, he wasn't able to put his primacy beyond dispute until he out-pointed the Filipino Small Montana, in 1936. The following year, he took on the up-and-coming 19-year-old English boxer, Peter Kane, who was being hailed as the heaviest hitter among flyweights since Jimmy Wilde, and who went on to become world champion himself. The fight was hyped by the newspapers, with one describing them as the most destructive flyweights in the world. That encouraged a massive 40,000 crowd in the Glasgow Shawfield Stadium arena. They were told the two would 'tear into each other like wildcats.' Benny Lynch must have read and believed the papers. He stormed out of his corner and assailed his opponent with the classic hook to the body and a right uppercut and hammered him to the canvas. Somehow Kane survived the count and made it to the end of the round. After that, it was an exchange between the experience of the champion and the raw courage of the teenager. The result was never in doubt. At the bell for the start of the twelfth round, Benny Lynch clearly decided enough was enough. He battered the contender to the floor twice and had him holding on to be saved by the bell. He finished it in the thirteenth, brutally and clinically. A left hook sent Kane crashing to the canvas. He struggled to his feet after a count of seven and was immediately floored again by another hammer blow. This time he wasn't able to beat the count. The fight was described as 'the best flyweight contest of all time.'

After reigning as world champion for three years, Lynch was robbed of the title not by a better opponent but, ironically, by alcohol-induced weight problems…ironic because he died of malnutrition only eight years later. In his last fight in defence of his title, he actually knocked out the American contender in the twelfth round but then was disqualified because he was found to be a half-pound over the eight-stone weight limit. Keeping his fighting weight subsequently proved too much of a problem and he retired the following year at the ripe old age of 25! He battled for the rest of his life with alcoholism and its disastrous side effects. He was still popular around Glasgow and was never short of an enthusiastic fan eager to buy him a drink, which he of course couldn't refuse. Eight years later, the combination of alcohol, pneumonia and malnutrition proved too much for his weakened system. He died in abject poverty in 1946. *The Ring* magazine described him as 'the greatest fighter that Scotland has ever produced.' He was inducted into the International Boxing Hall of Fame in 1998.

The same Peter Kane who had suffered so badly at the hands of Benny Lynch fared no better with Jackie Paterson (born Ayrshire, 1920–66), the first southpaw to win the World Flyweight Championship. Paterson took the title from him in a brutally brief 61-second encounter in the cauldron of Glasgow's Hampden Park in 1943. Jackie Paterson's route to the top was tough but well-managed. He started boxing at the Anderston Club in Glasgow when he was 13. He worked briefly in the Clydeside shipyards and then in a butcher's shop but turned professional as soon as he could – at 17. His first pro fight, in Greenock in 1938, was won in ten rounds. Over the next two years, he fought at the now unthinkable rate of once a month and won a remarkable 17 of his 18 bouts around Scotland, Northern Ireland and the north of England. Orthodox boxers couldn't cope with his southpaw stance or his lethal two-handed punching. His record won him a crack at the British flyweight title in 1939, in front of a Glasgow crowd, and he grabbed the chance and disposed of the defending champion, Paddy Ryan, with a knock-out in the thirteenth. He had joined the RAF at the outbreak of the war but was able to continue with his boxing and in 1940 he took the Commonwealth title after a points decision against the holder. Both titles were on the line when he had a rematch with Paddy Ryan at Nottingham in 1941. He won after the referee stopped the fight in the eighth round to save Ryan from further punishment.

Paterson had a stocky figure and in a weight division where every ounce counts, he had constant difficulty making the eight-stone limit. He decided to have a go at bantamweight but failed in an attempt to win the Commonwealth title and promptly returned to his original flyweight. After winning the world flyweight title in 1943, he again defended his British title and succeeded in taking a prized Lonsdale Belt (Britain's oldest boxing trophy, awarded for three championship wins). In 1945, he again drifted up to bantamweight and this time he did take the title; a year later he added the European bantamweight belt but lost it in the rematch, which saw him knocked out in the fourth round. In early 1947, he took the British bantamweight title with a tough scrap in which he had the defending champion on the canvas four times before knocking him out in the seventh round. Later in the year he scored a fifth-round knock-out victory in defence of both his British and Commonwealth bantamweight titles.

Like Benny Lynch, he didn't so much lose his world flyweight title as give it away: in July 1947, he put so much effort into making the weight for a defence fight that he collapsed at the weigh-in. He was stripped of the title. During his career he was estimated to have earned around £100,000 – about £3 million by today's standards. While a fair amount would have gone on management and other costs, all too much of it went to the bookmakers: he had an addiction for greyhound racing! When he finally retired from the ring he went to live in South Africa, where he ran a hotel. When that didn't work out, he became a lorry driver. In 1966, he was hit with a broken beer-bottle during a drunken brawl. He died from his wounds. He was 46.

MOTOR RACING

In the high-octane world of motor racing, Scotland has produced two Formula One champions – Jim Clark won the title twice, in 1963 and 1965, and Jackie Stewart went one better by winning in 1969, 1971 and 1973 – plus a fair number of race winners in the fastest sport on earth.

Jim Clark (born Kilmany, Fife, 1936–68) is very firmly established in the annals of his sport and so much has been written about him that I need do little more than acknowledge his astonishing record which, the *Times* has said, made him 'the greatest of all Formula One drivers.' He was certainly the dominant figure of his era. In taking the titles in 1963 and 1965, he won 25 Grand Prix races, more than any other driver up to that time, and had taken pole position 33 times, also more than any other driver. He was second in the 1962 championship and third in 1964 and 1967. He also competed in the gruelling Indianapolis 500 five times and became the first driver to win that and the world championship in the same year. He was second in 1966, as he had been in his debut in the race in 1963, when he was named Rookie of the Year.

He started racing in his teens – despite his parents being decidedly against the idea – driving his own Sunbeam Talbot in local rallies and hill climbs. His first major competition was in 1956, when he drove the German-made DKW Sonderklasse at the Crimond circuit in Aberdeenshire. By 1958, he had joined the Border Reivers team, raced Jaguar D-types and Porsches and won 18 races in the season. In one race he was second behind Colin Chapman, founder of Lotus Cars; it was then he was invited to join the famous marque and a brilliantly successful partnership was born. In the Lotus 25 he won his first Drivers' World Championship in 1963. He won seven out of the ten races and that also gave Lotus its first Constructors' World Championship. The following year, he was within a few laps of retaining his crown but an oil leak robbed him of the title. He roared back and won the championship again in 1965, and also the Indianapolis 500 in the Lotus 38. In his Indianapolis 500 win, he was in front for 190 of the 200 laps and drove at a record average speed of more than 150 miles per hour to become the first non-American winner in nearly 50 years. His last race was not in Formula One but in Formula Two. In a Lotus 48, he veered off the track at the Hockenheimring and smashed into the trees. He suffered a broken neck and a skull fracture and died before he reached the hospital. As a tribute to his closest friend, Colin Chapman changed the traditional green-and-yellow Lotus badge to black for a month. When teammate Graham Hill won the 1968 World Championship, he dedicated it to Clark. There is a life size statue of him in Kilmany, the village where he was born.

The first Scot to win a major F1 event was Innes Ireland (born Mytholmroyd, Yorkshire, 1930–93), who was driving for Lotus when he took top spot in the American Grand Prix in 1961. He was a dashing hero who sent young Scots' hearts pulsing with pride, but although he had twice beaten Stirling Moss in the previous season, he lost his place in the team only weeks later – to Jim Clark. He retired soon afterwards and became sports editor of *Autocar* magazine. He later took part in the London-Sydney Rally and wrote a book about it – *Marathon in the Dust* – in 1970. After that, he ran a small trawler out of Kircudbright, but resumed his journalism in the mid-1970s. He was president of the British Racing Drivers Club from 1992 until his death in 1993.

The flag-blue livery and the saltire emblazoned on the panel-work were the epitome of national pride when the Ecurie Ecosse made its F1 debut at the British Grand Prix in 1952. Behind the wheel of the team's Cooper T20 was founder David Murray (born Edinburgh, 1909–73), proprietor of a garage and motor showroom in Merchiston Mews, Edinburgh. Sadly, it was only the start of what was to be the team's ill-starred participation in Formula One: he had to retire early in the race because of engine problems. In the 1953 race, Jimmy Stewart (elder brother of Sir Jackie) drove the Cooper but spun off the track and Ian Stewart (born Edinburgh, 1929) in the second car, a Connaught A-type, had to retire with engine problems. In 1954, Leslie Thorne (born Greenock, 1916–93) did drive the Connaught all the way round... but had intermittent ignition trouble and finished unplaced. He later competed in several non-championship events but resumed his career as a chartered accountant. With that, the Formula One dream finally ended for David Murray and his partner and mechanic Wilkie Wilkinson.

However, undaunted, they switched their attention to sports-car events – and with dramatic results.

At the first attempt, Ron Flockhart (born Edinburgh, 1923–62) and co-driver Ninian Sanderson (born Glasgow, 1925–85) stormed to a famous victory in the 1956 Le

Mans 24-hour race in an ex-works Jaguar D-type, and this against the multiple teams from each of Ferrari, Aston Martin, Mercedes-Benz and Jaguar! Ron Flockhart was a professional (with 14 F1 drives behind him) but Ninian Sanderson was a car dealer with a bent for driving sports cars. Proving that it wasn't beginner's luck, Ron Flockhart and Ninian Sanderson split up for the 1957 event – and finished first and second! Flockhart's co-driver was Londoner Ivor Bueb (who had won in 1955 co-driving with Mike Hawthorn). Ninian Sanderson took the lead in the second Ecurie Ecosse car, with Jock Lawrence (born Cullen) as co-driver. First and second places in the world's greatest endurance test was an amazing achievement and the Ecurie Ecosse team tried in vain to repeat that success each year until it ran out of money and withdrew from competitive racing, after the 1962 event.

Among those who have driven for the Ecurie Ecosse marque at one time or another are Jack Brabham, Innes Ireland, Jim Clark and Jackie Stewart.

Following the death of David Murray, the team was disbanded in 1971 but the name was revived in the 1980s by Hugh McCaig, who organised and ran motor racing at the Ingliston circuit just outside Edinburgh and he continues as patron of the team. Even at school, Hugh McCaig had been a racing enthusiast, running the motoring club at Fettes College. In 1951, one of his coups was to persuade David Murray to bring the famous Ecurie Ecosse trailer and the flag-blue Jaguar D-type to the school! Under his patronage, the team won Group C2 at the World Sports Car Championship and developed the factory Aston Martin AMR1 team. It also won the British Touring Car Championship for Vauxhall and helped support some of Scotland's most successful modern racing drivers including F1's David Coulthard and 2007 Indianapolis 500 winner Dario Franchitti (born Bathgate, 1973).

The fastest Scot on two wheels was Bob McIntyre (born Glasgow, 1928–62), who broke the one-hour motorcycle speed record (147 miles) at Monza in 1957. The same year, he became the first to complete a lap at more than 100 miles per hour, winning both the Junior and Senior titles at the Isle of Man Golden Jubilee TT races. The following year he again won the Isle of Man 350cc race, was second in the 500cc and second in the Ulster Grand Prix. In 1959, he won the Isle of Man 500cc. In 1960, he was first in both the 350cc and 500cc at Mallory Park and first in the 350cc at Oulton Park. In 1961 he took first in both 350cc and 500cc in the North West 200 event and at the Ulster 250cc Grand Prix, but had to retire in the Isle of Man 250cc event when he was leading in the last lap. Soon after winning the Belgian Grand Prix in 1962, he was seriously injured in a crash at the Oulton Park circuit and died nine days later in hospital. He was 33.

CRICKET

Cricket has never been especially popular in Scotland but even so, it has thrown up the occasional world-class player... very occasional, it has to be said. But there was Leslie Balfour-Melville (born Edinburgh, 1854–1937). He was an opening batsman and wicket-keeper and had the glory of captaining Scotland to victory over Australia in 1882! Sadly, it hasn't happened again.

In those days of 'gentlemen and players' LBF was definitely a gentleman – an amateur who played for the love of the game. He led by example: he hit a remarkable 73 against what even then was a ferocious Australian attack spearheaded by bowler Fred Spofforth, known as 'the Demon'. The same Australian touring side beat England at The Oval and drew at Lords, in the match that led to the establishment of The Ashes tests.

In a career that stretched over 36 years, Balfour-Melville played in 18 international matches and hit 46 centuries. He played for the MCC and touring side I Zingari (whose governors later included fellow Scot Sir Alec Douglas-Home). He was the first president of the Scottish Cricket Union to still be playing for the national side – at the age of 55. Yet cricket was only one of his sporting passions. He also played rugby and won his first Scotland cap when he was just 17, in 1872. He played golf and won the British Amateur Championship at St Andrews in 1895, when he was 45, after having been runner-up six years earlier. He played tennis and won the Scottish championship in 1879. He played billiards and was the Scottish champion in 1881. He was also a competitive skater, a curler and a long-jumper. He was president of the Scottish Rugby Union, president of the Scottish Cricket Union and captain of the R&A Golf Club (1906). In between, this consummate all-rounder was a distinguished lawyer.

My inclusion here of Douglas Jardine (1900–58) as a contender for Scottish Empire status is debatable. Some of the record books claim him as an *English* cricketer although he was born in Bombay of Scottish parents and was at one point invited to captain the Indian XI. My defence is that *he* described himself as a Scot. Undoubtedly, he was not only an England cricketer but captain of the England team during its well-reported Ashes tour of Australia during 1932–33. He was the architect of the much-discussed 'bodyline' bowling used to counter the elegant skills of Don Bradman and his Aussie colleagues.

His fierce rivalry with the Australians went back to his days playing for the Oxford University XI in 1921. He had scored 96 when the tourists' skipper refused to allow play to continue beyond the scheduled time, which would have possibly allowed him to complete his century. He was also given a rough ride when he played for England during the 1928–29 tour of Australia. It seems his Indian Raj background may have made him just a touch too much of a gentleman for the local crowds and they jeered his every stroke. Some might think, therefore, that it was poetic justice when he returned as skipper in 1932 having devised what he called his 'fast leg theory' to neutralise Don Bradman. This involved bowling short deliveries on the line of the batsman's leg stump, to a carefully set leg-side field with a leg trap. It was the press that termed it 'bodyline'. Whatever it was called and by whomever, the tactic clearly worked. Don Bradman was contained to a test series average of 56.7 (against his astonishing career average of 99.4) and England returned home 4-1 winners of the Ashes. One Australian commentator described Douglas Jardine as 'the most notorious Englishman since Jack the Ripper.' When he returned to Britain, he married Isla, the daughter of the Scottish accountant Sir Harry Peat whose company has grown into the current KMPG partnership. He gave his four children Scottish names: Fianach, Marion, Iona and Euan. When he died of cancer at the age of 57 in 1958, his ashes were scattered at Loch Rannoch.

TENNIS

On one of the hottest days on record and in the gladiatorial arena that is Wimbledon's Centre Court, in July 2013 Andy Murray (born Dunblane, 1987), won tennis's most prized trophy and title: Wimbledon Champion. What made it even sweeter was that his opponent was the man ranked above him at number one in those world rankings, Serbia's Novak Djokovic. In what turned out to be the final game, we had to suffer as three match points slithered tantalisingly from his grasp, but sheer Scottish grit and stubbornness kicked in and he recovered from Djokovic's two advantage points to finally smash his way home in straight sets: 6-4, 7-5, 6-4. He was the first British winner since Fred Perry in 1936, the Wimbledon crowds – and no doubt most of the 17 million watching on TV – were ecstatic and the commentators had a field day. Fame and fortune are secure, as is his place in the Scottish Empire.

A year earlier, Andy has shed tears of frustration as he lost to then world number one Roger Federer but made up for that when he took Olympic gold in the men's tennis singles after beating who else but Roger Federer. He was the first British tennis medallist in more than a century and he underlined his change in fortunes by also taking silver in the mixed doubles. In further spectacular evidence of his growing popularity, he came third in the BBC's sports personality of the year contest for 2012. More importantly, he gained his first grand slam title at the US Open in September of that year, and moved up to number two position in the world rankings in spring 2013. The No 1 spot gets tantalisingly closer.

7

THE COLONIALS

 'No people so few in number have scored so deep a mark in the world's history as the Scots have done. No people have a greater right to be proud of their blood.'
— *James Anthony Froude*
(19th-century English historian)

To the Scots' tally of nine British prime ministers, we can add eight more brave souls who left their native heath to seek – and find – their political fortunes in the colonies: four served in the highest office New Zealand, two Australia and two in Canada. There were also 20 others who served as premier in the state or provincial legislatures and a raft of British-appointed governors.

AUSTRALIA: THE SETTLERS

The first person to officially use the name Australia – in 1817 – was Major General Lachlan Macquarie, the Scot who had to pick up the pieces after William Bligh's benighted governorship of New South Wales, the first of the colonies down under. The career soldier, from the tiny island of Ulva in the Inner Hebrides, took up his post in 1810. His articles of appointment from Lord Castlereagh, the colonial secretary, were clear and succinct: 'The great objects of attention are to improve the morals of the colonists, to encourage marriage, to provide for education, to prohibit the use of spirituous liquors, to increase the agriculture and stock, so as to ensure the certainty of a full supply to the inhabitants under all circumstances.' Countless books and reports are testament to how well he fulfilled these instructions over the 12 years he served in office and that allows me to pass on swiftly with this briefest of acknowledgments of the 'Father of Australia.'

Australia as we know it is a relatively new democracy. It wasn't until 1901 that the six states finally came together as a federation with a single constitution, forming a new nation of about four million people. The founding fathers, inevitably including a number of Scots, knew they had a clean sheet of paper and were determined to avoid some of the defects of the old-world system. They wanted Australia to be 'harmonious, united and egalitarian.' They had progressive ideas about human rights and were idealistic in their determination to observe the democratic procedures. The Aussie role in the modern world is evidence of the quality of those early foundations. At the general election for the first federal parliament, the leader of the Free Trade party was George Reid from Johnstone in Renfrewshire. He had previously served five years as the premier of New South Wales, but after winning only 25 of the 67 seats, he had to settle for the job as leader of the Opposition. Within three years, however, he had seen off the first three prime ministers before taking the top job himself in 1904. Unfortunately, he fared little better than his predecessors and was defeated exactly ten months and 17 days later. During that time, he had relied on an uneasy alliance with the Protectionists' Alfred Deakin (who had himself been top dog briefly) and that enabled him to push through the 1904 Conciliation and Arbitration Act which established a court for settling industrial disputes. Said to be one of the most significant pieces of legislation in federal history, it embraced economic and social policy and transformed the country's industrial relations.

Reid was a son of the manse, one of seven children of a Presbyterian minister. When the family emigrated, he attended Melbourne Academy (which later became Scotch College) before moving to Sydney, where he began working as an office boy when he was just 13. He then joined the civil service and worked his way up through the system the hard way. In 1864, he started as a lowly clerk in the Colonial Treasury in Sydney, graduated to accountant and by 1878 – when he was 33 – he had become the head of the accountant general's office. Rather than settle for the civil servant's lot, however, he made a dramatic switch to the law and qualified as a barrister. Once again he found success, and went to work in the Crown Law Office as secretary to the attorney general. He then turned to front-line politics and, in 1880, he was elected as an independent to the New South Wales Legislative Assembly, where he again launched himself on an upward trajectory. Three years later, when fellow Scot Sir Alexander Stuart became the state premier, he was offered the plum job of colonial treasurer, but his memories of working as a civil servant in that department mustn't have been all that good. He turned it down and instead opted to take the less-senior job of minister for public instruction. He was a key member and helped launch the Free Trade party in 1889 to counter the forces of the protectionists, who wanted to maintain tariffs. He became leader two years later and spoke against federation at the 1891 Federal Convention, because he feared it would force New South Wales to surrender its free trade policies. In 1894, he led his party to electoral triumph and became both premier and treasurer of the state. Within two months, however, he changed his mind about federation and earned the nickname of 'Yes-No Reid.' Undeterred, he proposed a second convention to re-examine the proposals. After three meetings, a series of state referenda were staged and all came up with a Yes vote with the exception of his own state, where the majority was too small to carry weight. He promptly suggested amendments that would make federation acceptable to New South Wales and it was finally agreed in 1899. Unfortunately, in the meantime, the debate had cost him support among his own voters and he was forced to rely on Labour party backing to continue in government. That was always going to be tricky: they pulled the plug on him and he resigned in September 1899.

While in opposition, and before switching to the federal parliament, he sought to broaden the base of the Free Trade party and became an ever more vocal critic of both the Labour party and the Protectionists. In the end, he took his members into the 1906 election as the Anti-Socialist party and the year after his retirement as leader, it became the Commonwealth Liberal party (with an ideology very different to that of the British Liberals). Although he soldiered on as leader of the Opposition for three years, he delegated more and more responsibility while he rebuilt his legal practice and became a King's counsel. Soon afterwards he took up his appointment as Australia's first high commissioner in London, where he served for six years. At the outbreak of the Great War in 1914, he persuaded Lord Kitchener to have Australian forces trained in Egypt to help acclimatise them for the European winter. On the completion of his term as high commissioner, he accepted the offer of a seat in the House of Commons and he was returned unopposed for a London seat in a by-election. He died two years later, two months before the end of the war.

As George Reid was taking his leave of the Australian parliament, another Scot was emerging as a party leader. Andrew Fisher (born Ayrshire, 1862–1928), who had worked down the mines when he was just ten, became Labour party leader in 1907 and prime minister the following year, going on to serve three separate terms. His first day in office was 13 November 1908 and he decided then that he would also act as treasurer. Among his achievements were the launch of the government-owned Commonwealth Bank, the introduction of invalidity benefits and maternity allowances, compulsory accident insurance for public employees, the raising of the first Australian Imperial Force and the building of the new federal capital of Canberra. When a colleague suggested that the new federal capital be called Fisher in his honour, he laughed it off as a joke. At the outbreak of the Great War in 1914, only months after he began his third term, he reluctantly sent his soldiers to fight at Gallipoli and on the Western Front but with the ringing endorsement: 'We will defend the Mother Country to the last man and the last shilling.'

Fisher was born in Crosshouse, a village near Kilmarnock, and was one of a family of seven whose miner father was incapacitated by pneumoconiosis. The family's financial circumstances meant that, despite the law restricting child labour, he went to work in the coal mines when he was ten. His initial education was pretty cursory but he also went to night school, despite the long hours at the mine. His father and some other miners had set up a cooperative scheme (which later became the Scottish Wholesale Cooperative Society) that included a library and reading room, and the young Andrew proved a voracious reader. He also began to take a keen interest in union affairs and by the time he was 17 he was secretary of Ayrshire Miners' Union. Inevitably, that got him blacklisted as a troublemaker by his employers and that in turn led to long periods of unemployment. In the end, frustration fuelled his decision to emigrate, and he and his younger brother left for Queensland in 1885. There he found work first as a coal miner and then, in 1890, in the gold mines. He also continued his voluntary union work and when he led a strike against the conditions, history repeated itself and he was again sacked as a troublemaker. Undeterred, he deepened his involvement with the Labour movement. In 1891, he was president of the Amalgamated Miners Association and of the local branch of the Workers' Political Organisation (Labour party).

In 1893, he won a seat in the Queensland Legislative Assembly. He lost it at the next election but then regained it in March 1899. Ten months later he joined the world's first Labour government as minister for railways and public works... it lasted just six days before the government collapsed.

He moved on to federal politics and in the first general election of 1901 he won Queensland's Wide Bay seat (which he went on to retain through five elections) and, with the other successful candidates, formed the new Commonwealth Labour party. The *Australian Dictionary of Biography* says his political philosophy 'contained no concept of class warfare. His ideas were based on his background in Ayrshire, his experiences as a miner and his habits of reading and study.' Although Labour won 26 seats at the 1906 elections, he took the view that it was better for the party to continue to support the now minority Protectionist prime minister, Alfred Deakin, and he led the demands for concessions on tariffs, old age pensions and other social issues. When his own party leadership became vacant the following year, he took on and defeated two other candidates. As the Labour leader and no doubt inspired by fellow Scot Catherine Spence (from Montrose), he argued at the 1908 Federal Conference for the place of women in the Australian parliament: 'I trust that not another Federal election will take place without there being a woman endorsed as a Labour candidate for the Senate.' Catherine Spence, since named as 'The Greatest Australian Woman' and commemorated on 2001's five dollar notes, emigrated to Australia in 1839. She was a teacher, author, journalist and leading suffragette who was the country's first female political candidate in 1897.

When Deakin and his Protectionists failed to deliver on their promises on pensions and tariffs, Andrew Fisher withdrew his support and the government collapsed. By the time he took on the dual role of prime minister and treasurer in 1908, Fisher had developed a very clear picture of Australian society as having 'a labouring class and a speculating class,' quite different from the British working class-middle class divide. He also had his own solutions: they were, as the *Australian Dictionary of Biography* notes, 'to provide parliamentary reforms in banking, industrial safety, workers' compensation, land and employment and so elevate the living standard of the labourer. A graduated income tax, control of monopolies and state ownership of certain enterprises would conversely lessen the power of the speculating class.'

He also set the ball rolling on creating a new seat of government at Canberra, launched a bounty scheme to reward iron and steel manufacturers who paid fair wages, commissioned three naval destroyers and put the Australian Navy at the disposal of the Royal Navy. But the fragility of Australian politics was against him. He lost a vote of confidence in parliament and sought dissolution. He was rebuffed by the governor general but resigned anyway and was out of office for ten months. He was vindicated by voters at the general election in 1910 and his party won 43 of the 75 seats. With this mandate, he launched a three-year programme of development and reform unmatched by any government until the 1940s. In 1913, he lost the election to a Liberal party with a one-seat majority and settled down to concentrate on being an effective leader of the Opposition and waiting for the inevitability of another government defeat. That came after 15 months and he resumed the premiership for the third time in 1914. It was during that election that he made his promise to support Britain in the war and he was unlucky enough to be in charge when Australia, with other Empire countries, had to send troops into battle.

Although still only 53, the strain of high office affected his health and he stepped down for the last time in October 1915. He replaced George Reid as high commissioner in London, where he served for six years. When he returned to Australia, he resisted attempts to get him back into parliament and back at the head of the party. He went home to Britain in 1922 and died there six years later. He is buried in London's Hampstead Cemetery, where a memorial was unveiled in 1930 by Ramsay MacDonald.

Before Australia's federation (in 1901), each state had its own legislature and premier and there too émigré Scots played their parts in the development of their adopted country. Queensland, for example, can boast no fewer than seven premiers hailing from Scotland (another four were second generation Scots), Victoria has had six, New South Wales two and Western Australia, South Australia and Tasmania one each.

Queensland

Once separated from New South Wales and established as a colony, Queensland set up its own Legislative Council in 1859 and the state's second premier was Arthur Macalister, a solicitor who had emigrated from Glasgow when he was 32. He served on three separate occasions for a total of four years. After having been a member of the New South Wales parliament, he was elected for the Ipswich division of Queensland and took on an important role as chairman of committees. In March 1862 he was appointed secretary for public lands and works. He became state premier after Robert Herbert resigned. He took office in February 1866 but as was far from unusual, he did not see eye to eye with the British governor and he resigned after only six months. As was again the norm, he bounced back and resumed office after two months and went on to serve until 1868 (when he was replaced by Robert Mackenzie – see below). He reverted to his old job as secretary for public lands and works but with added responsibility for the state's goldfields. Two years later, he was elected speaker but then lost his seat at the 1871 election and was out of government for two years. He was re-elected in 1873 and the following year became premier for the third time. In 1876, he stepped down and took up the job of Queensland's agent general in London. He served for five years before failing health forced his retirement.

During Macalister's second spell out of office, he was replaced by another Scot, Robert Mackenzie, from Coul in Ross, whose term as premier and treasurer lasted 15 months. He had arrived in Sydney in 1832 with £750. He was 21 and full of enterprise. He joined his older brother James and spent two thirds of his capital buying sheep. All went well for several years until he overstretched himself buying a sheep station and speculating in land deals with money borrowed from relatives back in Scotland. He went bust and was declared bankrupt in 1844. With his enthusiasm undiminished, he worked off his debts and was discharged from bankruptcy after two years. By the following year, his reputation had been sufficiently restored for him to become a magistrate. His interest in politics led to him to being elected to the new Queensland Legislative Assembly in 1859 and, almost immediately, appointed colonial treasurer. When Arthur MacAlister resigned for the second time in 1868, he formed a government and took on the dual role of premier and colonial treasurer. He resigned on 25 November 1869. A month later, his brother died and he inherited the family baronetcy. Three years later as Sir Robert he returned to live on the family estate in Scotland.

The third Scot to become premier was Thomas McIlwraith, from Ayr. He was the state's first Conservative leader when he took office in 1879 and became one of the most dominant figures in Queensland politics over a period of quarter of a century. His first term in office lasted for four years and he then had two six-month terms in 1888 and 1893.

He graduated as a civil engineer at Glasgow University and emigrated in 1854, when he was 19. When he first arrived in Australia, he worked as an engineer with the Victoria Department of Railways, before moving on to Queensland in 1862 and developing a range of business interests. As his influence grew, he started to take an interest in politics and was elected to the Legislative Assembly in 1868. His first government appointment was as minister for public works and mines in Arthur Macalister's cabinet in 1874, but he resigned within months. When the country suffered a series of severe droughts in 1879, the government fell and McIlwraith was elected premier. He made it his priority to restore the state's fragile economy and was successful enough in developing local government and establishing better postal services.

Like other colonial politicians, he became jittery about German expansionist policies in the region, and tried to pre-empt their annexation of New Guinea in 1883. The British colonial secretary, however, decreed that he did not have the authority to annex other colonies. It was this incident that sparked off the discussion about the Australian states coming together in a federation. That same year, there were allegations of corruption over the building of the transcontinental railway. Opposition attacks had a telling impact, he was forced out of office and retired from politics in 1886, receiving a knighthood the same year.

McIlwraith came back in 1888, but only briefly. Like so many Australian politicians he had an uneasy relationship with the British governor and tried but failed to win the state's right to have a say in the gubernatorial appointments. That and his failing health were the causes for his resignation. When he returned to Australia after extended recuperative travel in China and Japan, he was again seduced back into the political arena and, almost inevitably, he allowed himself to be talked into becoming premier for the third time in 1893. The strain told very quickly and he had to step down within six months. He struggled on as the government's chief secretary for more than a year, but when the economic depression came in 1985 he lost much of his business empire and he resigned from parliament in order to try to stench the flow of losses.

The fourth Scottish premier was another Ayrshire man, Hugh Nelson, who left his native Kilmarnock when he was 18. He was educated at the Edinburgh High School and went on to read philosophy under the noted metaphysician Sir William Hamilton at Edinburgh University. His studies were cut short in 1853 when the family migrated to Queensland. Initially he worked in a merchant's office in Ipswich but then moved on to work in farming and became a station manager in the Darling Downs region and then in Dalby, about 200 kilometres from Brisbane. After new local government laws came into effect, he was elected a councillor in 1880 and soon became the chairman. He was elected to the Legislative Assembly in 1883 and five years later he became secretary for railways, serving under two premiers. He formed a coalition with Thomas McIlwraith in 1893 and became premier in the same year. He was knighted in 1896 and, when he stepped down from the premiership in 1898, he became president of the Legislative Council, and five years later he was appointed lieutenant governor of the state.

Robert Philp, twice premier (1899–1903 and for three months in 1907), was the son of a Fife mill owner. He migrated with his family to Brisbane in 1862, and went to work for a shipping company at the age of 12. He stayed with them for more than ten years until he was able to afford a partnership in a trading company that acted as agent for the sugar cane and agricultural industries. His company used South Pacific islanders as labourers and it was when the Liberal government decided to end the practice that he became involved in politics. Initially, he provided financial backing to the opposition but he was elected to the Legislative Assembly in 1886. Again, he was moved by self-interest and supported North Queensland separatists in their unsuccessful attempts to gain independence, while continuing to pursue his business interests. He was a serial speculator and in 1893 he ran up serious debts that forced him to resign from the board of his company. That gave him more time for politics and later in the year he accepted the post of minister for mines. Between then and 1899 he held a number of other ministerial posts, including in the railways, public works and treasury.

In 1899, when two premiers fell in quick succession (one lasted only a week), he was the choice of his colleagues to take over, and he was re-elected at the 1902 election.

With the economic downturn worsening, relations between ministers became fractious and he was voted out in 1903. Opposition politics didn't suit him – he didn't seem to have the stomach for attacking the government, so much so that when there was an opportunity to be re-elected premier, his colleagues wouldn't back him. He got a further chance in 1907 but, being in a minority in the Assembly, his party couldn't sustain him for longer than a few months. He did remain in the Assembly but was more than happy to hand over the Opposition leader's job so he could spend more time with his business interests. In his continuing parliamentary role, he also helped found the University of Queensland (1912), but lost his seat in 1915. He died in Brisbane in 1922.

Although William Kidston started his political life in the Labour party, by the time he became Premier in 1906, he had been responsible for reviving the Liberal party. His first term lasted about ten months, his second in 1908 ran to three years. He was the son of a Falkirk ironworker and he followed his father into the foundry as an apprentice when he was 13. After 20 years around furnaces and hot iron, he decided to look for something better. He migrated to Queensland, where he became a bookseller in 1883. It's hard to imagine anything more removed from the iron industry, but he never forgot his background.

When the state was beset by strikes, he was a volunteer in the local militia, and when he was ordered to deploy against striking sheep-shearers, he simply said no… and then had to face a court martial. The trade unions lost the battle but it drove the labour movement to aim for political representation in the Legislative Assembly, and Kidston found himself in the forefront of the campaign to repeal anti-striking laws. He joined the Australian Labour Federation (ALF) and in the fight for electoral reform he wrote a poem 'The Ballot is the Thing', which attracted extensive publicity. He was unsuccessful as a separatist candidate in the 1893 elections but then won as a Labour candidate in 1896. He found himself treasurer in that first Labour government of 1899, but the glory lasted exactly a week before it became clear that Labour couldn't maintain a majority in the Assembly. That convinced Kidston of the need to seek a wider alliance of political groups. It worked, and when a coalition gained a majority in 1903, he was rewarded by being made treasurer once more. However, his readiness to cooperate with other politicians brought criticism from some of his Labour colleagues and when the party formally endorsed a socialist programme it proved the parting of the ways.

By the time he became Premier within the coalition, he was ready to move on: he re-formed the Liberal party in 1907 and was delighted when some of his Labour friends joined him. He ran into difficulties with the Legislative Council, which rejected too much of his programme, and then with the British governor, who refused to do anything about it. He had no option but to resign and regroup. He won the next election, in 1908, and this time had established a strong enough platform to sustain him for three years. He also took the opportunity to limit the Legislative Council's powers to thwart the Assembly and introduced electoral reform and wages boards – with the solid endorsement of the Labour party. The pendulum swung the other way when he set up private railway construction and he had to seek the support of other members including former premier and fellow Scot, Robert Philp. When he called an election in 1909, his Liberal party won comfortably. His most successful fight was against the federal government, when he demanded Queensland's rights to receive customs and excise revenue and won after a long, hard battle. In 1911, he resigned to become president of the Land Court and retained that job until his death in 1919.

The last Scot to be Queensland's premier was Glaswegian William Forgan Smith (born Invergowrie, 1887–1953), whose father's intended role for him was as a Presbyterian minister rather than a Labour cabinet minister. He held the job for a then record-breaking ten years from 1932 and was one of the few in the tough Aussie milieu who was able to step down at a time of his own choosing – in 1942. Rather than go into the church as his father wanted, he took an apprenticeship with a Glasgow painter and decorator. He worked around the city's working-class areas, saw the poor conditions, especially in the shipyards, and developed a strong interest in Labour politics. He was 25 when he emigrated to Australia and settled in Mackay, about 700 miles north of Brisbane and the centre of the sugar cane industry, and resumed his involvement with the trade unions and the Labour party. Within three years – in 1915 – he was elected to the Legislative Assembly. He quickly settled into the parliamentary routine and when the Federal prime minister called for the introduction of conscription, he was one of the foremost critics. That raised his profile in the state and he was made the influential chairman of committees in 1917. Four years later, he went into cabinet as a minister without portfolio and effectively chief assistant to the premier. He moved in 1922 to become minister for public works, where he introduced unemployment benefit and earned the respect of the unions. He was also elected to the powerful Central Executive of the Labour party and in 1925, after only ten years in parliament, he became deputy premier.

After Labour lost the 1929 election, he was elected leader. That was also the beginning of the worldwide Great Depression and as opposition leader he had to work hard to hold the party together and devoted himself to winning the 1932 election. He was rewarded with a seven-seat majority and took on the role of treasurer as well as that of premier. To counter some of the impact of the economic recession and fund his unemployment relief efforts, he raised taxes on the wealthy and the business community. At the same time, he used the relief work programs to build infrastructure and other capital works projects, including an upgrade of Mackay Harbour and a new building for the University of Queensland at St Lucia (which bears his name).

He was not always popular and upset the newspapers when he introduced laws that inhibited their reporting of new legislation. They said he was 'authoritarian and dictatorial.' That was exacerbated when his Transport Act of 1938 allowed the government to declare a state of emergency in any part or all of the state, for any time and any reason, and again when the 1940 Public Safety Bill gave the government wide powers during wartime. At the same time, he was a doughty defender of the state in its constant battle with the federal government, and he resisted all temptation to move on to the federal parliament. He also maintained his general popularity through his clever use of radio to reach a wider audience. He won the 1941 election with a comfortable majority and was able to plan his retirement from politics the following year. He became chairman of the Sugar Board and chancellor of the University of Queensland.

Victoria

James McCulloch, who left Scotland in 1853 to set up a Melbourne branch of the soft goods business in which he was a junior partner, was Victoria's fifth premier and served on four separate occasions for a total of eight years between 1863 and 1871.

His government was said to be the strongest the state had experienced and he was never afraid to flex his political muscle. He was constantly in battle with the conservative landowners, who dominated the legislative council. They were free-traders. He was a protectionist. In 1865, the council not only rejected his tariff bill but also "denied supply," cutting off the government's funds. However, he just happened to be a director of the London Bank and extraordinarily was able to lend his government nearly a million pounds to cover debts and running costs. When this failed to break the deadlock, he called and won an election in February 1866. Despite a large majority in the assembly, the council again rejected his tariff bill. He resigned in frustration and left a vacuum no one seemed ready to fill. It was only after lengthy wrangling and prolonged negotiations that McCulloch agreed to resume office and the council passed a modified tariff bill and granted supply.

Born in Glasgow and with no more than a basic primary school education, he had arrived in Australia just ahead of the gold rush and his business was one of the beneficiaries of the bonanza. He made enough money to develop a portfolio of bank interests that brought several directorships and, in 1856, the presidency of Melbourne's Chamber of Commerce. He was elected to the state's Legislative Council in 1854. He was knighted in 1870, the year before he retired from the office of premier.

James Service, from Kilwinning in Ayrshire, was the state's twelfth premier. He served briefly in 1880 and then had three years in office between 1883 and 1886. He had moved to Melbourne as a salesman for a Glasgow tea-importer in 1853 but just a year after his arrival he opened his own business as an import and wholesale merchant. He was very successful and diversified across a number of businesses, including banking. Four years after arriving in Australia, he could afford to pursue his interest in politics and he was elected first to the local council and then to the state Legislative Council, where he sat as a moderate liberal and a strong advocate of free trade. He was appointed president of the Board of Land and Works in 1859 and treasurer in 1875 but his attempt to reduce tariffs was so unpopular that it caused the collapse of the government.

After five years in opposition, he stepped in to form a minority government in 1880, but he had to admit defeat within a couple of months and called an election. He lost and again was out of office, this time for three years. He bounced back in 1883 and, as was common among state premiers of the time, decided that he would take responsibility for the Treasury as well as the premiership. He had three busy years during which he brought in laws that prohibited political patronage in the public services, a new Factories Act and a new Lands Act. He also helped set the ball rolling towards federation. He carried the proposal through the Victoria parliament in 1884 but his colleagues in the other states were less enthusiastic. Once again, the strain of political office took its toll and, with his health failing, he stepped down in 1886 and died the following year without seeing the fruits of his federation proposal.

Service was succeeded as the state's third Scottish premier by Duncan Gillies, who served from 1886 to 1890. He was the son of a market gardener and left Glasgow High School when he was 14 to work in a city office. Four years later, he embarked on the long voyage to Australia and arrived in Melbourne in 1852. His first job was as a storekeeper in Geelong but he quickly moved on to become a miner in Ballarat, where the first gold had been found in 1851. It's clear he won the respect of his fellow miners because he was elected a member of the local mining court and, in 1858, a member of the first Ballarat Mining Board, which was responsible for arranging independent surveys and the all-important registering of claims. He became a partner in a working mine and as he grew more prosperous he bought shares in a much bigger holding company, took up several directorships and moved to live in Melbourne.

There, he turned to politics. He was a conservative with a small c and in 1861, when he was 27, he won a by-election to become one of the 68 members the state's Legislative Assembly. His first government job was as president of the Board for Land and Works but he held it all too briefly. Three months into his new office, the government fell in a no-confidence vote and at the ensuing election he lost his own seat. He showed his resilience by returning at another by-election in 1870. He then held a series of posts in railways, lands, surveys and works until 1875, when James McCulloch made him minister for agriculture. He reverted to looking after railways and land when James Service became premier in 1884. He was promoted to minister for public instruction (i.e. education) two years later.

When he became premier in 1886, he also took on the railways portfolio and that of treasurer, and later added mining to his personal responsibilities.

During his term, Victoria enjoyed an economic boom triggered by the gold rushes and he comfortably won the 1889 election. However, with no regulation of the banking or investment sector, things got out of hand. Land prices became inflated and boom turned to bust. As the man in charge of the government, he had to face the music: when a group of his supporters, led by James Munro, turned against him and he lost a confidence vote, he had nowhere to go. He resigned. To make matters worse, he was one of the investors hit by the recession and he had to withdraw from politics to try to put his business empire back together. When he resurfaced, he was elected speaker of the Assembly and remained in office until his death in 1903.

James Munro became the third Scot in a row to become premier, days after he led the opposition to his former friend Duncan Gillies. However, he too became embroiled in the land and property crash and had to resign within two years, as his personal business empire collapsed leaving him with – at the time – breathtaking debts of £700,000. He was declared bankrupt in February 1893 and a few weeks later he was attacked by one of his ruined investors and left unconscious in a Melbourne street.

Munro was born in Sutherland in 1832. After a village school education, he worked for an Edinburgh publisher before settling in Melbourne in 1858 and setting up a printing business. From the success of that company he expanded into banking, promoting building societies and, in 1865, he founded the Victorian Permanent Building Society, which he ran for 17 years. With his personal wealth assured, he too turned to politics and won election to the Legislative Assembly in 1874. He served briefly as minister for public instruction in the Liberal government but he stepped down when he found himself drifting to the right in political terms. He then concentrated on developing his business interests, especially in the Federal Bank and the Federal Building Society, through which he was able to reap the benefits of the land boom.

After that, he returned to politics and 1890 he emerged first as leader of the Opposition and then premier. When the financial crash came, his bank had to suspend trading. He ended deeply in debt and resigned as premier. He persuaded his cabinet colleagues to appoint him as Victoria's agent-general in London. By the time the news got out, he was already on the ship for Britain and there was an outcry from investors. His actions, they said, did not fit his reputation as a God-fearing Christian nor his earlier denunciation of Duncan Gillies. He was recalled to Melbourne. He never recovered his good reputation but he did face up to bankruptcy and when he was finally discharged, he went to work as an estate agent.

Victoria's fifth Scots-born Premier was Allan McLean, who always said his family were frozen out of the old country by an exceptionally severe Highland winter. He was a Liberal and held the top job for just a year (1899–1900) before moving on to become a member of the first Australian federal parliament in 1901. He initially worked on his father's sheep station and then dabbled a bit as a journalist for a local paper before, in 1870, he was able to take the lease on his own station on the shores of Lake Wellington.

Once established as a farmer, McLean became a local councillor and then in 1880 he was elected to the Legislative Assembly, where he sat as a conservative. His first government job was as president of the Board of Land and Works and he doubled as minister of agriculture (1890–91), before moving to become chief secretary (1891–93). In 1894, he accepted a post in the Liberal government and served for four years before falling out with the premier. After that, he moved and led a vote of no confidence in the premier, which allowed him to take his place. He had little time to establish himself and after just 350 days in office was defeated in the 1900 election. Although a declared opponent of federation, he was persuaded to stand for the new Australian parliament in 1901 and he became a supporter of the Protectionist party. Despite that, when Free Trade leader George Reid formed another minority government in 1904, he accepted an invitation to serve as minister for trade and customs. He worked so well within the cabinet that it was often described as the Reid-McLean government. He lost his seat in 1906 and as his health started to deteriorate he decided to step down from politics and refused all blandishments to return to the fray. When he died in 1911, George Reid said of him: 'No public man in Victoria was more widely or more affectionately esteemed.'

The last of Victoria's six Scots-born premiers was Jack McDonald, who served under the Country party banner from June 1950 until December 1952... except for an extraordinary four-day gap in the middle when he was temporarily unseated by an Electoral Reform candidate. Like William Kidston, he was born in Falkirk and educated at the local school. When his father died, his mother decided to emigrate and she took him and his brother and two sisters on the long voyage to Australia in 1912. He was 14. They settled on a farm at Shepparton in Victoria but were devastated by a drought that wiped out their dairy herd in 1914, just at the outbreak of the Great War in Europe. He lied about his age so that he could join the army when still underage. A year later he was serving on the Western Front with the Australian Imperial Force when he was shot in the chest and lost a lung. Still not 20, he was invalided out of the army and returned to Shepparton, where he established an orchard with his brother. He proved to be a very successful fruit grower and as his business flourished he became more and more involved with community affairs and the agricultural organisations. He became president of the local Irrigators' Association, vice-president of the Fruit Growers' Association and the Australian Canning Fruit Association and a member of the Fruit Marketing Authority. He bought shares in the new Shepparton Preserving Company, joined the board and eventually served five years as its chairman.

He also found time to be a local councillor and then in 1936, he was selected as the Country party candidate in a Legislative Assembly by-election. He won; within two years he was a party whip and later, in 1943, minister for water supply and electrical undertakings. After his party's defeat in the 1945 election, he was elected leader. In 1947, he entered a coalition with the Liberals and when they won, he became deputy premier. However, the arrangement was too uncomfortable and it inevitably fell apart. He tried another coalition – with the Labour party – in 1950 and this time it lasted for two years, apart from that hiccup towards the end of 1952. He had asked for a dissolution of parliament and when it was refused he resigned. The Electoral Reform group tried to form a cabinet but admitted failure after three days and McDonald resumed as premier, but only for a few weeks. He was defeated at the polls by Labour and his problems deepened when electoral reforms meant the disappearance of his seat. The war wounds he had hidden for so many years started causing him health problems and he stepped down at the 1955 election and resumed his business and farming interests. He was knighted for his political services in 1957.

New South Wales

Alexander Stuart from Edinburgh was New South Wales' first Scots premier when he served from 1883–85, despite suffering a debilitating stroke in 1884. After leaving Edinburgh High School, he went briefly to Edinburgh University but didn't graduate and instead went to work, first in an office in Glasgow and then in a linen mill in Northern Ireland. Something of a rolling stone, he went to India when he was 20 but the climate didn't suit him so he moved on to New Zealand and finally, in 1851, to Australia. He tried gold prospecting and didn't have much luck, but when he went to work in a Sydney bank he struck gold metaphorically, rising to become secretary and inspector of branches for the Bank of New South Wales within just two years. He consolidated his position when he investigated a case of embezzlement of funds which saw one of the branch managers sentenced to five years hard labour. (The man's father described the institution as the 'Convicts' Bank' and went to jail for six months for criminal libel.) He went on to become a partner in a merchant company and a successful man-about-town. He was also a lay member of the Anglican Synod and when he spoke out in favour of denominational schools, his bishop suggested he stand for election to the Legislative Assembly. He was elected in 1874 and again success came quickly: two years later his financial background earned him the job of treasurer. He resigned from the Assembly in March 1879 to take up the plum job of the state's agent-general in London, but his business suddenly ran into financial trouble and within a month he was on his way back to Australia to stave off bankruptcy.

Within a year, he had bounced back, returned to the Assembly at the 1880 general election, and became leader of the Opposition. Two years later, Stuart became premier. He had a bumpy ride. He overcame tough opposition to pass a land act but suffered from constant sniping about his ownership of mineral lands. The strain told and he had a stroke, after which he went to recuperate with his brother in New Zealand. He resigned shortly after his return. He was knighted in 1865, joined the Legislative Council and was appointed commissioner to the Colonial and Indian exhibition in London shortly before he died.

The only other Scot to be premier of New South Wales was George Reid, who went on to be federal prime minister in 1904 (see earlier in this chapter).

South Australia

South Australia's only Scottish premier was Dr John Cockburn from Corsbie in the Borders, who was also the first family doctor to hold the office. He served for just over a year in 1889 before succumbing to the almost inevitable no-confidence vote that was so prevalent in early Australian politics.

He took his MD (with first class honours and gold medal) at King's College London and practised for several years before emigrating in 1879 and setting up in Jamestown, where he later became mayor. When he moved up to state politics, he was elected to the South Australian House of Assembly in 1884. His progress from then on was swift. In his first term he was able to initiate land tax legislation, he was promoted to minister of education in 1885, and two years later he was premier. However, his demise was equally swift and he survived only four months before being ousted. He stayed on in the Assembly and played a key role in representing South Australia in the confederation conferences in 1890 and 1891. He was also reappointed education minister (1893–98) and added the agricultural portfolio to his responsibilities. When he stepped down from the Assembly he took the well-worn path to Britain as agent-general, but he resigned in 1901 when the position was downgraded after federation. He was knighted and stayed on in London, where he acted as a kind of roving trade ambassador and became more involved in Freemasonry as president of the International Masonic Club.

Tasmania

Edinburgh-born Frederick Innes served all too briefly as Tasmania's only Scottish premier, but he did serve in the key role of treasurer and was said to have kept four other premiers out of economic trouble. His experience in the top job was limited to nine months in 1872–73. He was the son of an army officer and left school to work in his uncle's law office. There were too many cobwebs for his liking and so he took the ship from Leith to Hobart when he was 17. He was probably too young to settle and he caught another boat back to Britain, where he worked as a journalist in London, where he also contributed to the famous *Penny Cyclopaedia*. With a bit more experience under his belt, he allowed his wanderlust to take him back to Tasmania, where he flexed his journalistic muscle working in Hobart on the *Observer* and any other papers that would buy his copy. That was around the mid-1840s and there clearly weren't enough of them to sustain body and soul, so he took up farming.

His move into full-time politics came in 1856 when he was elected to the Tasmanian House of Assembly. The following year he was appointed Treasurer at a time when the economic outlook was bleak. He successfully steered the government – and four premiers – through the storms for the next five years before he moving to the Legislative Council, where he became colonial secretary in 1863. He was chairman of committee and then president of the council (1868–72) before he returned to the Assembly as premier. After being ousted, he remained in the Assembly and, to some people's surprise, accepted appointment as treasurer in 1875. He retired in 1886, was re-elected to the Legislative Council in 1878 and was made president again in 1880.

Governors in Australia

At this safe historical distance, it would be easy to imagine the life of the early colonial administrator to be comfortable and ordered, with servants on hand to look after your every need. The tales of some of the Scots who filled these posts offer a somewhat different insight. They all had to make perilous journeys to the other side of the world, many of them were welcomed with anything but open arms by ferociously independent settlers and belligerent local politicians – quite a few of them Scottish – and almost all of them suffered from isolation, poor communications with their British masters and a consequent tendency to be autocratic. They were, after all, the representatives of their Britannic Majesties. For good or bad, they also had considerable influence in their respective corners of the Empire.

New South Wales

The oldest constitutional office in Australia is that of governor of New South Wales, which followed the first settlement there in 1778. Initially, those appointed were the captains of the ships delivering convicts to the penal colonies at the behest of the home secretary, Lord Sydney. Sandwiched between the rebellion-prone Captain William Bligh (of mutiny on the *Bounty* notoriety) and Lachlan Macquarie ('Father of Australia') as New South Wales' fifth governor in 1809, was soldier and botanist Colonel William Paterson from Montrose. Unfortunately his botanical and military journeys around the globe had played havoc with his health and he had to retire after little more than a year in the job. He died aboard ship on his way home to Scotland.

He trained in horticulture at London's Syon House and at just 21 he was commissioned by the rich and eccentric Countess of Strathmore to collect plants in Africa. He arrived at Table Bay in 1777 and made four expeditions into the interior. He returned briefly to Britain, where he joined the army and was sent to serve in India for four years. When he returned once more to Montrose in 1785, he took time out to write about his botanical adventures in Africa. With his journals up to date, he embarked on another military expedition, this time to New Holland (as Australia was then known). He arrived in 1791 as a captain in the MacLeod Highlanders (later the Highland Light Infantry). By 1794 he had been promoted to lieutenant colonel commanding the New South Wales Corps and in that capacity he upset the then (naval) governor by ceding more land and the right to use convict-labour servants to the army. In 1801, he also led an expedition to the Hunter Valley and up what was later named the Paterson River by another governor.

His finest hour probably came when he was the first governor of Van Diemen's Land (later Tasmania), 1804–08. He combined leadership of the settlement with exploring and plant-collecting. He led an expedition to Port Dalrymple (briefly called Patersonia), sailed up the Tamar River and managed to get closer to the source of the North Esk River than any earlier explorers. He also collected numerous new species of plants, which he sent back to Britain. Paterson was appointed governor of New South Wales in January 1809 but due to the decline in his health he was replaced by Lachlan Macquarie at the end of the year. He left Sydney on 12 May 1810, but died on board ship while off Cape Horn just a few weeks later.

As evidenced earlier in this chapter, Lachlan Macquarie stamped his tremendous personality on both New South Wales and the whole of Australia. He was governor from 1810 to 1821 and during that time, he transformed the penal colony into a thriving, free settlement that had a crucial influence in shaping the whole country. His name is also stamped indelibly on the geography of Australia and takes up several pages of the country's gazetteers. For example, there's Macquarie Island (between Tasmania and Antarctica), Lake Macquarie, Macquarie River, Lachlan River, Port Macquarie and Macquarie Pass. In and around Sydney there's Macquarie Street (home of the New South Wales Legislative Council), Macquarie Place, Macquarie Lighthouse (Australia's first and longest operating navigational light), Fort Macquarie, Macquarie Fields and Lachlan Avenue. In Tasmania there's Macquarie Street in Hobart, and in Evandale, the town he founded, Macquarie Harbour, as well as the town of Lachlan, Macquarie River and Macquarie Hill. Institutions named after him include Macquarie Hospital and Macquarie University, both in Sydney, and the national Macquarie Bank. And as if afraid they may have been in danger of overdoing it, the Aussies occasionally used his wife's name for a bit of a change: Mrs Macquarie's Chair (a rock near Mrs Macquarie's Point, a peninsula in Sydney Harbour at the end of Mrs Macquarie's Road). Her maiden name was Elizabeth Campbell so there are numerous Elizabeth Streets, bays and rivers. There's a Campbelltown in New South Wales and a Campbell Town in Tasmania. That's some small evidence of his huge impact on Australia.

When he finally stepped down as Governor in 1821, Macquarie left some big shoes to fill. Luckily Major General Sir Thomas Brisbane, from Largs, was on hand and he came on the recommendation of none less than the Duke of Wellington. He had a remarkable career as a soldier... and stargazer! He read astronomy and mathematics at Edinburgh University and, in 1808, built an observatory at his family home and employed two assistants to help with his studies. (He took them and all his instruments to New South Wales, where he built another observatory.) His career choice, however, was the military. He took a commission in the army and served with distinction in Europe, the West Indies, Spain and North America. He served under the Duke of Wellington. In 1813 he was promoted to major general and the next year went to command a brigade in America. When he moved into the governor's mansion, Brisbane built on the solid foundations established by Lachlan Macquarie. He worked to improve the land grants system, reformed the currency, encouraged the experimental growing of tobacco, cotton, coffee and flax, set up Australia's first agricultural training college and was the first patron of the New South Wales Agricultural Society. In 1823 he sent one of his officers north to find a new settlement for recidivist convicts. The officer discovered a large river flowing into Moreton Bay (named by Captain Cook in honour of the Scottish Earl of Morton, then president of the Royal Society) and both the river and the new settlement were given the name of Brisbane.

From a journalist's point of view, one of his most remarkable experiments was in the introduction of freedom of the press after the launch of the new newspaper, *The Australian*, in 1824. Bearing in mind the febrile nature of colonial politics, it was a courageous decision and one that paved the way for today's Rupert Murdochs. He also had the foresight to create a locally-elected Legislative Council which would help reconcile the often conflicting interests of the governor and the politicians. That, however, did not give him immunity from the personal animosities that had beset so many of his predecessors. In one particularly bitter incident, he was falsely accused of conniving at female convicts being used for immoral purposes. Although he was completely exonerated, it brought a tragic end to what had been a successful diplomatic career and he was recalled from his post by the colonial secretary, Lord Bathurst.

He returned to Scotland to pick up the pieces of his life. He managed his country estate, attended mess dinners with his old regiment and continued with his lifelong interest in the stars. In 1828, he won the gold medal of the Royal Astronomical Society and the Brisbane Crater on the Moon was named in his honour. In 1832, he succeeded Sir Walter Scott as president of the Royal Society of Edinburgh. In 1833, he was elected president of the British Association for the Advancement of Science. He was knighted in 1836 and offered the role of commander-in-chief of the army in Canada. He declined and did so again when he was offered the same role in India two years later. He had had more than enough travel. He died at home in Largs in 1860.

The only early governor to die in office was Sir Robert Duff from Stonehaven. After being appointed by Gladstone, he took up his duties in May 1893, but became ill on a visit to Tasmania, was diagnosed with septicaemia and died in Government House on 15 March 1895. Sadly, that was not before he too had suffered the usual disaffection of some members of the Legislative Assembly.

He was born in Fetteresso Castle but educated in London and joined the Royal Navy in 1848. He rose through the ranks until his retirement from the service in 1870. He had also been elected Liberal MP for Banffshire in 1861 (and remained so until 1893 when he left for Australia) and inherited his uncle's extensive estate in Kincardineshire in 1862. He served as a party whip for Gladstone (1882–85), was made civil lord of the Admiralty in 1886 and appointed as a privy councillor in 1892.

His term in Sydney, however, didn't get off to the best of starts. He inadvertently got embroiled in a row about gerrymandering and was accused of being partisan. When he refused to approve the appointment of ten defeated ministers to the Legislative Council, he was severely harassed by the retiring premier George Dibbs. In a note to the colonial secretary in London, he said: 'I am sorry to have to report Dibbs' conduct in attempting to intimidate me by writing a memo full of false statements censuring my conduct and then offering to withdraw it, if I would accede to his request.' He later reported a more amenable relationship with the new premier, fellow Scot Sir George Reid. He was buried with full military honours at Waverley Cemetery, Sydney.

Victoria

The tale of Scottish soldier James Loch offers a different insight. In the name of Queen Victoria, he was governor of Victoria for the seven years (1882–89) but he might so easily have not even made it to Australia, which underlines the fact that empire-building carries its pitfalls. James Loch was serving as military attaché on Lord Elgin's mission to China in 1860 when, despite carrying a flag of truce, he was captured by

Emperor Xianfeng, imprisoned in a filthy Peking dungeon, tortured for three weeks and narrowly escaped execution.

Son of the MP for Midlothian, he joined the Royal Navy and served for two years before joining the British East India Company with a commission in the Bengal Light Cavalry in 1842. He then served in the first Anglo-Sikh War (1845–46) before returning to Britain. At the outbreak of the Crimean War, he raised an irregular Bulgarian cavalry troop which he commanded throughout the campaign. It was in 1857 that he signed up to Elgin's mission to the East. He took part in the capture of Canton in the second Opium War and later helped secure the Treaty of Yedo with the Japanese. He was again with Lord Elgin in 1860 when they ran into serious trouble during so-called peace talks with the Chinese emperor. He learned that treachery was planned and he rode out to warn the outposts. On his return, he found his men trapped and he rode in under the flag of truce to try secure their release. Instead, he too was captured and ended up in the Peking jail, where most of his men died. He was only released after extensive negotiations and later learned that he had walked out of the prison only ten minutes before the arrival of his death warrant, signed by the emperor. He was feted with the award of a CB, a knighthood and a job in the Home Office.

His arrival in Victoria in 1882 must have seemed like another sinecure. He served as commissioner for woods and forests before becoming governor of the territory during the premierships of fellow Scots James McCulloch and James Service. In 1889, he was appointed governor of Cape Colony and high commissioner for Southern Africa, where he had to deal with the restless Boers and managed to achieve agreement over Swaziland with their truculent president, Paul Kruger. A long serious of agreements and counter-agreements ensued – during which he was ennobled as Baron Loch – until war became inevitable. When, in 1899, it finally came he was 72 but personally raised his own cavalry unit – Loch's Horse – and led it into battle against the Boers. After the war, he returned to London and died the following year.

The twelfth governor was the Scottish aristocrat Sir Thomas Gibson-Carmichael (later Baron Carmichael) who served for the three years, 1908–11. He was the eldest son of a church minister and took his MA at St John's College, Cambridge, then almost immediately went into the civil service. After serving as private secretary to two secretaries for Scotland, he became chairman of the Scottish Board of Lunacy in 1894 and then, in 1895, he replaced Gladstone as Liberal MP for Midlothian. His other public appointments were as a trustee of both the National Portrait Gallery (1904–08) and the National Gallery (1906–08 and 1923–26). He was knighted on his appointment as governor of Victoria in 1908. From Australia, he went on to be governor of Madras (1911–12) and then, after being made a peer (as Baron Carmichael) in 1912, he was appointed the first governor of Bengal (1912–17). When he retired to Scotland, he was appointed Lord Lieutenant of Peeblesshire in 1920 and continued in the role until his death in 1926.

Queensland

During his travels as an imperial administrator acting on behalf of King and country, William MacGregor, from Aberdeenshire, had to overcome near disasters and serious privations before he arrived in Australia to be governor of Queensland, where he served from 1909 to 1914 and made his notable contribution to the empire.

The eldest son of a farm labourer, he was born in 1846 in the tiny parish of Towie, to the west of Aberdeen. He was lucky enough to go to a nearby village school and even luckier that his teacher recognised that he was especially bright. A bursary was found that – supplemented by working on the land during his breaks – allowed him to study medicine first at Aberdeen University and later Glasgow University, where he gained his MD in 1874. With his new qualifications, he took to the high seas and headed for the Seychelles, where he became the islands' assistant medical officer. His next port of call was Mauritius and a job as resident at the local hospital and superintendent of the island's mental hospital. There he met the island's governor, who just happened to be Sir Arthur Gordon, son of the Earl of Aberdeen. When Sir Arthur moved on to his next posting in Fiji, MacGregor went with him in the much-improved position of chief medical officer. He was 29. One of his first emergencies was a full-scale epidemic of measles that swept the country and despite his valiant efforts killed more than 50,000. Shortly afterwards, he showed commendable courage of a different kind when a ship ran aground and he personally saved several people from drowning. Although he never mentioned this in his official reports, he was awarded the Albert Medal (forerunner of the George Cross). His responsibilities were also widened beyond the purely medical and he stood in for the governor occasionally.

His first formal appointment was in 1888 as administrator for British New Guinea, where he had to try to avoid bloodshed among the very warlike tribes. He obviously made a decent fist of that and he was promoted to lieutenant governor in 1895 before stepping up in 1899 to governor of Lagos, where he launched a campaign to drain the swamps and try to destroy the malaria-carrying mosquitoes. That won him a medal from the Society of Tropical Medicine. His next appointment was as governor of Newfoundland (1904–09), where again used his medical experience, this time to combat tuberculosis. He was knighted in 1907. He arrived in Australia towards the end of 1909 to take up the key job as governor of Queensland, where the premier was yet another Scot, William Kidston. Unusually, the two got on well and he was able to play a major role in the inauguration of Queensland University. He acquiesced in the handing over of Government House to be its first home, and one of his first acts was to attend the dedication ceremony on 10 December 1909. He also became the first chancellor, and took great pride in the early development of the university.

When he retired in 1914, he returned to Scotland and lived in Berwickshire. He was made a privy councillor and during the Great War he lectured on his experience of German rule in the Pacific. He died in 1919 and was buried in Towie. The Brisbane suburb of Macgregor is named in his honour.

Western Australia

As well as being Western Australia's first and longest-serving governor (1828–38), Sir James Stirling, from Coatbridge, helped to establish the Swan River Colony when he was a naval officer there in 1826. It later became the state capital of Western Australia, Perth. It gives some indication of the communication problems with Britain that he served for three years without pay and without formal authority.

But he had the background to cope. He was born in 1791, one of 15 children – eight boys, seven girls – and with a grandfather and an uncle who were both admirals, it was almost inevitable that he should join the Royal Navy. He did so when he was just 12. He signed on as a first-class volunteer, embarking on his long career with a maiden voyage to the West Indies. He enjoyed rapid and regular promotion: midshipman when he was 14 (he was reported to have been killed in action at Montevideo), lieutenant at 19 and flag lieutenant to his uncle in 1811, at 20. He got his first command shortly after his twenty-first birthday and saw plenty of action during the Napoleonic Wars against both the French and Spanish fleets. He was then put in command of a small fleet sent by the then governor of New South Wales to explore and report on the viability of the west coast for settlers. It didn't take long for him to see the possibilities of the land around the Swan River. If a colony were to be established there, he said, it could easily defended 'with just a few cannons.' When he got back to Britain, he persuaded the Admiralty and the Colonial Office to allow him to recruit a group of industrious pioneers, whom he led back to the Swan River where they laid the foundations not just of Perth, but also Fremantle and Surbiton (now a suburb of Perth).

He became de facto governor, but was missing some key elements of the gubernatorial gubbins – as he declared dryly: 'I believe I am the first governor who ever formed a settlement without Commission, Laws, Instructions and Salary.' The paperwork and the money didn't catch up with him until 1831 but the oversight was no doubt ameliorated when he was knighted the following year. With the settlement well and truly settled, he returned to Royal Navy duty in 1838 and served in the Mediterranean Fleet, collecting a knighthood from the King of Greece during his peregrinations. He was promoted to rear admiral in 1851 and pushed paper at the Admiralty for a couple of years until he was appointed naval commander-in-chief in China and the East Indies (1854–56). During that tour of duty, he signed Britain's first treaty with Japan (the Anglo-Japanese Friendship Treaty) without the usual authority. Fortunately, his initiative was commended. He was promoted to vice admiral in 1857 and admiral in 1862. In Perth, the suburb of Stirling is named after him. The Royal Australian Navy's Indian Ocean Fleet is based at HMAS *Stirling*.

There were two further Scottish governors of Western Australia: Sir James Fergusson (1868–73), who went on to be governor of New Zealand (see later in this chapter), and the Earl of Kintore (1889–95). The Earl of Kintore was born in Edinburgh and was educated at Eton and Trinity College, Cambridge. After standing unsuccessfully as a Conservative parliamentary candidate, he became the 9th Earl on his father's death in

1880 and sat in the House of Lords. He held a number of government appointments and was Captain of the Yeomen of the Guard (deputy chief whip) for three years before he went to Australia in 1889. When he returned to Britain, he was made a privy councillor and became deputy speaker in 1913.

Tasmania

Tasmania's only Scottish governor – and commander-in-chief – was Shetland islander Sir Robert Hamilton. He served for five years, 1887–92. Before going to Tasmania, he was the senior civil servant who recommended that Ireland was given home rule. A son of the manse, he went to the local grammar school before going on to read law at King's College, Aberdeen, where he obtained first a masters degree in 1857, then a doctoral degree in law in 1885. He worked in the legal section of the War Office and then served in the Crimean War as a commissariat clerk (responsible for supplies). After the war he held a number of civil service administrative posts, published a book on bookkeeping in 1868, and became an accountant in the Board of Trade. In 1869, he became accountant general of the Royal Navy and ten years later he served on the Royal Commission on Colonial Defences. In 1882, he was promoted to be permanent secretary of the Admiralty. He then became permanent under-secretary to the Irish administration, where his distinguished service earned him his CB and a KCB. He lost his job, of course, after recommending home rule for Ireland and his appointment to Tasmania was seen as compensation. As governor, he encouraged industrial development and the construction of new roads and railways. He was a proponent of federalism and presided over the Federal Council of Australasia, held in Hobart, 1887–89. He also helped found the University of Tasmania and numerous schools, colleges and museums. When he returned to Britain, he re-joined the civil service, worked with various royal commissions and served on the Board of Customs.

GOVERNORS GENERAL OF AUSTRALIA

When the six states joined together as the new Australia in 1901, the first British-appointed governor general was the Earl of Hopetoun. He took office just before federation but dramatically resigned only two years later when the Australian government refused to raise his expenses to cover the costs of official residences in Sydney and Melbourne.

The Earl, born in South Queensferry in 1860, appeared to have impeccable credentials for the role. He went to Eton and Sandhurst, managed his family estates in Fife, served as a Conservative whip in the House of Lords, was Salisbury's paymaster general and had been lord chamberlain. More importantly, he had been a popular governor of Victoria for six years. His major task was to appoint the first interim prime minister of the new commonwealth government and he fell down the hole between protocol and common sense. Because the appointment was to be effective before elections took place, he decided it was diplomatically appropriate to offer the job to Sir William Lyne, premier of the largest of the states, New South Wales. The problem was that Sir William had fiercely opposed federation. In a foretaste of what was to be a regular pattern in Oz politics, the other premiers, who had fought for federation refused to serve under him. The situation was only resolved by Sir William declining the invitation. The hapless governor general then got it in the neck because he had brought his own secretary with him to handle communications with the British government. The Australians didn't want their official business handled by an Englishman. While they were at it, they also expressed their dislike of the pomp surrounding the governor general and nor were they happy about the expense of his office. It all came to a head when they refused to increase allowances for the gubernatorial residences. The Earl resigned in May 1902 and was soon on the ship back to Britain. His chances of fulfilling an ambition to be viceroy of India also disappeared. It was an inglorious end to the diplomatic career of a man who was still only 42. The only consolation was that he was created the first Marquess of Linlithgow and made secretary of state for Scotland.

The wartime governor general was Sir Ronald Munro Ferguson (later Viscount Novar of Raith), clearly a man who had learned to say 'no': he had declined Asquith's offer of a peerage in 1912, as he had done the invitations to be governor of South Australia in 1895 and governor of Victoria in 1910. When he arrived in Canberra he was not universally welcomed, with some politicians mumbling about him being a reject from the British House of Commons. The *Australian Dictionary of Biography* however, is much more positive, saying he 'was soon to prove himself the ablest of the early governors general.' After Sandhurst and the Grenadier Guards (1879–84), he was elected Liberal MP for Ross and Cromarty (1884–1889) and Leith Burghs (1904–1914) and became parliamentary private secretary to the prime minister, Lord Rosebery. With such patronage, Munro Ferguson might have expected to enjoy more government roles but he was overlooked by fellow Scot Sir Henry Campbell-Bannerman, who became prime minister in 1905, and he languished on the backbenches. He was made privy councillor in 1910 and sent to Australia in 1914.

Aware of the fractiousness of Australian politics, he said from the outset that he would maintain British parliamentary principles of fairness and balance to maintain the prestige of the infant commonwealth. That was tested early when he denied but then acceded to the then prime minister's request to dissolve parliament in the hope that he could improve on his precarious majority. The crisis was only averted and the opposition appeased when a general election came and the opposition won, but he did continue to have to tread delicately, especially through the complex relationships created by the Great War and Japanese activity in the Pacific. On his return to Britain, he accepted a peerage, prime minister Bonar Law made him secretary for Scotland in 1922 and he chaired the committee reviewing political honours in 1925.

William Morrison, from Argyllshire, had a long and distinguished political career, including serving as speaker of the House of Commons (see chapter 5: The power) before he became governor general in 1961. However, he was already ill when he arrived in Canberra to replace Sir William Slim and he died in office exactly one year and a day later.

SETTLERS IN CANADA

Canada's early politics seem to have been dominated by Scots and four in particular have earned special mention in the history books. The new dominion's first prime minister in 1867 was Glasgow-born John Alexander MacDonald, who is acknowledged as the 'Father of Canada', and he was succeeded in 1873 by a former stonemason from Dunkeld, Alexander Mackenzie, who established voters' right to a secret ballot. The other two didn't make it to the top job but each had a great influence on how the new nation shaped up. George Brown, from Alloa, came within a hair's breadth – he was co-premier of Canada West for all of four days in 1858 – and was one of the principal architects of confederation. Falkirk-born Tommy Douglas got as far as the premiership of Saskatchewan when he was 39, was the architect of the country's healthcare system and was voted the 'Greatest Canadian' in a 2004 poll by the Canadian Broadcasting Company. (John MacDonald was eighth in the list and Alexander Graham Bell, who developed the telephone while working in Canada, was ninth.)

John Alexander MacDonald – known affectionately as 'John A' – was not only the first but also the longest-serving of Canada's prime ministers. He won six general elections and was in office for six years between 1867 and 1873 and for a further 13 years between 1878 and 1891, earning the soubriquet: 'the perpetual premier.' Although he was initially against confederation because he feared that forcing disparate provinces together would weaken what was then British North America, he became one of its staunchest proponents and used all his legal and political skills to help shape a constitution that would be robust enough to overcome the inter-province tensions. He recognised that more than ideology was needed and he set out to give the new nation a backbone by creating the transcontinental Canadian Pacific Railway. He opened the prairies to settlers and made treaties with the native Indians, and he ensured law and order by creating the Royal Canadian Mounted Police. Having read law at Oxford, John MacDonald took an early interest in politics. When he had established himself in a successful practice in Ontario, he was elected to the provincial Legislative Assembly in 1844 as a Liberal-Conservative. He was 29. Three years later, his feet were firmly on the ladder when he was appointed receiver general. He became attorney general in 1854 and in the same year helped to establish a new Canadian Conservative party that created an effective alliance with French Canadian interests. He was elected leader in 1856 and the following year he became premier of Upper Canada, which proved to be a tough apprenticeship for his longer term ambition of leading the new Canada, and he worked tirelessly in helping to hammer out the constitution for confederation. In the first general election of 1867, his Conservatives won just 71 of the 180 seats but he became prime minister with the support of 29 Liberal-Conservatives. His first job was to try to pull together the warring factions and work with the French Canadians to overcome language, religious and cultural differences. In 1872, he was even more dependent on the Liberal-Conservatives and scraped home with only four more seats than the Liberals. Only months later however, he was caught up in a scandal in which he was accused of giving multi-million-dollar railway contracts to his political supporters (including fellow Scot, Sir Hugh Allan). His dreams of leading 'a great united nation' came tumbling down and he was humiliated in the ensuing election of 1873, which saw Alexander Mackenzie's Liberals win a 60-seat majority in the now 206-seat parliament.

At that point, most politicians would have gone to spend more time with their family but he was made of sterner stuff. Out of office, he led the Conservative party into a rethink of its policies and strategy and devised what he shrewdly labelled his National Policy, a series of high-tariff trade barriers against US imports designed to protect and therefore stimulate Canadian industry. His flag-waving strategy worked and he was able to put the so-called 'Pacific Scandal' behind him. In an astonishing turnaround of fortunes in 1878, he was returned to power with a handsome majority. He continued to try to balance the multiple interests of the different parties and provinces and his leadership was sorely tested in the ebb and flow of the resulting tensions. He advocated a model democracy in which Canada was an independent entity within the British Empire, and a bastion against what he suspected were America's expansionist tendencies. Canadian democracy was, he said, an antidote to American values. At the same time, he also used his National Policy of protectionism to encourage US companies to set up shop in Canada, in order to avoid the tariffs.

While he suffered many setbacks, he retained enough popularity to keep him in office until he died in 1891. In a show of respect, a special funeral train carried his remains across the country. The irony of using Canadian Pacific as his cortège would not have been lost on him.

When MacDonald had fallen from grace in 1873, he was replaced as prime minister by Alexander Mackenzie, who had been leader of the Liberals for little more than a month before the election. The euphoria of a substantial majority was seriously offset by both the problems inherited from the Conservatives and those in his own backyard. Not only had Mackenzie been leader for just weeks but he had taken over the reins of a demoralised party that had been literally leaderless and without direction for all of the five years since its founder, George Brown, had failed to win a seat in parliament in 1867. Alexander Mackenzie had, in fact been a back-room man for more than 20 years, first with the Reformers, who then became the Clear Grits (meaning tenacious or dedicated as in 'true grit') and finally emerged as the Liberal party. He was not a natural leader. When he became prime minister, he certainly needed the grit and he must have been grateful for his tough upbringing in Scotland. He was one of ten children and when his father died he had to give up school and go to work. He was 13 and a stonemason, packing in as much education as he could through reading into the night after his long working day.

He emigrated mainly to get away from the depression in Britain and it's ironic that avoiding such a situation should have been his major concern when he became prime minister in his adopted country. In order to bear the heavy burden of MacDonald's commitment to build the transcontinental railway, he reduced costs by slowing down the construction programme. During his five years as prime minister he did drive Canada forward. It was his unshakeable belief in honest government responsible to parliament – and through it to the people – that led to the introduction of the secret ballot and the creation of a Supreme Court. He also tried to ensure financial probity by setting up an independent Auditor General's Office. Another of his major proposals was to establish free trade with the United States but he couldn't get enough support, and when he refused to raise tariffs to increase income, it only weakened his already weak position and proved to be his undoing. He lost the 1878 election and then faced further pressure from within his own party. He stepped down as leader of the party in 1880 but remained an MP until his death in 1892.

Newspaper editor George Brown never became prime minister of Canada, but nevertheless played a crucial role in its development as an independent nation. Brown was another Father of the Confederation and although he was a fierce opponent of John MacDonald he served alongside him in laying the foundations for the new Canada. He migrated to New York in 1834, when he was 15, and worked in the print industry there with his father, before moving on to Toronto in 1843. Within a year, he launched *The Globe*, which quickly became the newspaper of the Reformers, and that gave him considerable influence. In 1848, he headed a Royal Commission to examine accusations of misconduct by officials at Kingston Penitentiary, but when he reported that there was enough evidence of abuse of prisoners to justify sacking the warden, he was criticised by John A MacDonald (then attorney general in the provincial Legislative Assembly). Brown retaliated by using *The Globe* to establish his own political agenda.

After writing about slavery, he founded the Anti-Slavery Society, helped former American slaves to escape to Canada and won widespread support from the country's liberals. Encouraged, he stood as a Reformer and won a seat in the Legislative Assembly in 1851; from then, he crossed swords more regularly with MacDonald. He became unhappy about the organisation of the party and worked with Alexander Mackenzie to reorganise as the Clear Grit party in 1857. As leader, he established a platform that included smaller government, the separation of church and state and the annexation of the Northwest Territories. More importantly, he wanted to resolve the inequity of representation which gave large and small provinces the same number of seats on the assembly. He launched a campaign that was popularly known as 'Rep by Pop' – representation based on population. For four days in August 1858 he sought to exploit a successful no-confidence vote against MacDonald (then premier) but in the end he was outwitted by his wily opponent.

When Brown was putting together a new cabinet to replace the Conservatives, he had to comply with the law that said new ministers had to resign and seek endorsement at a by-election. As soon as he started to do that, he immediately lost his majority and his chance of high office. While he played a leading role in the confederation plans, he never really recovered from that setback, and when he led his party into the election for the new parliament in 1867, he failed to win his own seat; his misfortune was compounded when he also lost his seat in the Legislative Assembly. Still regarded as the party's elder statesman, Brown continued to provide advice and support for Alexander Mackenzie and his other elected colleagues. When Mackenzie became prime minister, Brown was appointed to the Senate and made a trade ambassador in Washington. His death the following year was bizarre: he died from an infected wound after being shot by a disgruntled employee of *The Globe*. He was 62. His home, which is now a major conference centre, was declared a National Historic Site in 1974. A Toronto college was named in his honour and there is a monument to him in the city's Queen's Park.

In the official history of Canada, Tommy Douglas is listed as having served five terms as premier of Saskatchewan, but in the country's folklore, he is 'the best prime minister that Canada never had.' So many books and articles have been inspired by his commitment that there is little that needs to be said about him, but I am keen to fix him securely within my Scottish Empire and so hope I might be forgiven for repeating what many readers will already know.

With his parents, Tommy Douglas migrated from Falkirk to Canada, where he trained and was ordained as a Baptist minister. At the time Canada was struggling with a deep economic depression; Douglas saw its savage impact at very close quarters and conducted funeral services for at least two of his congregation who had died because they couldn't afford medical treatment. He vowed then that he would devote his life to improving living conditions for the poor people of Canada. In the shorter term, he tried to help his parishioners cope with the angst of the most difficult years by offering them spiritual solace but, in the end, he knew that this was not enough and he decided to take an active role in politics.

In 1934, he stood in a by-election as a Farmer Labour party candidate for the federal parliament but was unsuccessful. Shortly afterwards, a new party was launched by another Scot, William Irvine from Shetland. This was the Co-operative Commonwealth Federation and he joined up, fought the 1935 election under its banner and won. He became one of the party's seven MPs, pushing an unashamedly socialist programme of public ownership of key industries, the creation of a welfare state with pensions and health care for everyone, child allowances and unemployment benefits. Progress was painfully slow. In the 1940 election the party won only one additional seat and was having little influence on the Liberal government, so Douglas turned his attention to what he thought might be achieved within Saskatchewan. He stepped down from the national parliament and became leader of the provincial CCF, going into the 1944 Saskatchewan Legislative Assembly elections with a brilliantly organised campaign. He shrugged aside accusations of being a communist, took 47 of the 52 seats, won more than 53 per cent of the popular vote, and emerged as premier. He was still only 39.

Almost immediately, he started making good on his promises. His first major reform was to ensure pensioners had free access to all medical, dental and hospital services and that patients suffering from cancer, mental illness and tuberculosis were also given free care. By 1948, he extended the health service to free hospital care for everyone in return for an annual payment of five dollars. By 1956, he was able to introduce universal Medicare, including preventative care. He then turned his attention to another great social concern: the cost of heating and energy. His government created the Saskatchewan Power Corporation. Until then, only a small handful of rural homes had power. By 1964, the figure had soared to more than 65,000... and every one of them testament to a man who kept his word. When he died in 1986 at the age of 81, an obituary described him as 'a man who did good deeds in a naughty world.'

GOVERNORS IN CANADA

Although there was not the same proliferation of Scottish governors as in Australia, Canada had its fair share of Caledonian colonial administrators. The first was lieutenant general Peter Hunter from Perth. He served as governor of Upper Canada and commander of military forces from 1799. He was a military veteran who had been in the army since joining up as an ensign at the age of 21. He served in the Mediterranean, West Indies, Nova Scotia and in British Honduras, where he was superintendent (1789–91) and spent a year as military governor of Ireland. During his term in Canada, he built Government House, improved postal services, established a public market in York (now Toronto) and acquired a fire engine for the city.

He died suddenly in 1805, when he was 59, and was replaced temporarily by a fellow Scot, Commodore Alexander Grant from Glenmoriston, Inverness-shire (1734–1813). As a Royal Navy officer, Grant had served in Northern America and then fought in the Seven Years War which enveloped most of Europe between 1756 and 1763. After working as naval superintendent at the Detroit dockyards, he turned successfully to shipbuilding and had soon amassed enough money to make himself a major land-owner in New York. In the early years of the American Revolution, he continued to prosper, but as it wore on his fortunes turned, and by 1780 he had lost more than 12,000 acres of land and the associated income. He had to pull out of his ship building company. He did recover well enough to be appointed a magistrate in 1786 and then to a series of other government and political appointments. He became a member of the Executive Council of Upper Canada and the Legislative Council. In 1799, he was appointed deputy superintendent of Indian Affairs. When he was made acting governor, he continued the policies of his predecessor.

Charles Lennox, Duke of Richmond and Lennox was appointed governor general of Canada (or British North America, as it then was) in 1818 but he too served for only for a year. He died after a bizarre incident in which he was bitten by his pet fox and contracted rabies. He was the grandson of the 2nd Duke and son of General Lord George Lennox and was born at Gordon Castle in Aberdeenshire. A keen cricketer, he was an accomplished batsman and wicketkeeper and a founder member of the MCC. He was one of the guarantors when Thomas Lord created his first cricket ground (the forerunner of Lords and the home of cricket) in 1787. After joining the army, he was promoted to captain and was regarded as one of London's dashing young blades. In 1789 he was notoriously a combatant in at least two duels, including one with the Duke of York, who had accused him of ungentlemanly behaviour. Unabashed, he went off to do battle with the French in the West Indies and Gibraltar but was dismissed after unseemly conflict with his superior officers and sent home. He then succeeded his father as MP for Sussex (1790–1806) and then became a Duke on the death of his grandfather in 1806. He was Lord Lieutenant of Ireland (1807–13), with Arthur Wellesley (later Duke of Wellington) as his private secretary.

His successor, the Earl of Dalhousie, who was governor general for eight years (1820–28), also had personal connections with the Iron Duke. He was a general under his command at Waterloo. Although he was following his father's footsteps in the colonial service, he had previously endured a baptism of fire in his first administrative appointment, as governor of Nova Scotia. After attending the Royal High School and Edinburgh University, he became a career soldier and served around the world, reaching the rank of major general in 1808. Wellington promoted him to lieutenant general and made him commander of his 7th Division in 1812. He fought in Spain and France and was knighted in 1813 and was thanked for his valiant services in both houses of parliament. Like many of his fellow officers, he joined the colonial service when he left the army and in 1816 he went to Nova Scotia, where he served as governor for four years. His term in Halifax did not run entirely smoothly: in shades of the Australian tensions, he had numerous clashes with the House of Assembly, especially over control of the province's finances and his demands to reorganise and reinforce the military garrison. The situation became so fractious that he declined the presentation of a ceremonial sword at the end of his term.

He did, however, leave behind the foundations of what was to become Dalhousie University. He arrived in Quebec during a general election and he was able, therefore, to settle into his new role quietly and comfortably. But the tranquillity didn't last long and, try as he might to be independent – 'I am acting a frank, fair and candid part with them, free from intrigue and free from guile,' he said – he again became embroiled in the tensions of the rapidly-growing country. He was all too often caught in the crossfire between Catholic and Protestant, French-speaking and English-speaking, and even more often he thought he detected intrigue when there was none. His term of office could never be described as boring.

Lord Greenock (later the Earl of Cathcart), who served as governor general of the Province of Canada (an area in the east of modern-day Canada, covering parts of Ontario and Quebec) for less than two years from 1845, was yet another Waterloo veteran. He was Wellington's quartermaster general and had three horses shot from under him in 1815. He joined the Life Guards as a cornet when he was 17 and saw early service in Naples and Sicily during the first Peninsula Campaign. He was also part of the ill-fated British Expeditionary Force sent to capture Antwerp in 1809. He spent eight weeks on the mosquito-infested island of Walcheren, just off the Dutch coast, and caught malaria (which killed more than seven thousand soldiers in that campaign). He, however, recovered and was again in action as a lieutenant colonel at the Battle of Barossa, where his bravery won him a medal. He won further medals, including the CB, at Waterloo.

After the war, he returned to Britain, joined the Royal Staff Corps and developed his interest in science, which eventually led to the discovery of a new mineral – a sulphate of cadmium – during excavations in a tunnel near Port Glasgow. It was named Greenockite. After serving in Canada, he returned to take up the post of governor of Edinburgh Castle and commander of the army in Scotland (1837–42). He succeeded to the title of Earl of Cathcart in 1843. He again served in North America as commander-in-chief of the British Army there (1846–49) and held further home posts before retiring from the army in 1854.

He was succeeded in 1847 by the Earl of Elgin, who successfully negotiated the free-trade agreement with the United States in 1854. He was a career colonial administrator who redefined the role of the governor general and went on to be high commissioner in China, where he saw the end of the Opium Wars and sealed trade agreements with Japan, and viceroy of India. He had previously been governor general of Jamaica (1842–46). His time in Canada was momentous. After signing the Rebellion Losses Bill (to compensate French Canadians for losses suffered during the uprising of 1837), he was embroiled in riots in Quebec, saw the parliament building burned down by an angry, English-speaking mob and was personally attacked. To add insult to injury, the French-speaking minority in the parliament tried to have him sacked. Then, in a second riot in Bytown (later renamed Ottawa) the following year, one man was killed and another seriously injured before the army broke it up. After all that, it's hardly surprising that he took the first real steps toward establishing independent government in Canada. When moderate reformers won the 1848 elections in both Canada East and Canada West, he asked them to form a unified government. Once that had been established, he stepped back from any direct involvement with the legislature and established governor's role simply as the symbolic representative of the Queen. After finalising the free-trade treaty with America, he stepped down in 1854.

Of the four Scots who served as Canada's governor general after confederation in 1867, three were aristocrats, as was the custom of the time, and the fourth was among the great literary figures of the day. The first was the Marquess of Lorne (later the 9th Duke of Argyll) who, at 33, was also the youngest. His wife was Princess Louise, the fourth daughter of Queen Victoria, which might just have had something to do with his appointment. His term of office (1878–83) coincided with a significant easing of the economic crisis and he arrived to find Canada enjoying a new optimism. That allowed him to concentrate more on the social life of the country and he and his influential wife concentrated on meeting a very wide cross-section of the people. They encouraged the establishment of the Royal Society of Canada, the Royal Canadian Academy of Arts and helped select some of the first paintings for the new National Gallery of Canada. He was also able to indulge in his own writing and he produced several works about the natural beauty of the country. Persuaded by her daughter, of course, he named the Saskatchewan capital Regina in honour of Queen Victoria. Before going to Canada, he had attended Edinburgh Academy, St Andrews University and then Cambridge. He was the Liberal MP for Argyll, 1868–78 and 1895–1900 (when he inherited the title of Duke of Argyll). When he returned to Britain in 1883, he was appointed governor and constable of Windsor Castle from 1892, a post he held until his death in 1914.

When the 7th Earl of Aberdeen was appointed governor general in 1893, he faced a much more complex and difficult situation, with Canada's politics again in a state of considerable flux: during his five-year term, there were no fewer than four prime ministers. He did, however, have what almost constituted a home advantage. He and his wife had toured Canada a few years earlier and had so enjoyed their visit that they bought a ranch in British Columbia and called it 'Guisachan' (after his wife's family estate in Scotland). He had to contend with the fall-out from the abolition of separate French schools in Manitoba, but he did see the completion of the Canadian Pacific Railway and the discovery of gold in the Yukon.

One of his favourite duties was to regularly tour the country, because he enjoyed meeting ordinary Canadians from every walk of life. Among those he met was fellow Scot, Alexander Graham Bell, and on one trip he was made a chief of the Blackfoot. He, too, tweaked the formal role of governor general and sought to develop better communications with Britain and trade links with overseas, especially Australia and New Zealand. When he returned to Britain, he was made lord lieutenant of Ireland and his wife served as president of the International Council of Women.

His replacement was another Scottish peer with previous experience of Canada. In fact, when the Earl of Minto had served with distinction as a military aide-de-camp during the North-West Rebellion of 1885, the then prime minister, John A Macdonald had told him. 'I shall not live to see it, but some day Canada will welcome you back as governor general.' The prediction came good in 1898 and he served for six years until 1904, a term which saw some healthy muscle-flexing by the Canadians and a consequent increase in the natural tension with big brother America. He followed what was now the gubernatorial routine of travelling widely and endeared himself to the military by revisiting the battlegrounds on which he had fought. For one trip, he hitched up with the North West Mounted Police to ride through the Quebec countryside.

He had a keen sense of history and was instrumental in creating the National Archives and in widening the school curriculum to include the recent history of the young country. When the people faced a health crisis from tuberculosis, he promptly set up an association for the prevention of tuberculosis and promoted the development of the great national parks. He was one of the few men the Mounties didn't get. He was offered command of the North West Mounted Police but declined and instead became viceroy of India, 1905–10. In appreciation of his long service to the crown, he was made a Knight of the Garter.

It's appropriate that the last chapter of Scottish vice-regal service to Canada should have been completed by the distinguished writer and journalist, John Buchan. When he was appointed in 1935, he was raised to the peerage as Lord Tweedsmuir and served until his death in 1940. Born in Perth, he read classics at Glasgow University and law at Oxford. He was called to the bar in 1901 but almost immediately went to South Africa, in the aftermath of the Boer War, and spent two years as an assistant secretary to the high commissioner. It was an experience that gave him what he described as 'a lifelong attachment to empire' and one of his best-known novels (published in 1910) was *Prester John*, a prescient tale of African risings. On his return to Britain, he became director of a publishing company, a shrewd move for a writer. During the Great War, he went to France as correspondent for the *Times* and still found time to publish *The Thirty-Nine Steps* (which Alfred Hitchcock later turned into a gripping film). He returned to public service in 1917 when he became the government's director of information, working under the Canadian Lord Beaverbrook (then newly-appointed minister for information). After the war, he worked in the Foreign Office and became its nominee director on the board of Reuters, the international news agency (then part-guaranteed by the government) and became the Conservative MP for the Scottish Universities in 1927.

Eight years later, he was raised to the peerage as Lord Tweedsmuir and dispatched to Quebec as King George V's representative in Canada. He made it his priority to persuade both the American president (Franklin D. Roosevelt) and the Canadian prime minister (Mackenzie King) to use their influence in trying to avert another war. He also tried to preserve a feeling of normality, visited every part of the country, continued to write his books and sought to encourage a distinctly Canadian culture. He created the Governor General's Literary Awards (still highly regarded as marks of literary merit) and his wife launched what she called the 'Prairie Library', in which she used the governor's residence as a distribution centre for more than 40,000 books that were sent to readers in the most remote areas of the country.

He had the ultimate vice-regal experience when, in 1939, he organised Canada's first royal visit for the new King George VI and Queen Elizabeth and then escorted them throughout the dominion. In February 1940 he suffered a stroke and collapsed while having his morning shave and died from the head wounds he received in the fall. In a radio tribute, prime minister Mackenzie King said, 'the people of Canada have lost one of the greatest and most revered of their governors general and a friend who, from the day of his arrival in this country, dedicated his life to their service.'

SETTLERS IN NEW ZEALAND

The first Scot to take the top political spot in New Zealand was Edinburgh-born Edward Stafford, who became New Zealand's prime minister in 1856, when he was just 37. He went on to enjoy three terms, although, on reflection, *enjoy* may not be quite the right word. His contemporaries described him as 'pragmatic, logical and clear-sighted,' and he certainly needed to be pragmatic because these were tumultuous times in what might have been regarded as a political backwater. He served around 40 years before political parties were established in New Zealand (the Liberal party was launched in 1891) but that didn't mean the politicians were anything like genteel in their politicking. Democracy was as new as the country itself and the parliament, created four years earlier, was still a fledgling and had an unusually short three-yearly electoral cycle. Relationships between the settlers and the Maori were still tense from an earlier grim incident known as the Wairau Massacre, in which more than a dozen Europeans were reported shot or clubbed to death after having surrendered. The governor of the day decided to let the Maori perpetrators go unpunished and one of his fiercest critics was Edward Stafford. He had taken in an interest in provincial politics after arriving from Scotland in 1843 and readily joined the growing clamour for self-governance. By 1850, he was well enough established to start demanding universal suffrage.

He was highly thought of in political circles but he resisted pressure to stand for election when the new national parliament was created in 1851 and, instead, opted to become the first superintendent when the Nelson Province was established in 1853. Remembering his own privileged background of high school in Edinburgh and university studies at Trinity College, Dublin, he used his new position to create a free, compulsory education system in Nelson that was later used as the basis for the rest of the country. It wasn't until 1855 that he finally became the MP for Nelson and when the national premiership was created the following year, he again declined invitations to compete. He may have had a premonition about the difficulty of the job because its first two holders each only lasted an unlucky 13 days! He had also shrewdly declined offers to join either of their teams and therefore remained untainted by the rows. It was only once the dust had settled and he was being promoted as the only realistic candidate that he deigned to take on the nation's top job.

Once in office, he immediately set about defining relationships between central and provincial government and created a fuss by establishing a cabinet that met independently of the hitherto all-powerful governor's executive council. The governor, already disdainful of the two 13-day wonders, wasn't happy and relations plummeted further when the new prime minister refused responsibility for paying for any decisions not approved by parliament. He also clashed with the governor over who should be responsible for relations with the Maori and that caused him to pursue his demands for democratic self-government with renewed determination. He spent a lot of time travelling abroad to establish New Zealand's place in the world and to develop international trade relations. Without the discipline of a party system, some of his MPs took advantage of his absence and agreed with the governor that the Maori should be forced to sell land at Waitara. While Stafford railed against the proposals on both economic and moral grounds, his opponents accused him of weakness and when he forced the issue in parliament in July 1861, he lost a confidence vote by one!

His replacement as prime minister lasted just a year and he once more had the courage to say no to those who tried to persuade him to return to office. His reasoning was that he could not accept a situation in which parliament's decisions could be blocked by the governor. Showing remarkable single-mindedness, he refused the job a year later, again a year after that and yet again in 1864, as three others failed to make things work. Finally, when stress and illness caused the third resignation, he accepted a second term in October 1865. To counter the excesses – as he saw them – of his predecessors, he called for new efficiency and tighter budgets. He also pursued his enthusiasm for wider democracy and introduced votes for Maori men over 21 and, as a trial, promised there would be four Maori MPs (out of 70) after the 1866 general election. He won.

Sadly, Her Britannic Majesty's governor was as unmoved by this flexing of the democratic muscle as the prime minister was by the imperialism exercised in the name of Queen Victoria. Relations between the two continued to deteriorate. At the centre of it always was the Maori problem and, in particular, who should bear responsibility both for dealing with rebel tribes and for paying the costs. In the end, it was the stiff upper lip that gave way to Scottish cussedness. Britain ceded responsibility to the New Zealand parliament... but not without a final imperial flourish: London demanded compensation for the costs of its various military actions. Edward Stafford counter-claimed for the losses suffered by settlers and the battle raged for two long years but this time there was no winner. Both sets of claims were dropped.

The New Zealand government went on to establish good relations with the Maori but there were still those who were unhappy about reconciliation and their unhappiness was inflamed by the support of the governor. Frustrated, Edward Stafford decided to go to the country and called a general election in 1869. This time, he lost. Three years later he was back in office, but with a very small and unworkable majority. He wanted to hold another election but his friendly governor refused permission and after just a month there was another confidence vote, which he lost.

He tried his hand at opposition politics but was never comfortable in that role. He also declined the occasional offer of a ministerial post. When a former governor, Sir George Grey, was elected prime minister in 1877, it was too much for him. He was only 58 but he retired from politics and spent much of his time back in Britain attending to business matters. He was knighted and someone who clearly didn't know him too well offered him first the job as governor of Madras and later as governor of Queensland. True to his principles, he declined both. He died in London in 1901.

The continuing volatility of New Zealand politics is evidenced in the career of Robert Stout, a lawyer and teacher who emigrated from Scotland as a 19-year-old and was the only man to serve both as the country's thirteenth prime minister (1884–87) and fourth chief justice (1899–1926). Like Edward Stafford, he cut his teeth in local politics, and when he was elected to the Otago Provincial Council many colleagues were impressed by his energy and directness, although some saw it as abrasiveness. When he did move on to national affairs in 1875, it was also as an independent.

He was born in Lerwick in 1844 and is said to have retained a strong and life-long attachment to the Shetland Islands. After what he described as a 'good' education, he qualified first as a teacher and later, when he was still only 16, as a surveyor. As was the tradition on the islands, his extended family regularly met to discuss the key issues of the day and he developed into a free thinker with a broad interest in politics. He emigrated to New Zealand in 1863 and soon after arriving in Dunedin, he found himself attracted to the 'Freethought' group, whose participants held the philosophical view that beliefs should be formed through logic and not overly influenced by emotion, dogma or even tradition.

His first intention was to find a job as a surveyor in the goldfields but that bonanza escaped him and he turned to his teaching skills. He held a series of posts in the city's high schools, but after three years he found that wasn't enough for his restless mind and he decided to go into the law. After working in a solicitor's office and studying in his spare time, he was called to the bar in 1871 but delayed going into practice to instead become one of the first students at New Zealand's first university – at Otago. He studied political economy and the theory of morality. One of the dons was a fellow Scot, Duncan McGregor; he was a graduate of Aberdeen University and it quickly became apparent that the two shared a love for a good philosophical argument. For Stout, this constant sharpening of his wits led to him becoming a highly successful trial lawyer and, for a time, the university's first law lecturer. McGregor went in a very different direction and became inspector general of lunatic asylums in 1886! Once he had made the transition to national politics by being elected MP in 1876, Robert Stout's progress was swift and successful. Within two years, George Grey (the ex-governor-turned-prime minister) appointed him attorney general and four months later gave him the additional portfolio of lands and immigration. Stout was an advocate of land reform and worked towards the nationalisation of land with the objective of then leasing it back to the farmers. He was keen to avoid the development of a powerful landed gentry as there was in Britain. Then, still only 35, he had to give it all up. While he'd been increasingly involved in politics, he had left his partner to look after their law practice. That was still his main source of income and when the partner became ill, he had no option but to resign from both the government and parliament. It was 1879. Out of parliament, he of course maintained many of his old friendships and, away from the political coalface, he could more clearly see the advantages of a party system. He explored the idea of creating what he called 'a united liberal front' to counter the conservative forces at work in New Zealand.

It proved too difficult to achieve and when he returned to parliament in 1884, it was again as an independent. He did try to coordinate a group of like-minded MPs and seemed to be making some headway... enough to successfully muster a no-confidence vote against the conservative prime minister. So, within a month of his return, he became the new prime minister. However, such was the volatility of the country's politics that he was back on the backbenches within two weeks, this time the victim of a no-confidence vote rather than the instigator!

If August in 21st-century UK is regarded as the 'silly season' for politics, in 19th-century New Zealand it can only be described as an exceedingly silly season: it took the pendulum just five days to swing his way again. This time, Stout was able to form a stable government and introduce a programme of real reforms that streamlined the civil service, created more much-needed secondary schools and instigated the building of a major new railway line. At the same time, however, the country's economy hit the buffers and all his attempts to avoid recession came to nought. He was knighted in 1886 but in the general election of 1887 he lost his seat. Feeling badly bruised, he turned away from parliamentary affairs and became active in trying to establish better relationships between the trade unions and employers.

When, in 1891, the Liberal party was finally launched by the new prime minister John Ballance (who had been Stout's minister for native affairs in 1884), he promptly signed up as a member. Two years later, Ballance became seriously ill and urged Stout to return to the fray, with a view to replacing him. He succumbed to temptation but his friend died six weeks before he was able to return to parliament at an 1893 by-election. By that time, however, the deputy was ensconced in the prime minister's office and – on the promise of an early vote – had assumed leadership of the Liberal party. When the promise was not fulfilled, Robert Stout mounted a challenge, but his opponents convinced others that his views were too extreme for the great New Zealand electorate and he was left adrift on the backbenches. There he stayed but continued to play a fairly active role both in parliament and in the Liberal party and he did succeed in eventually winning the case for votes for women in 1893. By 1898, however, he had had enough and finally retired from the political arena.

He was only 54 at the time, and his colleagues knew New Zealand would be a poorer country for the loss of his energy and commitment. They found the perfect role for his brand of independence. In 1899, they made him chief justice and he held that post with distinction for 27 years He was made a privy councillor in 1921 and appointed to the Legislative Council the following year. From 1903 to 1923, he was chancellor of the University of New Zealand and then played a key role in the founding of Wellington University, where there is now a Stout Research Centre and a Robert Stout Building. He died in Wellington in 1930.

In the same 1887 election that Robert Stout lost his seat, Edinburgh-born Thomas Mackenzie became the new MP for the rural constituency of Clutha and was launched on a political career that took him to the top. He became prime minister in 1912, 'almost accidentally' according to contemporary reports, and for an all-too-short three months.

After emigrating from Scotland with his parents and settling in Dunedin, he initially worked as a surveyor like his brother James (who became the country's surveyor general) and that took him to many of the most spectacular areas of both North Island and South Island. It must have been a bit of a shock when, still only 23, he decided to settle down and bought a general stores business in Balclutha (which translates from the Gaelic as 'town on the Clyde'), a small town halfway between Dunedin and Invercargill. The *Encyclopaedia of New Zealand* describes him as a 'modest, hardworking man who made his way by diligence and businesslike methods.' This disciplined application to his new business clearly paid off. He expanded and developed until he was able to sell up for a handsome profit nine years later. This, combined with his membership of the local council, gave him a strong reputation and when he stood for election as an independent MP in 1887, he was duly elected. However, he didn't let his parliamentary duties get in the way of his other abiding passion: exploring his adopted country. His first expedition had been a couple of years earlier and took him to the Tautuku forest along the Otago coast, but now he ventured into the wilder Fiordland country. He took what is now called the Milford Track and dubbed 'the finest walk in the world' by poet Blanche Baughan. In the spectacular mountainous terrain, he discovered the Sutherland Falls – at nearly 2,000 feet, the highest in New Zealand. He also discovered a pass between Lake Manapouri and Hall's Arm and was the first to map the overland route from Dunedin to Dusky Sound (1896), the most south-westerly point of South Island.

He had, of course, continued to sit in the parliament and had worked on developing trade with Britain. In 1896 he hung up his walking boots, resigned from parliament, returned to the UK and for three years assiduously represented the interests of New Zealand's farm cooperatives. Only when he felt he had helped establish a fair trade did he return to New Zealand and once more take up his role as an MP. He joined the first Liberal government of Sir Joseph Ward in January 1909, when he took on an astonishingly broad range of responsibilities: minister of industries and commerce, tourist and health resorts, scenery preservation and state forestry departments. As if that wasn't enough, a few months later he added the role of minister of agriculture, with a seat in the cabinet. He was then successively minister of customs, minister of education, postmaster general and finally, in May 1912, he became the prime minister.

That happened when the unfortunate Sir Joseph was sustained in a confidence motion only by the vote of the speaker, and felt compelled to step down. Thomas Mackenzie was elected leader of the Liberals and duly accepted the invitation to form a government. As was far from unusual in the febrile politics of New Zealand, his glory was short-lived. Mackenzie was in office but so far little more than a caretaker when the ferociously independent-minded MPs ousted him in yet another no-confidence vote. He had survived for just under three months. That was the last straw for him as far as national politics was concerned. Although still only 58, he stepped down and shortly afterwards accepted the role of high commissioner in London.

He was knighted in 1916 and was New Zealand's representative at various peace conferences in 1919, as well as at the League of Nations, and was a member of the Dardanelles Commission. He retired in 1920 and returned to New Zealand, where he was appointed to the Legislative Council the following year and served until his death in Dunedin in 1930. His entry in the *Encyclopaedia of New Zealand* said his political career was based as much on administrative ability as on his power as a speaker although he could always marshal facts effectively. 'He reached the highest office briefly and almost by accident but did not disgrace it. His work as wartime high commissioner was the most valuable phase of his career.'

New Zealand's longest-serving prime minister and founder of the country's Labour party was former dock labourer Peter Fraser from Easter Ross. He was the fourth Scot to hold the office. He served from 1940–49 and is regarded as one of the major figures in the country's political history. He came from a poor family whose dire financial straits meant he had to leave school when he was 12. He got himself an apprenticeship with a local carpenter but unfortunately he developed a serious eye condition (which was to trouble him throughout his life) and had to give it up. That was a double blow because reading was one of his favourite activities. Even at that early stage, politics was in his blood. He became secretary of his local Liberal Association when he was 16. Later, after he left Scotland to work in London and aged 24, he joined the Independent Labour party of Keir Hardie and Ramsay MacDonald. Those were hard times in the city and he couldn't find a job so, in 1910, he emigrated to New Zealand because, he said, 'it had a strong progressive spirit.'

He may have changed his mind a little when he arrived in Auckland and the only work he could get was as a wharfie in the city's bustling docks. If there was any compensation, it was that he was able to more easily indulge his interest in politics. Having swung away from Liberalism, he thought the closest group to his own beliefs were the New Zealand Socialists, a Marxist party that had been founded by British migrants at the beginning of the twentieth century. He became campaign manager for one of their leading candidates, Michael Savage, who he would later succeed as Labour prime minister. He was also a leading figure in the Federation of Labour, the union organisation that had emerged from the coming together of the Federation of Miners and the various waterfront unions. It represented nearly a quarter of the country's workers, but to the ultra-conservative Kiwis he and his colleagues inevitably became known as the Red Feds. His federation work eventually meant he moved to Wellington, where, following the 1913 Unity Conference of trade unions, the left-wing Socialist party and the moderate United Labour party, he helped found the Social Democratic party.

The SDP had a short and traumatic history.

It got off to a great start by winning two by-elections but then quickly found itself mired in controversy. Ignoring the pleas of more moderate voices, the miners and the dockers went on strike and clashed head-on with the Reform party prime minister, William Massey. Farmer Bill, as he was known, showed no patience. He very heavy-handedly quashed the strike and had three of the SDP leaders – including Peter Fraser – arrested on charges of disturbing the peace. The party descended into chaos and went into the 1914 general election with little pre-planning and virtually no organisation. The two by-election winners managed to keep their seats and four other candidates from assorted leftist parties benefited from the lingering anger over the government's handling of the strike and the fears about the looming Great War, but it was not the great opposition that Peter Fraser and his political friends had hoped for.

He was one of the strongest critics of New Zealand's participation in that conflict and branded it 'an imperialist war fought for narrow national interests' rather than for principle, but no one seemed to take much notice. Frustrated with the way things were working out, he called for a new strategy. He advocated a move away from the kind of direct action that had caused so much grief and a concentration on winning more influence in parliament. He managed to use the weakened SDP to pull together his like-minded colleagues and in 1916, they formed the Labour party and he became campaign manager for the leader, Harry Holland, the former Australian socialist who had settled to New Zealand. However, later in the year, his outspoken comments about the war got him arrested again; he had demanded an end to conscription and this time the charge was sedition. He went to jail for a year.

When he got out, he worked as a journalist for the Labour party newspaper and resumed his role as the leader's campaign manager. He finally came out from the back room when he won a parliamentary by-election in 1918 and became the MP for Wellington Central. That was also the beginning of his drift away from the hard left. Having initially been supportive of Russia's Bolshevik Revolution, he now rejected Marxism and went as far as calling for communists to be excluded from the Labour party. Having been burned before by direct action, he tried and, despite the opposition of the party leader, succeeded in moving the party towards the moderate centre. When Holland died in 1933, Fraser contested the leadership but lost out to Michael Savage; nonetheless the two worked happily together and between them they broadened the appeal of the Labour party.

Two years later, they won the general election to form New Zealand's first Labour government, and Peter Fraser threw himself into ensuring its success. In the new cabinet, he took on a hefty package of portfolios: minister of health, minister of education, minister of marine and minister of police. He often worked 17 hours a day, seven days a week. With his background, he inevitably took a particular interest in education, which he knew was vital for social reform. He appointed Dr Clarence Beeby (later acknowledged as the architect of the country's education system) as the department's director and between them they introduced the ethos that 'every person, regardless of background or ability, has a right to an education of a type for which they are best suited'. In his determination to end poverty, he also introduced the 1938 Social Security Act. He was reported to have insisted that 'every citizen has a right to a reasonable standard of living and it is a community responsibility to ensure that its members are safeguarded against the economic ills from which they cannot protect themselves.'

He won a three-way contest to become the prime minister when Michael Savage died in 1940, but in doing so had to concede that the party would have the right to elect members to the cabinet without his prior approval. Although he had strongly opposed it in the Great War, he now acknowledged that conscription was vital to the Second World War effort. He also imposed censorship (in the interests of national security) and wage controls, to the outrage of his former left-wing friends. He tried to establish a unity government for the duration of the war but resistance both from within his own party and from the opposition National party made it impossible. He also had to face battles with Britain over New Zealand troops fighting in Europe: he insisted that they were not just an extension of the British Army and that their commanders must report back to his government. When Japan entered the war, he had another dilemma: to follow Australia's lead in pulling troops back to the Pacific or to leave them in Europe, where Winston Churchill said they were desperately needed. He decided to support Churchill. After the war, he took a much keener interest in international affairs and, in particular, the creation of the United Nations. He tried to stop the major nations having the power of veto within the Security Council and was a constant advocate for the smaller countries. Domestically, he was slow to remove wartime rationing and his insistence on retaining compulsory military training in peacetime damaged him politically. Support dwindled among the war-weary voters. He lost the 1949 general election. While he continued as leader of the opposition, his declining health meant he was unable to play any further significant role in New Zealand's affairs. He died in Wellington the following year. A statue of him stands in the Government Buildings Historic Reserve in Wellington.

GOVERNORS OF NEW ZEALAND

The role of governor of New Zealand became something of a family affair for the Fergussons of Edinburgh. Sir James held the post only briefly, in 1874, but his cousin (David Boyle) was appointed 1892–97, Sir James' son Charles served as governor general 1924–30, and his grandson Bernard took office 1962–67.

Sir James Fergusson, the first Scot to take on the job, was an officer in the Grenadier Guards during the Crimean War (1854–56) and also held the parliamentary seat of Ayrshire 1854–57 and again 1859–68. When he left parliament, he was made a privy councillor and appointed governor of South Australia for the five years to 1873. In his honour, the Australians named Jamestown after him. Although he stepped down from the New Zealand post, he remained within the colonial service and became governor of

Bombay in 1880. He remained there for five years and when he returned to Britain, he re-entered the House of Commons as the MP for Manchester North East. He was killed in an earthquake during a visit to Jamaica in 1907.

Arthur Hamilton Gordon (later Baron Stanmore), son of the Earl of Aberdeen, the one-time British prime minister, was a serial colonial governor. He served in New Zealand for three years (1880–83) after having been governor of New Brunswick (1861–66), Trinidad (1866–70), Mauritius (1871–74), and Fiji (1875–80). When he left New Zealand, it was to go to Ceylon as governor (1883–90). He went to Trinity College, where he had been president of the Cambridge Union Society in 1849. After graduating, he had worked as an assistant private secretary to his father while he was prime minister (1852–55), before moving to the Foreign Service.

David Boyle, the 7th Earl of Glasgow, was governor from 1892 to 1897. He had previously been a career Royal Navy officer who had seen action in the Crimea (1854–55) and in the Second Opium War in China (1857). In New Zealand, he inherited the uneasy relations between his office and the government resulting from an earlier row about appointments to the Legislative Council. However, his naval expertise was invaluable and he was always consulted on defence matters – although there were continuing debates about his formal role as commander-in-chief of the forces. His diplomatic skills avoided any major problems and he survived his five years in what was described as a congenial atmosphere. A suburb of Wellington was named Kelburn (after his family estate in Scotland) in his honour. When he asked to be relieved from the post in 1897, it was because he found himself 'unable to uphold the dignity of the office on the salary provided.'

Although the finer points of it escape me, the title of the office was upgraded to governor general in 1917 and the first Scot to benefit was Major General Sir Charles Fergusson (son of Sir James) who held the post 1924–1930. He, too, was a military veteran. He joined the Grenadier Guards after Eton and Sandhurst and served with the Egyptian Army under Kitchener. He fought in the Sudan campaigns of 1896–98 and rose to be adjutant general of the British Army (1900–03). He was promoted to major general in 1912 and given command of 5th (Irish) Division. In the Great War, he commanded 2nd Army Group and then 17th Army Group in France. By the end of the war, he was military governor of Cologne (1918–20). When he returned from New Zealand, he became chairman of the West Indies Closer Union Commission in 1933 and was lord lieutenant of Ayrshire 1937–51.

His son, Sir Bernard Fergusson (later Lord Ballantrae), governor general 1962–1967, also came to New Zealand with a proud reputation as a distinguished soldier, as well as being well-known as a writer. He was commissioned into the Black Watch in 1931 and for two years was aide-de-camp to General Archibald Wavell (later Field Marshal Lord Wavell, whose biography he wrote). In the Second World War he served as an intelligence officer in Palestine and Turkey and then fought the Vichy French in Syria. He was commanding officer of 2nd Black Watch at the Siege of Tobruk in North

Africa in 1941 and led his men in a dramatic break out to the skirl of the bagpipes played by Pipe Major Robert Roy. Two years later, he was in Burma joining in the deep-penetration sorties of Colonel Orde Wingate's Chindits. After the war, he served in Palestine and then became colonel of the Black Watch. He took part in the Suez operation of 1956, commanding two brigades in succession and retiring from the army in 1958. He became Lord Ballantrae in 1972 and was chairman of the British Council 1972–74. He published two books about his experiences in Burma, *Beyond the Chindwin* and *The Wild Green Earth*, plus his biography of Wavell and his own autobiography, *Trumpet in the Hall*.

8

SCOTLAND AND THE STARS AND STRIPES

 'Every line of strength in American history is a line coloured with Scottish blood.'
— *Woodrow Wilson*

There are indelible Scottish fingerprints – and footprints – all over America, from sea to shining sea. Scots were an integral part of the migrating huddled masses and have contributed significantly to the history of the most powerful nation in the democratic world. Just how relevant and how significant can be assessed from the 2000 US Census, in which the number-crunchers counted nearly five million people of what they call 'Scottish heritage', not that far short of the number currently living in Scotland. Fortunately, in the hope of completing this commentary in my lifetime, I have long since determined that I would concentrate on those actually born in Scotland and who made their impact through the run-up to independence and onwards. While that dramatically reduces the scale, it has still left me with a near-impossible task and I offer this chapter as a best effort of idiosyncrasy and not as an attempt at being comprehensive.

Having thus made my excuses, let me start somewhere near the beginning. There were countless Scots on the crowded ships that sailed with so much hope and determination to find a new life in the New World in the eighteenth century. They had made dangerous voyages on storm-tossed seas, risking icebergs and pirates and the horrors of yellow fever and scurvy and dysentery and all manner of privations. Not all survived and ships' logs are filled with the names of those poor souls who ended their journey in hessian body-bags

When the lucky ones eventually set foot on dry land, they infiltrated, they adapted, adopted and absorbed the culture of the time, they fought for, they fought against (quite often they did both in the same battle) and they fought alongside, they were part of the great welding exercise that forged the new nation and helped shape the very nature of its democracy, they became more Western than many cowboys and were equally happy to marry into the native American tribes, they explored and they settled and then they explored some more, they built bridges, both physical and metaphorical, they crossed the prairies and scaled the mountains, they made fortunes and lost fortunes and more importantly, they eagerly gave of their talents, energy and commitment and provided much of what the emerging nation needed, they created new communities, sometimes too inward-looking to survive, more often extrovert enough to still be on the map today, they helped reinvent the world, and they used the bagpipes and kilted swagger to inspire or intimidate as the occasion decreed. There was no United States then... just a collection of 13 colonies and 13 clocks ticking towards the overthrow of a British king and an imperialist parliament.

The ticking began around 1763 when the Seven Years War ended and the British sought to recover some of their costs by taxing their colonial subjects for the privilege of being part of the Empire (which had just got bigger as a result of the war) and by imposing a raft of inhibiting laws. Because the colonies did not have elected representation in the British parliament, many colonists considered the tax demands and the new laws illegitimate and a violation of their rights. As tension mounted, the colonists – through their patriot groups – created committees of correspondence and then effectively replaced the British control apparatus with their own provincial congresses. In 1774, the 13 colonies united at the Continental Congress and the following year the tension erupted into war. In 1776, representatives of the 13 colonies voted unanimously to adopt the Declaration of Independence. It was written by Thomas Jefferson and included the famous line: 'We hold these truths to be self-evident, that all men are created equal, that they are endowed by their Creator with certain unalienable rights, that among these are Life, Liberty and the pursuit of Happiness.' In a speech during the debate that effectively established the United States, New York Senator Gulian Verplanck said he traced the origin of the Declaration to the National Covenant of Scotland. Certainly there is evidence of some strong Scottish influence. Of the 56 signatories, two were Scots: lawyer James Wilson of Ceres in Fife and the Reverend John Witherspoon, a Presbyterian minister from Gifford in East Lothian (six others were Presbyterians of Scots descent). Both are said to have made key contributions to the process and both also contributed to the later framing of the constitution.

James Wilson (born Caskerdo, Fife, 1742–98) went to America when he was 22 but was already an established politician and legal expert in the run-up to independence. He served two terms in the Continental Congress and his legal expertise made him a key figure in drafting the constitution. George Washington rewarded his sterling efforts by appointing him as one of the six original judges of the Supreme Court of the new United States. He had a background ideally suited to the arduous struggle for a new life in his adopted land. He was one of seven children in a Presbyterian farming family and was reading law at St Andrews University when he hit his first brick wall: his father died in 1764 and he had to leave before graduating. While lesser men might have buckled, he sailed for Philadelphia… with a letter of introduction to wealthy lawyer and politician John Dickinson, who was to have a profound impact on his career. He worked for several years as a legal assistant to Dickinson – who went on to be a congressman – and unsurprisingly became absorbed in the politics of the time. He also qualified as a barrister, moved on to set up his own lucrative practice and became one of the most prominent lawyers in Pennsylvania. After that, it was only a matter of time before he followed Dickinson into the political arena, where his legal expertise proved invaluable. In 1774, he published a pamphlet denying the authority of the British parliament over the colonies. When he was elected to the Continental Congress in 1776, he argued even more forcibly for independence and was soon acknowledged as the leading advocate for the case. A colleague said of him: 'Government seems to have been his peculiar study, all the political institutions of the world he knows in detail and can trace the causes and effects of every revolution from the earliest stages of the Grecian commonwealth down to the present time.'

After signing the Declaration of Independence in 1776, he served on the Committee on Spies with John Adams, Thomas Jefferson, John Rutledge and Robert Livingston and helped define treason. He was embroiled in what became known as the Fort Wilson Riot in 1779, when militia protesting about food shortages, price regulation and inflation marched on his house in Philadelphia. He and 35 colleagues barricaded themselves in (hence 'Fort Wilson') and in the ensuing conflict, five soldiers died and nearly 20 people were injured before rescuing forces arrived. He was later elected to the Committee of Detail, which produced the first draft of the United States Constitution in 1787. He argued that the president and senators should be elected by the people and he devised the extraordinary 'Three-Fifths Compromise', which gave slave owners representation based on three-fifths of the total number of slaves they owned (the compromise was between the wishes of the slave-owning southern states, who wanted slaves to be counted in full for tax-distribution and representational purposes, and the north, which preferred to count only free men and thus avoid southern domination of the House of Representatives). Wilson is reported as having addressed the convention more than 150 times and was described as having a vision of an almost unlimited future for the United States. Another colleague said his mind was as 'sharp as one blaze of light.'

When he became a Supreme Court judge, he also found time to launch – in 1790 – a series of law lectures at the College of Philadelphia and these were so successful that they led to the eventual establishment of The University of Pennsylvania Law School. Sadly, his waning years were far from happy. His land investments ran him into heavy debt and twice he found himself in jail for non-payment. He moved to North Carolina to escape other creditors, but there caught malaria and died after a stroke in 1798. In 1956, his biographer Page Smith wrote: 'Tracing over the events of Wilson's life, we are impressed by the lucid quality of his mind. With this went a restless energy and insatiable ambition, an almost frightening vitality that turned with undiminished energy and enthusiasm to new tasks and new ventures. Yet, when all has been said and despite our probing, the inner man remains an enigma.'

John Witherspoon (born Gifford, East Lothian, 1723–94) was 45 and already a highly regarded preacher when he went to America in 1768. Just eight years later, he was the congressman for New Jersey and only clergyman to sign the Declaration. He was from strong Presbyterian stock, the eldest child of a kirk minister, who ensured he was well educated. He went to Haddington Grammar School, took an MA at Edinburgh University in 1739 and then stayed on to study divinity. As a young man, he was unfashionably opposed to the Jacobite uprising of 1745 and after the Battle of Falkirk he was imprisoned at Doune Castle. While that did nothing to diminish his convictions, it did have a deleterious and long-term effect on his health. After his ordination, he was minister in Beith until 1758 and then at Paisley's Laigh Kirk, 1758–68. He wrote extensively on theology and in the satire *Ecclesiastical Characteristics* he was highly critical of fashionable philosopher Frances Hutcheson (professor at Glasgow University), but that did nothing to impede the award of doctor of divinity from St Andrews. It was in Paisley that he met two American Christians who persuaded him to go to America in 1768. They were Benjamin Rush and Richard Stockton (who both were also later signatories of the Declaration) and the lure was the top job at the Presbyterian College of New Jersey. So, at the age of 45, he took his family to America, where he became the sixth president of the college that would later become Princeton University.

He is said to have modelled his syllabus on what he had seen at St Andrews and his most important course was moral philosophy, which he insisted was de rigueur for ministers, lawyers and anyone intending to go into government. In addition he offered eloquence or belles lettres, chronology (history) and divinity. His success at Princeton can be seen from even the most cursory glance at a list of his former students, who include President James Madison (served 1809–17), Vice President Aaron Burr (served under Thomas Jefferson, 1801–05), 37 judges, including three who went on to the Supreme Court, 12 members of the Continental Congress, 28 senators and 49 congressmen. The main raison d'être of the college was, of course, to train ministers and as evidence of his success in that area, a head count at the General Assembly of the US Presbyterian Church in 1789 showed that 52 of the 200 delegates had studied under him; this offers some idea of how his influence spread in the new republic.

When he became aware that the British troops were marching in the direction of Princeton, he immediately evacuated the college but the main building was badly damaged and all his records and personal papers were destroyed. He rebuilt it after the war, largely at his own expense. He went into politics with the same sort of zeal and energy with which he ran Princeton and from 1776 to 1782, he served in Congress, where he was described as 'a workhorse of prodigious energy.' He served on more than a hundred committees, including the key standing committees, the Board of War and the foreign affairs committee. He helped draft and later signed the Articles of Confederation in 1778, organised the executive departments, helped shape foreign policy; and devised guidance for the peace commissioners. Sadly he went blind in 1792 and died two years later at the age of 71.

There are statues in his honour at Princeton University and outside the University of West Scotland, Paisley (both bronzes by Scottish sculptor Alexander Stoddart), and in Washington. In Princeton there is the Witherspoon dormitory, built in 1877, and the street outside the main gate and the local public middle school also bear his name.

If we claim Scots had an influence in the achievement of independence, it must be said that they may also have contributed to the unrest that led to it. Of the colonial governors sent from Britain to the American colonies before the revolution, more than 20 were Scots. The first was The Earl of Orkney, who was appointed in 1714 but appears to have distinguished himself by not bothering to even visit the colony. He was the British Army's first field marshal in 1736.

The most prominent was Robert Dinwiddie from Glasgow, who is referred to in some history books as the 'Grandfather of the United States'. He was lieutenant governor of Virginia during the Seven Years War (known in America as the French-Indian war) of 1751–58. He created the first all-colonial professional military unit, the Virginia Regiment, in which one of his young officers was 21-year-old George Washington. Although colonials had served in the British Army and there were various part-time militias, the regiment was the first to wear a common uniform and to train regularly. In the continuing absence of the governor (a not unusual occurrence), Dinwiddie was effectively in control of the colony and when the French started making threatening noises from neighbouring Ohio, he dispatched Washington and an eight-strong group of soldiers to warn them off. The journey, in the winter of 1753, was in vain and the French refused to withdraw. The determined Dinwiddie sent Washington back, this time with 400 soldiers, to put the French in their place. The two sides clashed at Fort Necessity, where the unfortunate president-to-be suffered the only military defeat of his illustrious career. When Dinwiddie sent an even greater army to take on the French, Washington was aide-de-camp to the commander, General John Forbes (from Pittencrieff in Fife). In what was later described as 'a feat worthy of Hercules,' the general led his men, including the Scots Greys, across prairie wilderness and over mountains to capture Fort Duchesne. After routing the French, the one-time medical student established a new settlement that he called Pittsburgh in honour of Prime Minister William Pitt, the Elder. It was the beginning of a great conflict that occupied Robert Dinwiddie for the rest of his time in office as he rallied the other colonies against the French. The appreciative Virginians named Dinwiddie County in his honour.

The other Scots who served as British governors of Virginia were the Reverend Dr James Blair from Banffshire (1740–41), the Earl of Loudon (1756–58) and the last of the crown-appointees, the 4th Earl of Dunmore (1771–75), who had earlier been governor of New York (1770–71). Dr Blair played a major part in developing education in America and was founder of the William and Mary College in 1693 (see later in chapter). The Earl of Dunmore gave his name to a series of campaigns against the

Indians. 'Lord Dunmore's War' – waged mainly against the Shawnee – was supposedly to strengthen Virginia's claims to territory in Ohio country but others saw it as a loyalist action aimed at depleting the militia in fear of a colonial uprising. He is credited with the first mass emancipation of slaves through 'Lord Dunmore's Proclamation' (issued on 7 November 1775) which gave freedom to those who joined his Ethiopian Regiment. He clearly had a degree of prescience because the tensions between the British and the Colonial Assembly heightened and he retreated to his hunting lodge well away from Williamsburg. When the Revolutionary War broke out, he had to seek refuge on a Royal Navy warship in the York River and when he realised he could not regain control in Virginia, he returned to Britain in July 1776.

New York had six Scottish governors prior to the end of the American War of Independence. General Robert Hunter (born Edinburgh, 1666–1734) served simultaneously as governor of New Jersey throughout his ten years in office (1710–1720) and appears to have at least tried to live up to his belief that 'the true interests of the people and the government are the same.' He began his career as an apprentice to an apothecary but then joined the army in 1689 and eventually won a commission and rose to the rank of general. He fought with the Duke of Marlborough at Blenheim in 1704 and Ramillies in 1706 and it was presumably for this service he was appointed lieutenant governor of Virginia in 1707. However, en route to his new billet, he was captured by the French and spent two years in a French jail. On his release in 1709 he was sent to New York. He was a man of few words and his first address to the Assembly lasted barely two minutes, which he excused with a neat phrase: 'If honesty is the best policy, plainness must be the best oratory.'

Colonel John Montgomerie (born Giffen, died 1731) also served both colonies from 1728–31. He was an officer in 3rd Foot Guards before succeeding his father as the MP for Ayrshire (1708–22) and serving as master of the mint in Scotland. Cadwallader Colden (born to Scottish parents in Ireland, 1688–1776) was lieutenant governor for four periods between 1760 and 1775. He was a distinguished academic who tried to develop the resources of the state. A son of the manse, he went to Edinburgh Royal High School and then to Edinburgh University intending to follow in his father's footsteps and become a minister. However, he became interested in medicine and went back to study physics, anatomy, chemistry and botany. When he qualified, he went to live with an aunt in Philadelphia, where he established a general practice in 1710. After marrying back home in Scotland, he took his new bride to America. During his second term as governor, in 1765, he was faced with a mass protest against the Stamp Act which took on personal overtones when a mob carried his effigy. They also stole his coach and burned it and the effigy at the end of the protest. He later served as the first colonial representative to the highly successful 1775 Iroquois Confederacy and was so impressed with the level of debate that he wrote *The History of the Five Indian Nations*, the first book on the subject. Edmund Bailey O'Callaghan in his *Documentary History of the State of New York* says: 'Posterity will not fail to accord justice to the character and memory of a man to whom this country is most deeply indebted for much of its science and for many of its most important institutions, and of whom the State of New York may well be proud.' His grandson, David Cadwallader Colden, was the state's elected governor from 1818 to 1821.

After the 4th Earl of Dunmore served as governor 1770–71 (see earlier mention as governor of Virginia), the next Scot in line was lieutenant general James Robertson (born Newbigging, Fife, 1717–1788), who had gone to the colonies as a major with Britain's American troops in 1756. He was promoted to lieutenant colonel two years later and was appointed barrack master in New York. At the outbreak of the war, he became a full colonel in command of the 60th Regiment of Foot in 1776. He commanded a brigade at the Battle of Long Island, the bloodiest of the conflict, in which more than 300 of Washington's men died and nearly 1500 were wounded. The action allowed the British to set up their key headquarters in New York, where he became governor in 1880.

Robertson returned to Scotland in 1783 and was replaced by Andrew Elliot from Edinburgh, the last colonial governor. His appointment was unusual in that he had gone to America as an 18-year-old apprentice before developing into a merchant and pillar of society in Philadelphia. He was a city councillor and trustee of the city college (now the University of Pennsylvania). When war broke out, he remained loyal to the crown and was appointed at various points head of the customs, superintendent general of police, commissioner for restoring peace to the colonies and then military governor in 1783. Within months, when it was clear the Americans had won, he joined the delegation that met with George Washington and other American envoys to broker the peace. Although he was assured that neither his life nor his property were at risk, he and his family returned to Scotland and he declined an invitation in 1790 to serve as British minister to America.

In New Jersey, Lord Neil Campbell, son of the 9th Earl of Argyll, was appointed governor in 1687 but 'meddled little in the affairs of the colony.' When he left, his deputy Andrew Hamilton (from Edinburgh) became acting governor. He was, according to contemporary reports, 'an active energetic officer, who rendered good service' and organised the first postal service in the colonies. His son John Hamilton was acting governor for a time while he moved on to be governor in Pennsylvania (1701–03).

Apart from the Hamiltons, Pennsylvania had another Scots governor: Sir William Keith, from Peterhead, who served for a record nine years (1717–26). He was a Jacobite and served in the exiled court in France but was allowed to return to Scotland under the amnesty granted by Queen Anne on her ascension to the throne in 1702. However, a year later he was arrested on suspicion of treason but not charged. He first went to America as the Conservative-appointed surveyor general in a district of Virginia in 1714 but he lost that job in a change of government in London and came home to learn his father was implicated in the '45 Rebellion and had fled once more to France. He again sailed for America, this time for his appointment in Pennsylvania. While serving as lieutenant governor, he was popular with the colonists and managed to organise a militia (no small feat in a Quaker colony) and established a high court of chancery. He also arranged peace conferences with the Indians and promoted laws allowing wives of sailors at sea to become 'femme sole traders.' He also encouraged a 17-year-old Benjamin Franklin, who was to become one of America's founding fathers, to set up his own printing business in Philadelphia.

The first governor of the Albemarle County colony (then still part of Virginia but later to become North Carolina) in 1664 was William Drummond from Perthshire. He became an early patriot martyr when he was executed for his part in the first rebellion in the colonies in 1676. The crisis began when settlers led by Nathaniel Bacon demanded action against marauding Indians and Governor Sir William Berkeley refused to intervene. William Drummond sided with the frontiersmen in 'an insurrection brought about by the insolence and pig-headedness of the governor' and the situation escalated. Bacon's followers first laid siege to and then took over Jamestown... for three months. It took the British navy to regain the capital and the governor's retribution was swift. William Drummond was among the first to be tried and executed.

In stark contrast, Gabriel Johnston (born Annandale, Dumfries, 1699–1752) was the longest serving of all the colonial governors and had Johnston County named in his honour. He served in North Carolina from 1734 until his death in 1752, when he was just 53. Before going to America, he was professor of oriental languages at St Andrews University, where he had originally studied medicine. He also spent several years in London as a political commentator. During his tenure as governor, he had to face economic problems, internecine rows between local politicians, threats from Spanish pirates and disagreements over land rights and taxes. While he dealt with those issues, he also encouraged thousands of immigrants – including many from the Highlands – to settle in North Carolina. He also managed to hold the balance between his loyalty to the British crown and the ever-growing demands for independence.

In South Carolina there were two Scots governors: James Glen (born Linlithgow, 1701–1777) served for 13 years (1743–56) and Lord William Campbell (c.1730–1778), brother of the Duke of Argyll, was the last colonial governor and served in 1775. James Glenn's most signal achievement as governor was to broker a peace deal between the warring Creek and Cherokee Indians. His reward was the grant of several thousand acres of land from the Cherokee and it was there he built Fort Prince George, an important outpost and trading centre. Lord William Campbell was the last colonial governor of South Carolina. He had lobbied hard for the job mainly because his wife was a native of the province but had the misfortune to arrive in the year the fighting broke out in the War of Independence. He tried to pacify the revolutionaries but was unable to stop the intimidation against British officials nor the public violence and even hangings. In the end, he fled from Charleston aboard a British warship. When he returned the following year as part of the military attack on Fort Moultrie, he received wounds from which he died two years later.

When Florida was ceded to Britain by the Spanish in 1763, the first governor of West Florida was Commodore George Johnstone (born Westerhall, Dumfries, 1730–1787) and he served for four years. He was an irascible character who was once court-martialed for 'insubordination and disobedience' while still a Royal Navy lieutenant (1755) and later challenged to a duel for insulting a government minister with 'shameless and scurrilous utterances' while he was an MP (1770). However, his record of bravery in action got him off the navy charge with nothing more than a reprimand. He rose to captain in 1762 and commodore the following year when he was also appointed to Florida. In keeping with his disreputable reputation, his main activity there appears to have been fathering four illegitimate children – three sons and a daughter – each of whom he acknowledged and supported financially. When he returned to Britain in 1767, he became an MP and, despite the duel which ended with both men unhurt, served in the Commons for 20 years – although he did represent four different constituencies in the period.

In a classic attempt at closing the stable door, the prime minister (Lord North) proposed in 1770 partially repealing some of those taxes that the colonials found intolerable. George Johnstone was asked to go back to America as a member of the Carlisle Peace Commission in 1778 to try to find a way out of the war. It was to no avail. He again had his character called into question when he was accused of bribery and the Continental Congress refused to negotiate with the commission. They would settle for nothing less than independence. Back once more in Britain and anxious to continue to serve the crown, he used his political influence to get command of a naval squadron patrolling the South Atlantic in 1779 and had moderate success in capturing a French frigate and winning the Battle of Porto Praya. After the war, in 1783, he became a director of the East India Company until poor health (he was suffering with throat cancer) forced him to retire from public life in 1785. He died two years later.

While these Scots were, largely, stoutly trying to protect the interest of King and Empire, there were others who just as strongly saw themselves as part of the new order in the New World – but that was a privilege that didn't come without a long and bitter struggle. When war became inevitable in 1775, it was the Scottish soldier Major John Pitcairn (born Dysart, Fife, 1722–1775) who is said to have fired the first shots in the first engagement between the British and the revolutionary forces. He had been serving with the occupation army in Boston and was in command of the advance party of Redcoats at Lexington on 19 April 1775. Two months later, he was one of nearly 230 British soldiers killed in the battle of Bunker Hill.

Lexington was the turning point for the colonialists and almost immediately after this outbreak of hostilities the powers of the crown governors drained away and a new democratic order was established with elected and directly-accountable governors. One of the new breed was Scotsman Edward Telfair (born Town Head, Dumfries, 1735–1807), who had emigrated from his native Kirkcudbright in 1758. He was one of the strongest supporters of independence and was Georgia's elected governor in 1786 and 1790–93. During his second term, he saw the ratification of the state constitution. He was previously a member of the Continental Congress, 1778–83. After attending Kirkcudbright Grammar School, he learned basic business skills in a commercial office and it was as the company's representative that he went to Virginia in 1758, when he was 23. Promotion took him on to North Carolina and then, in 1766, he moved to Savannah, where he joined his brother and another Scot in a partnership that developed into one of the most successful merchant trading companies in Georgia. As the business grew, he invested in land and established a major plantation (complete with a large number of slaves) in the Savannah River basin. Two years later and with his business future secured, he turned his attention to politics as a vociferous advocate of independence.

In 1768, he was elected to the Commons House of Assembly and became irrevocably involved in the revolutionary struggle. He was a member of the Sons of Liberty and when news of the fighting at Lexington reached them in May 1775, he joined a group that broke into the British arsenal and seized a large quantity of gunpowder. He was appointed to the Committee of Safety (1775–76), the Provincial Congress (1776) and the Committee of Intelligence (1776). He was elected to the Continental Congress in 1778 and, in the same year, he was one of Georgia's three signatories to the Articles of Confederation. Before the Articles were formally ratified, the British named him as one of the congressmen guilty of treason but did not seek redress. In 1783 he was appointed commissioner to deal with the Cherokee Indians and as Georgia's agent in settling northern boundary disputes.

When he was elected governor of Georgia, in 1786, it was for a one-year term and he had to spend most of that time trying to put the state's finances in order and staving off a war with the Creek Indians. During his second and third terms as governor (1790–93) he tried to balance the rights of the state against the necessary tax and judicial powers of the new federal government. When he died, he was buried with full military honours and Telfair County was created and named in his honour. The family home was later bequeathed to Georgia Historical Society and it was converted to the Telfair Museum of Art, the first public gallery in the southern states. In 2006, a new state-of-the-art building was added to the site.

In Virginia, it was Scotsman Colonel William Fleming, from Jedburgh, who briefly took over as governor when Thomas Jefferson's term of office ran out in difficult circumstances in 1781. When British forces took over in the colony, Jefferson and most of his legislative colleagues were forced to flee. Colonel Fleming was the most senior member left and he took on the role for just nine days, during which he called out the militia to repel the Redcoats, an action only legalised retrospectively.

Alexander McDougall (born Islay, 1732–1786) may have been something of a reluctant soldier but he rose to become commander of the key post of West Point (later to be home of the military academy), appointed by no less a figure than George Washington. Born in Islay, he was yet another émigré who found success in his adopted land, but not without a struggle. With his parents and a group of other colonists, he settled in Fort Edward, New York, and for a while earned a meagre living delivering milk. When he was 14, he signed on as a merchant seaman and survived the tough life of a deckhand, junior officer and skipper until he was eventually able to own his own cargo ship. At the outset of the Seven Year War in 1756, he fitted his ship with guns and became a merchant privateer (we would call him a pirate), captured several French ships and made his fortune selling off their cargo in America. In 1763, he decided to cash in his naval assets and soon established himself as a merchant of substance and an importer of considerable success. He then acquired extensive land holdings around New York but not quite enough to make him wholly acceptable to city society. His broad Scots accent and his clothes were both a trifle too loud, it was said!

Pragmatism, however, won the day. With the States in revolutionary ferment, McDougall's outspoken comments on the notorious (in America) Stamp Act were clearly welcomed by his business associates and when he joined the Sons of Liberty, he was soon appointed their leader in the city. In 1770, despite never being convicted but because he refused to put up bail, he spent five months in jail for the alleged libel of senators who had approved financial support for the British troops. His popularity was such that the jailers had to introduce an appointment system for his many visitors. In the end, he was released unconditionally and immediately resumed his role as leader of the protesters, notably in 1773, against the Tea Tax. When New York finally established its revolutionary government in 1775, he was elected to the Provincial Congress.

In the same year, he was also commissioned as colonel of the 1st New York Regiment and enjoyed spectacular success by being promoted to brigadier general in 1776 and a major general in 1777. He led a brigade in the inconclusive battles of White Plains and Germantown and was then given the key job of commanding officer at West Point, which Washington regarded as the most important posting in his army. When the war ended, McDougall returned to commerce and became the first president of the giant Bank of New York.

One of the most significant Scottish contributions to the patriot cause must have been that of John Paul Jones, who is acknowledged as the father of the US Navy, formed in 1778. Like Edward Telfair, he also came from Kirkcudbrightshire, where he joined the navy when he was just 13. His exploits as a British-pirate-turned-all-American-hero-turned-Russian-admiral are well tabulated and need little amplification here. But one story I hadn't heard before – and can only hope is true – is the tale of the Countess of Selkirk's teapot! Jones is said to have led a raid on the Earl of Selkirk's home, intending to capture him to exchange for American prisoners. His lordship was absent and his wife was having breakfast so Jones settled for taking the family silver – including the still-warm teapot. He later bought it back from his crew and, on his eventual return to America, returned it to the countess with a letter of apology.

Symbolic of the Scots' contribution to the independence struggle was the kilted general who commanded the military escort at the inauguration of George Washington as the new nation's first president on 30 April 1789. He was Brigadier General William

Malcolm (born Glenrothes, 1745–1791), who migrated to America in 1778 and enlisted to serve in Washington's army later in the same year.

One of George Washington's closest advisers was Alexander Hamilton. He was born in the West Indies but regarded himself as a good Scot (from his father, a laird from Ayrshire). He joined the militia in New York at the beginning of the war and became the General's senior aide-de-camp. After the war he served briefly in congress but then switched to the New York Legislature, where he was the state's representative in signing the new constitution. When Washington became president in 1789, he made Hamilton the founding secretary of the US Treasury. He served for six years, during which he advised the government to take on the national debt and established a national bank. He also founded the country's first effective national political group, the Federalist party. But he was dogged by controversy and had to quit his Treasury post in what must have been another first – the United States' first political scandal. He had a three-year affair with the wife of an army officer who eventually handed love letters to investigators. The man who exposed him was another Scot, James Callendar (see later in this chapter). In 1801, Alexander Hamilton founded the *New York Post* (initially as the Federalist broadsheet *Evening Post*), which continues today as part of the Murdoch news empire. In 1804, he was engaged in one of the most bizarre events in political history. His constant clashing with the vice president Aaron Burr boiled over and ended with two of the country's most senior politicians facing each other in a duel. Hamilton lost. He was mortally wounded by a pistol shot and died the next day from his wounds.

Life in the New World was not all about politics and power, however, and there were many Scots among those who cared more about health and welfare, education and culture. On the health front, there are far too many Scots doctors dotted through the American history books to include them all in this limited volume. One who had influence beyond his lifetime was Gustavus Brown. He emigrated in 1708 and settled in Maryland and called his family home Middleton, after his birthplace near Dalkeith, where his father had been the local laird. Hard as he worked personally, however, his major legacy was to ensure that both his son and grandson – both also called Gustavus – read medicine in Edinburgh and returned to look after the well-being of Marylanders. The grandson became surgeon general of the Revolutionary Army in 1775 and was later personal doctor to George Washington during his final illness.

Alexander Garden from Birse, Aberdeenshire, was the doctor who, in 1760, did much to stop the spread of smallpox among colonists in Charleston, South Carolina, by inoculating more than 2,000 people. While studying medicine at Edinburgh University, he formed a keen interest in the medical use of plants and this developed into a general interest in natural history, which he pursued alongside his medical practice. He examined every kind of species in what was then Cherokee territory and he kept British collectors supplied with samples of plants, birds, insects, fish, reptiles and amphibians, including the first electric eel seen in Britain. He was so highly thought of – for his 'benevolence, cheerfulness, and pleasing manners' – that the Swedish naturalist Carl Linnaeus named the gardenia flower in his honour. Enthusiastic as he was about life under the Carolina moon, he was still a British loyalist and when Lord Cornwallis routed the American forces at the Battle of Camden in 1780, he voiced his congratulations. That was his undoing: his no-longer-grateful neighbours had his property confiscated and he had to flee the country. Back in Britain, he tried to pick up the pieces of his former career and became vice-president of the Royal Society but he was dogged by ill-health and died of tuberculosis in 1791.

Another Scot who recognised the impact of the environment on his patients' health was Dr John Lining (born Lanarkshire, 1708–1760), who left his native country when he was 22 and settled in Charleston sometime around 1730. Although he started his medical career as a GP and developed a successful practice, he became so concerned about the endemic diseases of the area that he turned investigative clinician. He made the connection between poor sanitation and poor health and he was also a pioneer in relating illnesses to the climate. 'They [the illnesses] as regularly return at their stated season as a good clock strikes 12 when the sun is in the meridian,' he wrote in his notebook. He worked tirelessly, often acting as his own guinea pig in finding answers to key health problems and, in doing so, changed the face of the sick room from heavily-shuttered gloom and pessimism to bright and airy hopefulness which, he asserted, was more conducive to recuperation. He also studied and, in 1751, wrote about *The American Yellow Fever* and helped develop quarantine arrangements to stop further diseases being brought into the country. As evidence of the regard in which he was held, a local newspaper obituary tribute said he had 'possessed all the good qualifications that could render his loss great, as a physician, husband, father, master, friend, neighbour and companion.'

Yet another who linked health to the environment was Dr Lionel Chalmers (born Argyll, 1715-1777). He also practised in Charleston, for more than 40 years in his case, and he fought the ignorance and fears of his patients as relentlessly as he fought disease. He was horrified to learn that a local 'cure' for smallpox was the habit of stuffing the patient's feet in the abdominal cavity of a gutted bird while applying a throat poultice of dung and honey! He had taken his medical degrees in Edinburgh before emigrating in 1735. In Charleston, he combined general practice with extensive research. For example, he recorded his observations on the weather for the ten years between 1750 and 1760, and published the results in his *Treatise on the Weather and Diseases of South Carolina*. He also produced his *Essay on Fevers* (1767). When he died, they named a street after him but he would almost certainly have been more appreciative of the tribute paid by the town mayor: 'He left behind him the name of a skilful, humane physician.'

Dr James Craik (born Dumfriesshire, 1731–1814) was yet another associate of George Washington. He was physician general to the Revolutionary Army, 1798–1800, an appointment that stemmed from his close friendship of 40 years with the president. He was his doctor during Washington's last illness and, with the younger Gustavus

Brown and another doctor, was at his bedside when he died in 1799. Born in 1731, he was said to be the illegitimate son of an MP, who coincidentally employed the father of John Paul Jones. He studied medicine in Edinburgh and, after graduating, joined the British Army as a surgeon. He served in the West Indies, where he resigned his commission to go and set up a private practice in Norfolk, Virginia. Much to his father's disgust, he became a committed Yankee and fervent supporter of the colonists and the two never spoke again. In 1754, he again went into uniform but this time as a surgeon in the Virginia Provincial Regiment. He served with such distinction that he was awarded £30,000 as a reward. It was around this time he first befriended Washington, who he later joined on surveying expeditions Pennsylvania in 1770 and what is now West Virginia in 1784. During the French and Indian War (known as the Seven Years War on this side of the Atlantic), he served at the Battle of the Great Meadows and the surrender of Fort Necessity and was with Washington in battles against the Indians in Virginia and Maryland. After the war, he returned to private practice, this time in Port Tobacco in Maryland, where he became a very prosperous family doctor until Washington summoned him in 1798 – at the age of 67 – to take up the post of physician general during further hostilities against the French. The following year, he was in attendance when Washington became seriously ill with a badly-infected throat and couldn't swallow medicines. With the other two doctors, he controversially treated the condition with bloodletting but it was ineffective and Washington died. In his will, the president described Dr Craik as 'my compatriot in arms and old and intimate friend.'

The man credited with introducing vaccination against smallpox to America was John Spence (born Edinburgh, 1766–1829). While he went on to read medicine at the city's university, his poor health prevented him from finishing his degree. So, at the age of 22, he left Auld Reekie behind and sought a new life as a private tutor in Dumfries, Virginia. There, the climate worked wonders on his health and he went back to his studies, qualified as a doctor and developed a successful practice. His work on vaccination – discovered in 1796 by Edward Jenner – was recognised by the Medical Museum of Philadelphia in 1806 and by the award of an honorary MD by the University of Pennsylvania in 1828.

Another Edinburgh graduate and medical pioneer was Peter Middleton, who conducted the first dissection of a body in America in 1750 and also helped establish the prestigious New York Medical School (now part of Columbia College) in 1767. He migrated to America in 1730 and became one of his adopted country's most eminent medical practitioners, working with fellow Edinburgh graduate Dr John Bard, president of the New York Medical Society. After setting up the new medical school, he was professor of pathology (1767–76) and when it was incorporated with King's College (now Columbia) he became professor of chemistry (1770–76).

Glasgow-born Granville Sharp Pattison made his major contribution to American medicine by creating the medical department at the University of New York City in the mid-nineteenth century... but not before a remarkable and somewhat questionable career. A biographer's description of him as a 'colourful and complex character' doesn't do him justice: during his student days reading anatomy at Glasgow University he was a body-snatcher, later had to defend himself in several pistols-at-dawn duels after a string of affairs, was named as the correspondent in a close friend's divorce case and was then accused of unprofessional conduct while working at the city's Royal Infirmary. He was born in 1791, the son of a well-to-do merchant, and the family lived in some style in Kelvingrove House, an eight-bedroom mansion close to the city centre (it was later the city's first municipal museum and the site of today's Kelvingrove Art Gallery and Museum, restored more recently in a £28 million project). He went to Glasgow Grammar School, then the city's only private school. He doesn't appear to have been a particularly bright pupil but when he was 15 and with the Napoleonic Wars creating a demand for military surgeons, he managed to enrol – there was no entrance exam – in the Faculty of Medicine at the university. He became a lecturer at the university in 1813, partly because he studied as hard as he played and perhaps because he had proved very successful in acquiring cadavers for research. At the time, such bodies had been made scarce because of strict laws and some students earned extra pocket money by scavenging the paupers' graves. He was arraigned but after spending a massive £520 on his defence, he was controversially acquitted. Scandal, however, continued to follow him. He went on to work at London University but was sacked after his students complained about his incompetence. He then moved to Philadelphia, where he is said to have brazenly kept his duelling pistols on his desk and hinted at little reluctance to use them. This clearly didn't endear him to the medical establishment and he moved swiftly on to Baltimore. There he seemed to redeem himself somewhat by helping to found an infirmary and slowly built a more amenable reputation.

Others on the long list of medico-migrants include Dr James McNaughton (born Aberfeldy, 1796–1874), one of the founders of the City Hospital, Albany, and surgeon general of New York State; Daniel McRuer (born Argyllshire, 1802–73), who ran the biggest general practice in Maine in the 1830s and was a military surgeon during the Civil War; James McLean (born Ayrshire, 1829–86), who combined medicine and politics and was elected as a Republican congressman in 1882; Dr. James Craig (born Glasgow, 1834-88), who was the first obstetrician to 'demonstrate hydriodic acid as a curative in acute inflammatory rheumatism'; and Professor Alexander Skene (born Fyvie, Aberdeenshire, 1837–1900), founder and first president of the American Gynaecological Society, inventor of a number of medical instruments and yet another Civil War Union Army doctor.

One of the many Scots who bought into the idea of America as the land of opportunity was engineer and pioneer of hydraulics, Robert Erskine from Edinburgh. He was a classic example of someone who not only benefited from a new start in the New World but also enormously appreciated the opportunity it afforded him and was determined to give something back. He showed that in the only way he knew how. He joined the struggle for independence and, in 1777, was appointed George

Washington's geographer and surveyor general, just six years after having left Scotland. In Edinburgh, where he graduated, he had been an engineer and inventor whose bright ideas outstripped his commercial acumen. He was a youthful leader in the field we now call hydraulics and invented the continual stream pump and platometer, a centrifugal hydraulic engine. He was also a public-spirited citizen, and the combination made him a highly respected figure in the city and he was elected a fellow of the Royal Society. However, that didn't stop him from being forced into bankruptcy in 1771. He took his responsibility seriously and it was his determination to pay off his creditors that decided him on seeking his fortune in America.

He settled in New Jersey where he helped turn round an ailing iron-producing company and was well rewarded. He was soon an iron-master and, this time round, a successful businessman. As war became imminent, he worried that he might lose his workers to the army. His pragmatic solution was to organise the men into a militia unit and served as captain in his own regiment in 1775. He also used his inventiveness to assuage one of the colonists' greatest fears. They were anxious that the British warships would use the Hudson River to attack northern forts and isolate New England from the rest of the colonies. He designed a marine barrier that would prevent ships from moving upriver. Washington was impressed and promoted him to the geographer's post, and he then immediately set about creating nearly 300 maps covering the northern sector of the war – with precise details of roads, buildings and so on – which proved invaluable to the general. He also kept his works in full operation to supply munitions and machines critical to the war effort. While out on a map-making expedition, he became ill and died from pneumonia. He was 45. New Jersey's Lake Erskine is named after him.

There is further evidence on today's maps of contribution made to the building of America by migrants from the auld country. A quick glance at the gazetteer reveals 14 Aberdeens, nine Dumbartons (plus the Dumbarton Bridge that connects the San Francisco peninsula to the rest of California), 13 Dundees, five Edinburghs (and another 12 without the final 'h'), 20 Elgins, 19 Glasgows (and one in Connecticut spelled Glasgo), 19 Hamiltons, 7 Invernesses, 7 Kelsos, 25 Montroses, 6 Paisleys, 4 Perths and 3 Stirlings. There are 22 Scotlands, eight Caledonias and six Albanys (from 'Alba', the Gaelic for Scotland) and clearly not a single state was without its settlers from the original Scotland.

In California, where more than half a million registering in the 2000 census claimed Scottish heritage, there's Loch Lomond, a beautiful man-made reservoir near Ben Lomond and not far from Bonny Doon and the Cheviot Hills. In Iowa, where 43,367 claim Scots heritage, there are more than 30 place names such as Armstrong, Ayrshire, Baxter, Blairsburg, Blairstown, Buchanan County, Coulter, Craig, Crawfordsville, Dundee, Dysart, Henderson, Hepburn, Lenox, Logan, McCallsburg, McCausland, McClelland, McGregor, McIntire, Maxwell, Malcolm, Montrose, Mount Ayr, Paton, Patterson, Ruthven, Scott County, Stuart and Tennant. Elsewhere there are hundreds of townships, rivers and lakes and mountains and valleys across every state honouring almost every clan and hundreds of Scottish villages and glens.

James Mackay, from Sutherland, didn't leave his name on the maps of America but he did make a major contribution to understanding its geography. He originally emigrated to Canada, where he was a fur trader and, from necessity, a keen map-maker. When he moved to America in 1794, he was hired by a group of Spanish merchants (the Company of Explorers of the Upper Missouri) in St Louis. They dubbed him 'Diego Mackay', commissioned him to build forts along the Missouri and to persuade the British to leave what had become Spanish territory. The following year, he set out on what would prove to be a two-year expedition during which he built Fort Columbus, discovered the main tributary (which he called Rochejaune or Yellowstone River) and produced the Missouri River Map, much used by later explorers. He also did manage to dislodge a few British settlers en route. He was the last commandant of the St Charles District of Louisiana under the Spanish and later served as a judge and legislator for the State of Missouri.

It was a Scot who completed the United States' first geological survey in 1809, left his name on a bay, a glacier, a lake and two mountains and, according to the history books, 'had an incalculable impact on American culture'. William Maclure (born Ayr, 1763–1840) is credited as being the 'Father of US Geology'. He was the son of a merchant successful enough to ensure him a good, private education and shrewd enough to provide exactly the right connections when the time came to consider a career. Through the lucky coincidence of sharp intelligence and family contacts, he began his successful business career at what most people would consider the top. He was just 19 when he secured a partnership in an American-owned but London-based merchant house trading extensively across Europe and the New World. That was in 1782. His new partners recognised his youthful energy and entrepreneurial potential. They grounded him solidly in the company's business and then let him loose on their customer base. He sailed to America in 1787 and thereafter criss-crossed the Atlantic on a series of voyages that today would put him at the top of the frequent-traveller list.

He didn't just visit. He lived, for varying periods, in France, Italy, Ireland, Switzerland and Spain and still found time to return to Scotland and America to see family and friends. He was a man of radical ideas and had the energy – and the money – to put many of them into practice albeit not always with success. During his time in Switzerland, for example, he became intrigued by the work of educational reformer Johann Pestalozzi, but he failed in his later attempts to set up a college – in Alicante in Spain – based on his educational philosophy. In France, he experienced the revolutionary fervour and the birth pangs of the new republic between 1789 and 1799. Despite his own growing wealth, he was clearly enthralled by the clarion call for 'liberty, equality and fraternity' and began a collection of pamphlets that was to grow to more than 25,000 and which equally clearly influenced his thinking. After several visits to New York, however, he decided that America was the land of opportunity. He became a citizen in 1796.

By 1803, Maclure had so effectively fitted into the American establishment that he was sent to Paris by the government to represent the interests of Americans who had suffered losses during the Revolution. There, between attending to matters of state, he also found time to indulge his growing passion for geology. He retraced his steps across the continent but this time he was not observing the still-fragile social conditions but searching out and collecting geological specimens. He returned to America in 1807 and allowed the scientist in him to gain the upper hand. He decided he would, at his own expense, conduct the first ever survey of the geology of his adopted country. He traversed the vast Appalachian mountain range, crossed and re-crossed the Allegheny mountains dozens of times, and examined the geology of almost every state. He published his findings in 1809. *Observations on the Geology of the United States* was presented to the American Philosophical Society and it was this that earned him the 'Father of' tag.

After that epic venture, he settled for a time in Philadelphia, which, according to the historians, was then known as the 'Athens of America' because of its 'cosmopolitan egalitarianism and its many learned institutions.' He added to that reputation in 1812 by helping to found and becoming a key member of the Academy of Natural Sciences of Philadelphia, whose purpose was 'for the encouragement and cultivation of the sciences, and the advancement of useful learning.' (The academy's 21st-century website says: 'The unique aspect lies in the word "useful", a mandate the Academy has continuously redefined through research and education that reflects the societal needs of the times.') Most people would have settled for the honour of being elected president of the Academy (a position he held for the rest of his life), but not Maclure. He still had too much energy to sit back from the fray.

In 1825 and at the age of 62, he launched his most ambitious venture. He decided to partner Robert Owen in his utopian dream of developing the perfect society. He contributed $150,000 to buy up what became the town of New Harmony in Indiana. Perhaps more importantly, he persuaded a large number of intellectual friends and professional associates to join the project. They gathered in Philadelphia and joined him aboard the keelboat *Philanthropist* for an extraordinary trip down the Ohio River. Among the distinguished passengers were naturalists Thomas Say (later to be described as 'Father of American Entomology') and Frenchman Charles-Alexandre Lesueur. Almost inevitably, the boat was dubbed the 'boatload of knowledge' even as it sailed into the history books. One historian says: 'Robert Owen and his followers, especially geologist William Maclure, had an incalculable impact on American culture and thought from their outpost on the Wabash River. They experimented with educational techniques, abandoning training in classical languages for a philosophy that combined mental and manual skills.' As they were joined by intellectuals from far and wide, the pair founded the first kindergarten in America, started the first public school system and established around a hundred free libraries in Indiana and neighbouring states.

Sadly the heady utopian days lasted only four years before disharmony broke out. One of the disillusioned participants, Josiah Warren, wrote: 'Most of the experimenters left in despair of all reforms and conservatism felt itself confirmed. We had tried every conceivable form of organization and government. We had a world in miniature. We had enacted the French revolution over again with despairing hearts instead of corpses as a result. It appeared that it was nature's own inherent law of diversity that had conquered us. Our united interests were directly at war with the individualities of persons and circumstances and the instinct of self-preservation... and it was evident that just in proportion to the contact of persons or interests, so are concessions and compromises indispensable.'

It was only failing health that finally curbed Maclure's enthusiasm for radical and dynamic change. In 1827, when he was 65, he retired and sought the quiet life in the warmer climes of Mexico. He never lost interest in the New Harmony project and in 1838, he returned once more, staying long enough to set up a working men's institute and endow it with a library and museum. He died at San Angel in 1840, but his memory lives on in California's Mount Maclure (12,967 feet), Maclure Glacier, Maclure Creek, Maclure Fork, Maclure Peak, Maclure Lake and Maclure Bay.

There can be nothing more American than the symbol of its wealth, the famous dollar sign – $ – and it comes courtesy of the Scottish printer, Archibald Binny, who emigrated from Edinburgh to Pennsylvania in the late eighteenth century. According to typography historian Daniel Berkley Updike, Binny first used the symbol in his publication of *The American Printer* in 1797. Binny and his partner, James Ronaldson, also from Edinburgh, established themselves as America's first type-founders in Philadelphia. Until then, US printers had depended on European font-makers.

Equally iconically American is bourbon. While I don't claim anything other than that he was an early producer, there are many who regard Dr James Crow from Edinburgh as the father of the modern bourbon industry and he certainly gets an honourable mention for developing the sour-mash process.

Dr Crow – and the Dr is important because chemistry was one of his specialties – graduated from Edinburgh University when he was 21 and shortly afterwards set sail for the United States, settling in Kentucky around 1825. It's not clear why he went into the bourbon business but he emerged as the master distiller for Oscar Pepper in the late 1830s and gave the company the cutting edge over its competitors by using his skills as a chemist. His system 'controlled the introduction and growth of foreign bacteria and yeasts that could damage the whiskey [note the 'e' to distinguish it from Scotch] and improves the consistency and quality of the liquor so that every bottle tastes as close to the same as possible.' So now you know! The customer certainly appreciated the result and, in a marketing man's dream, at least three presidents – Andrew Jackson, Ulysses S Grant and William Henry Harrison – became devotees. He died (suddenly, at work) in 1856, and the company later built the Old Crow Distillery and made Old Crow Bourbon there until 1985.

Improbably, Ramsay Crooks (1786–1859), from my home town of Greenock, became one of the United States' biggest fur traders. He successfully established himself as a confidant of the Indians whose Chief Black Hawk described him as the 'best paleface friend the red men ever had.' He was still a teenager when his father died and his mother took the family to live in Canada (where his brother later became an MP). He got a job in the fur trade in Montreal. After learning as much as he could about furs, he slipped over the border to America and set up a small trading post on the Great Lakes in partnership with another Scot. He earned a reputation for shrewd but fair trading and, in 1811, he accepted a lucrative invitation to join the Pacific Fur Company.

On one memorable trip to Astoria in Oregon territory, his trading expedition ran into difficulties trying to cross the Rocky Mountains in deepest winter. When one of his men, John Day, became delirious with fever, he opted to stay behind to look after him while the others forged on. He was reduced to trying to make a soup from minute scraps of vegetation, boiling bits of leather and chewing it, and somehow the pair managed to survive until they were found and rescued by Indians. They were later reunited with the rest of the expedition. John Day made a remarkable recovery and went on to be one of the region's most famous hunters: two townships, the City of John Day and Dayville, plus a river and a dam are all named in his honour. Not bad for a man who could so easily have been left to die in the frozen wastes but for the steadfastness of Ramsay Crooks.

Crooks saw out the winter by establishing a trading post and, when the weather allowed, he led a small party overland – through what was later to become the Oregon Trail – back to base. By 1817 he had become the general manager and a shareholder in Jacob Astor's American Fur Company. He built the company into the dominant force in the US fur trade and when Astor retired in 1834, he bought the company. He continued to trade successfully until 1842, when the European market in furs collapsed. He wound up the major company and opened a small fur business in New York, where he lived quietly until his death at 72.

With John Paul Jones having effectively created the US Navy, it was another Scot who provided it with some of its early warships. Henry Eckford, who had started his working life as an apprentice ship's carpenter in Irvine, supervised the building of ships for use in the second war against the British (1812–15). After attending grammar school in Irvine, Erskine had taken an apprenticeship as a ship's carpenter in the local yards. When he had qualified and gained experience, he emigrated to Canada in 1800, when he was 25.

His key expertise, vital to the war effort, was his knowledge of techniques that allowed accelerated construction or adaptation of ships for use on the Great Lakes. One of his first successes was in converting a merchant schooner into USS *Ohio*, which then operated as a flagship on Lake Erie for Captain Oliver Hazard Perry. Perry's victory over the British earned him the nom-de-guerre of the 'Hero of Lake Erie'. After the war, he designed and built a second USS *Ohio* in 1820. When it was launched, one of its officers declared: 'I never supposed such a ship could be built – a ship possessing in so great a degree all the qualifications of a perfect vessel.' Following that success, he was appointed naval constructor at Brooklyn Naval Yard and was responsible for the design of all US Navy ships. In 1822, he built the steamer *Robert Fulton* (named after the American designer of Napoleon's *Nautilus*), which made the first successful steam voyage from New Orleans to Havana.

Eckford lost his job because of an alleged affair and went to work for the Sultan of the Ottoman Empire in Constantinople, where he died in 1832.

Allan Pinkerton (born Glasgow, 1819–1884) gave America – and eventually the world – the private eye after setting up his famous detective agency in Chicago in 1852. He foiled an assassination attempt on Abraham Lincoln just before his 1861 inauguration and then accepted the president's personal invitation to set up the US Secret Service in 1862. He acted as head of the service throughout the Civil War. Pinkerton agents are also credited with having hunted down scores of dangerous outlaws, including Frank and Jesse James.

All that represented something of a dramatic career change for the man born in the notorious Gorbals district of Glasgow in 1819. He had trained as a barrel-maker but had fled Scotland in 1842, when the city police set out to arrest him for agitating for workers' rights. When he arrived in Dundee, Illinois, he supplemented his meagre earnings by acting as a police informant. He graduated to deputy sheriff of Cook County before setting up his agency with the slogan 'We Never Sleep' and the black-and-white eye logo that led to the term 'private eye.'

He is buried in Chicago's Graceland Cemetery, where the epitaph on his headstone reads: 'A friend to honesty and a foe to crime, devoting himself for a generation to the prevention and detection of crime in many countries. He was the founder in America of a noble profession. In the hour of the nation's peril he conducted Abraham Lincoln safely through the ranks of treason to the scene of his first inauguration as president. He sympathised with, protected and defended the slaves and laboured earnestly for their freedom, hating wrong and loving good. He was strong, brave, tender and true.'

For me, one of the most enduring images of America's early days is the gun-toting, star-wearing sheriff beloved of old movies (and especially of my Saturday morning matinees at the Regal Cinema in Greenock) in which the baddies wore black hats, the goodies sported white Stetsons and both were as tough as the leather of their boots. But the Scotsman who wore the badge in Marion County in the mid-nineteenth century doesn't quite fit the image. Archie Carmichael, from Appin in Argyllshire, was universally known as 'kind-hearted Carmichael' because of a generous trait that was so strong it led him to being locked up in his own jail for 20 months for refusing to help loan sharks. If he'd been depicted in the old films, he would certainly have worn a white hat!

After emigrating to South Carolina, he was elected sheriff for his first four-year term in 1841 at a time when the United States were suffering a savage economic depression. Debt was widespread and all too many people, unable to raise money through the banks, resorted to borrowing from loan sharks. Sheriff Carmichael was deeply concerned that his local community would be overwhelmed by the financial catastrophe. He point-blank refused to execute recovery orders and nor would he allow the repossession of homesteads. Unfortunately, the money men made their money talk. They claimed the law was on their side, that borrowing arrangements had been entered into voluntarily and that it was the Sheriff's duty to help them. The magistrates agreed and when he still refused to comply, Carmichael was sent to jail – his own – for 20 months.

However, he successfully held that, having been elected by the people for four years, he couldn't be stripped of office. So he stripped *his* office, and moved the desk, chair and filing cabinets into the cell next door while his family set up home in the cell next to that! From there, he announced business as usual. For the full 20 months he carried out his responsibilities, although he had to occasionally use deputies to make arrests and then share the cell with those arrested. He also used his influence with the debtors to ensure that the lenders did eventually get their money back. So everyone seemed to be happy... although there is no record of what his wife said when their first son was born in the jail! He certainly became a local hero. He completed his sentence and then his term of office. The system didn't allow him to seek re-election until four years later but when he did, his badge was overwhelmingly restored... and, presumably, his white stetson!

The biggest test for the burgeoning nation came in 1861, with the outbreak of the Civil War between the southern Confederate States and the northern Unionists and, as might be expected, there were Scots on both sides. The war was essentially about slavery, with the Confederate South – led by Jefferson Davis and his commander-in-chief General Robert E. Lee – determined to uphold the rights of the slave-owners to own slaves and the Union – Abraham Lincoln and the Republican party – equally determined to abolish the trade.

The Scots who fought for the Confederacy appear to have done so out of expediency rather than principle. The biggest contingent, first and second generation, served in 1st Virginia Infantry Brigade and the pragmatism of their rationale was underlined in a history of the regiment: 'Generally, they thought the idea of the Union was a good one but Virginia was their home. Virginia, as the mother of this new nation, was their country, not the United States. Consequently, the Valley men set out to defend their homes and homeland and cast their lots with the new Confederacy.' Those who signed up to the Union, on the other hand, could claim the moral high ground in fighting for the emancipation of the slaves. Said to be the only Civil War memorial outside the United States, there is a monument in Edinburgh's Old Calton Cemetery to them and it is signed by a grateful Abraham Lincoln: 'In memory of Scottish-American soldiers: to preserve the jewel of liberty in the framework of peace.' It also includes the legend: 'Suffrage – Union – Education – Emancipation.' There are only five names inscribed on what is known as the Emancipation Monument but they serve as representative of the Scottish diaspora: Sergeant Major John McEwan of 65th Illinois Voluntary Infantry; Lieutenant Colonel William Duff of 2nd Illinois Regiment of Artillery; Robert Steedman of 5th Regiment Maine Infantry Volunteers; James Wilkie of 1st Michigan Cavalry; and

Robert Ferguson of 57th New York Infantry Volunteers. All returned home after the war and died in Scotland.

The background to the memorial is that in 1892 John McEwan's widow asked the American Consul in Edinburgh (then Wallace Bruce) if she might be entitled to a pension because of her husband's service. She also mentioned that he had been buried in an unidentified grave. She got the pension and Scotland got the monument. It was unveiled in 1893 and although it is dedicated to the Union soldiers, Consul Bruce sought to bridge the one-time chasm with these conciliatory lines from a poem he wrote for the unveiling: 'One song unites the Blue and Gray, One glory binds the garnered sheaf – War's cruel reaping kindly sealed By brothers of the martyred field.'

Unlike the men commemorated on Edinburgh's monument, however, the majority of Scots who fought for the Union were migrants who had settled permanently in America and their commitment was to their adopted country and the ideals of Lincoln. The level of their commitment is shown in the 24 Medals of Honor (the closest equivalent of the British VC) that were awarded to Scots during the bitter fighting. The Roll of Honor gives few personal details but it does list each of the following as having been born in Scotland.

Signal Quartermaster Matthew Arther (27) was serving aboard USS *Carondelet* at the attack on Forts Henry and Donelson (6–14 February 1862) and other actions: 'Carrying out his duties as SQM and captain of the bow gun, he was conspicuous for valour and devotion, serving most faithfully, effectively and valiantly.'

Captain of the Foretop James McLeod (40) was serving on USS *Pensacola* during the attack on Forts Jackson and St Philip and the capture of New Orleans, 24–25 April 1862. 'Acting as gun captain of the rifled howitzer aft which was much exposed, he served this piece with great ability and activity, although no officer superintended it.'

Private John Gray (25) was serving with 5th Ohio Infantry at Port Republic, Virginia on 9 June 1862, when the citation says: 'He mounted an artillery horse of the enemy and captured a brass six-pound piece in the face of the enemy's fire and brought it to the rear.'

Bosun's Mate John McDonald (45) and Bosun's Mate Charles Robinson (31) were on USS *Baron De Kalb* during the Yazoo River Expedition, 23–27 December 1862. Proceeding up river with the object of capturing or destroying the enemy's transports, the ship found the steamers *John Walsh*, *R. J. Locklan*, *Golden Age* and *Scotland* sunk on a bar where they were ordered burned. Continuing up the river, the *Baron De Kalb* was fired on, but upon returning the fire, caused the enemy's retreat, and 'returning down the Yazoo, she destroyed and captured large quantities of enemy equipment and several prisoners.' Both citations added: 'Serving bravely throughout this action, they distinguished themselves in the various actions.'

Sergeant Major John Farquhar (32) was with 89th Illinois Infantry at Stone River, Tennessee on 31 December 1862: 'When a break occurred on the extreme right wing of the Army of the Cumberland, this soldier rallied fugitives from other commands and deployed his own regiment, thereby checking the Confederate advance until a new line was established.'

Seaman Andrew Brinn (25) was serving on USS *Mississippi* when the ship was damaged during a battle at Port Hudson on 14 March 1863. After orders to abandon ship, he remained on board and under enemy fire for more than two and a half hours while the rest of the crew reached safety: 'He was finally ordered to save himself and to leave the *Mississippi*, which had been deliberately fired to prevent her falling into rebel hands.'

Sergeant David Dickie (27) and Private William Fraser (23), both with 97th Illinois Infantry, and Sergeant James Jardine (26) of 54th Ohio Infantry were at Vicksburg, Missouri on 22 May 1863 and all three were cited for 'gallantry in the charge of the volunteer storming party.'

Five days later, two more Scots won their medals on USS *Cincinnati* during the attack on the Vicksburg batteries and at the time of her sinking. They were Bosun's Mate Henry Dow (23) and Quartermaster Thomas Hamilton (30). Both citations said: 'Engaging the enemy in a fierce battle, the *Cincinnati*, amidst an incessant fire of shot and shell, continued to fire her guns to the last, though so penetrated by enemy shell fire that her fate was sealed.' Henry Dow's also said: 'Serving courageously throughout this action, he carried out his duties to the end on this proud ship that went down with her colours nailed to the mast.' John Hamilton's added: 'Conspicuously gallant during this action, Hamilton, severely wounded at the wheel, returned to his post and had to be sent below, to hear the incessant roar of guns as the gallant ship went down , her colours nailed to the mast.'

Private Benjamin Thakrah (24) was serving with 115th New York Infantry near Fort Gates, Florida on 1 April 1864 when 'he was a volunteer in the surprise and capture of the enemy's picket.'

Musician James Snedden (22) of 54th Pennsylvania Infantry was serving at Piedmont, Virginia on 5 June 1864, when 'he left his place in the rear, took the rifle of a disabled soldier, and fought through the remainder of the action.'

Private Robert Reid (24) of 48th Pennsylvania Infantry was serving in Petersburg, Virginia on 17 June 1864 when he was responsible for the 'capture of flag of 44th Tennessee Infantry.'

Coxswain David Warren (28) was on USS *Monticello* during the reconnaissance of the harbour and water defences of Wilmington, North Carolina, 23–25 June 1864: 'Taking part in a reconnaissance of enemy defences which lasted two days and nights, Warren courageously carried out his duties during this action which resulted in the capture of a mail carrier and mail, the cutting of a telegraph wire and the capture of a large group of prisoners. Although in immediate danger from the enemy, he showed gallantry and coolness throughout this action which resulted in the gaining of much vital information of the rebel defences.'

First Lieutenant Andrew Davidson (24) was with 30th US Coloured Troops, during an attack on a mine at Petersburg, Virginia on 30 July 1864. He was 'one of the first to enter the enemy's works, where, after his colonel, major, and one-third the company officers had fallen, he gallantly assisted in rallying and saving the remnant of the command.'

Three Scots were awarded the Medal of Honour for their actions in 'braving the enemy fire said by the admiral to be one of the most galling he had ever seen and aided in rescuing from death ten of the crew' of the torpedoed *Tecumseh*, in Mobile Bay on 5 August 1864. Captain of the Forecastle John Harris (27) and Seaman James Avery (39), serving on USS *Metacomet*, were in the rescue party. Both their citations said they had 'elicited the admiration of both friend and foe.' During the same action, Captain of the Forecastle John Brown (38) on board USS *Brooklyn* won his medal during action against rebel forts and gunboats: 'Despite severe damage to his ship and the loss of several men as enemy fire raked her decks from stem to stern, he fought his gun with skill and courage throughout the furious battle which resulted in the surrender of the prize rebel *Ram Tennessee* and in the damaging and destruction of batteries at Fort Morgan.'

First Sergeant Thomas Meagher (31) of 158th New York Infantry was serving at Chapin's Farm, Virginia on 29 September 1864, when 'he led a section of his men on the enemy's works, receiving a wound while scaling a parapet.'

Seaman Charles Hawkins (30), on USS *Agawam*, was in a volunteer crew of a powder boat which exploded near Fort Fisher on 23 December 1864: 'The boat, towed in by the *Wilderness* to prevent detection by the enemy, cast off and slowly steamed to within 300 yards of the beach. After fuses and fires had been lit and a second anchor with short scope let go to assure the boat's tailing inshore, the crew again boarded the *Wilderness* and proceeded a distance of 12 miles from shore. Less than two hours later the explosion took place, and the following day fires were observed still burning at the forts.'

Coxswain John Dempster (26) was on USS *New Ironsides* during attacks on Fort Fisher, 24–25 December 1864 and 13–15 January 1865: 'The ship steamed in and took the lead in the ironclad division close inshore and immediately opened its starboard battery in a barrage of well-directed fire to cause several fires and explosions and dismount several guns during the first two days of fighting. Taken under fire as she steamed into position on 13 January, the *New Ironsides* fought all day and took on ammunition at night despite severe weather conditions. When the enemy came out of his bomb-proofs to defend the fort against the storming party, the ship's battery disabled nearly every gun on the fort facing the shore before the cease-fire orders were given by the flagship.'

First Lieutenant Allan Dougall (29) was adjutant of 88th Indiana Infantry at Bentonville, North Carolina, on 19 March 1865, when 'in the face of a galling fire from the enemy, he voluntarily returned to where the colour-bearer had fallen wounded and saved the flag of his regiment from capture.'

One of the Union's most unlikely cavalry officers was James Wilson (born Edinburgh, 1832–1914). He was a scholarly man of letters whose family emigrated to New York before settling in Illinois. In 1857, he founded the *Chicago Record*, an arts journal. He joined the war late in 1864. He became a major, commanded 4th US Cavalry, served with 'great distinction' and rose to brigadier general before the he left the army in 1865. He returned to New York where he became an equally distinguished biographer (his subjects included General Ulysses S. Grant) and co-editor of *Appletons' Cyclopaedia of American Biography*. He was president of the Society of American Authors and of the New York Genealogical and Biographical Society.

At the start of the war, James Geddes (born Edinburgh, 1827–1887) enlisted as a private in the 8th Iowa Infantry. He was rapidly promoted to captain, lieutenant colonel and, in 1862, to colonel of volunteers. He fought at Shiloh, where he was wounded and taken prisoner before being exchanged and returning to action at Vicksburg and Jackson. In October 1863, he took command of a brigade and went to Brownsville, Texas, before serving as provost marshal of Union-occupied Memphis. He commanded a brigade in the Mobile Campaign and fought with distinction at the Battle of Spanish Fort. In 1865, he was promoted to brigadier general and commended for his war service. When he left the army he became principal of the Iowa College for the Blind at Vinton, and until his death was connected with the Iowa College of Agriculture at Ames, being military instructor and cashier (1870–82), acting president (1875–77), librarian (1877–78), vice-president and professor of military tactics (1880–82), and treasurer (1884–87). He wrote a number of popular war songs, including 'The Soldiers' Battle Prayer' and 'The Stars and Stripes.'

One man who knew the Civil War was coming before most was Paisley-born William Phillips. After emigrating with his parents in 1838, he worked as a journalist with the *New York Tribune* and had interviewed John Brown about slavery in 1859, when Brown had declared: 'Nothing but war can settle the question.' Phillips was also a lawyer and was admitted to the bar in 1855, when he set up practice in Kansas. He was the first state Supreme Court judge appointed under the Leavenworth Constitution that effectively outlawed slavery and anti-black discrimination. In 1858, he was the founding-father of Saline, a small city on the River Saline in the heart of Kansas. When the war broke out, he was quick off the mark in raising troops and was appointed colonel and commanding officer of the Cherokee Indian Regiment within the Union Army. After the war, he served as prosecuting attorney of Cherokee County, was elected to the state House of Representatives in 1865 and was attorney for the Cherokee Indians in Washington. He sat as a Republican in Congress, 1873–79.

Another Scot who fought in the war and later became a Republican congressman was Glaswegian Clinton Dugald MacDougall. He joined 75th New York Volunteer Infantry as a captain in 1861 and as a reward for his 'gallant and meritorious service' he rose to major general before serving in Congress (1872–77). He had emigrated with his family to the US and settled in New York. When the war started, he served in the Army of the Potomac, first as a brigade commander and then as commander-in-chief of 1st Division of II Corps. He fought in the (Virginia) Peninsula Campaign, including the Battle of Williamsburg and the Seven-Day Battles in the summer of 1862. After the war, he became the postmaster in Auburn, New York (1869–73) and was then elected to Congress as a Republican in 1873. He refused to serve as US treasurer or as commissioner of internal revenue in 1876 and stepped down from politics in 1877. Instead, he served as US Marshal for the Northern District of New York for eight years until 1885. Three years later, he again turned down a major invitation – this time from President Rutherford – to be ambassador to London or Paris. Instead, in 1901 and aged over 70, he resumed his job as marshal and served for a further ten years!

Curwen McLellan was just 20 when he emigrated from Wigtownshire in 1849 and enlisted as a private in the US Infantry. He worked his way through the ranks to first sergeant in 1854. When he wanted to join the US Cavalry, he had to revert to private but by the time the war started he had again risen to sergeant. He was then commissioned as a 2nd Lieutenant in 3rd Cavalry and quickly promoted to Regimental Adjutant with 6th Cavalry. For his 'gallant and meritorious service' in the Battle of Williamsburg (1862), at Gettysburg (1863), and Dinwiddie (1865) he went to lieutenant, brevet captain and brevet major. After the war, he was saw action against the Indians around the Red River Valley, when his bravery again won him promotion, this time to brevet lieutenant colonel. He finally retired as a full colonel in 1893.

In addition to the individuals who served across the range of American military and naval units, there were two regiments in the Union Army that bore the nickname the 'Scotch Regiment' because they were made up of more than three-quarters Scotsmen: 12th Illinois Infantry in Cairo and 65th Illinois Infantry in Chicago. Both were formed in 1861.

The first, 12th Illinois, was under the command of General John McArthur, a former blacksmith from Erskine, Renfrewshire. He emigrated to the United States when he was 23 and settled in Illinois, where he became manager of the Chicago Iron Works. He also served in the Chicago Highland Guards militia and at the outbreak of war he became colonel of a volunteer regiment. He was promoted to command 1st Brigade in General Charles Ferguson Smith's Missouri Division and saw action at Fort Donelson. He was then made brigadier general and led 2nd Brigade at Shiloh, where, on the first day of the battle, he was wounded leading a breakout of the Confederate encirclement. Once recovered, he led his men in the sieges of Corinth and Vicksburg and helped counter the Missouri Raid in 1864. He then transferred to Tennessee, where he fought in the battles of Nashville and Fort Blakely. He was less successful after the war and his various business ventures were all unsuccessful.

The second 'Scotch' regiment was the kilted 65th Illinois Infantry under the command of Brigadier General Daniel Cameron, from Berwick-upon-Tweed. He had taken his family to America in 1851 and settled in Wheeling, Cook County, before moving to Chicago, where he became a newspaper publisher in 1853. He enlisted in the Union Army at the outbreak of the war and, in 1861, he raised the regiment in which more than three-quarters of the recruits were Scots living in Chicago and Cook

County. He was commander of Camp Douglas until he was then ordered to join the Army of the Potomac and the defence of Washington. In his *Compendium of the War of Rebellion*, Frederick H. Dyer wrote: 'The 65th Illinois Regiment fought passionately with an unyielding commitment to their cause. These men were determined to help their cause, and they were willing to die to prove themselves to their new country. This type of dedication was crucial to the Union's victory in the war and showed how much the immigrants in America wanted a place in American society.' The regiment served until 26 July 1865, fighting at the battles of Iuka, Corinth, Resaca, Kennesaw Mountain and Nashville. It took part in the siege of Atlanta in 1864 and then joined Sherman's March to the Sea (from Atlanta to Savannah). One officer and 30 soldiers were killed in action but nearly a hundred died of disease during the campaign. Daniel Cameron retired from the army at the end of the war and in 1870 went into politics; he was elected as a Democrat to the Constitutional Convention for Illinois.

There was also 79th New York Highlanders Volunteers, formed as part of the state's National Guard two years before the war. It was supported by the city's Caledonian Club and St Andrews Society and modelled on the Cameron Highlanders and was made up of migrant Scots and Scottish-Americans with some Irish and English. They wore kilts in Cameron tartan, black glengarries with red, white and blue dicing around the headband, and red-trimmed navy-blue dress jackets. That would certainly have set them apart from other regiments. When the war broke out, the 79th was increased in strength from four companies to nine. During the campaign they faced 17 major battles and earned the respect of both sides in the conflict. After one battle, General Sherman said: 'I have never seen regular troops that equalled the Highlanders in soldierly bearing and appearance,' while the *Charleston Mercury News*, reporting on the Battle of Secessionville, said: 'Thank God Lincoln had only one 79th Highlander Regiment.'

There were also several Scottish militia companies on the Confederate side. In Charleston, this included the ironically named Union Light Infantry. They were formed in 1807 at the Carolina Coffee House, to mark the centenary of the union of Scottish and English parliaments, and they wore Lowland military dress with trews in Black Watch tartan. Inevitably, the two 'Scottish' regiments faced each other: it was at the Battle of Secessionville in June 1862 and, in an incident that could have been penned by a Hollywood scriptwriter, two Scottish brothers fought against each other... albeit unknowingly.

They were James and Alexander Campbell, who migrated from Argyllshire to America in 1860 and both settled initially in Charleston, South Carolina. James got a job as a drayman and clerk and, with war looming, joined a militia unit of the Union Light Infantry (also known as 42nd Highlanders after the Black Watch Regiment). Alexander worked as a stonemason and served briefly in the Home Guard, but he left Charleston just before the outbreak of hostilities and moved to New York, where he worked on the building of the new US Customs House. In March 1862, the Union Infantry was consolidated into the regular army and James found himself embroiled in the bitter war and fighting for the Confederacy. In New York, Alexander, who had joined the 79th Highlander regiment, likewise found himself in the war, fighting for the Union and marching towards Charleston and his brother. In a letter to his wife, he wrote: 'We are not far from each other now. This is a war that there never was the like of before... brother against brother.' Little did he know just how close they came to meeting face-to-face.

On 16 June James was the lieutenant in charge of the troop defending a key battery. Alexander was a colour sergeant given the job of planting the Union flag on Confederate territory. However, it wasn't until after the fierce clash that they became aware of each other's parts in the battle. James wrote to his brother: 'I was astonished to hear from the prisoners that you were the colour bearer of the regiment that assaulted the battery at this point the other day. I was there during the whole engagement doing my best to beat you but I hope you and I will never again meet face to face as bitter enemies on the battlefield but if such should be the case you have but to discharge your duty for your cause for I can assure you I will strive to discharge my duty to my country and my cause.'

Alexander wrote to his wife in New York, enclosing James' letter: 'It is rather bad to think that we should be fighting, him on the one side and me on the other for he says he was in the fort during the whole engagement. I hope to God that he and I will get safe through it all and he will have his story to tell about his side and I will have my story to tell about my side.' Later in the war, Alexander was one of five Highlander colour bearers wounded during the second Bull Run. He never fully recovered and although he was promoted to second-lieutenant, he left the army in May 1863 and established himself as a businessman in Connecticut. James continued to fight for the Confederacy but he too was wounded and then captured in 1863. He remained a prisoner of war until 1865, when he returned to Charleston to manage a plantation. The brothers continued to write to each other throughout the war and were on good terms when it ended.

There were, of course, many other examples of brother fighting brother and father fighting son. Such was the nature of the Civil War.

James Campbell apart, it isn't as easy to identify Scots fighting for the Confederacy as to trace those who fought for the Union. Although thousands settled in the Southern states in the eighteenth century, it was the second and third generations who were of an age to enlist when the Civil War broke out and the picture is blurred further by the Ulster-Scots tag beloved of so many American historians. Nor were there many medals to be won and there are few rolls of honour to search. Certainly there are lots of Scottish *names* in the military archives of the Confederacy: of the generals serving with Robert E. Lee (who claimed Robert the Bruce as an ancestor), ten were said to be of Scottish heritage: Jeb Stuart, Albert Johnston, Joseph Johnston, John Bell Hood, John C Breckinridge, John Magruder (who claimed to be descended from Rob Roy MacGregor), Charles McArthur (a politician and journalist), George McCall, Charles Smith Hamilton and John Brown Gordon.

Scots-born Confederate officers included Major Henry McIver, born at sea on Christmas Day 1841, grandson of the McIver clan chief, and educated in Edinburgh. He had a colourful military career that included service during the Indian Mutiny when he was just 16, with Garibaldi in Italy, Don Carlos in Spain and Napoleon III in France. He was described by a contemporary as 'a soldier of fortune who, of all his brothers in arm, is the most remarkable.' In post-war reports, he was said to be 'an officer of great gallantry' variously on the staff of Stonewall Jackson, Jeb Stuart and Kirby Smith.

One of the first soldiers to die in the war was James Younger (born Perth, 1836). He was serving in the army of General Beauregard and fell in the first hour of the first battle – at Fort Sumter – in 1861. He was 25.

William Watson, an Edinburgh Scot living in Baton Rouge, was a reluctant recruit to the Confederate Army. He later wrote: 'Our firm would have been regarded with suspicion had we not contributed at least one man to the service. I had been an active member of the town's volunteer riflemen and to have withdrawn would not have been very creditable to me or my countrymen.'

John Scott (born Glasgow, 1841) had only been living in Virginia for two years when he got caught up in the anti-Union fervour. He was working on a plantation and was one of those nominated to sign up with 1st Virginia Infantry. He didn't demur and was reported as saying he was proud to wear the Confederate uniform. He was killed in the Battle of Winchester. He was 22.

The privation suffered by the Confederate soldiers is revealed in a letter John Beaton, from Inverness, wrote to his sister: 'You can tell Ma I am very well and weigh 175 pounds, about as much as I can easily travel with. You ask me what I want and my answer will be nothing. I have gone through the winter barefooted and can surely hold out in the spring until Lee's army is supplied. Then will come my time to draw from government what we need. I hope we may be ordered back. The service is lighter and you receive better attention in the field than around Richmond.' John Beaton got his wish. His unit went into action at the Battle of Drewy's Bluff, in Chesterfield County, Virginia, in May 1862. But he didn't get much time to enjoy his new boots. He was killed in action and his officer wrote to his sister: 'He was a noble soldier much beloved by the company and all who knew him. He fell during a charge on the enemy, who were concealed in woods behind a stockade they had thrown up during the night previous.' He was buried 'in a lot in the Hollywood cemetery at Richmond for all the Portsmouth Soldiers to be interred in case their relatives in future times may wish their removal.'

James Duff, who had emigrated from Aberdeen in the 1840s, signed up to the Confederate cause by forming an irregular unit of 23 officers and 300 men in San Antonio, Texas. It gloried in the name of 'Duff's Partisan Rangers' before it eventually became the nucleus of 33rd Texas Cavalry mustered in April 1863. Duff had emigrated to San Antonio and was a successful merchant whose wagons were used to carry a huge meteorite (the Wichita County Iron) to Austin and to remove the Commanches to designated Indian territory in 1859. His Partisan Rangers were used to disperse

Union sympathisers among German immigrants who looked like joining up with the Northern troops. The tactics used were so heavy-handed that he was accused of terrorising people. On his return from that assignment, his unit was expanded into 33rd Texas Cavalry; one of the regiments rostered to protect the Texas ports on the Gulf of Mexico and the key Confederate garrisons along the Rio Grande. He was also responsible for keeping essential trade – in cattle and cotton exports – moving and for buying arms and ammunition.

George Gordon, another Aberdonian, had become a regular soldier when he emigrated to the deep south of America. He was a major in 13th Georgia Battalion at the beginning of the war and was given the job of creating the new 63rd Georgia Volunteer Infantry out of various militia and regular units. Mustered in Savannah, the 63rd – with a strength of more than a thousand soldiers – served as a coastal defence unit and fought at Charleston and on Thunderbolt and Rosedew Islands, where Colonel Gordon ensured the Union forces were repelled. But later in the war he found himself a victim of the growing confusion within the Confederate Army. On 16 April 1864, he was ordered by General Lee to join the Army of North Virginia but days later that was countermanded by another general and was sent to join the Army of Tennessee. By May, his orders changed again and he joined General Johnston in North Virginia for what remained of the war.

Around the same time, 58th North Carolina Infantry was facing the Union troops in the Battle of Rocky Ridge, high in the bleak mountains above Crow Valley. The regiment's sergeant major was veteran James Inglis, from Tayside. He had emigrated in the mid-1850s and worked as a carpenter in Caldwell County, but signed on as a soldier before the war. At Rocky Ridge, he was responsible for trying to maintain the men's flagging morale. It was no easy task. High casualties and bad weather conditions had played havoc and even the general described the mood as 'despondent'. James Inglis was killed in the battle but was afforded little recognition. The only mention of him I could find was in a memoir by Confederate Major George Washington Harper: 'A number of casualties occurred in the Fifty-eighth. Among the killed was Sergeant Major James Inglis, a Scotch-man by birth, whose death was deeply regretted by his comrades.' The sergeant major is buried at the Confederate Cemetery in Dalton but the memorial lists him twice with his name spelled wrongly in both instances: 'Inglish' and 'English'. General Alexander Reynolds described the battle in which he died in a letter to his sister from Dalton, Georgia on 29 February 1864: 'The Battle of "Stone Side" [Rocky Face Ridge] was my own fight, I was in supreme command. I selected the field and my troops alone gained the victory. My command consisted of my Brigade, and 3rd Regt. of Gen Clayton's Alabama troops, in all 2500 men and opposed by Granger's Army Corps, Yanks, about 7000 men. The fight began about nine o'clock in the morning, our skirmishers having engaged them about six a.m. The enemy advanced in three lines with great confidence and expected to overwhelm me. The battle raged furiously all along my line. The thunder of cannon and clatter of musketry was deafening, yet our boys stood fast and pounded in their volleys with terrible effect. I ordered an advance. Shouts went up which rent the air and the Yankees broke. They soon reformed and again came to the charge. We met them again and drove them back. Being reinforced, they made their third and heaviest attack. The lines swayed to and fro for some time. I rode forward and ordered a charge and this entirely routed them. I never felt so glorious in my life. It was a complete victory and thank God. I am proud of my brave boys.'

The commanding officer of 50th Georgia Volunteer Infantry was a Scot with a chequered career. Colonel Peter Alexander McGlashan from Edinburgh was the son of a Waterloo veteran and grandson of the last chief of the McGlashan clan. He emigrated initially to Georgia but joined the California Gold Rush in 1849 with little success and returned none the richer to Georgia. He left again in 1856 to serve as a mercenary in William Walker's ill-fated Nicaragua expedition. When Walker, who had declared himself president of the South American state, was summarily executed in 1869, Peter McGlashan beat a hasty retreat to the US... just in time to sign up for service in the Civil War. His regiment was mustered at Savannah and was made up of recruits from the southern part of the state. He led it in battles including South Mountain, Sharpsburg and Gettysburg, the siege of Petersburg and then, in the final days of the war, at Sayler's Creek in Virginia on 6 April 1865. There, the South's troops were overrun. Of 11,500, more than 7,500 were captured, including Peter McGlashan. The rest surrendered. He was released three days later, when the war finally ended after four long, hard years.

America's railroad played a crucial part in the Civil War and one of the key figures in its building was Renfrewshire-born Daniel McCallum (1815–1878). He was an architect and engineer who transformed the system into one of the biggest and most efficient in the world. After emigrating and settling in Rochester, New York, he turned his ingenuity to new ways of building railway bridges. In 1851 he patented an inflexible arched truss and by 1855 he was superintendent of the Erie Railroad. When President Lincoln took wartime control of the railroad system, it was Daniel McCallum (already a colonel of volunteers) who was appointed military director and superintendent of railroads, reporting directly to the secretary of war. He had his headquarters in the quartermaster general's office and was able to take over the complete system 'to hold and use all locomotives, equipments, appendages and appurtenances that may be required for the transport of troops, arms, ammunition, and military supplies needed by the Union armies.' That wasn't quite as big a deal as it sounds. At the time, the government ran just one seven-mile rail line from Washington to Alexandria, Virginia. By the end of the war, however, he had built it into a major operation with nearly 420 locomotives and more than 6,000 railcars. His reward was to be made brevetted brigadier general of volunteers in 1864 and major general the following year.

When the war ended and the railroads were returned to private ownership, he became director and general manager. An executive order of 8 August 1865 returned all railroads appropriated for military use during the war to their original owners. The position of director and general manager was abolished on 31 July.

Another Scot involved with the complex logistics of the war was John Robertson from Banffshire, who served as Michigan's adjutant general, responsible for all army personnel and administration, throughout the war and beyond. He always wanted to be a soldier, but the uncle he thought would find him a commission instead arranged for him to work in the General Post Office in Edinburgh. He arrived in the capital when he was 15 and survived four years before becoming so frustrated that he decided to go to America to join the US Army. However, the ship in which he took passage disgorged him in Montreal. Undeterred, he set off across the border on foot, and more than 70 weary miles later found a recruiting post in Burlington, Vermont. In Spring 1834, still only 19, he finally became a private in 5th US Infantry. His enthusiasm and commitment soon paid off and by the time his seven-year term finished, he had risen to regimental sergeant major. He then went to work for a Detroit merchant, most of whose business was with the army, and again his commitment paid off. Within a couple of years, he went to run the company's business in Mexico and after returning to headquarters was made a partner. When the war broke out in 1861, the Michigan state governor appointed him adjutant general of the state and, according to his military masters, he served 'with zeal and energy'.

He later recorded his experiences in a series of books: *The Flags of Michigan*, *Michigan in the War* and *Roll of Honor*.

Away from the battlefields, a pioneer of American education was the Reverend James Blair (mentioned earlier as governor of Virginia, 1740–41) from Banffshire. He was sent to Virginia by the Bishop of London as part of the church's determination to bring what they called 'enlightenment' to the colonies. He founded the William and Mary College in Williamsburg in 1693, and the distinguished historian Professor Moses Coit Tyler, later said of him: 'probably no other man in the colonial time did so much for the intellectual life of Virginia.' A son of the manse, he was educated at Marischal College, Aberdeen, and Edinburgh University. In 1679, at the age of 23, he followed his father into the Church of Scotland. Two years later, he became embroiled in the arguments about the direction of the kirk and refused to support the Catholic Duke of York's claim to the British throne. As a result, he was removed from his Edinburgh parish and, in frustration, went to London, where he was ordained in the Church of England in 1685. Shortly afterwards, he was sent to America to 'revive and reform' the church in Virginia and began his mission as rector of a parish church. He took to his new task with relish quickly making friends and building up a strong reputation. He became part of the state establishment when he married the daughter of a prominent politician and by 1687 had become the commissary – the highest-ranking religious leader – of the state.

One of his responsibilities was to try to educate the Native Americans, with the aim of thus encouraging them in their enlightenment to join the church. He worked assiduously on the project and, in 1693, was granted a charter from King William and Queen Mary to found his college – in Middle Plantation, a high point equidistant between the Rivers York and James – and promptly named it in their honour. When the state headquarters in Jamestown was burned down for the third time in 1698, the legislature sought refuge in the college. The following year, Dr Blair and five of his students formally petitioned senators that Middle Plantation, then in the process of being renamed Williamsburg, should be the state capital. They agreed.

Having served as president of the Governor's Council, he exerted considerable influence in the state and as a man of the cloth, he determined to exercise his power with responsibility. He worked hard at improving conditions of the people and was quick to defend them against the excesses of the royal governors – he ensured the recall of at least three of them. In 1710, he became the rector of Bruton Parish Church in Williamsburg and happily served there until his death in 1743 at the age of 87. At the College of William and Mary there is a Blair Hall, a large portrait and a statue of the founder. There are two James Blair Middle Schools, one in James City County and the other in Norfolk. In 1943, the US Navy commissioned a victory ship *James Blair* in his honour.

Taken from Campbeltown to America by his parents when he was a lively five-year-old, Hugh Brackenridge grew up to be a classic frontier citizen in the tough environs of Pittsburgh, Pennsylvania, and he too was an educational pioneer and founded an academy that later became Pittsburgh University. He was also an army chaplain (in the War of Independence), a Supreme Court judge, politician, journalist and writer. Despite an early background of self-education, he was head of a free school when he was 15 and won a place at what is now Princeton University when he was 19. Although he was reading religious philosophy and divinity, he took a keen interest in politics and, with future president of the United States James Madison, was a founder of the American Whig Society. He also found time to write and in 1770 he and fellow student Philip Freneau were co-authors of *Father Bombo's Pilgrimage to Mecca*, the first novel ever written in America (it was only published by Princeton University more than a century later in 1875). In a show of support for the growing Independence campaign, the pair also wrote *The Rising Glory of America*, a poem of a united nation that would rule the New World from the Atlantic to the Pacific Ocean.

When Brackenridge graduated in 1772 he settled for the role of headmaster at a small academy in Maryland, with Freneau as his assistant. He returned to Princeton to take an MA, but then joined George Washington's army as a reputedly fire-and-brimstone chaplain. He emerged unscathed from his military service and in 1778 he made a dramatic switch to journalism and, again with his friend Freneau, he launched the *United States Magazine* in Philadelphia. He didn't seem to have his finger on the readership's pulse, however, and the early sales quickly drained away. His response was to return to university, where this time he took a law degree and was admitted to the bar in 1780, at the age of 32.

Philadelphia was not to his liking and he responded to the urge to go west and try his luck in Pittsburgh, then a small frontier community with a population of around 400, many of whom were Scots. There, he found enough confidence to have another go at journalism and he became a central community figure when he established the *Pittsburgh Gazette* (still published today as the *Pittsburgh Post-Gazette*) in 1786 and was elected to the state assembly in the same year. He was a strong supporter of a federal constitution and it was partly because of that that he won endowments to establish his Pittsburgh Academy. However, he failed in his bid for re-election and was also soundly beaten when he later ran for Congress. He was appointed as a judge in the Pennsylvania Supreme Court in 1799 and six years later completed *Modern Chivalry*, a satirical novel later described by author Henry Adams as 'a more thoroughly American book than any written before 1833.' He died in 1816.

A near contemporary and fellow educationist of Brackenridge was Aberdonian William Smith. He was said to be one of the greatest influences on American education. In 1755 he founded – with a little help from his associate Benjamin Franklin – what was to become the Ivy League University of Pennsylvania and then went on to also establish Washington College. Having been encouraged in his youth by Pennsylvania's then governor, Sir William Keith from Peterhead, Founding Father and polymath Franklin clearly enjoyed the company of Scots: as well as working with William Smith, he founded the American Philosophical Society in partnership with James Alexander and was co-publisher of the *Pennsylvania Gazette* with David Hall – both were from Edinburgh.

After attending the local parish school, William Smith graduated from Aberdeen University at the age of 20 and worked as a teacher before emigrating in 1751 to America, where he was a personal tutor to the sons of a rich merchant in Long Island, New York. Two years later, he was ordained into the Anglican Church and religion became a cornerstone of his life. He had significantly greater aspirations than to be a tutor and a local preacher, however, and in his spare time he mused about the kind of school at which he might one day teach. He carefully recorded his thoughts and eventually produced a pamphlet and had the audacity to send it to Franklin. Despite its grandiose title – *A General Idea of The College of Mirania, with a Sketch of The Method of Teaching Science and Religion, in The Several Classes; and some account of its Rise, Establishment and Buildings* – Franklin was intrigued by its contents because it chimed with his own ideas for creating new academies. The young Scotsman dreamed of a school fit for the new world, a school that would meet the needs of both the 'learned' and the 'mechanic' professions, a school that would both encourage scholarship and provide opportunities for a 'useful' education. Within a year of the exchange of correspondence, William Smith – just 27 – was appointed professor of ethics of the new Philadelphia Academy and College, and in 1755 he was appointed to be the first provost.

For the next quarter of a century, he translated his utopian 'Mirania' into reality and won the acclaim of his peers. He received honorary divinity doctorates from Oxford, Aberdeen and Dublin and in 1768, he was elected to the American Philosophical Society. He may have seen out his days in this ivy-clad eyrie had the turbulence of the Revolution not disrupted his idyllic, academic lifestyle. As a man of deep conviction and conservative politics, he felt honour-bound to voice his support for Britain and its king and thus found himself in direct conflict with Franklin and the liberals. In 1758 he was jailed briefly by the Provincial Assembly for his criticism of its military policy. Rather than languishing in the cells, he famously taught classes from the tiny jailhouse. In the ensuing bitterness, he was constantly accused of subversion and with the War of Independence raging at its most intense in 1779, he was stripped of the licence for his beloved academy.

In despair, he fled Pennsylvania and settled in Maryland where, ever inventive, he wasted little time in establishing another academy and became the first president of the non-denominational Washington College. Hardly surprisingly, he developed a curriculum not all that different from that of the College of Philadelphia. He also found time to pursue his religious leanings and was instrumental in reviving the Anglican interests in America by establishing the Protestant Episcopal Church and developing a new American prayerbook. He was president of the 1780 convention that created the new diocese of Maryland and was elected as the state's first bishop but was never consecrated. In 1789, when the angst of the war had dissipated and the political climate changed, he was invited to return to Philadelphia and was reinstated as provost. Two years later, the General Assembly established the University of Pennsylvania, into which the college was merged. Sadly, however, he was not made principal although he did continue as provost until he retired to his country estate, where he died in 1803.

Much further west, a university drop-out from Inverness was helping to shape California… literally. In between helping to reform the education system and framing new laws, Hugo Reid was a member of the Boundary Commission and heavily involved in determining the borders when California made the transition from a Mexican province to one of the United States of America. It was, however, a long and emotionally painful journey – including a twice-broken heart and two changes of citizenship – from the Scottish Highlands via Peru to America's golden state.

After doing well at his local school, Reid won a place at Cambridge University and in his second year seemed to be heading for a good degree… until he fell hopelessly in love at the ripe old age of 18. Sadly, his adoration was not reciprocated and in time-honoured fashion, he turned his back on his academic studies, packed away his broken heart and ran off to sea in 1828. He had no particular destination in mind but the first ship from Liverpool was heading for Peru so that's where he went. Once ashore in Lima, he was lucky enough to inveigle himself into a partnership with the English merchant Henry Dalton. The business went well and after a couple of years he was commissioned to set up a branch in Hermosillo, Mexico. Once that was firmly established and running profitably, his natural restlessness again took hold. This time, aboard one of the company's ships, he sailed further north to California, then still a province of Mexico, and set up a trading post in San Pedro. He was a popular figure among the Mexican traders, who gave him the nickname of 'Scotch paisano' (peasant).

On a visit to Los Angeles, he met an American merchant from Massachusetts and once more his energy and enthusiasm proved infectious. After some thought, he settled in LA, a new partnership was formed and that led to the opening of a general store in the main square. Working in the store, he met a beautiful young Indian woman and, with his teenage heartache long forgotten, he again allowed himself to fall head-over-heels in love. However, he again faced painful frustration. Like his first love, this lady was also called Victoria and not only was she married but she was the mother of three children and pregnant with a fourth. Able only to worship from afar, he once more he felt he had to turn his back on angst. In 1836, he retreated to the familiarity of Hermosillo, took a job as a schoolteacher and threw himself into encouraging his pupils. Just as he was beginning to feel settled again, he heard that Victoria's husband had died from smallpox. In unseemly haste, he returned Los Angeles only to learn she would not contemplate marriage. She was a Catholic and he wasn't. His immediate response was to convert, but rather than follow the church's tradition of taking a baptismal saint's name, he instead chose 'Perfecto' and was soon 'Don Perfecto' to his friends and neighbours. His proposal was finally accepted, the couple married in 1837 and at long last he felt able to put down firmer roots. He became a Mexican citizen and was then able to claim the right to acquire public land. Soon he had a huge spread of 13,000 acres (of which he didn't gain the formal title for another eight or nine years) and turned it into a highly profitable ranch. In 1839, with the help of the local Indians, he built an adobe-style home for his newly acquired family. It also became the headquarters of his thriving business. He grew wheat, raised cattle, planted fruit trees, developed 10,000 grapevines and established a stable of fine horses. Thus contented, he was able to play an ever-growing part in community affairs, helped to establish a local school and worked hard at improving conditions for the Native Americans. But despite his domestic bliss, despite the success of his ranching activities and despite his civic responsibilities, he still suffered from the travel bug. In 1842, he succumbed and took the long voyage to China, leaving his family with promises of exotic gifts on his return. It was two years before he arrived back in Los Angeles but, true to his word, he came laden with diamonds and pearls and fine silks and, by way of making further amends to his wife, he also redoubled his work on behalf of the Native Indian community.

With renewed vigour, he picked up the reins of his still-growing empire. His vineyards more than doubled their output of red and white wine and his fruit trees gave him peaches, lemons, pomegranates, oranges, pears, figs, blood oranges, plums, olives, apples and walnuts. In recognition of his importance in the community, he also became a magistrate and in 1845, the governor finally granted him title to the land he had tended so judiciously for the best part of a decade. It was soon afterwards that the uneasy relations between Mexico and America boiled over into open warfare. Hugo Reid, caught between conflicting loyalties of his citizenship and commercial aspirations, didn't play any active part in the war, although many of his fellow merchants did revolt against the Mexicans. With peace imminent in 1849, he did, however, use his influence with the Americans to ease the situation of the Mexican governor who had been so helpful in his land acquisition. To his credit, he was instrumental in gaining permission for the governor to remain in California as a private citizen. Almost as a reward for his diplomatic skills, he was elected as one of the 48 delegates to the California Constitutional Convention. He was still not 40 but was regarded as an elder statesman and for more than two months he played a leading part in establishing the state's first constitution and framing its liberal laws as it became part of the United States.

Those laws were, perhaps, less liberal towards the Native Americans and in 1852 he launched a series of letters to the local newspaper, the *Los Angeles Star*, in which he was highly critical of the Franciscan mission system in its treatment of the Gabrieliño Indians. In railing against their contemporary circumstances he also presented a vivid picture of their culture and their language. In a single year there were more than a score of letters and many editors might have got very fed up with such a barrage of reader's correspondence, but instead this sympathetic and shrewd man persuaded him they should be made into a book – *The Indians of Los Angeles County: Hugo Reid's Letters of 1852* – that formed an important historical record of the Gabrieliño lifestyle. Sadly, Hugo Reid didn't live to see the book. In December of that year, he died from TB. He was 42. His influence, however, is likely to continue long into the future. In the LA Arboretum, his original design of a single-storey adobe building that was once his home and headquarters of his business operation is now a popular visitor attraction. Just north of LA, between Arcadia and Ventura, there's the Hugo Reid Park and in Arcadia, there's the Hugo Reid Elementary School on Hugo Reid Drive. He would, no doubt, be pleased with the tenets of good character still handed down to today's young pupils: 'trustworthiness, responsibility, respect, citizenship, caring, and fairness.'

Another Scottish Reid – this time James, from Edinburgh – also played a key role in developing the infrastructure of the new country. He earned the accolade of 'Father of the Telegraph' after having supervised the construction of many of the most important telegraph lines in the United States. Born in 1819, James Douglas Reid emigrated to Canada with his parents when he was 15. When he was 18, he moved to America and became a post office clerk in Rochester, New York. There he met Irishman Henry O'Neil, the former newspaper editor who had become the city's postmaster. They enjoyed an instant rapport and within months Reid was the great man's assistant and – still in his teens –was assigned the key job of supervising the new telegraph line between the Pennsylvanian townships of Lancaster and Harrisburg. He then worked for various companies, sometimes with Samuel Morse (who became a good friend and mentor), and erected more than 8,000 miles of cable. By 1856, he was superintendent of the New York, Albany and Buffalo Telegraph Company, and when that was absorbed into the Western Union, he became the country's most senior telegrapher. Morse described him as 'a pioneer whose unwearied labours early contributed so effectively to the establishment of telegraph lines.'

In his spare time, he created and edited the *National Telegraphers Review* and was the originator of the telegraphic signal of fraternity. He suggested that the number 73 should be the telegrapher's sign-off equivalent to 'Best regards' and it quickly became universal as the greeting of goodwill and friendship. In 1877, he published his first edition of *The Telegraph in America* and shortly afterwards was appointed a professor at Rochester University. After he retired at the age of 70, in 1889, President Benjamin Harris sent him home to Scotland to act as American consul in Dunfermline. He was confirmed in the post by President Grover Cleveland in 1892 and did not return to America until 1897.

When he died in 1901, a close friend from their days as telegraph messengers together – steel magnate and fellow Scot Andrew Carnegie (see later in this chapter) – contributed half of the $3,000 costs of a monument in Mount Hope Cemetery, Rochester, and signed his farewell message with '73'. The rest of the money for the eight-foot statue was donated by fellow telegraphers.

The survival of one of America's great icons owes much to the efforts of Scottish rancher James Phillip. Known universally as *Scotty* and *The Man who saved The Buffalo,* he bought just five of the endangered animals in 1881 and gradually built up a herd of more than a thousand. By 1906, he was able to persuade the US Congress to lease him 3,500 acres at a peppercorn rent to continue his dream. The buffalo now freely roaming the great national parks are said to be descended from his herd. Scotty was born in 1858 in Moray, son of an Auchness cattle farmer, and left there when he was 18, intent on making his fortune in America – 'the great and growing western country', as he called it. Somehow, after a long and hazardous transatlantic voyage and an even longer trek across country, he reached Wyoming in 1876 and became a cowboy in Cheyenne. That job clearly didn't satisfy him and with stories of gold being found in the Black Hills of Dakota, he decided to head north and try his luck as a panhandler. He spent just one winter in the grim mining camps. He didn't find gold, but this was also the land where the buffalo roam, and he fell in love with the giant beasts, which even then were heading for extinction.

However, fed up with his lack of success as a prospector and the need to feed himself, he recrossed the border to Wyoming and took a government job as a teamster working out of Fort Laramie. He gave that up and his curriculum vitae became ever more like the script for a Hollywood western when he signed on at Fort Robinson and became an army scout in the long campaign against the Sioux Indians led by Chief Sitting Bull. At the end of hostilities in 1877, he went back to riding the range as a cowboy. He remained in the saddle for the best part of two years before finding a new and even less comfortable seat… on a freight wagon thundering through the Black Hills to and from Deadwood! Somewhere along the line, he managed to find time to meet and fall in love with Sarah, daughter of a French Canadian father and a Sioux mother. In time-honoured fashion, he married in 1879, gave up his travels and returned to the less frenetic lifestyle of cattle-farming.

In an ironic twist for the one-time army scout, his new wife's Sioux blood meant he was allowed to ranch on the rich reservation pastures from which palefaces were otherwise barred. He took full advantage of his good fortune and his success is well documented in the state's annals. In 1915, just four years after his death, the *History of Dakota Territory* by George Kingsbury records: 'There are those... whose names deserve to be honoured and their memory perpetuated throughout all the years to come while this Commonwealth endures. They are those who penetrated into the frontier regions, met the hardships, difficulties and privations of pioneer life and aided in planting the seeds of civilization which are now coming into rich fruition.' Foremost among them, of course, was Scotty Philip: 'There was a time when almost every stockman, from the owner of large herds down to the humblest cowboy of the northwest, knew him, and he went through every experience of life on the plains from the period of early settlement here to the present age of advanced civilization.'

While he was building up his stock and becoming the cattle king of the north-west, he remembered the roaming herds of buffalo. When he learned that a handful of calves had been saved from what was later called the 'Last Big Buffalo Hunt', he determined he would buy them and help in efforts to save the magnificent beasts as a contribution to that 'advanced civilisation.'

He slowly built up the herd and when his success was tangible and his head count reached more than 400, he was able to persuade Congress to grant him 3,500 acres so that he could continue the expansion. The cattle king became the buffalo boss. Although it's for this that he gets a mention in the history books, he also played a very significant role in developing the state's infrastructure. He helped build railroads west of the Missouri, was a strong advocate of irrigation to enrich the farmland and actively supported the commercial and industrial development around Fort Pierre. He established the county board of commissioners and, for two years, 1898–1900, he served on the state senate. At one time, he was also a director of the major cattle company, the Stock Growers Bank and the Missouri River Transportation Company. As Kingsbury wrote: 'He had the confidence of thousands of business men as well as plainsmen and nowhere that he went was he without friends and acquaintances. Physically he was a man large of stature and in any gathering of people he was a conspicuous and prominent figure.'

When he died suddenly, just 53, in 1911, his local paper in Fort Pierre, the *Capital Journal*, said of him: 'He was known from Mexico to Canada and in all the stock yards of the country. His herds of cattle at times numbered many thousands and for more than a quarter of a century, no round-up from the Black Hills to the Missouri was complete without the presence of this cattle king. At every shipping season his business was eagerly sought by the railroad companies.' He was buried in a cemetery near his buffalo grazing land. It is said that as the funeral procession passed, some of the bison came down out of the hills, 'showing their respect to the man who had saved them,' according to one local newspaper. Somehow, one desperately wants that to be true! The small South Dakota city of Philip (population 885 at the 2000 Census) is named in his honour.

The governor of Wyoming while Scotty Philip was at his peak was a fellow Scot, from Arbroath. He gloried in the name of General Thomas Moonlight, a surname that came from an ancestor who had been abandoned as a baby and found in the moonlight.

He clearly overcame the raised eyebrows about his name, rose through the ranks of the US Army, had a successful political career and went on to be US ambassador to Bolivia (1887–89).

He was born into an impoverished farming family in 1833 and by the time he was 12 had decided he could find a better life elsewhere. He ran away to sea and found a cabin boy's berth on a ship bound for New York. He jumped ship when it arrived in America but his early experiences of the New World were not much better than those of his days on the farm in Scotland. For seven years he scraped a living as an itinerant labourer on a series of farms up and down the east coast, before he enlisted in the army... and began a glittering career. He joined 4th Artillery Regiment, which tended to have smaller companies, and he rose swiftly through the non-commissioned ranks and served for five years as a first sergeant. At the outbreak of the Civil War (1861–65) he raised 1st Kansas Volunteer Artillery Battery and was commissioned as its captain. He fought against pro-Confederate bushwhackers and border guerrillas, most notoriously Quantrill's Raiders. The Raiders were quasi-military but operated well beyond army norms. In 1863, they massacred more than 200 men and boys, some only seven years old, at Lawrence in Kansas. Captain Moonlight was detailed to hunt them down but they managed to escape across the border to Texas, where they were sheltered by the Confederate Army. Despite that, he was promoted the following year to colonel and given command of the 2nd Brigade of 1st Division in the Army of the Border and led it at the Battle of Westport, where he was commended for his bravery. By the end of the war, the one-time private had become a brigadier general. He left the army in 1865 and returned to what he knew best, farming and developed a successful holding. That and his army credentials gave him a sound basis from which to launch himself into politics and once again he was successful. He won a seat in the state senate and served for a time as secretary of state for Kansas, before being appointed to his ambassadorial role in Bolivia in 1887.

Reputed to be the richest man in America (and almost certainly, therefore, in the world), Andrew Carnegie – the Steel King – gave the lie to the cliché of the tight-fisted Scot. So much has been written about him that I want to do little more than acknowledge his astonishing philanthropy and his place in the history of the land of opportunity. In 1881, he gave $56 million to build more than 2,500 free libraries throughout the English-speaking world and another $300 million for other charitable purposes, including huge educational endowments to Scottish universities and the purchase of hundreds of organs for the country's churches.

His humble beginnings underline his tremendous tenacity. He was born in Dunfermline but left for America in 1848 after his father was made redundant from the weaving trade. His first job was as a bobbin boy in a Pennsylvania cotton factory, where he earned just over a dollar a week. He later became a Western Union telegram boy on two dollars a week (which is where he met James Reid) and then held various jobs, rising to superintendent, with the state railway company. Frustrated by poor wages, however, he took out a bank loan to invest in the company that introduced sleeping cars on the railway. By 1868 he was able to lay the foundation of his steel conglomerate and in 1899 finally consolidated that as the Carnegie Steel Company. When he retired in 1901, the company became the giant United States Steel Corporation. This demonstration of America as the ultimate land of opportunity has, not surprisingly, been the subject of countless books and has more than 760,000 mentions on the world wide web! By the time he died, Carnegie had donated more $350 million to a wide range of charities; he had lived by his own philosophy that 'the man who dies thus rich dies disgraced.' Carnegie was a long way from being disgraced and few would argue with his description as the 'Father of Philanthropy'.

It was another Dunfermline man, Andrew Smith Hallidie, who invented the steel-wire haulage system and earned yet another soubriquet for Scotland as 'Father of the Cable Car' after building San Francisco's first cable-car link, which ran from the city centre to Nob Hill, in 1873. He was born just plain Andrew Smith, son of an inveterate inventor whose patents included the steel-wire that was to make the young man's fortune. He took on the Hallidie not in an act of self-aggrandizement, but, as he put it, to honour his famous uncle and godfather. Sir Andrew Hallidie had been physician to two monarchs, King William IV and Queen Victoria.

Andrew Smith (as he still then was), was apprenticed in his father's machine shop and then the drawing office but left Scotland with his family in 1852. He was 16 and determined to join the California Gold Rush. His father had joined him in prospecting but had soon had enough and quit after a year. Undeterred, Andrew worked on for five long, hard years as a placer-miner (panhandler) and occasional blacksmith. In his own words, he earned 'just enough to starve on.' He was, however, able to use his limited engineering experience to provide essential services for the mining industry: when he was 19 he sowed the seeds of a new career when he successfully built a wire suspension bridge over the American River in the Sierra Nevada Mountains.

Two years later, with tough working conditions having got the better of him, he abandoned the gold fields and settled in San Francisco, where he eventually managed to start a small firm making wire cable. This time he used his mining experience to devise a hoist system that soon became the norm in mine shafts across the goldfields. In 1867 he invented and patented the Hallidie Ropeway, a cable system, to haul the heavy ore from the mines. It was a great success and was used right across America and then exported to Mexico, Canada, New Zealand and Japan. Through his hard work, he quietly amassed life savings of $20,000. Rather than leave it in the bank, he decided to invest it in an idea that had been building in his febrile mind for several years. Having watched the horses pull the trams up the steep gradient of the city's Clay Street Hill – and collapsing in exhaustion on one occasion – he set out to create a cable system to replace the horses. In 1873, the first cable car trundled from Clay Street all the way up to Nob Hill pulled by Hallidie's cable system. The émigré from Scotland had arrived. His patent on the system made him a rich man.

Dunfermline was the birthplace for yet another Scottish contributor to the America we all know and love from the titanic battles on lush, green, manicured golf courses. John Reid, who emigrated when he was 16, is regarded as Father of American Golf after establishing the first club at Yonkers in New York in 1888. On its current website, St Andrew's Golf Club (distinguished from the Royal and Ancient by the apostrophe) describes how it started: 'John Reid and several of his friends took an armful of clubs, some balls and hearts full of enthusiasm to a pasture in Yonkers for a friendly round of Gowf [sic]. There, in front of a gallery of bemused cows, they knocked the balls around a three-hole course. Before long, these golfing pioneers had commandeered their own clubhouse – an old apple tree from whose gnarled branches they hung their coats and obligatory flasks of fine Scotch.' The founder is honoured in the club's John Reid Room, where there is a priceless collection of his early clubs and balls and even a branch from the apple tree! Originally, the members of this far-from-august establishment were known as the Apple Tree Gang. Photos of the time suggest that, far from the closely shaven surfaces of modern US courses, they putted across uneven, poorly-cut grass and even across cart tracks. The Gang's creation stems from the schoolboy friendship of John Reid and Robert Lockhart, who had both left their home town to find their way in the New World in 1866. One prospered as a steel founder and the other was a successful linen merchant, but they remained firm friends. Robert's business meant that he took regular trips back to the Scottish mills and with his linen samples often brought back stories about the golf. When he brought a set of clubs and a few balls, he easily persuaded John and his son to try their hand in Central Park. John Reid liked it so much that he started playing in the field next to his house and invited his friend and a few others – including Andrew Carnegie – to join him. He expanded the course from three to six holes and the essential 19th was moved from the shade of the old apple tree to his front parlour. As membership grew, so the club developed. He gave a medal, the first prize ever put up for competition in America, for a 36-hole stroke competition and it has been played for ever since. The course, needless to say, has changed dramatically.

Another major contributor to the development of American golf was Donald Ross, from Dornoch. He earned the reputation as one of the greatest golf-course architects in American history. During the first half of the twentieth century, he designed more than a hundred courses including the famous Pinehurst in North Carolina, the British at the Bobby Jones Golf Complex in Sarasota, Florida, the Chevy Chase in Maryland, the Washington Country Club, the South Course at Daytona Beach in Florida and the championship course at Columbus Country Club in Ohio. He was an apprentice with one of the golfing greats, Old Tom Morris (the four times Open champion) at St Andrews, before investing his little savings on a passage to America in 1899 when he was 19. He didn't let the grass grow under his feet and within the year he was appointed club professional at Pinehurst. He developed the course there and soon became the man all the big golf clubs wanted to shape their sport. He was a founding member and first president of the American Society of Golf Course Architects in 1947. He died in 1950 and was admitted to the World Golf Hall of Fame in 1977.

Brothers William and Henry Chisholm from Fife both made their mark in the booming steel industry of their adopted city of Cleveland. While younger brother William made his name as an innovator and inventor, Henry was the businessman par excellence and earned, you've guessed it, the title of 'Father of Cleveland'.

William went to work when he was 12. He was apprenticed to a dry-goods merchant in Kirkcaldy but three years in a dusty office was enough and at 16 he signed on as a sailor and enjoyed life at sea for seven years. In 1847, then 22, he weighed anchor, and with his brother emigrated to Canada and became a builder and contractor in Montreal. Five years later he was on the move again, this time to Cleveland, where his brother had settled. His restlessness took him soon afterwards to Pittsburgh. He worked there until 1857, when he returned to join his brother in the rolling-mills. Three years under the shadow of his big brother again proved enough and he decided that he preferred the nuts and bolts rather than the big picture of management. He stayed within the steel industry but as an inventor able to indulge his instincts and ideas. He worked out how to make screws from the new Bessemer steel and that was so successful that, ironically, he had to establish his own company to make them in 1871. From his earlier experience, he had learned not to get bogged down in the paperwork and continued coming up with new ideas for both machinery and products. By 1879, he had to open a factory and three years later he began to make steam engines, which he adapted for hoisting and pumping, and transporters for carrying coal and ore between vessels and railroad cars.

Big brother Henry also left school at 12 but he started work as a trainee carpenter and completed his apprenticeship before going to Montreal, where he too set himself up as a contractor and quickly established a reputation. His first visit to Cleveland was in 1852, when he was contracted to build a breakwater. He did a good job and he was invited to invest in a company whose main output was the replacement for worn out railway rails. He persuaded them to reuse the old rails and soon he became the senior figure in the company. By 1858, the company was producing more than 50 tons of re-rolled rails every day. He recognised the key importance of a strong and contented workforce. He created jobs for thousands of migrant workers, built houses for them and developed a company store to reduce the cost of their shopping. He also knew that steel was the metal of the future and ensured his ironmasters kept up to date with developments, including the emergence of Bessemer steel. By 1858, his plant was the fifth biggest in the country. He was able to compete successfully, spread his investments into blast furnaces in Indiana and iron ore in Lake Superior, and to diversify into making smaller components like the nuts and bolts his brother disliked so much!

The scale of the company's operation can be seen from a clipping from the *New York Times* with the Cleveland dateline of 24 November 1879. The reporter described his purchase of Chisholm's partner's shares for $1.4 million dollars as 'one of the most important business transactions which ever took place in this city.' He died suddenly in 1881. He was just 59. His workers showed their affection for him by contributing to a handsome monument for him in Lake View Cemetery. It bears the legend: 'Erected by 6000 employees and friends in memory of Henry Chisholm, Christian, philanthropist, and everyone's friend.'

Initially he was worth barely a footnote in history but since the Florida vote recounts of 2000 (in the presidential election between George Bush and Al Gore) Glaswegian John McTammany merits a mention for having invented the first voting machine used in many American state and local elections. He emigrated to America in 1863, when he was 18, and served with the Ohio Volunteers in the Civil War. He was wounded at the Battle of Chattanooga and was invalided out of the army and became a music teacher. He also played in a band, sold pianos and organs and invented a player piano with perforated music rolls. From there, it was only a small step to the voting machine that eventually led to the drama of Florida 2000.

The Hollywood movie has given us a picture of the District Attorney figure as a sharp-suited legal expert: the good guy dedicated to nailing the bad guys. Hugh Maxwell, originally from Paisley, fitted the bill perfectly. He was tall, elegant, perfectly turned out and with a mind like a razor. He was one of New York's early DAs. He was elected in 1819 and his dazzling courtroom successes ensured he held the plum post for a then record-breaking ten years. His family left Paisley for the New World when he was in his early teens and he went to Columbia College in New York until he was 21. He then went on to study law and was admitted to the bar in 1811. He was clearly a very bright advocate and within three years he was appointed assistant judge advocate general in the United States army. Five years later and now in a smart civilian suit, he was elected DA for New York. (The nearest UK equivalents, although appointed rather than elected, are the Crown Prosecutor in England, Wales and Northern Ireland and the Procurator Fiscal in Scotland.)

His forensic skills as a prosecutor were noted in the *New York Times*, which described him as one of 'the most venerated and venerable of lawyers of his day' before recording that 'perhaps the greatest case ever tried in the DA's office… was when a large number of eminent merchants, inadvertently, became involved in a prosecution for violating the statutes of the State. As they were all influential men, there was great public excitement and great efforts were made to prevent the cases being tried but Mr Maxwell performed his duty as DA, contending successfully against the most eminent talent of the time.' These particular bad guys were convicted of conspiracy to defraud. He went on to become a leading politician and held the influential post of collector (of import duties and taxes) of the Port of New York for the three years 1849–52.

If it wasn't a Scot who invented Father Christmas, James Edgar (born Edinburgh, 1842–1930) came quite close. He was the world's first in-store Father Christmas. A tall but chubby figure with a natural long white beard, he pulled one of many crowd-pulling stunts in his Brockton, Massachusetts, dry goods store by donning the now-traditional red outfit and ringing a hand-bell, offering the children all the joys of a department store Christmas in 1890.

He had something of a reputation as a man who loved children and was always out to find ways of attracting them and their free-spending parents to his store. On Saturday mornings, he would often clamber onto the store's roof and shower coins on them. Every Independence Day, he hired the town's trolley cars to take every child on a picnic to the neighbouring county. When he heard of any child who was sick, he ensured a doctor would call at his expense. 'My life in Scotland was a poor one,' he once told an associate, 'when I came to this country, I had to scratch to get by. I never really had a childhood. I was always out working. I think that is why I enjoy children so much. I'm trying to make up for the childhood I never had.' I'm sure his customers – young and not-so-young – would agree that he surely did.

One of the many great wonders of California is the magnificent Yosemite National Park: 1,200 square miles of magnificent mountain terrain about 200 miles the east of San Francisco. It was designated the United States' first wilderness park in 1890 thanks to the determination of John Muir, from Dunbar.

It earned Scotland another Father of…credit: Father of America's National Parks. A description by one of the park's guides suggests it was well-earned: 'I have seen people of emotional temperament stand with tearful eyes, spellbound and dumb with awe as they got their first view of the valley from Inspiration Point, overwhelmed in the sudden presence of the unspeakable, stupendous grandeur.' Abraham Lincoln, too, was overawed by Yosemite and, as president, signed a Bill giving it to the State of California in 1864 so it would be better protected. When John Muir first saw it, he said: 'No temple made with hands can compare with Yosemite' and he described one of its most stunning features, the Sierra Nevada, as 'the most divinely-beautiful of all the mountain chains.'

A look at his background shows that his interest and appreciation in nature can be traced back to Scotland. Born in 1838, he was one of eight children and was clearly a precocious child in educational terms. He went to Dunbar Grammar School when he was just three and then to university when he was 11. That, however, doesn't appear to have interfered with a normal boyhood. He later recalled fighting in the school playground, enacting the great battles of Scottish history and trying to keep ahead of his pals in the number of bird's nests he could find. However much he enjoyed school, he often opted out of classes in favour of exploring the great outdoors. In *The Story of My Boyhood and Youth* (1913), he recounts his early adventures in Scotland: 'I was fond of everything that was wild… I loved to wander in the fields to hear the birds sing and along the shore to gaze and wonder at the shells and the seaweeds, eels and crabs in the pools when the tide was low; and best of all to watch the waves in awful storms thundering on the black headlands and craggy ruins of old Dunbar Castle.'

Soon after arriving in Wisconsin, he went back to university and studied botany and geology. When he left, before graduating, he didn't make use of his new learning, but instead turned his attention to his many inventions… wooden clocks, thermometers, barometers, a combination lock and even a bed that tipped him onto the floor to wake him up in the morning! His restlessness took him through a fistful of jobs (between inventing things) and all across America and Canada. He was at various times a mechanic, a saw-mill operator and an engineer. While working in a factory in Indianapolis, he had an accident that nearly cost him his sight. A metal spike pierced his eye and left him temporarily blind, but he recovered after four weeks in a darkened room

In 1867, the great outdoors called him again and he set out to explore his new country. He walked more than a thousand miles from Indiana to the Gulf of Mexico, sailed to Cuba and Panama and then up the west coast of Central and North America to San Francisco. The following year, he discovered the Sierra Nevada and was later, in 1892, to co-found and become president of the Sierra Club (which continues to play its part in preserving the parks). In 1880, he married Louisa, whose parents owned a 2,600-acre ranch and fruit orchards near San Francisco. For ten years, he worked assiduously in managing the family ranch and vineyards, which he built into a successful, money-making enterprise.

That didn't deter him from also taking on the mantle of the preservationist and he was especially concerned about the future of Yosemite. He saw it as 'inviolable territory' and warned that the most serious threat was from the free-roaming livestock and especially sheep, which he called 'hoofed locusts.' In 1889, he went on a camping trip with an editor of the influential *Century* magazine and showed the damage sheep had done to the grassland. The editor, Robert Underwood Johnson, immediately invited him to write for the magazine and, even more importantly, agreed to use his political clout to introduce a bill to Congress to make Yosemite into a national park. It took just a year for Congress to pass a bill that essentially followed Muir's recommendations, but to his chagrin it left the valley in state control.

It took more than 12 years for him to ensure more effective legislation and that was only through his relationship with President Theodore Roosevelt. He took the president on a stagecoach trip through Yosemite and used that to repeat his concerns about state mismanagement and exploitation of the valley's resources. That and the wonders of the area convinced the president that it should be taken into federal control and he shortly afterwards followed his host's advice. Yosemite was taken into federal control in 1906, and became the first National Park in 1916.

John Muir valued nature for its spiritual and transcendental qualities. In an essay he referred to the National Parks as 'places for rest, inspiration, and prayers.' He often encouraged city dwellers 'to experience nature for its spiritual nourishment.' There is a very beautiful statue of him feeding birds in Dunbar.

A perhaps less-welcome natural feature of California, the San Andreas Fault, was identified and named in 1895 by Anstruther-born academic and earthquake expert Andrew Lawson. Later – following the 1906 San Francisco earthquake – his *Lawson Report* showed that the fault stretched well into southern California when it had been thought it was confined to the Bay area. He had emigrated to Canada with his parents and graduated from Toronto University in 1885. He worked for the Geological Survey of Canada before becoming a consulting geologist in Vancouver. In 1892, then aged 31, he moved to Berkeley in California where he became Professor of Mineralogy and Geology. He was later a consultant on the construction of the Golden Gate Bridge in the 1930s. He gave his name to the mineral Lawsonite and the Franciscan Complex of rocks. His Berkeley home, designed to withstand earthquakes, is now an officially designated local landmark.

The history of journalism and the media is an endless fascination for me (it's been my life for longer than I'm going to admit) and the Scots in America offer a very rich vein for my jottings. They were in on the beginnings of some of the world's great papers and spawned news headlines, foreign correspondents, cartoons, the gossip column and the financial pages. More importantly for me, they fought for and won the right of the freedom of the press and established the journalist's role at the heart of democracy.

John Campbell of Islay perhaps wins the prize for the best scoop of all: he produced the country's first regular newspaper, *The Boston News-Letter* on 24 April 1704. It might not be much of a match for today's heavyweight newspapers, however: it was only a single page, had a limited circulation of 300 and tried to ape the *London Gazette,* with much of the content lifted from the British press. Campbell had emigrated with his parents and was following in his father's footsteps as a bookseller and postmaster. He was more of a collator of information than a journalist and the *News-Letter* title was quite apt. Over the years, however, he seems to have learned something of the trade of popular journalism and clearly developed an eye for a good story. One of his later issues would have done today's tabloids proud. In 1719 he printed a graphic report on the death of the notorious pirate Edward Teach – known universally as Blackbeard – at the hands of Lieutenant Robert Maynard. The young naval officer had been instructed by Virginia Governor Alexander Spotswood to hunt down and eliminate the pirate. He did just that and John Campbell splashed it in his paper: 'Maynard and Teach themselves begun the fight with their swords, Maynard making a thrust, the point of his sword against Teach's cartridge box and bent it to the hilt. Teach broke the guard of it and wounded Maynard's fingers but did not disable him, whereupon he jumped back and threw away his sword and fired his pistol which wounded Teach. Abraham Demelt struck in between them with his sword and cut Teach's face. In the interim, both companies engaged in Maynard's sloop. Later during the battle, while Teach was loading his pistol he finally died from blood loss. Maynard then cut off his head and hung it from his bow.' The story was illustrated with a line drawing of the gruesome head hanging from the bowsprit of Lieutenant Maynard's ship. John Campbell retired from the editorship in 1722 but the paper continued until 1776, shortly before the last British troops were evacuated from Boston.

With American journalism still in its infancy, it was an Edinburgh lawyer who successfully defended a newspaper printer accused of libelling the British governor of Pennsylvania and thus firmly established the principle of the freedom of the press, which we hacks still cherish today. It was not simply a victory for journalism and newspaper publishing. It was a victory for free speech and all that means in a democracy. The celebrated 1735 court case established that truth is a defence against accusations of libel and is often cited as 'the beginning of America's liberty.'

The hero of the piece was Andrew Hamilton, a distinguished politician and lawyer who had arrived in America as an itinerant 25-year-old in 1701, but went on to a glittering career of high politics. For such a historically important figure, his early background is all too vague. We know he was born in 1676 but know nothing of his family or their circumstances in the Scottish capital. Nor do we know of any training or specific qualifications he might have had. His first job after emigrating was as a steward on a Virginian cotton plantation. His fortunes changed somewhat when he married the widow of the plantation owner and at one stage he opened a school and taught classics, which suggests he had a good education back in Edinburgh. His wife obviously also provided influential connections and he was able to train as a lawyer and then set up in practice. From there, it was success all the way as he became one of the state's most sought after attorneys. He was appointed as state attorney general in 1717 and to the Provincial Council in 1721. It's significant that he had sufficient clout to insist that he would only serve as long as it didn't interfere with his legal work. He then moved effortlessly on to two terms as speaker of the state's House of Representatives (1729–32 and 1734–38) and a seat in the Supreme Court. He also designed and helped commission the famous and appropriately named Liberty Hall in Philadelphia (where the Declaration of Independence was later signed).

By 1735, Hamilton had retired from front-line legal affairs. It was then that a group of fellow Scots and a German émigré printer careered into his quiet life. The Scots, led by James Alexander, a very distinguished lawyer from Edinburgh, had invested in the small *New York Weekly Journal* as a vehicle to voice opposition to continuing British rule. John Peter Zenger was the printer. When the British governor could no longer stand the constant taunts, he used the full weight of his royal position: he accused the printer of 'seditious libels which with utmost virulence have endeavoured to asperse his Excellency and vilify his Administration.' Seditious libel is a criminal as opposed to a civil offence so Zenger was arrested, refused bail and thrown in jail, where he languished for ten months before the case came to court. The governor was able to appoint the judge sympathetic to the crown and when James Alexander sought to plead Zenger's innocence, he was promptly disbarred from all legal practice! At this point the matter became a cause celebre. A very frustrated James Alexander appealed for help from fellow Scot Andrew Hamilton, then in his late seventies but still a much-respected figure. After carefully studying the case papers, the elder statesman agreed to come out of retirement.

He reasoned that the articles in the *Weekly Journal* suggested no more than the truth: that the liberties of the people were in danger from their government and that the governor had interfered with the rights of trial by jury. This, he said was the use of lawless power and he said the love of liberty was the only defence against such tyranny on the part of reckless rulers: 'Power may justly be compared to a great river which, while kept within its due bounds is both beautiful and useful, but when it overflows its banks, it is then too impetuous to be stemmed. It bears down on all before it and brings destruction and desolation wherever it comes. If this then is the nature of power, let us at least do our duty and like wise men use our utmost care to support liberty, the only bulwark against lawless power.'

He underlined his commitment to the case by acting *pro bono publico* (without fees) to plead Zenger's case – that everything printed was true. The judge would have none of it. He cited British law at the time: 'You cannot be admitted to give the truth of a libel in evidence.' In other words, as the printer had admitted publishing the offending material, he was guilty of libel. When Hamilton tried to counter, he was told brusquely: 'You are not permitted to argue against the opinion of the Court.' Lesser advocates might have buckled under this courtroom tyranny but not Andrew Hamilton. Undeterred, he pointedly ignored the judge and thereafter talked directly to the jury: 'The question before the court and you, gentlemen of the jury, is not of small nor private concern. It is not the cause of the poor printer or of New York alone. It may in its consequence affect every freeman that lives under a British government on the main of America. It is the best cause. It is the cause of liberty... the liberty both of exposing and opposing arbitrary power by speaking and writing the truth.' The jury got the message and quickly returned a not guilty verdict. There was riotous jubilation among those of Zenger's supporters who were packing the court and the judge threatened to jail them all for contempt. Andrew Hamilton was duly feted. He was given the freedom of New York and the symbolic keys to the city were presented in a magnificent gold box. His success in the case gave rise to the popular American expression, 'Philadelphia lawyer,' when referring to someone who can achieve the seemingly impossible.

The result was welcomed in all the colonies (and by not a few people in Britain). Former New York Chief Justice Lewis Morris later referred to him as 'the day-star of the Revolution.' Andrew Hamilton returned to Philadelphia to enjoy his retirement until his death in 1741. Zenger continued to print the *New York Weekly Journal* as it went from strength to strength. James Alexander later joined Benjamin Franklin as one of the founders of the American Philosophical Society.

Another close associate of Benjamin Franklin and a contributor to the development of the press was Edinburgh-born printer and publisher David Hall. When the pair teamed up to launch the *Pennsylvania Gazette* in 1748, they established a very positive style of journalism that is said to have become the foundation for modern American news coverage. They also introduced the political cartoon as an original and acerbic way of making political comment. David Hall, born in 1714, learned the printing business in Edinburgh before moving to London, where he worked alongside fellow Scot, William Strahan, then a journeyman but later master printer to the King. Strahan was a friend of Benjamin Franklin and it was through him that the *Gazette* partnership evolved. The company also printed the paper money issued by Congress during the Revolutionary War.

The other key Hamilton in America's press history, Alexander – the one who died after being shot during a duel with the vice president (see earlier in chapter) – launched the *New York Post* in 1801. It's the country's oldest daily, its sixth biggest and now part of Rupert Murdoch's News Corporation. He funded it with $10,000 from a group of investors, including other members of the Federalist party, such as his old army and university friend, Robert Troup, and former secretary of the treasury, Oliver Wolcott. The first meeting of the group took place in the weekend villa of Scottish shipping magnate Archibald Gracie (from Dumfries). The building later housed the Museum of New York and then became the official residence of the city's mayor.

Despite the fact that I've already overused the phrase in this chapter, I'm glad to say that it was James Gordon Bennett from Lanarkshire who earned the soubriquet 'Father of Modern Journalism' and was a towering figure in the growing newspaper industry. He launched the *New York Herald* in 1835 and was the first to introduce a regular financial report, a society page and a European correspondent. He was born in 1795, son of a poor farmer in Newmill, Moray. After going to the local school, he decided to train as a minister but then, on a whim, he emigrated in 1819 to Nova Scotia, where he taught bookkeeping. That clearly wasn't to his liking and he soon moved on to Portland, Maine, and just as quickly to Boston. In 1820, he worked as a proofreader and bookseller before edging that little bit closer to journalism. The *Charleston Courier* employed him to translate Spanish news reports. He then, somehow, landed the post of Washington correspondent for the *New York Enquirer*, a party paper supporting aspiring and later serving President Andrew Jackson. (It should not to be confused with the *National Enquirer* of 20th-century origin and notoriety: see later in this chapter.) When it merged with the rival *Morning Courier*, he became associate editor, but his own personal views became ever more trenchant and in 1832 he was dismissed.

Having tasted the high life of New York from afar, the lure of the Big Apple finally got him and he moved to the city in 1823, where he took a number of jobs which allowed him to assiduously learn the business side of publishing. At last, in 1835, he launched the *New York Herald*. He had only $500 working capital, his office was in a cellar and his desk was a wooden plank supported by two flour barrels. Out of necessity, he wrote every word of the paper himself. Almost immediately, he made a success of it.

My journalist colleague Gerald Isaaman wrote a very nice piece about Bennett in the *Scottish Review* of May 1996, in which he said, 'he more or less invented the gossip column, the interview and financial reporting for the masses. He introduced news from abroad and used the extension of the railroad to put his *Herald* on every breakfast table.' He later featured sensational sex-and-crime stories, made heavy use of pictures and posted correspondents to far-flung regions. The following year, he shocked and excited his readers with his sensational front-page coverage of the murder of a prostitute and the subsequent trial. His was the most complete reporting and unlike other papers, who tended to take sides, he was sceptical about the guilt of the accused and after the 19-year-old man was found not guilty, Bennett got the first ever newspaper interview with him. He wasn't balanced enough, however, not to exploit the lurid nature of the case, and he introduced the use of illustrations produced from woodcut blocks. In 1839, he pulled off yet another remarkable the scoop when he secured the first ever exclusive interview with an American president. He was allowed into the confidence of President Martin Van Buren, the first New Yorker to hold the office. Despite that, he maintained a fairly neutral stance in politics, although he did endorse candidates he believed to be of exceptional calibre. He was just as shrewd in business terms as he was in journalism. He made advertisers pay upfront and thereby avoided defaulters. He also kept himself at the cutting edge of technology and was quick to use new techniques in news-gathering, printing and communications, all of which helped to make his paper profitable.

When he retired in 1866, the *New York Herald* was the city's brightest and most popular read and had the highest circulation of any paper in America. He gave his name to the New York Fire Department's highest award for bravery, the James Gordon Bennett Medal, and he is also honoured in the name of a street and park in Washington Heights. Sadly, his son James Gordon Bennett Junior, was not exactly a chip off the old block. He had none of his father's skills or charms. It was his ineptness that gave us the time-honoured expression of exasperation and disbelief ... *Gordon Bennett!* Initially the younger Bennett raised the paper's profile when he backed Henry Morton Stanley's 1869 expedition into Africa to find the Scottish missionary, David Livingstone, in return for the exclusive account of Stanley's progress. That success did not last, however, and the paper was eventually merged with its arch-rival, the *Tribune* to give today's *Herald Tribune*.

Next, yet another Scottish Father of... but this one somewhat less glorious than the others. James Callender, from Edinburgh, earned the unfortunate title of Father of Yellow Journalism through his acrimonious attempts to, as he saw it, cut the rich and famous down to size. The founding fathers were easy targets for his phlegm but he operated under a cloak of anonymity: hence the yellow.

Born in 1758, he had no formal education but got a job as a junior clerk in an Edinburgh law office. In his spare time, he wrote and published what at first were satirical pamphlets, with Samuel Johnson as one of his early victims. When he moved to take on the politicians, his tone became more savage and, inevitably, he lost his job. With more time on his hands, he widened his attacks and initially amused some of the more liberal landed gentry and he enjoyed their patronage for a time. As his writing became ever more scurrilous and he accused public figures of corruption, his backers backed off and he was forced by threats of legal action to slip over to Ireland. When his political pursuers looked like catching up with him, he fled to America in 1793. There he slotted into the febrile political debate by writing for the highly partisan newspapers, and sniped away at George Washington, John Adams and even the man who had given him patronage, Thomas Jefferson.

As a freelancer, Callender's earnings were sporadic and he lived barely above the poverty line, which only served to increase his bile. His writing was described as 'a mix of reasoned argument, satire and personal invective.' It was the invective that added to his notoriety. In one of his pamphlets, *History of 1796*, he exposed the affair of Federalist party leader, Alexander Hamilton but the following year he went one further and accused him of corruption. It was a libel too far and proved to be the beginning of the end of his turbulent career. In 1798, he suffered the trauma of his wife's death from yellow fever, his earnings dried up, he was forced to seek poor relief and then departed Philadelphia in such a state of despair and disarray that he left his children behind. Federalist John Adams became so angered by his harassment that he had him charged with seditious libel. He had reached Richmond, Virginia, when the law caught up with him in 1800. He was fined $200 and sent to jail, where he stayed until he was pardoned by the incoming president, Thomas Jefferson, in March 1801.

He was appointed editor of the *Richmond Recorder*, a Federalist newspaper, and used his position to continue his attacks on the politicians. Despite the pardon he had granted and his earlier support, Callender exposed President Jefferson's liaison (after his wife's death, when he was only 39) with his mixed-race slave, Sally Hemmings, and accused him of an earlier attempt to seduce a neighbour's wife. After the Jefferson controversy, he fell out with the newspaper owner over his salary and was, once again, unemployed. His demise was especially inglorious. He drowned after stumbling into the James River while staggering home in a drunken stupor. He was the subject of the novel *Scandalmonger*, by *New York Times* columnist and Pulitzer prize-winner William Safire, published in 2000.

When Daniel Cameron, a journalist from Berwick-upon-Tweed, emigrated to America in 1851, he certainly didn't let the grass grow under his feet. He was just 23 but he quickly found his feet in the cut-throat milieu of the Chicago press. Within a year he was in business talks with Cyrus Hall McCormack, inventor and boss of the giant International Harvester Company. A year later, the two formed an unlikely partnership to launch not one but two newspapers: the *Chicago Herald* and the *Chicago Times*. It proved to be a mutually profitable arrangement. Daniel Cameron gave McCormick a strong enough grounding in newspaper production for him to act as editor of the *Times* for six or seven years. In return, McCormick taught him about the volatile world of balance sheets and business enabling him to become a highly successful publisher. At the outbreak of the Civil War in 1861, Cameron immediately joined the Union Army and helped raise the 65th Illinois Infantry, or Scotch Regiment. The rest of his tale is told earlier in this chapter.

The first to spot an opening for a major magazine to serve the ever-growing American finance and business market was, of course, Bertie Forbes. He gave his name to *Forbes Magazine* in 1917 and was editor or editor-in-chief for the rest of his life, establishing his own fortune in the process. Born in New Deer, Aberdeenshire, in 1880, he decided early in life that he was going to be a journalist and got off to a good start as a reporter with the *Dundee Courier*. He quickly established a reputation and spent his twenty-first birthday en route to Johannesburg where he had taken up the offer to be involved in the launch of the *Rand Daily Mail* in 1902. Two years later, he emigrated to New York and became financial editor of the *Journal of Commerce*. He was a columnist with Hearst newspapers (1911–13) and business and financial editor of the *New York American* (1913–16). It was, of course, this last job that sowed the seeds of his determination to launch his own magazine. As a financial journalist he spent much of his time chasing the wealthy looking for information that he could turn into stories. Part of his beat in his search for news about the country's major businesses was William Rockefeller's Jekyll Island, summer haunt for many of Wall Street's emerging millionaires. Among these, JP Morgan was probably the dominant figure and, far from being irritated by the attentions of a reporter, he saw the advantage of making friends. He was soon feeding the hungry journalist with stories, carefully spun by self-interest, of course. The arrangement worked well for both of them because for Bertie Forbes, it led to his launch of *Forbes Magazine*, America's first specialist magazine for anyone interested in business and businessmen. He got the idea for using his own name on the masthead from his spell on *Leslie's Weekly*, the illustrated literary magazine named after its founder, Frank Leslie.

A second Scot to recognise the potential of this lucrative market was Malcolm Muir from Kelso. He founded the highly influential *Business Week* in 1929… just seven weeks before the disastrous stock market crash that signalled the beginning of the Great Depression. Eight years later, he became president and editor-in-chief of *Newsweek*, America's second-largest current affairs magazine. Prior to the launch of his new publication in 1929, he had been appointed president of the ever-expanding publishers McGraw-Hill and, despite the gathering economic gloom, he had confidence in the new magazine. He wrote: '*Business Week* will never be content to be a mere chronicle of events. It aims always to interpret their significance. It always has a point of view, and usually a strong opinion, both of which it does not hesitate to express and all the way through, we hope you will discover it is possible to write sanely and intelligently of business without being pompous or ponderous.' In its first issue on 7 September 1929 he forecast: 'Business will gradually and steadily recover as businessmen regain their perspective and go back to work.'

To show his own confidence and optimism, he established four new magazines in 1930, opened a West Coast office, set up a huge book depository in San Francisco and expanded into the trade-book market. He also commissioned a new office building in New York in 1931. The Great Depression, though, turned out to be much more severe than he had thought: in 1933 he was forced to slash personnel and salaries and even then ended the year facing a then huge deficit of nearly a quarter of a million dollars, leaving him with no choice but to sell press machinery and equipment. However, both he and the company survived, and in 1937 he moved on to take over management of one of the country's great magazines, *Newsweek* (then called *News-Week*). As editor-in-chief for 22 years, he transformed it into a cutting-edge commentary on current affairs and introduced international editions. Soon after he retired, the magazine was bought by the *Washington Post* and he was made honorary chairman of the board in 1961.

Iain Calder looks like a genial bank manager. In fact, the man who left school at 16 to become a reporter on his local paper in Falkirk was editor of America's sensational *National Enquirer* for 23 years (1971–94). He boosted the shocking tabloid's circulation from around 700,000 to the US's biggest. The 1977 edition with Elvis Presley's coffin on the front cover sold more than six million copies.

Iain Calder came from a poor family. His father was a factory hand and he grew up in a mining village. 'We were poor but too stupid to know we were poor because everyone else was the same. Half the boys at my school went straight down the mines.' His decision to become a journalist was borne out of bloody-mindedness. He had been offered two jobs: one as a bank clerk and one as a reporter on the *Falkirk Sentinel*. The reporter's job paid less but his father told him to take the bank job. 'That influenced me not to. The other reason I became a reporter was because I thought it would sound better when a girl at a dance asked you what you did.' He must have had second thoughts about his choice of career when the *Sentinel* closed down just six months after he joined. However, he shrugged that off and turned his hand to freelance journalism, feeding the big papers in Glasgow, Edinburgh and London with snippets from his local beat.

When he was 21, he was invited to join the *Daily Record*, Scotland's biggest tabloid (sister paper to the *Daily Mirror*): 'I was quaking. Only three reporters in 30 years had made it from Falkirk to Glasgow.' As it happened, he arrived in the middle of a fierce circulation battle with the *Scottish Daily Express* and the rivalry – not always friendly – served to sharpen his wits. Skills learnt in Glasgow during that frenetic period proved invaluable when he became a reporter for the *National Enquirer* in London in 1964. At that time the paper was still black and white and was best known for its lurid photos of headless bodies and its 'human interest' stories. With an offer he couldn't refuse, he transferred to the New York office in 1967. Five years later he was appointed editor and almost immediately started improving what was then a more seedy than sensational paper.

He injected British tabloid talents and offered readers an improved diet of celebrity gossip and scandal. He also very shrewdly moved the whole editorial and print operation from high-price New York to Lantana, Florida. When the owner died in 1989 and the paper changed hands for $412 million, Iain Calder was not only retained by the new management but given a chunk of the equity that turned him into a millionaire. As editor-emeritus in 1997 – in an article under the headline 'The man who made a monster' – he told the *Independent* that people wanted gossip: 'It is a human need. Once, they got scandal from their corner shopkeeper about the people in the street or village. Now they live in the suburbs and don't know their neighbours so they gossip about TV stars, the people they know now.' His autobiography *The Untold Story: My 20 Years Running the National Enquirer* was published in 2004.

One of the pioneers of the American motor industry was Arbroath-born David Buick. He set up one of the earliest factories in 1902, invented a new style of engine, gave his name to one of the world's most famous cars and sowed the seeds of the giant General Motors. These are formidable achievements for a man whose earlier experience was in the plumbing industry, where he invented the lawn-sprinkler and a new galvanising process to cover metal bathtubs with porcelain.

He went with his parents to America, where his father initially worked in Detroit as a plumber but was able to establish a small company. He served his apprenticeship in the family business and eventually inherited the company when his father retired. He worked hard, used his imagination and skills to invent a series of plumbing applications and was able to sell the business in 1899 for $100,000. That gave him enough to establish the Buick Auto-Vim and Power Company and he began building engines for small boats and farm equipment. Three years later, he dipped his toe into the still murky waters of car-making when he launched the Buick Manufacturing Company. However, his designs were too advanced for the time and the costs were too high to fit into the growing market for assembly-line production. He struggled for a couple of years but then his small team had success with their development of the valve-in-head engine, which proved to be the strongest and most reliable as soon as it hit the market. Eventually, the other manufacturers caught on and used the same form. Sadly, the success did not accrue to David Buick. Inevitably, his company was swallowed up by the mighty General Motors. They kept him on for his engineering genius but he knew he was never going to adapt to mass production and he left the company in 1906. He died penniless in 1929 although, of course, the name lives on in a long line of classic cars.

In Hollywood, Scots have had more than the odd walk-on part in the ultra-glamorous world of the silver screen. Even before it had gained its 'Tinseltown' tag, Glaswegian Frank Lloyd was rubbing shoulders with emerging stars, big-name directors and movie tycoons. Even before the Academy Awards were called Oscars, he was named best director for his first film *The Divine Lady* at the very first awards ceremony, in 1929, and went on to collect three more of the coveted awards. He was one of cinema's most prolific actors and directors. He appeared in 50 movies but really came into his own as director of more than 130 films. He was one of the 36 founders of the Academy of Motion Picture Arts and Sciences (initiated by Louis B Mayer of MGM) and was president, 1934–35.

He arrived in the United States in 1913, fresh from the British theatre, just as the first big Hollywood studios were being created by the likes of Cecil B De Mille, whose *The Squaw Man* was the first feature film made there in 1914. The stars of the day included Lillian Gish, Mary Pickford and Lionel Barrymore and they were soaring into the stratosphere as a result of their early successes on celluloid. His own first screen appearance was in the 1914 crime drama, *The Invisible Power* and he made his directing debut in 1917, with the first film version of the Dickens classic, *A Tale of Two Cities*, starring William Farnum, the biggest box office name of the day. The *Yahoo*

Movies website says of it: 'In spite of the difficulty in translating the finer points of English literature to the silent cinema… it is, perhaps, the truest rendition of Dickens's masterpiece. In this lavish production the set pieces maintain an excellent historical accuracy, the mob and battle scenes of the French Revolution are handled with great dexterity, and every plot twist and turn is played out for maximum dramatic value.' He then went on to direct *Les Miserables* in 1918 and, for good measure, managed to make in the same year two Zane Grey westerns: *Riders of the Purple Sage* and *The Rainbow Trail*. In the 1920s, his films included *Oliver Twist,* with Lon Chaney as Fagin and Jackie Coogan as Oliver; and, of course, his award-winning *The Divine Lady.* He is the only person ever to win a best director award for a film not nominated for best picture. The star, Corinne Griffith, who made her name in silent films, also won a nomination. Amid a host of big-screen successes, he won two more Oscars – for best director and best picture – for his 1934 version of Noel Coward's *Cavalcade,* about life upstairs and downstairs in Victorian London.

The following year, his *Mutiny on the Bounty* won a record eight nominations including, for the only time, best actor nominations for three actors in the same film. Clark Gable (as Fletcher Christian), Charles Laughton (the sadistic Captain Bligh) and Franchot Tone (Midshipman Roger Byam) were each nominated and Lloyd won his fourth Oscar for best picture. After that he went on to direct *Under Two Flags* (1936), *If I Were King* (1938) and *The Last Command* (1955).

It's a long way from the rough, tough British comedy circuit to the glitzy elegance and big sets of the Hollywood musical. Jack Buchanan, a one-time stand-up comic who survived the notorious Glasgow Empire, made it… to dance with Fred Astaire and Cyd Charisse in one of MGM's greatest musicals, *The Band Wagon,* in 1953. Born in Helensburgh in 1893, he was the son of an auctioneer who could afford to send him to Glasgow Academy. When he left school he tried to follow in his father's footsteps, but soon found the saleroom was not for him. In what can only be described as a dramatic twist, he became a music-hall comedian! Equally surprisingly, he took the stage name of Chump Buchanan. By the time he was 19, he had made it to London's West End, where his debut was in the comic opera *The Grass Widow* at the Apollo Theatre. Chump was no more: Jack, the star, was born. When Britain went to war in 1914, he failed the medical, was declared unfit (with back problems that dogged his career) for military service and instead entertained the troops waiting to be posted to the Front. Despite his Scottish-ness, he created the persona of the quintessential Englishman and made his screen debut in 1917 in the silent movie *Auld Lang Syne* (set, counter to the suggestion of the title, in the English Lake District). In the 1921 revue *A to Z,* he starred alongside Gertrude Lawrence and among his numbers in the show was Ivor Novello's 'And her mother came too.' It became his signature song and the show transferred successfully to give him his first appearance on Broadway in 1924.

Soon he was a much-in-demand leading man and starred in the title role in *Bulldog Drummond's Third Round* (1925) and as Count Zorro in *Confetti* (1927). Between films, he found time to cross and recross the Atlantic to appear on Broadway and in the West End, firmly establishing himself as an elegant song-and-dance man. He was famous for 'the seemingly lazy but most accomplished grace with which he sang, danced, flirted and joked his way through musical shows … the tall figure, the elegant gestures, the friendly drawling voice, the general air of having a good time.' He actually moved to America in 1929 and starred in two early screen musicals, Cole Porter's *Paris* (with French music hall star Irene Bordoni) in 1929, and *Monte Carlo* (with Jeanette MacDonald) in 1930. In 1938, he had the unique experience of starring in the London stage musical *This'll Make You Whistle* while making the film version at the same time. He was on the film set in the mornings and afternoons (except when he had a matinee, of course) and then raced to the West End for his evening stage performances. When the film was released, the stage show was still running so the two productions competed with each other. After *The Sky's the Limit* (1938), which he directed, and *The Gang's All Here* (1939), he went on to produce several films including *Happidrome* (1943). He continued to work on Broadway and the West End and took roles in several Hollywood musicals, including the career-topping *The Band Wagon* (1953), with Charisse and Astaire, the biggest names in musicals. More than 40 years later, in 1995, the film was selected for preservation in the US National Film Registry as being 'culturally, historically and aesthetically significant.'

Despite the outward show of the English man-about-town, Buchanan never forgot his origins. He enthusiastically invested in the genius of another son of Helensburgh, John Logie Baird, for whom he provided financial backing for the early development of television. He was also said to be 'generous towards less prosperous actors and chorus performers.' He indulged his interest in horse-racing by regularly cancelling whatever he was supposed to be doing on Grand National Day. He would, instead, charter a train to take the cast and crew for a day at the races. He provided food and drink all the way. His final film was *As Long as They're Happy* in 1955. It had a cast list that read like a who's who of British cinema and television: Janette Scott, Jeannie Carson, Diana Dors, Athene Seyler, Joan Sims, Dora Bryan, Joan Hickson and TV's Gilbert Harding (in a cameo role as himself). It was written by Alan Melville. All this despite painful suffering from what had eventually been diagnosed as cancer of the spine. He died in London in 1915, when he was 66 years old.

Born in Dundee in 1906, James Macdonald is virtually unknown outside the tight professional world of Hollywood but he has been heard – and instantly recognised – as the voice of Mickey Mouse in hundreds of cartoon films. He took over the part from Walt Disney himself in 1946 and squeaked his way to celluloid stardom for 30 years. For good measure, he also gave a voice – of sorts – to the Chipmunks, Dopey of the Seven Dwarves and Mickey Mouse's favourite dog, Pluto! He emigrated with his parents and settled in Philadelphia, where he took an engineering degree through a correspondence course. He then moved to California where he worked as an engineer… until, just like a Disney cartoon character, he fell down a manhole on which the cover was missing! His injuries, however, were far from funny and he was forced to give up the tough manual work. He fortuitously decided to become a musician and that led to an invitation to provide a soundtrack for a Mickey Mouse cartoon. That was in 1934 and he was 28. It might not seem like work for a grown man, but he turned out to have expert timing in matching the music to the cartoon action and suddenly he had a brand new career for life. He joined the ever-inventive sound effects department and as well as his famous voices, he created the gadgets that produced so many Disney brilliant sound effects.

His credits track the history of Disney: *Peter Pan, Cinderella* (he was the squeak of both mice, Jaq and Gus), *The Lady and the Tramp, Snow White* and *Fantasia* and after he came out of retirement, *The Rescuers* and *The Black Hole*. Such was his enthusiasm that he was still working – and was due to contribute sound effects for Disney parks in Tokyo and Florida – just before he died in 1991. He was 84.

Helensburgh-born Deborah Kerr was the world's most popular actress after her starring role alongside Yul Brynner in the 1956 film *The King and I*. She won the Golden Globe award and was the toast of Hollywood. In 1994, the Motion Picture Academy gave her a lifetime achievement award for 'a film career that always represented perfection, discipline and elegance.' Daughter of a Great War soldier, she learned her trade in Scotland, where she trained as a dancer before turning to acting. She did very well and won her first film part when she was just 20. She appeared in George Bernard Shaw's *Major Barbara*, which starred Wendy Hillier and Rex Harrison. She played three roles in *The Life and Death of Colonel Blimp* (1943) and then starred in several other British films including playing Sister Clodagh in *Black Narcissus* (with Flora Robson and Jean Simmons) in 1947. By the time she was 26, she had been lured to Hollywood and the MGM studios, where because of the confusion over the pronunciation of her surname, Louis B. Mayer billed her as 'Kerr rhymes with Star!' She appeared in *The Hucksters* with Clark Gable and Ava Gardner; *Quo Vadis,* for which Peter Ustinov won a Golden Globe for his portrayal of Nero (1951); and, in 1953 *From Here to Eternity* with Burt Lancaster and Frank Sinatra. She was also successful on Broadway – in *Tea and Sympathy* – before playing Anna in *The King and I* in 1956. More success followed in *Heaven Knows, Mr Allison* (1957), *An Affair to Remember* (1957), *Separate Tables* (1958), *The Sundowners* (1960), *The Innocents* (1961) and *The Night of the Iguana* (1964). She stepped out of the limelight in 1968, appalled, she said, by the explicit sex and violence in films of the day. After some stage and TV work in the 1970s and 1980s she retired from acting altogether. She was given an honorary Oscar for her screen achievements in 1994.

I knew her brother Ted Trimmer (the family name was Kerr-Trimmer: he dropped the Kerr; she dropped the Trimmer) when he was head of news and current affairs at Central Television in the 1980s and I worked at BBC Pebble Mill. Despite his flamboyant trademark bow-tie, he was a quiet, genial character. He died in a tragic road-rage incident in 2004.

A number of other Scots have continued to win the plaudits of the Hollywood cognoscenti including David McCallum (born Glasgow, 1933), best-known as Illya

Kuryakin in *The Man from U.N.C.L.E.*; Dougray Scott (born Glenrothes, 1965), played Moses in *The Ten Commandments* (2006); and Ewan McGregor (born Crieff, Perthshire, 1971), who turned down the role of James Bond in *Casino Royale* (2006) because he didn't want to be typecast.

Scots had a strong influence in many areas of American life in the first half of the twentieth century. David and James Forgan, for example, played a crucial part in the development of Chicago's banking and financial system, with both of them having served as president of the First National Bank. They hailed from St Andrews, and younger brother David had started his career as a messenger boy with the Clydesdale Bank in Edinburgh, while James worked for the Bank of Scotland before the pair emigrated to Nova Scotia. Both worked their way up from these lowly beginnings in the banking hierarchy and, after making First National into one of the most powerful bank in the States, James moved on to be president of the even more influential Federal Advisory Council of the Federal Reserve for six years (1914–20). He was also a director of Equitable Life Insurance and a host of other companies. David, who was just 18 when he left Scotland, served as president of the North Western National Bank in 1898 before following his brother at First National.

On the other side of the capitalist-labour coin, Douglas Fraser, who moved from Glasgow to Detroit when he was 18, was president of the powerful United Automobile Workers of America from 1977 to 1983. He started on the factory floor before becoming a union activist, and went on to become the first labour leader to sit on the board of a major American corporation – Chrysler, 1980–84. He helped Chrysler restructure labour costs while still getting a good deal for his union members. His role in the rebirth of the company, a modern industrial miracle (before the 2009 economic crisis, of course) proved significant. He died in 2008.

Equally importantly, Scots still play an impressive role in the boardrooms of America – see chapter 11, Waiting in the wings, for more on their triumphs.

Americans clearly appreciate the Scottish connection because they have been celebrating National Tartan Day – 6 April – since 1998. It has its roots in a one-off celebration of the 200th anniversary of the repeal of the Act of Proscription, which forbade Scots to wear tartan (or '*plaid*', as the Americans have it). That was in 1982 and the unlikely progenitors were New York Mayor Ed Koch (not a Scots bone in his body) and state governor Hugh Carey (born and bred in Brooklyn). Since 1998, the day – in fact a Scotland *Week,* in some states – has been officially recognised by the United States Senate as a day 'for celebrating the contribution made by generations of Scots-Americans to the foundation, freedoms and prosperity of modern America.'

I have some personal experience of how friendly the Americans are to Scots. On my first visit to New York in the 1960s, I arrived in mid-December, dressed for a British winter, and had to make a hurried visit to a Fifth Avenue store to gear up for the much more savage winds of Manhattan. After I had bought a very heavy coat, the salesman, having heard my accent and raved about Scotland and all things Scottish, threw in a pair of lightweight snow boots and a pair of snow gauntlets. During the same visit, I couldn't resist the allure of Tiffany's on Fifth Avenue and bought my wife an expensive (for me) gold bracelet. The salesgirl asked for my passport so that I could avoid city tax of about $50. I didn't have it with me but that was no problem: they would deliver it to the hotel and check my passport there. They did… and also sent a bottle of champagne to compensate for 'the inconvenience suffered after having travelled all the way from Scotland!' On another occasion, I found myself the victim of a credit card stretched to its limit as the crashing pound hit parity with the dollar. When a senior executive of Burger King heard me muttering into my beer, he promptly invited me to dinner… not at his own establishment but at one of Los Angeles' most expensive restaurants.

Today and on a more global scale, it's clear the US fascination with all things Scottish continues. New Yorkers, for example, turned out in their thousands for the 2002 'Tunes of Glory' parade, which featured more than 10,000 pipers and drummers marching down Sixth Avenue to Central Park. Equally, Scotland's politicians take America's annual Tartan Day celebrations seriously. In 2005, William Wallace's sword left Scotland for the first time in 700 years for an exhibition in New York. In 2008, the original manuscript for 'Auld Lang Syne' was loaned by the Mitchell Library in Glasgow.

'Let anyone scrutinize the list of names of distinguished men in our annals; names of men eminent in public life… in medicine, surgery, education, trade, commerce, invention, discovery… in all the arts which add to the freedom, enlightenment and wealth of the world… and he will be astonished to find how large a proportion of these names represent men of Scottish birth.' – *Charles Dinsmore, US historian*

9

REACHING FOR THE TSARS

 'To come from the north side of the Tweed is the best recommendation a man can bring to St Petersburg.'
— *English engineer, 1809*

From the quiet, correct backwaters of a small Presbyterian town in south-west Scotland to the opulence and, some might say, outrageous decadence and intrigue of Tsarist Russia is quite a journey. For one young doctor from the small community of Lochmaben to make the transition is remarkable enough. For three to do so is extraordinary and beyond normal speculation.

Lochmaben's population is currently around 3000 and was almost certainly even smaller in the eighteenth century. The town is four miles west of Lockerbie and about eight miles east of Dumfries. It's a pretty place but, if the local people will forgive me for saying so, there's little remarkable about it. On its website its most ambitious boast is that 'facilities include a number of shops, a bank with an ATM which does not charge, a post office, a chemist, branch library, public houses, cafes, and take-away food shops... a community centre, primary and nursery school, a church, doctors' practice and a small geriatric hospital.' Sounds fairly normal - and yet it was from here in the late 1700s, despite what may have seemed impenetrable language barriers and more than 1200 miles, that Russian courtiers chose to recruit three medical advisers over a period of 30 years. How Dr Matthew Halliday, Dr James Mounsey and Dr John Rogerson found themselves transported from Dumfriesshire to St Petersburg is something of a mystery.

I occasionally make the journey from the English Midlands to that corner of Scotland and even in a fast car on today's roads it can take the best part of seven wearying hours. From there to St Petersburg... in the eighteenth century? No planes or trains or buses? One young man who travelled to Russia at the time described it as a 'perilous journey.' Perilous and extremely long.

Neither deterred the first of the Lochmaben trio, Dr James Mounsey. I came across his name in one of my old spiral notebooks ('Reporter's Notebook' it says on the front cover) alongside a dodgy shorthand note that says something like 'Minister of Health, Russia 1760-ish'. Very interesting, but surely unlikely? Several days of painstaking research later, I had fleshed out the story... but only a little. I still don't know why he went to Russia, how he got there or how long it took. En route, however, he must have studied whatever Russian-English texts were available extremely conscientiously. When he arrived in 1736, still just 26, he appears to have been fluent enough to win appointment as a medical officer in the Russian Navy.

He then had a peripatetic role in Moscow and St Petersburg, where one of his patients was a fellow Scot, Field Marshal James Keith, then serving in the Russian Army. A gunshot wound in the military man's leg had become so badly infected that the local doctors wanted to amputate, but Mounsey stopped them and advised other treatment. It worked, the Field Marshal was clearly relieved and grateful, and the young Mounsey soon thereafter became physician-in-chief to the army and later personal physician to the Tsarina of All Russia, Elizabeth, daughter of Peter the Great.

In the citation which marked his 1750 election as a fellow of the Royal Society in London, mention is made of his role with the army 'which marched through Bohemia and Poland to the assistance of the Allies.' He is described as 'a gentleman of extensive learning, curiosity and knowledge' and his value as a fellow was underlined: 'Residing in a country where it is very difficult to obtain any satisfactory information, he is likely to prove a desirable and useful member.' The Russians clearly shared that view and when Peter the Third briefly became tsar in 1761–62, Dr Maunsey's stock was enhanced even further. He was appointed director of the Medical Chancery and the Medical Faculty throughout the Russian Empire. That effectively made him the minister of health and a very important political figure.

When Catherine the Great usurped her husband to take the throne later in 1762, Dr Mounsey found himself out of favour and he swiftly retired to Scotland. His closeness to the Russian crown and the secrets of the court is evidenced by the fact that for the rest of his life he was said to be in fear of Russian agents determined to silence him. Tellingly, no one accused him of paranoia. From the reports of radiation poisoning of Russian dissidents in London in 2006, we know almost anything is possible in that murky, power-hungry milieu. However frightened Dr Mounsey may have been, though, he still found time to take with him the seeds of a plant he had used in his medical practice. He gave them to the Royal Physic Garden (now Royal Botanic Garden) in Edinburgh... and thus Britain was introduced to rhubarb!

Despite the abrupt and unhappy ending of his days in Russia, Dr Mounsey was replaced in the imperial household by the second of the Lochmaben trio, Dr Matthew Halliday. I've found it impossible to get more than the scantiest of information about Dr Halliday (1732–1801) other than that he married a Russian lady called Anna Regina, had several children and that he served Catherine from 1762–68. He was succeeded by yet another Lochmaben doctor. John Rogerson, 24 years old, just a year out of Edinburgh University with the ink hardly dry on his MD degree, had decided that he too would seek his fortune in Russia and made the long, long journey to St Petersburg.

It's not clear what he did there when he first arrived in 1765, but after three years practising in the city, he came to the notice of Catherine by giving life-saving treatment to one of the young royals. He became court doctor, looking after Catherine's wider retinue. Then in 1776, he was promoted to body physician to the tsarina. His services must have been more than satisfactory because he was also appointed a councillor of state. That clearly gave him considerable political status and allowed him to socialise on equal terms with the Russian elite.

As it happened, there were a number of other Scots around St Petersburg and Moscow at the time – one estimate puts the figure at more than a hundred – and Dr Rogerson mixed with the likes of Sir Samuel Greig (see later in this chapter), the Inverkeithing naval officer with the unenviable job of updating Catherine's navy, and the British ambassador, Sir James Harris (later the Earl of Malmesbury). He obviously schmoozed well in diplomatic circles and in 1797, the year after Catherine's death, he was elevated to privy councillor by Tsar Paul.

The Lochmaben three were not the first Scottish clinicians to serve at the Russian court. That honour, it seems, goes to Robert Erskine (1677–1718), who Peter the Great appointed president of the Medical Chancery and of the whole Medical Faculty throughout the Russian Empire. After taking his first medical degree at Edinburgh, Erskine went on to further his studies in Paris (where he read chemistry, 1697–99) and Utrecht (biology, 1700). He returned to London to practice and became a fellow of the Royal Society in 1703 (when he was still only 26). He was already, then, a distinguished doctor when he arrived in St Petersburg the following year. His initial appointment was as physician to Prince Aleksandr Menshikov (who later acted as de facto ruler during the short reign of Catherine II 1725–27) but he was soon chief physician to Tsar Peter, who appointed him to the most senior of medical roles in 1714.

He supervised the setting up of Russia's first botanical garden in St Petersburg and, also in 1714, he became the first director and chief librarian of the newly established Kunstkamera (museum of rarities). Two years later, he was appointed state councillor and became a member of Russia's hereditary nobility. He had a reputation as a great scholar, reader and collector. His library of more than 2,000 specialist books became the core of the library of the Russian Academy of Sciences. When Erskine died at the early age of 41, Tsar Peter accorded him a full state honours, carried a torch at his funeral and arranged his internment in the same monastery as his favourite sister.

Glasgow-born Dr John Bell, who went to St Petersburg 'in search of adventure,' also eased his way into the service of Peter the Great via spells as surgeon on ambassadorial expeditions to Persia (1715–18) and China (1719–21). He read medicine at Glasgow University but soon after graduating set out for Russia, where – through the good offices of another Scot – he was appointed as travelling doctor to the entourage of the new ambassador to Persia. After three years there, he trekked through Siberia and the Tartar deserts to an embassy in China, where he served until 1721. He must have gained a reputation as a fine surgeon because he was scarcely back in St Petersburg when Tsar Peter decided he personally needed him on an expedition to Russia's most ancient and southernmost city, Derbent, gateway to the Caucasus. He survived several changes of royal patron and in 1738 Tsarina Anna sent him on a mission to Constantinople. Although he returned briefly to St Petersburg, it appears that he then established himself as a merchant in Turkey, where he married in 1746. The following year, he retired with his new bride to the family estate of Antermony, where he spent the remainder of his life. He died in 1780 and is buried in Campsie Glen. His account of his early journeys appeared in 1763 as *Travels from St Petersburg in Russia to Various Parts of Asia* and was so popular that it was translated into French and sold widely across Europe.

My note on Dr Matthew Guthrie (born Edinburgh, 1743–1807) is decidedly sketchy and I know little more than that he was physician to Catherine the Great for nearly 30 years. She was said to have especially enjoyed his sharp wit and intellect. He had worked for the East India Company and first visited Russia in 1770, but continued to serve in the Royal Navy until 1776, when he returned to Russia and settled in St Petersburg. There he became chief medical officer of the Corps of Noble Gentlemen before being promoted to Catherine's physician. His influence on her seems to have been considerable. She had a reforming zeal and responded readily to new ideas and, in 1763, he was involved in establishing Russia's College of Medicine and then first teaching hospital. He was elected a fellow of the Royal Society of London 1782, a member of the Societies of Antiquaries of both London and Edinburgh and wrote on subjects as diverse as scurvy, the plague, music and history.

The most influential doctor in 19th-century Russia, serving three tsars (Paul, Alexander and Nicholas II), was Sir James Wylie from Kincardine-on-Forth. He was director of the Russian Army Medical Department, effectively head of the country's medical profession, for more than a quarter of a century. Ironically, he had failed to get his medical degree from Edinburgh University and instead became apprenticed to a group of specialists including the chemist Joseph Black. He went to St Petersburg when he was just 22, joined the Eletsky Regiment as regimental surgeon and served at the Siege of Warsaw in 1794 and Krakow in 1795. Within five years he had become surgeon to the Russian imperial court, where a simple but dramatic operation made his reputation. One of the Tsar's favourites was on the point of death and Wylie drained the abscess that threatened to suffocate him. He continued in active military service and he was present at the Battles of Austerlitz (1805), Jena (1806) and Borodino (1812), in which the Russian army lost 45,000 men. When he died, he bequeathed his fortune to Tsar Nicholas and the Russian nation for the construction of a large hospital in St Petersburg, to be attended by the pupils of the Medico-Chirurgical Academy. In 1859, a life-size statue of him was erected in the grounds of the academy.

Just as they played a key role in the pacific practice of medicine, so did Scots have a strong influence on the way tsarist Russia went to war against most of its neighbours at one time or another. In the mid-seventeenth century, Sir Alexander Leslie, from Auchintoul in Aberdeenshire, recruited and established a then-modern army for Tsar Aleksei; in 1689 another Aberdonian, General Patrick Gordon, played a key role in establishing the reign of Peter the Great and helped him launch the Russian Empire in 1721; and 50 years later, Samuel Greig from Inverkeithing, was celebrated as the 'Father of the Imperial Russian Navy', which he modernised for Catherine the Great.

In traditional mercenary style, there appear to have been some Scottish soldiers in Russia during the Livonian War (1558–82). Initially they were said to have fought for Ivan the Terrible but later turned against him during the long struggle between Russia and a host of its neighbours (including Denmark, Norway, Lithuania, Poland and Sweden) for control of territory that makes up present-day Estonia and Latvia. But it was Sir Alexander Leslie who is first formally recorded as taking the Tsar's rouble (at four times the going rate) in May 1633, with a brief to rebuild his army along British lines. He was granted a warrant (referencing him as 'Generall Colonel of the Forrain forces of the Emperour of Russia') by the Privy Council of Scotland allowing him to recruit 200 trained men from his homeland. These were in addition to an earlier 200 signed up by fellow Scot, Captain James Forbes.

They were especially welcomed by Aleksei, who had expelled English citizens from his empire in retaliation because they had 'done a great wickedness by killing [their] sovereign, King Charles, for which evil deed they cannot be suffered to remain in the realm of Muscovy.' Sir Alexander also recruited thousands of infantrymen from Sweden and bought the services of supporting blacksmiths, wheelwrights, carpenters and other essential craftsmen. The new blood and his organisational skills enabled Sir Alexander to establish cavalry and infantry regiments, both of which were commanded by Scots and both of which had a Scottish company. He quickly established the worth of this new-style army – now swollen by more than 50,000 mercenaries – in the Smolensk War (1632–34): he led the army to recover territory lost earlier to Poland and was made governor of the key garrison city.

His initial small band of soldiers from Scotland increased in number each year and, by the later part of the seventeenth century, there were around a thousand in total and no fewer than 15 had reached the rank of general. One of these was General Tam Dalyell of Binns, West Lothian. He travelled to Moscow where he entered Tsar Aleksei's imperial service, helped train the Russian Army, fought with them against the Tartars and the Turks... and because of his heroic leadership, earned the nickname of 'The Muscovite De'il.'

He had joined the army in Edinburgh when he was just 13 and fought in Ireland in the 1640s. A committed Royalist (who never shaved after the death of Charles I), he served in the Scottish Army at Worcester (1651), where he was captured by Cromwell's forces and sent to the Tower of London. He was one of the few to ever escape from the Tower and fled with the king to France, from where he went on to Russia. When he returned to Britain, the king rewarded him with appointment as a privy councillor and made him commander-in-chief of the army in Scotland. There he found himself unhappily embroiled in the battle between the Covenanters and Cromwell. While he was called 'Bluidy Tam' for his relentless pursuit of dissenters, he resigned his commission in protest at the treatment of innocent women and children and stayed out of public life for more than ten years. However, he remained an ardent loyalist and in 1679 he resumed his army career because of the renewed threat to the Crown. In 1681, he raised a new regiment, the Royal Scots Greys (from the unusual colour of their uniforms, chosen to act as camouflage).

The foremost Scot of the day was, however, General Patrick Gordon, whose shrewd manoeuvrings helped establish the reign of Peter the Great and then, in 1721, helped him create the Russian Empire. He was one of the Tsar's most trusted advisers, again restructured and modernised the army and even took control of Muscovy during his absence. Born into the Aberdeenshire Gordon clan in 1635, he went to parish schools in Cruden and Ellon where he had what he later described as a competent education. When he was 15, he resolved to travel abroad to seek a new life, 'not caring much on what pretence or to which country I should go, seeing I had no known friend in any foreign place.' Having read Latin at school, his initial inclination was to enter a Jesuit college in Poland but then he had second thoughts: 'My humour would not endure such a still and strict way of living.' He decided to return to Scotland... on foot! He got as far as Hamburg, where general poverty and hunger forced him to join the Swedish army as a mercenary in 1655. During a battle, he was captured by Polish troops and immediately changed sides, only to reverse matters two years later when he was caught by the Swedes.

It was in 1661, still only aged 25 but with considerable fighting experience, that Patrick Gordon joined the Russian army as a major. It was not an auspicious start to what would become a glittering career in the service of Tsar Aleksei and his three successors, including Peter. He and a few other Scots officers were, he wrote, perceived 'as strangers to be looked upon as a company of hirelings and at the best, necessary evils.' It was made clear he could expect no preferment and only a limited command. There would be no 'marrying with natives.' They were looked on by the upper echelons of imperial society 'as scarcely Christians and by the plebeians as mere pagans.' Despite this hostility, he and his fellow Scots distinguished themselves in wars against the Turks and the Tartars and he was promoted from major to colonel and, in 1678, to major general. The following year, he was made commander-in-chief at Kiev and was quartermaster general during successful campaigns in the Crimea. In the internecine and revolutionary atmosphere of Moscow in 1669, he used his military wiles to assure the accession of Peter over his older brother, Ivan, and his sister, Sofia Alekseyevna, who had been acting as regent. His reward was promotion to general-in-chief and a free hand in rebuilding the army along British lines. As part of that, he also supervised the creation of the Tsar's Life Guard regiment.

His most significant civilian achievement was getting permission to build the first Catholic church in Russia. He also found time to act as a special correspondent for the *London Gazette* and to write his diary (published some time after his death) His diary entries for 1698 make grim reading and act as a sharp reminder of the brutality of the times. On 8 April he wrote about growing discontent in the ranks of the Life Guards: 'These were the first distant mutterings of the tempest. There was to be a lull of two months before it broke.' By 19 June, the storm had indeed broken and retribution was swift: 'The greater part of the influential men and others being examined, it was frankly confessed that some had been the ringleaders and guilty rebels. Those that were found good we put on the one side, the bad on the other.' The 'bad' were given some sort of trial and he revealed the verdict on 22 June: 'Twenty-four individuals were found guilty, on their own confession, of the most shocking crimes and of having designed, when they got to Moscow, to massacre certain Boyars… On these we pronounced sentence of death… They were confined apart and directed to confess, receive the eucharist and prepare for death.' The 23 June entry was stark: 'Those condemned yesterday were beheaded.'

The pattern was repeated throughout the summer and somewhere along the way around 200 soldiers were executed by beheading or hanging. On 14 November, 'orders were issued [by the Tsar] not to give support to any of the wives or children of the executed soldiers.' By this time, Patrick Gordon's health was failing and it's perhaps not surprising that the final entry in the diary – on 31 December – is a religious confession: 'God be praised for his gracious long suffering towards me in sparing my life so long. Grant, gracious God, that I may make a good use of the time that thou mayest be pleased yet to grant me for repentance.' The following year, his condition deteriorated and he became so weak he was unable to leave his bed. The Tsar was a constant visitor and was with him when he died. It was reported that 'His Majesty stood weeping by his bed as he drew his last breath; and the eyes of him who had left Scotland a poor unfriended wanderer were closed by the hands of an Emperor.'

When Tsar Peter founded St Petersburg as his new capital in 1703, it was yet another Scottish mercenary who gave him succour against the Swedes (under Karl XII), who had a highly-efficient and well-drilled army and had inflicted a series of heavy defeats on him when he had ventured into their Baltic provinces during the Great Northern War. They made Peter look anything but great as they routed an imperial Russian army four times their number. Soon after that, Field Marshal George Ogilvie, who had earned his spurs as a young cornet in the British cavalry, was given responsibility to deal with the Swedes at the siege of Narva (in Estonia) in 1704 and then at Grodno (then under Polish control but now also in Estonia) in 1706, when he once more outwitted the enemy with his superior tactics.

It was another of the Aberdeen clan – Admiral Sir Thomas Gordon – who helped underpin both Tsar Peter's greatness and the security of the Russian Empire. He led the creation of a formidable fleet that proved more than a match for would-be marauders. He was appointed admiral of the Imperial Navy's Red Division in 1717 and went on to serve Peter's four successors until he died in 1741. Born the son of a doctor in 1658, he originally served in the merchant navy and was a qualified master by the time he was 30. He captained a merchantman that logged voyages to the Mediterranean, Norway, Sweden and Holland. He transferred to what was then the Scots Royal Navy in 1703. He was commissioned as a captain and for the next ten years he was responsible for protecting coastal waters from pirates. When the Scots navy was merged with the Royal Navy (after the Act of Union), he was given command of the 50-gun *Leopard* and distinguished himself against the French. However, he refused to take the oath to King George I on accession in 1714, and resigned his commission. Three years later he went to Holland, where he joined Peter the Great's navy. It was a propitious time to arrive because several of the old officers were due for retirement and an admiral was languishing in a Finnish prison after having been captured in battle. Thomas Gordon also had the added advantage of being able to speak several European languages and was fluent in Russian. Despite the inevitable jealousies about foreigners attaining high rank, Tsarina Catherine I gave him command of a third of the Imperial Navy (Red Division) and, in 1727, the new Tsar Peter II made him commander-in-chief at the Baltic Fleet's base in Kronstadt. He was far from an office-based warrior and ended the Siege of Danzig in 1734, when he commanded the 100-gun *Peter I* at the head of a fleet of 14 battleships, five frigates and usual flotilla of support vessels. It took him just ten days to force the city to surrender. He never forgot his native city and he was made a freeman of Aberdeen in 1736; the citation read: 'This brave man, when in the British navy, strenuously defended the commerce and ships of this city from pirates and enemies of every kind; and that he, being an account of his great valour deservedly promoted to the highest honours by the Empress of Russia, still befriends this city.'

Never one to do things by halves, Catherine the Great didn't simply promote Samuel Greig to the rank of admiral: she named him 'Admiral of all the Russias', commissioned him to take on the mighty armada of the Ottoman Empire and to make her as powerful at sea as she was on land. He did.

The man from Inverkeithing first distinguished himself in the Battle of Chesma (1770), with an extraordinary act of personal courage. He had joined the Royal Navy as a boy and quickly been recognised not just for his skills but for his 'zeal and attention to the discharge of his duty.' Once commissioned, he swiftly rose to lieutenant and when Catherine asked for the help of British officers to strengthen her navy, he was immediately seconded to her service. The senior Russian officers were equally impressed by his naval performance and, with war raging against the Turks, their chauvinistic tendencies were set aside and he was rapidly promoted to captain. His was one of just nine Russian ships that sailed from the Baltic to the Mediterranean, where he found himself facing a Turkish fleet of 16 battleships, a full support group of smaller vessels and fire power of more than a thousand guns. This was the embodiment of the might of the Ottoman

Empire which then, at its height, spanned three continents, controlling south-eastern Europe, the Middle East and North Africa from its power base in Constantinople. Its power lay in its key position between the Eastern and Western worlds and its long-established armada of warships.

All Captain Greig saw, of course, was an enemy waiting to be outwitted and that's what he did. He engaged in a minor skirmish with enough ferocity to force the Turks to retreat to the safety of their home base in Chesma Bay and the additional protection of the shore batteries. He then waited for nightfall before he and another British officer scrambled aboard their two fireships – packed with explosives – and stealthily sailed them into the very centre of the Turkish vessels. They lit the fuses, hastily dived overboard and swam back to their own ships as explosions ripped through the entire flotilla and marksmen tried desperately to shoot the arsonists. Back on his bridge, Greig then led the fleet in for the kill and destroyed what was left of the enemy ship, before turning his attention to the shore batteries and the base fortifications. The Turks never recovered from this body blow and an uneasy peace was established soon afterwards. Greig became a firm favourite of Catherine, was promoted to admiral and commissioned to rebuild her navy.

He immediately set about strengthening the fleet, remodelling its codes of discipline and 'by his example infusing a spirit into every department of its economy, which finally made it one of the most formidable marines in Europe.' He was appointed governor of Kronstadt and continued to serve Catherine well by protecting her against hostile neighbours. For example, he took on the Swedes at what proved to be the beginning of another protracted conflict, the Russo-Swedish War (1788–90). He commanded the fleet and led it to victory in the Battle of Hogland, but as he sailed homeward in triumph he was 'attacked by a violent fever.' When Catherine heard of his condition, she immediately asked her personal physician, Dr John Rogerson (see earlier in this chapter), a fellow Scot and good friend, to go and look after him. It was to no avail. The admiral died on 26 October. He was just 53. Such was Catherine's respect and affection for her chief sailor that she accorded him a state funeral. She also paid for his tomb in the main church in Tallinn and that is now one of the key milestones on the tourist map of the Estonian capital.

In the nineteenth century, it was another soldier with Scottish blood in his veins who led the Russian army against Napoleon's invasion of 1812. Michael Andreas Barclay de Tolly's reward was to be promoted by Tsar Alexander I to field marshal, then to minister for war and, later, ennoblement as Knyaz (Prince) Mikhail. He was born in what is now Estonia, where his family - members of the Clan Barclay from Banffshire – had settled and had been accepted enough for his grandfather to have been Mayor of Riga and his father admitted into the Russian nobility. He took a commission in the Russian Army in 1786 and then had a distinguished career, serving in the Tsar's campaigns against Turkey (1788–89), Sweden (1790) and Poland (1792–94). In 1806, he fought and successfully resisted Napoleon at Pułtusk in Poland and the following year he was wounded in the bloody but inconclusive Battle of Eylau (in which as many as 25,000 men on each side are thought to have died).

He was made lieutenant general in 1808 and was commander of Russian forces against the Swedes in Finland. After a successful tour of duty, he was promoted to be the Tsar's minister for war and served for two years before returning to active service when Napoleon relaunched his invasion. He took supreme command of the Russian 1st Army of the West and as a last resort and against overwhelming numbers, he fell back on the notorious scorched-earth tactics against the rapidly encroaching Grande Armée. To the fury of many of his officers and many of the Tsar's courtiers (already opposed to the appointment of a foreign general), Barclay de Tolly launched a drastic policy that had as serious an effect on the civilian population as it did on Napoleon. As he steadily retreated to Moscow, he laid waste to the Russian farms and villages behind him. His objective was to prevent anything useful falling into French hands, but by many he was branded a coward, and to others he was seen as nothing less than an agent of Napoleon. Reluctantly, the Tsar sacked him but after his replacement was forced to adopt the same tactics, he was reinstated (with the title of Count thrown in for good measure) and sent to fight in Germany.

He led his men deep into France in 1815 and while there may well have introduced the French to the 'bistro'. It simply means 'quickly' in Russian and reflected his impatience when being served his food! After that, he was elevated to Prince but soon afterwards, his health began to deteriorate and he retired from the army. In 1837, nearly 20 years after his death, a well-known Russian sculptor designed a magnificent bronze statue in his memory, which still stands at the front of the Kazan Cathedral in St Petersburg.

Russia's military and naval might was as dependent on its superior equipment as it was on the men who led it with such vigour, and there again the Scots played a vital role in supplying the imperial needs – as well as making their own fortunes. One key example was Charles Baird, who initially set up munitions factories at the invitation of Samuel Greig before going on to set up his own St Petersburg shipyard, from which he launched Russia's first steamship, the *Elizaveta*, in 1815. He was born at Westerton, near Falkirk, and his father was superintendent of the Forth and Clyde Canal. After leaving school, he became an apprentice at the Carron Ironworks in 1782. Within three years, he had been promoted to foreman in the company's gun department and, still only 24, he went with a senior manager to set up two major plants in Russia: a gun factory and a cannon-ball foundry at the naval base at Kronstadt. In 1792, he set up Baird Works to produce steam-driven machinery for major government concerns including the Imperial Arsenal, the mint and glassworks. His company supplied the ironwork for several bridges in St Petersburg and Moscow (including the first cast-iron arch bridge in Russia in 1805) and provided technical advice in the design of the dome for St Petersburg's famous St Isaacs Cathedral. He not only built the *Elizaveta* but operated it between St Petersburg and ports such as Kronstadt, also developing his own loading wharves around the Baltic. He even owned a sugar-refinery which operated using his own new methods. His achievements were recognised both in Britain and in Russia. In 1841, he was made a member the Institution of Civil Engineers in London and a knight of St Vladimir in St Petersburg. A 2002 article in the *St Petersburg Times* credited him with helping to 'create a great industrial kingdom' in the city. He died in 1843 and is buried in the Smolensk Lutheran Cemetery.

Although Murdoch Macpherson didn't join the Russian Navy, he did play an important part in personally keeping Tsar Nicholas afloat – as engineer in charge of his personal yachts. He was also the founder of the giant Baltic Iron Works and Shipyard, and effectively shipbuilder to the Tsar.

Born at Perth in 1813, Macpherson studied engineering at Glasgow University and later owned a small shipbuilding yard on the Clyde. His interest in Russia began in 1839 when he won the tender to build a yacht for Tsar Nicholas. On completion, he sailed with it to St Petersburg in order to hand it over personally. Clearly pleased with both the service and boat, the Tsar immediately offered him a job as the imperial engineer. He took it and became responsible for the four royal yachts. From then on, he was engineer-in-charge whenever and whichever yacht the Tsar chose to sail for the next 12 years. He launched his shipbuilding giant in St Petersburg, in partnership with another British businessman, in 1856. His orders included, of course, yet another imperial yacht – the *Lavadia* – for the Tsar's use in the Black Sea. Macpherson also did his bit for strong Scottish-Russian relations. He married a 17-year-old Scots girl whose parents were living in St Petersburg and they had ten children – five daughters, five sons – who all lived, worked and married and had similarly large families in Russia. One grandson became a prominent member of the Russian Stock Exchange and patron of the city's yacht, rowing and tennis clubs. Another returned to Britain to serve in the Great War and was at one time an aide to Lord Kitchener. Murdoch Macpherson died in St Petersburg in 1879.

The Tsars lived in some splendour, with winter and summer palaces, town houses, great country estates and public buildings of every kind, and many of their courtiers tried hard to emulate the grandness of their emperors. The result was extremely good business for Europe's leading builders and architects, and one of the earliest beneficiaries was Christopher Galloway from Haddington. In 1621, he was commissioned by Tsar Mikhail, the first of the Romanovs, to help reshape Moscow's Red Square by working on the Saviour's Gate. This was and is one of the most famous landmarks in the city, centre-piece of hundreds of ceremonial occasions and official entrance to the Kremlin. Built by an Italian architect towards the end of the fifteenth century, the clock tower over the gate was to be redesigned to Tsar Mikhail's extravagant specifications, a project Christopher Galloway took five years to complete. The clock stretched over three of the tower's ten storeys and had two faces with gold numerals in Old Slavonic and Arabic on a blue background, decorated with silver stars. Its hands were more than three metres long and the chimes could be heard across Moscow. It survived for more than two centuries before being replaced in 1852 and it was Joseph Stalin who added the red star on top in 1935.

Christopher Galloway trained in Scotland as a clock-maker before going on to become an engineer and architect and it was these combined skills that made him eminently suited for Tsar Mikhail's needs. His reputation was such that he was recommended by no less a personage than King James (VI of Scotland, I of Great Britain), who was then trying to more firmly establish diplomatic and commercial relationships with Russia. He also repaired the fire damage caused by an assumed arson attack on the Kremlin shortly after he had finished his work in 1626. Next, he restored another fifteenth-century building, the Cathedral of the Assumption, then used his engineering skills to design and construct a new water-pumping system for the Kremlin, and then built a steeple over the city's Printing House.

In the later part of the eighteenth century, Russia's most fashionable architect and builder was yet another Scot: Charles Cameron of Aberdeen. He designed and built palaces for Catherine the Great of Russia for the 17 years between 1779 and 1796. It was he who laid the foundations of the 1,500-acre park and the Palace of Pavlovsk as her sumptuous summer residence outside St Petersburg. Cameron was invited to St Petersburg by Catherine's agents and in a letter of 1779, she wrote: 'At present, I am very taken with Mister Cameron and we are fashioning here with him a terraced garden with pools beneath, an arcade beneath; this will be beautiful, beautiful.' When she became more familiar with him, 'Mister Cameron' became Karl Karlovich. They made a natural partnership. She had a natural flair and taste for beautiful buildings and he, said to be a master of interior design and a brilliant draughtsman, had the creativity to translate her ideas into reality.

He initially studied under his father, a master builder in Aberdeen, and then went to Italy in 1767, where he is thought to have been on the fringes of the Stuarts' Roman court. Five years later, it was clear that whatever politicking he might have done, he had also been conducting an in-depth study of Rome's famous and ancient baths. He turned his survey into a book, *Roman Thermae*, published in 1772. It had a very limited circulation (no more than 50) but one of them found its way into Catherine's hands, no doubt via a courtier who knew of her fascination with baths. She invited Cameron to St Petersburg and persuaded him to join her imperial household. One of his first jobs was... to build new public baths. That was more important that it might first seem: the baths were where the ministers of the day would often meet to debate state business while enjoying the relaxing atmosphere. The idea of the Palace of Pavlovsk came from Catherine's heir, Paul, because he had outgrown his old house. Charles Cameron was 'graciously loaned' for the project to build a new residence and create a park in what was then a tangled forest. He spent two years on his designs and drawings and supervised the laying of the foundation stone of the palace in May 1782, but it was not to be completed until long after his death in 1812. When Catherine died in 1796, he lost his royal patronage and, now receiving commissions for only minor buildings, he returned to Britain, where he lived and worked quietly for five years, effectively sitting out the reign of Tsar Paul. He returned to work for Tsar Nicholas in 1801 and, ironically, was on hand to help with the restoration work when the Palace of Pavlovsk was badly damaged in a fire of 1803. The following year, he joined the team designing and building Kronstadt Cathedral but he somehow fell out of favour and, at the age of 65, he was replaced by a younger man. He died in 1812.

He was followed into Tsar Nicholas's service in 1820 by Edinburgh-born Adam Menelaws. He became architect to the imperial household and was hailed as the finest designer in the empire in 1825. He was already in his late 70s and had been working in Russia for more than 40 years. Information about his early life in Scotland is fairly sketchy. He was born in 1748 into a family of builders and he is thought to have begun his career as a stonemason. He moved on to become a landscape designer and architect and was already a highly regarded professional when he read an advertisement in the *Edinburgh Evening News* in 1784. It was ostensibly placed by Catherine the Great, but more likely it was the work of Charles Cameron, who was then looking for construction workers for his great Tsarskoye Selo (royal village) project – and where better to look than his native Scotland? When Adam Menelaws applied, he was signed to a three-year contract that included training Russian workers. During his work there, Cameron described Menelaws as one of the finest stonemasons he had ever come across and called him his 'vaulting master' for the work he did on various roofs. Despite also working alongside and training local craftsmen, he and a group of other British workers fell foul of an anti-foreigner mood (we were actually taking their jobs!) and his contract wasn't renewed.

His reputation, however, was such that by the beginning of the nineteenth century he had considerable success as the designer of homes and parks for aristocrats one-step removed from the imperial household. His clients included the president of the Russian Academy of Arts, Alexander Strogonov, a favourite of Catherine the Great. He also built a palace for Field Marshal Count Kirill Razumovsky on the banks of the River Moika in St Petersburg, and a string of exotic gardens. He decided to retire in 1803 but discovered he didn't have enough money to provide an adequate pension and was more or less forced to carry on working. One of his commissions took him back to Tsarskoye Selo, where he built a towered house for the Tsar Alexander's chaplain, and when the Tsar saw his work at first hand he was then commissioned to redevelop Alexandria Park. Menelaws then designed and built a series of new buildings including the magnificent Egyptian Gates and three pavilions and renovated the menagerie. In 1821, he started on the White Tower, a self-contained home for the Tsar's children.

When the new Tsar Nicholas ascended to the throne in 1825, Menelaws was well into his seventies. Despite that, the Tsar, perhaps more aware of his reputation than his age, lured him into the imperial household and became what was described as 'his most appreciative patron.' Indeed, his final and, appropriately, most important commission was to design and develop a 300-acre park and yet another new summer residence, given the inappropriate (in English terms) name of 'The Cottage'. In reality, it was a huge neo-Gothic three-storey palace. The only thing it has in common with what westerners think of as a cottage is that the roof tiles are the colour of thatch! In a project reminiscent of painting Edinburgh's Forth Bridge, the project grew to include a farm, a sanctuary for retired work horses and an elephant pavilion! Adam Menelaws died in Saint Petersburg during the cholera epidemic of 1831. He was 83.

Another Scot who successfully replied to the advertisement in the Edinburgh paper was William Hastie. His early career had also been as a stonemason, before moving on to engineering and architecture. After completing his contract at Tsarskoye Selo, he became Tsar Alexander's head architect and bridge-builder and was said to have been responsible for much of the Russian urban development of the early nineteenth century. He built the first iron bridges in St Petersburg in 1808 and, as a mark of the affection in which he was held, he was given the Russian name of Vasily Ivanovich Heste and became what was effectively the boss of the Tsar's town-planning schemes. In 1814, he began to draw up the plans to rebuild Moscow (sacked by Napoleon's troops) and with a team of architects, he designed the Garden Ring, a 16-kilometre avenue around the city centre. Within the ring, the roads were widened into 17 elegant boulevards and each linked a range of squares. Having set the planning in progress, he went to Kiev in 1815 and was commissioned to build the Contract House, Ukraine's Stock Exchange. It was one of the most important buildings to emerge from the terrible fire that had reduced much of that city to ashes the previous year. He died in 1832 at the age of 69. He was the last in a line of Scots who left their mark on Russia.

10

Messages and Messengers

 'Communication is not only the essence of being human but also a vital property of life. Words are, of course, the most powerful drug used by mankind.'
— *Rudyard Kipling*

No empire can survive without effective communications. John Reith (born Stonehaven, 1889–1971) got it right when he made the BBC's raison d'être: 'Nation shall speak unto nation.' Communication is the essence of empire, and in the case of this Scottish Empire, my countrymen have again been pre-eminent. They have, around the globe, carved out major roles in what has become the glue of my thesis.

It's therefore ironic that my first stumble into writer's block should happen on this of all chapters. Usually such a state of abject misery is brought about when there's a dearth of ideas, when the great muse deserts the hapless victim. In this case, the exact opposite is the cause of my despair. I have so much to recount that I am at a total loss as to where to start because in all the myriad forms of communication, Scots have made such considerable and often unique contributions. I fear I will not do justice to my fellow journalists. All I can do is offer a series of brief portraits that illustrate more the wealth of their talent rather than its depth, again in the hope readers will be encouraged to dig further. My mind is additionally confused because of my long employment with the BBC and my long-term campaigning for freedom of the media – these facts must colour my views.

The creation of the BBC – by John Reith – and the invention of television – by John Logie Baird – are seminal moments in the development of electronic communication and have led to today's wireless wonderland and the universal 24/7 news services. But a couple of centuries earlier two other Scots, Andrew Hamilton (born Edinburgh, 1676–1741) and James Alexander (born Edinburgh, 1691–1756), were also in the forefront of establishing the fundamental freedom of the press in a legal ruling that changed the way we live and even think (see chapter 8, Scotland and the Stars and Stripes). Whichever route I take, I'm safe in the knowledge that I will be meeting towering personalities and not a few super egos, so in the end, a toss of the coin decreed that I should go with chronology and start at the beginning!

Andrew Hamilton, the Scottish lawyer whose win in the Zenger case (documented in chapter 8, Scotland and the Stars and Stripes) established the very principle, is quoted as saying: 'Freedom of the press... is the best cause. It is the cause of liberty both of exposing and opposing arbitrary power by speaking and writing the truth.' Safe in their new fireproof status as the voice of the people, journalists used Hamilton's hard-won freedom to expand their endeavours around the globe and, inevitably, Scots once more found what they regarded as their rightful place: out in front as reporters, correspondents, editors, publishers and proprietors.

Journalism has been around in one form or another since ancient times but it was not until more recently – since the reign of Queen Victoria – that, thanks to both increased literacy and the advent of technology, it could claim to be *popular*. Thus the preponderance of my snapshots is from then on, although a couple of eighteenth-century examples were irresistible. Of course, whatever period one looks at, it's abundantly clear that there is not exactly a dearth of erudite editors and journalists with their roots in Scotland. I hope, therefore, I will be forgiven for ever-briefer brevity. I also hope the snatches of information will lead diligent readers to further research that can put more flesh on the bones. I can promise any such endeavours will bear rich fruit. The journalist's life can be colourful!

As examples of the tenacious and brave editor go, there's none finer than James Perry (born Aberdeen, 1756–1821). He battled against the might of the establishment of King George III, consistently suffered the ire of an irate prime minister and spent three months in jail for contempt of Parliament. For good measure he also engaged in a bitter circulation battle but that saw him swallow the opposition. And all that from a decidedly shaky start that saw him unemployed or having to settle for humdrum jobs throughout his formative teens. He went to Marischal College, Aberdeen, when he was 15 with the intention of reading law and becoming a barrister. However, the family building business failed in 1774 and he had to abandon his studies. Instead, he went to Edinburgh with 'the humble hope' of procuring employment as a clerk. His humility was apparently justified. He tried for weeks to get a job of any description but was then forced to contemplate the long road to England. In Manchester, he found work in a counting house. It was far from what he wanted but he proved diligent and stayed for two years.

His recreation was the city's debating society and his oratorical skills were good enough to attract admiration in influential circles. This was enhanced by his literary deftness, which he demonstrated with a stream of erudite essays. When he finally set out for London in 1777, he had a bagful of letters of introduction and recommendation. This, of course, was pre-Fleet Street, when media baronies were not yet a gleam in the eyes of the predecessors of Northcliffe, Harmsworth, Beaverbrook, Thomson and company. There were no corporate HR departments and the only route to employment was via the hard-nosed proprietors personally. In this tough atmosphere, his high hopes for a launch into a career were again seriously frustrated. London was no more receptive to his applications than had been Edinburgh. But the young James Perry was dogged.

He virtually laid siege to the *General Advertiser*. One of his letters of introduction had been to the paper's proprietor and so Perry kept him supplied with a daily diet of essays and followed that up with regular personal visits, always with the same question: 'have you got a job for me?' One morning, he found the now-friendly proprietor engrossed in a manuscript. 'If only you could write like this…' he said on being disturbed, 'you could start here immediately!' Even looking at it upside down, James Perry knew the man was reading his writing and he just happened to have the sequel to it in his pocket as final proof of his talent. His career was launched at last.

The very next day he became a journalist and was paid a guinea a week to work for the *General Advertiser* and half as much again for writing for the sister paper, *London Evening Post*. The legal knowledge he had gained in Aberdeen now stood him in good stead. He became a court reporter and was credited with raising sales in 1779 with his reporting from the Portsmouth trial of Admirals Keppel and Palliser. He went on to establish *The European Magazine* in 1782, leaving it a year later to make his first foray into the stormy waters of eighteenth-century editorship when he joined the small-circulation *Gazetteer*. It was little more than an advertising platform for London's booksellers and he was paid a paltry four guineas a week. Soon, however, he turned it into a radical, campaigning newspaper that openly supported the Whig opposition under Charles Fox. While his stance – the *Gazetteer*, he claimed, was now the 'paper of the people' – may have caused him a great deal of angst, it also attracted readers and circulation boomed.

With that success behind him, he went one better when, in 1790, he became proprietor and editor of the *Morning Chronicle*. Proving he was still a reporter at heart, however, he forsook the safety of his office to go to Paris, from where he filed reports on the French Revolution during 1791–92. Back in London, his influence and talent were strong enough for Pitt the Younger and Lord Shelbourne to each offer him a parliamentary seat. His political convictions, however, were also strong. He refused. His Fox journalism (a very long way from today's Fox TV journalism) made senior government politicians very uneasy and he became a regular in the law courts. In 1792, he was prosecuted for printing an advertisement for a meeting of the Society for Constitutional Information. He was acquitted. Six years later, he made a repeat appearance in court charged with libelling the Parliament. He went to jail for three months. He continued to edit the paper until his death at the age of 65.

His successor was another Scot, John Black (born Duns, 1783–1855). Having also tasted the bitterness of unemployment and talents unrecognised, the new editor of the *Morning Chronicle* was naturally sympathetic when dealing with aspiring journalists and one of the beneficiaries was a young man called Charles Dickens. Dickens, still only 20, had barely shrugged off the privations of poverty when he turned up at the offices of the *Morning Chronicle* just as Black himself had done 20 years earlier. He did have the advantage of some modest experience of reporting and John Black took him in and dispatched him to Westminster to chronicle the antics of the political classes. The two also became good friends and Dickens described the older man as 'Dear Old Black: my first hearty out-and-out supporter.' That support allowed Dickens the freedom to develop his more imaginative writing. This led to *The Pickwick Papers*. The rest of that story is, as they say, history.

John Black had a tragic childhood. His father, a farm labourer, died when he was three. Before he was 13 both his mother and younger sister died and he was taken in by an uncle, another farm worker. He was sent to the parish school at Duns and as soon as he was old enough was apprenticed to a local writer. This was an environment in which he flourished. He became a daily visitor to the subscription library and began a love affair with books that was to become an obsession. Like his predecessor James Perry, John Black had a hard time getting into journalism. He moved to Edinburgh and worked first as a clerk for the British Linen Bank and then in a city accountant's office so that, in his spare time, he could attend lectures at the university. He also helped with translating German material for David Brewster's *Edinburgh Encyclopaedia*. During this time, he became friends with a fellow student, William Mudford, who, as well as contributing to *Blackwood's Edinburgh Magazine*, was a successful London journalist (he also later edited the *Morning Chronicle* and the *Courier*, and one of his books, *The Iron Shroud*, was to influence Edgar Allan Poe in *The Pit and the Pendulum*). When Mudford became editor of *Universal Magazine*, Black was invited to freelance, writing articles on Italian and German literature, but when his engagement was broken off in 1809, he suffered an emotional breakdown that affected his personality. His friend's solution was to invite him to join him in London. He also found him comfortable lodgings with the publisher and fellow Scot Robert Cromak. Even with good contacts, it was three long months later that Black was taken on as a reporter for the *Morning Chronicle* by James Perry. He worked diligently in his new job and showed his appreciation by being ready to help wherever and whenever necessary. Perry was suffering from long-term poor health and Black became his right-hand man.

In 1817, Perry's health deteriorated to the point where he felt he couldn't carry on in the high-profile role and he handed over editorial responsibility to the now 34-year-old John Black. Black remained faithful to Perry's political antipathy to the Tory government and was swift and forceful in his condemnation of its use of the cavalry against anti-poverty protesters at the Peterloo Massacre in 1819. He also aligned the paper against Queen Caroline during her House of Lords trial in 1820 and he was punished by a savage drop in circulation. However, he survived a subsequent change of ownership in 1821, although the newspaper continued to lose readers in the face of growing competition. By 1834, the circulation had plunged to a mere 800 copies a day and in something of a forced sale the paper again changed hands, but once more Black survived as editor. Encouraged by the new proprietor, he rebuilt the readership towards a more acceptable 10,000 daily. But the savage stress of the circulation battles began to take its toll and, as Black approached 60, the proprietor decided to replace him with the paper's foreign editor... who just happened to be his son-in-law. It was only then that John Black realised he had not made provision for a decent pension. His only asset was his beloved library of around 30,000 books, built up over his lifetime. He had to sell the collection and, with a little extra help from the proprietor of the paper, he realised an annuity of £150. He also had to depend on the considerable charity of his fellow editor and friend, Walter Coulson, who allowed him to stay rent-free in his country cottage. He lived there for the rest of his life, gardening and studying Greek.

One of the biggest scoops in journalistic history was achieved by William Jerdan (born Kelso, 1782–1869). He was a 30-year-old jobbing reporter who happened to be in the lobby of the House of Commons when Prime Minister Spencer Perceval was assassinated on 11 May 1812. He was also close enough to be the first to catch the assassin. Apart from the tragedy and trauma, it was a journalist's dream; the shrewd Jerdan took full advantage of it and revelled in the massive headlines that ensued. Within twelve months, his celebrity earned him the editor's chair of *The Sun*. Not the *Sun* as we know it but then an evening broadsheet and the semi-official organ of the Tory party. During his four years as editor his most significant contribution was his commissioning of articles from the literati of the day, including Samuel Taylor Coleridge and William Wordsworth. The Scot again showed he was shrewd by syndicating the best items to the provincial newspapers, the first service of its kind.

That was to stand him in very good stead when he had a row with the *Sun*'s proprietor and was sacked in 1817. He moved seamlessly into the editor's chair at the *Literary Gazette*, a new publishing venture by Henry Colbourn. He was in his element. As the launch editor, he devised the full title – *The Literary Gazette and Journal of Belles Lettres, Arts and Sciences* – to ensure he had a broad canvas. He was able to establish the magazine's ethos and he wrote as many of the articles on as many matters as he chose. He enjoyed the lifestyle so much, he stayed for 34 years. During that time he acquired shares and eventually ownership. Sadly, somewhere along the way he had lost his Scottish shrewdness. He retired in a distinctly impecunious state. His friends came to the rescue. A testimonial raised £900 and the prime minister – and fellow Scot – the Earl of Aberdeen granted him a government pension of 100 guineas a year. That allowed him the retirement time to write his autobiography and then later a collection of reminiscences entitled *Men I Have Known*. Before breaking into journalism in 1806, William Jerdan had worked in an Edinburgh solicitor's office, a London counting house and aboard HM Guardship *Gladiator* as surgeon's mate to his uncle.

A later editor – and eventual proprietor - of the *Sun* was Murdo Young (born Inverness, 1790–1870). He proved himself well up to the cut-and-thrust of Fleet Street and was described by fellow newspapermen as an adventurer and 'an active, shrewd, calculating Scotsman'. He remained very firmly in charge for 37 years (1825–62), until his retirement at the age of 72.

His father was a printer and bookseller who, in 1807, had also launched the *Inverness Journal* as the first newspaper north of Aberdeen. He sold it on Fridays for sixpence and made the paper's objectives plain enough: 'Interested in everything that relates to the prosperity of a district of country to which we lie under so many obligations, it shall be our earnest desire to introduce into the *Inverness Journal* every topic that may tend to its improvement and advantage.' No need, therefore, to wonder where the 17-year-old Murdo got his inspiration to become a journalist rather than a printer. Like so many Scots, however, he found the pages of a local broadsheet were not broad enough for his ambitions and so he found his way to London, where he quickly earned a reputation as an energetic and committed reporter.

He was a veteran of 35 when the chance came to sit in the editor's chair at the *Sun* and he had no hesitation in taking up the challenge. His shrewdness also meant he was able to acquire 25 per cent of the shares. The major shareholder was a fellow Scot, Patrick Grant of Glen Urquhart. Mr Grant didn't share his partner's canniness and when he spread his investments in other publishing ventures too widely, he ran into financial difficulties and was declared bankrupt. In lieu of the £8,000 owed to him, the courts ceded sole ownership to Murdo Young in 1838. He celebrated by brightening up the newspaper and broke new ground by introducing his daughter Catherine (1826–1908) as one of the first female reporters in Fleet Street. She was still in her teens when he called on her services but he was obviously careful not to show her undue favour and proved a hard taskmaster. As she later wrote: 'He was very particular and did not think so much of the style as others did. He would never let me write the principal article.' As in all the best stories, she only got her chance when some war news broke and she was the only one in the office!

Murdo Young was also ahead of the opposition when he produced another Fleet Street first: a commemorative four-page gold-coloured supplement to mark the coronation of Queen Victoria. The front page was dominated by a striking new portrait of the Queen – by none other than the talented editor himself. It clearly caught the mood of the moment. It ran to 20 reprints and sold more than 300,000 copies. A copy of the front page is held in the National Gallery archive and the central portrait of Victoria is attributed to him. I'm sure he would see that as a fitting memorial.

When confronted with demands for an early version of dumbing down at his beloved newspaper, *Atlas*, Robert Rintoul (born Tibbermuir, Perthshire, 1787–1858) showed his courage as an independent editor and resigned. He retaliated by launching the *Spectator* in 1828, and declared his intent to maintain standards: 'We will provide the whole news of the week and we will provide full and impartial exhibition of all the leading topics of the day.' While today that may be seen as a statement of the obvious for a lively news journal, then it came in the face of his former employers' urging to 'vulgarize' the respected radical newspaper.

Equally outraged by the suggestion was fellow Scot Joseph Hume (born Montrose, 1777–1855), the Tory-turned-Radical MP. He was one of the key founders of *Atlas* as 'the organ of Benthamite thought.' He readily gave his political and financial support. The new enterprise offered readers 'instruction and entertainment at the same time and a section devoted to literature... independent criticism of new books... dramatic and musical criticism... scientific and miscellaneous information.' Rintoul promised that the *Spectator* would be 'the voice of educated Radicalism' and he kept his promise throughout his 30 years as editor. During the controversial parliamentary debate about the Reform Bill, he famously declared: 'The bill, the whole bill and nothing but the bill.' However, my favourite quote from him comes from when he was speaking about the relationships between journalists and politicians: 'The tone in which newspapers are usually mentioned in the House is absurd. Men who cannot breakfast without one, in the evening pretend to be hardly cognisant of the existence of such things. Men who in private life look to them for their sole stock of opinions are found in public sneering at their contents.' He sold the paper in February 1858 and died a few weeks later.

Politicians were not slow to appreciate the ever-growing influence of the press. While the history books (and indeed chapter 7 of this book) quite rightly concentrate on the statesmanship of two great Scottish founding fathers of Canada, George Brown (born Alloa, 1818–80) and John Macdonald (born Glasgow, 1815–91), my interest in the pair for this chapter is that they also had a hand in establishing Canada's early newspapers and very much enlivened the political scene by slogging it out in the public prints.

First to recognise the power of the press was George Brown. After his education in Edinburgh, he had migrated with his family to New York at 15 and worked with his father in the print industry. At 25, he decided to go north, to Canada. Within a year of arriving in Toronto, he was deeply immersed in politics and in 1844 he matched his political passion with his printing skills. In support of the Reformers, he launched the *Globe* and this quickly gave him considerable influence. Clearly not enthusiastic about the Auld Alliance between Scotland and France, he was unashamedly anti-French and he often gave vent to these chauvinistic feelings in his newspaper. There's little doubt that he contributed to the divisions that persist in Canada.

Although it was his clear intention to use the newspaper as a platform for his political ambitions, the shrewd Scot soon discovered the Canadians had a very healthy appetite for news and were more than happy to pay the cover price for his weekly outpourings. Within five years, the four-page *Globe* had developed a healthy independent editorial stance and switched from weekly to daily publication. Brown also took advantage of the railroad system to massively increase distribution and turn his newspaper into the country's first national morning paper.

Watching this success closely was Brown's fellow Scot but fierce political opponent, John Macdonald, who had become Canada's first prime minister in 1867. He was clearly feeling insecure towards the end of his first term of office and, in 1872, with an election in the offing, he launched Toronto's *Mail* to give the Liberal-Conservatives their own voice and bolster his chance of remaining prime minister. Like George Brown, however, he found that, as powerful as the power of the press might be, it didn't win him a further term. He lost the 1873 election and was then able to spend more time with his newspaper. This spell was much more successful in influencing *Mail* readers and Macdonald was returned to office in 1878, remaining as prime minister until his death 13 years later.

Ironically, George Brown's *Globe* and John Macdonald's *Mail* merged in 1936. While the two Scots politicians might have turned in their graves, the two newspapermen would undoubtedly be pleased that their press legacy to Canada was a flourishing newspaper with a 21st-century circulation of nearly a million a day!

In Britain, another Scot, Peter Borthwick (born Midlothian, 1804–52), revelled in that heady mix of press and politics which runs through this chapter. He was the MP for Evesham (1835–37 and 1841–47) and editor of the London *Morning Post* from 1848 until his death. That death might have come somewhat earlier had there been a different outcome to the duel – thought to be the last in England – that he fought with the politician who beat him in the 1937 election. In the event, although shots were exchanged, neither hit their target and both men were uninjured. Borthwick did have the ultimate satisfaction, however, when he regained his parliamentary seat from his opponent at the following election. His journalistic career was severely curtailed by poor health. When he left parliament in 1848 he became editor of the *Morning Post*. Two years later he bought the paper and used it to support aspiring prime minister Palmerston, himself a journalist-turned-politician. Borthwick did not live to see his man take office. The evening after writing his usual fiery leader for the paper, he died of an acute attack of pleurisy. His son, Algernon, took over the paper and when he was later given a peerage, in honour of his father, he took the Scottish title of Baron Glenesk.

I'm sure that, like most successful journalists, many of my compatriot scribblers have sailed close to the wind but not too many have ended up in jail. One who found himself a guest at the notorious Newgate in London was Robert Alexander (born Paisley, 1795–1854), when he was editor of the city's *Morning Journal*. I should add immediately that his sojourn behind bars had nothing to do with excesses of the flesh or the Victorian equivalent of phone-hacking; he found himself on the wrong side of the law over the inflammatory question of Catholic emancipation and a right royal fall-out in the upper echelons of the Tory party. As one contemporary report said, 'so severe were the strictures on men and measures, so fearless and pungent the denunciations of the torturous policy of Peel published in the *Journal*, that the Government took advantage of unadvised expressions which had escaped, no doubt injudiciously but almost unconsciously, in the heat of argument and vehemence of invective.' Robert Alexander had had the temerity to question the Catholic Church, was found guilty of libel and promptly dispatched to jail.

The son of a builder, he had attended Paisley Grammar School and then tried his hand at commerce first locally, then in Ireland and finally in Glasgow before the penny dropped that he wasn't cut out to be a businessman. He decided to try writing and, in particular, journalism. He got a job on a local paper and by the time he was 25 found himself in charge of the *Clydesdale Journal*, a Conservative-sponsored weekly. He did well there, and the party promoted him to a larger publication, the *Glasgow Sentinel*. That appeared to stretch the party coffers too much and it was discontinued. Like so many other Scots, he then headed south and tried his hand as a jobbing journalist around London. He was lured to Exeter as editor of the *Western Luminary*, but the lights of the capital burned too brightly and he returned after a year to edit the Conservative-owned *Watchman*. He had been encouraged to think the paper would be converted to a major daily but the plans came to nothing and so he made the fateful move to the editor's chair at the *Morning Journal*. In 1829 he wrote a leader too far and the attorney general dropped on him decisively. The indictment was that the article had been written 'upon principles of the basest personal feeling and with a hostility unqualified by the least regard to honour or truth.' So much for the Georgian view of freedom of the press. On 10 February 1830 Robert Alexander was punished with a fine of £300 and a year's imprisonment in Newgate. The greater punishment was the collapse of the *Morning Journal*. It closed three months later. When he was freed, Robert Alexander decided he'd had enough of London and the political classes. He moved to Liverpool where he worked for the city's *Standard* for five years. He then launched the rival *Liverpool Mail* and happily edited it until his death in 1854.

There was obviously a typically Scottish restless streak in George Buist (born Forfar, 1804–60). After attending St Andrews and Edinburgh universities, he became a journalist and was appointed editor of the *Dundee Courier* in 1874. But he swiftly moved on to launch a new paper, the *Dundee Guardian*, later the same year. Within months, he was off again to edit the *Perth Constitutional*. He lasted two years there before moving on to edit the *Fifeshire Journal*. But holding four local editorships in five years wasn't enough to sate his wanderlust. In 1839, he set sail for India. There he became editor of the *Bombay Times* and found a contentment in that role that kept him in the one place for 18 years. In 1858 he was off again – but only down the street – to launch his own newspaper, the *Bombay Standard*. The very next year, however, he abandoned journalism to settle for life in the Indian civil service as superintendent of the Government Printing Press in Allahabad. He stayed in that job until his early death two years later, at the age of 55.

Few have managed to combine journalism, economics and politics with the same fine skill as James Wilson (born Hawick, 1805–60). He founded *The Economist*, got himself elected as a Liberal MP, served in the cabinets of two prime ministers, made several fortunes but flirted with bankruptcy, founded what is now the Standard Chartered Bank and went to India to try to reorganise a chaotic tax system.

It's true that he had a good start in life. He came from a long line of successful sheep farmers and his father was a wealthy wool merchant. It was assumed he would become a teacher when he left school at 16, but he refused and instead went to work as an apprentice hatmaker! His plan was to start at the bottom and learn everything there was to know about the economics of the business. Once his father realised he was serious, he bought the company and handed it over to James and his older brother. They made a success of it but, frustrated by the constraints of life in the Scottish Borders, they both moved to London and set up a similar business with a third partner. That was less successful and James left to set up on his own in 1831.

Initially, he stuck to what he knew best, but as his new venture bore fruit he started to invest in property and on the stock market. When the country suffered a serious economic downturn in 1837, he was one of the victims. However, he avoided bankruptcy by selling off all his properties and eventually weathered the storm. In 1843, he diversified into publishing but played safe by making use of his business background: he launched *The Economist* to report and comment on the ups and downs of the commercial world. To make doubly sure of success, he himself sat in the editor's chair – and stayed there for 16 years.

Somehow James Wilson also managed to develop a career in politics and in 1847, he became MP for Westbury in Wiltshire. Within five years, he was in the Earl of Aberdeen's cabinet as financial secretary to the treasury; he stayed in the post under Palmerston and was then promoted to paymaster general in 1858. He remained as editor of *The Economist* but also employed Walter Bagehot, who later became not only the paper's editor but also Wilson's son-in-law. Now regarding himself as a proper journalist, he found time to pen trenchant economic pieces for the *Manchester Guardian*.

Incredibly, on top of all that he was able to launch the Chartered Bank of India, Australia and China, (the forerunner of today's Standard Chartered Bank) in 1853. His ultimate challenge was an invitation to join the Council of India in 1859. He promptly resigned his editorship, his parliamentary seat and his cabinet post and went to Calcutta committed to establishing financial stability in a country still reeling from revolution. So committed was he that he refused to head for the cooler climes of the mountains and stayed in Calcutta throughout the stifling summer. He almost inevitably caught dysentery and died at the age of 55.

Thomas Ballantyne (born Paisley, 1806–71) was both a political campaigner and a journalist so it seems almost natural that he should become editor (1839–46) of the prestigious and famously liberal *Manchester Guardian*. He was only 33 when he took up the role and he worked enthusiastically with Richard Cobden and John Bright, the leading figures in the Manchester-based Anti-Corn Laws League. In 1841 he published the *Corn Law Repealer's Handbook*.

As one might expect of a distinguished editor in the Victorian era, Ballantyne was well connected, and among his associates was writer and fellow Scot Thomas Carlyle (born Ecclefechan, 1795–1881). In February 1839, Ballantyne felt able to ask for the great man's advice on writing his autobiography and got a very helpful and detailed response: 'Why not try the undertaking; you will then see best of all whether you have a call to it. The written record can at least do no ill. To yourself it will infallibly do good and though written, it need not be printed till you see cause otherwise.' That's advice any writer would find comforting but Carlyle was not content to leave it there. He warmed to his theme and offered further encouragement to his journalist friend: 'Write what seems lucid, beautiful or significant to your own mind and believe always that the public will adjust itself to that, or at worst that you can do nothing else for the public.' He also showed great interest in Ballantyne's early life and experience in Scotland: 'Life in Paisley, in the workshops, at the firesides of the poor, this ought to be fully given; as a thing little known to readers and a thing well deserving to be known – perhaps of all others the most important thing in these days: and as for your own feeling about it, I greatly mistake you if those young Scottish years, with their thrift and rigour and necessitous affection and endeavour, are not the dearest to your heart of all you have seen or hope to see.'

When Ballantyne launched his new *Manchester Examiner* in April 1846, Carlyle was first on the mailing list and he returned the compliment with equal promptness: 'I am very glad indeed to see you get along so handsomely. Continue to tell a straight, manful story about what comes before you and people will not fail to listen. They are getting every day more prepared to hear one's full mind spoken about all manner of matters.' When the *Examiner* merged with the *Times*, he moved west to become editor of the *Liverpool Journal* and later of the *Liverpool Mercury*, then a strongly Liberal weekly newspaper. Later, he moved to London to edit *The Leader* and sometimes wrote for fellow Scot Charles Mackay (see below), then editor of the *Illustrated London News*. He also launched the *Statesman*, which he edited till its close, when he became editor of the *St James's Chronicle*.

In a world away from Thomas Ballantyne's genteel journalism, Charles Mackay (born Perth, 1814–89) spent a turbulent three years (1862–65) as the *Times* correspondent covering the American Civil War. He replaced the famous William Howard Russell, whose reportage had so outraged the Unionists that he was effectively expelled from the country. Mackay's was an appointment that did little to pacify the Union leaders because he was an avowed supporter of the Confederates. Somehow, he survived the political onslaught and only returned to Britain when the Civil War ended.

The son of a sometime naval officer and army infantryman, Charles Mackay first went to London to further his education at the improbably named Caledonian Asylum, an establishment set up in 1815 to provide a home and schooling for Scottish children orphaned in the Napoleonic Wars. He qualified on the basis that his mother had died shortly after his birth. His route from there to the *Illustrated London News* was circuitous. He finished his education on the continent then returned to London, and when he was 21 launched his journalistic career as a reporter for the *Morning Chronicle*. He pounded the Fleet Street beat for seven years before being recruited as editor of the *Glasgow Argus* in 1844. His three years there were clearly productive because he also found time to study for his literary doctorate at Glasgow University. He returned to London as political editor of the *Illustrated London News*. He covered the Westminster scene for four years before he moved became editor in 1852 and was later made general manager. That experience led him to leave in 1859 to launch his own *London Review and Weekly Journal,* through which he sought to publish material from his literary friends.He also found time to indulge his own literary interests and he published various collections of songs and poems, including this well-known verse:

> *You have no enemies, you say?*
> *Alas, my friend, the boast is poor;*
> *He who has mingled in the fray*
> *Of duty, that the brave endure,*
> *Must have made foes! If you have none,*
> *Small is the work that you have done.*
> *You've hit no traitor on the hip,*
> *You've dashed no cup from perjured lip,*
> *You've never set the wrong to right,*
> *You've been a coward in the fight.*

That, of course, could not be said of Charles Mackay. During his spell as the *Times* correspondent in America, he not only covered the war from the front line but he also uncovered details of a Fenian conspiracy. On the strictly personal front, he had an affair with his housekeeper and became the father of her illegitimate child, Margaret. She grew up and followed in his literary footsteps. Her pen name was Marie Correlli.

Another Scottish veteran of the American Civil War was Alexander Gardner (born Paisley, 1821–82). Some of the most vivid newspaper images of the war came from his camera after he won the role of photographer – and the honorary rank of captain – in the Union Army of the Potomac in 1862. The astute professional used his friendship with fellow Scot Allan Pinkerton (see chapter 8, Scotland and the Stars and Stripes), then Lincoln's intelligence chief, to find his way through the labyrinth of army command. He was made chief photographer, oddly, within the US Topographical Engineers, but he quickly moved on to be staff photographer to General George B. McClellan, commander of the Army of the Potomac. He photographed the Battle of Antietam in September 1862, developing photos in his travelling darkroom, and his pictures were used in newspapers across the globe. He also photographed Lincoln and then was an official observer at the execution of the conspirators to the President's assassination.

Alexander Gardner left school and went to work as an apprentice silversmith in Glasgow when he was 16. It wasn't a trade that suited him and instead he followed his interest in the utopian socialist experiment at New Lanark and Robert Owen's cooperative movement. Determined to develop the philosophy in America, he and his brother led a group that bought land in Iowa with the intention of establishing a cooperative community. This was more costly than Gardner had estimated, so he returned to Scotland to raise more funds. While back in Glasgow, he learned that a local newspaper was for sale and promptly invested in becoming the proprietor and editor of the *Glasgow Sentinel*. He gave himself the role of specialist writer on art and science!

He first became interested in photography when he saw the work of the American Mathew Brady at the Great Exhibition in London in 1851. Enthused, he studied every aspect of taking and producing photographs. When he returned to America in 1856, he found that tuberculosis had decimated the community in Iowa and it was slowly disbanding. Instead he stayed in New York and there initiated contact with Mathew Brady to see if there might be a photographic job for him. Coincidentally, the American's eyesight was deteriorating and he was finding it ever more difficult to keep pace with the growing demands for his services. He welcomed the Scotsman with open arms. Over the five years he was with Brady, Gardner became the chief assistant and then was rapidly promoted to take charge of the company's Washington studio. In the end, however, he was frustrated that all his work was distributed under the copyright byline 'Photographed by Brady'. In 1863, Gardner finally snapped and he and his brother James opened their own studio in Washington. Later the same year, he was at the Battle of Gettysburg and the following year witnessed the Siege of Petersburg. He claimed to have been the last to photograph Lincoln, just four days before his assassination.

Donald Mackenzie Wallace (born Boghead, Dunbartonshire, 1841–1919) started out determined to be a scholar and studied law, metaphysics and ethics at universities in Glasgow, Edinburgh, Berlin, Heidelberg and Paris, but he was pressed into service as a foreign correspondent and ended up giving *The Times* one of its greatest scoops. In 1878, he attended the Berlin Congress and then sewed the details of the sensitive treaty (to end the Russo-Turkish war) into the lining of his overcoat, smuggled it back to Brussels and then on to Printing House Square. For a period, he was political officer to Tsar Nicholas II during his tour of India and then became private secretary to the viceroy of India (the Earl of Dufferin). When he finally returned to London, he was made director of *The Times*' foreign services and was editor of the tenth edition of *Encyclopaedia Britannica*. He reported on the Russian Japanese peace conference (in the US) in 1905 before returning to study and travel. Or so he thought. King George V had other ideas: he 'commanded' Wallace's assistance on a world tour and then assigned him to assist the Tsar on his visit to London. He was twice knighted: once for his services to India, and then he was made KCVO by Edward VII for his services to the Crown.

Hard work is not unusual in journalists. It's a great job and at its best, it's exciting and fulfilling. Sometimes it doesn't even seem like work. But Angus Reach (born Inverness, 1821–56) took his commitment to excess and worked himself into an early grave.

Reach (pronounced *ree*-ack) started writing reports for his father's *Inverness Courier* when he was 16 and still at Inverness Royal Academy. After university in Edinburgh he moved to London at 20, and took Fleet Street by storm. He followed in the footsteps of Charles Dickens as the parliamentary reporter for the *Morning Chronicle* and then became an early investigative reporter, producing mould-breaking commentaries on the social condition of his day. He developed what has been described as 'picturesque reporting' and influenced a generation of journalists. One perceptive critic wrote: 'He had the power to bring a vivid picture before the reader, a practice associated with the novelist rather than the journalist. Under his influence the public saw what he saw, heard what he heard and shared all the emotion and excitement of a spectator at the scene.' In 1849, when the editor decided to launch an investigation into 'the condition of the labouring classes,' he picked a team that included Angus Reach, fellow Scot Charles Mackay (see earlier in this chapter), and the man who was to become Reach's best friend – Shirley Brooks. Reach's assignment took him into the homes of working people, previously uncharted territory for journalists. He visited many of the key industrial towns and cities in the Midlands and north of England and his reports in the *Morning Chronicle* underpinned his reputation as one of Britain's leading journalists.

He was invited to write extensively for other national newspapers, which he did with undiminished erudition. Every month he also wrote two very funny columns – 'Town Talk' and 'Table Talk' – for the discerning *Punch* magazine. And still he found time to edit *The Man in the Moon* magazine which was described thus: 'a monthly review and bulletin of new measures, new men, new books, new plays, new jokes and new nonsense; being an act for the amalgamation of the broad gauge of fancy with the narrow gauge of fact into the grand general amusement junction.' Inevitably, he started to show the strain of this volume of work, but he ignored all the health warnings and added to his phenomenal output by producing books at an astonishing pace: *The Natural History of Bores* (1847), *The Natural History of Humbugs* (1848), *A Romance of a Mince-Pie* (1848), *Clement Lorimer* (1849) and *Leonard Lindsay: The Story of a Buccaneer* (1850). In 1854, when he was just 31, he suffered a brain haemorrhage. It left him unable to work and therefore unable to provide financially for his family. His friends rallied round. His colleague Shirley Brooks took over his work for the *Morning Chronicle* and paid all the earnings to Reach's wife. Another friend, the author Albert Smith, organised a benefit performance at a London theatre which included readings of Reach's work. In the sell-out audience was Charles Dickens. The event was repeated at the Drury Lane Theatre and was attended by Queen Victoria and Prince Albert. Angus Reach died a year later. His tombstone was paid for by William Makepeace Thackeray.

Before he established himself as a serious writer and long before Peter Pan soared across the West End skies, J.M. Barrie (born Kirriemuir, 1860–1937) was a humble journalist. He started his career as a £3-a-week leader writer on a provincial newspaper. He had taken his MA at Edinburgh University and announced his intention to become a writer. His more worldly sister, prompted by an ad in the *Scotsman*, pointed him in the direction of Nottingham, where he became a jobbing journalist on the city's *Journal*. For two long years he laboured at the coalface and proved himself prolific by turning out a 1000-word leader every day and also writing book reviews and other articles for the weekend supplement.

Barrie's journalistic career was curtailed when the paper bowed to its competitor and closed down. He tried for other jobs, even travelling to Liverpool on one occasion, but he was unsuccessful and had to return to Scotland. It was a year before anything else happened. In 1885 he was 25 and still determined to be a writer so he jumped at the chance when he was offered a regular column in the *St James's Gazette*. He dusted down his portable typewriter and caught an early train to London. He wrote weekly for the *Gazette*, used up more of his boundless energy by also writing for a string of papers and magazines and still found time to produce cricket reports for the Edinburgh *Evening Despatch*. His first book, *When a Man's Single*, was published in 1888 and he was lost to journalism! The rest is history: *Quality Street*, *The Admirable Crichton*, *Peter Pan*, a knighthood in 1913, the Order of Merit in 1922, and the chancellorship of Edinburgh University in 1930.

America has proved a very happy stamping ground for Scottish journalists since scribbling became a profitable business and David Baillie (born Glasgow, 1845–1902) was one who found a comfortable berth as editor of the *Los Angeles Herald*.

He cut his teeth on local papers around his native city before emigrating at the age of 25 and settling initially in New York. He held several high-profile jobs including political correspondent for both the *New York Tribune* and the *New York World*. That was in the *World*'s pre-Joseph Pulitzer days (he didn't buy it until 1883) and the paper was reportedly losing money. It's not clear if that fuelled Baillie's urge to go west, but he arrived in Los Angeles with his eyes clearly set on breaking into the editorial hierarchy and he chose the *Los Angeles Herald* from an array of lively newspapers on the West Coast. When he retired in 1910, he went with strong praise ringing in his ears and congratulations on 'the work he [had] been doing so well and with such signal originality and ability.' These weren't exactly unbiased words, of course: they referred to him as 'Clansman Baillie' and came from the chieftain of the Cameron Clan in California who added, 'we congratulate him on the great work and on the honours he has shed upon the clan and all the Scottish people… during the years he has been on *The Herald*.'

He was once described as 'the ambitious Glaswegian' and Kennedy Jones (born Glasgow, 1865–1921) certainly lived up to that reputation. He talked the Harmsworth brothers into buying the London *Evening News* in 1894, turned it into a roaring success and then set the tone for today's popular journalism with the creation of the *Daily Mail*. KJ – as he was universally known – had initially hoped to buy the paper himself but realised he wouldn't be able to raise the necessary capital, so he applied his persuasive tongue to convince the empire-building brothers of the value of what was, for them, a small investment. He had left his local high school and dived straight into journalism as a junior reporter on Glasgow's *Evening News* when he was 16. His ambition was obvious from the start and he was quickly given the additional responsibility of sub-editing the paper. Fleet Street clearly beckoned. But he only got there in stages. He worked for newspapers in Birmingham and Leicester and when he did eventually get to London, it was only in hope. There was no job offer on the table and he had to tout his services around the capital. Still in his mid-twenties, he had a long hard look at the penny broadsheets on offer on the newsstands and was convinced the reading public was ready for something different.

In 1892, he helped launch a ha'penny newspaper, *The Evening*. It didn't quite work and when, in 1893, the *Sun* was launched as a non-political literary journal – but still selling every evening for the magic ha'penny – he clambered aboard and was soon the paper's chief subeditor. That seriously whetted his ambitious appetite and when he heard that the *Evening News* was in financial difficulties he and a colleague moved quickly to take an option to buy it. They didn't have the £25,000 needed but they knew a man who did – Alfred Harmsworth. The journalists' grapevine told them he was keen to get into the lucrative London daily market and although ailing, the *Evening News* still had a circulation of more than 100,000, which offered a solid base upon which to build. A deal was done, Harmsworth acquired the paper in 1894 and the two journalists each got a fair percentage of the profits.

At last, the dynamic KJ became an editor and was able to put into action his ideas for a new kind of newspaper. The *Evening News* immediately looked different, with a typographical make-over and an attractive mix of news and features, better sports reporting, competitions and even a daily episode of popular fiction. KJ had changed the face of journalism and the readers loved it: within months the *Evening News* set a new world record for daily circulation, with 394,000 copies sold on 15 November 1894. The new-look paper proved so profitable that Harmsworth confidently described it as 'the gold brick' of his empire and he took the 'ambitious Glaswegian' into the heart of his management team.

When the now gruff and somewhat abrasive Scot returned to Glasgow in 1895, it was to buy the *Daily Record* and add it to the Harmsworth stable. There's no telling where this acquisition culture may have led, because the following year came the launch of the *Daily Mail* and that required all KJ's considerable energies and skills. He was now too embroiled in management to take on the editorship but it was his vision of a national ha'penny paper aimed at the ever-growing middle classes that was at the heart of the enterprise. He had an oversight of style and content and his instincts for what Middle England wanted ensured that the paper was successful. The early print runs seemed ambitious at 100,000, but within three years the *Daily Mail* was selling more than half a million copies every day. It was through KJ that *The Times* was bought and drawn into the Harmsworth empire in 1908. He was said to have conducted negotiations with considerable subtlety and is credited with returning the paper to profit.

After bringing so much to the table, including further innovations, he had expected to be made a director of the paper, but it was not to be. Perhaps because of his brusque demeanour, he was not elected to the board and nor was he offered any editorial influence. He was not the sort to suffer such a slight readily and when he became seriously ill and had to have a major operation, he decided enough was enough. Still only

47, he walked away from journalism and turned his attention to politics. He stood as an independent in a 1916 parliamentary by-election in Wimbledon. He got a respectable vote but not enough to win the seat. A year later, he was returned unopposed as a Unionist in another by-election in Hornsey. Within months, Lloyd George had given him a junior ministerial job in the Ministry of Food, where his ingenuity was again put to good use in helping the war effort. KJ died of pneumonia in 1921.

Although a career diplomat, Sir William Allardyce (born Aberdeen, 1861–1930) additionally distinguished himself by editing the Western Pacific native newspaper, *Na Mata*, for nearly ten years up to 1899. He was high commissioner at the time and later went on to become governor of the Falkland Islands (1904–14), the Bahamas (1915–20), Tasmania (1920–22) and Newfoundland (1922–28). He was knighted in 1916.

Hamish Blair (born Dingwall, 1872–1935) travelled to the far side of the world to find fame and a modest fortune. Son of the local headmaster, he went to Glasgow High School and became a journalist when he was 18. After a three-year stint as a subeditor on the Birmingham *Daily Argus,* he felt the need for a more exotic beat. Within three years of arriving on the Indian subcontinent, he was editing – without irony – the *Englishman* in Calcutta (1896–1906). The paper had been launched in 1811 by Robert Knight, the founder and brilliant editor of the *Times of India,* and had a circulation of more than 100,000. In 1906, his entrepreneurial urges got the better of him and he launched the *Empire*, acting as both editor and managing director of the business. He ran the paper for six years before he succumbed to the blandishments of the proprietor of one of India's most important newspapers, the *Statesman*. He set up the new Eastern bureau and became the joint editor and director of the company. After he had retired, his old paper, the *Englishman,* was merged with the *Statesman* and continues to be the leading English language newspaper in Calcutta and West Bengal.

When he retired, he clearly had no inclination to return to Scotland. He is often quoted in collections of poetry for his lines, 'Best bloody place is bloody bed,|With bloody ice on bloody head,|You might as well be bloody dead,|In bloody Orkney.' Instead he stayed on and lived in Wellington in the Nilgiri Hills (now in Bangladesh) and continued writing articles and short stories for the Indian press, He also produced three novels: *1957, Governor Hardy* and *The Great Gesture.*

It was Scotsman Douglas MacRae (born Aberdeen, 1861–1901) who famously, with a stroke of marketing genius, first printed the *Financial Times* on pink paper. The one-time printer's apprentice came up with the idea when he was battling to confound the opposition in the ferociously competitive arena of finance and business journalism in the 1890s. It may seem an innocuous device today, but then it was little short of sensational and it had an equally dramatic impact on MacRae's career: he switched from printing to journalism as editor of the paper.

The young MacRae was taken from his Aberdonian roots when the family moved south. He finished his education in London and became an apprentice in the print industry. But he was fascinated by journalism and when he wasn't devilling in the print room, he spent his limited free time seeking to emulate some of his journalistic heroes. He wrote for any journal that would take his material, including the misleadingly titled *Cricket* magazine (it was about natural history, not sport) and papers in South Africa. His head, however, was not turned so much that he ever took his eye off the ball. In fact, he progressed so well in the shadowy world of hot-metal printing that he was able to establish his own publishing operation. Among his subsequent acquisitions – from the later-notorious financier and disgraced MP, Horatio Bottomley – was the *Financial Times*, then battling against the well established *Financial News*.

It seems extraordinary today that there were two financial dailies, but both were successful because of the huge interest in the money markets. Douglas MacRae took his new responsibility very seriously. He gave up all his printing and other publishing interests to concentrate on the *FT*. That included travelling the world to study finances and financial customs, commerce, industry and especially mining. Then, barely 30, he took on the editorship in fulfilment of his dream to be a journalist. He later wrote: 'I took a great deal of trouble in order to be in a position to judge intelligently the affairs in which our readers are interested.' He forecast what became known as the 'Kaffir Circus', a huge interest in the burgeoning gold mines of South Africa that saw frantic buying and selling on the London Stock Exchange, where business sometimes spilled onto the surrounding streets. His paper went from success to success and the once-ferocious competition with the opposition settled down to a fierce but friendly rivalry. Mr MacRae would surely have smiled when, in 1945, the two rivals merged and it was decided that it would be the other, slightly older paper that disappeared. He would undoubtedly smile even more broadly at the contemporary success of his newspaper.

While he served for more than 30 years as a civil servant, Ernest Bendall (born Edinburgh, 1846–1924) also established himself as one of the country's leading drama critics before becoming something of a poacher-turned-gamekeeper: he joined the Lord Chamberlain's Office as a censor or, less pejoratively, an 'examiner of plays'.

A product of Edinburgh Academy, he went to London to work as a clerk in the paymaster general's office in 1866. The work there was clearly not unduly taxing and the young Scot was soon writing play reviews for the London *Figaro*. He graduated to theatre critic for the *Observer* and with his reputation soaring, he also found time to write for several other newspapers without taking his eye off the civil service ball. In 1912, his government masters rewarded his diligence and appointed him to the censorship role in an executive office in St James's Palace. Of course, he finally had to retire from the newspaper scene in order to recycle his critical faculties as a censor. He was further rewarded by being made a Member of the Victorian Order in 1917.

If you ever wondered what *News of the World* reporters did in between their weekly efforts to ensure the paper could live up to its strapline – 'All human life is here' – you probably didn't guess how the hard-nosed Glaswegian Howie Milligan (1871–1940) passed the time: he wrote comic songs for Harry Lauder! During the duller patches in salacious court cases, Howie was penning daft songs for Scotland's greatest comic actor and singer. Perhaps pertinent to this tome, he gave us 'Pin your faith on the Motherland: Song of Empire', and then came 'The Kilty Lads' and a host more to meet Edwardian tastes. But the one that outweighs both Howie's long stint as the chief reporter of the *Scottish Daily Express* and his days on the *NoW* crime beat was surely Sir Harry's biggest hit, the sentimental love song, 'Roamin in the Gloamin'! Soft thing.

A journalist who had left school at the age of twelve and then educated himself from the books in Glasgow Public Library had a significant influence both in the making of the Australian Constitution and on the political leaders of the early Commonwealth. James Edmond (born Glasgow, 1859–1933) edged his way into journalism by a very circuitous route and ended up with more power and influence than he could ever have imagined back when he sat among those regimented rows of books instead of playing football with his mates.

The son of a carpet maker, he became an avid reader and spent hours in the stuffiness of the library that would have intimidated most twelve-year-olds. However, when he was old enough to work, it was as a lowly clerk with an insurance company. Frustrated with his lot, he emigrated to New Zealand when he was 19 but his bid for fame and fortune only took him as far as a sweet factory and he spent little more than five years there before it all got too much for him. He upped sticks again and moved to Australia. He was 25 and becoming ever more anxious about the lack of any career path. In the end, he resorted to a touch of fabrication. He saw an advert for a proofreader, was fortunate that his claims to appropriate experience were never tested, and joined the staff of the *Morning Bulletin* in Rockhampton, Queensland.

Reading all the material produced by the reporters, he reckoned he could do that job as well as any of them. He must have caught the editor on a good day and soon James Edmond was on the ladder that would eventually take him to the top of his purloined profession and see him rubbing shoulders with the leading politicians. With his bookish background, he was more interested in magazine writing than newspaper reporting, and he started commenting on the news in short pieces he sent to *The Bulletin* in Sydney. The owner and editor at the time was the great J.F. Archibald and he particularly liked the way Edmond could write entertainingly about politics and finance. His style suited the magazine's unconventional reputation and he joined the small but illustrious staff. 'Jimmy's the only man I know who can get fun out of a balance sheet,' said the Archibald of his newest recruit.

With his feet under what he now felt was the right desk, the boy from Glasgow – who never lost his broad accent – set to with a will and produced an endless stream of commentary that was contemporaneously described variously as lucid, cogent, dry and pungent and which helped to characterise the ironic flippancy that defined the *Bulletin's* style. It worked wonders for the circulation and he established a reputation that meant he was not only appreciated by his boss but also listened to by the politicians. They, at the time, were engaged in writing Australia's constitution and it is said that Edmond's influence in a series of finely honed articles in 1900 helped pave the way for the new

Commonwealth. He argued against overseas borrowing, writing in *A Policy for the Commonwealth* that fiscal self-sufficiency was essential. Published as a series of *Bulletin* leaders, that work was later reissued as a pamphlet. When the irrepressible Archibald's health broke down in 1902, he readily handed the editorship to James Edmond. He held the stressful post for more than ten years until exhaustion and ill-health caught up with him too. He was just 55.

One of the most remarkable newspapermen at the turn of the twentieth century was Bertie Forbes (born New Deer, Aberdeenshire, 1880–1954), who helped establish the *Rand Daily Mail* in South Africa and then went to America where, in the ultimate show of ego and self-confidence, he launched the renowned financial journal *Forbes Magazine*. His magazine (still the centre of a family dynasty), a host of books and countless newspaper columns leave little to be said here about a man whose early days were spent as an odd-job farmhand around what he always called a 'wee Heilan' hamlet.'

He went to the village school until he decided to learn shorthand when he was 13. He might have aspired to be a journalist but even his local paper wasn't ready for a 13-year-old reporter so he settled for a job as an apprentice compositor and worked in hot metal for three years before the *Dundee Courier* gave him a break and the princely wage of a pound a week. It was an early lesson in financial management. He also took night classes at University College and that helped him with his first move up the journalistic ladder to become a senior reporter, subeditor and occasional leader writer. He firmly established his personal byline: B.C. Forbes, though his proper name was Robert.

When he came of age, he decided to strike out for bigger and better things. He emigrated to South Africa, where he found himself in the middle of the Boer War and somehow talked his way into becoming the war correspondent for *Johannesburg Standard and Digger's News*. At the end of the war, the paper's print works were requisitioned by the British government so young Bertie promptly took his talent to the new *Rand Daily Mail* which was coincidently being established in the city at the time. Another new boy was the young Edgar Wallace (whose first job had been selling newspapers in Fleet Street at the age of 11). The two effectively took editorial control of the fledgling newspaper and quickly established it as the country's strongest liberal voice.

With the job well done, Bertie returned to Scotland but stayed barely a year before striking out for New York. Although he was still only 24, his background and experience landed him a job with the prestigious *Journal of Commerce*. Within a year he had become the financial editor. It was clear his future lay in the business sector. He moved on to Hearst's *New York American* where he wrote a syndicated business and finance column that continued long after he had left to found his own magazine. He joined forces with an experienced publisher and 1917 saw the first issue of *Forbes: Devoted to Doers and Doings*. It was perhaps not the slickest of titles but it sold… and the rest is well-documented history.

During the grim days of the First World War, censorship and its impact on freedom of the press was a major issue for journalists around the world, and at the forefront of the campaign was Scotsman Robert – later Sir Robert – Donald (born Banffshire, 1860–1933). He was chair of the Empire Press Union from 1915 to 1926 and took on the world's most senior politicians in tense debates about the role of the press. Among them, of course, was Lloyd George. Initially the two were good friends but, as it became clear that Robert Donald was no yes-man and had very strong views on freedom of the press, he suffered the wrath of the prime minister. The effective role he had played in ensuring Lloyd George replaced Asquith in 1916 was of nought. He was consigned to the outer darkness of political circles and, worse, felt compelled to give up his job as editor of the *Daily Chronicle* when Lloyd George headed the consortium that bought the paper!

Back when there was still a warm glow between them, Lloyd George had commissioned Donald to write a report on government propaganda. He completed it in less than a month. His reward was an appointment to serve alongside John Buchan in the secret War Propaganda Bureau and as an advisor to the Department of Information at the very heart of government. A year later, the department became the Ministry of Information under Lord Beaverbrook. Lord Northcliffe was director of propaganda and Robert Donald was director of propaganda in neutral countries.

It was all a long way form Robert Donald's roots. The son of a stonemason, he had to work as a clerk while trying to break into journalism. He peddled bits and pieces to his local paper and as his confidence grew he got a job as reporter on the *Evening News* in Edinburgh. The lure of London was strong and he started the long journey south more in hope than expectation. En route he worked briefly for the *Northampton Echo* but then turned freelance again for his assault on Fleet Street. In 1888 he landed a job on the *Star*, then revelling in its gory coverage of the Whitechapel Murders and its dubbing of Jack the Ripper. Such lurid scribblings were not for Robert. He decided to specialise in the under-reported world of town hall politics.

He had accidentally struck journalistic gold. Local government was a huge sector and it had hitherto gone unreported in any depth in the popular press. He worked hard investigating municipal murk but clearly the subject didn't stand a chance against the gruesome details of the Whitechapel Murders.

Frustrated, he used his extensive contacts book to good effect and created a remarkable legacy that he could scarcely have imagined. In 1893, he launched the specialist *Municipal Journal*, still after more than a century the bible for Britain's town halls. For good measure, he also launched the *Municipal Year Book*, described today as 'the authoritative source book for local government data and developments.' After that, he surprised colleagues by going into public relations as publicity manager for a group of hotels. That dalliance lasted for five years.

But Robert was still hungry for success in the mainstream of journalism. In 1906, he succumbed to temptation. He took on the job of editor of the ailing Liberal newspaper, the *Daily Chronicle*. Winning new readers was a long, hard struggle but after eight years he had turned the paper into the most successful in Fleet Street. His circulation was greater than the combined sales of all his competitors including *The Times*, the *Daily Telegraph*, the *Morning Post*, the *Evening Standard* and the *Daily Graphic*. There was therefore no surprise when he was appointed managing director and a year after that his status within the profession was acknowledged and he became chair of the powerful Empire Press Union.

Donald had carefully positioned the *Chronicle* to support the progressive wing of the Liberal party and that meant backing the aspiring Lloyd George over prime minister Asquith. His reward, in February 1918, was the propaganda job. In taking it, Robert Donald was careful to cover his journalistic back. He issued a press release: 'I could not undertake work of this kind if it interfered with my editorial responsibilities or my political independence or if it did not give me liberty of action within the sphere allotted to me. After all, this is a newspaperman's job. It consists simply of presenting the British case in neutral and allied countries in a form which is at once interesting and informative.' After just two months, however, he resigned. He cited pressure of work but his close colleagues knew he had concluded that propaganda and journalism were incompatible.

It was, of course, that determined independence that led to the schism between the editor and the prime minister. When an army general was sacked for publicly accusing Lloyd George of misleading Parliament over the number of serving soldiers, Robert Donald promptly gave the man a job as his military correspondent. An already angry Lloyd George went ballistic, and took his revenge quickly and brutally. He persuaded the Scottish MP and newspaperman, Sir James Dalziel, and a group of associates to form a consortium to buy the *Daily Chronicle*. The deal was concluded on a Thursday, the new management moved in on the Friday and Donald resigned immediately.

In its editorial the next day, the *Star* said bravely, 'Fleet Street knows the prime minister does not spare those who cross his path,' and the *Morning Post* was equally upfront: 'just as there are other ways of killing a cat than choking it with cream, so there are other ways of silencing newspaper critics than by conferring on them the Order of the British Empire.' A former Liberal MP, Walter Runciman, sent Donald a personal note: 'It is a matter for pride to your friends to have seen the dignified and emphatic manner of your departure from the *Daily Chronicle*. The whole transaction bears the mark of the hands which devised the scheme of political influence from which political opinion has suffered during the last two years.'

Robert Donald was not one for licking his wounds. Within a year he had bought the *Globe* and installed himself once more as the editor. It was to be but a short interlude, however. In 1921, he sold out to the owners of the *Pall Mall Gazette* (which soon afterwards merged the two papers). Probably because it was important to his status within the Empire Press Union, he took on the editorship of the *People*, but also launched into another career as an author of well-received books on the Great War.

Between times, his drift to the political left earned the friendship of Ramsay MacDonald and he was happy to help publicise the nascent Labour party's cause. In 1931, he joined National Labour and edited its party newspaper: the *News-Letter* (which later became *Everyman*). He died two years later at the age of 73. Evidence of how grand the grand old man had become is the title of fellow journalist Henry Taylor's book: *Robert Donald: Being the Authorized Biography of Sir Robert Donald, G.B.E., LL.D., Journalist, Editor and Friend of Statesmen.*

Charles Beattie (born Aberdeen, 1875–1952) was another Scots journalist who made a significant contribution towards the development of Lord Northcliffe's Associated Newspapers empire. Beattie became a journalist after attending Robert Gordon's College and Aberdeen University and, inevitably, made his way to Fleet Street, where he spent most of his career working for the *Daily Mail*. He briefly edited the London *Evening News* after replacing long-time editor Walter J. Evans in 1922, but more importantly he became a long-term confidant of Northcliffe, soon after becoming night editor of *The Daily Mail* in 1915. He developed a close working relationship with Lord Northcliffe, exchanging regular late-night telephone calls keeping him abreast of the paper's fast-moving content. He also ensured the paper reflected his master's voice. His reward was a lucrative directorship of Associated Newspapers.

The serendipitous nature of the journalist's life is epitomised in the crazy career path of William Lang (born Glasgow, 1888–1923). He went from being a trainee lawyer to a journalist, back to the law and then again to journalism, before ending up in the right place at the right time to become a joint editor of the celebrated *Financial Times*. Educated at Dundee High School and then the city's Harris Academy, William trained initially as a lawyer but ducked out of that profession when he was still only 18 and was able to grab a reporter's job on *The Times*. After experiencing the rough and tumble of Fleet Street, he clearly thought he'd made a mistake and went back once more to the dusty law books. This time, however, he kept his options open by doing a bit of freelance journalism. In the end, the lure of the newspaper life got the better of him and in 1912 he took up the post as editor of the Manchester *Weekly Times*.

Three years later, after the start of the Great War, he joined the navy and served with the Grand Fleet during the Battle of Jutland. When he was demobbed in 1919, he wrote a well-received book *A Sea Lawyer's Log* and then various political and economic books. In 1920 he joined the *Liverpool Chronicle* as a leader writer and theatre critic. The following year, he was surprisingly appointed joint editor of the *Financial Times*. He worked alongside the more experienced William Doman. He was in charge during the night and Doman was editor by day. Sadly, he died within two years. In his book *City of London*, social historian David Kynaston wrote: 'He had a good sense of humour beneath his Presbyterian front and was both liked and respected.'

The British Broadcasting Company sprang into life in November 1922 after the government had licensed a group of radio manufacturers to provide a new broadcasting service, and at the helm of a tiny workforce – of four people! – was the pioneering

Scotsman John Reith (born Stonehaven, 1889–1971). It's unclear what the politicians expected of Mr Reith but they certainly got more than they bargained for. He was a towering, glowering influence in the creation of what is, arguably, still the greatest media operator in the world. He is very firmly placed in the pantheon of greats and his record has been examined and re-examined in minute detail in hundreds of books and so again needs little more than a passing reference. I've already declared my 25-year dalliance with Auntie but that is sufficiently removed from the Reith days to allow me to assert my objectivity. In any case, all the great BBC Scots I knew will get a mention in my final chapter, 'Waiting in the wings'. There can be little doubt, anyway, that Reith's role in creating the BBC – and establishing its very definite separation from the political executive – had a seminal influence on journalism and has led inexorably to today's 24/7 news coverage. But that's another book.

Significantly, it was the BBC journalists' impeccably balanced coverage of the General Strike of 1926 – Reith described it as the BBC's 'baptism of fire' – that firmly established the wireless as a source of news. The reward came quickly. Within months of the end of the strike, the *Company* was dissolved and the British Broadcasting *Corporation* was formed, with a royal charter and an august Board of Governors to protect the public interest. For John Reith, that meant he was installed as Corporation boss with the appropriately grand title of director general. His, and it was very much *his*, radio service attracted listeners in ever-increasing numbers throughout the 1930s, developing beyond news into music and drama and becoming central to the British way of life. With a strong whiff of an imperial past, Reith set out to conquer the world by introducing the Empire Service (precursor of the BBC World Service), and when fellow Scot John Logie Baird (born Helensburgh, 1888–1946) successfully demonstrated his newfangled television that was quickly annexed by the BBC. Baird was ranked 44th in a BBC poll of the 100 greatest Brits in 2002 and he was among the ten Scottish scientists inducted to the National Library of Scotland's Science Hall of Fame in 2006. Of Baird's invention, Reith said: 'I think it will be admitted by all, that to have exploited so great a scientific invention for the purpose and pursuit of entertainment alone would have been a prostitution of its powers and an insult to the character and intelligence of the people.'

It was, perhaps, the realisation of the huge power that would be wielded by television as an information medium that led to Reith's demise. He was never short of critics and in the House of Commons, one MP railed: 'The BBC is an autocracy which has outgrown the original autocrat. It has become despotism in decay, the nearest thing in this country to Nazi government. If I talk to any employee of the Corporation, I am made to feel like a conspirator.' Against such criticism, Reith defended himself in the combative royal-we style later adopted by Margaret Thatcher: 'It is occasionally indicated to us that we are apparently setting out to give the public what we think they need and not what they want. But few know what they want and very few what they need. In any case, it is better to overestimate the mentality of the public than to underestimate it.' There would be no dumbing down on his watch.

In 1938, having clashed with successive prime ministers, he was unceremoniously deposed. He was the first – but certainly not the last – public figure to be sacked because his profile threatened to overshadow that of his political masters. It was Neville Chamberlain who wielded the axe, although he sought to limit the damage by appointing him, apparently without irony, chairman of Imperial Airways! Soon after the war started, he was given a seat in the House of Commons and was appointed minister of information. When Churchill arrived at Number Ten in 1940, he went one better and promoted Reith to be minister of transport. Almost inevitably, however, Churchill – himself not short of ego – regretted his generosity, found the fiery Scot too difficult to work with and dispatched him to the House of Lords.

Meanwhile, back at the BBC the poor souls charged with finding Reith's replacement were well aware of the enormity of their task. A newspaper of the day described the Corporation as having grown to 'overwhelming imperial importance' The corporation was deeply entrenched within the British establishment. On the domestic front, it produced and broadcast radio programmes to over eight million British homes and uniquely also broadcast a shortwave service to the far-flung outposts of the Empire; and, of course, there was a fledgling television service that would eventually come to fully exploit Logie Baird's invention.

Out of a ruck of possible candidates, the board of governors chose another Scot, Frederick Wolff Ogilvie (born Edinburgh, 1893–1949), to succeed Reith as director general. He was described by the newspapers as the 'dark-horse candidate' for the £37,500 job, but the board had previously decided that they wanted an academic – an educator, they said – and the 45-year-old Professor Ogilvie clearly met their requirements. He was a distinguished economist and academic who had lectured at Oxford and Edinburgh before becoming president and vice chancellor of Queen's University, Belfast. He was also a First World War veteran who has lost an arm in battle. Despite that, wrote the clearly admiring journalists, 'he drives an automobile, flies a plane and plays a fair golf game.' They seemed unperturbed that he had never broadcast and the nearest he'd so far got to the BBC was when his 12-year-old son had written a play that won a spot on a Northern Ireland children's programme. *The Times* said: 'Director General Ogilvie comes to the BBC at a time when there is talk of spending millions to double Broadcasting House facilities, when the daring television venture needs careful nursing, when BBC's critics are calling for a return of the human element to their efficient but relatively austere radio machine.'

Professor Ogilvie shrewdly declined to forecast what he planned to do in his new job: 'I am not director-general until October and I hope to be in cold storage until then,' he said. For the *Daily Mail*, of course, that seemed evidence he would perpetuate the Reithian tradition of 'aloof frigidity'; it carped, 'we do not want any more sphinxes at Broadcasting House. The BBC is an organisation paid for and designed for the ordinary listener and is not an Egyptian desert.' But in Belfast the DG-to-be had a very unsphinxlike reputation. When the 80 bricklayers, plasterers, painters and sundry other craftsmen and labourers had completed extensive renovation work on the elegant residence he was to occupy as vice chancellor, they and their wives were his first guests! He further established an excellent reputation for his people skills by getting to know the first names not just of his professors but all the assistants and researchers too. He held regular receptions and 'always provided really good dance music'. At weekends he could be seen on the touchline at the Gaelic football matches cheering on the university's teams. All that clearly outweighed his controversial (in the tense days immediately before the outbreak of the Second World War) pacifist convictions and his refusal to let the university's officers' training corps take part in the Armistice Day celebrations. A note in the BBC Archives records that under him the corporation 'caught the mood of the nation and forged stronger bonds than ever with audiences.' While he didn't have quite the same impact as Reith, he did introduce new foreign language services which helped the BBC to establish 'an unrivalled reputation as a source people could trust.'

He also made what was later described as an inspired appointment. For the job of head of the German service, he recruited an academic colleague and fellow Scot, Lindley Fraser (born Edinburgh, 1904–63). Fraser was given leave of absence from Aberdeen University. He spoke German fluently – with a distinct Edinburgh accent – and soon won a large following among listeners in Germany. By the end of the war he had become a national institution to his German audience. He was so convinced the BBC's German service could play a valuable role in the rebuilding of post-war Germany that he resigned his chair at Aberdeen University in 1945. He was promoted to director of the German service in 1947 and head of German programmes in February 1948. He died of cancer in 1963.

Andrew Caird (born Montrose, 1870–1956) lived up to many Sassenachs' image of a Scot – dour and tight-fisted. He was night editor of the *Daily Mail* in the 1920s and it has to be said there was much of the night about him: he bestrode the editorial floor dressed in a black morning-coat, pipe clenched firmly in his mouth and a constant glower on his face. He saw himself as Lord Northcliffe's man and scrutinised every aspect of expenditure, acting, as he saw it, as 'the brake man on his lordship's generosity.' He clearly wasn't too subtle in his fiscal management and 'indulged in a vulgarity and brusqueness the boss didn't appreciate.' Lord Northcliffe apparently even talked with his brother (Lord Rothermere) about getting rid of him in 1909, but ultimately stayed his hand… and clearly had cause to rejoice. Two years later he said Caird was one of the strongest members of his team and chose him to accompany him on the British War Mission to the United States. When Northcliffe returned, Caird stayed behind to head the administration of the mission's New York Office. He acquitted himself so well that he came home to a knighthood! Soon afterwards and now Sir Andrew, he resumed his prowling tenure of the *Daily Mail* night shift until, in 1922, an ailing Lord Northcliffe made him managing director and vice chairman of Associated Newspapers. He stayed on for four years after Lord Northcliffe's death. In 1927, he left the UK to become editor and managing director of the *Statesman* in Calcutta.

Johnny Campbell (1894–1969) was yet another Paisley boy who, as editor of the *Daily Worker* (now the *Morning Star*), combined politics and journalism in a heady mix. He was a Communist activist and in 1924, he was charged over the publication of a letter, seen by many as an incitement to mutiny among the armed forces. In what was called *An Open Letter to Fighting Forces*, published on 25 July 1924, an anonymous writer called on the armed forces to unite to form 'the nucleus of an organisation that will prepare the whole of the soldiers, sailors and airmen, not merely to refuse to go to war, or to refuse to shoot strikers during industrial conflicts but will make it possible for the workers, peasants and soldiers and airmen to go forward in a common attack upon the capitalists and smash capitalism for ever and institute the reign of the whole working class.' In what became known as the Campbell Case, the publication of the letter had dramatic consequences. Labour's first prime minister Ramsay MacDonald engineered withdrawal of the prosecution of Campbell, then refused to allow an inquiry, went on to make it a matter of confidence in his fledgling government and crashed to defeat after just nine months in office. Stanley Baldwin added to the political drama when he made it a key issue in his Conservative manifesto at the ensuing general election. He wrote: 'The refusal to allow any inquiry inevitably suggests that the result of such investigation would only have been to emphasise the conclusions that the course of justice had been deflected by partisan considerations and to increase the public anxiety.' He had a landslide victory.

Johnny Campbell was only 18 when he joined the British Socialist party in 1912. At the outset of the First World War, he joined the Navy; he was wounded in action and won the Military Medal 'for bravery in battle.' After the war, he returned to Scotland and joined the Clyde Workers Committee and for three years edited its newspaper, the *Worker*. He was a founder member of the Communist party and served on its Central Committee from 1923. Shortly afterwards he and fellow Clydesider Willie Gallacher (later Britain's only Communist party MP) were elected as joint secretaries of the British Bureau of the Red International of Labour Unions. In 1924, he went south to London to edit the *Workers' Weekly*.

The Campbell Case did nothing to diminish his left-wing determination. He continued to write and publish aggressive articles and within a year he was one of twelve CP members in the dock of the Old Bailey. Once again the charge was brought under the Incitement to Mutiny Act. This time the verdict was guilty and Campbell was sentenced to six months in prison. He was saved from the full term by the 1926 General Strike and, undeterred, he joined the executive of Communist International in 1928, became foreign editor of the *Daily Worker* in 1932 and editor in 1939.

When war was declared, Johnny Campbell was confused by the emergence of the Hitler-Stalin pact and when he spoke against labeling it 'an imperialist war between two equally-guilty capitalist nations,' he was booted out of his editor's job. It wasn't until Hitler invaded the USSR in June 1941 that he was reinstated as a force within the party and another eight years before he again became editor of the *Daily Worker*.

During his ten years at the helm, he supported the 1956 Soviet invasion of Hungary but he condemned invasion of Czechoslovakia in 1968.

When James Drawbell (born Falkirk, 1899–1979) was appointed editor-in-chief of William Berry's *Sunday Chronicle* in 1925, there were many raised eyebrows. He was just 26 and the youngest senior executive ever to reach such dizzy heights since 23-year-old James Delane had taken over *The Times* 80 years earlier. It was a spectacular achievement, but then, Drawbell had journalism in his blood. His maternal grandfather was owner and editor of the *Bo'ness Journal* and he was brought up among the thundering presses. More than that, he had amazing life experience. He was one of a family of six and had had to fend for himself from an early age. His father was over-fond of the booze and the family suffered constant marital conflict and teetered on the edge of poverty. When his father suddenly disappeared to the colonies the family was uprooted and moved to Edinburgh, where the young James was able to attend a decent school, although university was never an option. In 1916, already two long years into First World War and as soon as he was old enough, James enlisted in the Royal Scots Fusiliers and cheerfully served for the duration.

Back in Edinburgh, he found it impossible to find a job in newspapers so he and a friend decided to emigrate to Canada. He must have got his wires crossed because he ended up in Montreal where jobs for journalists who couldn't speak French were in short supply. Still undaunted, he crossed the border to America and headed for New York. There his luck changed. He worked for various newspapers and discovered his reporter's status also gave him access to the heady world of celebrity. He rubbed shoulders with Noël Coward, F. Scott Fitzgerald and a host of others then on the equivalent of today's A-list.

He had packed a lot into a short period, so, at the ripe old age of 23, he felt ready for Fleet Street and recrossed the Atlantic. His first job was not in newspapers but with the popular if somewhat jingoistic *John Bull* magazine. The editor at the time was Geoffrey Williamson. He was also an author, his wife was descended from Welsh kings and he was at the heart of the British establishment. Once again the young Drawbell found himself surrounded by the elite. He enjoyed this association with big names and it was to be a hallmark of his career. He was in exactly the right place when Edward Hulton (the founder's son) sold the *Sunday Chronicle* to Allied Newspapers and they moved the printing from its original Manchester base to London, bringing with it a vacancy for an editor. The new owner, William Berry (later Viscount Camrose) was looking for someone to enliven the newspaper, which despite its title was published on Saturday and Sunday! James Drawbell – with his American experience, his substantial contacts book and his abundance of youthful energy – seemed to fit the bill. For his part, the very young Scot was determined to prove himself. He saw the Sunday newspaper as the ideal canvas: 'On Sunday, half the day is spent in an examination of all the papers and the other half is the necessary unwinding of the human machine.' It was the chance he'd been looking for. He revelled in his elevated status as editor-in-chief and set about revitalising the newspaper. He wanted it to be contemporary and relevant to its readers' lifestyles. He wrote: 'The one fatal thing for a journalist is aloofness or detachment. His greatest strength is an awareness of current activities, trends, prejudices, discontents and satisfactions.'

He was ready to be provocative when the occasion demanded and readily threw his pages open to a very wide range of contributors. That's where his contacts book came in very handy. In addition to American friends like Scott Fitzgerald, it now included George Bernard Shaw, D. H. Lawrence, Margot Asquith, Winston Churchill and Leon Trotsky. All graced his pages at one time or another.

When Jacob Epstein, later said to 'take the brickbats for modern art', scandalised the art world with his interpretation of *Rima* in London's Kensington Gardens, James Drawbell was alone in offering him column space to explain his work. However, D.H. Lawrence's *Lady Chatterley's Lover* was a step too far. Soon after it was published in Florence in 1928 and while it was still banned in Britain, Drawbell was sent a copy, presumably in the hope of finding some understanding from the adventurous editor. Despite their friendship, the Scot seemed outraged by the blurring of class boundaries and damned the book as 'a falsification.'

He encouraged Monica Dickens in her literary aspirations and he bought the rights to dancer Isadora Duncan's memoirs. He paid her a handsome £300, thereby funding her love for fast cars and long scarves! There was, of course, a much more serious side to the newspaper too, and the editor-in-chief engaged directly with British and world politicians all the way to Adolf Hitler. Although Churchill was in the political wilderness at the time, the *Sunday Chronicle* urged its readers to take heed of his warning about Nazi Germany and campaigned for rearmament for an inevitable war. The paper's anti-Nazi stance was formidable and the likes of Trotsky were wheeled in to dispel the notion – held by too many of the establishment – that Herr Hitler harboured no ill will towards Britain. Drawbell firmly endorsed his Berlin correspondent's warning: 'Hitler is fanatical and ruthless . . . he is a real menace to the British Empire and to world peace.'

James Drawbell spent 21 years in the editor's chair, but in 1946 he felt the need for a change and became managing editor and consultant to a magazine publishing group. He also published a series of books and once more took advantage of his contacts to reflect on a fascinating journalistic career which had taken him through war and peace.

Ian Fleming couldn't have invented a character like Robert Bruce Lockhart (born Anstruther, 1887–1970). He claimed ancestry from half a dozen clans including the Bruces and the Wallaces and often asserted, 'there is no drop of English blood in my veins.' He was variously a rubber planter in Malaya, a diplomat in Moscow and Prague, an author, a spy who rubbed shoulders with Trotsky, a propagandist and a footballer who won a medal in the Russian championship. But he appears in this chapter because he was also a brilliant journalist and close confidant of Lord

Beaverbrook. At one stage he claimed to be writing more than 400,000 words a year for the *Evening Standard*, the *Daily Express* and *Sunday Express*, but was seemingly finding few of his Fleet Street colleagues to his liking: 'This is no place for me. With very few exceptions, I loathe and despise everyone connected with it… and the exceptions are the failures.' Nor was he especially enamoured of the job and often railed: 'I feel nailed to my desk.'

It's fair to say that journalism hadn't been part of his game plan. After a hair-raising lifestyle, he seemed to have settled on becoming an author and it was in that capacity he was invited to write the memoirs of Lord Beaverbrook in 1926. In the course of the subsequent conversations, Beaverbrook inveigled him into writing occasional paragraphs for the *Evening Standard*'s 'Londoner's Diary' gossip pages. These proved to be very amusing and very popular with the readers. His reward was a massive £2,000 a-year offer to be a leader writer on the *Daily Express*. He declined.

Beaverbrook, of course, was not prepared to accept defeat. Bruce Lockhart became editor of the Londoner's Diary and found himself also writing leaders. He only escaped four years later by becoming Beaverbrook's chief propagandist in his epic Empire Free Trade Crusade (for which he added the famous crusader logo to the masthead of the *Daily Express*). He produced all the leaflets and provided all the data to make the Free Trade case. That could have been the end of Lockhart's journalistic career, but when his successor as editor of the Londoner's Diary resigned in 1931, he succumbed to pressure and returned to the fray. He soldiered on for six more years. But, emotionally exhausted, he resigned in the summer of 1937 and later wrote: 'I left Fleet Street – I hope – forever.'

Robert Bruce Lockhart was educated at Fettes College and at the Sorbonne in Paris. From there he headed east to Malaya where he found rubber-planting wasn't as easy as it had sounded. He didn't stay long and beat a retreat to the Foreign Office, whence he was swiftly posted to Moscow as a vice consul. His term there had seriously comic overtones. Somehow, he got tangled up in the CV of his brother John, a Cambridge rugby blue. Unaware of the difference between rugger and soccer, the Russians pressed him into playing for a Moscow factory team. Ever the diplomat, he bravely turned out in baggy shorts and the shirt of Morozaov FC and in true boys'-own-adventure style, helped them win the championship and collected a medal for his efforts. It may, of course, have been part of his plan to keep a close eye on the revolutionary ferment of the time. He was acting consul general during the first uprising of summer 1917 but was then recalled to London before the October Revolution. It was Lloyd George who sent him back to Moscow as our first envoy to the Bolsheviks and with a brief to counter the growing influence of the Germans. He was charged with persuading the Soviets to accommodate the Japanese army as a bulwark on the Eastern Front. When straightforward diplomacy didn't work, Bruce Lockhart resorted to an alternative approach… and was revealed as a spy implicated in a plot to assassinate Lenin. As he waited in the Kremlin to meet his fate, he was dramatically saved by skilful diplomacy and exchanged for Maksim Litvinov, a Russian being held in London. He later recounted some of these experiences in his autobiography, *Memoirs of a British Agent*, published in 1932.

After giving up the grind of daily journalism in 1937, he resumed his favourite role as a full-time author, although he was lured back to the *Evening Standard* to produce expert pieces on Czechoslovakia and the Munich crisis. When war broke out in 1939, he rejoined the Foreign Office as director general of the Political Warfare Executive and later acted as liaison officer to the Czech government-in-exile. It was for these wartime services that he was knighted in 1943. After the war, he again returned to writing books but added further strings to his bow: he lectured and – for ten years - presented a weekly programme about Czechoslovakia on the BBC World Service. He died in 1970 at the age of 83.

It's never easy following in the footsteps of the great but that didn't deter David Pendrigh (born Edinburgh, 1868–1932) from taking on the top job at world-famous Reuters – and doing it his way. He changed the reporting style laid down by Julius Reuter, having worked his way up from the newsroom floor to the top spot as editor-in-chief.

He told the staff he was fed up with their tendency to wait to see what the newspapers were reporting as they had been doing for the previous 80 years and more. He issued an edict demanding 'an end to telegrams beginning with the formula [used since the founder's days], "*Le Matin* says... "' Luckily for him, he had the full backing of his chairman, Sir Roderick Jones, who said of him: 'It is difficult to envisage the editorial department without Pendrigh. He was one of the most brilliant men at his task it has ever been my privilege to meet.' After Heriot-Watt College, David Pendrigh became a reporter on the *Edinburgh Evening News* but then, like so many young Scottish journalists before him, he headed for London when he was 26. Instead of joining any of the Fleet Street papers, however, he joined Reuters as a night editor, though in the 24-hour-a-day operation it was sometimes difficult to work out what 'night' meant. When he was promoted to dominions editor, he set about sharpening up the missives from his reporters in far-flung places. He went on to become associate editor and in 1931, joint managing director, just a year before he died.

They say today's news is tomorrow's history. One story proving the point is that of Francis Low (born Aberdeen, 1893–1972). He had a front-row seat in what we now know to be a turning point in the history of the British Empire. As editor of the *Times of India* between 1932 and 1948, he charted the nation's rocky path to independence and reported every eventful day leading up to the sub-continent nation's self-determination. He clearly immersed himself in India's affairs of state and managed to make himself amenable to nationalist leaders and British politicians alike. As an unofficial go-between, his sources were impeccable and he was able to translate that into brilliant journalism and in those days of ferment was also able to consolidate the *Times'* reputation and build it into the biggest-selling newspaper on the sub-continent.

He arrived in Bombay in 1922 and became a lowly subeditor on the *Times of India*. His talent and energy were quickly spotted and the following year he was promoted to edit the sister paper, the *Evening News of India*. After two successful years in charge, he returned to the morning paper in the key post of news editor, fulcrum for the fast-flowing reports that plotted the pains and the pleasures of the birth of a new nation. From his early journalistic days in India, he had seen and reported on the growing demands for swaraj (self-rule). By 1932, when Low became the *Times*' editor, he knew many British politicians were already convinced India should develop as a self-determining dominion within the Empire. He also knew there were too many others of a different view and he had to report on too many conferences begun in hope that later ended in stalemate. He saw the beginning of the non-violent, non-cooperation movement led by Gandhi and watched it growing ever stronger despite the determined opposition of Winston Churchill, who described him as a 'half-naked fakir'. He charted every twist and turn through to independence in 1947. He was still in the editor's chair when Gandhi was assassinated in January 1948.

Educated at Robert Gordon's College, Francis Low had joined the *Aberdeen Free Press* as a reporter in 1910 and worked assiduously learning the rudiments of journalism. After wartime service in the Gordon Highlanders, he picked up the pieces with the *Free Press* and within a year had been promoted to chief reporter. In 1922, however, he got itchy feet and struck out for India. Like all great editors, he sought to be part of the community within which he lived and worked. He was particularly pleased to be elected as president of Bombay YMCA (1943–48) and his chairmanship of the Indian region of the Commonwealth Press Union underlined his pre-eminence in the region's journalism. When he returned to the UK in 1948 he collected a well-earned knighthood and wrote his memoirs, *Struggle for India*, published in 1955.

Considering the reputation earned by journalists, one unfortunate Scot might be considered unlucky to have lost his job due to persistent drunkenness in the strange pre-war years of the 1930s! Gerald Aylmer Vallance (born Partick, 1892–1955) was editor of the liberal *News Chronicle* for three years before he resigned after pressure from his own subeditors, who presumably got fed up covering his back with the paper's proprietors, the non-drinking Cadbury family. His less-than-enthusiastic support for the Liberal party (the paper's normal alignment) probably didn't help much either. (He later revealed his own political instincts when he named his son Tito, after the communist leader of Yugoslavia.)

However, when he first joined the paper in 1933, he did as every new editor should. He shook things up. He openly criticised Oswald Moseley and exposed many of his well-known supporters in the British Union of Fascists. He also spotted the talents of a young Geoffrey Cox, who he sent to Madrid to report on the Spanish Civil War, working in partnership with Arthur Koestler. While Koestler was using his correspondent's role as a front to spy on the Franco regime, Geoffrey Cox was honing the skills that would take him to be editor-in-chief of ITN and creator of its *News at Ten* bulletin. Vallance had a strong reputation before joining the *News Chronicle* – he was assistant editor on the *Economist* for three years – and that obviously survived the displeasure of the Cadbury family because he went on to be finance editor of the *New Statesman* and wrote regularly for the London *Evening Standard*.

For most people, being shipwrecked by an enemy torpedo and tossed about in an open boat on the icy-cold Atlantic Ocean would have been a grim experience. For journalist James Bone (born Glasgow, 1872–1962), however, it was just another day at the office. He had a story to tell and he filled his notebook with a detailed account of that time during the Second World War when, he wrote, 'the line between wives and widows was very close.' Bone was returning from a visit to the United States and was aboard the MV *Western Prince* when it was pounced on by the German *U-96*. In the initial attack, eight crewmen and six of the 60 passengers were lost. The casualty list could have been much greater but the U-boat captain held off his second strike until he could see the rest of the passengers and crew were in the lifeboats. Despite his parlous situation, James Bone reverted to his reporter's role and made assiduous notes that were to later appear in the *Manchester Guardian*.

He had begun his working life in a Glasgow shipping office until he was able to escape and join his father on the *North British Daily Mail*, Scotland's first daily paper, launched in 1847. Sadly, in 1901 it was absorbed into the *Daily Record* and he had to go job-hunting. Like so many others, he was forced south of the border. It took him nearly a year before he landed what turned out to be, literally, the job a lifetime. It was in the bosom of the London office of the *Manchester Guardian*, where he stayed for the rest of his career. Not long after his thirtieth birthday he was made the London editor. He worked assiduously at keeping provincial readers au fait with the happenings in the capital and his London Letter became the most influential of all the regional epistles. He was rewarded with a directorship in 1919. He retired at the end of the war and was appointed a Companion of Honour in 1947. His younger brother was Sir Muirhead Bone (1876–1953), Britain's first official war artist, whose knighthood, also in 1947, was for services to art.

Briefly the editor of the *Daily Telegraph* in 1923, Fred Miller (born Dundee, 1863–1924) was almost as keen a golfer as he was skilled a journalist. Sadly, an accident on the links seriously curtailed his career. In what proved to be a very expensive round, a stray ball hit him full in the face and caused him to lose an eye. That was in 1885, soon after he had been appointed chief subeditor on the paper, which he had joined from the *Scotsman*. The high-stress top table of a national newspaper was no place for someone with a serious disability and his sympathetic editor, the great Sir John Sage, found him a less-demanding role as a roving reporter. When that didn't really work out, he was brought back to the newsroom as assistant to the editor. Overcoming all the problems associated with his limited sight, he became Sir John's right-hand man, with the title of chief assistant. But that's not a role likely to satisfy any journalist and Fred Miller tirelessly strove to get back into the front line… literally.

Nearly 20 years after his accident, in 1914, he was appointed assistant editor and immediately after the outbreak of the First World War, he went to Paris to organise the paper's war reporting. Although he continued to distinguish himself on the paper's behalf, he was in the wrong place at the wrong time: in the shadow of Fleet Street's longest-serving editor. He had to wait until Sir John finally retired – after 40 years – in 1923 before becoming editor. By then he was already 60, and he died suddenly just a little more than a year later, before he could put his own stamp on the paper.

One of the most distinguished of Britain's war correspondents was Kilmarnock-born Alexander Berry Austin (1903–43), who was killed by a German shell on Italy's notorious Road of Death. His last report was published in the *Daily Herald* the day before news of his death reached the paper. Austin – known as AB – joined the London *Morning Post* straight out of Edinburgh University. Initially he was an assistant librarian but he quickly became a reporter and during the next twelve years he graduated to being a parliamentary sketch writer. When the paper was merged with the *Daily Telegraph* in 1837, he left and worked as a reporter on the *Daily Herald* until the outbreak of war. He was commissioned into the RAF and became a wing-commander in the press section of Fighter Command. After the Battle of Britain, he rejoined the *Herald* as its air correspondent and later war correspondent. He took this job very seriously and went through training with the Commandos. He was the only journalist with them on the Dieppe raid in 1942 and his graphic reports on the front-line fighting earned him respect around the world. His book about it – *We Landed at Dawn* – was a best-seller.

In 1943, he joined the First Army and stayed with it throughout the Tunisian campaign. He transferred to the Fifth Army, landed at Salerno and joined the trek to Naples. This was along the 'Road of Death,' as he described it in his final dispatches, which also recorded the 'relentless courage' of the foot soldiers. He was with a press group when they arrived at the town of Scafati, only 15 miles from Milan, behind the advancing troops. They waited while the infantry cleared the side streets of straggling Germans. When church bells rang out and the townsfolk emerged to cheer the British troops, Alex Austin watched the celebrations with two other reporters, Stewart Sale of Reuters and William Munday of the *News Chronicle*. As BBC correspondent Frank Gillard recalled, 'things looked absolutely safe.' Suddenly, a German tank appeared from nowhere and opened up with its heavy gun. The reporters scattered. For Alex Austin, standing casually at a street corner and soaking up the atmosphere with the two other correspondents, it was too late. A shell exploded among them and all three died instantly. They were buried alongside each other in Salerno war cemetery and a memorial service for them was held a month later at St Dunstan-in-the-West Church in Fleet Street. St Bride's, the newspapermen's church next door to Reuters HQ, had been left roofless by German bombing.

Peter Ritchie Calder (born Forfar, 1907–82) was yet another journalist who found it easy to mix his job with his political passions. He went to the local academy and opted to go into journalism at the age of 15 when he became a junior reporter on the *Dundee Courier*. After a stint with the DC Thompson Group's Glasgow office, he went to London to work variously for the *Daily News*, the *Daily Chronicle* and the *Daily Herald*. As a socialist, he was most at home with the *Herald* and he stayed there from 1930, specialising in writing pioneering articles on popular science and sociology. Then he wrote vividly about the Blitz and published *Carry on London* about the courage and stoicism of the city's beleaguered people. In 1941, he joined the Foreign Office's top-secret foreign propaganda unit, the Political Warfare Executive (PWE) and a year later he was appointed director of plans and campaigns working with Robert Bruce Lockhart, who called him 'one of the best brains in the organisation.' He helped develop radio propaganda at the BBC, including for key military initiatives such as Operation Torch (the allied invasion of north-west Africa) and Operation Overlord (the D-Day landings). His wartime work earned him the CBE in 1945.

After the war, he returned to Fleet Street as science editor for the *News Chronicle* and happily stayed there for more than ten years writing about science, internationalism and the peace movement. He broke the story of the discovery of the structure of DNA. His political and sociological interests took over in 1956 and he joined fellow Scot John Boyd-Orr at the UN's Food and Agricultural Organisation and travelled throughout Africa and south-east Asia on special projects aimed at easing world hunger. In 1960, he became only the third Briton to win UNESCO's Kalinga Prize for the popularisation of science. He was following in the mighty footsteps of Julian Huxley (1953) and Bertrand Russell (1957). Later recipients include Arthur C. Clarke, Fred Hoyle, David Attenborough and, in 1972, Ritchie Calder's own son Nigel. The following year he became professor of international relations at Edinburgh University and, later, president of the National Peace Council and president of the CND. In 1966, he was made a life peer and went to the House of Lords with the glorious title of Baron Ritchie-Calder of Balmashanner in the Royal Burgh of Forfar.

Before he rose to the dizzy heights of the editorship of Reuters, arguably the world's greatest news-gathering operation, Doon Campbell (born Annan, 1920–2003) distinguished himself as one of the youngest and bravest of the reporters who covered the Second World War from the front line and the first allied war reporter ashore on D-Day. He got himself attached to Lord Lovat's Commandos in the invasion of Normandy in 1944 and found himself in a landing craft that crashed through surging waves onto Sword Beach. His huge commando backpack carried a portable typewriter amid his survival gear. He said he took a deep breath to calm his jangling nerves and then, trying to ignore German shell and mortar, plunged into the water – careless of the handicap of having had only one arm from birth – and scrambled ashore.

He was just 24 and the sight that met him on the beach was horrendous. In his first dispatch, which he datelined 'a ditch 200 yards inside Normandy', he wrote: 'It was a sandy cemetery of the unburied dead, where bodies lay scattered with arms or legs severed.' Later, he wrote, 'it is a miracle that I am alive to write this story, that I have survived 24 hours on this bridgehead bag of wicked tricks. Bombs, shells, bullets and mines to say nothing of booby traps, make each hour an age of grim experience… Most of my 24 hours have been spent lying flat out on my front burrowing into sand or earth, the good earth.' That and all his other reports were rushed back across the Channel by the navy and these added to his ever-growing reputation. He became a legend in his own wartime. From Normandy, he hitched a lift with the elite US 17th Airborne Division and flew through heavy enemy flak perched on boxes of grenades in a glider that crash-landed on the far side of the Rhine. For that escapade, the Americans awarded him their distinctive Glider Wings and Combat Star.

Doon Campbell was the younger son of a Dumfriesshire church minister and went to school locally before going on to George Watson's College, Edinburgh. Instead of university, he became a reporter when he was just 18, working on the *Linlithgowshire Gazette*. He then went on to the *West Lothian Courier* and the *Edinburgh Evening Dispatch*. In 1943, he couldn't resist the lure of London and a job at Reuters, offered by a burly, charismatic fellow Scot, Walton Cole, who was then the agency's managing editor but went on to become general manager. In the confusion of war, young Doon rose spectacularly through the reporters' ranks and within the year was a frontline war correspondent. After the German surrender, the still-hungry Doon headed east to find out what was happening in China in the struggle between nationalists and Communists. Reminding himself that if you don't ask you don't get, he spectacularly asked and wrung out a rare interview with Mao. The more pedestrian old hands in China were left flat-footed and not amused by his pugnacity. As the world's attention shifted to India in early 1948, so did Doon Campbell's and he was in the country when Gandhi was assassinated. He wasn't an eye witness but he was quickly on the telephone to an Indian reporter who was. That enabled him to send a dispatch that was later regarded as a classic of international news agency journalism: 'FLASH Double Urgent Gandhi shot four times at point-blank range worst feared.' After that he headed back to London – via a short spell in Paris – to inevitable promotion into the management structure at the Fleet Street headquarters.

In 1963 and still only 43, he became editor of the global news-gathering agency. At the time, Reuters was growing and developing into a business empire, but as Campbell later wrote in his autobiography *Magic Mistress – A 30-year Affair with Reuters*: 'The only thing that ever mattered to me was the story. The news – how to convey even a detail of the mighty mosaic – transcended everything.' When the agency was floated as a public company, he left to join another great Scot, Lord Barnetson at United Newspapers, of whom more below. Campbell was made an OBE in 1984 and died in 2003.

Bill Barnetson was a remarkable Scottish journalist and responsible for the post-war launch of one of Germany's greatest newspapers and, partially, the career of an ambitious young German called Axel Springer, whose media empire became the biggest in twentieth-century Europe. Barnetson (born Edinburgh, 1917–81) was 28 and a veteran of five years in the Anti-Aircraft Command when he was summoned to the War Office soon after the end of the Second World War and asked to help restart West Germany's shattered newspaper and publishing industry. The history books tell it all: he found Axel Springer, pointed him in the right direction and lit the blue touch-paper on a revolution in post-war German journalism. But as dazzling as that was, it didn't outshine Bill Barnetson's own career. From being a 19-year-old freelance correspondent in the Spanish Civil War, he climbed through the ranks of journalism to leader writer, editor, managing director, proprietor, chairman of the *Observer*, chairman of Reuters and chairman of Thames Television. That's only a very rough outline of his career, during which he also managed to hold regular lunches at London's Savoy, where the guests included royalty, cabinet ministers, diplomats, financiers, academics and fellow newspapermen. The lunches were part of his journalist's instinct to develop 'contacts' and they became an established part of the London social scene. I could only watch from afar with envy. Whatever he did, he retained his newspaperman persona. He kept a battered typewriter in his office and was often seen battering the keyboard, writing articles and speeches through the fug from his ancient briar pipe.

Bill Barnetson attending Edinburgh's Royal High School but interrupted his studies at Edinburgh University to hone his journalistic skills in the Spanish Civil War. After Spain, he returned to Edinburgh with just enough time to complete his degree course and get married before he was off again – this time to join the army and serve as an artillery major. After ensuring Axel Springer was the 'fit and proper person' the War Office wanted to revive the German press, he returned to Edinburgh in 1948. He joined the *Evening News* and was successively leader writer, editor and general manager. In a further display of his phenomenal energy and enthusiasm, he lectured at the university and became a regular pundit on radio and television.

He was very much an early bird and one morning he had barely settled behind his typewriter in the still-deserted offices when he was surprised by a visit from an equally bright-eyed businessman. Just off the night sleeper from London, Harley Drayton was a financier and proprietor of United Newspapers, and he had a proposition. He was keen to expand his newspaper interests and he thought Bill Barnetson was the man to help him. Happily, Bill agreed. He became a director of United Newspapers in 1962 and over the following four years, developed plans for the conglomerate of evening and weekly papers around the country. He caught the acquisition bug. After his partner died in 1966 he became chairman, and within three years had doubled the size of the company through the takeover of the *Yorkshire Post* and *Punch* magazine.

He became chairman of Reuters in 1968 and during his 11 years in charge the agency's turnover rose more than tenfold and the company developed into a worldwide business and economic information service that caters for almost every financial market in the world. He sat on numerous boards including Argus Press and the Press

Association. From 1973 he was a member of the *Times* Trust, became chairman of the *Observer* in 1976 and chairman of Thames Television in 1979. He also found time to serve on the Press Council and the boards of the Open University, English National Opera and the Queen's Silver Jubilee Appeal. Bill Barnetson became Sir William in 1972 and three years later went to the House of Lords as Baron Barnetson. He died in 1981.

11

WAITING IN THE WINGS

'The moment you doubt whether you can fly, you cease for ever to be able to do it.'
— *J.M Barrie*

With the disintegration of the British Empire in mind, one has to ask of the future of this Scottish Empire, to which I've hopefully given some historical substance. Have we seen the best of our restless race? Has our course been run? Do we doubt our ability to fly? I think the answer is a resounding *no*, because there is no shortage of prominent Scots in the latter part of the twentieth century and the beginning of the twenty-first. However, because they have not yet been subjected to the brutal test of time, I have listed them only as probable greats with some clearly more probable than others. Nowhere is my caution more justified than in the banking and financial sector, where high-octane careers have been hitting the bumpers since 2008. The febrile political world has also provided proof that we need the passage of time before we commit our perceived heroes to the history books. I hope this final chapter, which in many areas bears a striking resemblance to the first, will reinforce my thesis that there will always be one Scot or another, untroubled by doubt and making history or being made by history in the twenty-first and future centuries.

While at home the bruising argument about Scotland's place within the UK gathers pace and passion ahead of the 2014 referendum, there are Scots continuing to play key roles in almost every aspect of contemporary endeavour on the world stage and I am happy to use this final chapter to nominate a few of *tomorrow's* great Scots. Argue if you will but marvel at their achievements from this closer historical perspective – the last half century – and then add your own nominees… for a future edition! Again, the numbers are so great that I can only seek to whet the appetite with brief notes and name checks to highlight the richness of talent ready to take its place in tomorrow's history books. En passant, I apologise to all those Scots whose fame and fortune is yet to emerge internationally. We can have every confidence it will. Reinforcement for that confidence comes from the distinguished academic Dr Brian Long (born Edinburgh, 1945), former vice chancellor of the University of St Andrews (2001–08) and chief executive of the British Library (1991–2000): 'Scotland has 0.1% of the world's population. Despite that, Scotland is responsible for the publication of 1% of the world's scientific papers. Scotland is third in the world for research publications per head of population.' In a speech to the World Bank, he also said: 'As a small country on the edge of western Europe, the ability to interact with international partners and participate in the world economy is critical... we want to be confident that Scotland and Scots are making a difference for the better, no matter where in the world they might be active.' The essence of this chapter is to illustrate that the essentially outward-looking Scots continue to punch well above their weight.

BUSINESS AND PUBLIC LIFE

That is certainly true in the coalition government formed after the 2010 general election. There were six Scots in the 22-strong cabinet: four Conservatives – Michael Gove (born Edinburgh, 1967), Liam Fox (born East Kilbride, 1961), Iain Duncan Smith (born Edinburgh, 1954) and Lord Strathclyde (born Glasgow, 1960) – and two Liberal Democrats – Danny Alexander (born Edinburgh, 1972) and Michael Moore (born Ulster but educated and brought up in Galashiels, 1965). Michael Gove has been an often controversial education secretary since his appointment in 2010. In April 2013 he suggested the end of school half-term holidays and gave as one of his reasons the fact that there was no longer a need for a 'tattie holiday' (the period when Scottish children earned extra pocket money from harvesting the annual potato crop) in October. Before election to government he had served as the shadow secretary of state for children, schools and families (2007–10). Dr Liam Fox lost the 2005 leadership battle to David Cameron but was nevertheless appointed defence secretary in 2010. He resigned the following year over allegations that he had improperly given a close friend and lobbyist access to the Ministry of Defence, allowing him to join official trips overseas. He had previously held ministerial roles in the Major government and was a frontbench spokesman in opposition and party chairman (2003–05). Iain Duncan Smith, a captain in the Scots Guards whose six years' service included postings in Northern Ireland and Rhodesia, was elected leader of the Conservative party in 2001 but stepped down after only two years. He has been work and pensions secretary since 2010 and has introduced dramatic reforms of the benefits system. Lord Strathclyde, was leader of the House of Lords from 2010 until he stepped down in January 2013. He had previously been opposition chief whip (1994–97) and leader of the Opposition in the Lords (1998–2010).

Danny Alexander, was a surprise choice as chief secretary to the treasury after the sudden resignation of David Laws, who had been caught up in the expenses scandal.

He had been chief of staff to Nick Clegg and was the principal Liberal Democrat author of the Coalition Agreement. Michael Moore replaced David Steel in his Borders constituency in 1997 and has proved an able and shrewd secretary of state for Scotland. He introduced the Scotland Act 2012, which grants further devolution to Scotland ahead of the independence referendum.

One step away from Cabinet are Alistair Carmichael (born Islay, 1965), proving to be a redoubtable deputy chief whip; Norman Baker (born Aberdeen, 1957), promoted to transport minister in 2010 with a reputation as a formidable backbencher who, in his first three months in the Commons, had asked more questions than his Tory predecessor had done throughout his 23 years as an MP; and Jo Swinson (born Glasgow, 1980), the youngest MP when first elected at the age of 25 and now a rising star within the Liberal Democrats – she is the coalition's equalities minister.

If there are fewer globe-trotting adventurers these days, it's because the world is a smaller place and all the drive and energy is being channelled into new global challenges. There are Scots pushing the boundaries of science and technology, in key positions in business and industry, in major corporations, in the banks (although some may have been demonised beyond salvation by the economic downturn revelations), in public enterprises, in the new wave of official regulators (Ofcom, Ofwat, Ofgem, etc.) and consumer protection, in government, politics, religion, diplomacy, the civil service, the armed forces, global charities, broadcasting, journalism, trade unions, acting, writing, the fine arts and, of course, in sport. Though different in many ways from those of the past, the endeavours chronicled in this chapter still require that special something above and beyond the norm in terms of courage, commitment and, of course, achievement. This is the stuff of empire.

Accolades don't come much grander than Outstanding Young Person of the World, the title accorded Magnus Macfarlane Barrow (born Dalmally 1968) in 2005 for his work in helping to feed the world's hungry children through his charity, Mary's Meals (after the Virgin Mary). The award comes from the global network Junior Chamber International and Magnus is one of only a small group of Britons to receive it (Dame Evelyn Glennie was a winner in the 1980s). Mary's Meals creates feeding projects in some of the world's poorest communities, where hunger and poverty also prevent children from gaining an education. That in itself would make him a prime candidate as a citizen of our Scottish Empire, but to underline his achievement he was also named the *Sunday Mail*'s Unsung Hero of 2006, Rotary Club International twice gave him its top honour, the Paul Harris Award, he was named CNN's Hero of 2010, and he was awarded an OBE in the 2011 New Year Honours.

His story begins at the height of the Balkan conflict in 1992. Moved by the plight of ordinary people, Magnus (then 25) and his brother Fergus organised a local collection of blankets and food in Argyll, packed everything into an old Jeep and drove it to Bosnia. When they got home, they discovered a shed on the family fish farm had been pressed into service to store more and more donations. Magnus decided to take a gap year so that he could deliver the gifts... but they just kept coming so he abandoned his plans to join the family business and instead created the charity, then called Scottish International Relief. His next expedition took him – in the footsteps of David Livingstone – to Blantyre (now in Malawi), where he was so distressed by the impact of hunger and poverty on the country's children that he decided to sharpen his focus. One child told him what he hoped for in life was 'to have enough to eat and to go to school one day.' He immediately set up a temporary feeding station and was soon serving 300 meals a day. That was 2002. By 2012 the charity, now known as Mary's Meals, was providing more than 650,000 school meals a day in Africa, Asia, Latin America, the Caribbean and Eastern Europe.

Two Scots have been winners of the £1 million Templeton Prize, awarded for making 'an exceptional contribution to affirming life's spiritual dimension, whether through insight, discovery, or practical works.' Tom Torrance (born in China to Scottish missionary parents, 1913–2007), former moderator of the Church of Scotland, won in 1978, and George McLeod (born Glasgow, 1895–1991), founder of the Iona Community, won in 1989. Their citations describe them as 'entrepreneurs of the spirit.'

Tom Torrance went to Edinburgh University when he was 18 and, after winning the Blackie Fellowship in 1936, he went to study in the Middle East. He showed considerable sangfroid when he was accused of being a spy and then sentenced to death by the Iraqi judiciary! Fortunately, he was able to convince the authorities that he was simply studying theology and allowed to continue his travels before returning to Scotland. He became moderator in 1976 and is recognised as one of the first religious leaders to win the respect of both theologians and scientists. He sought 'to provide evidence of God through scientific reasoning.'

George, formally Baron Macleod of Fuinary, became a Church of Scotland minister in 1924 and made it his mission to work among the poor. When he was made rector of Glasgow University (1968–71), he was said to be 'a tireless campaigner against poverty and social injustice.' He founded the ecumenical Iona Community in 1938 – 'to encourage peace in the world' – with the help of a dozen or so out-of-work craftsmen and members of his Govan congregation. He was moderator of the Church of Scotland in 1957 and was made a life peer in 1967.

A Scot who may not have noticed the shrinking world is Professor Alan Watson (born Edinburgh, 1938), a cosmic ray hunter whose explorations extend the Scottish Empire into outer space and black holes. Now emeritus professor, he retired as reader in particle cosmic physics at Leeds University in 2003 and still scans the universe restlessly seeking the source of cosmic rays, admitting to being embarrassed about the lack of success! He helped create the world's biggest observatory in Argentina, on which work began in 1999. It covers an area the size of Luxembourg and has 1,600 particle detectors spaced at 1.5 km intervals, which it uses to gather data that has led to major discoveries in cosmic-ray astronomy.

If our empire was to need any global propaganda, the man to call on would surely be Lord Dennis Stevenson of Coddenham (born Edinburgh, 1945). He has combined his high-powered business career with board membership of the British Council, which aims to build trust between the UK and the rest of the world through cultural and educational work. Lord Stevenson has chaired the boards of HBOS (2001), Halifax plc (1999) and Pearson, the media giant that owns the *Financial Times* and the *Economist* (1997–2005). In 1999, the Press Association ranked him as number 24 in its top 50 powerful people list. In 2004, *The Times* ranked him eighth in its Power 100 list. He has been advising prime ministers as far back as Ted Heath in 1971. He was only 26 when the Tory prime minister sent him to negotiate major investments in Japan. More recently, in 1997, Tony Blair asked him to chair a commission on the role of IT in schools. Two years later he went to the House of Lords as an independent peer and in 2000 he became chairman of the Lords Appointments Commission and now vets all new members and selects other independent peers. He is also a member of the Bank of England Takeover Panel. He was chancellor of the London Institute when it became the University of the Arts in 2004. He was chairman of the trustees of the Tate Gallery Foundation (1988–98) and chairman (2002–12) then president (since 2012) of Aldeburgh Music.

Among the biggest beasts of global business, Scottish lions account for themselves in grand manner. They grace boardrooms around the world and are key players in a multitude of commercial matters. For example, as UK chief executive of the Amazon empire, Brian McBride (born Glasgow, 1955) helped change our book-buying habits. He gave us books at the click of the mouse and a breathtaking courier service that delivered his promise of next-day delivery. From 2006 to 2011, he led Amazon through its phenomenal high-growth period and extended its online retail operation into a host of different lines. He stepped down from the high-pressure job only because he was diagnosed with prostate cancer and needed urgent treatment. His recovery was rapid and within months, in April 2012, he joined the government's Digital Advisory Board and six months later he was recruited as chairman of another fast-moving online retail operation: ASOS, Britain's biggest multi-brand fashion online retailer (created in 2000 by Lord Ali Waheed). As well as its UK base, it has websites targeting the US, France, Germany, Spain, Italy and Australia and ships to more than 190 other countries. It is reported to have more than three million regular customers worldwide. To underline his return to robust good health, Brian McBride is also a non-executive director of the BBC, Celtic FC and several technology-focused organisations, and a director of the British Retail Consortium. Before joining Amazon, he worked for Xerox, IBM and Dell and was managing director of T-Mobile (2003–05).

A former pupil of Fettes College, Sir David Reid (born Aberdeen, 1947) held one of the toughest jobs in retailing. He was chairman of Tesco plc for seven years (2004–11), having been deputy chair and a board director since 1985 and helped steer the company to become the biggest supermarket group in the UK. He qualified as a chartered accountant in Aberdeen and held an early role with Peat Marwick Mitchell (now part of KPMG) in Paris (1970–73). He is now chairman of the Kwik-Fit group and deputy chairman and senior independent director of the publishing giant, Reed Elsevier Group plc. He is also a director of the Tesco Charity Trust and chairman of Whizz-Kidz, a charity helping disabled children. He was knighted in the 2012 for services to business and charity.

One of the most powerful corporate figures over the past half century has been Sir Denys Henderson (born Ceylon, 1932). He was chairman of ICI, the UK's third largest company (1987–95), chairman of the Zeneca Group from (1993–95), chairman of the Rank Organisation (1995–2001), chairman of the Crown Estate (1995–2002) and a non-executive director at Barclays Bank (1990–95), Rio Tinto Zinc (1990–96), Schlumberger (1995–2001), Market & Opinion Research International Ltd – better known as MORI – (2000–02) and QinetiQ (2003–05). After replacing the charismatic John Harvey Jones at ICI in 1987 he had to battle against an economic downturn, and then in 1991 he successfully beat off an especially hostile takeover bid by Lord Hanson.

Although he was born in Ceylon, where his father was a tea planter, Sir Denys' family returned to Scotland in time for him to go to school in Aberdeen and he took his degree at Aberdeen University in 1955. After training as a solicitor, he was a National Service conscript and served as a captain in the army's legal services unit. For 18 months, he was the prosecutor in a wide range of military trials including everything from fraud, assault and attempted murder to what he has described as 'various unnatural offences.' After that kind of experience he said he couldn't face the tedium of wills and small-debt summonses. Instead he became a scrubber in the company secretary's office at ICI. It was neither well-paid nor interesting but he stuck with it and slowly climbed the corporate ladder... to become chairman! Two years after the Hanson raid, he supervised the split of ICI and then chaired the de-merged Zeneca Group in its first two years. He was knighted for his services to industry in 1989.

The UK chairman of global consultancy Deloitte is David Cruickshank (born Anstruther, 1959), who was re-elected for a second four-year term in 2011. He also serves on the international board (since 2007) and provides advice to a number of multinational corporations. He qualified as a chartered accountant at the Edinburgh office in 1982, then moved to London in 1988, becoming a partner and then head of the firm's tax practice for eight years. He co-chairs the Education and Employers Taskforce, serves as a council member of Heart of the City and on the Appeal Committee of the British Heart Foundation's Mending Broken Hearts appeal, and leads the Business Support Group for Community Links. He is founder chairman of the 30% Club, the group of City chairmen committed to bringing more women onto UK corporate boards.

America still plays host to hordes of ambitious Scots and many of them play key roles in global boardrooms. One is Professor Gordon Hewitt CBE (born Glasgow, 1945), who isn't content to supervise the affairs of merely a single corporation: he is recognised as a world authority on international business and corporate strategy and is welcomed as a consultant by a portfolio of top names including Pfizer, Time Warner, Zurich, IBM, Honeywell, PWC, Shell, Credit Suisse, Mars Inc, and Standard Chartered Bank. When he isn't commuting between the United States, Asia Pacific and Europe (where he still keeps a home in Glasgow), he is the professor of business administration at the business school of Michigan University. When he was awarded a CBE in 2007 for his services to business, he said, 'the honour is for Scotland's internationalism.'

President of the Americas: it has a certain ring to it and chimes comfortably with ideas of empire. For Derek Blackwood OBE, it's more of a simple job description of the Texas-based role he took up in 1999 with global oil and gas conglomerate, Wood Group PSN. In 2011 he also joined the board of directors of WFS Technologies, a world leader in through-water and through-ground wireless technology for communication, navigation and power transfer, with its HQ in West Lothian. He began his career as an apprentice with BP Tanker Company and worked in a variety of roles in the oil and gas industry with companies including John Brown Engineering and Marathon Oil before joining Wood Group as managing director in Aberdeen in 1996. He moved to Texas three years later and took on responsibility for the group's engineering and production facilities in North and South America. In his current role, he is responsible for the group's businesses in Canada, USA, Latin America and the Caribbean.

Having served as president and chairman of US-based Disney Consumer Products (2000–11), Andy Mooney (born Whitburn) stayed in California, where he is now president and CEO of Quiksilver, one of the world's largest manufacturers of surfwear. At Disney, he trebled the company's retail operation to $36 billion and developed two of the biggest franchises, Disney Princess and Disney Fairies, through global outlets including Wal-Mart and Sears. Before Disney, he spent 20 years with another US major brand, Nike, where he held several senior positions before becoming chief marketing officer and head of the $3 billion organisation, with additional responsibilities for worldwide marketing strategies for the Nike and Jordan brands.

Described as one of the oil and gas industry's 'most tireless, passionate and effective emissaries', Peter Robertson (born Edinburgh, 1947) joined Chevron, the California-based global energy giant in 1973 and rose to be president of its worldwide petrol group in 2000. He was the group vice chairman from 2002 until he retired in 2009. He is a past chairman of the US Energy Association, co-chairman of the US-Saudi Arabian Business Council, a member of the powerful US-Russia Business Council and the American Petroleum Institute. He also served on the advisory board of the Global Business Coalition on HIV/AIDS, tuberculosis and malaria.

Liberty Mutual is one of America's biggest property insurers. With assets in excess of $113 billion, it employs 45,000 people in more than 600 locations around the world. As the senior vice president, Helen Sayles (born Kilmarnock, 1951) helped the global giant run with the highest efficiency. She was responsible for the company's lifeblood – its human resources. Before retiring in 2011, she had been responsible for the whole area of HR development across the company. Helen went to Kilmarnock Academy and took her BA in business at Edinburgh's Heriot-Watt University.

A one-time holiday arranger with Thomas Cook, Will Whitehorn (born Edinburgh, 1960) clearly has a yen for travel and when he got together with Richard Branson in 1987, he had in his mind only one direction – upwards. In 2004, he became president of Virgin Galactic and helped develop the possibility of space tourism for the paying public. He was awarded the Royal Aeronautical Society Space Medal for his services to the industry in 2010 and stepped down from Virgin Galactic the following year, having helped sign up more than 400 would-be astronauts and persuading them to invest more than $550 million for a place in the queue for a package trip on the VSS *Enterprise* to… somewhere out there! He also pursued other interests including the chairmanship (2004–11) of international PR organisation Next Fifteen Communications, which has offices in 19 countries, and other subsequent roles in the communications industry. He is a member of the UK government's Science and Technology Facilities Council, the Space Leadership Council and the Advisory Board of the National Space Centre.

Scotland's first billionaire, Sir Tom Hunter (born New Cumnock, 1961) gave the world a lead in philanthropy – putting even Andrew Carnegie in the shade – with his astonishing 2007 promise to give £1 billion of his hard-made fortune to charity. There was no transformational moment that drew him into such generosity, more a growing realisation that making money was 'only half of the equation', as he told Andrew Marr in a 2005 BBC TV interview. His business enterprise was born out of frustration at not being able to find a job when he graduated from Strathclyde University's business school. The alternative? Selling trainers and tracksuits out of the back of a van. It was a modest start which depended heavily on family support and the astute use of the bank's money to balance his books. The rest is history: Sports Division became one of Britain's biggest retailers, with more than 250 shops and somewhere around 7,000 employees. When he sold up in 1998, his personal stake was said to be worth £260 million! The same year, together with wife Marion, he set up the Hunter Foundation to manage what he calls his 'venture philanthropy'. I met Sir Tom when I was making a BBC series called *Enterprise*, about the country's best small businesses. As an aside, I invested heavily in a pair of his walking boots… which are still going strong after more than 25 years. He was knighted in 2005.

Having sold the tyre sales business he set up in 1964, Sir Tom Farmer (born Leith, 1940) took his profits to retire at the ripe old age of 29 and enjoy life in the United States. Within two years, he declared himself bored and returned to Scotland. From his base in Edinburgh, he built set up another venture fitting tyres – often doing the dirty work himself – and expanded into fitting exhaust systems. Kwik-Fit was born. Mainly through acquisitions, the operation developed across the UK and into the Netherlands in 1975. In 1985, his success was underlined when he was named Scottish Businessman of the Year. By the time he sold the company to Ford in 1999 for more than £1 billion, it owned 2,000 centres in 18 different countries. Ironically, considering the founder's heritage, in 2005 he was the first Scot to be awarded the Andrew Carnegie Medal for philanthropy! In 2009 he was appointed Commander of the Royal Victorian Order (CVO) for his work as chairman of the board of trustees of the Duke of Edinburgh's Award.

My favourite entrepreneur on BBC TV's *Dragons' Den* programme is Duncan Bannatyne (born Clydebank, 1949). He is a deliciously acerbic judge and, for a shrewd Scot, appropriately cautious about parting with his hard-earned money and never shy of calling a crackpot idea just that! He earned his place on the entrepreneurial judges' bench through an astonishing career that took him from selling ice cream from the back of a £450 van to selling a couple of his businesses for a cool £50 million . . . and still having a string of health clubs to his name, plus, as he declares on his website, an interest in 'hotels, media, TV, stage schools, property and transport'. On that same website, he recalls how it all began: 'I was raised in relatively modest circumstances. I was told by my mother she could not afford to buy me a bicycle, so I asked the local newsagents if I could start a paper round. Told I would need a list of 100 potential customers, I painstakingly knocked on many doors and eventually drew up a list of 100 names and addresses. I got the job, bought a bike and never looked back.' Had he not already made his fortune, he could have done so from his writing: 'I have written five books: *Anyone Can Do It* sold more than 200,000 copies; *Wake Up and Change Your Life* quickly entered the *Sunday Telegraph* top-selling books list, as did *How to be Smart with Your Money*. My fourth book, *How to be Smart with Your Time*, provides practical advice on making the best use of your most valuable asset, and my most recent book, *43 Mistakes Businesses Make*, explains how to avoid those costly mistakes that can waste time, cause embarrassment or even endanger the future of a business.' It's not all business for Bannatyne, of course: he was made an OBE for his contributions to charity. He is heavily involved with Comic Relief and UNICEF and is a passionate anti-smoking campaigner.

Fed up with bras that never seemed to fit comfortably, Michelle Mone (born Glasgow, 1971) decided to do something about it. She not only designed and patented a new shape that created more cleavage but also set up a company, MJM International, to market it around the world. When she launched her Ultimo bra at Selfridges in London in 1999, it was a huge success. More than 50 photographers were there to snap the first model, Penny Lancaster, showing more of her cleavage and the store sold out its entire stock in a single day. The following year she staged a US launch at Saks in New York, and when Hollywood superstar Julia Roberts flaunted her cleavage in an Ultimo OMG plunge bra in the 2000 film *Erin Brockovich*, it was clear Michelle was going to be a business superstar. In 2001, she was named World Young Business Achiever in America, Business Woman of the Year in London and was presented with a best newcomer award by the Princess Royal at the British Apparel Export Awards. In 2003, *Management Today* voted her one of the top three female entrepreneurs in the UK (the other two were Martha Lane Fox and Stella McCartney). In 2005, she shared a memorable speaking engagement with Bill Clinton and Mikhail Gorbachev. She produced her third design – the Ultimo Miracle Backless Body – in 2003. The following year the company launched a new lingerie brand, Michelle for George, with Asda; in 2006 came Adore Moi for Debenhams and in 2007 she entered the diet market with her Trim Secrets pill. She is a member of the Scottish council of the Prince's Trust. She was awarded an OBE for her contribution to business in 2010.

In an obituary for Jean Muir (born London to Scottish parents, 1928–95) in the *Independent*, Sir Roy Strong wrote that she was 'a tough and resilient Scot; the bravery that represents epitomises the courage of a woman who was never anything other than definite.' He also said Muir, who preferred to describe herself simply as a dressmaker despite being one of our world-ranked designers and a hard-headed businesswoman, was an original: 'Her passions were strong, for quality, finish, training, discipline, cleanliness, order, all ingredients she expressed in her own art, that of clothes, but ones that she regarded as fundamental to any professional career. For her, the role of creative designer and efficient businesswoman ran in tandem. She was fervently patriotic, dedicated to furthering the cause of British design, furious at government, the art colleges, the fashion industry or anything or anybody who was seen to be responsible for any form of lapse or slip downwards in standards.' She was renowned for designing 'a look for the professional woman [on her way] to the top'. It is said that her style depended on drape, cut and craftsmanship. Beatrix Miller, then editor of *Vogue*, described her as 'the English Madeleine Vionne, the feted French architect among dressmakers.' Muir lobbied consistently for improvements to training in design and craftsmanship and was awarded the CBE for services to the fashion industry in 1984.

Among the rising stars of our putative Scottish Empire is another fashion designer, Henrietta Ludgate (born Dingwall, 1979). She established her own label in 2009 and it is now being sold as far afield as Kuwait and Japan, though the majority of stockists are in Europe. Her dresses regularly make headlines when worn by celebrities including Downton Abbey star Elizabeth McGovern, Colin Firth's wife Livia Giuggioli, supermodel Laura Bailey and singer Emeli Sandé. She says her emphasis is on quality of design and Scottish craftsmanship and her ambition is to build a couture house of the future and create classic pieces that are handed down through the generations. During her first appearance at London Fashion Week, she won the Ethical Fashion Forum's Fashion Innovation Award (for Spring/Summer 2010) and she was Young Designer of the Year at the 2011 Scottish Fashion Awards. She says an ethos of supporting Scottish craftsmanship is central to her work, with all fabrics sourced from within the British Isles. Included in my reading is the *Business Insider* and I was delighted to see one of my selected Scottish Empire candidates featured in its focus on 'the people who will be shaping the future of business in Scotland over the next 25 years.' Leigh Wilson (born Ayrshire, 1976) is proprietor and CEO of the high-flying Jetlogic, providing a jet charter service for a worldwide who's who of celebrities and senior business figures. Reflecting her Scottish heritage, Leigh has a keen eye on the global market, with offices in Los Angeles, New York and India and plans to expand in the Middle and Far East. When she left Napier University, she spent four years fundraising for the Marie Curie Cancer Charity before striking out into the luxury business sector as an international yacht manager. She was headhunted by the boss of a chartered planes business and it was while working for him that she spotted a gap in the market.

The Perth brother and sister team of Ann Gloag (born 1942) and Sir Brian Souter (born 1954) have shown empire-building enterprise and made a significant contribution to the UK's transport system through their Stagecoach Group, which includes major bus services and rail franchises. After a 20-year career in nursing, Ann Gloag borrowed £25,000 of her father's redundancy payout to buy two small buses and launched Gloagtrotter in 1980 with her then-husband, Robin Gloag. Initially, the company offered a cheap service between Dundee and London and the frills included hand-cut (by her and her mother) sandwiches, tea and blankets to keep the passengers warm. As business grew, her brother joined the company and it became Stagecoach Express Services and then the Stagecoach Group. By 2006, the *Scotsman* was able to describe her as one of Britain's wealthiest women, worth £200 million. Although she remains a non-executive director of the group, she now devotes much of her time to charity, for which she was awarded the OBE in 2004. She also funds the Jonathan Gloag Academy in Nairobi, in memory of her son, who died when he was just 28.

As well as playing a key role in expanding the business, Sir Brian Souter (formerly a chartered accountant with Arthur Anderson) has also been supportive of the SNP and gave them a donation of £500,000 in 2007. He made world headlines when he reportedly spent £1 million on a campaign and private national referendum aimed at preventing the repeal of a law that forbade local authorities from 'promoting homosexuality'. None of this distracted from the Stagecoach Group's continued growth: when it was floated on the London Stock Exchange in 1993, it was valued at £134 million and the capital raised was used to expand overseas, especially in America and Canada. In 2009, his bonus was £1.6 million but he donated most of it to the Souter Charitable Trust and the rest to the group's staff pension fund. He was knighted in 2011 for services to transport and the voluntary sector. He stepped down as chief executive and became chairman of the group in May 2013.

Having cut his teeth in the dynamic Scottish chemicals sector, Mark Bamforth (born Glasgow, 1963) spread his wings and took America by storm in 2012. In a multimillion-dollar venture, he set up Gallus BioPharmaceuticals in Boston and within a year was developing a $20 million drugs manufacturing plant in St Louis. Underlining his reputation in global business, he is also a director of Massachusetts Biotechnical Council (MassBio). The not-for-profit organisation represents 600 biotech companies, universities, research hospitals and other groups involved in life sciences. It is committed to 'advancing the development of critical new science, technology and medicines that benefit people worldwide.' Mark had ten years (1988–98) in global business as senior vice president for corporate operations with the Genzyme Corporation. There he had responsibility for 12 manufacturing sites in America and Europe and a staff of 3,600. Through organic growth and shrewd acquisitions, he invested $2 billion and achieved 200 per cent growth. He previously worked in the whisky industry and as a petroleum engineer exploring for North Sea oil.

While Standard Life is Edinburgh-based it has more than six million customers around the world and I think that qualifies David Nish (born Barrhead, 1960) for a place in our empire's who's who. He's been the chief executive since 2010, having previously been the group financial director for four years. He is also deputy chairman of the Association of British Insurers, a director of the UK Green Investment Bank plc and a member of the Strategy Committee of TheCityUK, a membership organisation for the financial services industry.

Another senior figure in global banking is John McFarlane (born Dumfries, 1947), who has banking experience in more than 50 countries and was chief executive of the Australia and New Zealand Banking Group (ANZ) for ten years (1997–2007). He is now chair of the UK's biggest insurance company, Aviva plc. While based in Melbourne, he was also president of the International Monetary Conference, chairman of the Australian Bankers Association and a government advisor on foreign affairs, regulation, and financial literacy. He was also a director of the Business Council of Australia and the Australian Graduate School of Management. In the UK he has been a director of the London Stock Exchange, the Auditing Practices Board, and The Securities Association Conference. In 1992 he produced the McFarlane report on 'The Future Development of Auditing in the United Kingdom and Ireland'. He was awarded the OBE in 1985 and received both the Australian Centenary Medal and the inaugural Cranfield School of Management Distinguished Alumnus award in 2003.

Another Scot to run a major Australian bank is John Stewart (born Edinburgh, 1950), chairman of the FTSE 100 company Legal & General since 2010. He is also a member of the Court of the Bank of England (since 2009). In Australia, he was CEO of National Australia Bank Limited (2004–09), having served as MD of the bank's European operation (2003–04). He served on the prime minister's task group on emissions trading and the attorney general's business advisory group on national security. He was previously deputy CEO of Barclays plc (2000–03) and group CEO of Woolwich plc (1996–2000). Like David Cruickshank, he too is a member of the 30% Club, and he is also chairman of Guide Dogs for the Blind (since 2012).

After 25 years with the World Bank, the softly spoken Gerry Rice is now the public face and the Scottish accent of the all-powerful International Monetary Fund (IMF). As director of external relations since 2011, he fronts the regular media briefings and his responsibilities include 'strategy on external engagements with media and the Fund's key stakeholders, including legislatures and parliaments, unions, civil society groups and academics, as well as the Fund's internal communications.' Prior to that he was communications director at the World Bank. He returned to Scotland in 1999 to help with the international economic dimensions of devolution and published a book on the subject, *Scotland's Global Opportunity*. He was a Kennedy Scholar at Harvard and his PhD thesis on the US Peace Corps was published as *The Bold Experiment*. He has also been a visiting professor at Glasgow University, where he had earlier taken a PhD in modern history.

Surely another shoo-in for the empire is Sir Donald Cruickshank (born Aberdeen, 1937), who was chairman of the London Stock Exchange (2000–03) and before that director general of the independent regulator Oftel (now Ofcom, 1993–98). His extremely strong CV also includes three years as general manager of the *Sunday Times* (1977–80), managing director of the Virgin Group (1984–89), chief executive of the NHS in Scotland (1989–93) and chairman of the Scottish Media Group (1999–2004). He has been a member of the independent regulator, the Financial Reporting Council, since 2002 and was knighted in 2006.

Since starting his career ingloriously as a graduate trainee in the pet food industry, Adam Crozier (born Rothesay, 1964) has swept majestically through a series of high-profile jobs in high-profile boardrooms and since 2010 has been chief executive of the high-profile ITV plc (having replaced Michael Grade). Before that he was CEO of the Royal Mail (2003–10), CEO of the Football Association (2000–02) and, at just 31, CEO of Saatchi and Saatchi (1995–99). He was also a non-executive director of lottery organisers Camelot (2007–10) and a member of the president's committee of the Confederation of British Industry. In his short stay at the FA, he relocated the headquarters, appointed the first ever foreign England manager (Sven-Göran Eriksson), increased revenues, reduced the average age of staff to 32, chased the Wembley Stadium redevelopment and reduced the FA's ruling body from a 91-member board to a 12-member committee. When he moved to Royal Mail Group in 2003, he said his new job required 'the biggest corporate turnaround programme in the UK'. He delivered. He turned £1.5 million-a-day losses to £2 million-a-day in profits. He became CEO of the advertising giant following the traumatic departure of the Saatchi brothers, for whom he had worked for more than ten years. He took over ITV plc with a brief to increase advertising revenues which had slumped with the expansion of the TV market. From the number and length of today's commercial breaks, one can only assume he has been successful!

The Scottish connection at the Royal Mail was maintained when Donald Brydon (born Edinburgh, 1945) was appointed chairman in 2009. He is also chairman of the FTSE 100 engineering giant Smiths Group plc, the London Metal Exchange and the Medical Research Council. He was previously chairman and chief executive of AXA Investment Managers (1997–2009) and spent 20 years (1977–1997) with Barclays' investment arm, BZW, latterly as chairman and chief executive. He joined the state-owned Royal Mail at what was described as 'a challenging point in its history.' It was profitable for the first time in 20 years but was facing increasing competition from email and rival mail operators and the huge expense of modernising. He said: 'there is clearly a big challenge ahead but also great opportunities to meet our customers' needs and I look forward to a positive involvement which will benefit our customers, employees and the taxpayer.' Few will doubt Mr Brydon's ability to meet that challenge head-on. While he was chairman of the market research group Taylor Nelson Sofres, he was described as 'a bruiser' when he beat off a billion pound takeover bid. He was awarded an OBE for services to the financial industry in 1994 and a CBE in 2004.

We Scots like to think of ourselves as a hospitable bunch, but Guy Crawford (born Forres, 1952) has taken that to global heights. For ten years (2002–12), he was chief operating officer of the Dubai-based Jumeirah Hotels group. That includes the iconic Burj Al Arab (Tower of the Arabs), which claims to be the world's only seven-star hotel. It only has suites and guests are collected from the airport by Rolls Royce or helicopter. Guy Crawford was instrumental in developing Jumeirah into what is arguably the most successful of global luxury hospitality brands. His chairman said that he 'recorded consistently high levels of profitable growth and outperformed the market both commercially and in terms of guest satisfaction.' What that means in plain English is that he nurtured the fledgling company and created a portfolio of 20 five-star hotels, restaurants, spas and water parks around the world, and to be sure of maintaining a high calibre of staff, he established the Emirates Academy of Hospitality Management. Before joining Jumeirah, he had extensive experience as MD of McDonald hotels, MD of Heritage Hotels (a division of Forte) and worked variously in South America, Monaco, Germany, France, the United Kingdom, Morocco, the Bahamas and Belgium.

The boutique hotel is a comparatively new phenomenon and two Scots, Ken McCulloch (born Glasgow, 1948) and Robert Cook (born Peterhead, 1967) have been very much ahead of the curve. Ken McCulloch takes Scottish hospitality to new levels: he owned some of the best restaurants in Scotland in the 1970s and 1980s, created Glasgow's first boutique hotel (One Devonshire Gardens) in 1986, spread his wings to build the über-stylish and multimillion-pound Malmaison and Hotel Du Vin group (with 24 boutique hotels across the UK) in the 1990s, crossed the Channel in 1999 to show the continentals his style with the Columbus and Dakota operation in Monte Carlo and now runs the aptly named McCulloch Unique Hotels, which includes the self-descriptive air traveller's hotel, Aviator in Farnborough! One specialist magazine has said of him that 'everything he touches turns to gold' and he's won a fistful of industry awards including *Good Food Guide*'s County Restaurant of the Year in 1992, 1993 and 1997 (for Malmaison), UK Hotelier of the Year 1993, Egon Ronay Hotel of the Year Award 1994, a Michelin Star in 1996, and the European Hotel Design Award for Outstanding Achievement in 2002. En passant: he also won an award from a TV series – *The New Venturers* – which I produced for BBC Scotland in 1991.

Now chief executive officer of the De Vere Village Hotels, Robert Cook (born Peterhead, 1967) was born into the hotel trade – at the Swallow Hotel in Peterhead, where his father was the manager. He linked up with Ken McCulloch when he became general manager of the Newcastle Malmaison in 1997 and later moved up to director of regional operations with the company. He then went to McCulloch's Monte Carlo hotel and was appointed the UK MD for the Columbus and Dakota Group. He returned to Malmaison as CEO in 2004, when he managed the acquisition of Hotel Du Vin. In the AA Awards in 2006, he was Manager of the Year and Malmaison was named Hotel Group of the Year. In 2008 Hotel du Vin won the Small Hotel Group of the Year award and for the sixth consecutive year he also won a *Guardian/Observer* Business Travel Award.

As a journalist, I have met all conditions of public figures but it's Jimmy Reid (born Glasgow, 1932–2010) who stands out most in my memory. He became a worldwide hero when he led the 15-month Clyde shipyard work-in (June 1971 to October 1972). He and the other leaders of the Amalgamated Union of Engineering Workers (AEUW) were determined to prove the viability of the yard and to stop the government closing it down. His leadership earned him the title of the *Great Clydesider* and I've never heard anyone demur! Maybe it's the familiarity of the name Jimmy but I like to think that he and I became good friends… no, we were more than that: we were mates, and got on well enough to discuss the idea of collaborating on what would have been a fascinating biography. I said it should be an autobiography (and that I would help marshal the masses of material) but despite the astonishing riches of his past, he knew that it would never happen. It wasn't laziness, or any lack of enthusiasm. It was as if he saw it as the final chapter of a life that he was still too busy living. 'We should get round to it one day but not too soon,' he said on more than one occasion! Sadly we never did, but maybe there has been enough written about him over the years to serve the purpose of recording an astonishing life. His role in any telling of the modern history of the Scottish Empire is secure. I was one of the awestruck audience – the others were the latest cadre of participants in the Young UK Programme – when he talked theology with the former Bishop of Durham David Jenkins. He always tried to avoid getting involved in what he regarded as pointless arguments but he made an exception for the good Dr Jenkins. He rattled off biblical texts and continually outscored the bishop to the point of speechlessness and splutter. Afterwards, he asked me, 'was that wicked of me to argue so much about something the man believes in?' It was a rhetorical question. Wickedness would not have fitted Jimmy. He may have disputed that he had one, but his soul was surely pure.

Another Scottish trade unionist who became a working-class hero was Mick McGahey (born Shotts, 1925–99). He was a leading figure in the National Union of Mineworkers and his distinctive gravelly voice and pugnacious stance were central to the miners' strikes in 1972 and 1974. I was an editor at the BBC in the Midlands at the time and saw and heard Mick regularly – albeit from afar – in daily radio and television reports, as he displayed his full range of firebrand exhibitions. Those who knew him, however, say he was 'warm and companionable' and our reporters all said he could be very entertaining. Prime Minister Ted Heath and the coal bosses who were subjected to tirades in his rasping Scottish voice would not share that view. Nor would those inside the union movement who didn't share *his* views! In 2006, however, he was formally recognised as a working class hero when a memorial – in the shape of a pithead wheel – was unveiled in Cambuslang. Fellow trade unionist Rodney Bickerstaff said Mick had never lost touch with his roots and recalled one of his regular sayings: 'we are a movement, not a monument.'

A contemporary of Mick McGahey was Lawrence Daly (born Kelty, Fife, 1924–2009), who served as national secretary of the NUM for 16 years (1968–84) and was also a key figure in the miners' confrontations with Ted Heath. He was a very different sort of personality. He had joined the Communist party when he was 14 and was an assiduous student of the party's classes on Marxism and topped that up with a wide range of correspondence courses offered by the labour movement's colleges. He was also a member of CND and in the late 1960s served alongside Bertrand Russell and other intellectuals – including Jean-Paul Sartre, James Baldwin and Simone de Beauvoir – on a tribunal to investigate alleged American atrocities in Vietnam. He visited North Vietnam and Auschwitz and he is reported as saying the experiences haunted him for the rest of his life.

Sam McCluskie (born Leith, 1932–95) combined his role as general secretary of the National Union of Seamen (1986–90) with roles in mainstream politics as Labour party chair (1983) and treasurer (1984–92). He first contested the election for the union's key role in 1974, but lost to the charismatic Jim Slater and had to wait 12 years for him to retire. He served until the merger which formed the National Union of Rail, Maritime and Transport Workers (RMT) in 1990. In 1988, to the amusement of most of his colleagues, he and John Prescott recorded a fundraising single. It didn't make the charts!

A larger-than-life personality with a strong Ayrshire accent, Jimmy Knapp (born Hurlford, 1940–2001) was one of the dominant figures of the trade union movement in the 1980s and 90s. He was general secretary of the NUR from 1983 and then of the new RMT from 1990 until his death. He also served on the general council of the TUC and was president in 1994. Jimmy was born into a railway family and went to work on the railways as soon as he left school. By the age of 18 he was NUR branch collector and became branch secretary when he was 21. He rose through the union ranks and became a full-time official in 1971, moved to London in 1972 as NUR HQ organiser and in 1983, at the age of 43, he was elected general secretary of the union. When he died of cancer at just 60, he was the last person in Britain to be given a full railway funeral. In honour of the work he had done for rail workers, his coffin was carried by a special train from London to Kilmarnock for burial in August 2001.

One of the trade union leaders who went on to the House of Lords after Tony Blair became prime minister was Hector MacKenzie (born Isle of Erraid, 1940), general secretary of the Confederation of Health Service Employees (1987–93) and president of the TUC (1999). A former nurse at the Leverndale Hospital in Glasgow, he switched to being a full-time union officer in 1969 and worked his way up through the ranks. When the CHSE became part of Unison in 1993, he became an associate general secretary until 2000. He is now Lord MacKenzie of Culkein.

A worthy negotiator with the trade unions was Sir Campbell Adamson (born Perth, 1922–2000), who was boss of the bosses organisation – the Confederation of British Industry – for the seven years 1969–76. He was an economist who had studied under John Maynard Keynes at Cambridge before going into the steel industry, where he was in charge of labour relations. When he retired from the CBI, he became chairman of Abbey National Building Society and was instrumental in turning it into a bank.

The first chief scientific advisor to the European Commission is Professor Anne Glover (born Arbroath, 1956). She was appointed in 2011 to provide expert advice on science, technology and innovation to policymakers and the Commission's president, Jose Barroso. On appointing her, he said: 'Her outstanding background and calibre will bring invaluable expertise to the Commission.' Her appointment is a key part of the EU drive to harness science and research to tackle the key global challenges of our age – such as climate change, energy, health and demographic change – and to underpin a return to sustainable and balanced economic growth. He was particularly impressed with her strong track record as chief scientific adviser for Scotland from 2006 to 2011, when her role was to further enhance Scotland's reputation as a science nation. She holds a Personal Chair of Molecular and Cell Biology at the University of Aberdeen and honorary positions at the Rowett and Macaulay Institutes. She is a fellow of the Royal Society of Edinburgh, a member of the Natural Environment Research Council and a fellow of the American Academy of Microbiology. She was awarded a CBE in 2009.

A world authority in forensic anthropology, Professor Sue Black (born Inverness, 1961) was one of the key figures in the British Forensic Team in Kosovo in 1999 and more recently has been training the police and scientists of the UK National Disaster Victim Identification team. In February 2013 she was named one of the 100 most powerful women in the United Kingdom by *Woman's Hour* on BBC Radio 4. She is head of the Centre for Anatomy and Human Identification at the University of Dundee and has a police commendation for DVI training. She was awarded the OBE for her services in Kosovo and in 2008 she won the Royal Anthropological Institute's Lucy Mair Medal.

A shrewd practitioner of health politics, Dr Hamish Meldrum (born Edinburgh, 1948) was chairman of the BMA – often described as the UK's most powerful trade union – for five years (2007–12). He was ranked third in the *Health Service Journal*'s list of the top 100 people in the health industry and had a crucial voice in the NHS reform, which he described as a curate's egg: good in parts, bad in parts, unclear in parts and even internally inconsistent in parts. A senior colleague said of him: 'I've seen him in action. He's incredibly skilled and the BMA was stronger because of him.' He was chairman of the BMA GPs Committee (2004–07, having been a member from 1991) and was part of the team that negotiated a new contract for GPs.

Another Scot who helped shape the modern National Health Service was Alasdair Liddell (born Pitlochry, 1949–2012). In 1998, he masterminded NHS Direct, the telephone health advice line staffed by nurses. A White Paper at the time said the aim of the 24-hour-a-day service was 'to provide people at home with easier and faster advice and information about health, illness, and the NHS, so that they are better able to care for themselves and their families.' It worked. Within a year, it was reaching more than a million patients in England and Wales and that allowed the Department of Health to boast that the NHS was now 'the largest and most successful healthcare provider of its kind, anywhere in the world.' When a website was added a year later, it attracted more than 1.5 million visits a month.

Having joined the NHS straight from university, Alasdair Liddell became a senior manager in his 20s and was largely responsible for establishing the University College London Hospital Trust, the biggest in the UK. In central London, it incorporates seven major units including the Royal National ENT, the Hospital for Tropical Diseases, National Hospital for Neurology and Neurosurgery and the Heart Hospital. In 1990, he helped commission what became known as the 'Rubber Windmill', an exercise which tested proposed reforms to show how they might work in practice. It enabled managers and clinicians to test mechanisms and behaviours, and develop practices to ensure the new system worked. It achieved national notoriety following press reports that the new NHS market had crashed, although in reality it had been deliberately tested to destruction by withdrawing funding to the point where services could not be sustained. He was made a CBE in 1997.

Scots also continue to play key roles in the management of medicine. Finlay Scott (born Greenock, 1947) was chief executive of the General Medical Council (1994–99) and when he retired he was replaced by Niall Dickson (born Glasgow, 1953). Finlay Scott had previously been a permanent secretary in the Department of Education before becoming deputy chief executive of the Higher Education Funding Council for two years (1992–94). He was a member of the International Association of Medical Regulatory Authorities and chaired its working group on international exchange of information between doctors. Niall Dickson was the BBC's health correspondent (1988), then chief social affairs correspondent and social affairs editor (1995), regularly broadcasting on the *Today* programme on Radio 4 and on TV news bulletins. In 2004, he became chief executive of the independent health think tank, the King's Fund. He is a member of the NHS Modernisation Board and chair of the Department of Health's Direct Payments Steering Group. He sits on the University of Warwick's Faculty of Medicine Advisory Board and is a member of the Royal College of Physicians working party on medical professionalism. He is an honorary fellow of both the Royal College of Physicians and the Royal College of General Practitioners.

A former cancer specialist, Professor Sir Kenneth Calman (born Glasgow, 1941) was the chief medical officer for Scotland (1989–91) and then held the same position in England and Wales (1991–98), in a period that saw the BSE crisis. He was made a KCB in 1996 and is a fellow of the Royal College of Physicians, the Royal College of Surgeons and the Royal Society of Edinburgh. Sir Kenneth was a member of the Nuffield Council on Bioethics (2000–2008) and chaired its inquiry into the ethics of healthcare research in developing countries (2000–02). In 2006 he was elected chancellor of the University of Glasgow with around 60 per cent of the vote. He chaired the commission set up by the Scottish Parliament in 2008 and among his recommendations in the Calman Report of 2009, he argued that the Parliament should receive greater tax-raising powers, as well as control over the regulation of airguns, the administration of elections, drink-driving limits and the national speed limit. He has been president of the Boys' Brigade since 2007.

At the cutting edge of research into human genetics is Professor Nicholas Hastie, who has been director of the Medical Research Council's Human Genetics Unit since 1994. As evidence of his pre-eminence in the field, his unit at Edinburgh University won a major grant of £60 million in 2012. The money will help his team gain fresh insights into schizophrenia, cystic fibrosis, osteoarthritis, genetic eye disorders, and cancer. The unit, already one of the biggest in Europe, is a world leader and its role is to 'advance the understanding of genetic factors implicated in human disease and normal and abnormal development.' He says the funding will help turn the potential into reality. He is a member of the Scientific Executive Board of Cancer Research UK and chairs a number of scientific advisory boards, including the Sanger Institute. He was also one of the 20 UK International Scholars of the Howard Hughes Medical Institute in Maryland. He is a fellow of the Royal Society (2002) and was made a CBE in 2006.

The first chief executive of the Human Tissue Authority was former senior civil servant Adrian McNeil (born Edinburgh). He was appointed in 2005 as head of the watchdog aiming to bolster public confidence by licensing those organisations that store and use human tissue for research, treatment, post-mortem examination and teaching. It also approves organ and bone marrow donations. When he took up the post, he said: 'Our aim is to set standards that are clear and reasonable, and in which both the public and professionals can have confidence.' He was previously responsible for a range of policy and operational posts in the Department of Trade and Industry, the Department of Health Social Security and the Department of Health (where he was head of the Human Tissue Branch).

I would like to tell you why Sir Fraser Stoddart (born Edinburgh, 1942) is in my notebook of likely entrants in this chapter but I don't really have the language . . . nor the grasp of supramolecular chemistry and nanotechnology. However, I do know that he was the 2007 winner of the $200,000 King Faisal International Prize for Science and that's a very beefy prize not handed out lightly. A colleague at Chicago's Northwestern

University, where he was professor of chemistry, helps me out: 'Stoddart is one of the few chemists of the past quarter of a century to have created a new field of organic chemistry – namely, one in which the mechanical bond is a pre-eminent feature of molecular compounds. He has pioneered the development of the use of molecular recognition and self-assembly processes in template-directed protocols for the syntheses of two-state mechanically-interlocked compounds (bistable catenanes and rotaxanes) that have been employed as molecular switches and as motor-molecules in the fabrication of nanoelectronic devices and NanoElectroMechanical Systems (NEMS).' You don't have to take that single expert's view for it, though, because, in addition to the King Faisal Prize, Sir Fraser has won a formidable number of other awards including the Carbohydrate Chemistry Award of the Chemical Society (1978), the International Izatt-Christensen Award in Macrocyclic Chemistry (1993), the American Chemical Society's Cope Scholar Award (1999), the Nagoya Gold Medal in Organic Chemistry (2004), the Tetrahedron Prize for Creativity in Organic Chemistry (2007), the Albert Einstein World Award of Science (2007), the Foresight Nanotech Institute Feynman Prize in Nanotechnology (Experimental) (2007), the American Chemical Society's Cope Award (2008) and the Royal Society's Davy Medal (2008). He was one of 20 research scientists invited by the Royal Swedish Academy of Sciences to participate in the Nobel Jubilee Symposium on Frontiers of Molecular Sciences in Stockholm in 2001. He is an honorary fellow of the Royal Society of Edinburgh (2008) and the Royal Society of Chemistry (2011). He was knighted in 2007 for his services to chemistry and molecular nanotechnology. In 2010, he received a Royal Medal from the Duke of Edinburgh. He also holds honorary professorships at the East China University of Science and Technology (2005) and Jilin University (2012), and was the Carnegie Centenary Visiting Professor at the Scottish Universities in 2005. It is estimated that during his 42 years as a professor around 370 PhD and postdoctoral students have passed through his laboratories and 'have been inspired by his imagination and creativity.' Eighty subsequently embarked on successful academic careers.

Sadly, the intricacies of the Higgs boson and the Large Hadron Collider are also beyond my comprehension, but that the research was largely conducted at Edinburgh University shows the enormous achievement and global potential of Scotland's academics and scientists. Described as one of the greatest scientific landmarks of recent years, the discovery of the Higgs boson was made by Professor Peter Higgs (born Newcastle, 1929) during his research at Edinburgh (where he is now emeritus professor) in the 1960s. It suggests that the eternal restlessness of the Scot is catching! The professor's paper predicted the existence of the most keenly sought particle in modern physics, the so-called 'god particle'. It is crucial to scientists' understanding of physics as it explains why particles have mass. Its existence was finally established at CERN in Geneva in 2012. He won a number of major awards including the Dirac medal from the Australian Institute of Physics (1997), Israel's Wolf prize in Physics

(2004), the Oskar Klein medal from the Royal Swedish Academy of Sciences (2009), the Sakurai prize from the American Physical Society (2010), and the unique Higgs medal from the Royal Society of Edinburgh (2012). Stephen Hawking was reported as saying he should be awarded the Nobel prize for physics and he was made a Companion of Honour in the 2013 New Year Honours List.

Famous for the creation of Dolly the Sheep, the Roslin Institute is no longer involved in the cloning of animals, although many of the techniques developed as part of that research continue to be used in the Institute's development of genetic modification technologies and applications. It recently moved into a new £60 million state-of-the-art building on Edinburgh's Easter Bush campus. The Roslin is part of a consortium that is one of the world's largest groups focused on the biology of companion and production animals. Its website states that it 'undertakes basic and translational science to tackle pressing issues in animal genetics and genomics, development, health and welfare and their implications for human health.'

As chief engineer, Ken Cameron (born Inverness, 1953) was a key member of the Transglobe Expedition (1979–82). He was in Sir Ranulph Fiennes' team on the first circumnavigation of the world on its polar axis. He travelled the 100,000-mile route across the Sahara, through the jungles of Mali and the Ivory Coast, over vast unexplored crevasse fields in Antarctica, through the treacherous North West Passage and into dangers waters of the Arctic Ocean. Ken had the useful experience of having been brought up on his father's farm on the slopes of Ben Nevis.

Three Scots have held the rank of chief scout of the worldwide Scout Association (once spanning the British Empire now more modestly covering 'the UK and its Overseas Territories') since the Baden-Powell days. Lord Hector Maclean (born Duart, 1916–90) was 27th chief of the Clan Maclean and served with the Scots Guards during the Second World War. He was the Queen's lord chamberlain 1971–84 and in that role was responsible for the funeral arrangements of the Duke of Windsor in 1972. He was chief scout for sixteen years (1959–1983) but gave up responsibility for the UK in 1972. He was succeeded as chief scout for the UK by Sir William Gladstone (born Fasque, 1925), the great-grandson of the former prime minister. He served in the Royal Navy Reserve during the Second World War and was later headmaster of Lancing College (1961–69) before his ten-year spell as chief scout (1972–1982). Garth Morrison (born Edinburgh, 1943–2013), chief scout 1988–96, was destined to succeed in whatever he did. He captained the English Under-15 Schools Rugby XV, was captain of Cambridge University Golf Club in 1966 and, at the end of his naval training at Dartmouth, won the top prize, the 'Queen's Telescope'. As one of the high constables of Holyroodhouse, he later served in the Queen's ceremonial guard of honour in Scotland.

There can be no doubt that art historian and museum curator Neil MacGregor (born Glasgow, 1946) has already earned his place in this selection of names to illustrate the continuing strength of our Scottish Empire. He was director of the National Gallery in London for 15 years (1987–2002) and is currently boss of the British Museum (since

2002), where he is also chairman of world collections, a position created for him by the Labour culture secretary, James Purnell, in 2008. The generous minister also gave him £3 million to promote Britain's national collections from the British Museum, the Tate, the V&A, the British Library, the Natural History Museum and the Royal Botanic Gardens at Kew to the rest of the planet with no national boundaries to his endeavours. He has presented three television series on art and his BBC Radio 4 series, *A History of the World in 100 Objects* (broadcast in 2010), became a bestselling book. In 2013, he broke new ground by screening the British Museum's blockbuster Pompeii exhibition in more than 200 cinemas around the UK. He is said to have been inspired in his lifelong interest in art when he saw Salvador Dalí's 'Christ of Saint John of the Cross', then newly-acquired by Glasgow's Kelvingrove Art Gallery. He was nine. He declined the offer of a knighthood in 1999, reportedly the first director of the National Gallery to do so. In 2008, he also turned down the job of director of the Metropolitan Museum of Art in New York – because it charged visitors for entry. When he was made director of the British Museum in 2002, it was £5 million in deficit. He turned that around with ventures such as bringing a small collection of China's Terracotta Warriors for exhibition in the museum's Reading Room, and lending an ancient Persian artefact for exhibition in Tehran. He was appointed to the Order of Merit by the Queen in 2010.

In the academic world, Niall Ferguson (born Glasgow, 1964) can only be described as a superstar. In 2004, *Time* magazine named him one of the hundred most influential people in the world. That's a very high rating for an academic. But then Professor Ferguson is no ordinary university don. His curriculum vitae sweeps across some of the world's great educational institutions: professor of history at Harvard, senior research fellow of Jesus College, Oxford and of the Hoover Institute at Stanford, and the list goes on... Magdalen College, Oxford, Hamburg, Berlin, Christ's College, Cambridge, Peterhouse, Cambridge, the Stern School of Business, New York, Harvard Business School, London School of Economics. He's also been Houblon-Norman fellow at the Bank of England. He's rightly described as a controversialist – even a contrarian – and uses his intellect to lacerate politicians across the globe. He claims Europe's leaders have created an EU structure that's a disaster waiting to happen and Putin is putting Russia in a similar position to Germany under Hitler. He is currently (in 2013) working on the official biography of Henry Kissinger. Nor has he been shy of bringing history into our living rooms: he is a regular contributor to radio and television and his six-part series *Empire: How Britain Made the Modern World*, made for Channel 4 in 2002, promptly became a bestseller when turned into a book... as did later series, *The Ascent of Money: A Financial History of the World* and *Civilization: The West and the Rest*.

Formerly chief of staff to Prime Minister Gordon Brown, Stephen Carter (born Edinburgh, 1964) was the first ever chief executive of the communications industry watchdog, Ofcom (2003–07), and minister for communications (2008–09), before returning to the commercial world as managing director of a Paris-based telecommunications manufacturer, with a brief encompassing Europe, the Middle East and Africa. During his three years at Ofcom, he oversaw the restructuring of the wholesale telecoms market and the growth of broadband. As minister for communications, he wrote the 'Digital Britain' report which outlined the Government's strategic vision and led to the Digital Economy Act 2010. Having joined advertising giant J Walter Thompson straight from Aberdeen University in 1987, he rose to be UK CEO for six years (1994–2000). He then moved to become managing director of NTL, the UK cable TV operator (now part of Virgin Media) and took the company to a leading position in the broadband market. He was made a peer in 2008.

While he was most definitely not a regulator in the legal sense, Lord McGregor of Durris (born Kirkton of Durris, Aberdeenshire, 1921–97) did a very good job of licking the UK's newspapers into shape when he was the launch chairman of the new Press Complaints Commission That was the 'self-regulatory' body created in 1991 in response to the Calcutt Report, which had shown a loss of confidence in the Press Council. As executive director of the Association of British Editors at the time I was theoretically on the other side of the fence from him, but in honesty, it never seemed like that. He was a doughty defender of free speech and freedom of the press but was adamant that editors had to be grown up and responsible and cherish those freedoms rather than abuse them. I found it impossible to disagree. It's tempting to launch into a then-and-now comparison with the Levenson enquiry but that's for another time and another place. Lord McGregor exuded authority on the subject of press freedom and also agreed with one-time *Mirror* editor Hugh Cudlipp that good newspapers made important stories interesting. He had chaired the third Royal Commission on the Press for the three years 1974–77 and had been chair of one of the Reuters trusts since 1987. He also knew all about the murkier side of newspaper economics, having served as chairman of the Advertising Standards Authority (1980–90). He was happy to take on board the ministerial warning that journalists were 'drinking in the last chance saloon' and if he didn't make the PCC work, it would be replaced within 18 months by a statutory system. That this never happened is testament to his diplomatic skills with intemperate editors. In his obituary in the *Independent*, Robert Pinker wrote that, 'on the key issues of principle and strategy McGregor got it right. He ensured that the industry wrote, endorsed and gave total support to a code of practice that the Commission administered. He steered the Commission through its hazardous early years and restored the credibility of press self-regulation. The newspaper industry owes him an incalculable debt.' Some may wish he was on the case to smooth today's troubled relationship between editors and the politicians, who have now all but called last orders at that last chance saloon.

Diplomat Dame Anne Pringle (born Glasgow, 1955) was the first woman to be appointed British ambassador in Moscow (2008–11). Before that, while serving as ambassador to the Czech Republic (2001–04) the self-confessed 'rock chick' raised a few eyebrows when she offered the official residence as the venue for Mick Jagger's sixtieth birthday party. He was on a world tour at the time and he just happened to be one of her teenage idols. Her real job, of course, was helping to prepare the ground for the country's membership of the European Union. After Prague, she returned to London where she served on the FO Board as director of strategy and information for four years (2004–08). She graduated with a degree in French and German from St Andrews University and joined the diplomatic service in 1977. She was made a Dame Commander of the Order of St Michael and St George in 2010. She returned to London just as the government was developing its new regulatory regime for public appointments and she was made an assessor, charged with ensuring fairness and openness.

The first female chief executive of the Crown Estate (the royal property portfolio, worth somewhere close to £8 billion) since the reign of George III is Alison Nimmo (born Edinburgh, 1964). She was appointed in 2012 after five years helping to deliver the London Olympics. There, she was director of design (of all the venues) and regeneration (the legacy ambitions) and a member of the bid team. She had previously been project director of Manchester Millennium, the partnership set up to rebuild the city centre after the IRA bomb caused havoc in 1996. The success of the project led to the creation of four similar companies and she became CEO of Sheffield One.

Although Alison Nimmo is the first to be chief executive, the chairmanship of the Crown Estate was held by a string of distinguished Scots consecutively from 1962 to 2009. The Earl of Perth (born Strathallan, 1907–2002) was only the second chairman and he served 1962–77. He spent part of the Second World War in Paris working with Noël Coward on producing propaganda material. He later worked in the war cabinet office and was minister for colonial affairs in Harold McMillan's government (1957–62). He was followed by Lord (George) Thomson of Monifieth (born Broughty Ferry, 1921–2008) who was in office 1977–80. He was also chairman of the Independent Broadcasting Authority (1981–88, more of which later in this chapter) and of the Advertising Standards Authority (1977–80). He was Labour MP for Dundee East (1952–72), secretary of state for commonwealth affairs (1967–68) and chancellor of the Duchy of Lancaster (1966–67). After him came Scotland's premier earl and chief of Clan Lindsay, Robert Lindsay, Earl of Crawford and Balcarres (born 1927), who was chairman 1980–85. He was a Conservative MP (1955–74) and served in Ted Heath's government first as defence minister and then foreign minister. When he lost his seat in January 1975 he was made a life peer, but then inherited the earldom on the death of his father less than a year later. When hereditary peers were expelled from the Lords in 1999, he was able to continue because of the life peerage. A former officer in the Scots Guards who had served in Malaya, the Earl of Mansfield (born 1930) held the office 1985–95. He was a member of the British delegation to the European Parliament 1973–75 (in the period immediately before the election of MEPs) and was then a Conservative spokesman in the Lords before Margaret Thatcher made him Scottish Office minister in her first government in 1979. He was first president of the Federation of Hunting Associations of the European Communities (1977–79) and first president of the Scottish Association for the Care and Resettlement of Offenders (1985–96). Sir Denys Hartley Henderson (born 1932), mentioned earlier as boss of ICI, was chair 1995–2002. The last Scot to hold the post was Sir Ian Grant (born Perthshire, 1943). He served between 2002 and 2009 and has been chairman of the Scottish Exhibition Centre since 2002. He has also been chairman of the International Federation of Agricultural Producers (1984–89), president of NFU Scotland (1984–90), and chairman of the Scottish Tourist Board (1990–98). He was knighted in 2010.

ARTS

In the creative industries Scots have been industriously creative, making lasting impressions in writing, acting and in the broad area of popular entertainment. My bookshelves, regular visits to the cinema and theatre, assiduous listening to the radio and more than my fair share of watching television attest to this industry. It's for the reader to determine the quality but I feel reasonably relaxed in suggesting a few probable names for this element of the empire.

The first of those, however, is a painter, one dubbed by television's *South Bank Show* as the 'People's Painter'. Jack Vettriano (born Methil, Fife, 1951) has sold millions of prints of his most popular pictures to prove the point. However, his credentials as a much-admired artist are underlined by the £744,880 sale of his 'Singing Butler' at Sotheby's in 2004 and solo exhibitions in Edinburgh, London, New York and Hong Kong. He left school at 16 to become a mining engineer but a girlfriend triggered his serious interest in art with a twenty-first birthday present of a set of watercolour paints. He tentatively entered two pictures for Royal Scottish Academy's annual summer show in 1988. When both sold on the first day, he became a full-time professional artist. The following year, he sold three paintings at the equally prestigious Royal Academy Summer Exhibition in London. In 2003 he was awarded an OBE for services to the visual arts. His phenomenal success with the 'Singing Butler' was followed by sales of more than three million prints (a record) and an honorary degree from St Andrews University. He published his book *Studio Life* in 2008 and was commissioned to paint Sir Jackie Stewart and Zara Phillips as part of TV's Sport Relief. In 2010 he showed more than 40 new paintings at his *Days of Wine & Roses* exhibition, opened by Scotland's first minister, Alex Salmond, at the Kirkcaldy Museum & Art Gallery in Fife, before going to the Heartbreak Gallery in London. He is planning a retrospective exhibition at Glasgow's Kelvingrove Museum & Art Gallery, showing work from across 20 years as an artist, in late 2013.

The appointment of Britain's first female poet laureate, Carol Ann Duffy, was also a first for the Gorbals, Glasgow's toughest neighbourhood. When she was appointed in 2009, the BBC described her as 'the first woman, the first Scot, and the first openly

LGBT person to hold the position.' She had already established herself as a popular and accessible writer with a string of prestigious prizes including a Scottish Arts Council award for her collection *Standing Female Nude* (1985); a Somerset Maugham award for *Selling Manhattan* (1987); the Whitbread Poetry Award for *Mean Time* (1993), the T. S. Eliot Prize for *Rapture* (2005).

My bookcases would once have satisfied the most fastidious of librarians but now they resemble a hurriedly arranged jumble sale as I've worked through the volumes making notes and tabulating information. While I've never been conscious of buying or reading with a preference for Scots writers, my subconscious has obviously had this exercise in mind. At one end are the historical greats who need no elaboration. To back up the claim, let me offer the briefest of lists of names and the very substantial Scottish back-catalogue they provide, a more-than-credible literary who's who of celebrated authors. They include James Boswell (born Edinburgh, 1740–95), biographer of Samuel Johnson; Robert Burns (born Alloway, 1759–96), the country's unofficial bard; Sir Walter Scott (born Edinburgh, 1771–1832) who created the *Waverley* novels; Thomas Carlyle (born Ecclefechan, 1795–1881), author of the satirical *Sartor Resartus*; R.M. Ballantyne (born Edinburgh, 1825–94) and his *The Coral Island*; Robert Louis Stevenson (born Edinburgh, 1850–94), also inspiring would-be adventurers with *Kidnapped* and *Treasure Island*; Sir Arthur Conan Doyle (born Edinburgh, 1859–1930), creator of Sherlock Holmes; Kenneth Grahame (1859–1932) and his children's classic, *The Wind in the Willows*; Sir James Barrie (born Kirriemuir, 1860–1937), creator of *Peter Pan*; John Buchan (born Perth, 1875–1940) mentioned earlier as writer of *The Thirty-Nine Steps*; A.J. Cronin (born Glasgow, 1896–1981), who was responsible for *Dr Finlay's Casebook*; and Muriel Spark (born Edinburgh, 1918–2008), author of *The Prime of Miss Jean Brodie*.

Testing contemporary writers against that treasure trove is beyond my wit. So those books at the other end of my collection, accumulated in more recent years, are selected as best I can. Simply, these are the modern Scots I've personally enjoyed reading. Although I'm no critic, I feel that, without fear of contradiction, I can assert that creative writing is alive and well and finding multiple outlets – as e-books and for sale online and in the bookshops – in our global empire. Against that backdrop, forecasting which of today's writers will enjoy similar success to their forbears seems to me something of a fraught occupation and I venture onwards cautiously... in the safety of alphabetical order.

Iain – with and without an M – Banks (born Dunfermline, 1954–2013) was named in *The Times* 2008 list of the 50 greatest British writers since 1945. There's no argument from me but Iain gained even higher praise for his courage in the face of inoperable cancer. With only months to live, and with what he described as 'ghoulish humour', he asked his partner, Adele Hartley, if she would 'do [him] the honour of becoming [his] widow.' Adele, director of Edinburgh's international Dead by Dawn horror film festival, accepted the proposal, but Iain died less than two months after they married. His last book, *The Quarry*, is about a man dying from cancer, but it was not a reflection of his own experience. It was all but complete before he was told about his own condition in March 2013. Adele told the *Guardian* after his death: 'Had he known he had cancer, he would never have written about it.' In what proved to be his final interview, also in the *Guardian*, Iain himself said that on the day he was given the diagnosis, he was just ten thousand words from completion. 'Luckily, even though I'd done my words for the day, I'd taken a laptop into the hospital in Kirkcaldy and once I'd been given the prognosis, I wrote the bit where Guy says: *I shall not be disappointed to leave all you bastards behind.* It was an exaggeration of what I was feeling but... because I was feeling a bit kicked in the guts... I thought, *OK, I'll just give Guy a good old rant.*' Adele has described *The Quarry* as beautiful: 'It's a breathless read, laugh-out-loud funny, heart-breaking and fantastically sweary in a way that would definitely meet with the approval of Malcolm Tucker [the foul-mouthed Scot played by Peter Capaldi in TV series *The Thick of It*] – and all the more devastating because in the end, Iain came to know his character's story just a little too well. The vicious irony of the situation wasn't lost on either one of us.' Iain Banks' first novel, *The Wasp Factory* (1984), was initially very controversial because of its relentless violence. However a poll of readers in 1997 voted it as one of the best 100 books of the twentieth century. His *The Crow Road* (1992) was adapted as a BBC television series in 1998 and starred Joe McFadden, Bill Paterson and Peter Capaldi. For his science-fiction stories, he used his middle initial – M for Menzies – as a distinguishing mark.

Carol Anne Davis (born Dundee, 1961) comes with a terrific commendation for those who like the macabre. The *Bookseller* says she 'understands primal fears from the inside' and there's clear evidence of that in her first novel, *Shrouded*, about the fantasies of a trainee undertaker! Douglas, the would-be embalmer, runs into trouble when his girlfriends prove less docile than his charges in the funeral parlour. His lust cascades into murder and the slippery slope gets ever steeper as he wallows in self-justification. Like each of her first three novels, it's set in the Marchmont district of Edinburgh, where she once lived and which will be familiar to readers as the home of Ian Rankin's Inspector Rebus, Muriel Spark's Miss Jean Brodie and Alexander McCall Smith's Pat MacGregor. The book was also well received by the critics and four of them named it as their top debut novel of 1999. Writing on Amazon, one reader said Davis's world was particularly disturbing 'because it is fundamentally our world, with none of the twisted new rules dark fiction often asks us to accept. In many ways, the novel [*Shrouded*] addresses parenting and its ultimate effects, through the cast of socially maladjusted characters, all of whom are remarkable in their psychological realism. You know these people. You probably poke fun at them when they aren't in the room.'

Dorothy Dunnett OBE (born Dunfermline, 1923–2001) commands a complete bookshelf to herself and her fame requires no more than an acknowledgement from me. She had her own International Dorothy Dunnett Day in Edinburgh in 2011 to mark the 50th anniversary of the publication of *The Game of Kings*. That was the first in her six-volume *Lymond Chronicles* series (1961–75), about the life of Renaissance man Francis Crawford, a young Scottish nobleman and polyglot in sixteenth-century Europe. She followed up with the eight-volume prequel *The House of Niccolò* (1986–2000), about Crawford's ancestors. She also wrote a novel about the 'real Macbeth' called *King Hereafter* (1982) and, presumably because she didn't know what else to do, she produced a series of mystery novels whose central character was a portrait painter and spy. More formally Lady Dunnett – wife of Sir Alastair, one-time editor of the *Scotsman* – she was herself a distinguished portraitist and exhibited at the Royal Scottish Academy on many occasions. She was also a trustee of the National Library of Scotland and served on the board of the Edinburgh International Book Festival.

Muriel Gray (born East Kilbride, 1958) could be included in this empire-building exercise as an award-winning journalist or as gritty TV inquisitor (she has stood in for Jeremey Paxman) but her books are on my shelves and the great Stephen King regards her as a formidable writer, describing her horror novel, *The Ancient*, as 'scary and unputdownable'. Given such a review by the master of the genre, this seems the more appropriate place to reflect on her talents. Published in 2000, *The Ancient* was her third fiction story and the ancient of the title is the demon lurking within the depths of a huge cargo ship. The horror evolves slowly and with chilling effect. Her debut horror was *The Trickster* (1994) and she was rewarded immediately with a shortlisting for the British Fantasy Society's best novel prize. She turned up the heat with *Furnace* (1996), heaping horror upon horror in a small American town fortunately far from anywhere you or I might stumble into. Had I had the mind to, I would have found her first publication *The First Fifty,* tellingly sub-titled *Munro-Bagging Without a Beard* (1991) an invaluable guide to Scotland's rugged peaks. A self-styled 'eight-stone peroxide blonde', she makes light of conquering a hundred Munros, but as I never did have the mind to, I allowed myself to be readily put off… by the fact that I shave daily. Another peak in the redoubtable Gray's career is the rectorship of Edinburgh University – she is the only woman to have held the post.

Quintin Jardine (born Motherwell, 1945) has been penning novels since 1993, when his hero Bob Skinner was a detective chief superintendent in *Skinner's Rules*. He's so prolific I ran out of shelf-space for his books and was forced to contribute a dozen or so to my local charity shop. I think it was that first tale that did it. It was so good that it was nominated for the John Creasey award for best debut crime novel of the year. The one-time journalist, political spin doctor and media relations consultant was hooked. His lively website saves me the trouble of describing him as a 'crusty-but-urbane' Scot, a tag that I'd dearly like to hang round my own neck: it would cover my back from those who would label me a Grumpy Old Man! Mr Jardine was encouraged to write after a frustrating summer read of a novel he later described as 'absolute crap' – nobody spoils a Scot's hard-earned holiday and gets away with it. He said he could do better, set out to prove it… and did. He painstakingly created the character of Edinburgh-based Bob Skinner, not surprisingly a crusty-but-urbane policeman, slowly turned him into

'Britain's toughest copper' and took him – at a staggering rate of a book a year for 21 years – to the dizzy heights of chief constable, married to no less than Scotland's first minister.

Lest he should feel constrained to the environs of Edinburgh, he also created Oz Blackstone, a glamorous globe-trotting film star with a private eye background that allows him to find danger and intrigue across continents… and through nine novels from *Blackstone's Pursuits* (1996) to *For the Death of Me* (2005). Having allowed Oz to die quietly and off-stage, as it were, Mr Jardine skilfully slipped into the persona of Oz's ex-wife, the exotic Primavera, for *Inhuman Remains* (2009), the first of yet another series that also looks set to run into double figures. I'm further indebted to the author's website for the information – or is it hope – that a Skinner television series is a possibility: 'These hopes beat strongest in the breasts of the author's publisher and agents, the man himself having learned to believe, after a lifetime of following Motherwell Football Club, only in things that he can actually hold in his hand!' There speaks a cautious man.

James Kelman (born Glasgow, 1946) won the 1994 Booker prize with *How Late It Was, How Late*, written in the almost-impenetrable Glaswegian street dialect and including more than 4,000 uses of the f-word. It was clearly a controversial choice. One judge quit in protest saying it was a 'disgrace' and another English commentator described it as 'vulgar' and fellow author Michel Faber, writing in the *Guardian*, later described him as one the country's 'share of prickly, stubbornly anti-establishment authors.' However, most literary critics agree that the Glaswegian is one of the most important, politically-charged writers working today and Professor Kirsty Gunn, the New Zealander who runs Dundee University's creative writing department, goes even further: she says he is 'the greatest British novelist of our time.'

He says his background – in 'the housing scheme homeland' – is 'as normal or abnormal as anyone else's'. When he started writing, at the age of 21, the stories he wanted to write derived, in his own words, 'from my own background, my own socio-cultural experience. I wanted to write as one of my own people and remain a member of my own community.' His 1989 novel *A Disaffection* was shortlisted but didn't win the Booker prize. It did win the fiction award in the James Tait Black Memorial prizes (Britain's oldest literary awards, established in 1919). In 1998 he won the *Scotland on Sunday*/Glenfiddich Spirit of Scotland award and in 2008 he took home Scotland's most prestigious literary prize, the Saltire Society's Book of the Year award, for *Kieron Smith, Boy*.

James Kennaway (born Auchterarder, 1928–68) wrote his first and most successful novel *Tunes of Glory* in 1956 but he continued to hammer so effectively at his typewriter that that and two more books made it to the big screen and two were published posthumously… after he died of a heart attack when he was only 40. I have to be careful not to describe him as a Scottish writer. He insisted he was 'a writer from Scotland' although he too used his own background, as a young officer in the Gordon Highlanders, as a backdrop to his story of class consciousness and simmering regimental rivalries in the aftermath of the Second World War. Four years after it was published, the book was turned into what we had yet to learn to call a blockbuster film, with a glittering cast led by Alec Guinness, John Mills, Dennis Price, Kay Walsh, Susannah York and, not surprisingly, a raft of Scots including John Fraser, Duncan Macrae and Gordon Jackson. Kennaway wrote the screenplay himself and was rewarded with an Oscar nomination and then a BAFTA nomination. The film was the official British entry at the 1960 Venice Film Festival, where John Mills was named best actor and later in the same year, it was voted best foreign film by the Hollywood Foreign Press Association.

His second novel *Household Ghosts* (1961), set where else but in a Scottish country house, was turned into a three-act play in 1967 and then into the film 'The Same Skin', starring Peter O'Toole and Susannah York, two years after Kennaway's death. He followed up with *The Mindbenders* (1962) – about a secret research laboratory that played havoc with a scientist's psyche – and yet again struck cinematic gold with Dirk Bogarde and Mary Ure in the starring roles. One of his short stories, *The Dollar Bottom*, was also later adapted as a short film and won an Academy Award in 1981, while a stage version of his 1967 novel *Some Gorgeous Accident* (1967) was featured at the Edinburgh Fringe in 2010. The two novels published after his death were *The Cost of Living Like This* (1969) and *Silence* (1972).

A.L. Kennedy (born Dundee, 1965) is a creative polymath. In addition to being an award-winning novelist, she's a professor (of creative writing), a newspaper columnist and she regularly takes on the persona of the stand-up comedian at Edinburgh's The Stand Comedy Club and other dangerous places. When she published her first collection of short stories, *Night Geometry and the Garscadden Trains*, in 1990, the *Sunday Telegraph* was unequivocal, describing her as 'one of the most brilliant writers of her generation', and the American critic Richard Ford added, 'this woman is a profound writer'. For her first novel, *Looking for the Possible Dance* (1993), she won the Society of Authors' Somerset Maugham award and universal critical acclaim that's never since been in short supply. It also led to her being commissioned to write the screenplay for the 1994 British Film Institute film, *Stella Does Tricks*, featuring Kelly Macdonald as a young Glaswegian prostitute. She then won the £10,000 Encore award (for best second novels) for *So I Am Glad* in 1996 and in 2007 scored four-fold international success with the $150,000 Lannan Literary award, an honorary DLitt from Glasgow University, the Costa Book of the Year award (formerly the Whitbread) for her novel *Day*, and the Austrian State prize for European Literature! Her other novels are *Everything You Need* (1999), *Paradise* (2004) and *The Blue Book* (2011). In poacher-turned-gamekeeper style, she has acted as a judge for the Booker prize (1996), the *Guardian* First Book prize (2001) and the Orange Prize for Fiction (2002).

Ludovic Kennedy (born Edinburgh, 1919–2009) is one of those polymaths who defy categorisation. He was a journalist, broadcaster, author, a humanist and a ferocious campaigner for the abolition of the death penalty and later against miscarriages of justice. He was perhaps best known for his books re-examining cases such as the conviction and execution of Timothy Evans, Derek Bentley and Bruno Hauptmann (for the 1936 kidnapping and murder of Charles Lindberg's son). In *Ten Rillington Place* (1961) he contended the innocence of Timothy Evans, who had been executed for the alleged murder of his wife and baby in 1950. He argued that the murders were part of the serial killings of John Christie, who had lived at the address where six more bodies were found and who was hanged three years after Evans. After intensive campaigning, Evans was posthumously pardoned in 1966 and the abolition of the death penalty followed soon afterwards. In 1970, the book was turned into a film with John Hurt playing Evans and Richard Attenborough as Christie.

In 1985, Kennedy argued in his book *The Airman and the Carpenter* that Bruno Hauptmann did not kidnap and murder Charles Lindbergh's baby, a crime for which he was executed in 1936. In 1996, the book was made into the gripping film *Crime of the Century*, starring Stephen Rea and Isabella Rossellini. Throughout his lifelong campaigning, Kennedy constantly alleged – and often proved – that the miscarriages of justice were due to police failure and misconduct. He concluded that 'the adversarial system of justice is an invitation to the police to commit perjury, which they frequently do'. He said he preferred the inquisitorial system. I only met Ludo in his later years and I have to confess his curmudgeonly exterior took some breeching, but I found that talking about miscarriages of justice was like lighting the blue touch-paper. His passion and compassion seemed boundless. He was knighted in 1994.

Val McDermid (born Kirkcaldy, 1955) won the CWA Gold Dagger for *The Mermaids Singing* in 1995 but it is for her later novel *The Wire in the Blood* (1997) that she's best-known. She turned it into the intense and highly successful ITV programme that ran for six series (2002–2008). It starred Robson Green as a clinical psychologist who is able to get inside the head of even the most pathological killers. As seems appropriate from a scholar of St Hilda's College, Oxford, she took the title from T.S. Eliot's *Four Quartets*: 'The trilling wire in the blood |sings below inveterate scars |appeasing long-forgotten wars'. But I suspect that it was the journalist in her that recognised the potency of the title; as she herself says, 'who knows what Eliot meant. I've always taken it to be a metaphor for the thrill of adrenaline surging through the bloodstream. But we'll never know for sure.' That didn't stop Robson Green offering his own explanation: in an interview he said he took the line to mean 'a genetic kink, something impure and unusual in the blood, which leads to the kind of psychosis Tony Hill (his character) might deal with'.

In 2012, McDermid told the *Daily Record* that she had based 'psycho' Jacko Vance on Jimmy Savile. She said she had felt deeply uneasy when, as a young reporter in 1977, she met Savile and he later inspired one of her most sinister characters, who the *Record* describes as 'the TV celebrity with a secret lust for torture, murder and under-age girls... Vance, a former athlete, hung about hospitals and toured towns in a show called

Vance's Visits – similar to the *Savile's Travels* radio show.' McDermid told the reporter: 'People often asked me where I had got the inspiration for the character. They never guessed it was Savile. For a start, Jacko is handsome and charming. I assume Savile didn't recognise himself in that description.' She added: 'He was a deeply unpleasant man. He was all smiles and laughter for the audience but as soon as we were alone, he was different. Savile was very much in the front of my mind when I was creating Jacko.' Her work fits neatly into what is termed the 'tartan noir' genre!

Ian Rankin (born Cardenden, Fife, 1960) seems to me to have the perfect background for a novelist: a degree and then work as lecturer, grape-picker, pigman, taxman, alcohol researcher, hi-fi journalist, college secretary and punk musician. All that was en route to huge publishing success with his Rebus novels, another mainstay of tartan noir. Ten of his stories – more than half of the Rebus canon – have been made into the ITV series starring first John Hannah and later Ken Stott. For me, Mr Rankin has served not just as a cracking storyteller but also as an invaluable guide to my past. In every chapter he reminds me of my youth in Scotland. In *Mortal Causes* (1994), he brings back with astonishing vividness the inanities of Edinburgh's famous Fringe: 'There were jugglers and people with painted faces and a cacophony of musical disharmonies. Where else in the world would bagpipes and banjos and kazoos meet to join in a busking battle from hell.' Memories come flooding back of my first taste of festival madness and throughout each story, the drollery of John Rebus gives me back a language I had all but forgotten through living for so long in England. The inspector reminds me that I never had a 'mukker' called Hugh who wasn't better-known as 'Shuggie'. Now I remember being 'fair scunnered' by 'gallus' behaviour and indulging in slanging matches with such indelicacies as 'Awa' an bile yer heid' (get lost!) and 'Haud yer wheesht!' (belt up!).

Manda Scott (born Glasgow, 1962) follows in the footsteps of James Herriot as a vet-turned-writer but it's there any similarity ends. Instead of the gentility of homespun animal welfare, she plunged into a life of crime-writing with a vengeance. After her first book *Hen's Teeth* (1997), Fay Weldon said Scott was a 'new voice for a new age' and she was promptly shortlisted for the Orange prize. *The Times* then described her as 'one of Britain's most important crime writers.' Almost by way of research for her early writing, she studied at Glasgow University's august School of Veterinary Medicine. In an online review of *Hen's Teeth* – a crime thriller set on a farm near Glasgow – it was said 'she does a fantastic job with the science... the book is one of the few that includes it in an intelligent way without scaring the average reader.' It features a Glasgow psychiatrist, Kellen Stewart, who shrewdly decides that the heart attack that killed her ex-lover, Bridget, was in fact foul play. She becomes even more convinced that it was murder when she learns that the woman's brother had died in precisely the same manner after delivering some hens to Bridget's farmhouse... for safe keeping. The mystery deepens when the hens go missing. Suspicions spiral as Kellen Stewart follows evidence that is a tangled maze of hens, a house-breaking pathologist – as rare as hen's teeth, I'd have thought – poisoned eggs, disappearing bodies (snatched from the mortuary) and a feathery scattering of biomedical clues. Manda Scott was clearly satisfied with her first creation and repeated the formula with *Night Mares* (1998) and *Stronger than Death* (1999). Next, she changed tack and time frame to produce the Boudica series of four historical thrillers: *Dreaming the Eagle* (2003), *Dreaming the Bull* (2004), *Dreaming the Hound* (2005) and *Dreaming the Serpent Spear* (2006). She began her Roman spy-thriller series with *The Emperor's Spy* (2010) and followed up with *The Coming of the King* (2011), *The Eagle of the Twelfth* (2012) and *The Art of War* (2013). If that wasn't industrious enough, she also managed to write two other novels: *No Good Deed* (2001) and *The Crystal Skull* (2007), a dual-time thriller that has an historical thread that takes us into Tudor times and then into contemporary Cambridge.

Irvine Welsh (born Leith, 1958) has published seven novels but it's his first (published in 1996) that still grabs the headlines and defines his talents. Set in Leith, *Trainspotting* – the street term for shooting heroin – gave him cult status when Danny Boyle turned it into a critically acclaimed but unrelentingly brutal film set in the raw vernacular of 1980s Scotland. One reviewer said it was 'a wild, freeform, Rabelaisian trip through the darkest recesses of Edinburgh low-life' and another described it as 'the voice of punk, grown up, grown wiser and grown eloquent.' It starred Ewan McGregor, Robert Carlyle, Jonny Lee Miller and Ewen Bremner. The British Film Institute has ranked it 10th in its list of the top 100 British films of all time and it has clearly achieved cult status. Welsh is certainly a product of the punk era. He lived in an Edinburgh housing scheme (council estate) and left school at 16. He took a City and Guilds course in electrical engineering and got a steady job as a trainee TV repairman. However, his smart certificate didn't stop him from getting an electric shock. Thus shaken, he left the wires and circuits behind him and worked wherever he could at whatever he could. In 1978, he was lured to London by the heady excitement of punk music and he played guitar and sang with anti-establishment groups called The Pubic Lice and Stairway 13. Between gigs, he took what he thought was the road to easy money... petty crime. But his arrest record proved more disastrous than his punk records and when he was finally threatened with prison, he woke up to reality, spotted a new revolution and took a free Manpower Services Commission course in computing. This was the 'punk, grown up, grown wiser'! He then cashed in on the gentrification of north London by becoming a property speculator and enjoyed the rewards of renovating old properties and selling them at very new prices. He was on the capitalist ladder. By the mid-1980s, he was ready to come home. He got a place at Heriot-Watt University and won an MBA for his thesis on 'creating equal opportunities for women.' Life continued to be full of surprises and in an extraordinary interview in the *Daily Mail* in 2006, he revealed more about his growing up. He said he was 'not so much middle-class as upper-class.' He explained: 'I'm very much a gentleman of leisure. I write. I sit and look out of my window into the garden. I enjoy books. I love the density and complexity of Jane Austen and George

Eliot. I listen to music; I travel. I can go off to a film festival whenever I like.' Mr Welsh moves rapidly upwards. Watch this space.

As we move swiftly on, I should stress again that this selection of names owes much to my personal reading habits and, while it is intended to show the strength in depth of Scottish writing, it should not be regarded as an attempt to produce a definitive list of current Scottish writers.

The number of Scots actors and actresses who in recent years have been accorded star status on both small and big screens is so great that there's room here for no more than my truncated version of an A to Z list… but it's a list any self-respecting agent or casting director would kill for!

Ronnie Ancona (born Troon, 1968) was named best TV comedy actress at the 2003 British Comedy Awards for her work alongside Alistair McGowan in The Big Impression.

Ian Bannen (born Airdrie, 1928–99) was given the BAFTA Lifetime Achievement Award in 1996, following starring roles in *From Beyond the Grave* (1974) and *Tinker Tailor Solider Spy* (1979).

John Barrowman (born Glasgow, 1967) was third in *Broadcast* magazine's Hottest Commodity poll in 2006. He played Captain Jack Harkness in *Dr Who* and the spin-off series, *Torchwood*.

Stanley Baxter (born Glasgow, 1926) has long been an icon of British comedy acting. His one-man shows on television were lavish productions in which he often appeared in drag, and he gave the first television impersonation of the Queen, something which in earlier times might have been regarded as a treasonable offence!

Joseph Brady (born Glasgow, 1928–2001) was best-known for his long-running role as PC Jock Weir in the pioneering BBC TV drama *Z-Cars* (1962–78).

Gerard Butler (born Paisley, 1969) is a trained lawyer-turned actor. His latest part in 2013 was as American Secret Service agent Mike Banning in the highly successful *Olympus Has Fallen*.

Peter Capaldi (born Glasgow, 1958) was the uproariously foul-mouthed Malcolm Tucker in the hilarious BBC TV sitcom *The Thick of It* (a behind-the-scenes view of Whitehall and Westminster). It was written by fellow Scottish-Italian, Armando Iannucci. In August 2013, he became the third Scots actor to win the coveted role of Dr Who, in the BBC series' 50th anniversary year. In a break with tradition, the news was broken on a special live programme before an invited audience instead of simply happening within the series. He was cast by Steven Moffat (born Paisley 1961), the *Dr Who* writer-turned-executive-producer.

Robert Carlyle (born Glasgow, 1961) was the steelworker turned male stripper in the funny and poignant 1997 film *The Full Monty*.

Ian Charleston (born Edinburgh, 1949–90) played Olympian Eric Liddell in the Oscar-winning *Chariots of Fire* (1981). His was the first celebrity death from Aids and he asked for that to be publicised to create greater awareness of the disease.

Robbie Coltrane (born Rutherglen, 1950) started his showbiz career as a stand-up comedian and was part of TV series *A Kick Up The Eighties*, but is better known for playing Dr Fitz Fitzgerald in *Cracker* during the 1990s and more recently Hagrid in the Harry Potter films.

Billy Connolly (born Glasgow, 1942) and **Sean Connery** (born Edinburgh, 1930) need no further comment from me.

Tom Conti (born Paisley, 1941) played the starring role in 1976 BBC series *The Glittering Prizes* and won a Tony Award in 1979 for *Whose Life is it Anyway?* In 1986 he played the Greek café-owner in *Shirley Valentine*.

Brian Cox CBE (born Dundee, 1946) played Hannibal Lecter in the Michael Mann film *Manhunter* (1986) and has regularly played the villain ever since: a rogue general in *X2*, the tyrannical Agamemnon in *Troy* and a devious CIA official in the *Bourne* films. He won an Emmy Award in 2001 for his Hermann Göring in TV's *Nuremburg*.

Kenneth Cranham (born Dunfermline, 1944) starred in the title role in the popular 1980s comedy drama *Shine on Harvey Moon* and has a long string of credits in film, theatre, radio and television.

Annette Crosbie (born Gorebridge, Midlothian, 1934) is a highly acclaimed actress who played Catherine of Aragon in the BBC TV series *The Six Wives of Henry VIII* in 1971 and Queen Victoria in the ITV's *Edward the Seventh* in 1974. However, she is probably best known for role as Victor Meldrew's long-suffering wife in *One Foot in The Grave,* alongside Richard Wilson (see later in this chapter).

Andrew Cruickshank (born Aberdeen, 1907–1988) will be forever the crusty senior partner Dr Cameron in BBC's long-running *Dr Finlay's Casebook* (1962–71), in which the title role was played by Bill Simpson (born Dunure, Ayrshire, 1931–86).

Alan Cumming (born Aberfeldy, 1965) is something of a polymath . . . actor, singer, director, producer, author and most recently TV presenter. He was the Bond villain in *GoldenEye* (1995), won Broadway's 1998 Tony award as best musical actor for his role as the MC in a revival of *Cabaret*, appears in US TV's popular *The Good Wife*, and took his acclaimed one-man *Macbeth* – made for the National Theatre of Scotland – to the Lincoln Center Festival in New York in 2013.

Iain Cuthbertson (born Glasgow, 1930–2009) has a string of successful film and TV programmes to his credit but is best known as Charlie Endell in *Budgie*, the ITV series that starred Adam Faith, and its spin-off *Charles Endell Esq.*

James Donald (born Aberdeen, 1917–93) was the senior British officer in Steve McQueen's *The Great Escape* (1963), and in the film version of *Quatermass and The Pit* (1967) he played a senior colleague of the professor, himself played by Scot Andrew Keir (born Shotts, 1926–97).

Lindsay Duncan (born Edinburgh, 1950) played Servilia Caepionis in the 2005 BBC series *Rome*, Lord Longford's wife, Elizabeth, in the TV film *Longford*, and Margaret Thatcher in the BBC's *Margaret* in 2009.

Gregor Fisher (born Glasgow, 1953) will be forever known as *Rab C. Nesbit* – from the sitcom of the same name. He starred in the TV show *Naked Video*, which was where the Nesbitt character originated, along with the Baldy Man … later to feature in an advert in which he can't get a satisfactory passport photo from a photo-booth and lights up a Hamlet cigar to calm himself down!

Clare Grogan (born Glasgow, 1962) was working in a Glasgow restaurant when she was spotted by Bill Forsyth and cast for a role in the iconic *Gregory's Girl*.

John Hannah (born East Kilbride, 1962) had, for me, his most memorable role as Matthew, the partner of Gareth (Simon Callow) in the award-winning box office smash hit *Four Weddings and a Funeral* (1994).

Gordon Jackson (born Glasgow, 1923–90) won his first role in an Ealing comedy while he was a draughtsman for Rolls Royce. He was memorably the butler in television's *Upstairs, Downstairs* (1971–75) and the spy chief in *The Professionals* (1977–83).

Deborah Kerr (born Helensburgh, 1921–2007) was the Hollywood super star who famously played opposite Burt Lancaster in *From Here to Eternity* (1953) and Yul Brynner in the glorious *The King and I* (1956). A string of other films brought her six Oscar nominations, an honorary Oscar (1994), a Golden Globe award, three New York Critics awards, a BAFTA Special Award in 1 991 and the CBE in 1998. See chapter 8, Scotland and the Stars and Stripes, for more on her achievements.

Kelly Macdonald (born Glasgow, 1976) was a barmaid hoping to go to drama school when she heard about an open casting session for *Trainspotting* in 1996. She got the part… and forgot about drama school. For her performance in *The Girl in the Café* (2006), she won an Emmy and nomination for a Golden Globe. The following year she won the best supporting actress BAFTA award for her part in *No Country for Old Men*. Her other credits include *The Decoy Bride* (2010) opposite David Tennant and *Harry Potter and the Deathly Hallows – Part 2* (2011).

James McAvoy (born Glasgow, 1979) played the personal physician – a character he described as 'a completely selfish prick' – to Idi Amin in *The Last King of Scotland* in 2006. He won the BAFTA rising star award and the film was named outstanding British film of the year. His major breakthrough came the following year when he starred opposite Keira Knightley in *Atonement*. He won the *Empire* best actor award, and the critics' best British actor prize. In 2014, he will reprise his role in the 2011 hit, *X-Men: First Class*.

Ewan McGregor OBE (born Perth, 1971) is perhaps best known for three very diverse roles: as heroin addict Mark Renton in *Trainspotting* (1996), Jedi Obi-Wan Kenobi in three *Star Wars* films (1999–2005) and the poet in *Moulin Rouge!* (2001). He has also received critical acclaim for his starring roles in London West End productions of *Guys and Dolls* (2005–07) and *Othello* (2007–08). In 1999, he was ranked number 36 in *Empire* magazine's top 100 movie stars of all time. In 2012, he was the youngest person ever to receive a lifetime achievement award at an international film festival.

Fulton Mackay (born Paisley, 1922–87) was RADA trained and a distinguished Shakespearean actor, but he will be forever identified with his brilliant portrayal of a so-called hard-nut prison warden in the 1970s sitcom *Porridge*, alongside Ronnie Barker's Fletcher.

Mark McManus (born Hamilton, 1936–94) played the title role in *Taggart*, ITV's detective series for the 11 years up to his death. In a remarkable tribute, the programme continues with the same title although the tough detective chief inspector was given an on-screen funeral in 1994.

Peter Mullan (born Peterhead, 1959) is an actor-director who appeared in *Trainspotting* and *Braveheart*. He won the Golden Lion award at the Venice Film Festival as director of *The Magdalene Sisters*, which was based, he said, on stories about cruelty in the Catholic church, and brought strong criticism from the Vatican. In 2010, he directed *Neds*, about the 1970s Glasgow teenage-gang culture of hooliganism and violence. He won the San Sebastian International film Festival Best Picture award.

Chic Murray (born Greenock, 1919–85), named the Comedian's Comedian in 2005, was one of Britain's funniest men before turning actor to appear in the 1967 comedy version of *Casino Royale* and as Bill Shankly in the West End musical *You'll Never Walk Alone* in 1969.

Bill Paterson (born Glasgow, 1939) has had a distinguished career in film but is probably best known for his award-winning TV work, which has included *Smiley's People* (1982), *Auf Wiedersehen, Pet* (1986), *The Singing Detective* (1986), *Traffik* (1989), *Doctor Zhivago* (2002) and since 2008, *Law & Order: UK*.

Ian Richardson CBE (born Edinburgh, 1934–2007) was one of the foremost actors of his generation and strutted his stuff for more than 15 years as a leading member of the Royal Shakespeare Company. An obituary in the *Daily Telegraph* said: 'His magnificent voice, arresting stage presence and incisive delivery of verse brought authority to every role.' However, in mid-career he switched to television and produced equally-towering performances: as a double agent in *Tinker, Tailor, Soldier, Spy* (1979), Major Neuheim in the award-winning *Private Schulz* (1980), Sir Godber Evans in Channel 4's *Porterhouse Blue*, and Nehru in *Lord Mountbatten*. However, his most acclaimed performance – for which he won BAFTA's best actor award – was as the Machiavellian Francis Urquhart in Michael Dobbs' *House of Cards* (1990). His most famous line, 'you may very well think that: I couldn't possibly comment' was later used by John Major in the House of Commons.

Dougray Scott (born Glenrothes, 1965) starred as Tom Jericho, the young mathematician determined to break the Germans' codes in Robert Harris's *Enigma* (2001). In 2006 and 2007 he starred as Teri Hatcher's lover in the US series *Desperate Housewives* and the following year played both roles in *Dr Jekyll and Mr Hyde*. In 2011 he played Matt Busby in *United*, a BBC made-for-television film about Manchester United that starred David Tennant as the assistant manager, Jimmy Murphy. The same year he played Arthur Miller in *My Week with Marilyn* and took the lead in *Love's*

Kitchen, the romantic comedy which featured fellow Scot Gordon Ramsay in his first acting role!

John Sessions (born Largs, 1953) is best known for his part in the improvisational game show *Whose Line is it Anyway?* on Channel 4 (1988–98). He also used his skills as an impressionist on the savagely satirical ITV puppet show *Spitting Image* (1984–96). Between acting roles, he is a regular panellist on the BBC's *Have I Got News for You.*

John Gordon Sinclair (born Glasgow, 1962) was only 19 when he starred in Bill Forsyth's award-winning film *Gregory's Girl.* He reprised the role for *Gregory's Two Girls* (1999) and also appeared in Forsyth's *Local Hero* (1983). In 1995, he won the Laurence Olivier theatre award for best actor in a musical for *She Loves Me.* In 1992, he was Master of Ceremonies at Mike Oldfield's premiere performance of *Tubular Bells II* at Edinburgh Castle.

Sharon Small (born Glasgow, 1967) is one of the most recognisable faces on television with appearances in most of the major series, from *Taggart* to *Rebus* and *Downtown Abbey* to *Call the Midwife,* but she is probably best known as Detective Sergeant Barbara Havers in ITV's *Inspector Lynley Mysteries* (2001–07) and as Trudi in the BBC's *Mistresses* (2008–10).

Ken Stott (born Edinburgh, 1954) seems to have spent much of his recent career as a member of the Scottish constabulary. He was a detective inspector in ITV police drama *The Vice* (1999–2003), chief detective inspector in the BBC series *Messiah* (2001–08) and DI again in the title role of Ian Rankin's *Rebus* (2006–07). However, his other roles have included Adolf Hitler in ITV's *Uncle Adolf* (2005) and chancellor of the exchequer in the BBC's *The Girl in the Café* (2005). He plays Balin in the 2012 and 2014 adaptations of J.R.R. Tolkein's *The Hobbit.*

David Tennant (born Bathgate, 1971) was a devoted childhood fan of *Dr Who.* He says that's what inspired him to become an actor and he must, therefore have been in seventh heaven when he landed the title role as the tenth incarnation of the Doctor, from 2005–10. However, his long list of awards better reflects the breadth of his brilliant performances and his popularity with audiences. In 2005, he was sixth in the top ten poll by the *Stage* to find the most influential British television artists of the year (for his roles in *Blackpool, Casanova* and *Secret Smile* as well as *Doctor Who*). In December 2008, the *Stage* named him as one of the most influential people in show business, only the fifth actor ever to make the top 20 on a list dominated by producers and directors. One judge described him as 'the biggest box office draw in recent memory.' He won the National Television award for most popular actor in 2006, 2007, 2008 and 2010. In January 2006, readers of the *Pink Paper* voted the father of two the 'sexiest man in the Universe' (ahead of David Beckham and Brad Pitt). Later that year, *New Woman* polled more than 10,000 readers who ranked him twentieth in their top 100 men. At the 2006 Scottish Style awards he was voted 'Scotland's most stylish male'. In 2007, he was 'coolest man on TV' in a *Radio Times* survey. In 2008 he was voted sixteenth 'sexiest man in the world' in a *Cosmopolitan* poll and the same year was named 'greenest star on the planet' in an online poll for Playhouse Disney. In 2013, he was *GQ* magazine readers' third best-dressed man in Britain. Of his 2013 television performances, a critic in the *Guardian* wrote: 'The copper in *Broadchurch* explores the brooding, tragic notes that made Tennant a great stage Hamlet in a performance also thankfully preserved on film, while the thwarted minister in *The Politician's Husband* is positioned somewhere lighter – skittish, darkly comic, closer to the tone of his Doctor Who.'

Richard Wilson (born Greenock, 1936) is best known as Victor Meldrew in *One Foot in the Grave* (1990–2000). The programme won a number of awards, including the BAFTA for best comedy 1992. It was tenth in a 2004 BBC poll to find Britain's best sitcom and it featured in the British Film Institute's 100 greatest British television programmes. Wilson was awarded the OBE in 1994 and was elected rector of Glasgow University (1996–99).

It was the Aberdeenshire-raised singer-songwriter **Emeli Sandé** who finally beat The Beatles' record when her album *Our Version of Events* was in the top 10 for more than 63 weeks. That happened in April 2013, when she was just 26 years old, and followed a spectacular year in which she sang at both the opening and closing ceremonies of the Olympic games, won Brit awards for best album and best female solo artiste. She also took the German Echo award for best international female artiste and the Swiss Music award for best international artiste. These came in addition to more than a dozen other prizes she has won and she's probably added to that since this chapter was written. The only way seems to be up! As well as all her own music, Sandé has also written for leading singers including fellow Scot Susan Boyle, Rihanna, Leona Lewis, Alesha Dixon and Cheryl Cole. She was educated at Alford Academy, where her father was a teacher. It wasn't always easy for her. 'Inevitably it was part and parcel of my identity that I was Mr Sandé's daughter. No way could I muck about or get into trouble because it would've got back to him within minutes… and Dad was strict, let me tell you. I hated to be ill and to miss a day because I was so hungry to learn. I was very shy, nerdy and extremely well-behaved.'

Although she finished second in the contest, **Susan Boyle** (born Blackburn, West Lothian, 1961) shot to international stardom following her appearance on ITV's *Britain's Got Talent* in April 2009. She arrived on stage very shy, looking distinctly plain and somewhat dull. No one was prepared for her mezzo-soprano rendition of 'I Dreamed a Dream' from *Les Miserables*. She was given a standing ovation even before she had finished singing and within days of her appearance her performance had been viewed more than a billion times on the internet. When she released her first album, six months later, it was immediately among the best-selling in charts around the globe. Although she had taken singing lessons, attended Edinburgh Acting School and taken part in the Edinburgh Fringe, Boyle's experience had come from singing in her local church and in karaoke performances at pubs around her village. It was her mother who urged her to enter *Britain's Got Talent* after she had pulled out of an audition for

The X Factor because she thought contestants were being chosen for their looks. She was determined to seek a musical career in tribute to her mother, who died shortly before her appearance on the show. She is reported to have made £5 million from the *I Dreamed a Dream* album and its singles, and she followed it up with *The Gift* (2010) and *Someone to Watch Over Me* (2011). In 2012, she sang 'Mull of Kintyre' at Windsor Castle for the Queen's Diamond Jubilee Pageant. Her earnings were estimated at £22 million but she still lives in the family council house in West Lothian.

By their nature, popular performers – and their publicists – are not shy of promoting their talents, and Scottish musicians from the last 50 years therefore leave me with the need to offer only minimal reminders of their success, some in the pop world and some in the Scottish tradition.

Ian Anderson (born Dunfermline, 1947) was guitarist and front man for Jethro Tull, formed in 1967. His trademark is playing the flute while standing on one leg. The band had three hit singles in the 1970s: 'Living in the Past', 'Sweet Dream' and 'The Witch's Promise' and continue to play sell-out concerts.

Moira Anderson OBE (born Kirkintilloch, East Dunbartonshire, 1938) had her own television programme, *Moira Anderson Sings*, on BBC1 in 1968, starred at the London Palladium in 1969 and hosted a second television programme, *Stars on Sunday*, which ran for the decade 1970–80. She recorded a series of duets with Harry Secombe in 1981 and also joined Kenneth McKellar in a round of TV shows and concerts singing traditional Scottish songs.

The Bay City Rollers were the most screamed-at teeny bopper band in the world in the 1970s, at the height of what was called Rollermania. They were hailed as 'the tartan teen sensation from Edinburgh' when they launched in 1972. They were guitarist Eric Faulkner (born Edinburgh, 1953), lead singer – from 1973 – Les McKeown (born Edinburgh, 1955), guitarist Stuart Wood (born Edinburgh, 1957), bass guitarist Alan Longmuir (born Edinburgh, 1948) and drummer Derek Longmuir (born Edinburgh, 1951). They had a string of chart hits including 'Shang-a-Lang', 'Summer Love Sensation' and 'All of Me Loves All of You'.

Jack Bruce (born Glasgow, 1943) was the bass player in Cream with Eric Clapton and Ginger Baker. His playing was a sensation at the time and is said to have influenced younger musicians ever since. He has had a solo career, releasing many albums in the past 40 years. In 2003 he had to have a liver transplant but recovered for a series of Cream concerts with Clapton and Baker at the Albert Hall and New York's Madison Square Garden.

Brian Connolly (born Glasgow, 1945-97) was the singer with glam rock superstars The Sweet in the early 1970s and had massive hits with 'Wig Wam Bam', 'Blockbuster', and the legendary 'Ballroom Blitz'. He died of liver failure in 1997.

Barbara Dickson (born Dunfermline, 1947) became a household name through the 1970s TV comedy show *The Two Ronnies*, where she sang in the show's musical breaks. She had a hit with her 1985 duet with Elaine Paige, 'I Know Him So Well' from the musical *Chess*, and was again successful with 'Another Suitcase, Another Hall' from *Evita*.

Lonnie Donegan (born Glasgow, 1931–2002) was the crowned King of Skiffle and said to be a major influence on British music. *The Guinness Book of British Hit Singles & Albums* describes him 'as Britain's most successful and influential recording artist before The Beatles.' He had 24 successive top 30 hits – including 'Rock Island Line' – and was the first Brit to reach the US top 10 twice.

Sheena Easton (born Bellshill, 1959) sang the theme song for the James Bond movie *For Your Eyes Only* in 1981 and performed a duet with Prince on 'You Got the Look' in 1987. She also acted in the US television cop show *Miami Vice*. She now acts on Broadway and sings in Las Vegas.

Jim Kerr (born Glasgow, 1959) was the singer-songwriter and keyboard player who had huge success with Simple Minds and had a series of number-one hits from 'Sparkle in the Rain' (1984) to 'Real Life' (1991). The group held a concert at Wembley Stadium in 1988 to and released the record *Mandela Day* to mark the 70th birthday of Nelson Mandela and demanded his release. Twenty years later, Jim Kerr helped organise a ninetieth birthday party in London's Hyde Park, which Mr Mandela attended in person.

Mark Knopfler (born Glasgow, 1949) was co-founder and frontman for multi-platinum stadium rockers Dire Straits from 1977 until they disbanded in 1995. Their 1985 album *Brothers in Arms* has become a classic and has been described as one of the top albums ever made. Knopfler made Scots fans particularly happy when he played rousing finale of 'Going Home' on the soundtrack of the 1983 film *Local Hero*.

Annie Lennox OBE (born Aberdeen, 1954), solo artist and one-time member of Eurythmics, has won so many Brit awards that they call her the Brits champion of champions. Her other titles include the 'greatest white soul singer alive', one of the 100 greatest singers of all time (according to *Rolling Stone* magazine) and number 22 on VH1's 100 greatest women in music list. She's also been named as the most successful female artist in UK music history with estimated sales of more than 80 million records. Of her early days, she has said: 'I have had to work as a waitress, barmaid, and shop assistant to keep me when not in musical work.' She is also a political activist and philanthropist.

Kenneth McKellar (born Paisley, 1930–2010) took the best of Scotland's traditional songs to the world. With his glorious tenor voice, he produced the definitive versions of Burns' songs, which were hugely popular on his frequent tours of America, Canada, Australia and New Zealand in the 1960s and 1970s. He was the much-loved star of countless television and radio programmes, especially around Hogmanay. When he sang duets with Joan Sutherland for a Decca record, Sir Adrian Boult said he was 'the best Handel singer of the 20th century'.

Gerry Rafferty (born Paisley, 1948–2011) is best known for his 1978 hit 'Baker Street', regarded by many as one of the finest songs ever written. He also scored a double success when 'Stuck in the Middle With You' was a hit on both sides of the Atlantic, and the song experienced a revival when it was used for a scene in Quentin Tarantino's 1992 film *Reservoir Dogs*.

Eddi Reader (born Glasgow, 1959) was the lead singer with Fairground Attraction and reached number one in the UK charts with 'Perfect' in 1988. She went solo and won a Brit award for her ballad 'Patience of Angels'. In 2003, she released an album of Burns' songs.

Sharleen Spiteri (born Bellshill, 1967) was co-founder and lead singer of rock band Texas (1988–2008) and sold more than 20 million records worldwide before going solo in 2008 with the debut album *Melody*, which reached number three in the UK charts.

KT Tunstall (born St Andrews, 1975) made her live television debut in 2004 when she sang 'Black Horse and the Cherry Tree' on *Later... with Jools Holland*. She went on to win a Brit award, a Grammy nomination and an Ivor Novello award. Her singles 'Suddenly I See' and 'The Other Side of the World' both made the top 10. She performs regularly at major festivals including Glastonbury and T in the Park.

Midge Ure (born Cambuslang, 1963) is simply Midge Ure – rock star and co-founder with Bob Geldof of the incredible Band Aid/Live Aid charity project. In 1976 he was the singer with Scots band Slik and had a number one hit with 'Forever and Ever' but then moved on to be front man for Ultravox and had a stream of hits including 'Love's Great Adventure' and 'Dancing with Tears in my Eyes'. He toured with Thin Lizzy in 1979. He teamed up with Geldof in 1984 to write 'Do They Know It's Christmas' for Band Aid.

Wet Wet Wet was formed in 1982, when the original four members were still at Clydebank High School, and is made up of singer Marti Pellow (born Clydebank, 1965), drummer Tommy Cunningham (born Drumchapel, 1964), singer and bass player Graeme Clark (born Glasgow, 1969) singer and keyboard player Neil Mitchell (born Helensburgh, 1964), and singer and lead guitarist from 1983 Graeme Duffin (born Glasgow, 1956). Although they were successful throughout the late 1980s, their biggest hit was in 1994 when 'Love is All Around' stayed at the top of the charts for 15 weeks, having been used on the soundtrack to the Hugh Grant film *Four Weddings and a Funeral*. It was also included in their 1995 album *Picture This*.

One lady who presumably need not speculate about the future of our Scottish Empire is **June Field** (born Dundee, 1959). She was crowned the 2012 world psychic champion after an exhausting six-month competition run by Ukrainian TV (said to be watched by 34 million people). The judges included Uri Geller. She, no doubt, is fairly certain of the names that will translate into long-term fame?

One such name, possessed of the global attributes necessary to our empire is that of **Sir Alexander Gibson** (born Motherwell, 1926–95), who founded Scottish Opera in 1962. His reputation in Scotland is inestimable and there is little need for me to linger on his enduring legacy to the nation but report his key achievements I must. Few were better prepared for an illustrious career. He studied music at the Royal Scottish Academy of Music and Drama and in London, Salzburg and Siena. In 1957 he became the youngest ever musical director at Sadler's Wells in London and was an associate conductor of the BBC Scottish Symphony Orchestra at the same time. He returned to Glasgow two years later to become principal conductor and artistic director of the Royal Scottish National Orchestra. During his record 27-year tenure, he helped the orchestra achieve international status and took them to Vienna's Musikverein and New York's Carnegie Hall. Under his baton, Scottish Opera became one of the most respected companies in Europe and attracted international singers, directors and designers to Scotland. He received a CBE in 1967 and was knighted in 1977. He was principal guest conductor of the Houston Symphony Orchestra (1981–83) and also held operatic posts in Los Angeles and Kentucky.

In that high-octane world of opera and theatre, **Sir David McVicar** (born Glasgow, 1966), product of a Glasgow comprehensive, is variously described as 'the bad boy of opera' and 'a genius'. In 2002 the *Daily Telegraph* said of him: 'he's widely ranked the hottest talent on the international opera circuit; and his special genius is for telling stories on a big scale but with clarity and focus.' He has directed productions in all the great opera houses around the world – London, Glyndbourne, Paris, St Petersburg, New York, Houston, Salzburg, Copenhagen and Brussels – but also maintains close links with Scottish Opera. In the *Independent* in 2009 Christina Patterson wrote, 'it's clear he eats, sleeps and breathes opera. His nightly dreams about it add to his sense of artistic destiny but the destiny, he admits, is retrospective and was quite a long time coming.'

McVicar grew up in a lower middle-class suburb of Glasgow and only discovered opera when he saw Bergman's *Magic Flute* on television. He had been interested in theatre since his teens and was a regular at Glasgow's Citizens Theatre, but when he left Williamwood High School he went to art college for a year, before switching to study acting at the Royal Scottish Academy of Music and Drama. He graduated in 1989 with the self-knowledge that he wasn't destined to be an actor. However, a shrewd head of department pointed him in the right direction… that of directing. He's been doing that ever since and with dramatic effect. His enthusiasm and energy have led him to direct as many as five operas in a year since the early 1990s, and all to astonishing critical acclaim. Astonishing to him, that is! Interviewed by Michael White of the *Daily Telegraph* in 2002, he said: 'I still begin rehearsals for a new show in a blind panic, because I never really know what I'm going to do – I work from instinct, from gut reaction to whatever's around me – and I'm always afraid this will be the show where everyone discovers I'm a fraud and not so intellectual or artistic as they want me to be. But that's OK. If you don't feel that insecurity and think, well, actually I know nothing, I've no right to be doing this job, and this is where I hit the wall, the whole thing's not worth doing. In any case, I'm not an intellectual. I'm an innocent. It's my greatest virtue. I blundered into this business and I blunder on.' In 2007, he was named as one of the 100 most influential gay people in the UK. He was knighted in 2012.

Journalism and Broadcasting

One of the earliest superstars of British television was the redoubtable Lady Isobel Barnett (born Glasgow, 1918–80), who, with her upmarket glamour and husky voice, enchanted viewers and critics alike in her weekly appearances on the BBC's most popular programme of the 1950s and 1960s, *What's My Line?* She was feted wherever she went and on one occasion a London bookshop had to close its doors because the number of people who piled in wanting her autograph threatened the load-bearing capacity of the floor. She won the nation's affection and adulation with her constant poise and charm and she became a byword for sophistication. She wore the courtesy title – derived from her husband's knighthood – comfortably and without pretension. An unlikely showbiz figure, she won an amazing double set of awards when, in 1956, she was named the *News Chronicle* top woman personality and top variety artist. Her reaction was typically modest: 'My husband will be as amazed as I am to hear that I have joined the variety profession. I don't do an act. I couldn't. I am simply myself and I enjoy myself on television and I hope some of that gets through to the audience.' It did. Award piled on award and in 1961 the *Daily Mail* hailed her as one of Britain's 'indestructible' personalities. Those were the days when people liked to look up to their stars, when idols were still secure on their pedestals. Lady Isobel had a solid background that added to that security. She was the daughter of a Glasgow doctor and went to the city's university when she was just 17. She was the youngest of only 19 girls among more than 200 first-year medical students. At 21, she was the youngest Scot to ever qualify as a doctor and specialised in obstetrics. She gave up that career when she married into the English squirearchy. Only weeks after her husband was knighted in the 1953 Coronation Honours list and she gained that useful 'Lady' appendage, she appeared on an obscure regional television programme in Birmingham. A backstage sound-engineer thought her rich, deep voice was that of a man and called her Mister Barnett. She laughed uproariously and thus endeared herself to the audience. Television was still developing and the nascent critics were quick to pounce on what they described as a sparkling performance and by someone with a posh title. A star was born.

While that was to be the major element of her life, there was a darker side that few knew about. Her Presbyterian upbringing and a Quaker education gave her firm resolve but her obsessive self-discipline clearly gave way to anxiety and insecurity, which in turn led her shockingly into shoplifting. It's an inexplicable lapse and it had a devastating effect. I wrote a biography of Isobel (*Portrait of a Lady*, 1982) and found the business of assembling her credentials a very sad affair: taking me from the glittering heights of television stardom to the depths of despair when she was finally charged with shoplifting. When caught, she opted to go for trial by jury and appeared in the dock, charged with stealing a carton of cream and a tin of tuna. She was found guilty. Four days later, alone in her large home, she killed herself.

A Scottish journalist with two very different claims to fame was Fyfe Robertson (born Edinburgh, 1902–87). While working with *Picture Post*, he exposed the notorious Tanganyika groundnut scheme that cost taxpayers millions of pounds and later, like Isobel Barnett, became one of the most popular faces on the BBC TV *Tonight* programme. The 1950s groundnut scheme was a major government project to cultivate tracts of land with peanuts. No one in Whitehall seemed to realise that the humble peanut needed an average annual rainfall of 20 inches and Tanganyika was subject to drought! The Tory opposition made effective use of Robertson's report in the Commons debate. He became an improbable and idiosyncratic favourite when he entered television. His lugubrious features, topped by an ancient trilby, a very hesitant Edinburgh accent and his stock intro of 'Hellooo... therrre. I'm standing...' made him a joy for comic parodies by funny men like Bill Pertwee and Graeme Garden and endeared him to millions of viewers.

Looking at the wider history and development of radio and television, particularly at the BBC, is in itself something of a Scottish who's who. Every schoolboy and schoolgirl knows John Logie Baird invented television in 1926 and many will also know that John Reith was the man who invented the BBC in 1922. Less well-known is how the Corporation has been sustained by a line of Scots throughout its short history. Having been an inmate there from 1966 to 1990, I had the privilege of working for or alongside many of them. I wasn't exactly bosom buddies with the big boys in London but through my role as head of network radio at the Pebble Mill studios in Birmingham, I was allowed the privilege of calling most of them by their first names rather than by the dreaded initials so beloved of bureaucrats. Believe it or not, there was once an EIEIO (Engineering Information, External Information Officer) and a GOD (General Overseas Director)!

I lasted much longer in the allegedly elitist organisation than I was entitled to expect as a working-class lad from Greenock: I survived and prospered (at least to a degree) for a quarter of a century. The incomparable Hugh Carlton Greene (brother of novelist Graham Greene) was the director general when I started as a lowly news producer in Birmingham so I only clapped eyes on him once. I served under five DGs and my favourite by far just happened to be the fiery, bagpipe-playing Scot: Alasdair Milne (born India to Scottish parents, 1930–2013), who had also been controller of BBC Scotland (1968–72).

Surprisingly, I think, he was the first television producer to reach the top of the pile when he was appointed in 1981. He had an unrivalled programme record – *Tonight*, *That Was The Week That Was*, *The Great War* – and as director of programmes was instrumental in bringing the entire Shakespeare canon to the television screen, as well as one of the BBC's most acute and best-loved comedies, *Yes Minister*, and breakfast-time TV. His landmark broadcasting events included *Live Aid* (1985), the massive pop event precipitated by a BBC news report on famine in Africa. He joined the BBC in 1954 following a two-year National Service commission in the Gordon Highlanders. He was a graduate-trainee in a cadre of astonishing talent that included Robin Day, Richard Dimbleby, David Frost, Cliff Michelmore, Ian Trethowan and Huw Wheldon.

But when he became DG, he quickly found just how hot the hot seat could be. Crises and controversies seemed to come along as regularly as London buses. Popular with the lower ranks (including me), he stood up for the BBC's independence in a series of rows with government: he insisted coverage of the Falklands War should be impartial, Margaret Thatcher didn't like the coverage of the 1983 general election and nor was she pleased about the reporting of the miners' strike (1984–85). On top of all that he had to face the possibility of the licence fee being abolished. He told the Peacock Committee it was 'the best bargain in Britain… by far the cheapest form of paying for a high standard of broadcasting', and the fee survived. But if the constant battles had not got him down, they did the BBC governors. In an unprecedented step, the governors asked Milne to step down in 1987, believing 'a change of direction was needed.' He was the first director general not to be knighted. His 1988 autobiography, *DG: The Memoirs of a British Broadcaster*, was described by the publisher as 'the most authoritative account of the age of television.' Few would disagree.

There have been many more Scots prominent in the upper echelons of the Corporation and on both sides of the screen and microphone and in this sphere as in so many others, this small nation has punched well above its weight. Not content with inventing the medium and establishing the BBC's initial commitment to educate, inform and entertain, Scots have continued to play an important part in the development of broadcasting. Their accents and faces have been readily recognised both on camera and on microphone, and their credits are on an enormous list of distinguished programmes – in drama, light entertainment and, of course, journalism. The austere Lord Reith has, I believe, left an indelible legacy that gave me a deeply personal commitment to the ethos of the BBC as a public broadcaster. I worked for Auntie for half of the last half-century and I think I was there through especially exciting times, when the Corporation was a hotbed of creativity, energy and breathtaking artistic freedom. I am lucky enough to have been a producer when the producer was king. I made more than a thousand programmes – mainly for Radio 4 – and each was a programme I *wanted* to make. I never had to meet quotas or to fill the time and space and nor was cost ever a constraint. That's not to suggest we were in any sense profligate. Far from it: I never once overspent the allocated budget and when I was a programme head over a period of 20 years, neither did any of my staff. It didn't stop us winning a comforting array of awards. In those glorious days before the bean-counters inhabited – and, sadly, inherited – the Corporation, the routine was that we offered up our ideas to the network controllers and they were assessed on their audience appeal and their creative merits. However, it's much too early to determine whether or not this is a fair assessment of what I think was a golden period. Only time will tell.

I was too late to meet Lord Reith. He had long since departed from the BBC but his influence was still tangible. When I started producing programmes in 1966, I learned – almost by osmosis – about the dos and don'ts that had been laid down by him. Blasphemy, swearing, sexual innuendo, scatological jokes, overt mention of physical or mental disabilities and colour or class distinction were all taboo. That may sound somewhat inhibiting but I can honestly say I never saw it as a problem. In any case, it was quite useful having the old man glowering in the background whenever any of the brighter young sparks wanted to test my managerial mettle. One of Reith's characteristics, according to a biographer, was that he could not get on with authority and I often used that to massage my ego when relations with my bosses were under strain, as did happen from time to time!

One of the key pioneers of post-war television was the BBC's Jimmy – later Sir James – Redmond (born Falkirk, 1918–99) who joined the Corporation as a £3-a-week trainee and rose through the ranks to be director of engineering (1968–78). He was one of the team that made possible the development of live outside broadcasts, satellite transmission, 625-line television, colour television and BBC2, and he helped create the Eurovision Network and the Open University. He also initiated digital technology and the Ceefax service. After school, he went to the Caledonian Wireless College in Edinburgh, gained a first-class certificate in radio telegraphy and at 17, joined the Merchant Navy working for the Marconi Company on Canadian Pacific passenger liners. He came ashore in 1937 and joined Post Office Engineering until he landed a trainee post with the BBC in Edinburgh. A year later he went to London to work as a vision-mixer in the fledgling television service at Alexandra Palace. When television closed down during the war he joined the Blue Funnel Line as a radio officer in the Far East. He retired in 1979 and was knighted in that year's New Year Honours list. He then joined the board of the Open University (1981–95) and the council of Brunel University (1980–88). He was succeeded as director of engineering by fellow Scot Bryce McCrirrick (born Galashiels, 1927) and radio's chief engineer during my period at the Corporation was another Scot, Duncan McEwan.

An improbable controller of television programmes (1962–64) was Stuart Hood (born Edzell, Angus, 1915–2011). Alasdair Milne, who worked with him as a producer, described him as a 'strange private man' and others said he was 'enigmatic', although he went on to become a professor of film at the Royal College of Art and something of a media guru. He joined the BBC World Service as a news producer before switching to television programme-making. He recognised the different needs of radio and television audiences and created separate news services (brought together again only in 2012) and also introduced Nan Winton as the first woman television newsreader. The DG who promoted him to head the television service was Hugh Carleton Greene, who positively encouraged him 'to seek to test the limits of viewer tolerance and interest'. This resulted in the gloriously satirical *That Was The Week That Was* (directed by Ned Sherrin and presented by David Frost) and paved the way for ever more cutting-edge programmes. However, he never seemed at ease among the corporation suits and he left suddenly in 1984 to go to Rediffusion (then the London weekday service of ITV). Soon afterwards, he left there, set himself up as an independent producer and was finally able to effectively disown the establishment.

He became active in the industry's trade union and underlined his left-wing tendencies when he joined the Workers Revolutionary party (1973–78). During the war, he had been an army intelligence officer and a prisoner-of-war in Italy until he escaped and worked with the local partisans (1942–43). His memoir of the time, *Pebbles from my Skull*, was published in 1963 and described as 'a major piece of twentieth-century war writing'. He later wrote several critiques on broadcasting, including *A Survey of Television* (1967), *The Mass Media* (1972) and *Behind the Screens: The Structure of British Television* (1994).

The man who brought breakfast TV to a bleary-eyed Britain in 1983 was Ron Neil (born Glasgow, 1942), who had earlier been the first editor of the *Six O' Clock News*. He had a glittering career that saw him rise from deputy editor of *Tonight*, to editor of *That's Life* and then *Newsnight*, overall editor of TV news (1985–87), to director of news and current affairs (1988–89), managing director of regional broadcasting (1989–96) and chief executive of BBC Productions (1996–98).

The man who was keeping the BBC ahead of the digital curve in the 1990s was David Docherty (born Glasgow, 1956). As the BBC's deputy director of television (1996–99), he was responsible for the management of online services and ensuring that the Corporation was able to play its usual pioneering role in the new digital world. He joined the BBC in 1984 as a research fellow at the Broadcasting Research Unit in London. He left in 1999 to become MD of broadband at the cable company Telewest. Since 2009 he has been chief executive of CIHE, a network of blue-chip companies working with universities to develop the UK's knowledge-based economy. He has served on government committees on the future of media and technology. He also writes thrillers and specialist books about the media.

The man who kept the BBC on the straight and narrow legal path was John McCormick (born Ayrshire, 1944), the highly influential secretary of the BBC (1987–92) and later controller of BBC Scotland (1992–2004). A former teacher, he joined the BBC as an education officer in Scotland in 1970 and served as secretary and head of information before taking the lead role north of the border. When he retired in 2004, then DG Greg Dyke said: 'As BBC secretary he was a key member of the team that began negotiations leading to the successful renewal of the current BBC Charter... and was a source of unrivalled wisdom and common sense to successive chairmen and director generals.' The BBC's national governor for Scotland, Sir Robert Smith, said: 'His vision, his inspiration and his commitment to public service have set standards for BBC Scotland that will serve to define the organisation in the years to come.'

One of the great influences on me as a young producer was Charles Maxwell (born Fife, 1910–98). Although he'd been around for some time, he was appointed chief producer of Radio 4 light entertainment in 1966 (just as I was arriving to take up my news producer post in Birmingham). His name was spoken with reverence and his pedigree stretched back through the mists of time. He originally qualified as a solicitor but somehow caught the theatre bug and abandoned the dusty legal tomes for a career as an actor. Between acting roles, he signed up as an announcer on Radio Luxembourg and found himself presenting a gramophone record programme. He then moved to Radio Normandy, where he met Roy Plomley (later of *Desert Island Discs* fame). When he finally joined the BBC after wartime service in the RAF, he produced a string of successful programmes such as *Take it from Here* (with Jimmy Edwards, the singer Alma Cogan, June Whitfield and, of course The Glums) which was announced as 'half an hour of laughter… every minute packed with seconds!'

After becoming the Light Entertainment boss in 1966, he raided the Cambridge Footlights to bring in the bright new talents needed to create the long-running *I'm Sorry I'll Read That Again* (1964–73): John Cleese, Tim Brooke-Taylor, Bill Oddie, Graeme Garden and David Hatch, who in time would himself become managing director of BBC Radio. He did much to fire both my imagination and my hitherto limited ambition and he showed there was plenty of scope for being different.

Charles Maxwell knew better than anyone that the catchphrase was an essential element of success in radio entertainment and often quoted George Elrick (born Aberdeen, 1903–99) for his natural-sounding signing-off line: 'this is Mrs Elrick's wee son George saying thanks for your company – and cheerio!' Elrick's Aberdeen accent endeared him to listeners and the former dance band drummer, initially hired as a two-week stand-in, stayed for more than 20 years. He later became an agent and among his clients was Mantovani.

It's difficult to know how best to describe George Chisholm (born Glasgow, 1915–97). Jazz-lovers will say he was a brilliant trombonist, pianist, composer and arranger, and so did Fats Waller, Louis Armstrong, Duke Ellington and Humphrey Lyttelton. But many of us will remember him more as the cheeky chappie who made us laugh when he stepped out from the band to join Spike Milligan, Harry Secombe, Peter Sellers and company to take part in the glorious idiocies of *The Goon Show*. In an obituary in the *Independent*, Steve Voce neatly summed up his sparkling career: 'Can one say anything better about somebody than that he really did bring happiness wherever he went and that the sight of him was enough to make people burst out laughing? George Chisholm's career lasted more than 60 years and for most of it he was the finest jazz trombonist in Europe. As well as being the first British jazz musician to rank with the American giants, he was a spontaneous and inspired comedian. His extrovert humour and jazz playing covered a shy and extraordinarily modest personality. He was universally loved and nobody ever had any reason to say anything unkind about him.'

When I graduated to documentary-making, one of my London bosses was a tall craggy Scot called Archie Gordon (born Aberdeen, 1913–84). He was a vaguely aristocratic soul and some people – mockingly, I thought – called him Lord Archie. It was only later that I learned he had inherited the family title to become the fifth Marquess of Aberdeen in 1974 and was thus fully entitled to his lordly title! For 20 years he had produced *The Week in Westminster* and many party political broadcasts, but when I arrived in 1966, he was head of radio talks and documentaries (1967–72).

One of the richest voices I ever heard on the radio belonged to Derek Cooper (born Portree, 1925), long-time presenter of *The Food Programme* on Radio 4 and one of the icons of broadcasting. I had the great joy of working closely with him for several years. He sounded as if he gargled in his much-loved malt whisky every day – and that could well have been the case, because Derek was a connoisseur of fine whiskies and one of the best writers on the subject of the national drink. He introduced me to the delights of Talisker and other island brands when we made *Offshore Britons*, a Radio 4 series that took us from Jersey to Orkney. Derek served in the Royal Navy during the Second World War and then spent a long stretch working for Radio Malaya, before returning to the UK in 1960. In addition to a long string of radio and television programmes for the BBC, he helped found the Guild of Food Writers and was later chairman and then president. He received the OBE in 1997 and two years later he was awarded an honorary DLitt by Queen Margaret University College, Edinburgh.

At Broadcasting House, radio's HQ, the editorial corridors were stalked by a bevy of Scots and one was Andrew Boyle (born Dundee, 1919–91), who in 1965 created one of BBC Radio's most successful current affairs programmes, *The World at One*. He persuaded one of the giants of Fleet Street – William Hardcastle, previously editor of the *Daily Mail* – to present and it quickly gained a reputation as one of the best-informed programmes and won an audience of four million. His biography of Brendan Bracken won the 1974 Whitbread prize and it was his book *The Climate of Treason* that exposed Anthony Blunt as the fourth man in the Cambridge Soviet spy ring.

I met the redoubtable writer-performer Armando Iannucci (born Glasgow, 1963) in the late 1980s, when he was producing Radio 4's *Quote, Unquote* and brought the show to my local arts festival. We ran into the inevitable hitch and Armando had to go out front and entertain the audience while the technicians sorted things out backstage. It was his first taste of audience appreciation and he clearly enjoyed it. More recently, of course, he has earned a reputation as one of the country's sharpest satirists and his string of credits include the brilliant political sitcom *The Thick of It* for the BBC and the spin-off film *In the Loop*. While there is every likelihood that his star will continue to rise, I think he's already well-qualified to help our epic empire-building.

Further up the food chain, Scots were firmly ensconced in key positions in programme management and engineering. From 1976 to 1978, the controller of Radio 1 and 2 was Charles McLelland (born Glasgow, 1930–2004). He then oversaw the separation of the management of what were then the most popular networks and, continuing as controller of Radio 2, went on to launch it as a 24-hour station. He had previously been head of the BBC's Arabic Service. He left the BBC and became director general of the Association of British Travel Agents in 1987.

Ian McIntyre (born Inverness, 1931) was controller of Radio 4 (1976–78) and then of Radio 3 (1978–87). When he left the BBC, he became an associate editor of *The Times* and wrote a number of books including a biography of Lord Reith, *The Expense of Glory*, in 1993.

After I left the BBC and was working as an independent producer in 1990, the new controller of Radio 4 James Boyle (born 1946) proved to be such a new broom that, despite my extensive experience and a portfolio of award-winning programmes, I was excluded from the magic circle of producers allowed to pitch ideas! I didn't have the right experience, he said. After four years he returned to Scotland in 2000 to be chairman of the Scottish Arts Council and more recently he has been chairman of the National Library of Scotland.

In recent years, the broadcasting air has been thick with Scottish accents and it's safe to say a fair number of them are likely contenders for our empire. At the sharp end of current affairs, Nicky Campbell (born Edinburgh, 1961), a former Radio 1 DJ, has been presenter of the Radio 5 Live Breakfast Show since 2005 and BBC TV's *Watchdog* (2001–09). Gavin Esler (born Glasgow, 1951), formerly the BBC's chief correspondent in America, is one of four presenters on *Newsnight* (since 2003). Alan Little (born Edinburgh, 1953) is one of the BBC's special correspondents, following the news around the globe. He won a Sony award for reporter of the year in 1992, and in 1994 he was named Bayeux war correspondent of the year. He is married to Sheena McDonald (born Dunfermline, 1954) former presenter with Radio 4's *The World at One* and Channel 4 News. In 1995, she won the first Woman in Film and Television Award. Sally Magnusson (born Glasgow, 1955), the daughter of Magnus, was one of the original presenters on the BBC's *Breakfast Time,* worked for *Panorama* and *Songs of Praise* and now presents *Tracing Your Roots* on Radio 4. Eddie Mair (born Dundee, 1965) is a Scottish presenter on national BBC radio and television. He presents BBC Radio 4's daily news magazine *PM* and was a stand-in for Jeremy Paxman on *Newsnight* and for Andrew Marr while he was absent through illness from his flagship Sunday morning programme on BBC One. He was news journalist of the year at the 2005 Sony/Radio Academy awards and his prizes include a Sony award for speech broadcaster of the year and the best breakfast show. In a 2005 poll by *Radio Times*, he was listed as the 5th most powerful person in British radio. James Naughtie (born Milltown of Rothiemay, near Huntly, 1951) has been a presenter on Radio 4's flagship *Today* programme since 1994. Kirsty Wark (born Dumfries, 1955) has been a regular presenter of *Newsnight* since 1993, as well as hosting its weekly arts section, *The Review Show*. Kirsty Young (born East Kilbride, 1968) presents Radio 4's *Desert Island Discs* (since 2006) and BBC TV's *Crimewatch* (since 2007).

Even the weather forecast seems brighter for Scots accents, Ian McCaskill (born Glasgow, 1938) joined the Met Office in 1978 and for the next 20 years was the familiar face of the BBC TV weather forecasts. He gained his skills when he was in the RAF at Kinross and first joined the Met Office at Prestwick Airport, but his on-camera the style was all his own: heavy-rimmed specs, bubbling enthusiasm and flailing arms. He was hugely popular with viewers – and with the satirist who gave him his own *Spitting Image* puppet! Carol Kirkwood (born Morar, 1960) of BBC TV *Breakfast* programme was named best TV weather presenter in 2003, 2008 and 2009 (the only presenter to win it three times) by the Television & Radio Industries Club.

On the sports scene and following in the great footsteps of Bill McLaren (see later in this chapter) are: Andrew Cotter (born Irvine, 1973), golf and rugby commentator since 2004; Dougie Donnelly (born Glasgow, 1953), who commentates on snooker, golf and bowls; and Alec Hay (born Edinburgh, 1933–2011), the softly authoritative voice of golf. Hazel Irvine (born St Andrews, 1965) was one of the first women to breech what were then the almost impenetrable realms of sports broadcasting. Her Scottish charm soon had the sportsmen eating out of her hands and she has been able to establish a formidable reputation as a top commentator. Shirley Robertson (born Dundee, 1968), the 2000 and 2004 Olympic sailing gold medallist, is now a reporter on BBC *Grandstand*.

In the particular corner of Auntie's empire that I inhabited – BBC Pebble Mill as it then was – there were distinctive Scottish voices all around me. The two successive heads of engineering while I was there were both Scots: Eddie Deighton (a gentleman engineer of the old school) and John Jarvie (an enthusiastic piper who helped us celebrate… often). The head of personnel and administration was John MacQueen, who over the years had built up the most splendid wine cellar in the Beeb. Jack Johnstone (born Glasgow, 1930–96) was an especially tough Midlands news editor and later the first manager of BBC Radio Birmingham, where the chief engineer was Stuart Miller. Archie McPhee (born Edinburgh) was the editor of agricultural programmes who, during the 1972 Cod War, got us all into trouble when he landed in Iceland without prior permission and was thrown into jail while the diplomatic wheels ground slowly! Gavin Davies was the senior television designer and his wife Ann managed the press office. The engineer-in-charge at the key Sutton Coldfield transmitter station was Tom Douglas.

A regular conductor of our Midlands Radio Orchestra was Iain Sutherland (born Glasgow, 1936), who was a great favourite on Radio 2's *Friday Night is Music Night*, where he was the principal guest conductor. In the 1980s, he became principal conductor of BBC Radio Orchestra. He had previously been conductor of the BBC Scottish Radio Orchestra until it disappeared in the Corporation's re-organisation of music services in 1981.

Scots were instrumental in creating daytime television's popular *Pebble Mill at One*. Tom Ross (born Glasgow, 1947) was an assistant editor, while one of the launch presenters was the larger-than-life Donny B. McLeod (born Stornoway, 1932–84). Tom Ross, an old boy of Hutchenson's Grammar School in Glasgow and a history graduate of Glasgow University, joined the BBC as a journalist trainee alongside the likes of war correspondent Brian Hanrahan, and had been well blooded in radio and television current affairs before arriving at Pebble Mill in 1984. He quickly caught the enthusiasm of the programme and one of his coups was to broadcast live from HMS *Ark Royal* somewhere in the English Channel. He moved on to be editor of *Top Gear* (then also produced from Pebble Mill).

Donny – who had got used to including the B to distinguish himself from the many other Donny McLeods at his Hebridean school – was a great charmer and played a crucial role in establishing the programme's immediate popularity and creating the perfect platform for the development of daytime television. He had previously spent two years on the equally popular *Nationwide*. While working in newspapers in Scotland, he was also the Liberal parliamentary candidate for the Western Isles in 1959 and 1964. He came second on both occasions. He died from cancer at the age of 52. Overlapping with Donny was Paul Coia (born Glasgow, 1960). He worked on the programme for three years before returning to Scotland in 1987 to present his own chat show on Grampian Television.

Even that most English of institutions, Radio 4's long-running soap opera, *The Archers*, owes much to its Scottish connections – but here I must tread warily: as head of the network radio output from Pebble Mill, I was responsible for the daily serial for about 20 years (1970–90) and I was always getting confused between the characters and the actors who played them. One of the early writers was John Keir Cross (born Carluke 1914–67), an amazing personality who quickly became part of the Ambridge folklore. As an enthusiastic young writer, he had set out in 1935 to seek fame and fortune and left home on his bike with two ventriloquist dolls in the saddle bag. He made an early unplanned stop for a night in the cells of Paisley jail after being arrested on suspicion of murder! In good soap-opera style, he beat the phoney rap and continued his journey into broadcasting history. He joined the programme in 1962 and was described by William Smethurst in his *The Archers: The True Story* as "a writer of thrillers and a specialist in the macabre." His scripts were said to be "full of quirky life." That was hardly surprising because his previous work had been an odd mix of horror, black magic, detective yarns… and children's stories. These included *The Children's Omnibus* (1945) and an adaptation of Masefield's *Box of Delights* for radio's Children's Hour. He inherited two Scots characters, the local GP, Dr MacLaren, and Angus, the Archer family's stockman (played at one time by the late Andrew Faulds, who went on to become an MP). He then created a third in the shape of Andrew Sinclair, the Ambridge Estate manager. He became ill in 1968 and died in January 1969.

The Scottish influence continued when Julia Marks (born Glasgow, 1934) played the Irish barmaid Nora McAuley (1972); Crawford Logan (born Stirling, 1957) first played Alan Fraser (1982), SAS boyfriend of Caroline Bone and later GP Dr Matthew Thorogood (1986); Michael Deacon (born Glasgow, 1933–2000) played the local vicar Jerry Buckle (1987); and since 2000, Glasgow-born Ryan Kelly has played Jazzer McCreary, a one-time petty criminal turned lady's man, sensitive soul and occasional folk singer.

There were also Scots in key places in ITV and right at the top of the industry was the ebullient Lord (George) Thomson of Monifieth (born Broughty Ferry, 1921–2008). He was chairman of the Independent Broadcasting Authority – then the all-encompassing regulator, transmitter, franchising authority and arbiter of taste for commercial television – for the seven years 1981–88. Whenever I write about him, I allow myself the journalistic excess of reminding people that he had once been editor of the *Dandy* (away back in 1939 when he was only eighteen) even ahead of all his other heavyweight roles, including a cabinet post in Harold Wilson's government. But I'm equally keen to balance that inanity with a quote from his time as the European commissioner responsible for Europe's worst-off areas: 'I am on the side of the underprivileged, and it doesn't matter which country they work in.' In what have been described as 'eight turbulent years' at the IBA, he constantly clashed with Mrs Thatcher's government. He had a rocky ride overseeing the controversial launch of Channel 4 and TV-am and paving the way for satellite television. At the tail end of his tenure, which might have been longer had he been more compliant, he stoutly rejected Foreign Secretary Sir Geoffrey Howe's appeal to ban the Thames documentary *Death on the Rock*. The film raised questions about an official account of how SAS men shot three would-be IRA bombers in Gibraltar. When Mrs Thatcher railed against his decision, he incensed her even more by saying she was 'grossly overreacting'. She proved his point when her revenge was to put all the ITV franchises up for auction and to severely limit the IBA's role. It was subsequently subsumed into various successor bodies, culminating in today's Ofcom.

Before the IBA, Lord Monifieth had a distinguished political career in first the Labour party and more recently with the Liberal Democrats. After wartime service in the RAF, he became assistant and then editor of the Scottish Labour weekly *Forward* and earned a reported £10 a week. He was blooded as a parliamentary candidate in Glasgow Hillhead, where he was ritually drubbed by the Tory Tam Galbraith. He was then selected for a 1952 by-election in the Labour-held marginal seat of Dundee East. He doubled the majority and remained the MP for 20 years. He was Harold Wilson's chancellor of the Duchy of Lancaster (1966–67). He was promoted to secretary of state for Commonwealth affairs (1967–68) and during that short tenure was confronted by Rhodesia's UDI and the Nigerian civil war. He was appointed a European Commissioner in 1972, confusing the stuffy Eurocrats by serving the drinks at formal receptions and insisting that he was 'just George', and in 1977 he went to the House of Lords, where he sat as a Liberal Democrat from 1989. Before taking the chair at the IBA, he was chairman of the Advertising Standards Authority (1977–80), where he caused waves over a vodka ad that showed a girl wearing a lifebelt labelled SS *Titanic*.

The pioneer who created Channel 4 television in 1981 was Jeremy Isaacs (born Glasgow, 1932), producer of some of the finest British television programmes of the 1960s and 1970s and among the most respected figures in the industry. He was director of the Royal Opera House at Covent Garden (1987–96), president of the Royal Television Society (1997–2000) and is currently chairman of Sky Arts. He began his television career with Granada in Manchester in 1958 and was responsible for series such as *World in Action* and *What the Papers Say*. He also worked for the BBC (on *Panorama*) in the 1960s but moved to Thames Television in 1973 to produce the 26-episode *The World at War* and became Thames' director of programmes from 1974 to 1978. When he launched Channel 4 in 1981, he determined the network would be high-brow and should cater for less mainstream tastes (much more so than today). He featured opera and foreign language films alongside the pop-music series *The Tube* and the soap opera *Brookside*. He commissioned an epic production of *King Lear* (1983) starring Laurence Olivier in the title role and pinched a few programmes from his time at Granada, including *What the Papers Say*. He appointed an old Pebble Mill colleague of mine, David Rose (he created *Z-Cars*, the first live drama on TV) as the commissioning editor for fiction, encouraged the channel's involvement with the 80s revival of the British film industry via the Film on Four strand, and in 1986 broadcast a four-hour dramatisation of an early Percy Bysshe Shelley gothic horror novel, *Zastrozzi*. He later said that it was among the ten programmes of which he was most proud. When handing over responsibility for running the channel to Michael Grade in 1987, he is reported as demonstrating a touch of Glaswegian diplomacy... by threatening to throttle him if he betrayed the trust placed in him to respect the channel's remit!

Journalism continues to be a strong suit for Scots and there is a respectable handful of great byliners from the past 50 years. For me – and perhaps betraying my liberal tendencies – the first among equals was Alastair Hetherington (born in Wales to Scottish parents, 1919–99). He was at the helm of one of UK's finest newspapers for nearly 20 years (1956–75), transforming the *Manchester Guardian* into the highly respected London-based *Guardian*. In what is surely a tribute to Alastair, his successors have clearly valued their inheritance and the paper today is produced in the distinguished left-of-centre vein he developed. He was the son of a professor and went to Oxford in 1938, but his studies were interrupted by the outbreak of the war. He was called up and served in the Royal Armoured Corps as a tank commander. He ended up as a major in the Intelligence Corps and in one of those mysterious military ways, was offered a demob posting to Germany to be managing editor of *Die Welt*, alongside fellow Scot Bill Barnetson (see Chapter 10), based on his three months as a trainee subeditor on the Glasgow *Herald*. He enjoyed the experience and returned to Glasgow to write on defence before moving to the *Manchester Guardian*, where he was rapidly appointed foreign editor (1953). Three years later, the proprietor Laurence Scott asked him to do the necessary to transform the provincial paper into a national daily. Only weeks after taking over the editor's chair, he was hit with the biggest story of his career: the Suez Crisis. Bravely, he decided to test whether or not the pen really was mightier than the sword and he denounced Britain's involvement as 'an act of folly'. He took a lot of flak from the politicians (and not a little from his readers) but was, of course, vindicated when we later withdrew.

He continued in the same determined style and campaigned for social justice, for bridging the poverty gap between the north and south of the country, and for nuclear disarmament, and appeared for the defence in the Lady Chatterley trial. He was rewarded with the title of journalist of the year in the 1971 National Press Awards and a circulation that had grown to a healthy 350,000.

When he talked of giving up the editor's chair in 1975, most of us thought he would be taking up a post in academia so his move to the BBC (to become controller of BBC Scotland) came as something of a surprise. It proved to be something of a culture shock for him too. Having been used to complete editorial freedom, the often bureaucratic BBC proved an uncomfortable fit. He expected autonomy to do what his new title suggested – to control the BBC's activities in Scotland. He set about doing what he knew best: stimulating creativity, stretching the sinews of the news operation and bringing in fresh faces including heavyweights like Helen Liddell (later to go into politics). His BBC Scotland wanted and fought for prime time slots on the main networks. However, all that costs money and when he started banging on appropriate doors, the London-centric bosses were less than cooperative and he had testing clashes with the director general. In the end, the compromise reached in 1978 was that he stepped down from the controller's post and took to the quieter pastures of Radio Highland. He enjoyed the change but four years later he did make the move into academia – as professor of media studies at Stirling University – and in 1984 he became chairman of the Scott Trust (owners of the *Guardian*). In 1989 he retired to the Isle of Arran to concentrate on writing.

In the days when the *Daily Express* and the *Sunday Express* were part of Beaverbrook's crusading empire, there were several Scots who seemed to meet the Beaver's high expectations and contributed to the greatest period for both papers. John Gordon (born Dundee, 1890–1974) was editor and later editor-in-chief at the *Sunday Express* (1928–1952). When he joined the paper – initially as co-editor, but not for long – the circulation was around half a million. When he stepped down, it had reached an all-time high of more than four million. He succeeded in building circulation because he had a strong sense of readers' aspirations and expectations. He knew the middle classes and he cashed in on the Royals' popularity when he commissioned a horoscope for the birth of Princess Margaret. It was so well-received that he turned it into the first regular horoscope in a national newspaper. He also started his famous and irreverent 'Current Affairs' column in 1940 when another contributor let him down, and he then kept it going every week for more than 30 years.

John Gordon never knew anything but newspapers. He was 14 when he began work on the *Dundee Advertiser* in 1904. His keenness oozed from every pore and rapid promotion took him up the ladder to editorship of the group's highly successful *People's Journal*. The trek south came in 1911 when he transferred to the London office of the *Advertiser*, then the London office of the Glasgow *Herald*. When war came in 1914, he joined the King's Royal Rifle Corps, served for the duration and on his demob worked for the *London Evening News* until 1922. He moved to become chief subeditor of the *Daily Express*, but a few years later there was a mix-up over a promised pay rise and he promptly resigned. However, keen to retain his services, Lord Beaverbrook intervened and gave him editorship of the *Sunday Express*. In 1952, close to retirement age, he was made editor-in-chief but that meant he no longer had day-to-day influence on the paper's content and he instead concentrated on his weekly column.

Following hot on the heels of John Gordon was Sir John Junor (born Glasgow, 1919–97), who took up the editorship of the *Sunday Express* in 1954 and put in a record-breaking stint of 32 years in the Fleet Street hot seat. Like John Gordon, he found time to edit and write his trenchant 'JJ' column for the *Sunday Express* (1973–90) and then for *the Mail on Sunday* (1990–97) right up to the week before he died. In the column, he was the self-styled 'Sage of Auchtermuchty' (his version of the 'man on the Clapham omnibus' test) and his catchphrase for debunking hypocrisy was 'pass the sick bag, Alice.' Junor read English at Glasgow University where he was also president of the University Liberal Club. During the Second World War, he was a pilot in the Fleet Air Arm and launched the magazine *Flight Deck*. He joined Beaverbrook in 1947. He was knighted by Margaret Thatcher in 1980. He published his memoirs, entitled *Listening for a Midnight Tram*, in 1990 and his daughter, Penny, gave a torrid account of the great man's private life in her biography *Home Truths*.

According to an obituary in the *Guardian*, Ian McColl (born Glasgow, 1915–2005), editor of the *Daily Express* (1971–74), 'personified the eclectic causes and Presbyterian values that underpinned the success of the Beaverbrook newspaper empire in its heyday.' He had endeared himself to Lord Beaverbrook when, as editor of the *Scottish Daily Express* (1961–71), he made the paper so popular it was said to be read by half of the adult population. The Scottish titles were very much Lord Beaverbrook's personal creation, founded, in 1928, in honour of his father, a former Church of Scotland minister. Apart from war service in the RAF, Ian McColl spent all his adult life working for the Beaver ever since somehow managing to get one of the coveted cub reporter jobs at the *Scottish Daily Express* when he was 18. He sunk his teeth into his new profession and never let go. He wasn't over keen on joining the trail south and at one stage hankered after a career in politics. He twice stood as a Liberal parliamentary candidate: finishing third in Dumfries in 1945 and second in Greenock in 1950. However, he could not resist the Beaver's constant blandishments and finally accepted what was then regarded as the best job in Fleet Street (following in the footsteps of great editors like the legendary Arthur Christiansen). Then, scoops were the red meat of journalism and his greatest coup was undoubtedly the tracking down of the Great Train Robber, Ronnie Biggs, in Brazil. However, although his reporter got a terrific exclusive he was unable to persuade the robber to return to face his punishment in Britain. When he retired, he returned to Scotland as chairman of Scottish Express Newspapers, as a member of the Press Council (1975–78).

Over at *The Times*, two Scots made their mark: Charles Douglas-Home (born Perth 1937–85), a one-time encyclopaedia salesman and nephew of Prime Minister Alec Douglas-Home, was editor for three short years up to his death in 1985, when he was replaced by the pugnacious Charles Wilson, a former Royal Marines boxing champion. Douglas-Home had an appropriate background: Eton College (where he was a King's Scholar), a commission in the Royal Scots Greys and service as aide-de-camp to the Governor of Kenya. When he returned to the UK, he rather fancied working in television but television was not enamoured of his posh accent and he was ever-so-politely turned down. Although he had absolutely no journalistic training, nor any appropriate experience, he talked his way into the Glasgow newsroom of the *Scottish Daily Express*. Astonishingly, despite having openly said how dull he found the daily grind of news-reporting, he was promoted (possibly to get him out of the news editor's hair) and sent to London as deputy to one of the most respected figures in Fleet Street, *Daily Express* defence correspondent Chapman Pincher. Suddenly the light went on and he was fascinated by the intrigue that went with the job. He decided journalism was to be his profession after all.

Within 18 months, his impeccable private contacts with the establishment landed him the role of political and diplomatic correspondent. However, he couldn't agree with paper's intransigent opposition to British entry to the European Community and in 1965 he fled to the more liberal confines of *The Times* as defence correspondent. He relished covering the Arab-Israeli Six Days War and the 1968 Soviet invasion of Czechoslovakia and impressed his masters in the process. Two years later he became features editor, then home editor in 1973 and foreign editor in 1978. He might have become editor when William Rees-Mogg stepped down in 1981 but was pipped to the post by Harold Evans. He only had to wait a year before the almost-inevitable falling out of Evans and proprietor Rupert Murdoch. He therefore inherited a much-weakened paper and had to set about restoring morale before instigating improvements to the news coverage. He asserted his total commitment to *The Times* tradition of impartial news reporting, regardless of the Conservative bent of the leader column. He was just 48 when he died of cancer.

Charles Wilson (born Glasgow, 1940) could not have been more different from Charles Douglas-Home, whose deputy he'd been for three years before taking up the editorship in 1985. Journalism was in his blood and even the forthright Andrew Neil (see later in this chapter) described him as tough.

He had come up through the ranks the hard way, with jobs in Glasgow, Manchester, London and even, briefly, in Chicago, and en route had endured bitter clashes with the print unions. The ring-craft he learned in the boxing arena must have stood him in good stead. He was undoubtedly feared by many of those who worked for him but equally respected by others, including the former MP and columnist Matthew Parris, who was quoted as describing him as 'an inspiration in the craft of journalism.' He must have thought himself lucky when he got his first Fleet Street job for the *News Chronicle* in 1959... only to see it close months later. He was lucky, however, because he switched to the *Daily Mail*, where he learned all the executive tricks of the trade, including a stint as deputy night news editor, sports editor and deputy northern editor in Manchester. He returned to London as *Evening News* assistant editor in 1974, only to head north again two years later to be editor of the Glasgow *Evening Times* and the Scottish *Sunday Standard* (1976–1982) and crossed the pond as editor of the *Chicago Sun-Times* in 1984. Wilson is a keen horse-racing fan and must have especially enjoyed being MD and editor-in-chief of *Sporting Life* (1990–92). He became editorial director of Mirror Group Newspapers (1991–92) and MD of the Mirror Group (1992–98). He managed to sandwich a two-year spell as editor at the *Independent* (then part-owned by MGN) before handing over to Andrew Marr in 1996. He was made chairman of judges for the 2006 British Press Awards as part of an effort to promote transparency and fairness in the judging process. He was also a member of the Newspaper Panel of the Competition Commission (1999–2006). Proving – as is sometimes necessary – that there is life beyond newspapers, he was a trustee of the Royal Navy Museum (1999–2009), a board member of the Countryside Alliance (1999–2005) and the senior non-executive director of Chelsea and Westminster Hospital NHS Foundation Trust.

Fellow journalist Andrew Neil described Sir Alastair Burnet (born Sheffield to Scottish parents, 1928–2012) as 'Britain's greatest broadcaster' and his CV more than supports that view. He was ITN's news anchor for 15 years (1976–91), won BAFTA's Richard Dimbleby award three times (in 1966, 1970 and 1979) and was knighted in 1984 for services to journalism and broadcasting. He had previously been editor of *The Economist* (1965–74) and the *Daily Express* (1974–76).

Another Fleet Street heavyweight to be lured by the bright lights of television is the said Andrew Neil (born Paisley, 1949), who was the fearsome editor of the *Sunday Times* (1983–94) and grew up to be a media baron as one-time proprietor of the *Business* and the *European,* editor-in-chief of Barclay Brothers Press Holdings (including the *Scotsman)* and with stakes in sundry other industry groups including the *Spectator.* He set all that aside, however, to be the regular host of BBC's *Daily Politics, This Week on BBC One* and *Straight Talk with Andrew Neil.* His profile and diary leave me gasping. But that's nothing new. When I reviewed his book *Full Disclosure* for the *British Editor* in 1996, I wrote: 'Unexpectedly, almost shockingly, Mr Neil's book jolted me out of middle-aged complacency. He made me realise I had stopped thinking for myself, that my critical faculties were in the same sad shape as my ageing body. When it thumped on my desk for review, I groaned and made the assumption that the tome would be a classic example of name-dropping. Without reading it, I just knew proprietors, prime ministers, presidents and personalities with a capital P would be scattered through the pages like autumn leaves. I thought I was about to wade through the ultimate in self-justification and I had my poison pen poised to prick the prick (if you'll forgive the vulgarity). I put it away, the poison that is, before I got to the end of the second chapter. The book turned out to be a cracking read, as you would expect from such a consummate gossip. His ego occasionally did get in the way but it was still a great piece of journalism . . . chronicling the Shah Wars, the Battle of Wapping and a string of other key incidents of the eighties and nineties. Like it or like it not, it's a piece of modern media history told from the inside by a journalist who not only witnessed it but often made it happen.' Mr Neil continues to make things happen and is another shoo-in for the empire.

A former graduate trainee on the *Scotsman*, Murdoch MacLennan (born 1949) has been the boss of the Telegraph Media Group since its acquisition by the Barclay brothers from Conrad Black in 2004. Before that, he had been group MD of Associated Newspapers (the *Daily Mail* group) and held senior positions with the Mirror Group and Express Newspapers. Underlining his eminence in the news media, he has been chairman of the PA group, the UK's major news agency, since 2010 and is vice chairman of the World Association of Newspapers.

Cartoonist Alex Graham (born Dumfries, 1915–91) introduced his most famous character, Fred Basset, to readers of the *Daily Mail* in 1963 and the strip is still running today – more than 20 years after Graham's death. He based it on the antics of his own dog, Frieda, and he sustained the jokes through 8000 strips. Most of the names and general backgrounds came from places and people he knew in Scotland. His daughter Arran is one of the team producing new cartoons since his stockpile ran out around 1993. Alex originally created the cartoon for the *New Yorker* magazine in 1953 and it was syndicated around the world – as *Wurzel* in Germany, *Lillo il Cane Saggio* (Lillo the wise dog) in Italy, *Lorang* in Norway, *Laban* in Sweden and *Koiraskoira* in Finland. He also gave us the phrase 'take me to your leader', which he first used in another strip cartoon for the *New Yorker*.

Another long-running feature in the *Daily Mail* has been the *Mac* cartoon created by Stan McMurtry (born Edinburgh, 1936), started in 1971 and still running daily as one of the most popular elements of the paper. Although he began sketching cartoon figures in the margins of his schoolbooks, he was 25 when he was first published – in *Today* in 1961. It was another four years before he finally took the dive into the precarious world of the freelancer. At first he drew strips for a string of comics and the occasional joke cartoon for *Punch* and the *London Evening News*. In 1968, he joined the *Daily Sketch* as a topical cartoonist until it was merged with the *Daily Mail* in 1971 when he used the abbreviated *Mac* for the first time. The rest is history. In 2003 he was awarded an MBE for services to the newspaper industry. When he received the medal from the Queen, she is reported as saying she particularly liked his cartoons when they featured her corgis.

A key influence on the progress of this tome from conception to its publication has been my good friend Kenneth Roy (born Falkirk, 1945), one-time columnist for the *Observer* and 1994 columnist of the year in the UK *Press Gazette* awards. He has smiled occasionally, raised eyebrows often and encouraged consistently whenever he's seen my scribbles. He never goes as far as offering advice but I am always conscious of being pointed in the right direction. However, this Old Pals Act is not what secures his place in the Scottish Empire. Since 2000, he has presided over the Young UK and Ireland Programme, a remarkable project through which he helps develop the communication skills of people in the early stages of their working lives. It works brilliantly. I've seen fragile, uncertain young folk arrive nervously for the residential course and then emerge a few days later, full of self-confidence and determination and ready to grow their careers. The programme aims to encourage the research, writing and presentational abilities of delegates, helping to build confidence and dispelling insecurity as well as enhancing the talents of more experienced participants. Kenneth is also editor of the successful online *Scottish Review*, which has more than 25,000 subscribers.

There's a fairly crass modern saying, 'if you've got it, flaunt it', and Gail Porter (born Edinburgh, 1971) appears to have taken the advice. In 1999, a rear-view of her naked body – taken for men's magazine *FHM* – was famously screened in the most public of places. A well-named marketing company, Cunning Communications, beamed an enormous projection of her posterior on the exterior of the Houses of Parliament, canvassing votes for her in the magazine's '100 Sexiest Women in the World' poll. The stunt worked. She came eighth (not far behind Catherine Zeta-Jones and Cameron Diaz) and the imagery flashed around the globe. More usefully, as a television presenter Gail refused to hide under a wig when she lost her hair because of alopecia, and became a patron of the Little Princess Trust, the charity that helps children with hair loss. Her grit could be invaluable in the empire stakes.

SPORT

Sport has a powerful emotional impact on the Scottish psyche. As a small nation, we are invariably underdogs in international competition. We are always the Davids against the Goliaths. That doesn't make the all-too-common defeat any the less painful, but it does make the successes particularly sweet. When our sportsmen and women win at the highest level, each against-the-odds victory can induce a sense of euphoria that binds Scots together, wherever they are in our global empire. Such then is my state as I try to record the events in London in the summer of 2012.

Andy Murray (born Dunblane, 1987), frustrated by his recent loss in the Wimbledon final to world number one Roger Federer, all but made up for that when he took gold in the men's tennis singles after beating who else but Roger Federer. He was the first British tennis medallist in more than a century and he underlined his change in fortunes by also taking silver in the mixed doubles. In further spectacular evidence of his growing popularity, he came third in the BBC's sports personality of the year contest for 2012. More importantly, he snagged his first grand slam title at the US Open in September of that year, and moved up to number two position in the world rankings in spring 2013.

That, however, was never going to be enough. On one of the hottest days on record in the gladiatorial arena that is Wimbledon's Centre Court, in July 2013 Andy Murray won tennis's most prized trophy and title: Wimbledon Champion. What made it even sweeter was that his opponent was again a man ranked above him at number one in those world rankings, this time Serbia's Novak Djokovic. In what turned out to be the final game, we had to suffer as three match points slithered tantalisingly from his grasp, but sheer Scottish grit and stubbornness kicked in and he recovered from Djokovic's two advantage points to finally smash his way home in straight sets: 6-4, 7-5, 6-4. He was the first British winner since Fred Perry in 1936, the Wimbledon crowds – and no doubt most of the 17 million watching on TV – were ecstatic and the commentators had a field day. Fame and fortune are secure, as is his place in the Scottish Empire.

Like the rest of the UK and most of the world, I was enthralled by the 2012 London Olympics and Paralympics and the Games proved my point when Scots, competing with the world's finest sporting figures, won 25 medals, ten of them gold. Their places in sporting history are surely safe. The most outstanding of them all was, of course, Sir Chris Hoy (born Edinburgh, 1976) who upgraded his place in the record books when he won two cycling gold medals, taking his total Olympic haul to six. He had already been knighted for his achievements in the 2008 Games in Beijing (see chapter 6, And the glory) and it was a surprise when he decided to retire while still at the top of his sport in April 2013. He went in style: not just with his collection of medals but with the title Britain's greatest Olympian. It's a record that won't be easily surpassed and it has made the Scottish Empire the more plausible.

Rower Katherine Grainger (born Glasgow, 1972) bettered her silver medals at the previous two Olympics by taking gold in the women's double skulls; Heather Stanning (born Moray, 1985) added another rowing gold in the women's pairs; Tim Baillie (born Aberdeen, 1979) brought home gold in the canoe slalom; and Scott Brash (born Peebles, 1985) shared gold as part of the GB showjumping team. David Florence (born Aberdeen, 1983) won silver in the canoe slalom; Luke Patience (born Aberdeen, 1986) silver in sailing; Michael Jamieson (born Glasgow, 1982) was awarded silver in the 200m breaststroke. Daniel Purvis (born Dundee, 1990) took bronze for his performance in the artistic gymnastics team final; and Laura Bartlett (born Glasgow, 1988) and Emily Maquire (born Glasgow, 1987) both collected bronze as part of the GB hockey team. That's a very respectable haul by any standards. In the Paralympics, the small team of 27 Scots outperformed expectations and brought home three gold, six silver and two bronze medals. This exceeded the eight-medal haul from Beijing and the target of nine medals set by Sport Scotland. Neil Fachie (born Aberdeen, 1984) won a cycling gold, as did Craig Maclean (born Grantown, 1971), acting as pilot to Anthony Kappes; David Smith (born Dunfermline, 1978) won rowing gold in the mixed pairs. The six Scots taking home Paralympic silver medals were Aileen McGlynn, OBE (born Paisley, 1973), Karen Darke (born Inverness, 1971) and, again Neil Fachie, all in cycling events; Sam Ingram's silver was in judo; Stef Reid (born New Zealand to a Scots father, 1984) was second in the long jump; and Libby Clegg (born Bollington, 1990) also won silver in the 100 metres. To make it a family affair, her brother James (born 1994) took bronze in the 100-metre butterfly in the Olympic pool, while Aileen McGlynn completed the Scottish haul with her second medal, a cycling bronze.

It wasn't only in the sporting arena that Scots excelled at the London Olympics. Musician Dame Evelyn Glennie (born Aberdeen, 1965) collaborated on the soundtrack to the opening ceremony and performed live in the stadium, while Sir Charles Allen (born Lanark, 1957) and Sir Craig Reedie (born Bridge of Weir, 1941) played key management roles in bringing the Games to London and in delivering the mammoth spectacle. Sir Charles (knighted in the New Year Honours that followed the Games) was honorary mayor of the Olympic Village and Sir Craig (who led an earlier bid to bring the Games to Manchester) was vice president and the only Briton on the executive of the International Olympic Committee.

Dame Evelyn is, of course, renowned as one of the world's finest percussionists, despite losing her hearing when she was eight. Much has been written about her exceptional career and her fortitude in overcoming her profound deafness, so all I need do here is enter a reminder of some of her awards and achievement. She won a Grammy award for best chamber music performance in 1989, *Rhythm Magazine*'s best studio and live percussionist in 1998, 2000, 2002, 2003 and 2004, *Musical America*'s instrumentalist of the year 2003, and the Sabian (instrument-maker) lifetime achievement award in 2006; she joined the Percussive Arts Society's Hall of Fame in 2008 and was also named Scot of the year in 1982 and Scotswoman of the decade in 1990. She holds 15 honorary doctorates from UK universities, was awarded an OBE in 1993 and made a dame in 2007.

Chairman of the successful Commonwealth Games of 2002 in Manchester, Charles Allen had been vice chairman of the bid and then chairman of the London Organising Committee for the Olympic and Paralympic Games (LOCOG) Nations and Regions Group, responsible for developing the nationwide benefits of the Games. He also served on the Audit and Ceremonies Committees is now chairman of the Join In Trust. He has long been a major player in Britain's media industry. He was CEO of Granada Television and instrumental in the takeovers of London Weekend Television and Yorkshire Television. When that group merged with Carlton to become ITV plc, he was appointed chief executive and served for 15 years until he stepped down in 2006. He is currently chairman of the UK's biggest commercial radio group, Global Radio (which includes the Heart Network). He is also a senior advisor at Goldman Sachs, a non-executive director at Virgin Media and chairman of the Two Sisters Food Group. He was appointed chair of The British Red Cross at the end of 2012.

Sir Craig, knighted for his services to sport, is a former international badminton player and was chair of the British Olympic Association until 2005. He suffered the frustration of leading an earlier failed bid to bring the Games to Manchester but that experience meant he was a pivotal figure in the bidding and organising phases of London 2012. He has served on the influential 15-member executive board of the IOC since 2009. He was also on the Evaluation Commission that awarded the 2016 Olympics to Rio de Janeiro and has been leading the evaluation of the three short-listed contenders for the 2020 Summer Olympics: Istanbul, Madrid and Tokyo from which Tokyo emerged triumphant. Sir Craig has enjoyed a long career in sports administration: as president of both the Scottish Badminton Union and the International Badminton Federation, he was responsible for the admission of the sport to the Olympic programme in 1985. He became chairman of the BOA in 1992 and led it through the Games in Atlanta, Sydney and Athens and the Winter Games of Lillehammer, Nagano and Salt Lake City. Rio de Janeiro beckons.

Football

Scotland's national sport is still football and if, perhaps, we don't shine so brightly as a team on the world stage, as a nation our contribution to the game is still remarkable. It must be something in the porridge because there are a host of Scots ensuring the development of modern soccer both on and off the field, playing for or managing many of the top English Premiership clubs, which are arguably amongst the best in the world. Although we may have struggled with our management of the national team (fingers crossed for the 2013-appointed Gordon Strachan), Scottish managers – some, it has to be said, dour-but-committed, others charismatic – have had great success at club level south of the border.

Manchester United, for my money the greatest and certainly the richest football club in the world, owes most of its success over the past 60 years to two undeniably great Scottish managers and one rather more controversial one, and the baton has now been passed on to yet another man from Govan. Sir Matt Busby (born Bellshill, 1909–1994) laid the foundations of the club's formidable reputation (1945–71); Tommy Docherty (born Glasgow, 1928) revived its fortunes during his three-year stay (1973–77); Sir Alex Ferguson (born Govan, 1941) consolidated and built its phenomenal global success in the 26 years before his retirement, at the end of the 2012/13 season; and David Moyes (born Govan, 1963) is set for a sturdy defence of the Man U reputation.

Comparing the achievements of the United giants Matt Busby and Alex Ferguson is very difficult. Both have towering reputations. Sir Matt (knighted 1968) managed the team for nearly a quarter of a century and Sir Alex (knighted 1999) comfortably overtook that record. Former English international Johnny Giles, who joined Matt Busby's team when he was just 15, summed it up in a newspaper article: 'We cannot speak of an age of Busby and the era of Ferguson. The line… is obliterated in a football phenomenon sealed with blood and glory.'

It was Matt Busby – a former player with Manchester City (1929–36) and Liverpool (1936–39) – who picked up the pieces of a club wrecked by the Second World War, during which its famous Old Trafford ground had been bombed by the Luftwaffe. Within two years he had won both the FA Cup and the League Cup and within ten had built one of the best teams in football. All the players had come up through the club's unique academy and the newspapers (the word media was not then in popular usage) dubbed them the 'Busby Babes'. When they won the League Championship in 1956, the average age of the team was 21. They won the title again in 1957, but the following year tragedy struck again. As has been written about in numerous books and on every sports page in the world, Manchester United suffered the disaster of the air crash at Munich in 1958. Eight players, all under 23, died and Matt Busby was so seriously injured that he was given the last rites twice.

Against the odds, he recovered and rebuilt the team, won the League in 1965 and 1967 and then the European Cup in 1968. His place in history was secured with a knighthood the same year. After retiring, he served as a director and president of the club and was a member of the Football League Management Committee. He published his autobiography, *My Story*, in 1957. There is a statue to his memory outside Old Trafford and the Sir Matt Busby Way leads to the ground's south entrance. His close friend Bill Shankly (see later in this chapter) paid tribute to him, saying he was 'the greatest football manager ever.'

The club suffered a slump in the five years after Sir Matt retired and it was the fast-talking Glaswegian Tommy Docherty who did his bit of reparation by dragging the club out of the second division, back into the top flight and winning the FA Cup in 1977. The Doc, as he was universally known, was born in the Gorbals in 1928. He was a player and serial manager. His claim was to have had 'more clubs than Jack Nicklaus' and he has the CV to prove it: Chelsea (1962–67), Rotherham (1967–68), Queens Park Rangers (for just a month in 1968 but again 1979–80), Aston Villa (1968–70), Manchester United (1972–77), Derby County (1977–79), Preston (for six months in 1981), Oporto (1981–84) and Wolves (1984–85). He also managed the Scottish national team for a short spell in 1971. He was less promiscuous in his playing days, appearing for just four teams: Celtic (1947–49), more than 300 games, including the 1954 FA Cup final, for Preston North End (1949–1958), Arsenal 1958–61, and a handful of appearances for Chelsea (1961–1962). He was capped 25 times for Scotland.

The outpouring of respect and admiration that greeted the announcement of Sir Alex Ferguson's retirement underlines how football has transcended sport and become an international business. He made the headlines in almost as many of the business sections as sports pages. When he made his way through Manchester in the team bus for the last time, the police had to close one of the best vantage points – appropriately Sir Matt Busby Way – outside the Old Trafford stadium, when the crowd reached 20,000! That was despite the weather, which the *Guardian* described colourfully and succinctly: 'There was wind, there was hail. There was thunder and lightning and sideways rain. But a bit of bad weather failed to deter the tens of thousands of United fans who jostled for position to bid farewell to the most successful manager in British football history.'

Sir Alex was born in Glasgow on Hogmanay 1941 and that birthday serves to make him even more defiantly Scottish. When he left school he became an apprentice toolmaker in a Clyde shipyard but his passion was football and he signed as an amateur for local club Queen's Park in 1957, when he was 16. He scored the winning goal in his first match and for three years he was able to turn his back on the clamour of the shipyards every Saturday afternoon. When he turned professional, he played more than 300 games for several clubs – including Rangers – and notched up somewhere around 170 goals. His first taste of management was at East Stirlingshire, where he briefly had a part-time contract for £40 a week! At the end of the season, he couldn't resist the challenge of a full-time post with St Mirren (1975–78), taken up on the advice of his friend, Jock Stein. He transformed the club's fortunes, taking them from the lower regions of the second division to champions of the first division in 1977. The average age of his first team was 19 and the skipper was 20. However, he fell foul of the club chairman, who said he had 'no managerial ability'!

He therefore headed north to Aberdeen (1978–1986), where he replaced the great Billy McNeill, who had gone to manage Celtic. The Scottish game was then still dominated by Rangers and Celtic and although the Granite City club was a major contender, it hadn't won the league since 1955. Alex Ferguson led his team to the semi-final of the Scottish Cup and the final of the League Cup, but lost both and finished fourth in the league. In 1979, they lost another League Cup final but he managed to raise their performance in the second half of the season and finally broke the 15-year stranglehold of the Old Firm to win the league title. After the club's win in the 1982 Scottish Cup, he was able to turn down an offer to manage Wolverhampton Wanderers. The following season they went on to the European Cup Winners' Cup, where Aberdeen beat Real Madrid to become only the third Scottish team to lift a European trophy. They topped that by retaining the Scottish Cup with a win over Rangers. The following year the team retained the cup and won the Scottish League and Ferguson was awarded the OBE in the Queen's Birthday Honours. He was also offered jobs with Rangers, Arsenal and Tottenham Hotspur. He stayed put to win the Scottish League title again in 1985 and the League Cup and Scottish Cup double the following year, and he was appointed to the board.

When Jock Stein died suddenly, he took over as manager of the Scottish national team and took them through the final stages of 1986 World Cup. He then rejected further offers from Spurs and Arsenal but finally took on the Manchester United job in November 1986. For several years he struggled to change United's fortunes, and it wasn't until the 1990s that he turned the corner. Once he did, of course, he made 'Man U' the most successful football club in the world.

Following his retirement, Sir Alex continues to be involved at United, taking up a position on the club's board and acting as an ambassador for the club. More importantly, I think, he plans to keep out of the hair of his young successor and let him get on with the job. He is the one who recommended David Moyes (born Govan, 1963) for the job and he was fulsome in his praise: 'He's hard-working and has an integrity about him. He's got a work ethic and he's a serious football man. He's also got perseverance: look at what he's done at Everton.' After taking over at Everton in 2002, David Moyes was named the Premiership's manager of the year in 2003, 2005 and 2009. He too is a former player, with a career that spanned more than 600 appearances with clubs including Celtic, Dunfermline Athletic and Preston North End.

It was at Preston that he began his managerial career, working his way up from coach to assistant manager and then manager in 1998. In his first season, he helped the team avoid relegation from the second division, took them to the play-offs the following year and to the second division title and promotion in 2000. He then led them to the first division play-offs in 2001. Since then, he has put a stop to the see-saw performance that saw Everton in the top half of the league one season and struggling to avoid relegation the next. In 2004/05, he took them to fourth in the Premiership and a place in the Champions League and the UEFA Cup. Coincidental with the retirement of Sir Alex, his contract was due for renewal at the end of the 2012/13 season, so his transition to Manchester United was seamless. He got off to a great start with his arrival unanimously welcomed by the players. One of the most senior, Rio Ferdinand, was quoted as saying: 'He couldn't be walking into a healthier situation. The young players here are hungry and want to win stuff. The senior players have won a lot of things but have still got the desire and the work ethic that the manager has instilled into us. I think that's vital for the future of the club.'

If anyone can be said to have become – in the journalistic jargon – a legend in their own lifetime, one of the most likely must be Bill Shankly (born Glenbuck, Ayrshire, 1913–81). How else can one explain the way the press hung on the Liverpool boss's every word and immortalised him in his own quotes? I could write a chapter on his glorious bon mots. After an emotion-packed Anfield thriller against Celtic in 1966, he asked Jock Stein: 'Jock, do you want your share of the gate money or shall we just return the empties?' When it was suggested he had used an away game with a lowly league side as a special wedding anniversary celebration with his wife, he said: 'Of course I didn't take my wife to see Rochdale as an anniversary present. It was her birthday.' He was renowned for gritty determination and commitment and he expected the same of his players: 'if a player isn't interfering with play or seeking to gain an advantage, then he should be!' When Adidas wanted to present him with its Golden Boot award for services to football, Bob Paisley took the call and told him they wanted to know his shoe size; Shanks shouted back: 'if it's gold, tell them I'm a 28.' And always there was pride in his team: 'there are two great teams in this city: Liverpool… and Liverpool Reserves.' To rub salt into the wounds of his local rivals, he added, 'if Everton were playing at the bottom of my garden, I'd pull the curtains.' Referring to a player he had just offloaded, he said, 'he's got the heart of a caraway seed.' But the best, for me, was his most famous comment, made to a *Sunday Times* journalist: 'Some people think football is a matter of life and death. I can assure you it's much, much more serious than that.' When I first read that, I simply thought it was a very funny, off-the-cuff remark, but on reflection and to paraphrase the man himself, it's much more serious than that. It barely disguised the raw, Scottish passion he had for the game. It positively oozed from every pore.

His cracks were but a sideshow, however, to his massive contribution to football. From the first time he kicked a ball in the village street, he was destined to be a pivotal figure in the game, and yet Liverpool didn't seem to realise his potential when they turned him down for the manager's job in 1951! He was another Scot who used football as an escape route from the pits. He had a decent career as a player but it might have flourished more if it hadn't been savagely disrupted by the war. The leagues were suspended for the duration and matches were sporadic. During those uncertain times, he played occasional games for a number of teams, including Liverpool (where he played alongside Matt Busby and began a lifelong friendship), Arsenal, Cardiff City, Bolton Wanderers, Luton Town and Partick Thistle. He won seven wartime caps and helped Preston to victory in the 1941 FA Cup final, and when normality was restored in 1946-47, he rejoined his old club. By then, of course, he was 33 and he retired three years later.

In 1949, he began a new phase in his life. He was appointed manager of Carlisle United and two years later he applied for the Liverpool job. He was told he didn't meet their needs and settled for a job at Grimsby. From there he moved on to Workington in 1953 and then quickly to Huddersfield Town, where, as proof of his sharp eye for soccer talent, one of his signings was the 15-year-old Denis Law, who he gave a first-team place within a year. He finally joined Liverpool just before Christmas in 1959. The team was languishing in the second division, the stadium was crumbling, the training facilities were poor and the team hadn't exactly been setting the world alight. Even worse, they lived in the shadow of Everton. That was the challenge and to help meet it, Shanks brought in a group of backroom staff including Bob Paisley. He insisted on regular fitness training and introduced communal meals to develop team spirit... and to check on the players' diets! It worked. They started winning games and he was able to make new signings including Ian St John and Ron Yates. In just three seasons, Liverpool were back in the first division. Two seasons later the team won the league championship and had the emotional bonus of taking the title from Everton!

The following year they won the FA Cup and reached the semi-final of the Champions' Cup. They beat Inter-Milan at Anfield but lost the away leg and went out on aggregate. In 1966, he again led the team to the League Championship and the final of the European Cup Winners' Cup, which they lost to Ajax. After finishing second in the first division in 1969, Shankly restructured the team: he brought in Kevin Keegan and tried for Lou Macari but lost out to the chequebook of Manchester United. In 1973 he repaid the faith of the Kop by again winning the first division Championship (the club's eighth title) and then he finally got his hands on his first Euro trophy, the UEFA Cup. The next season was to be his last as the boss of Anfield. Although he had to settle for second place in the League Championship, he took the team to Wembley and saw them beat Newcastle United 3-0 to collect the coveted FA Cup. Later in the year he was awarded the OBE and, having reached his sixtieth, he retired while still at the top and with a final quote: 'I was only in the game for the love of football... and I wanted to bring back happiness to the people of Liverpool.'

When he died in 1981, at the age of 68, the Labour party conference stood for a minute's silence. His old friend Matt Busby was so upset he refused to take calls from journalists asking for his reaction. At the first game after his funeral, the Kop fans unfurled a huge banner that said 'Shankly Lives Forever'.

Although he made only the briefest of sorties outside Scotland and so, strictly speaking, shouldn't be included in this book of empire, Jock Stein (born Burnbank, 1922–85) earned such towering esteem throughout the football world that I have no hesitation in making him an exception. He was the first British manager to take a team into the heart of Europe and come away with the trophy. When his Celtic side beat Inter-Milan to win the European Cup in Portugal in 1967, they won universal respect and accorded their own epithet: the 'Lisbon Lions'. Although Celtic had won the Scottish League title and the League Cup in the two preceding seasons, Inter – twice winners in the Cup's then 11-year history – had been the clear favourites to win, but as Jock Stein said, his team weren't there just to make up the numbers. After the win, Bill Shankly told him: 'You're immortal now!' In a 2003 poll by the *Sunday Herald,* he was voted Scotland's greatest football manager.

Apart from a short spell in America, George Graham (born Glasgow, 1944) has spent his career in England, where he took on some of the toughest jobs in football. When he became manager in 1983, Millwall were bottom of the old third division. When he took over in 1986, Arsenal hadn't won a trophy for seven years. When he joined Leeds United in 1996, they were struggling with relegation. When he went to Tottenham Hotspurs in 1998, they were becalmed mid-table. In each instance, he had major impact.

At Millwall, he first avoided relegation and then took them into the second division in 1984. When he moved on in 1986, he left them in such good shape that they went into the first division the following year. At Arsenal, he took the Gunners to the top of the League by mid-season but then ended in a very creditable fourth place. He took them to the League Cup final the following year, and in his third season he took them to their first League title since 1971. In 1993 Arsenal became the first team to win the League and Cup double and the following year they won the UEFA Cup Winners' Cup. When he joined Leeds United in 1996, the team scored twice as many goals as in the previous season, finished fifth in what had become the Premiership and qualified for the UEFA Cup. He moved to Spurs and within months had taken them to a League Cup victory and a place in the UEFA Cup. He was sacked after a disagreement with the club chairman in 2001.

Kenny Dalglish (born Dalmarnock, 1951) won everything it was possible to win as a player including the title of Player's Player of the Year (1983) and twice the Football League's Player of the Year (1987 and 1983). He played for Celtic (1971–77) when he was just 20 and became captain within three years. He was a prolific goal scorer and was the first to score a hundred league goals in both Scotland and England. At Liverpool, the fans called him King Kenny and he was a runaway number one in the poll of 'Players Who Shook the Kop'.

After that golden playing career, he turned to club management. He became Liverpool's player-manager in 1985 (in the wake of the Heysel Stadium disaster) and continued to more than satisfy the success-hungry Scousers. In his first season in charge, he led the team to the League and FA Cup double. During the next five years he won three more league titles and two FA Cups. In 1991, he made a surprise move to the unfashionable, second-division Blackburn Rovers and, with a little bit of help from his millionaire chairman's chequebook, turned them into Premier League winners in 1995. Two years later, he moved on again, this time to Newcastle United. The team were Premier League runners-up at the end of his first season but faltered in the next year and he was unceremoniously sacked at the beginning of 1998/99. He was appointed Celtic's director of football and had a short spell as caretaker manager but yet again left in some acrimony. He left football in 2000 to concentrate on the breast cancer charity established by his wife, making a brief return first as caretaker then permanent manager of Liverpool in 2011–12. They won the League Cup and reached the FA Cup final, but eighth place in the Premiership was not the standard the club had come to expect and he left after one and a half seasons.

After a successful playing career (mainly with Liverpool, Blackburn Rovers and Newcastle United), Graeme Souness (born Edinburgh, 1953) had a somewhat torrid time managing some of the biggest clubs in Europe: Rangers, Liverpool, Benfica, Galatasaray, Blackburn Rovers and Newcastle United. He began his career as a 15-year-old apprentice at Tottenham Hotspurs in 1968, and within four years he was playing in the American summer league and winning his place in the All-Star team of 1972. He returned to Spurs for the winter but played only one game before being transferred to Middlesbrough for £30,000. He helped them to win the second division title and automatic promotion to the first division, with a hat-trick in the 8-0 victory over Sheffield Wednesday in the final game of the season. He joined Liverpool in 1978 and during his seven seasons was part of the squad – including Alan Hansen and Kenny Dalglish – that won an astonishing five League Championships, three European Cups and four League Cups! In 1984, he joined the Italian club Sampdoria for a £650,000 transfer fee and in his first season helped them win the Coppa Italia for the first time in their history. After two seasons he returned to Scotland as player-manager for Rangers. He embarked on what became known as the Souness Revolution, with signings of English players including Terry Butcher, Trevor Francis and Gary Stevens.

In Graeme Souness' first season in charge (1986/87), Rangers won the Championship and the League Cup, beating Celtic 2-1 in the final. He restored the club to the fore of Scottish football and, despite controversy about his style, won two more championships and two League Cups. When he returned to Liverpool as manager (1991–94), his success was more in developing new talent than adding silverware to the trophy case. Although his early days at the club were blighted by heart problems, he did lead the club to triumph in the FA Cup in 1992. Despite undergoing major surgery days before the final, he left hospital to lead his players out at Wembley. They repaid him by beating Sunderland 2-0. In 1998 he was included in the Football League's 100 Legends, and in Liverpool's 100 Players Who Shook The Kop poll, the fans named him the ninth most popular player in the club's history. He was inducted into the English Football Hall of Fame in 2007 and he is one of only 70 players in Rangers' official Hall of Fame.

Before moving into management, Gordon Strachan (born Edinburgh, 1957) also had an illustrious playing career. His most recent success was at Celtic, where he was in charge for four seasons (2005–09) during which he won the Scottish Premier League title three times. As a player, his string of clubs included Aberdeen during most of the highly successful Alex Ferguson years (1977–84); Manchester United (1984–89); and Leeds United (1989–95). With Aberdeen, he won premier division medals in 1979–80 and 1983–84; Scottish Cup winners' medals in 1982, 1983 and 1984; and the UEFA Cup Winners' Cup and Super Cup winners' medals in 1983. He won a medal with Manchester United in the FA Cup in 1985, and at Leeds United his medals included second division winner 1989/90, first division winner 1991/92, FA Charity Shield 1992. He was also named Player of the Year in 1991. He was appointed the Scottish team manager in 2013.

Another of Liverpool's ex-stars-turned-pundits is the stylish Alan Hansen (born Alloa, 1955). He acquired his trademark forehead scar by running into a glass door at school. It took 27 stitches to put him together again but it never deterred him from being a tough central defender. After a successful career that included no fewer than seven League Championships, a number of cup medals and 26 Scottish caps, a serious knee injury forced him to retire in 1991. He declined offers to manage and opted instead to become a commentator, first with Sky and then with the BBC, where he is a Saturday regular. He also features regularly in TV commercials.

It will be fascinating to watch the next generation of young players and managers come through the ranks. The list of great Scottish players is formidable by any standards and in a bid to contain this book to readable proportions, all I can do is indulge my own whimsical preferences and name a few of the men whose performances have thrilled me down the years. Two or three are mentioned earlier as managers and fortunately the record books pay justifiable tribute to the others.

Few, I suspect, would quibble about putting the incomparable Denis Law (born Aberdeen, 1940) at the top of that list. From the moment he caught the eye of Bill Shankly at Huddersfield in 1950, Denis was destined for stardom and he was named as Scotland's greatest ever player in a 2003 poll to mark the 50th anniversary of UEFA. In the intervening years, he won everything in sight – including the cap that made him Scotland's youngest international just short of his nineteenth birthday and the accolade of European Footballer of the Year in 1964.

Pat Crerand (born Gorbals, 1939) was one of those granite-hard Glaswegians who displayed his toughness at Celtic Park for six years before the almost-inevitable drift south to Manchester United in 1963. He always controlled the midfield and was renowned for being the feed for Bobby Charlton and George Best. He helped United win the league championship in 1965 and 1967, the 1963 FA Cup and the 1968 European Cup. He played 16 games for Scotland. He is now a regular commentator on Manchester United's radio and TV stations.

Rejected by Arsenal and Chelsea because he was too small for their liking, Billy Bremner (born Stirling, 1942–97) showed that what he lacked in stature he made up for in a fiery spirit during nearly 800 games for Leeds United. The *Sunday Times* once described him 'as ten stone of barbed wire.' Leeds fans adored him, voted him their greatest ever player and erected a memorial statue of him – hands gloriously aloft in triumph – outside the Elland Road stadium, where he was an almost permanent feature of Don Revie's team for more than 15 years. He was made captain in 1966 and led the side through its most successful period: they won the League Cup and the Fairs Cup in 1968 and, finally, the League Championship in 1969, after losing only two of the season's 42 games. During his career he played in four FA Cup finals but collected just the one winner's medal. He also had one hand on the European Cup Winners' Cup in 1973 (but lost late in the game to AC Milan) and another on the European Cup in 1975 (but lost out to Bayern Munich). When he finally retired from the game, he comfortably settled into the media and after-dinner circuit. He died after a heart attack in 1997. He was 54. In their first match after his death, Leeds had two players sent off and the fans sang: 'We've got nine men and Billy!' The team held out for a draw. The club song, 'Glory, Glory Leeds United', has a verse that sums up his place in the fans' affections: 'Little Billy Bremner is the captain of the crew |For the sake of Leeds United he would break himself in two |His hair is red and fuzzy and his body's black and blue |But Leeds go marching on.'

Motherwell-born Ian St John (born 1938) started setting records from the moment he walked on the pitch for his hometown club in 1959. He scored the fastest hat-trick on record – in just two and a half minutes – to stun the then-formidable Hibs. At the end of the following season, he left Motherwell for Liverpool for a fee that doubled Anfield's previous highest spend. He made the same locomotive start when he scored another three goals against Merseyside rivals Everton in the Liverpool Senior Cup final, and went on to score an average of 20 goals in each of his first three seasons. He helped Liverpool out of the second division, helped them win the League Championship in only their second season in the top flight and headed home the winner to give the club its first FA Cup success in 1965. He ranks at 21 in the Kop's all-time favourites poll. After retiring from playing and dabbling in management he moved into television as part of the hugely-successful ITV show *Saint and Greavsie* (with Jimmy Greaves). He now also has his own programme on the fans' Radio City.

Rugby

Television has transformed rugby into a truly global sport with the Six Nations, the World Cup, the Lions and the Barbarians brought into our living rooms and countless bars around the world. The Scottish XV has had mixed fortunes over the past half century but there has been a string of individual players who have shown courage and ability the equal of any in the crunching world of rugby. However, no account of the game in the 20th century would be complete without mention of the most popular contributor to the game. I hope, therefore, I'll be forgiven for this short, indulgent memoir not about a player, but about the man who brought rugby alive for me: Bill McLaren (born Hawick, 1923–2010), the most respected of sports commentators, whose BBC career spanned 50 glorious years. Exceptionally, he was awarded three honours: the MBE in 1992, OBE in 1996 and CBE in 2003. He was the commentator in 1936 when 'Scotland beat a Rest of the World XV by the runaway score of 70-3.' Sadly, you won't find that staggering statistic in the record books. It was but a figment of his febrile imagination. He was only 13 at the time and his fictional commentary was written to pass away the hours while he was convalescing from tuberculosis. The disease, which nearly killed him, robbed him of playing his beloved sport and he had to settle for the vicarious thrills of the onlooker... but that's when he discovered another way of taking part. He discovered he was a natural commentator. 'There must have been something inside me that wanted to describe rugby to people,' he has said. It was the colour of his descriptions of all the great moments of twentieth-century rugby that endeared him to an audience far beyond the confines of rugby supporters. He made the game exciting and accessible for those, especially many Scots, who had thought it was a middle-class game for big girls! He became known as the 'Voice of Rugby' – and what a voice and what language! In the sometimes painfully partisan world of sports journalism, he was a beacon of fair-minded objectivity. He oozed a deep love of the game and all those who played it. He was unconcerned by the colour of the shirt, only that the player had good red blood coursing through his veins. He extolled exciting rugby wherever and by whoever it was played.

Although a loyal Borderer (he once said 'a day away from Hawick is a day wasted'), he was never partisan and never disparaging, but he did allow himself the odd moment of saying exactly what he meant and many of his bon mots still make me laugh:

'He kicked that ball like it was three pounds o' haggis'

'That one [a missed goal kick] was a bit inebriated . . . just like one of my golf shots.'

'Big? He must have born when beef was cheap' (of a South African forward)

'He's like a demented ferret up a drainpipe'

'He's like a raging bull with a bad head'

'He's as quick as a trout up a burn'

'Those props are as cunning as a bag o' weasels'

'The All Blacks look like great prophets of doom'

'I'm no hod-carrier but I'd be laying bricks if he [Jonah Lomu] was running at me!'

And of course, there's his most famous line, delivered when he was extolling the virtues of one or another local hero: 'They'll be dancing in the streets of [one Borders town or another] tonight!'

In her tribute on his retirement, the Princess Royal (patron of Scottish Rugby) said: 'He has passed on his love for the game and all it represents to everyone he has met or spoken with. His unique contribution to the commentator's art has been applauded by both his peers and listeners alike the world over.' When he made the last commentary of his career at Cardiff's Millennium Stadium in 2002, a huge banner claimed: 'Bill McLaren is Welsh.' It was the ultimate tribute from rugby's most passionate supporters for the game's most compassionate Scotsman.

On the pitch, the 1971 Lions were a roaring success Down Under and eight Scots played their part in ensuring the Aussies and New Zealanders knew they had been in some rugby matches. The tourists, led by their Scottish manager, Dr Doug Smith, racked up their best ever performance with their first series victory against the mighty All Blacks. The seven Scottish players were Rodger Arneil (born Edinburgh, 1944), who had been in South Africa in 1968; Frank Laidlaw (born Hawick, 1940), Gordon Brown (born Troon, 1947–2001), Sandy Carmichael (born Glasgow, 1944), Ian McLaughlin (born Tarbolton, 1942), who gloried in the nickname the Mighty Mouse, Alastair Biggar (born Edinburgh, 1946) and Chris Rea (born Dundee, 1943). It shows the strength of the party that it also included Ireland's Willie-John McBride, Fergus Slattery and Mike Gibson; Wales' Gareth Edwards, JPR Williams, Gerald Davies and Barry John and England's David Duckham and Stack Stevens.

Doug Smith (born Aberdeen, 1924–98) had a dual role on the tour because he was able to double as the team doctor. He had been a moderately successful player as wing in eight games for Scotland during the dog days of the early 1950s and joined the Lions' first post-war tour to Australia and New Zealand in 1950. He broke his arm early in the tour so had to content himself with enjoying the sunshine for most of the three months. It was when handling the organisational elements of the 1971 tour that he came into his own. For a start, he made sure the press pack were kept onside by encouraging them to match the players in all their off-pitch pleasures, notably in a marathon pub crawl during the stop-over in Hong Kong. When the team looked jaded in losing 11-14 to the Queensland state side in their first match, he explained that they were suffering from 'chronic circadian dysrhythmia'. The equally jet-lagged journos were too tired to disagree. He only had to explain away one more defeat, when the All Blacks won the second test. That time there was no play on words: 'We were beaten by the better side and must do better if we are to win the series.' They did so... famously!

Since then, there have been a host of Scottish names gracing the team-sheets of the British and Irish Lions and most of the great Barbarian travelling sides. In addition to those already mentioned, the names that leap out at me include Jim Renwick (born Hawick, 1952); Andy Irvine (born Edinburgh, 1951); Ian (now Sir Ian) McGeechan (born Leeds, 1946), who was also coach to the Lions in 1989, 1993, 1997, 2005 and 2009; Billy Steele (born Langholm, 1947) who gave the Scottish team its 'Flower of Scotland' anthem; Jim Aitken (born Penicuik, 1947), who captained the Scottish Grand Slam side in the 1984 Five Nations Championship; Gavin Hastings OBE (born Edinburgh, 1962), who captained the Lions in New Zealand in 1993; his younger brother Scott Hastings (born Edinburgh, 1964); Gary Armstrong (born Edinburgh, 1966) of whom Jonny Wilkinson said, 'I've never met anyone as tough as him', and who was the architect of Scotland's 1990 Grand Slam; Craig Chalmers (born Galashiels, 1968); and Mike Blair (born Edinburgh, 1981) the only Scot to have ever been nominated for the IRB International Rugby Player of the Year in 2008.

Cricket

Scotland and cricket don't readily go together so it was almost inevitable that Mike Denness (born Bellshill, 1940–2013) would suffer from the nickname Haggis during a long career which, improbably, saw him captain the English Test side for 17 matches, including tours of the West Indies (1973–74) and Australia (1974–75) and the home tests in 1976. Overall, he won 28 Test caps, scored 1,667 runs at an average of nearly 40, and was named the 1975 *Wisden* cricketer of the year. He first played cricket for the Ayr club and won the first of ten Scottish caps in 1959 when he was just 18. Three years later, he moved south and turned professional with Kent. There he helped the county become a dominant force. They won the Gillette Cup in 1967 and the 1970 County Championship. He was made captain in 1972 and led them to victory in the Gillette Cup again, the Benson and Hedges Cup and three One-Day League trophies. In 1977, after 15 years, he moved to Essex and helped them to the County Championship in 1979. He won his first England cap in 1969 against New Zealand at the Oval and quickly became a fixture in both Test and one-day sides, replacing Ray Illingworth as captain in 1973. While captain, he was successful in holding the formidable West Indies side to a 1-1 draw (1973–74) but that joy was short-lived when in the following year he came up against the formidable Aussie bowling team led by Dennis Lillee and Jeff Thomson. Those two put the visiting batsmen to the sword and won the first three Tests. But, as a colleague said in Denness's obituary, 'he had a happy disposition and bore it cheerfully.' He was also ready to take the blame and famously dropped himself from the fourth game in the series. He returned for the fifth match and scored a brave half-century but the Aussies still made it five wins in a row. A whitewash seemed inevitable but in the sixth and final Test, he showed his batsmen the way by hitting a match-winning 188 that gave England an innings win. Haggis became Captain Marvel! Sadly the Australians came back to form for the 1975 first Test at Edgbaston. After being put into bat (to cries of despair from the commentators), they exploited a soggy pitch to score an innings win. Captain Marvel was sent off to lick his wounds… and never played Test cricket again. After retiring from playing, he served as an ICC match referee until 2002.

Golf

Universally known as Monty, Colin Montgomerie, OBE (born Glasgow, 1963) won a record eight European Tour Order of Merit titles, including a streak of seven consecutively from 1993–99. He has won 31 European Tour events, the most of any British player, placing him fourth on the all-time list of golfers with most European Tour victories. He won three consecutive Volvo PGA Championships at Wentworth (1998–2000) and was runner-up on five occasions in major championships. He has a spectacular record in the Ryder Cup and is hailed as the all-time greatest player of the tournament. He never lost a singles match and helped Britain win the Cup in 1997, 2002, 2004 and 2006. He won again as non-playing captain in 2010 and was named coach of the year in the BBC Sports Personality of the Year awards. He also captained Great Britain and Ireland against a Europe team in the four matches for the Seve Trophy – awarded in tribute to Seve Ballesteros. His team lost in 2000 but won in 2002, 2003 and 2005. He was also captain of the winning European Team in their 2010 and 2011 wins against Asia in the Royal Trophy. His career-high world ranking is second. He was awarded an OBE in 2005 and inducted into the World Golf Hall of Fame in 2013. Scotland's first minister, Alex Salmond, made him an ambassador for the junior golf programme 'clubgolf' in 2012.

Sam Torrance OBE (born Largs, 1953) was one of the leading players on the European Tour from the mid-1970s to the late 1990s. He had 21 Tour wins. He was also a member of European Ryder Cup teams that won four out of the eight matches between 1981 and 1995. He was the winning non-playing captain of the European Ryder Cup team in 2002. He was awarded the MBE (1996) and OBE (2003), for his outstanding contributions to golf.

Sandy Lyle MBE (born Shrewsbury to Scottish parents, 1958) won the Open in 1985, the first British winner since Tony Jacklin years earlier. Three years later he became the first European to win the famous green jacket at the US Masters, after an almost perfect bunker shot onto the final green. He played in five European Ryder Cup teams (1979–87) winning in 1985 and in 1987, Europe's first ever win in America. The same year he won the prestigious Tournament Players Championship in America. He spent more than three years in the top ten of the world rankings (1986–89) and topped the European Tour's order of merit in 1979, 1980 and 1985. He was elected to the World Golf Hall of Fame in 2011.

Bernard Gallacher OBE (born Bathgate, 1949) took up golf at the age of 11 and was only 20 when he became the youngest ever member of the Ryder Cup team. He went on to play eight times and was non-playing captain of the European Team in 1991, 1993 and 1995, losing the first two but winning the third. He now plays on the European Seniors Tour. His daughter Kirsty is a presenter on Sky Sports News.

Paul Lawrie MBE (born Aberdeen, 1969) was the first qualifier to win the Open at Carnoustie in 1999, after a record final-round comeback of ten strokes and a dramatic three-man play-off in driving rain. He won with a birdie on the fourth hole after Frenchman Jean Van de Velde got tangled up in the deep rough and the American Justin Leonard found the water. Although he had won the Qatar Masters earlier in the year, he was ranked 159 in the world and had to qualify for Carnoustie. Winning the biggest prize in golf gave him an automatic berth in Europe's Ryder Cup team and a place in the US Masters. That year he finished ninth in the European Tour Order of Merit and moved up to 6th when he won the Dunhill in 2001. At the 2009 Open at Turnberry, he scored only the eighth albatross (double eagle) in the competition's

150-year history. He won the Andalucia Open in 2011 and the Qatar Masters for the second time in 2012. He played in that year's Ryder Cup in Chicago and won his single match but lost both foursomes in Europe's one-point win. His Paul Lawrie Foundation has taught thousands of youngsters to play golf and in 2012 he also created the Paul Lawrie Golf Centre in his home town, which, according to the *Golf Club Management* magazine, makes him the 37th most powerful person in British golf.

Curling

It was in Salt Lake City in 2002 that the Great Britain women's curling team – made up entirely of Scots – won the first British Winter Olympic gold medal since Jayne Torvill and Christopher Dean danced to *Bolero* in 1984. Scotland's then first minister, Jack McConnell, was there to welcome them home and Prime Minister Tony Blair was also quick to congratulate them. In a fax message he said: 'You have captured the imagination of the whole of the UK.' He was right. The drama had been played out under the all-seeing TV cameras and the world stood still as millions improbably cheered on a small group of women brushing furiously as they tried to steer their stones towards the target. They waged an extraordinary battle against the firm favourites, Canada, in a match decided on the very last stone. This, we learned, was 'chess on ice' because so much strategy is involved and the 'roaring game' because of sound the stone makes as it speeds over the ice.

Curling is another Scottish invention and dates back to the Middle Ages. It's first mentioned in a 1620 poem by Henry Adamson of Perth, but a stone found in Paisley was inscribed 1511 and another, in Dunblane, was marked 1551. Kilsyth Curling Club, formally constituted in 1716 and still going strong, is thought to be the oldest in the world and claims to have the oldest purpose-built curling pond. The Salt Lake City gold-medallists – the first Scots on the podium at the Winter Olympics since 1936 – were skipper Rhona Martin (born Ayrshire, 1966) and her team of Fiona MacDonald (born Paisley, 1974), Janice Rankin (born Inverness, 1972), Debbie Knox (born Dunfermline, 1968) and the reserve, Margaret Morton (born Mauchline, 1968). Even years after the event, the team was still attracting strong media interest. In 2010, Patrick Burnham of the *Guardian* wrote: 'The unlikely triumph of four ordinary Scottish women in a sport most English people had never heard of was a sensation. They were feted as housewife superstars. Flag-waving crowds gathered at Heathrow to welcome them home, they were awarded MBEs and summoned on to Richard and Judy's sofa. There was talk of a Hollywood movie.' To date, the movie hasn't happened. 'In a sense, they became the Susan Boyles of their day: celebrated but also slightly belittled by some of the media coverage,' wrote Burnham. 'They were athletes who had mastered a fiendishly challenging sport while holding down ordinary jobs, yet the talk was of housewives with brooms. Did they feel patronised? "No, because we'd had it for years," says Martin. Locally, there was a lot of recognition and affection. "I still have customers who recognise me. That's quite nice," says MacDonald.'

Rhona Martin was a full-time housewife and mother of two when her final stone clinched the Olympic victory. She was still recovering from knee surgery in 2001. She is now coaching the Scottish junior team and is part of UK Sport's elite coaching programme. Janice Rankin had already been the world junior champion in 1992, a silver medallist with the women's team at the world championships in 1994 and again at the 1998 European championships. She is now an administrator in the recruitment industry. Fiona MacDonald, the youngest of the team, was another former world junior champion, having won her gold in 1993. Shortly after joining the senior ranks she was just edged out of the medals in 2000. Her husband, Ewan, was in the unsuccessful men's team in Salt Lake City. She is now working as an accounts manager in the family insurance business. Debbie Knox was the only one in the team with previous experience of the Winter Olympics. She competed in France in 1992, when curling was only a demonstration sport. She was a gold medallist in the Scottish championships in 1992 and 1999. She went to Utah as the reserve but was promoted to third player with the coach saying it was to 'help team dynamics.' Margaret Morton, who was working at the time for a debt-recovery company, played the important role as second in command but made only a brief appearance on the ice, in the earlier round-robin stage.

Motor racing

There was clearly racing in his blood. His father was a motorcycle racer (in between running his Jaguar car dealership) and his big brother Jimmy was a driver with the Ecurie Ecosse racing team. Jackie Stewart (born Milton, Dunbartonshire, 1939) grew up around cars and was an apprentice mechanic. Now of course Sir Jackie, he is a distinguished figure in the motor racing world and needs nothing more than an acknowledgement of a brilliant career, throughout which he displayed his Scottishness by emblazoning his helmet with a band of Stewart tartan!

Because his parents weren't keen on their second son taking up motor racing, his early ambition was to be an Olympic marksman. However, on his 21st birthday, he failed to qualify for the clay-target team in the 1960 Games and concentrated instead on his apprenticeship. All that changed in 1963 when a customer of the family garage invited him to test a Formula Three car at the Oulton Park track. His skill clearly impressed onlookers and he was subsequently invited by Ken Tyrell to join Cooper's Formula Three team. In 1964, he easily took the *Express & Star* Formula Three championship, winning all but two of his 13 races. He clearly enjoyed the experience and has been quoted as saying: 'It was fantastic winning all those races against some top names, and I think it really sent me on my way.'

After his successes in Formula Three, he joined Graham Hill's BRM Formula One team and his first F1 race was in the South African Grand Prix in 1965, when he earned an invaluable championship point by finishing a creditable sixth. His first win came in just his eighth race – the Italian Grand Prix at Monza – and by the end of the season he was third in the World Championship, behind Jim Clark and Graham Hill. Things didn't go so well in 1966. His BRM didn't stand up to the rigours of the Indianapolis 500 and a pump problem when he was in the lead wrecked his chances. Then a real wreck caused him physical problems. In the Belgian Grand Prix torrential rain made the track dangerous and he was one of the drivers who inevitably spun off. He ended up in a ditch and was trapped inside the car by the steering wheel. It took nearly half an hour to get him out and there were further delays in getting him to hospital. During the time he spent on a stretcher in great pain, he determined that he would try to do something about improving race safety. It became one of his enduring commitments to the sport. Despite his injuries he resumed driving and ended the season in a creditable ninth place. He then went to rejoin Ken Tyrell in his new Matra International F1 team. He moved up the drivers' table to second place in 1968, despite nursing a fractured wrist. In winning the championship in 1969, he won seven of the 14 races and was also named the British F1 Champion.

Car problems meant that his 1970 season was seriously curtailed. Tyrell was able to prepare the car for only three of the Grands Prix and, frustrated, Jackie left to drive for the March team, winning enough points to finish seventh in the championship. By the beginning of the 1971 season, the Tyrell team had managed to build him a new car and he rejoined them and won his second championship. The following year, he again hit problems, this time with his health. Stomach ulcers meant he missed a couple of races, but he persevered and still ended the season in second place. In 1973, he won his third world championship before announcing his decision to retire after nine years and 99 races. It would have been a hundred had he not pulled out of the final Grand Prix in New York after his teammate François Cevert was killed during the qualifying round.

His record of 27 wins and 360 championship points stood for 15 years. When he gave up driving, he became a television commentator and held consultancies around the sport and was even involved in developing new generations of F1 engines. He also opened a shooting school at Scotland's famous Gleneagles Hotel in 1985 and took on several business directorships. In 1997, he returned to Formula One with a vengeance: he joined his son to form Paul Stewart Grand Prix Racing in partnership with Ford, and they signed up Rubens Barrichello and Jan Magnussen. Sir Jackie managed the team for their first season and Barrichello gave them a very creditable second place in the Monaco Grand Prix. Two years later, the team won the European Grand Prix and he sold the company to Ford for a reputed £60 million but stayed on as a consultant. The team morphed into Jaguar Cars in 2000, with Paul Stewart as CEO. Jackie Stewart was knighted in 2001 for his services to British motor racing.

Scotland's most successful F1 driver since Sir Jackie is David Coulthard (born Twynholm, Kirkcudbrightshire, 1971), who retired in 2008 after 14 years, around 250 Grand Prix races and 13 individual wins. He had driven for three of the leading teams: Williams, McLaren and Red Bull. Despite never having won the championship, he is fifth on the all-time points list and the top British scorer. Coulthard began racing go-karts when he was 12 and moved up to Formula Ford in 1989 when he was 18. He showed his steely determination and competitiveness by winning the first McLaren-*Autosport* young driver of the year award in the same year. Despite breaking his leg in a racing accident in 1990, he won the Formula Three Macau Grand Prix in 1991. He was third in the Formula 3000 series in 1993, and then moved up to F1 as the test driver for the Williams team. Following the death of Ayrton Senna, he was promoted to partner with Damon Hill. His first major win was the Portuguese Grand Prix in 1995, his best championship placing was second (to Michael Schumacher) in 2002 and his last podium finish was third in the 2008 Canadian Grand Prix, just before he retired. He published his autobiography, *It Is What It Is*, in 2007. He continues as a consultant to the Red Bull team and also acts as a pundit on BBC's F1 television coverage.

Another Scot who tried to make a fist of Formula One was the aristocratic Johnny Dumfries (born Rothesay, 1958), who appears in A&C Black's *Who's Who?* as the '7th Marquess of Bute, Sir John Colum Crichton-Stuart, Earl of Dumfries', with the total number of his other hereditary titles running into double figures! He had only one season – 1986 – in the hottest of hot seats, but it was remarkable in that he partnered Ayrton Senna in Team Lotus, completed all 16 Grands Prix and picked up three championship points. When Lotus started to use Honda engines in 1987, he had to give way to a Japanese driver and he reverted to Formula Three. When he was driving in Formula Three, he won the British Championship and was second in the European Championship in 1984. He won the 1988 Le Mans as lead driver in a Jaguar XJR-9 and then drove for Toyota in 1989–90.

The Americans bill it as the 'greatest spectacle in racing' and it attracts an annual crowd of 400,000. That surely underlines the amazing achievement of Dario Franchitti (born Bathgate, 1973) in winning the Indianapolis 500-mile race three times (2007, 2010 and 2012). Jackie Stewart describes him as 'a top-flight talent' but he has chosen to race in America rather than on the Formula One circuit. Racing is in his blood. He was only 11 when he started his high-speed career as Scottish junior kart champion in 1984. That was followed by British junior champion 1985 and 1986 and Scottish senior champion in 1988. He joined the Paul Stewart team with aspirations to follow his teenage idol Jim Clark into Formula One. He was the Vauxhall junior champion in 1991, the McLaren/*Autosport* young driver of the year 1992 and the Formula Vauxhall Lotus champion in 1993. He spent three years competing in Formula Three and German Touring Cars before trying his luck in American CART racing in 1997. Two years later, he was the series runner-up. He suffered a serious back injury in a motorbike accident in Scotland in 2003 and it looked as if his career was over but, despite the odds, he fought back to fitness, only to win his first Indy 500 in 2007. He says his inspiration is still Jim Clark and there's a room in his house decorated with memorabilia of the two-time Formula One world champion. Sir Jackie Stewart says of him: 'He's never lost his

Scottishness, his accent, or any of his values. He hasn't changed at all with his fame. He's one of the nicest men I know.'

Rally driving

Britain's first world rally champion was Colin McRae (born Lanark, 1967–2007), who – at 27 – was the youngest ever winner of the title in 1995, was second in 1996, 1997 and 2001 and third in 1998. As was reported around the world, he died in a helicopter crash near his home in Lanarkshire in 2007. He was 40.

The son of five-time British rally champion Jimmy McRae (born Lanark, 1943), Colin often said he first sat in the driving seat when he was only two, but his first experience of high-speed was on two wheels. As a teenager, he won several motorbike trials competitions. He was still only 18 when he made his rally debut, and combined driving with his work in the family heating and plumbing business. He joined the World Rally Championship circuit in 1987 and won his first event, the Tweedies Rally in the south of Scotland, the following year. His co-driver was his future wife Alison. He was the Scottish rally champion in 1988 and British champion in 1991 and 1992. When he joined up with a former world champion in the new Subaru team he came second in the Swedish rally, despite a puncture on the final day. His first win was in New Zealand the following year. He secured his world champion title in some style by beating twice-champion Carlos Sainz at the final event of the 1995 season in Britain, in front of hundreds of thousands of his most enthusiastic fans! In all, he won 25 world rallies and climbed onto the podium on 42 occasions. In 1996, he was made an MBE for services to motor sport. He published his autobiography *The Real McRae* in 2002. When he asked why so many Scottish drivers had achieved world success, he said, 'it's a reflection of the fact that the Scots are, by and large, a very determined group of people. Determination is a quality that motor sport demands in abundance, so maybe that serves us well and drives us on.'

Scottish driver Louise Aitken-Walker (born Duns, 1960) was the first Briton to win the Ladies' World Rally Championship in 1990. She began competitive driving almost by accident: in 1979, her brothers secretly entered her in Ford's Find a Lady Rally Driver competition… and she won from an entry of two thousand. Her first major drive was in the 1981 RAC Lombard Rally and she finished nineteenth overall. Her most successful year was 1990: in addition to winning the world championship, she also won the Coup des Dames at Monte Carlo (11th overall) and the Ladies Cups at the New Zealand Rally, Rally Australia and the Rally of Italy. She survived her car somersaulting into a deep lake in Portugal, then went on to win the Asia Pacific Ladies Rally Championship and the driver of the year award from the Guild of Motoring Writers. She retired from driving after being awarded the MBE in 1992.

Boxing

It was in 1966 that Walter McGowan (born Hamilton, 1942) won his flyweight title in a 15-round thriller at Wembley. He won the points decision over the Italian holder, despite suffering a cut above his eye in the seventh round. It was his susceptibility to cuts that was to haunt and finally end his career. He managed to avoid most of the potential damage, however, because of his innate skills in the ring. His footwork was brilliant and he used the ring to its full extent –something more than evident in his career statistics. As an amateur he lost only two of his 124 bouts and was the ABA flyweight champion in 1961 at the age of 19, after which he turned professional. He had a terrific debut. His first pro bout – in Kelvin Hall, Glasgow – was stopped in the third round because his opponent couldn't carry on. In only his tenth pro fight, in 1963, he took on the defending champion (fellow Scot Jackie Brown, born Edinburgh, 1935) and knocked him out in the twelfth round to claim both the British and Commonwealth flyweight titles. He was not quite 21.

He defended the Commonwealth title in 1963 and won a technical knock-out decision in the ninth round. Six months later he challenged the Italian holder, Salvatore Burruni, for the European flyweight title, but he lost on points in Rome's Olympic Stadium, having gone the distance with the champion. It was Salvatore Burruni that he fought for the WBC world flyweight championship in 1966. This time the fight was at the Empire Pool, Wembley, and this time he won the 15-round points decision to gain the title. Once again, however, he had to fight the last eight rounds nursing a badly gashed eye. Later in the year, having again gone up a weight, he fought Alan Rudkin for the British and Commonwealth bantamweight titles. This time he didn't suffer any cuts until the tenth round and again won on points. It was another cut – this time on the nose – that robbed him of the world title. He and his seconds were unable to stench the flow of blood and the referee was forced to stop the fight and hand the title to the Thai challenger. In a rematch ten months later, he yet again suffered cuts around his eyes and the fight was stopped in the seventh. His last championship fight was in May 1968, when he lost his British and Commonwealth bantamweight titles. Despite that, in a final show of his indomitable spirit, he went on boxing for another 18 months and won all of his last six fights!

He was the first Scottish boxer to be awarded the MBE and he was inducted into the Scottish Sports Hall of Fame in 2002.

In comparison with the stick-thin flyweights, Ken Buchanan (born Edinburgh, 1945) was a positive bruiser: a nobody-kicks-sand-in-my face, nine-stone-nine package of muscle and grit. Many say he was Scotland's best ever boxer. He started boxing when he was eight and won a medal in his first year. By the time he was 18 he had earned a reputation as an accomplished and stylish boxer and was selected to take part in the European championships in Moscow in 1963 and Berlin in 1965. In the same year, he won the ABA lightweight title. Shortly afterwards he turned professional and won his first fight with a second-round knockout. In 1967, he took the vacant Scottish lightweight title when he out-pointed John McMillan over ten rounds. He fought his way into contention for the British lightweight title after winning no fewer than 23 consecutive fights. His reward was a match with the holder, Maurice Cullen, in 1968. He knocked him out in the tenth round.

That put him on the road to the world title but it wasn't a smooth road. He won his first three fights but lost his fourth, in Madrid to Miguel Velazquez (who was later the world welterweight champion), after a 15-round points decision. With that blip behind him, he continued his winning ways, and when he defended his British title he knocked out the contender in the fifth round. In 1970 he confounded the experts by acclimatising himself to the gruelling heat of Puerto Rico for his world title fight with the South American holder, Ismael Laguna. He went the full distance and won by a unanimous points decision. Soon after that he was a victim of internecine wrangling between the British and US boxing authorities and found himself unable to box in the UK... so he fought and won in America and successfully defended his title after another tough, 15-round battle.

When the suits stopped quarrelling and he was able appear again in the UK ring, he defended his title against former champion Carlos Hernández and won after an eighth-round knockout. In the rematch with Laguna in New York, he again won on points. In 1972, he lost his world title in a controversial encounter with the legendary Roberto Duran in New York's Madison Square Garden. On (some say *after*) the bell ending the thirteenth round, Buchanan was caught by a heavy punch to the midriff, which his corner claimed was below the belt. The blow left him unable to come out for the fourteenth the referee ruled that a technical KO and awarded the fight to the Duran. Duran, from Panama, one of the greatest lightweights of all time, always said Buchanan was his toughest ever opponent.

Undeterred by the loss of the title, Buchanan returned to New York later in the same year and dispatched three-time world champion Carlos Ortiz by knocking him out in the sixth. The next year, in what was their only ring meeting, he went the full distance with fellow Scot Jim Watts and won the points decision that gave him back the British lightweight title. With wins in the United States, Canada and Europe, he took on and beat the European title-holder on points after 15 rounds. After defending and retaining the title in Paris, he went to Japan to try to win back his world title . . . but lost the points decision. He successfully defended the European title with a knockout in the twelfth round and then hung up his gloves in 1982. He was inducted into the International Boxing Hall Of Fame in 2000.

Like Jackie Paterson (see chapter 6, And the glory), Jim Watt (born Glasgow, 1948) was another southpaw, but he fought in the lightweight division. Where he was born, in the city's East End, boxing was second nature for many of the lads but he preferred football. But in the it's-an-ill-wind mode, his soccer ambitions were severely curtailed by a savage winter that left pitches unplayable. Determined to expend his youthful energies, he joined the boxing club in Maryhill... and a champion was born. He was just 20 when he won his first major title. In 1968, he became ABA lightweight champion by knocking out Londoner John H Stracey (the future British, European and world welterweight champion) in the first round. His success as an amateur earned him selection for the British boxing team for the 1968 Olympics in Mexico.

He shocked many by declining the opportunity because he had already decided to turn professional (and the Olympics were then still amateur). He fought most of his early pro fights at the National Sporting Club in London and strung together a steady stream of stylish victories. He earned a crack at the Commonwealth lightweight title and travelled to Lagos to do battle with the reigning champion, Nigerian Jonathan Dele. Although he took him the full distance, he lost on points. In 1972, he had a tough fight in South Africa and beat the Springbok Andrew Steyn. Later in the year, he won the British lightweight title, lost it a year later to Ken Buchanan and then regained it in 1975.

He won the European title in Madrid in February 1978 with a points decision over the Spanish former world champion, Perico Fernadez. When Roberto Duran (who had snatched the title from Ken Buchanan in 1972) finally moved up a division and left the world lightweight title vacant in 1979, Jim Watt was matched with Columbian Alfredo Pitalua and regained the crown for Scotland with a twelfth-round knock-out. It wasn't an easy victory. Early on he was hit by what he said was 'the single hardest punch I ever took in the ring' and had to survive a barrage of heavy blows before countering with his own southpaw artillery, to the delight of the Kelvin Hall crowd.

Having won the crown, he held onto it tenaciously. He defended it a record four times... on each occasion in his own backyard of Glasgow. In January 1980, in the Kelvin Hall, he stopped American Sean O'Grady (who later won the title), in the twelfth after a gash below the eye. There was some controversy over whether the cut was caused by the head or the glove but the referee was unequivocal. Two months later, he climbed into the ring to defend his title against the high-voltage assault of Ulsterman Charlie Nash. Watt found himself on the canvas in the first round but quickly bounced back and turned the heat on Nash. He floored the Irishman four times before the referee called a halt in the fourth round. When American Howard Davis (the 1976 Olympic gold medallist) arrived in Glasgow to challenge for the title just three months after that, he made the arrogant mistake of asking: 'Jim who?' In the rain in front of a packed Ibrox stadium, he got his answer: 'Jim Watt, that's who!' – and the very same Jim Watt out-boxed him over the 15 rounds! After his record run of defences, he finally lost the title to the 'Explosive Thin Man', Nicaraguan Alexis Arguello (former world champion in featherweight and junior lightweight divisions), on points in London's Wembley Arena in 1981. He retired with a record of 38 wins (including 27 knock-outs) and just eight defeats. He was awarded an MBE in 1980 and given the Freedom of Glasgow in 1981. Since retiring from boxing, he has been a commentator and boxing analyst for ITV and Sky Sports and is also a popular after-dinner speaker.

Following his father and uncle into the ring, Pat Clinton (born Croy, Dunbarton-shire, 1964), yet another southpaw, outdid both of them by winning his world title in 1992. His father, who was the Scottish professional flyweight champion in 1940 and had made an unsuccessful bid for Jackie Paterson's world title in 1941, died relatively young in 1980. This convinced Pat to abandon boyhood aspirations to be a jockey and take his boxing seriously, in tribute to his father. What he hadn't absorbed from his father and his uncle Jimmy (ABA flyweight champion in 1944 and 1947), he picked up battling with his five brothers (he also had four sisters) and the locals at the miners' boxing club in Croy. It was a tough school and he clearly learned his ring-craft well. He shrewdly decided to take the long route through the amateur ranks. In 1984, when he was not quite 20, he became ABA flyweight champion and went to the Los Angeles Olympics as part of the British team but missed out on the medals.

In 1985, after successfully defending the ABA title, he turned professional and in 1987 picked up his father's old title when he became the Scottish flyweight champion. He made an unsuccessful bid for the European title in 1989, taking the champion, Eyüp Can of Turkey, the full distance, but sustained hand injuries that would cause problems throughout his career. He successfully defended his British title by stopping Welshman David-Alyn Jones in six rounds but that fight was followed by a long lay-off due to injuries, and it wasn't until the following year that he was fit enough to have a shot at the European title again. This time, the defending champion was the Italian Salvatore Fanni and the fight was in his hometown on Sardinia. It was a tough clash and Clinton was down in the tenth round and was nursing a damaged tendon in his right hand. But he more than survived and was declared the points winner. The European the title was his.

He made his challenge for the world title in the cauldron of Glasgow's Kelvin Hall in March 1992. He stood toe-to-toe with the defending champion Isadore Perez and after 12 hectic rounds the judges were divided... two-to-one in favour of the Scot. The only thing that detracted from the occasion was the absence of his father. Six months later and again in Glasgow, he easily fended off the challenge of Englishman Danny Porter with a unanimous points decision, having previously stopped him in five rounds in a British title fight. Like most of the flyweights, Clinton had a perpetual struggle to keep inside the eight-stone limit and he suffered from a series of hand injuries. He wasn't in the best shape, therefore, to defend his title against the South African 'Baby' Jake Matlala in 1993. Over seven rounds, the judges were split: one for, one against and one draw. But all that changed in the eighth when the referee stepped in and gave the win to the challenger. Pat briefly considered fighting at bantamweight but that idea slipped away and he retired from the ring.

There have been a number of Scots who have held boxing titles at British and Commonwealth levels, and no fewer than four contemporary world title holders – Murray Sutherland (born Edinburgh, 1954), 1984 super middleweight champion; Paul Weir (born Irvine, 1967), 1993 light flyweight champion; Scott Harrison (born Bellshill, 1977), 2002 featherweight champion; and Alex Arthur (born Edinburgh, 1978), 2004 super featherweight champion – are waiting in the wings for history to assess their achievements.

Horse racing

Scotland's most successful jockey is Willie Carson (born Stirling, 1942), five times British champion and winner of 17 Classics (including the Derby three times). He rode his first winner in 1962 and notched up a hundred (or more) winners in a season on no fewer than 23 occasions. He was champion jockey in 1972, 1973, 1978, 1980 and 1983 and amassed a career total of 3,828 wins, making him the fourth most successful jockey in Great Britain. His best season was 1990, when he rode 187 winners, including riding the winner of every race on a six-race card at Newcastle. He was awarded the OBE in 1983 for his services to horse racing. He was 54 when he retired in 1996.

Roaring into contention as Scotland's new leading rider is Ryan Mania (born Galashiels, 1989) after his spectacular nine-lengths win at 66-1 in the 2013 Grand National on the 11-year-old Auroras Encore. Less than 24 hours after his Aintree triumph, he was airlifted to hospital after a crunching fall at Hexham. He had a fractured vertebra and soft-tissue and ligament damage to his neck but he was given the all-clear and left hospital two days later to return to the saddle. He has since won a string of other races but missed out on the double when he pulled up on Auroras Encore in the 2013 Scottish National at Ayr. The pairing had been second there the previous year. It's early days yet but he has given me a good reason to watch the form-books!

Snooker

Every time the snooker comes on television, I'm haunted by memories of my misspent youth – of days spent in darkened rooms above Burtons (the tailor's), waiting impatiently for a table to come free so that I could make a fool of myself yet again. The lure of the bright lights and the green baize was irresistible. I never aspired to the multiple-ball wizardry of today's geniuses but contented myself with the attempted mastery of three-ball billiards. I kidded myself that it was helping me with physics and maths and I remember talking with pseudo-erudition about angles, weight, stun and spin. I also dropped in historical snippets about how Mary, Queen of Scots, ended her days wrapped not in a shroud but in the cover of her billiard table; that Shakespeare had Cleopatra compete with her eunuch; that Marie Antoinette played when she wasn't telling the peasants to eat cake; and that other historical figures who waved a cue included Mozart, Mark Twain, General Custer and Charles Dickens. Much good did it do me. I invariably lost my pocket money on side bets and often had to stand and watch my schoolmates enjoy extra games at my expense while I waited for the next hand-out from my mother.

All that makes me an unashamed fan of Stephen Hendry (born Edinburgh, 1969), who in 1990 at just 21 became world snooker champion, the youngest ever to win the title… and went on to do it all over again in 1992, 1993, 1994, 1995, 1996, 1999. This genius of the green baize turned professional in 1985, when he was just 16, and within the year he had won the Scottish championship. He holds the record for the most titles – nine – won in a season, which was 1991. He was awarded an MBE in 1999 and an honorary degree from the University of Stirling in 2000. He helped Scotland win the World Cup in 1996 and the Nations Cup in 2001. He is described as the greatest player of all time in Luke Williams and Paul Gadsby's *Master of the Baize*.

There are a number of other Scots likely to appear in a future edition, including: John Higgins (born Wishaw, 1975) with three world titles; Alan McManus (born Glasgow, 1979), nicknamed 'the Angles'; Graeme Dott (born Larkhall, 1977), who reached number two in the world rankings; and Stephen Maguire (born Milton, 1981), winner of the 2004 European Open.

Shooting

Scotland's most successful shooter is Alister Allan (born Freuchie, Fife, 1944) who, in 20 competitive years (1974–94), won three gold, three silver and four bronze medals in five Olympic Games, and six Commonwealth Games and the World Championship (of 1976). Two of the silver and a bronze were gained in the 1986 Games in Edinburgh. He also scored a perfect 600 points at the 1981 European championships held in Titograd, in the former Yugoslavia. He was shooting in the prone position at a target 50 metres away and hit dead centre – an area no bigger than a five-pence piece – 60 times out of 60! He said modestly: 'I performed to my maximum.' In the 1988 Olympics, he set a new record of 1181 points in the qualification round of the 50-metres rifles (three positions), beating his GB team-mate by a single point, Unfortunately, he lost by a single point to the same GB shooter in the final and had to settle for silver. He was awarded an MBE in 1989 and was elected to the Scottish Hall of Fame in 2002.

Shooting for the British team in 2006, Matthew Thomson (born Edinburgh, 1986) became the world junior men's prone champion by recording a score of 593 in very tricky conditions. He also led the team to victory in the junior men's competition, Britain's first rifle team gold for nearly quarter of a century. In the two previous years he had been Scottish prone champion and he took the title again in 2008. At the 2012 International Shooting Competition in Hanover (ISCH), he won a team silver and an individual bronze medal. He began his career as a schoolboy with the Watsonian Shooting Club and also shot for the University of Edinburgh rifle club.

The first woman for 70 years to win the Queen's Prize (gold medal) at Bisley was Joanna Hossack (born Edinburgh, 1980) in 2000. Facing competitors from 14 countries, she was then still a student at the University of Edinburgh and at twenty, was the second youngest ever to have won the premier prize in world shooting. In the final, she beat the South African champion Johan Ahrens with a dramatic final shot. From 1000 yards, she hit the bull and in the sport's tradition, was carried off the range in the champion's chair. Earlier in the year, she was a member of the Scottish team unbeaten in a tour of Australia. She took up the sport when she was 12. Her father, David, who died in 2012, was Scotland's former target-rifle shooting captain and a British international.

Bowls

Having tried it only once, I am happy to simply be mesmerised watching bowls – both lawn and indoors – on television. While it looks the most tranquil of games to play, the competitiveness of the players and the committed and expert commentary gives it a real edge that makes for fascinating viewing. This is a sport also clearly suited to the Scottish temperament and our small nation has fostered no fewer than seven male and six female world champions, who have amassed no less than 23 individual world titles and too many other doubles, triples and fours honours to comment on adequately.

For example, since the World Indoor Championships began in 1979, Scots have won 16 of the men's titles against England's ten, with three to Wales and one each to Ireland and Australia. In a record-breaking run, Alex Marshall (born Edinburgh, 1967) has taken an astonishing five of the world titles: in 1999, 2003, 2004, 2007 and 2008. He has a similar array of gold medals in pairs, fours and team events. He comes from a bowling family: his mother, father, sister and brother (a Scottish international indoor and lawn player) are all players of the game. 'It was a family thing,' he says in glorious understatement! He started winning when he was ten years old, taking the Edinburgh Schoolboys title against fellow world champion Richard Corsie. 'We're now very good friends,' he later said. His first senior cap was in 1988 and he won three gold medals – in the pairs (with Richard Corsie), the fours, and the team event – at his first World Outdoor Championships in 1992. He won another gold in the team event in 1995 and silver in the pairs in 1996 World Outdoor Championship, together with wins in the 1999 World Indoor Championships and the 2000 World Indoor and Outdoor Championships. As well as his world trophies, he also won Commonwealth gold (pairs in lawn bowling) in 2002 and again in 2006. He was awarded an MBE in the 2007 New Year Honours.

Many say the best bowls player to come out of Scotland was Richard Corsie (born Edinburgh, 1966). He won three world titles – in 1989, 1991 and 1993 – and would have been likely to have won several more if he hadn't retired in 2003 (at just 37) because he wanted to concentrate on his business. The BBC commentator David Rhys-Jones described him as 'the most naturally gifted player I have seen.'

He clearly recovered from losing to the young Alex Marshall in 1977 and won the Scottish Junior Championship when he was 17 in 1983 and again in 1989, when he also added the British Isles junior title. He made his debut as a Scottish international in 1984 and was the team's dominant player for the next 14 years. In 1986 and still only 19, he picked up a Commonwealth bronze medal in the singles, repeated the feat in New Zealand in 1990 and finally hit gold in Canada in 1994. Earlier, in 1989, of course, he won the first of his three world titles, when he beat his mentor and fellow Scot Willie Wood (born Haddington, 1938) in the final. Two years later he beat Australia's Ian Schuback before adding a record-equalling third title in 1993 when he enjoyed victory over fellow Scot Jim McCann (born Blantyre). David Rhys-Jones, who followed

Richard Corsie's progress throughout his career, said: 'When in the mood and firing on all cylinders he was a joy to behold and I count myself privileged to have watched and commentated on most of his principal triumphs.' Five-time champion Alex Marshall said of him: 'His was the best delivery of a wood in the world, smooth and relaxed in everything he did. I tried to take my game off him. He had won everything in the game and was a fantastic sportsman.' He was awarded the MBE and retired from the sport in 2003.

Darts

Scotland's only world darts champion has been Jocky Wilson (Kirkcaldy, 1950–2012), who took the title twice: in 1982 and 1989. Before turning professional, he both delivered coal and worked as a miner. With the closing of the pits, he was thrown out of work and it was while on the dole that he entered a holiday camp darts competition ... and won £500. That was a small fortune in 1970 and it set him on a new path that led him to taking the British championship a record four times – in 1981, 1983, 1986 and 1988. In 1982, he won the world championship, then still in its infancy, and repeated the feat again seven years later, when he famously recovered from being 5-0 down. He was in the British team that won the Europe Cup in 1978 and he also won the BBC Bullseye championship in 1980 and 1981, the British Open in 1982, the Autumn Gold Masters 1984, the Finland Open 1986 and the Denmark Open Pairs in 1981, 1983 and 1984. He stopped playing in 1995 and became something of a recluse before his death in 2012.

... And also

Don't be misled by the sub-heading. This short tailpiece, not just to the sports section but to this saga of global enterprise, is for those successful Scots who don't necessarily fit into the neat boxes proscribed by previous sections, but whose achievements still illustrate all the strength of character that it takes to make the Scottish Empire.

Scots have sailed round the world and flown around the world, but Mark Beaumont (born Edinburgh, 1983) was the first to do it on a bike, in 2008. He did it in style, covering the 18,000-mile journey in 194 days and 17 hours, a staggering 82 days less than the previous record. He turned the epic journey into a BBC documentary, *The Man who Cycled the World* and used the same title for his follow-up best-selling book. A year later, he set out on his second eye-watering expedition: to cycle the length of North and South America: not content to cycle 13,000 miles, he also climbed the highest peaks in the two continents. His earlier exploits included cycling across Scotland when he was 12 and then going from Joan O'Groats to Land's End when he was 15.

As another example of utterly dogged Scots determination, take Sir Chay Blyth (born Hawick, 1940). He is one of the world's greatest, most successful sailors. He sailed the high seas in every direction, often on his own, he rowed across the North Atlantic, he broke records, won great prizes... and left lesser beings in his wake. In 1971 he was the first to sail solo non-stop around the world, westward against the prevailing winds and currents. After leaving his local high school, he joined 3rd Parachute Regiment at 18 and was a sergeant by the time he was 21. He was still in the army in 1966, when he and Captain John Ridgway rowed across the Atlantic in an open, 20-foot dory. It took 92 days and earned him the British Empire Medal. He had no sailing experience but that didn't stop him competing in the 1968 *Sunday Times* Golden Globe race in a 30-foot yacht. He got as far as the Cape of Good Hope before being forced to retire. Undaunted, he set sail yet again – and again solo – on the 59-foot yacht *British Steel* in 1971, and became the first to sail non-stop westwards around the world. That took 292 days and earned him the CBE. In 1973, he skippered a crew from the 3rd Paras and took line honours in the Whitbread Round the World Yacht Race. In 1978, his crew were the outright winners of the Round Britain Race. He won (with Robert James) the first double-handed *Observer* Transatlantic Race in record time in 1981, beating off the competition from a hundred other yachts. In 1985, he was co-skipper with Richard Branson on *Virgin Atlantic Challenger* in the attempt on the fastest crossing of the Atlantic. The boat sank off Land's End. The following year however – in *Virgin Atlantic Challenger II* – they broke the record created in 1950, but were denied the famous Blue Riband because they had refuelled in mid-Atlantic and because the boat didn't have a commercial use! He was knighted for his services to sailing in 1997.

Going one better than Chay Blyth in the rowing stakes, SAS man Tom McClean (born Mallaig, 1943) was the first to cross the Atlantic single-handed, in 1969. He was brought up in orphanage from when he was five until he left school at 15 and then went into the Parachute Regiment before transferring to the SAS. With toughness overlaid by more toughness and convinced that life was all about the survival of the fittest, he set out to survive in style! Before he launched himself onto the cold waters of the Atlantic, he had no previous knowledge of sea conditions. He took just 70 days to row himself indelibly into the record books. His next major endurance test was in 1982 when he decided to make the 3,000-mile voyage in the world's shortest yacht – just nine feet and nine inches long. In 54 days he established another world record. But unfortunately it didn't last long: just three weeks behind him was an American whose boat was eight inches shorter! Not to be outdone, he cut a whole two feet off his boat and hurled himself against the Atlantic again the following year. During the voyage, he hit a thunderstorm in the Bay of Biscay and emerged mastless and with serious steering problems. Nevertheless, he made it, and recaptured the world record.

In 1985, he did it for Britain: he set up a precarious camp on the uninhabited island of Rockall in the middle of the Atlantic and stayed there for 40 days in a tiny survival unit. Why? To underpin British sovereignty, not just of the island but of the potential oil and gas that lies beneath the Rockall Bank. Unfortunately, the status of the riches is still uncertain. In 1987, when most middle-aged men have bowed to the inevitable, 44-year-old Tom McClean again climbed into a 20-foot rowing boat, determined to recover his transatlantic record from a Frenchman. This time he had to overcome 50-foot waves that capsized the boat and tipped all his essential equipment into the murky depths. He made it in 54 days. I suspect that even now he is not yet done with rowing and sailing and pitting himself against the sea.

Dougal Haston (born Currie, 1940–77) climbed his way into the record books in 1975 by being one of the first two Britons to make it to the summit of the world's highest mountain – the hard way. He and his climbing partner Doug Scott made the first ascent of the south-west face of Mount Everest. Haston had cut his teeth on Scotland's Ben Nevis almost as soon as he was able to lace up his climbing boots. In 1966, he climbed the north face of the Eiger (by a direct route) and was in Chris Bonnington's team which conquered the south face of Annapurna in 1970. He was first to climb Changabang in India (1974). After his success in reaching the Everest summit, later in the year, his team also made the first ascent of the south-west face of Mount McKinley in Alaska. He was director of the International School of Mountaineering at Leysin in Switzerland and it was there, in January 1977, that he was killed by an avalanche while skiing alone on the north-east face of La Riondaz. Of the majesty of mountains and mountaineering, he said: 'In winter, the mountains seem to regain their primitive, virginal pride and no more do the howling, littering summer masses tramp their more accessible slopes.'

So I end my own faltering attempt at scaling a mountain and bring to a close what, for me, has been an epic journey in which I have tried to contain the energy and enterprise of a restless, uncontainable nation. One kindly editor has described this journalistic compilation as a masterwork and a diligent reporter could ask for no better compliment. It assures me that I have remained reasonably detached - when often I was lured towards hubris - in chronicling our small nation's contribution, as Voltaire saw it, towards civilisation. For me, this is the beginning of a new chapter in the chronicles of Scotland's Global Empire.

'If one took the Scots out of the world, it would fall apart'
— Dr Louis B Wright, National Geographic Magazine

Bibliography

Encyclopaedia Britannica
Multiple editions

Pears Cyclopaedia
Multiple editions
Penguin Books

Chambers Biographical Dictionary
Volumes I and II
W&R Chambers Ltd, Edinburgh 1974

Oxford Dictionary of Political Biography
Edited by Dennis Kavanagh
OUP 1998

Who's Who?
Multiple editions
A&C Black

Debrett's People of Today
Multiple editions
Debrett's Peerage Limited

Who's Who in the Media 1998
European Editions Ltd

The Journalist's Handbook (multiple
    editions)
Carrick Media

*The Encyclopaedia of the British Press
    1422-1992*
Edited by Denis Griffiths
Macmillan Press 1992

The Scotsman
Multiple issues
plus *Scotsman.com*

The Herald (Glasgow)
Multiple issues

The Daily Record
Multiple issues

The Sunday Post
Multiple issues

The Daily Mail
Multiple issues

The Independent
Multiple issues

The Guardian
Multiple issues

The Daily Telegraph
Multiple issues

The Times
Multiple issues

Roget's Thesaurus
Multiple editions

Oxford English Dictionary
Multiple editions

Wikipedia Free Encyclopaedia (Internet)
and numerous other websites

Scotland.org
Website

The Scottish Review (online journal of the
Institute for Contemporary Scotland)

Multiple editions*Baxter's Book of Famous
    Scots Who Changed the World*
Bill Fletcher

Lang Syne Collins Gem *Famous Scots*
HarperCollins

Scotland's Mark on America
George Fraser Black
Biblio Bazaar 2007

Who's Who in the Liberal Democrats?
Editor Jock Gallagher
Multiple editions
PCA Books

The Mark of the Scots
Duncan A Bruce
Carol Publishing Group 1997

Twelve Days on the Somme
Sidney Rogerson

Whiskies of Scotland
Derek Cooper
Pitman 1978

Against Goliath
David Steel
Wiedenfeld & Nicolson 1989

Burns Poems and Songs
Editor: James Kinsley
Oxford University Press

Crowned Masterpieces of Eloquence
International University Society 1911

Full Disclosure
Andrew Neil
MacMillan

DG: The memoirs of a British broadcaster
Alasdair Milne
Hodder & Stoughton 1988

Jo Grimond: Memoirs
Heinneman 1979

The Past Masters
Harold Macmillan
Macmillan London Ltd 1975

Promise Me You'll Sing Mud
Ian Wallace
John Calder 1975

*The Penguin Book of Twentieth Century
    Speeches*
Edited by Brian MacArthur
Viking 1992

A Question of Leadership
Peter Clarke
Penguin 1992

Book of Firsts
Patrick Robertson

The Van Gogh Assignment
Kenneth Wilkie
Paddington Press 1978

Isobel Barnett: Portrait of a Lady
Jock Gallagher
Methuen 1982

The Tartan Pimpernel
Donald Caskie
Birlinn, Sept 1999

*Miss Cranston: Patron of Charles Rennie
Mackintosh*
Perilla Kinchin
NMS Publishing, May 1999

*Mungo Park: Writer Surgeon and West
African Explorer*
Mark Duffill
NMS Publishing, May 1999

*Livingstone's Quest: A Journey to the Four
Fountains*
Aisling Irving and Colum Wilson
House of Lochar, April 1999

Scottish Inventors
Alistair Fyfe
HarperCollins, April 1999

They Called it Passchendaele
Lyn Macdonald
Michael Joseph 1978

The Gentle Lochiel
John S Gibson
NMS Publishing Oct 98

Elsie Inglis
Leah Leneman
NMS Publishing Oct 98

Little Boss: A Life of Andrew Carnegie
James Mackay
Mainstream 1 Sept 1997

John Muir: From Scotland to the Sierra
Frederick Turner
Canongate July 1997

The Wilderness Journeys
John Muir
Canongate

The Marquis of Montrose
John Buchan
Prion

Robert Burns: The Tender Heart
Hugh Douglas
Alan Sutton Publishing

Scotland's Grand Slam 1990
Ian McGeechan, David Sole and Gavin
Hastings
Stanley Paul and Co.

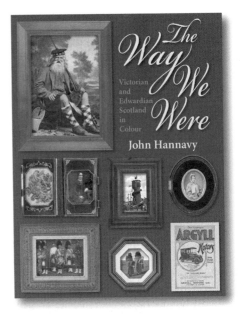
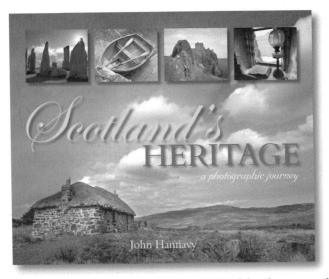

'...a new collection of Gunn's short fiction ... while set in the Highlands the [stories] deal with universal human preoccupations'.
The Scotsman

As featured in BBC Radio 4's **Afternoon Reading** show

An appraisal of Scottish nationalism through the lens of Neil M. Gunn's writings and its relevance to the modern debate and contemporary political development in Scotland.

Contributers include Dairmid Gunn, Michael Russell MSP and Ewen Cameron.

www.whittlespublishing.com

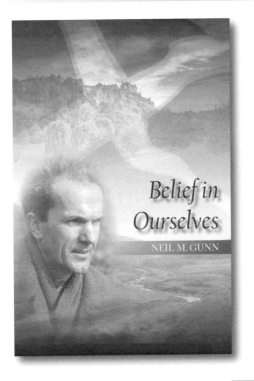